SMYTHE LIBRARY

Stamp this label with the date for return.
Contact the Librarian if you wish to renew this book.

D1336425

CALL TO ARMS

CALL TO ARMS

THE BRITISH ARMY 1914–18

Charles Messenger

WEIDENFELD & NICOLSON

Weidenfeld & Nicolson
The Orion Publishing Group Ltd
Orion House, 5 Upper Saint Martin's Lane, London WC2H 9EA

1 3 5 7 9 10 8 6 4 2

British Library Cataloguing-in-Publication Data
A catalogue record for this book is available from the British Library

ISBN 0 297 84695 7

Printed in Great Britain by
Clays Ltd, St Ives plc

www.orionbooks.co.uk

CONTENTS

LIST OF ILLUSTRATIONS

1. The Regular Army deploys to France.
2. 2nd/9th Londons (Queen Victoria's Rifles) on a lunch break, late 1914.
3. A Kitchener recruit undergoing a medical inspection.
4. The 6th (Service) Battalion the Lincolnshire Regiment parades in early September 1914.
5. Members of the University and Public Schools Brigade (18th–21st Royal Fusiliers) build their own hutted camp at Epsom, Surrey, October 1914.
6. The 8th Welsh Regiment carrying out miniature range practice at Bournemouth, December 1914 – January 1915.
7. The 16th Cheshires practise trench digging.
8. Palestinian volunteers for the 38th and 39th (Jewish) Battalions of the Royal Fusiliers, Jerusalem, summer 1918.
9. 2nd/1st Kent Cyclists Battalion TF ground their mounts while on training, 1915.
10. The Royal Scots Greys in France, May 1918.
11. Junior officers undergoing bayonet fighting instruction, Third Army School, Flixécourt, October 1916.
12. Frenchwomen producing camouflage netting for concealing roads from the air, September 1918.

13. Members of the staff of HQ XIV Corps at Meaulte, south of Albert, May 1917.

14. Cadets at the Royal Military College Sandhurst, November 1917.

15. Members of No. 1 Cadet School RGA at Trowbridge, Wiltshire, carry out gun drills on an 8-inch howitzer, November 1917.

16. Men of an Infantry Labour battalion on road repairs, Hamel, 1916.

17. South African Native Labour Corps, France, February 1917.

18. Bringing back salvaged rifles, La Boisselle, Somme, July 1916.

19. Members of the Calais Convoy of the First Aid Nursing Yeomanry (FANY) in early 1918.

20. QMAAC Camp No. 4, Rouen, probably autumn 1918.

21. 9th (Scottish) Division walking wounded at a battalion aid post, Meteren, 18 August 1918.

22. A ward in No. 32 Stationary Hospital, Wimereux, also known as the Australian Voluntary Hospital.

23. Francis Derwent Wood, one of the leading sculptors of his day, measuring a badly disfigured soldier for a face mask.

24. A returning supply column passes graves at Bernafay Wood on the Somme, September 1916.

25. Wounded horses and mules arriving at No. 5 Veterinary Hospital, Abbeville, April 1918.

26. Incoming mail being sorted at Dernancourt, near Albert, September 1916.

27. Bread production in the ASC Field Bakery at Calais, March 1917.

28. The arrival of the leave train at Charing Cross, London.

29. A padre takes down the personal details of a wounded German soldier at an Advanced Dressing Station near Carnoy, 30 July 1916.

30. A Church Army canteen at Saint Omer.

31. The Diamonds, 29th Division's concert party.

32. The commander of the 56th Brigade (19th Division) presenting medals to his men.

INTRODUCTION

Much has been written and continues to be written about the British Army in the Great War, encouraged not least by the increasing interest in family history which has sparked curiosity in the background to relatives' service during 1914–18. There tend to be three broad categories of published works. The first concerns operations. Many of the books on these during the past twenty years have sought to add weight to the pioneering efforts by the late John Terraine to counter the 'Lions Led by Donkeys' school that became so popular in the 1960s. The second category is concerned with the life of the soldier, usually with emphasis on the Western Front. Books like John Ellis's *Eye-Deep in Hell*, Denis Winter's *Death's Men* and, most recently, Richard Holmes's *Tommy* have done much to improve our understanding of what conditions were like on the ground. Finally, unit histories continue to be published. Rather than the traditional approach of providing a straightforward account of a battalion's doings, a new school is growing up which is much more concerned over unit character, even going to the extent of creating large databases of individuals who served in it to analyse exactly how its nature, especially socially, changed during the course of the war. It is an approach which is beginning to yield fruit in the form of fresh insights.

What is missing is a study of the mechanisms used to mobilize a small regular army, supported by the part-time Territorial Force, for war and then transform it into the massive military machine that existed by the end of the war and one that was fighting an entirely different type of warfare, at least on the Western Front, to that which it had trained for. True, there have been some preliminary efforts in this direction. The papers contained in *A Nation in Arms*, edited by Ian Beckett and Keith Simpson in the mid 1980s, provide much interesting material on the nature of the Regular and New Armies, as well as the Territorial Force. Peter Simkins's account of the raising of the New Armies, *Kitchener's Army*, is now a standard work. Other valuable contributions include Ian Whitehead's *Doctors in the Great War* and K. W. Mitchinson's *Pioneer Battalions of the Great War*. There is, too, Ian Brown's deeply researched *Logistics on the Western Front*. Yet, many gaps continue to exist and the aim of this book is to attempt to fill at least some of them.

The main theme of the book is manpower. To my mind, irrespective of what happened on the battlefield, the army's greatest struggle during 1914–18 was obtaining and maintaining the necessary strength to meet increasing commitments, few of which had been envisaged prior to the outbreak of war. In particular, an ever-expanding munitions industry in what became a *matériel*-intensive conflict was as voracious in its demands as the army was, and had to be given its fair share. The nature of the war also resulted in a plethora of new specialities, which needed particular types of people and this compounded the army's manpower problems. At base, though, the infantryman was still the most important item and everything else was there to enable him to reach his objective. Much of the juggling with manpower was aimed at trying to maintain the infantry's strength, without prejudicing the needs of the other arms and services. I have treated this in the form of an examination of the four strands that made up the British Army – the Regulars, the Territorials, the Kitchener volunteers and the conscripts. Incorporated in these chapters are little-known dilemmas faced by the authorities, including how to treat those of alien parentage and others who were non-naturalized British, notably the Russian Jews, which itself is worth a full-length book.

One other problem which had to be confronted, and which has received little attention up until now, was military labour. In other theatres, indigenous workers were generally readily available, but on the Western Front the pre-war assumption that the French would provide much of the labour, especially in the field of transportation, was soon proved wrong. In spite of the War Office's constant efforts to provide sufficient, culminating in the formation of the Labour Corps, the hard-pressed infantry continued to find itself employed on working parties at the expense of rest and training. To this end, I have highlighted the history of military labour. A further aspect is the employment of women, whose potential the War Office was slow to tap.

Once a man had been enlisted, he had to be trained. The army's training organization went through several changes during the war and its evolution is often confusing. Again, this is something which has received little detailed coverage and I have sought to explain the changes that took place, especially with regard to the infantry. This is supported by an appendix which explains the wide variety of infantry units that grew up during the war. I have also included chapters on officer selection and training and how the staff was organized and inducted. Likewise, there is the question of home defence, which created new organizations like the Royal Defence Corps and Volunteer Force. Finally, once a man had become a soldier, his motivation had to be maintained. Discipline, good medical care, attention to his welfare, and awards and decorations all helped to achieve this. But none were without their controversies. That concerning those who were executed for military crimes is generally well known and, indeed, continues to this day. I have read much of the literature on this and have tried to give a balanced view. Less known is the army's attitude to active homosexuality or, indeed, the debate on Field Punishment No. 1. In connection with discipline, shell shock inevitably has to be reviewed, especially the difficulties that the Royal Army Medical Corps had in diagnosing it. Welfare, too, had its problems, not least that enthusiastic charity could show military administration and logistics in a poor light to the public at large. Likewise, the policy over awards and decorations came under much fire during the war and has been attacked ever since for the policy of giving what were supposedly combat awards to those who were nowhere near the firing line. I have shown that the problem was not as clear-cut as is popularly made out.

Inevitably, there have had to be omissions to make the book of manageable length. I have referred little to the Dominion forces, who, in any event, are generally well provided for in histories. Logistics and transportation are vast subjects on their own, as are aspects like press and censorship. Indeed, this book is devoted to the 'A' (administration of personnel) side of the army as opposed to the 'G' (operations) and 'Q' (logistics) aspects. In terms of theatres of war, it is very difficult not to concentrate on France and Flanders, since the bulk of the army fought there and developments on the Western Front tended to be taken up by other theatres. I have, however, not forgotten the other fronts. I have also included two further appendices on military acronyms and medical categories, both of which figure frequently in the book.

I originally started my research for this book by looking from the top downwards, but realized after a time that I was obtaining only a partial picture of what happened. I therefore decided that I should look through the other end of the telescope and read the personal accounts of those who served. As I expected, this provided me with a wealth of pointers which I could then use to re-examine the official records, held at the National Archives, Kew. These are, however, not as complete as one might expect. Weeding through the years has left some significant gaps and, in some cases, much lateral thinking has been needed to provide answers to questions.

A book like this cannot be undertaken without considerable external help. I would like to express my warm thanks to the staff of the National Archives, Kew, and to that of the West Hill Library, London Borough of Wandsworth, whose superb reserve collection contains much material on 1914–18. I am also much indebted to my friends and colleagues in the British Commission for Military History and London Branch of the Western Front Association both for providing perceptive comments on draft versions of chapters which I presented to them as papers and for valuable advice. The same goes for the Territorial Force Study Group, whose members have been generous with the fruits of their own researches. I would also like to pay particular tribute to Chris Baker, a former Chairman of the Western Front Association, and his *The Long, Long Trail* website. Not only does it contain a vast range of information on the British Army of 1914–18, but it has a thriving forum, a number of whose members have a remarkable specialist knowledge covering many aspects of the Great War. Rather than list all individuals who have assisted me by name and run the risk of inadvertently omitting some, I have specified people who have given me particular help in the source notes.

The gestation period for this book has been considerably longer than both my publisher and myself had intended and I am deeply appreciative of the patience and forbearance that Ian Drury, Weidenfeld & Nicolson's Publishing Director, has shown me. I would also like to thank Thomas Cussans for his very sympathetic editing. I am most grateful, too, to Penny Gardiner and her team for seeing *Call to Arms* through to publication. Penny's enthusiasm and, indeed, fortitude have my admiration. Finally, I hope that this book will add to our knowledge of the British Army in the Great War and encourage people to probe further, since it is very clear that there is much more to discover.

Charles Messenger
LONDON, OCTOBER 2004

one

THE BRITISH ARMY IN 1914

In 1914 the British Army had only recently undergone wide-ranging reforms brought about from the lessons learnt from the war in South Africa at the turn of the new century. While it was still oriented towards defence of Empire, by 1910 it was committed to the continent of Europe through an agreement with France that, in event of war with Germany, it would provide an expeditionary force to fight alongside the French. This provided an additional spur to modernization.

The reforms began with the establishment of the Committee of Imperial Defence (CID) at the end of 1902. Its purpose was to produce a coherent strategy for the defence of Britain and the Empire. Following hot on the heels of this was the setting up of a Royal Commission to examine the recent war in South Africa and draw lessons from it. The Elgin Committee, as the commission was named, made numerous recommendations, two of the most significant being the need to create a proper General Staff and for the army to be structured in such a way that it could be rapidly expanded in time of war, drawing on the resources of the Empire. During the early months of 1904 another committee, chaired by Lord Esher, developed the recommendation concerning the General Staff. It concluded that the post of commander-in-chief should be abolished and replaced by a chief of staff, who would act as the principal adviser to the Secretary of State for War. Simultaneously, it created an Army Council, which was chaired by the Secretary of State and included four military members – Chief of Staff, Adjutant General, Quartermaster General and Master General of the Ordnance. Furthermore, the Esher Committee recommended that a General Staff be created largely from graduates of the Staff College at Camberley. It was to devote itself to the solving of military problems and planning for war. To this end, it was to be separated from the administrative staff. Officers were to be appointed for tours of four years and this would qualify them for accelerated promotion. General Staff officers would not form a separate corps, but they would be given a distinctive uniform.

The Esher Committee recommendations were not put into immediate affect. Partly, this was because the committee itself antagonized senior officers, but also because the Conservative government of the day, preoccupied by other matters, lacked the necessary drive to ensure that the reforms were implemented. It was not until there was a change of government and the appointment of a new dynamic Secretary of State, Lord Haldane, that the wheels began to turn. For a start, following an overhaul of the CID designed to make it more effective, the Chief of Staff became the Chief of the Imperial General Staff (CIGS). Then, on 12 September 1906, a Special Army Order announced the establishment of the General Staff. Its tasks were 'to advise on the strategical distribution of the army, to supervise the education of officers, and the training and preparation of the army for war, to study military schemes, offensive and defensive, to collect and collate military intelligence, to direct the general policy in army matters, and to secure continuity of action in the execution of policy'. General Staff officers would be present in the Directorates of Military Operations, Staff Duties and Military Training at the War Office and in home commands and districts, as well as overseas. Accelerated promotion could be awarded for distinguished service in a staff post, though it was emphasized that this also applied to administrative posts. In fact, this benefited the General Staff as the more able officers opted to join it. They tended to regard logistics as the domain of specialists and this resulted in a gulf developing between the two. On the other hand, the General Staff did not become the elite that its German counterpart was. It was made clear that the exercise of command was not part of its brief, which implied that commanders did not necessarily need to have attended Camberley.

Director of Transport
sea and land, all forms of transp
Corps (ASC)

* The building is today known as the Old War Offi

Furthermore, many staff posts were not held by Staff College graduates, though in theory they should have been.[1]

In January 1907 the War Office staffs moved into a new building in Whitehall, the first time they had all been under one roof.* The organization within the War Office changed little over the next few years and by 1914 it was organized as three main staff branches: G, covering operations and intelligence (the province of the General Staff); A, covering administration of personnel; and Q, which dealt with *matériel*. The CIGS headed G branch, the Adjutant General A branch, and the Quartermaster General Q branch.

The branches themselves were subdivided as follows:

G branch

Director of Military Operations (DMO) – strategic and operational planning, intelligence

Director of Staff Duties (DSD) – war establishments, staff training and selection, training manuals, the Army Signal Service and formulation of principles governing the employment of aircraft

Director of Military Training (DMT) – home defence and training

A branch

Adjutant General's Branch (AG) – peace establishments, manning and recruiting, terms of service, war medals

Director of Personal Services (DPS) – discipline, ceremonial, education of non-commissioned ranks

Director of Mobilization (DM) – mobilization for war

Director-General, Army Medical Services (DGAMS) – medicine and health, selection and training of medical personnel including nurses

Q Branch

Director of Supplies and Quartering (DSQ) – accommodation, supply of food, fuel and light

~~sport~~ and Movements (DTM) – movement of units by

~~rt~~, administration of Army Service

of the Ministry of Defence.

Director of Remounts (DR) – supply of horses

Director-General, Army Veterinary Services (DGAVS) – animal health. Manned by Army Veterinary Corps (AVC)

Director of Equipment and Ordnance Stores (DEOS) – general stores, and supply of machine guns, small arms, and clothing. Administration of Army Ordnance Department (AOD)

There were three other branches of the War Office which fell outside the main G, A and Q categories. The Military Secretary's (MS) branch came directly under the Secretary of State and handled officers' promotions, decorations and awards. The department of the Master General of the Ordnance (MGO) ranked alongside those of the Adjutant General and Quartermaster General, with the MGO having a seat on the Army Council. His empire was varied and consisted of the following:

Director of Artillery (DofA) – provision of artillery weapons and stores, machine guns, ammunition (including explosives) and weapons trials, as well as administration of the ordnance factories. Manned almost entirely by the Royal Artillery.

Director of Fortifications and Works (DFW) – design and construction of fortifications, gun emplacements, barracks (less those allocated to DBC), and rifle ranges, electrical and mechanical engineering, provision of engineer stores, training of railway transport personnel. Manned by the Royal Engineers.

Director of Barrack Construction (DBC) – design and construction of barracks as ordered by the Army Council. Wholly civilian manned.

Director-General of Military Aeronautics (DGMA) – all aspects of military aviation.

When the ranks of the departmental heads are examined, it becomes clear that there was an obvious pecking order. G branch, with the CIGS, a field marshal, at its head, took precedence, while the Adjutant General was three-star appointment. The QMG was a major general. All on the Army Council, the army's go but at the outbreak of war was a mere substantive colonel, with the local rank of major general. Of the remainder, who were not Army Council members, the Military Secretary was a three-star appointment, while the DGMA was a colonel temporary brigadier general.

Two other senior posts in the 1914 army need mention at this point. These were the two inspectors general, who were not part of the War Office. In August 1914 Sir John French was Inspector General of the Home Forces, having swapped the post of CIGS with Sir Charles Douglas after the Curragh Mutiny. He had his headquarters at Horse Guards and had five subordinate inspectors under him, covering Cavalry, Royal Horse and Royal Field Artillery, Royal Garrison Artillery, Royal Engineers and the Infantry. Sir John's opposite number was Sir Ian Hamilton, who was Inspector General of the Overseas Forces. From his headquarters in Malta, he covered not only British garrisons (excluding India) but also the Dominion Forces. Their role, as laid down for the Inspector General Home Forces in *King's Regulations*, was:

a) By means of inspection ascertain whether the training, instruction, and preparation of the army for war, as laid down by regulations, are fully carried out in the various commands, and whether a uniform standard of efficiency is attained.

b) Advise as to regulations bearing on (a).

c) By inspection, either personally or through his subordinates, keep the Army Council informed of the state of the army at home as regards both personnel and equipment.

French and Hamilton reported directly to the CIGS on the state of the land forces. He, in turn, implemented their recommendations through the War Office or, in the case of Dominion forces, via the Committee for Imperial Defence (CID).

The army at home was organized in territorial commands: Aldershot (Sir Douglas Haig); Eastern (Sir James Grierson); Irish (Sir Arthur Paget); Northern (Sir Herbert Plumer); Scottish (Sir John Ewart); Southern (Sir Horace Smith-Dorrien); Western (Sir Henry Mackinnon); and London District (Sir Francis Lloyd), which equated to a command because it controlled the Household Division. Each command was divided into a number of administrative districts. The original theory, under a plan drawn up in 1901 by the then Secretary of State, St John Brodrick, was that each existing command would represent an army corps. Three – Aldershot, Southern Command and Ireland – would be all-Regular and would form an expeditionary force in time of war. Of the remainder, IV Corps (Eastern) would be half Regular, while V (Northern) and VI (Scottish) would consist largely of auxiliary forces and would be responsible for home defence. A Special Army Order of 4 March 1902 put this scheme into effect, with each corps consisting of three divisions, each of two brigades. But this needed a significant increase in manpower. The existing length of engagement was seven years' service with the Colours, followed by five on the Reserve. In the belief that a shorter term of active service would prove more attractive to recruits, a three-year engagement with the Colours, with nine on the Reserve, was introduced. This did not improve recruiting. Worse, once the soldier's six months' recruit training and his voyage out had been taken into account, units stationed abroad had little benefit of his service before it was time to send him home for discharge. It also meant that they were in a constant state of upheaval. Consequently, in November 1904 the engagement was set at nine years with the Colours and three on the Reserve, only to revert to seven and five just two years later.* At the same time, the army corps were renamed commands and it was decided that the Regular Army at home would consist of six infantry divisions, with only Aldershot Command, which had two divisions, providing any semblance of a corps in peacetime. But throughout the years leading up to 1914 there was confusion as to what an army corps was. Indeed, it was variously referred to as 'corps', 'army corps', and 'army'. As for the headquarters of the Expeditionary Force, this was called both 'GHQ' and 'Army HQ'.[2]

The army's active strength on 1 August 1914 was 247,798 all ranks. A significant proportion (just over 46 per cent) was serving overseas, however, and was not immediately available to form the Continental Expeditionary Force. Excluding the nine battalions of Foot Guards, which were tradi-

---

* There were variations among the arms in the length of engagement with the Colours. While for Cavalry, Foot Guards and Line Infantry it was seven years, RHA, RFA and RE recruits did six years and RGA eight. Services such as the ASC and RAMC were also on a seven-year term.

tionally based at home, half of the 148 Regular infantry battalions were abroad, as were twelve out of the thirty-one cavalry regiments. They were deployed as follows:

	Cavalry	Infantry
India	9	51
South Africa	2	4
Egypt/Sudan	1	5
Malta		5
Gibraltar		2
China		2
Hong Kong		1
Aden		1
Bermuda		1
Mauritius		1
Singapore		1

The units overseas were maintained up to strength at the expense of those at home under a system designed by Lord Cardwell in the early 1880s. Each two-battalion infantry regiment always had one battalion abroad, which the other kept supplied with drafts. It meant that the home battalion was always well below its establishment for war and relied heavily on reservists to bring it up to strength in time of war. Indeed, a survey carried out among the home commands in spring 1913 revealed that the six Regular divisions were on average 60 per cent below their war establishments in infantry and 55 per cent in artillery.[3] This shortfall had to be made good by reservists. In addition, the Regular Army faced a crisis in 1914 in that it was about to lose two batches of men at once to the Reserve – those who had enlisted on the nine-year engagement during 1904–5 and those who had joined during 1906–7 on the seven-year term.[4]

There were two main types of reserve in 1914, the Army Reserve and the Special Reserve. The Army Reserve was just over its establishment of 145,000 strong and consisted of Sections A, B and D.* Section A had a ceiling of 6,000 men and was likely to be called up during a partial mobilization. Men could opt for Section A during their first year on the Reserve and extend their time in it for a further year. Preference was given to soldiers

* There appears to be no discernable reason why there was not a Section C.

who had served abroad, were of good character and were second-class shots at least. They were entitled to one shilling per day, just one penny under the basic pay of a private soldier serving with the Colours, and were paid monthly. Section B covered all those who were doing their five years on the Reserve but were not in Section A. Section D men were those who had signed on for an additional four years on the Reserve. They could not be called up until the whole of Sections A and B had been mobilized. Both Sections B and D reservists received sixpence per day, paid quarterly.

The Regular Army could also draw on the Special Reserve, which had been created out of the old Militia and was another of Lord Haldane's reforms. The Militia itself was an ancient body which, by the latter half of the nineteenth century, provided the army with a partially trained Reserve. Men served for six years, carrying out a month's training every year at their nearest regimental depot. They could also join the Militia Reserve, which also supported the Regular Army. The officers of the Militia tended to be on the old side, however, and the men either very young or old. This was not satisfactory and Haldane replaced it with the Special Reserve, which was organized in formed units. Thus, the third battalions of most two-battalion Regular infantry regiments became the Reserve battalion, while, with one exception, four-battalion regiments had their fifth battalions designated Reserve battalions and sixth battalions Extra Reserve. Some two-battalion regiments also had Extra Reserve battalions, and the Royal Fusiliers had two Reserve (fifth and sixth battalions) and one Extra Reserve (seventh) battalions. Three of the Irish regiments also each had three Special Reserve battalions. Each soldier on joining carried out the full six months' recruiting training and did a month's annual training. He was paid at the same rates as his Regular counterpart when in uniform and also received an annual total of £4 in bounties. The Militia and Militia Reserve were invited to join the Special Reserve and over 80 per cent did so. By 1913, the Militia Reserve stood at a mere 636 officers and sixty-four men and it was allowed to die out naturally. The Militia itself did remain in existence in the Channel Islands, which provided five infantry battalions, together with coastal artillery and engineers.

The Special Reserve was also broken down into two sections, with Section A having a limit of 4,000 men who were prepared to serve anywhere in the world, but for a maximum of twelve months, unless any portion of the Special Reserve was put on permanent service. Section A men had to have attended at least two annual camps and were required to give three months' notice of their intention to resign. They were paid a retainer of sixpence per day. Section B encompassed the remaining members of the Special Reserve, but this was broken down into three sub-sections. Sub-category (a) covered the bulk of the Special Reservists, who were on a six-year term. It also included the South Irish Horse, whose members served just four years, the North Irish Horse and the King Edward Horse. Sub-category (b) represented Territorials who agreed to accept the Special Reserve liability, while (c) related to certain specialists – horse transport (HT) and mechanical transport (MT) drivers in the Army Service Corps (ASC) and Royal Flying Corps (RFC). They re-engaged every year up to the age of 50, received no pay unless mobilized, undertook no military training in peacetime and could not transfer to any other branch of the Special Reserve. They did, however, receive an annual bounty. One unique element of Section B (c) was the Wold Waggoners, who were part of the ASC Special Reserve. They were transport drivers from Yorkshire who were used to handling heavy draught horses. Their establishment was some 1,000 men of whom 780 would cross to France in August 1914, joining Nos. 1–6 Reserve Parks and Nos. 1 and 2 Bridging Trains RE. An officer who inspected them shortly after they had arrived in France described them as 'extremely shy in disposition'.[5]

Another source of potential manpower with some military experience was the National Reserve, which came under the umbrella of the Territorial Force even though it was 'supplementary to the army'.* The TF County Associations were tasked with maintaining a register of trained officers and soldiers who were under no further obligation to serve in the Forces of the Crown so that 'the military authorities' could 'keep in touch with men who would be able to render assistance in time of grave national emergency when additional personnel may be required, either for active duties with the home defence forces or for other services.' The National

---

* The National Reserve was formed in 1910, when it was known as the Veteran Reserve, and came under the Territorial Reserve, which also included the Territorial Force Reserve and the Technical Reserve (later section B (c) of the Special Reserve). Under AO 240/11, the Volunteer Reserve was retitled the National Reserve and later that year was made distinct from the TF Reserve. [With thanks to Jock Bruce]

Reserve was open to officers with at least one year's service, ex-naval ratings and Royal Marine other ranks, ex-Royal Naval Reserve and Royal Naval Volunteer Reserve members, ex-soldiers of the Regular Army, former members of the Militia, Imperial Yeomanry and Volunteers, as well as ex-members of the Royal Irish Constabulary and holders of a campaign medal.

The National Reserve was divided into three classes. Originally, Class I contained former officers under the age of 55 and other ranks under 45 who were physically fit enough to join a combatant unit in the field, while Class II represented officers aged 55 to 60 and other ranks aged 45 to 55 who were capable of garrison duty or administrative work. Those who did not fit these categories were termed 'honorary members' who were retained for 'social and influential purposes' and were placed in Class III. In 1913, however, the age limits were made more restricted. All members of Class I now had to be under the age of 42, while Class II accepted officers, warrant officers and sergeants under the age of 55 and junior ranks under the age of 50 for home defence and garrison duty. Class III was now split into three sub-classes: those qualified by age, but not medically fit for Class I; the same for Class II; and the honorary members who now found themselves in Class III (3). The strength of the National Reserve on 1 October 1913 was some 215,000 officers and men.[6]

The Continental Expeditionary Force was itself organized as three army corps, each of two divisions, and was drawn from home commands as follows:

Cavalry Division – 1st Cavalry Brigade at Aldershot, 2nd at Tidworth, 3rd at the Curragh in Ireland, 4th in Kent, but would only form as a division on mobilization. 5th Cavalry Brigade (HQ York) would act as an independent formation.

Aldershot Command
1st Infantry Division – HQ Aldershot, 1st and 2nd Brigades (Aldershot), 3rd Brigade (Fleet)
2nd Infantry Division – HQ Aldershot, 4th Brigade (London), 5th and 6th Brigades (Aldershot)

Southern Command

3rd Infantry Division – HQ Tidworth, 7th Brigade (Tidworth), 8th Brigade (Devonport), 9th Brigade (Portsmouth)

Eastern Command

4th Infantry Division – HQ Woolwich, 10th Brigade (Shorncliffe), 11th Brigade (Colchester), 12th Brigade (Dover)

Irish Command

5th Infantry Division – HQ Curragh, 13th Brigade (Dublin), 14th Brigade (Curragh), 15th Brigade (Northern Ireland)
6th Infantry Division – HQ Cork, 16th and 17th Brigades (Cork), 18th Brigade (Lichfield)

This gives a very clear indication as to the importance of the various commands. Aldershot was the 'jewel in the crown', providing two divisions and, indeed, the corps headquarters, under Douglas Haig, to control them. Irish Command was the next in importance, providing almost two infantry divisions and a cavalry brigade. However, in 1914 Sir Arthur Paget was aged 63 and considered too old for a field command. Southern and Eastern Commands were next in importance, although it was Sir James Grierson, rather than Sir Horace Smith-Dorrien, who would command II Corps in the Expeditionary Force, while Sir William Pulteney, GOC 6th Division, would be elevated to command III Corps. The other commands – Northern, Western, and Scottish – were largely made up of Territorial Force units.

Each infantry division consisted of three brigades, each of four battalions, three field artillery brigades, each of three batteries with six 18-pounder guns, a howitzer brigade with eighteen 4.5-inch howitzers and a heavy battery with four 60-pounders. In addition, the division had two field companies RE, a Signal company, a divisional ammunition column (DAC) based on an ASC mechanical transport company, a divisional train, which consisted of four ASC horse transport companies, and three field ambulances. The division also had its own integral reconnaissance element. This consisted of a squadron of cavalry and a cyclist company, the latter having been formed in May 1914 from infantrymen within the division.[7] There was no formed cavalry division prior to the outbreak of war and a cavalry brigade consisted of three regiments supported by a Royal Horse Artillery (RHA) battery armed with the 13-pounder gun. On mobilization, the cavalry division would be formed and would receive a field squadron RE, a signal section, which was manned by cavalrymen, rather than sappers, and a cavalry field ambulance for each brigade, as well as three ASC companies.

A word should also be said about the training of the army at home. This was organized as an annual cycle, which was split into two phases. The first – individual training – was to 'prepare the individual officer, non-commissioned officer or soldier for the duties he will carry out in war'. It usually lasted from mid October until the end of February and it was during this time that most annual leave was taken. Collective training began at squadron/battery/company level and progressed through battalion, brigade and divisional levels, culminating in army manoeuvres, which usually took place once the harvest had been gathered in so as to minimize damage to the countryside.[8] Underlying all training was the morale factor. *Infantry Training 1914* laid much stress on this:

> The soldier should be instructed in the deeds which made the British Army and his regiment famous … The privilege which he inherits as a citizen of a great Empire should be explained to him, and he should be taught to appreciate the honour which is his, as a soldier, of serving his King and country.

While home defence was considered mainly the responsibility of the Territorial Force, the Regular Army also made a contribution, especially in port security. Each home command, apart from Aldershot, was responsible for coastal defence within its sector and sub-commands were established specifically for this purpose. Thus, Southern Command had Southern Coast, responsible for the Defended Ports of Portsmouth and Portland, and South-Western Coast, responsible for those of Plymouth and Falmouth. The defence of the ports themselves was shared by the coastal artillery branch of the Royal Garrison Artillery (RGA) and the Royal Engineers (RE). The former was organized in companies, which manned batteries of coastal artillery, comprising elderly 6-inch howitzers with a range of little over 5,000 yards. They were augmented by TF companies of the RGA. The RE provided Fortress Companies, both Regular and Territorial, which were responsible for the maintenance of forts, in which many of the batteries were positioned and the construction of gun emplacements. There were also a number of Electric Light Companies RE (TF), which primarily manned searchlights. A similar organization covered ports around the Empire.

The Territorial Force itself came into being on 1 April 1908. This was another Haldane creation and replaced the old Volunteers,* who had been formed over a hundred years earlier when Britain faced the threat of a French invasion and whom the Norfolk Commission of 1904 had considered incapable of facing Regular troops in the field. Initially, Haldane aimed to use the Territorial Force to reinforce the Regular Army once it had mobilized and completed six months' training. However, from 1907 onwards he and subsequent war ministers placed increasing emphasis on home defence, although the CID concluded that the threat on Britain itself was more likely to take the shape of a major hostile raid than a full-blown invasion. Territorial soldiers enlisted for four years at a time and, provided they attended a fixed number of drills and annual camp, they were awarded an annual bounty. They were organized as fourteen infantry divisions, including supporting arms, and fourteen mounted brigades made up of Yeomanry. In August 1914 these were distributed as follows:

Southern Command: 1st and 2nd South Midland and 1st and 2nd South-Western Mounted Brigades; South Midland and Wessex Divisions

Eastern Command: Eastern and South-Eastern Mounted Brigades; East Anglian and Home Counties Divisions

Northern Command: Yorkshire, Notts and Derby, and North Midland Mounted Brigades; Northumbrian, West Riding and North Midland Divisions

Scottish Command: Highland and Lowland Mounted Brigades; Highland and Lowland Divisions

---

* One Volunteer unit did survive Haldane's reforms. This was the 1st Isle of Man Volunteers, which became the 7th Volunteer Battalion (Isle of Man) the King's Liverpool Regiment. On the outbreak of war it was attached to the West Lancashire Division TF. In 1915 it formed a service company, which was transferred to the 3rd Cheshires before serving with the 2nd Cheshires in Salonika. A second service company was formed to replace this, but was soon broken up.

Western Command: Welsh Border and South Wales Mounted Brigades; East Lancashire, West Lancashire and Welsh Divisions

London District: London Mounted Brigade; 1st and 2nd London Divisions

In addition, the Territorial Force possessed a number of Cyclist battalions for patrolling the coast.

Aldershot Command contained no Territorial troops and neither did Irish Command, since, for political reasons, the Territorial Force (TF) did not operate in Ireland. Territorial divisions and mounted brigades were organized in a similar way to their Regular counterparts. Much of the administration was carried out by the TF County Associations, while the Director-General of the Territorial Force (DGTF) at the War Office, Lieutenant General Edward Bethune, came under the Department of the Civil Member of the Army Council. This served to create a gulf between the TF and the Regular Army, although TF units did have Regular adjutants and NCO instructors and some commanding officers had seen service as Regulars.

On paper, the Territorial Force appeared formidable, but the truth was that by the outbreak of war it was significantly under establishment in terms of numbers. It should have had a strength of just over 316,000 officers and men, but on 1 August 1914 it was just under 270,000. Furthermore, a substantial number of these men had not attended camp and nearly 25 per cent were aged under 19 (the minimum recruiting age for Territorials was 17, as opposed to 18 for Regulars), which meant that they could not be sent overseas. In any event, although they were invited to take what was called the Imperial Service Obligation, the Territorials were not legally bound to serve abroad.[9] As it was, a little more than 7 per cent had volunteered to do so, with only five units – Northumberland Yeomanry, Dorset Fortress Company RE, 6th East Surreys and 7th and 8th Middlesex – having sufficient volunteers to enable them to be deployed overseas immediately on the declaration of war.[10] There was, too, a TF Reserve, which was pegged at one-third of the active establishment. It was not a success and by July 1914 had an overall strength of a little over 2,000 men.[11]

The Territorial Force also suffered from outdated equipment. The Regular Army had recently undergone an almost complete overhaul. Apart from receiving a new range of artillery weapons, the infantryman had a new rifle, the Short Magazine Lee-Enfield (SMLE) Mk III and web (as opposed to leather) equipment. Each infantry battalion also had two Maxim machine guns which were in the process of being replaced by the Vickers. The Territorial Force, on the other hand, had to make do with obsolete 15-pounder, 4.7-inch and 5-inch guns and leather equipment; it was also largely reliant on commandeering transport vehicles from civilian sources. The TF also had the old Long Lee-Enfield, which used different ammunition from the SMLE. The Territorial infantry battalions retained the old eight-company organization, while the Regulars had recently adopted the new four-company establishment, although the Reserve and Extra Reserve battalions did not actually do so until 5 August 1914, the day after the declaration of war against Germany. In terms of training, the TF could also not match the Regular Army. In his first year the Territorial was expected to attend forty drills, together with two weeks' annual camp. Thereafter he needed only ten drills and annual camp to gain his bounty.

At the end of 1909, a committee was set up to consider the additional duties and responsibilities which the War Office would have to bear in the event of general war. The result was the compilation of a War Book, which detailed the steps to be taken to mobilize the army, the additional duties of each branch and the extra staff required. The first edition was published in 1912; thereafter it was published annually.

There were three phases to mobilization: the precautionary stage; general mobilization; and the declaration of war. Partial mobilization was also covered. The precautionary stage catered primarily for the threat of war with another maritime power and had two objectives. These were to safeguard naval bases in Britain and to protect vulnerable points in the country. The latter were specified as 'magazines, stores and factories of war material', as well as communications, especially 'wireless telegraph stations' and the railways, particularly railway bridges. The majority of those involved in this task would be Regular troops, but a few Territorial members, especially in Scotland, where Regular units were thin on the ground, were also employed. These were designated Special Service Sections, which could be called out under direction of the Secretary of State for a period not exceeding one month, even though the TF as a whole had not been embodied. They were mainly deployed in ten-man sections at key signalling stations and cable landing points. Even smaller detachments were sent to guard oil-company premises, which provided Admiralty fuel reserves. In one case, a complete company was involved. This was the Ardeer Company TF, which was affiliated to the 4th Royal Scots Fusiliers. It was drawn from the workforce of the Nobel explosives factory at Ardeer on the Clyde coast and in time of war guarded its own workplace.[12]

Once the decision to institute the precautionary stage had been made by the Cabinet, it was passed to the Army Council by the Secretary for War, and then to the War Office branches concerned. A prepared cipher telegram would then be sent to home commands ordering them to deploy garrisons to ports and vulnerable points in accordance with previously issued instructions. Protection of ports was the role of the Reserve and Extra Reserve battalions. Close coordination with the police and railway companies was laid down for the guarding of vulnerable points. Likewise, the General Post Office had to keep some offices open day and night for the transmission of telegrams and to make arrangements for army postal service reservists in its employ to be readily available if and when mobilization was declared.

General mobilization was defined as 'the possibility, imminence or declaration of war with a first-class European Power which would entail the complete mobilization of the whole of the Naval and Military Forces of the Crown'. It could not, however, take place until the King had approved it and the Royal Proclamation was issued. This itself contained seven instruments: 1) a proclamation calling out the General Reserve and embodying the Territorial Force; 2) another to ensure continuance of service of all soldiers serving with the Colours; 3) and 4) a further one, together with an Order in Council, recalling the Jersey Militia Reserve to active service; 5) an Order in Council empowering the government to take over the railways; 6) an order by the King empowering the requisitioning of animals, vehicles, vessels (for inland waterway transport) and aircraft; and 7) an order by the King authorizing requisitions of civilian property for the billeting of troops.

The first action by the War Office was to issue the 'mobilization ordered' telegrams, which were sent to post offices where mobilization posters were to be prominently displayed. These posters were put up in

30

other public places under the direction of chief constables and mobilization notices were also published in the newspapers. Individual mobilization telegrams to Regular reservists would be distributed by the post offices, which were to stay open for 24 hours a day. Each reservist already had documentation instructing him where to report, with a railway warrant attached. Reservists were also issued with special money orders to the value of three shillings as advance pay, which could be cashed at post offices. Officers and men on leave were to report back to their units on seeing the mobilization notice. Those on leave from garrisons abroad were to report in writing to the War Office (officers) and their Records Offices (the remainder). In the meantime, all commands were ordered, also by telegram, to mobilize. The Declaration of War would be similarly transmitted both within the home commands and throughout the garrisons overseas. All coastal defences were placed on a war footing and additional defence works would begin to be constructed with the cooperation of the police.[13]

The general principle was that mobilization schemes were based on stations and barracks and not on units. Thus, when a cavalry regiment or infantry battalion changed stations it handed its mobilization scheme and stores over to the incoming unit. As far as the reservists themselves were concerned, the rule was that they first reported to their regimental depots, except in the case of Royal Engineers and Royal Army Medical Corps (RAMC) personnel, whose units in Britain seldom moved. The depots processed the reservists before despatching them to their units. That of the Leinsters was at Birr (today situated in County Offaly close to the Tipperary border), where the officer commanding had drawn up detailed instructions on how reservists were to be processed. NCOs were to be detailed to meet the trains arriving at the town's railway station and would then take the reservists to the barracks, where they would be directed to the gymnasium. Here they would be handed medical inspection cards and organized into twelve-man sections, each under an NCO, and allocated to a company. The next port of call was the hospital, where each man was medically examined, those found to be unfit for service being immediately discharged. The temporarily unfit would be placed on the Reserve, while those judged permanently unfit for service abroad would either be placed on the Reserve or retained for duty at home.

Any man rejected for immediate service would be provided with a railway warrant to get him home.

The remainder were then to be taken to the mobilization stores to be issued with their kit, including two sets of service dress and a greatcoat. The company commanders were exhorted to take the greatest possible care when it came to the fitting of boots. Finally, the reservists received their rifles, together with a strip of flannelette for cleaning them. The reservists were then taken to the company barrack room, where their kit was checked and signed for. (They had to make their own arrangements for disposing of their civilian clothes, it being at their own risk if they decided to leave them in the depot stores.) They would be fed and issued with two blankets each for the night. On Day 2 of mobilization the first special train would leave for the 2nd Battalion, which was based at Cork as part of the 6th Division. The latter would provide an officer and five NCOs to conduct the men and the depot itself also had to detail a captain and two subalterns for the same purpose. The same process of receiving reservists would continue on this day and another special train would leave Birr on Day 3.[14]

The infantry depots also had to mobilize their Reserve and Extra Reserve battalions. This, however, was not to take place until the fourth day of mobilization to enable them to first process the bulk of the Regular reservists. Special Reservists were sent individual telegrams in green envelopes marked 'Mobilization'. The Reserve and Extra Reserve battalions deployed to their war stations, which were largely ports, on the fifth day of mobilization. Their ranks would be swelled by Regular reservists who had been temporarily found unfit and serving Regular soldiers aged under 19, since they were not permitted to serve abroad.[15]

Apart from the calling up of reservists to bring units up to their war establishment, the various headquarters of the Expeditionary Force, renamed the British Expeditionary Force (BEF) following its deployment, also had to be expanded. HQ BEF itself had to be formed from scratch. Prior to the outbreak of war, its commander-in-chief had not been nominated – although it was generally understood that it would be Sir John French – and neither had his staff. The bulk was to be provided by the War Office, their places being filled by members of the Reserve of Officers.

The headquarters would actually form at the Polygon Hotel, Southampton.[16] While HQ I Corps was drawn mainly from the existing staff of Aldershot Command, II and III Corps had to create their staffs from scratch. In peacetime, an infantry division HQ had merely a GSO1 and a Deputy Assistant Adjutant and Quartermaster General (DAA&QMG). This was increased on mobilization by five additional staff officers, which were drawn from other posts in the army. Thus, 1st Infantry Division could expect a GSO2 from the Staff College, a GSO3 from the Staff Duties (SD) Branch in the War Office, an AA&QMG also from the War Office, and Deputy Assistant Quartermaster General (DAQMG) who was nominated by DADST Aldershot Command. Likewise, in peacetime brigades had only a brigade major to assist the commander. To bear the administrative staff burden, a staff captain was appointed, nominated by the brigade commander himself from within the units under his command.[17]

It was now that the deployment of the BEF to the Continent began. The underlying principle was to establish the lines of communication on the Continent before sending across the fighting troops. These would constitute two waves – the cavalry division and four mainland infantry divisions in the first, followed by the divisions based in Ireland. Crucial to the movement of the BEF from its peacetime stations were the railways, which, on the declaration of war, came under government control under the 1871 Regulation of the Forces Act. In 1912 the Railway Executive Committee was set up and drew up plans for bringing the railway companies under state control in the event of war, with the aim of 'ensuring that the railways, locomotives, rolling stock and staff shall be used as one complete unit in the best interests of the State for the movement of troops, stores and food supplies.'[18] The committee also drew up detailed timetables for the movement of troops on mobilization. In addition, there was the Engineer and Railway Staff Corps RE, which had been established in 1865. Sir Sam Fay, General Manager of the Great Central Railway, was a member and described it as

> a curious combination of prominent engineers and railway officials. It possessed a colonel and a number of lieutenant colonels and majors, but no rank and file. It was established for the purpose of rendering expert

assistance in time of war, and singularly enough was the only military or semi-military force not mobilized as such during the Great War. It exercised one function, that of having dinner, with members of the War Office staff as guests, once a year.[19]

In practice, the members of the Engineer and Railway Staff Corps were consulted individually and some sat on the Railway War Council, whose president was the Director of Movements and Quartering.

The first elements of the BEF to cross to the Continent were the advance parties of two ASC supply depots, each consisting of one officer and thirteen other ranks. Thanks to the Railway Executive Committee's timetables, they knew that they would catch the 8.23 a.m. train from Aldershot on Day 1, arrive at the port of Newhaven at 2.10 p.m., and then be embarked. The first 'teeth arm' units to move were five infantry battalions earmarked to secure the lines of communication. They would move on Day 2, with the HQs of the Cavalry Division and 1st and 2nd Infantry Divisions on Day 3. The last elements of the first wave were various stationary hospitals, which would move on Day 19.[20] To gain some idea of the scale of effort required, eighty trains were needed to transport one infantry division to its port of embarkation.

Similar railway transport arrangements were made for the collection of remounts, with unit grooms earmarked to collect them from all over the country prior to deployment across the Channel. Thus, on the morning of Day 1 of the deployment, additional horses for 108 Heavy Battery RGA would travel, escorted by three soldiers, from Farnham to Bournemouth Central and thence to Eastleigh, where they would change trains and travel onwards to their port of destination with 1st Royal Scots Fusiliers.[21] The scheme for obtaining remounts had been overhauled by General John Cowans, the Quartermaster General, during 1912–13. He created a voluntary Army Horse Reserve (AHR), whereby owners registered their horses with the Remount Department. In return for agreeing to them being requisitioned should any portion of the Army Reserve be called up, they would be paid an annual subsidy of £4 for each artillery horse and ten shillings for others. Furthermore, he arranged for military wagons to be modified so that, instead of being drawn by four light horses, two draught horses would be used, thus reducing, to a degree, the initial demand for extra horses.[22] Even so, 14,000 additional animals were needed immediately on mobilization. Likewise, the army required 900 motor vehicles of various types, but at the outbreak of war the ASC, which was responsible for them, possessed only 507, thirty-five of which were abroad. The remainder had to be requisitioned in the same way as the horses.[23]

The planners recognized that crucial to the speedy deployment of the BEF to the Continent was the smooth transfer of units, with their equipment, from their troop trains to the ships that were to take them across the Channel. Seven ports of embarkation had been earmarked – Southampton, Newhaven, Avonmouth, Liverpool, Belfast, Dublin, and Queenstown. Southampton was the main port, with motor transport and fuel being despatched from Avonmouth, supplies from Newhaven and further motor transport, together with frozen meat, from Liverpool. Embarkation at each port was to be controlled by an Embarkation Staff Officer, nominated by the War Office, with a number of assistants. These appointments were to be filled by Staff College students, a clear indication of just how vital this operation was considered. Southampton, the main port of embarkation and where the BEF HQ would form, was allocated no less than four embarkation staff officers and nineteen assistants.[24]

The BEF was given three French ports for disembarkation – Boulogne, Le Havre and Rouen. These would also act as bases, with Le Havre as No. 1 Base, Rouen No. 2 and Boulogne No. 3. From there, the troops would be taken by train to their concentration areas. The railway system, however, would remain under French control and there was a stark difference in the two philosophies for running a military railway system. The British believed in running medium-sized troop trains at speed, while the French ran very long trains at slow speed. This meant that a French troop train could lift one battalion but it took two British trains to do the same. Since the mobilization plans could not guarantee to put the two halves of a battalion on the same ship, it was decided that, on landing in France, units would remain in their port of disembarkation for some twenty-four or forty-eight hours to allow them time to come together again prior to being moved to the BEF's concentration area. To this end, each base had what was called a Large Rest Camp to accommodate the units while they were waiting.[25] All requests for trains were to be addressed to the French military and not the civilian railway authorities. It was laid down that only the three base commanders, a member of the Inspector General of Communications (IGC) staff at the advanced base and the AQMG at GHQ within the concentration area could submit requests. Under these conditions, it was accepted that the Director of Railway Transport (DRT) did not have a worthwhile role to play and so he was to remain in Britain for the time being. Instead, an Assistant Director (ADRT) was to be deployed, with the tasks of administering the railway organization, including the one railway company RE which was to be sent, and providing technical advice to the IGC, liaising with the General Staff at GHQ and generally becoming familiar with the French railway system. The mobilization instructions made it clear that the ADRT was not to interfere with the railway arrangements and was to keep strictly to his brief. To assist him, the ADRT was provided with six Deputy Assistant Directors (DADRT), three of them Staff College students. One would remain at Southampton, one would go to each of the three disembarkation ports, one to the advanced base, which was to be Amiens, and one to the concentration area. None, however, would be directly under his command. In addition, twenty-four Railway Transport Officers (RTO) would deploy to the concentration area – two each to the detraining stations which the BEF expected to use. They would liaise with the local French military authorities and assist with the billeting of the arriving troops. The majority of the RTOs were drawn from the Reserve of Officers, but there were also nine Staff College students detailed.[26]

Once the BEF had deployed to France, its *modus operandi* was governed by *Field Service Regulations 1914*, which came in two parts. Part I covered all operational aspects, while Part II included organizations and administration. An abbreviated version was contained in the *Field Service Pocket Book*. The army in the field was headed by the commander-in-chief and his staff, but his force was divided into two basic parts: the combat element, represented by the army corps, of which he was in direct command; and the lines of communication, which were the responsibility of the Inspector General of Communications. The IGC was the designated commander of all units on the lines of communication (LOC), apart from those charged with their defence, which were under the control of GHQ. The IGC was responsible 'for the disposition of all reinforcements, supplies, and stores on the LOC, and for sending up to within reach of field units all such requirements as are communicated to him from time to time'.[27] It was a concept which had been developed to cater for home-based forces fighting in wars around the Empire, when the lines of communication were inevitably very long and required an overall coordinator to act as a link between the home base and the army in the field. But the IGC operated partially in a vacuum. He was not part of GHQ and hence found it difficult to comprehend the commander-in-chief's future intentions. The result was that it was almost impossible for him to exercise that fundamental principle of logistics, foresight. He could only react to events, as he was soon to find out. Equally problematical was the fact that he had no say on the stores being shipped from Britain. These were province of the QMG at GHQ, who sent his requirements directly to the War Office. The flaws in this system had been pointed out at the annual CIGS's conference held at the Staff College, Camberley, in January 1914. Indeed, one critic of the system called the IGC a mere 'traffic manager'. However, Sir John French, the CIGS at the time, was not convinced that any change in the regulations governing the role of the IGC was needed.[28]

On 28 June 1914, Archduke Franz Ferdinand, heir to the Austro-Hungarian throne, was assassinated with his wife by a Serbian separatist in the Bosnian provincial capital of Sarajevo. This set in train a series of events which made a clash between Europe's two armed camps – the Central Powers and the Triple Entente – increasingly inevitable. Serbia resisted Austria–Hungary's demands for its officials to conduct an investigation of the outrage in Serbia itself. On 28 July, Austria–Hungary declared war on its small neighbour. Berlin then warned Russia not to go to the aid of its fellow Slavs, but two days later, as Austrian artillery bombarded Belgrade, a full Russian mobilization was ordered. This brought France in alongside her ally and on 3 August Germany declared war on her. Only Britain remained on the sidelines, but not for long. Indeed, steps were already being taken to prepare for the imminence of war.

two

THE REGULAR ARMY GOES TO WAR

The first active steps towards mobilization of the army came on the evening of 27 July 1914, when orders for Reserve officers to report to the Expeditionary Force headquarters units were posted. The GOC-in-C Southern Command was also ordered to place guards on vulnerable points in southern England. The following day, mobilization instructions were sent to Reserve officers who had wartime posts as cable censors and with the Railway Transport Home Defence.[1] Late that evening, the 3rd Rifle Brigade, which was carrying out training at Moore Park Camp, Tipperary, received warning that the precautionary period was to come into effect next day. However, the mobilization papers were back in the battalion's barracks in Cork, which necessitated the adjutant having to rush back to get them. These were crucial, since the 3rd Rifle Brigade had to supply guards for various key points. Lieutenant Billy Congreve had to take a detachment to a former fishing village near Queenstown. 'I found that my duties were to guard the tiny landing place, and patrol the coast – my first independent job!'[2] He remained there until relieved on 7 August. James Jack of the 2nd Scottish Rifles (Cameronians) had a similar task, preparing the defences of and guarding Fort Ardhallow on the River Clyde.[3]

On 29 July 1914, the Army Council met and agreed certain additional precautionary measures. All officers and men on leave were to be recalled and all leave stopped. Officers on leave from the garrisons at Malta and Gibraltar were to be sent back to their units, courses at the School of Gunnery at Shoeburyness were to be terminated, and the QMG was to requisition 'boarded out' horses and the services of certain veterinary officers on leave from Egypt. No action was yet to be taken on instructing the railway companies to place guards on railway bridges.[4] The Jersey Militia 'jumped the gun' and mobilized. They had to be stood down again and sent back to their homes.[5] The Special Service Sections TF were also deployed. The 4th East Yorkshires were at their annual camp at Deganwy in North Wales and received a War Office telegram at 6.10 p.m. on the 29th. It read, simply, 'Precautions Act'. The East Yorkshires' response was to parade its Special Service Section of two officers and fifty men, with volunteers taking the places of those not attending the camp. They entrained for the battalion's depot at Hull that night, arriving at just after 6 a.m. the following morning. After sharpening their bayonets and being issued with live ammunition, the section deployed in two detachments, one to guard a coastal battery and the other a signal station.[6] On that same day, 30 July, Sir John French was officially informed by the CIGS that he was to command the Expeditionary Force.

This time of year saw many Territorial units undertaking their annual camps. The War Office asked the government whether the deployments, which were by train, should go ahead. The hope was that they would be cancelled so that the TF could be employed in guarding the railways, which were so vital to the deployment of the Expeditionary Force. The Cabinet decided that the camps should go ahead, since to cancel them would indicate too openly that Britain was preparing for a war the government was still hoping could be averted. The only exception was that the TF coastal batteries in the Orkney Islands were mobilized to provide security for the Grand Fleet's wartime anchorage at Scapa Flow.* The next two days were spent in checking that the General Post Office was ready for its mobilization duties and ordering units who were out on training to return to their peacetime stations prior to mobilization. Some members of the GPO clearly became over-excited: the main post office at Exeter, for example, posted the order to mobilize on 2 August. The GPO had to instruct all its

* In 1915 this role was taken over by the Royal Marines and the Orkney RGA TF was disbanded.

offices to ensure that this was not repeated.[7] On 1 August, the Master General of the Ordnance (MGO) warned Asquith, who was acting as Secretary of State for War: 'Present ammunition in equipments and reserve have been held sufficient to meet the requirements of the EF [Expeditionary Force] in the field for six months, but unless orders are placed I cannot guarantee that there will not be a deficiency when the first six months of the war are over.'[8]

On Sunday 2 August, the QMG issued a memorandum warning that mobilization was dependent on the halting of the rail movement of Territorial Force units to their summer camps. If the order was issued by 2 p.m. on that same day, mobilization could be ordered for the following Tuesday. If the decision was delayed until Monday, mobilization could not begin until Thursday the 6th. Furthermore, he stressed that mobilization and the deployment of Territorial Force units to their home defence stations must be simultaneous, since to do otherwise would delay the deployment of the Expeditionary Force to France by several days. Captain H. O. Mance DSO RE was the Staff Captain Railway Transport in the Directorate of Transport and Movements. He was summoned to a 6 p.m. meeting at 10 Downing Street. Apart from the Prime Minister, the CIGS, Adjutant General and Winston Churchill (then First Lord of the Admiralty) were also among those present. 'I explained that owing to the Territorials being scattered at that moment all over the country it would not be possible to make the following day the "First Day of Mobilization".' The earliest it could be was 4 August. In the light of this, Asquith decided that all Territorial Force movement was to be halted and that mobilization was to begin on 5 August. However, any pretence of maintaining secrecy was destroyed when the intention to mobilize was announced in Parliament on Monday the 3rd. The Downing Street meeting also decided that, because of the need for the railways to return the Territorials to their peacetime locations, the deployment of the Expeditionary Force to France could not begin on the first day of mobilization, as was the pre-war intention, and would not now start until the fifth day.[9]

Later that Sunday evening, the order went out to all units on training – Regular, Special Reserve, and Territorial – to return to their peace stations. Some, however, had already received the order days earlier. The 2nd Royal

Welsh Fusiliers were carrying out musketry and field training at Bovington Camp in Dorset and were ordered late on 30 July to return to their barracks at Portland.[10] Rory Macleod, a subaltern with 80 Battery RFA at the Curragh, wrote to his father on that same day: 'We are ready to mobilize at a moment's notice. All officers on leave have been recalled and no more leave is to be granted. We have been studying the mobilization regulations, so that everything will go off smoothly.'[11] The Eton College Officers Training Corps (OTC) had begun its annual camp on 28 July. It was warned three days later that the camp might be terminated because the Regular officers running it would have to return to their units. Not, however, until early on 3 August was the order received to strike camp.[12] The 3rd Londons were ordered back to London while en route to their annual camp at Swanage. They were told to put their men into a YMCA establishment in Tottenham Court Road. Their adjutant recorded:

> Packing into the YMCA was a nightmare. We have a very large percentage of married men on our strength, and the wives wanted to get to their husbands inside and the latter to their wives outside. No one was allowed out of the building, and semi-hysterical women spent their time shouting and passing unlimited bottles of beer to their menfolk. The work of keeping order and endeavouring to get some method into the chaos of a battalion intended for peace and suddenly faced with war was enough to drive a saint silly.[13]

There were, however, exceptions to the order for an immediate return to barracks. Late on 2 August, two companies of the Royal Scots Special Reserve were ordered to the Clyde shipyards, where six battleships and cruisers were being built. The 7th (Reserve) Battalion the Royal Fusiliers was at annual camp at Felixstowe. Edmund Malone was commanding a company:

> ... though no war had been declared, I found, to my horror, that my company had to go on outpost duty on the seashore only 300 yards from the camp. This seemed a silly proceeding. I had to guard a front of 200 yards along the esplanade. There were no troops on either flank, or in fact anywhere else on the east coast as far as we knew. Beery sentries fully

armed, marched up and down the esplanade and terrified the inhabitants and trippers, who bolted indoors and barred their windows.[14]

Luckily, within a few days the battalion was ordered back to London.

On the wider screen, 3 August saw the German declaration of war against France and the issue of an ultimatum to Belgium to allow German troops unopposed passage through the country. Sir Edward Grey, the Foreign Secretary, warned Parliament, which had been hastily reconvened in spite of it being a Bank Holiday, of the British commitment to provide naval protection for France in the event of war. At the same time, under the 1871 Regulation of the Forces Act, the railways, which were owned by private companies, were brought under government control. The following morning, German troops crossed into Belgium. That afternoon, citing an 1839 treaty guaranteeing Belgian neutrality, the government sent an ultimatum to Berlin demanding that its troops be withdrawn from Belgian territory. If no satisfactory answer was received by midnight 4 August, Britain would consider itself at war with Germany.

In the meantime, the Cabinet now agreed that full mobilization could go ahead, and the King's Proclamation was signed at 11 a.m. on 4 August. However, it was not until 4.40 p.m. that the War Office sent out the mobilization telegrams. H. F. N. Jourdain, commanding the depot of the Connaught Rangers at Galway, received his telegram a little over two hours later. 'I walked at once to the orderly room, unlocked the safe, sent out telegrams throughout the Province of Connaught, and the whole machinery of mobilization began to move at once.'[15] Simultaneously, an Army Order was issued stating that all soldiers serving with the Colours were to be retained for the duration of hostilities. Thus, at a stroke, the problem that the Regular Army had of releasing two batches of men at once to the Reserve was overcome. Finally, at midnight on 4 August, with no German reply to the British ultimatum having been received, the government authorized the despatch of 'at war' telegrams.

Most units had completed much of the groundwork for mobilization during the precautionary period. Indeed, the 2nd Royal Welsh Fusiliers had already, albeit in error, sent out mobilization telegrams. They had also dug out their mobilization stores, but because they had recently returned from India and had not been affiliated to a particular formation they found the equipment not wholly satisfactory – 'the men had dixies instead of field-kitchens, better known as "cookers"; our machine guns were on heavy antique gun-carriages instead of the tripod mounting'. Not until the second half of September, when the battalion spent two weeks in GHQ reserve in the aftermath of the Battle of the Aisne, did it receive its proper equipment.[16] Robert Lucy recalled he and his fellows in the 2nd Royal Irish Rifles selling their review uniforms to 'visiting contractors, together with their civilian clothes.'[17] A further Army Order was issued stating that all men who were posted as deserters as at 5 August would be pardoned if they surrendered voluntarily.[18] Two Royal Welsh Fusiliers took advantage of this. One had deserted from the 1st Battalion to the Channel Islands two years earlier and made his way to the 2nd Battalion at his own expense, while the other had absented himself just before the outbreak of war.[19]

As for the reporting of reservists, the 3rd (Reserve) Battalion King's Own Yorkshire Light Infantry was in camp at Strensall. On 3 August it was ordered to return to its depot at Pontefract. It arrived on the following day, its men being billeted in the town. On 5 August, 790 men of Sections A, B, and D of the Army Reserve reported, together with two officers on the Reserve. A further 374 men reported on the following day, but at the same time 362 Section A and B men were despatched to the 2nd Battalion, which was stationed in Dublin. A draft of 274 followed the latter on 7 August and fifty more over the next few days. By this time the battalion had deployed to its war station at Sutton-on-Hull. The first new recruits, forty-six in total, were received at the regimental depot on 12 August.[20] Major Jourdain noted that by the evening of the fourth day of mobilization he had sent 621 reservists from the Connaught Rangers depot to the 2nd Battalion, which was part of the 2nd Division at Aldershot (the 1st Battalion was in India). Twenty-four hours later his other responsibility, the 3rd (Reserve) Battalion, was also complete and he was able to hand it over to its commanding officer. He then passed his duties to a member of the Reserve of Officers prior to taking on a new task – raising the first Service battalion of his regiment.[21] Lieutenant E. J. Needham with the 1st Northamptons noted: 'On the evening of the third day of mobilization, i.e., the 7th August, the whole Battalion, at full war strength, paraded at 5 p.m., complete with mobilized transport. It was a marvellous sight, and a truly wonderful piece of organization accomplished in three days.'[22] Indeed, the reporting by reservists to their depots took place more quickly than expected and a large number of infantry battalions were, like the 1st Northamptons, at full strength by the end of the third day of mobilization. Nearly 95 per cent of the available Regular reservists rejoined and less than 2,000 were discharged for medical or other reasons. Of the remainder, the majority were abroad and many of them were on their way home to join up. Only those residing in India were posted to units serving out there.[23]

Ben Clouting of the 4th Dragoon Guards at Tidworth wrote: 'Our first instructions were to let everything go rusty. Nothing was to be polished – buttons, cap badges, buckles, stirrup irons – anything that could reflect sunlight and so give notice of our presence in France.' He was also sent with six other troopers and two veterinary officers to a mineral water factory in Birmingham to commandeer heavy draught horses for the artillery and Army Service Corps (ASC). Once the horses had been passed fit and numbered, Clouting and his fellow troopers took them to the railway station and loaded them on board.[24] In Ireland, there was no requisition scheme in force. Consequently, as Lieutenant Trevor Horn, with the 16th Lancers at the Curragh, recalled:

> On mobilization a general order was sent out for horses aged from six up to ten years and between 15.2 and 16.0 hands and the Curragh Race Course was turned into a Remount Depot. The Government price was £40 for a Troop Horse and £60 for an Officer's charger … The horse was led or ridden in and if passed sound the man was given a chit and told to go to the Remount Board. All particulars were taken and a receipt given to the man, who was instructed where to leave the horse. The unscrupulous went off, put the receipt in his pocket and led the horse out of the exit gate, probably saying that the animal had not been passed. Next day the 'owner' was changed, also the horse's appearance, and again led in and passed. It took two or three days before this was realised – when all those passed were branded on the hoof this of course stopped the practice![25]

But not all went smoothly. Some Territorial units who had not yet departed for camp did not receive any order cancelling it. The 8th Londons (Post

THE REGULAR ARMY GOES TO WAR

Office Rifles) had set out by train for their annual camp at Eastbourne on the day war was declared. Their trains were stopped outside London and sent back to the metropolis.[26] The Highland Railway reported on 6 August that it could not carry on without its employees who were reservists. As a result they were temporarily stood down. In contrast, several reservists who were instructors with the Ulster Volunteer Force applied to be exempted from mobilization. This request was turned down.[27] There was also the case of the 1st Devons. The battalion was stationed on Jersey in the Channel Islands. On mobilization, a transport vessel would arrive to take the Devons to France, where they were to be one of the five battalions deployed on the lines of communication. The ship duly docked and the battalion boarded, but neither the master nor the CO had any idea of their destination. A telegram was sent to the War Office but apparently never arrived. Meanwhile, a TF battalion arrived on Jersey to take over the Devons' garrison duties, but still no instructions arrived for them. Not until some ten days later did General F. S. Robb, commanding the lines of communication in France, ask what had happened to the Devons, and hasty arrangements had to be made to get them across the Channel.[28] The battalion finally landed at Le Havre on 21 August.

Once they had cleared the Regular reservists, the Reserve and Extra Reserve battalions received their own men. They then left their regimental depots and deployed to their war stations. George Ashurst of the Special Reserve had just completed his annual month's camp with the 3rd Lancashire Fusiliers. He received a letter ordering him to report to its depot at Wellington Barracks, Bury, on 8 August. 'Crowds of people were outside the barracks. The public houses were doing a roaring trade to both men and women. There was a lot of hand-shaking, kissing, and good wishes; women were crying and laughing and quite a number of men were drunk.' Ashurst was given a medical that took just twenty seconds and was passed fit for active service abroad. He was then issued with uniform, equipment, and a rifle and bayonet, which 'I noticed with a thrill had been newly sharpened'. He was also given brown paper and string so that he could send his civilian clothes home. After a meal of bread and cheese, the battalion formed up and marched to the station, where it entrained for its war station at Hull, although the troops themselves were told nothing of their destination. The battalion would remain based in the Hull area for the rest of the war.[29] Edmund Malone with the 7th Royal Fusiliers was sent to Falmouth. His company occupied the house of a local Member of Parliament, whose family were still living in it.

> We have put it into a state of defence by orders of the local RE. Who on earth is going to attack? We have barbed-wire entanglements all round. We have loopholes in the kitchen-garden wall. But when I suggested we clear the foreground of hedges and banks, the RE said, 'You must imagine that has been done'. Will the Germans also imagine this? What a farce this active service is![30]

Many of the Regular officers and NCOs attached to the Special Reserve units were returned to their depots, since they would be needed as first line reinforcements for the Expeditionary Force. This added to the pressure on Reserve and Extra Reserve battalions which had two roles to perform – home defence and recruit training. At the outbreak of war they were still on the eight-company organization and, although the order to do so was issued on 5 August, most did not change to four companies until early September. By this time, however, their strength was swelling. The 3rd East Yorkshires, for instance, now had twenty-one officers and 2,000 other ranks and decided to form eight of the new large companies. A–D would be Service companies of trained men, who would carry out the defence role, while E–G were made up of recruits.[31]

On Monday 3 August, Field Marshal Earl Kitchener, the Sirdar of Egypt, had boarded a cross-Channel steamer at Dover, impatient to return to his post. The boat train from Victoria was late and his departure was delayed. While he waited, he received a telephone message from Herbert Asquith summoning him back to London at once. The Prime Minister had been acting as Secretary of State for War since the resignation of J. E. B. Seely in the aftermath of the Curragh Mutiny. He realized that, with war imminent, he could not bear the twin burdens himself for any longer. Kitchener enjoyed the status of national hero and indeed *The Times* of 5 August urged Asquith to make him Secretary of State. That afternoon this became fact and Kitchener attended his first council of war at which it was confirmed that the Expeditionary Force would cross to France. Pre-war staff discussions between the British and French had resulted in agreement that the BEF should initially concentrate in the Mauberge area. Kitchener, pessimistic about the French ability to withstand a German invasion, considered that this would leave the British too exposed and argued for Amiens. The following morning, the Cabinet bowed to Kitchener and agreed to Amiens as the initial concentration area. Such was Kitchener's presence. His suspicion of the French was also reflected in the decision to send only four infantry divisions and the cavalry division to France. The 6th Division would be moved from Ireland to England and, with the 4th Division, be held until the Territorial Force had deployed to protect England's vulnerable East Coast against German attack. Following the Cabinet meeting, Kitchener entered the War Office for the first time in his new post. He dominated from the outset and such was his conviction in the soundness of his military judgement, that Sir Charles Douglas, the CIGS, became a mere cipher, although the fact that he was a sick man did not help. The only occasion during the early part of the war that Kitchener was forced to back down was over the BEF's concentration area. At a meeting held on 12 August with French representatives he was compelled to accept that it had to be in the Mauberge area.

The War Office itself suffered a major upheaval because a number of its key personnel were required for Sir John French's headquarters. One of these was Henry Wilson, the Director of Military Operations (DMO). He appears to have appointed his own successor. This was Colonel Charles Callwell, who had retired in 1909 after service in the Second Afghan War and First and Second Boer Wars and earlier in 1914 had been removed from the Reserve of Officers after reaching the age ceiling for colonels. He was, however, qualified as a staff officer and also had a reputation as a published military historian. On the morning of 31 July Callwell received a letter from Wilson asking him to breakfast in London the following day. As it happened, Callwell had planned to go to Winchester to watch the Home Counties Division TF complete a march to Salisbury Plain and said that he would call at Wilson's house on Sunday 2 August. He arrived home in Fleet late on the Saturday evening to find a wire from Wilson telling him to come up to the War Office the following day. Wilson, who was to be Sir John French's sub chief of staff, told Callwell that he was to succeed him as DMO. It came as a complete shock to Callwell, especially since if he had still been on the Reserve of Officers he would have been appointed to a staff position in the home defence forces and also because 'after five years in civil life it was a large order to find myself suddenly thrust into such a job and to be called upon to take up charge of a War Office Directorate which I knew was overloaded'. Even so, he was at his desk the following day, Monday 3 August. He found his first week somewhat bewildering:

> There were huge maps working on rollers in my spacious office, and in particular there was one of vast dimensions portraying what even then was coming to be called the Western Front. During the week or so that elapsed before GHQ of the Expeditionary Force proceeded to the theatre of war, its cream thought fit to spend hours of suspense in creeping on tiptoe in and out of my apartment, clambering on and off a table which fronted this portentous map, discussing strategical problems in blood-curdling whispers, every now and then expressing an earnest hope that this was not a nuisance. It was a most intolerable nuisance, but they were persons of light and leading who could not be addressed in appropriate terms.[32]

But Callwell laboured under a more serious problem – the reduction of the DMO staff as a result of the need to bring the BEF up to strength. He lost a third of his staff officers in five out of the six Military Operations (MO) branches, and the whole of MO5.[33] This branch dealt with censorship, aliens, control of the press, international law and the Secret Service, some of these in conjunction with MT1, which was responsible for home defence. All required specialized knowledge, but Colonel George Macdonogh, who headed MO5, was earmarked to head the BEF's intelligence branch and took his subordinate staff officers with him. Callwell's comment was that the BEF post was one which many other experienced officers in the army could have effectively filled. The appointment at the War Office which he gave up was one which no officer in the army was so well qualified – nor nearly so well qualified – to hold as he was, and it was at the outbreak of war the more important of the two.[34] In compensation, MO4, which dealt with maps, performed prodigies during the first weeks of the war, especially during the retreat from Mons.

The BEF had gone to France with maps covering the area north of a line drawn between Le Havre and Luxembourg. They were organized in packs consisting of one strategic and thirty-six tactical maps and were expected to last the entire campaign. The problem was that a brigade's map allocation weighed three-quarters of a ton and no transport was available to carry it. Consequently, the packs were broken down and the maps issued to individuals, who soon either lost or damaged them. In addition, because its line of retreat from Mons took it south rather than west to the Channel ports, the BEF found itself in an area for which it did not have coverage and was soon demanding thousands of copies of maps stretching back to the rivers Seine and Marne, and then to Orleans and Bordeaux. Luckily, the Ordnance Survey had a comprehensive collection of printing plates, and MO4 was able to deliver new maps within twenty-four hours. The Printing Company RE deployed with the BEF also helped to make good the shortfall.[35]

In terms of staff, the field formations also had their problems. John Edmonds, the GSO1 of 4th Division, noted that the four staff officers appointed to bring the headquarters up to war establishment came from outside the division. One had just come from the directing staff at Camberley, but curiously was unable to write a proper operation order or understand how to draw up a march table. The newly appointed AA&QMG was not a Camberley graduate and also could not write an operation order. The third was temporarily sick, while the fourth, Captain Hugh Elles RE, the DAA&QMG, who would later command the Tank Corps, was a current student at the Staff College and, once the division had crossed to France, displayed far more interest in observing the fighting at close range than in staff work, and so spent little time at divisional HQ.[36] Colonel Charles Vaughan, commandant of the cavalry school at Netheravon, was appointed GSO1 of the Cavalry Division, the first staff post he had ever held, even though he was a Staff College graduate. Luckily, the GSO2 was to be Archibald Home, who, although he had not seen active service, had wide staff experience and came from 'a weary year as a teacher at the Staff College'.[37]

Another indication of lack of foresight concerned the intelligence branch directly. Macdonogh decided that he needed far more intelligence officers than were allowed on the establishment of the BEF. His plan was to form a corps consisting of a motorcycle section, a mounted section, a dismounted section, and a security duties section which was to be manned by Scotland Yard detectives. All he had were the names of a few Regular officers who were fluent in foreign languages. One was a relative of Macdonogh's, Captain Jamieson Torrie of the 27th Light Cavalry Indian Army, who happened to be home on leave at the time. On 5 August, Macdonogh told him that he was to command the Intelligence Corps which was to cross to France with the BEF. Another was Lieutenant James Marshall-Cornwall RFA, who was already qualified as an interpreter in six European languages. He was touring Peninsular War battlefields in Portugal when war was declared, but managed to get back to Britain on 10 August. Reporting to the War Office the following day, he was told that he was joining the new corps. He rushed back to RMA Woolwich, where he was an instructor, to collect his kit and then reported to Torrie at Southampton. Torrie asked him whether he could ride both a horse and motorcycle. 'Somewhat untruthfully, I replied in the affirmative, although I had never ridden a motorcycle. Being a field gunner I was fortunately allotted to the mounted section, and took over a fine chestnut gelding named Sunbeam, which had been requisitioned from the Grafton Hunt stables.'[38]

But the majority of officers for the fledgling Intelligence Corps had to be drawn direct from civilian life. One who tried to volunteer for this unorthodox band was Oxford undergraduate Stanley Casson. He had applied for a commission, citing his OTC experience. Not having any immediate response, he

> was put in touch with some secret department of the War Office which wanted special officer motorcycle despatch-riders for urgent service in France. I rushed up and was at once sent to be examined in French and German, two essentials of this strange job. The examination consisted in the polite exchange of compliments for the space of two minutes between me and two examiners at Burlington House, and I passed with honours.

Unfortunately, Casson was rejected because he had never ridden a motorcycle. He did, however, eventually receive a commission in the 3rd East

Lancashires.[39] Roger West was more successful. He had an engineering degree from Cambridge, spoke French and German, and was a keen motorcyclist. Indeed, his efforts to enlist took him on a ride of nearly 1,000 miles between Birmingham, London, Cambridge and the Royal Engineers at Chatham, who told him that they were full but that the War Office was looking for particular individuals. West raced back to London and was interviewed by a captain and was granted a commission for 'six months or the duration of the war'. He managed to purchase a second-hand uniform and on 12 August was at the quayside at Southampton with an army-issue Peerless motorcycle. Sigismund Payne Best, who had studied in Germany, had sent his name into the War Office before the outbreak of war. Like West, his efforts to enlist at various recruiting offices were in vain, but he then received a telegram ordering him to report to the War Office, where he was given a quick oral test in German and French and a brief ride on a motorcycle. He crossed to France on 23 August. In all, the initial strength of the Intelligence Corps contingent was thirteen Regular and Reserve officers, and forty-two 'scout officers', who compromised the civilian volunteers and the detectives.[40] But not all those who reported at Southampton went to France. A number appear to have been rejected, including 20-year-old John Lingemann. No reasons were given to the War Office, although the Intelligence Corps suspected that in Lingemann's case that it was because of his German-sounding name. He himself managed to get attached to the 7th Division as an interpreter and then attempted to get back into the Intelligence Corps, telling highly fanciful tales of his doings with the 7th Division. Because of this he was sent back from France and enlisted in the 16th Lancers in late October 1914. He appears to have remained with them until August 1915, when he was discharged with the comment 'free to take up a commission'. There is, however, no evidence that he did apply for one.[41]

The Cavalry Division, which was not formed until the outbreak of war and had to create a headquarters staff from scratch, had no establishment for an intelligence officer. Given that one of its prime roles was reconnaissance, this was a serious oversight. Edmund Allenby, who had been appointed to command the division, found a suitable man, Lieutenant Colonel George de Symons Barrow of the Indian Army, in the corridors of the War Office, and commandeered him. Barrow then formed an intelligence section consisting of a civil engineer, an Indian Army subaltern, a Dutchman and a Swede (taken on because of their foreign language skills), and two police detectives with bicycles. Later, during the retreat from Mons, the section was joined by two car-owning Englishmen who lived in Paris.[42]

The young officers of the Intelligence Corps had little idea of what their duties were supposed to be. James Marshall-Cornwall spent his first few days in France as an Assistant Military Landing Officer (AMLO), 'charged with boarding each ship as it berthed, and giving each unit instructions as to its assembly camp'. On 23 August, the day the Battle of Mons was fought, he finally joined GHQ, where he was tasked with interrogating German prisoners and translating captured documents. But that evening, with the BEF now in retreat, he was ordered to take the staff's chargers back to Compiègne. That accomplished, he was told to report to HQ 3rd Division for intelligence duties. 'My military status was designated as "Agent, 1st Class", so the rest of the staff invariably addressed me as "Agent".' Marshall-Cornwall was then put in charge of the divisional cavalry squadron, which had lost all its officers bar one.[43] Payne Best complained that the staff had little for the intelligence officers to do, and he and West found themselves being used as despatch riders. Roger West did, however, distinguish himself by blowing a bridge in the face of the advancing Germans and was awarded the DSO.[44] The truth of the matter was that Sir John French did not appreciate the value of intelligence and it was not given the importance that it merited. Indeed, when Barrow and another on the staff of the Cavalry Division established the progress of the German advance by the simple expedient of telephoning numerous places in Belgium from Mons railway station – including the fact that its right wing had extended much further westwards than thought – this was dismissed by GHQ.[45]

The Royal Engineers Signal Service also decided that it needed additional despatch riders, although the shortage had been identified at the beginning of 1914.[46] They recruited them in a similarly amateurish way. William Watson, who was an Oxford undergraduate, was on his way up to London to enlist when he read in the newspaper that the War Office was appealing for motorcyclists. After a medical, he and his fellow volunteers were sent down to Fulham where their particulars were noted and Watson marked as 'very suitable'. He purchased a motorcycle in Great Portland Street and returned home. That evening he received a telegram ordering him to Chatham. There he was given another medical and, on 6 August, was appointed a corporal in the Royal Engineers. Watson and three others (all linguists) were then sent to be interviewed at the War Office for possible employment as intelligence officers, but were informed that there were already sufficient. The next few days at Chatham were spent in being drilled, lectured and issued with kit. They were then told that they would join the 5th Division and crossed to Carlow in Ireland, where they became part of the 5th Divisional Signals Company and moved with it to France. Within two weeks of enlistment they were in the thick of the Battle of Mons.[47] The 2nd Royal Welsh Fusiliers came across them on 17 August in Amiens: 'Our billet was invaded by about 150 youthful enthusiasts with motor bicycles, a large percentage of whom had no idea of how to manage their mounts.'[48]

Even more bizarre was the recruitment of gentlemen chauffeurs and their cars. At the age of 47, Toby Rawlinson, brother of Henry, who would rise to command the Fourth Army in France, was no longer on the Reserve of Officers. The War Office had nothing to offer him, but he heard from the Royal Automobile Club that the army might be wanting civilian drivers and their cars to make BEF staff officers more mobile. Rawlinson himself had spent the past twelve years as managing director of the Darracq motor company, which had its main factory on the outskirts of Paris. Darracq was also one of the leading motor-racing teams, and Rawlinson had been much involved in their training in northern France and Belgium and hence, as well as being a French linguist, knew the BEF's area of operations well. Consequently, he put his name forward to the RAC Secretary and on 19 August was instructed to submit his car for an RAC technical inspection the following day. It passed, and Rawlinson was told to obtain a khaki uniform, without badges, and present himself at Southampton docks on the 21st. In all, the RAC provided twenty-five drivers and their cars. Among their number were the Duke of Westminster, Lord Dalmeny and C. d'A. Baker-Carr, all of whom subsequently distinguished themselves during the war. Officially titled the RAC Corps of Volunteer Motor Drivers, the cars reported to General Robb, the Inspector General of Communications. He allocated them to their duties, with six, including Rawlinson and Westminster, being sent to Sir John French's headquarters, then at Le Cateau. Rawlinson found himself driving French's staff officers to liaise with French and British units. This kept him busy during the retreat from Mons and the subsequent advance to the Aisne. He then joined his brother Henry, who was commanding IV Corps, and served during the operations to relieve Antwerp and the First Battle of Ypres. Paul Maze, an interpreter with the BEF, came across him just before the opening of the First Battle of Ypres and described him as 'an English civilian wearing grey flannels' in 'a white racing car, on the bonnet of which he had fixed a repeating rifle. He drove his car backwards and explained that in an emergency he could get away without turning.'[49] The RAC also supplied forty-six owner-drivers and their cars to support the Royal Naval Division in its abortive attempt to relieve Antwerp, as well as others to carry King's Messengers from GHQ in France to Boulogne and elsewhere. In 1915 the club established the RAC Owner-Drivers War Service, which operated for the remainder of the conflict under the aegis of the War Office and supplied cars for government ministries and the home commands.

Maze was in fact only an unofficial intepreter. French interpreters were essential to the BEF and the French had agreed to supply sufficient for the first five divisions, though thereafter the War Office had to find its own. One who volunteered was Ralph Hamilton, a former officer of the 3rd Hussars, who was now serving as the commander of the Essex Royal Horse Artillery TF and was a French and German speaker. Realizing that it would be some time before his battery would be sent on active service, he looked around for a job which would take him to France and discovered that the War Office was looking for interpreters. He found himself attached to one of the 7th Division's artillery brigades, in time for the landings by that division and the 3rd Cavalry Division at Zeebrugge. 'It was then, to my horror, that I discovered that neither French nor German was of the slightest use, as the language of the country was Flamande – a horrible mixture of bad Dutch and even worse German'.[50] Hamilton remained with the division during the First Battle of Ypres, during which he was wounded. He was, however, able to be of some use in liaising with French units, dealing with claims for damages by civilians and interrogating captured Germans.

Maze had got himself attached to the BEF under unusual circumstances. A French Anglophile artist, he was not liable for conscription because of his eyesight. Nevertheless, he was determined to play an active part in the war and made his way to Le Havre, where the BEF was disembarking, to offer his services. He managed to persuade the Royal Scots Greys to take him on as an interpreter. They supplied him with a khaki uniform of sorts and he took part in the Battle of Mons and subsequent retreat, at one point being arrested as a spy. General Hubert Gough, then commanding the 2nd Cavalry Division, took Maze under his wing and he remained with Gough until the latter was sacked from command of the Fifth Army in March 1918. Gough used Maze as his eyes, and also made full use of his talents as an artist, sending him out to sketch parts of the front. For the final part of the war, Maze fulfilled the same role in Rawlinson's Fourth Army.

Another who was taken on unofficially as an interpreter was Frederick Suzmann, who was of Danish descent and fluent in French, German and Portuguese. He had served a period in the Volunteers and had taken part, as a volunteer, in Greece's 1897 war with Turkey. He enlisted in the ASC in early September 1914 in the belief that he would be quickly sent to the Front as an interpreter or despatch rider. This did not happen and so on 29 September he wrote personally to Kitchener, complaining that he was being employed merely on fatigue duties. The War Office replied, enclosing two applications for the 'Interpreters Corps', but warned that there was a long waiting list. Suzmann was then taken on unofficially as an interpreter by Lieutenant Colonel R. G. I. Bolton, commanding the 2nd Scots Guards when it was rushed to Belgium as part of the 7th Division on 6 October. Bolton himself was soon captured and Suzmann, now without a patron, was returned to England. He appears then to have got himself discharged from the ASC, but continued, without success, to pester the authorities for a commission.[51]

The passage of the Expeditionary Force to France went remarkably smoothly. J. F. C. Fuller, later to become one of the prophets of armoured warfare, was a student at the Staff College and one of those detailed to join the embarkation staff at Southampton. Because he had been a railway transport officer on the Aldershot manoeuvres, Fuller was appointed as

Deputy Assistant Director of Railway Transport (DADRT), with the task of ensuring that each trainload of soldiers was conducted to the right wharf. He noted that only a single set of lines connected the station to the docks and that at the height of the deployment of the BEF a train arrived every four minutes. To assist him he was given 'a board about two-feet square with little slips of wood the size of narrow rulers, which could be pulled out and pushed in, and upon which small coloured labels could be pinned, each representing a train-load of troops'. Luckily he recognized it as the invention of a sapper, Major A. M. Henniker,* a railway transport special-ist whom Fuller had lived opposite in Aldershot and with whom he had played with this machine. He was also impressed by the efficiency and enthusiasm of the London & South Western Railway:

> The result was remarkable, for during August we had to deal with hundreds and hundreds of trains coming in from every part of the kingdom, and in one period of some twelve hours eighty, and yet there was never a delay, never a mishap, and when the first six divisions had left this country, the sole casualty was one horse killed – it kicked itself out of its slings whilst being embarked.[52]

There were minor frustrations for the embarking troops. The 2nd Royal Welsh Fusiliers were one of the first infantry battalions to cross – they were to deploy initially on the lines of communication. They entrained at Dorchester in two trains, starting at 6.30 a.m. on 10 August and arriving at Southampton at 10.30. They were ushered into a shed on the wharf and not permitted to leave it until called forward, 'but Boy Scouts did "good deeds" running for fags, etc.'. A and B Companies boarded a not very clean ship and, because there was no food on board, had to subsist on their iron rations – bully beef, biscuits and water. One of the officers spotted an old friend among the embarkation staff who told him 'under oath of secrecy, that we were the first Regular troops to embark, that we were going to Rouen, and were to be employed with three other battalions in passing the Expeditionary Force up-country'.[53] The 1st Irish Guards, who had entrained from Nine Elms, London, had an exhausting time on a hot day loading

---

* Henniker later wrote the volume of the Official History which covered transportation on the Western Front.

their vessel, whose bulwarks, because of the tide, were 25 feet above the quayside.[54]

Once across the Channel, the movement of the BEF to its concentration area went remarkably smoothly. The advance parties crossed on 7 August, the first to land in France being ASC elements who would set up the first supply base. The Railway Transport Establishment (RTE) embarked on the 9th, together with the commandants of the three bases to be established at the entry ports and their staffs, and those of the three Large Rest Camps. The staffs of these had mobilized at Southampton but were given little idea of their role. All they received by way of equipment were horses for the commandant and adjutant of each. No. 2 Large Rest Camp's staff disembarked at Rouen and took over four tented camps which had been set up by the French and then began to receive troops.[55] The first trains run carried supplies and the actual deployment of the troops began on the night of 14/15 August. Inevitably, not all went to plan. The base commandant at Rouen noted that troopships were sometimes arriving up to twenty-four hours behind schedule.[56] Even so, by the time the Battle of Mons opened on the 23rd, the first four divisions and the Cavalry Division were in place, and the deployment of the 4th Division and that of army and lines of communication elements was completed two days later. In all, 343 trains had been run over a period of thirteen days.[57]

The retreat from Mons wrong-footed the supply system, which had been geared for an advance into Belgium. This was aggravated by the fact that the BEF marched south, away from the Channel port bases. This called for a good deal of improvisation, though matters were simplified when the IGC was placed under command of Wully Robertson, the QMG. The crucial reason for this was that the practice of the QMG nominating the refilling point (RP) and the IGC then selecting the railhead and giving orders to the mechanical transport (MT) supply columns quickly proved unworkable. Communications problems, the ever-changing situation and the distance between the IGC HQ and GHQ made this so. Robertson therefore decided that he should nominate the railheads and issue orders to the supply columns.[58] So that the lines of communication could be better secured, on 27 August it was decided to move the bases from Le Havre and Rouen to Nantes and Saint-Nazaire, while the advanced base was already in the process of being moved from Amiens to Le Mans. The moves between ports were conducted largely by sea and were completed by the end of the first week of September. Yet in spite of this disruption, and the fact that the Railway Transport Establishment (RTE) was very much in the hands of the French over the availability of track and rolling stock, the supply system did hold up during the retreat.

Another problem was the feet of the reservists. They had had little time to break in their new boots before arriving in France and the uneven surface of the cobbled roads caused them agony. Indeed, Colonel E. H. Swayne, commanding the 1st Somerset Light Infantry, noted that his reservists, who made up more than two-thirds of the battalion, had been issued with boots without studs; it took much effort to put this right. He also observed that the reservists had had little time to settle in before going to France.[59] This meant that they were not as physically fit as those currently serving with the Colours. The 8th Brigade War Diary noted, for instance, that during the period 9–12 August its battalions had carried out route marches, but 5 miles was thought to be enough for the reservists.[60]

The early weeks of fighting in France soon brought to light deficiencies in the army's weaponry and equipment. The lack of heavy artillery was recognized almost as soon as the Battle of Mons had been fought. On 24 August 1914, the War Office ordered Southern Command to mobilize as soon as possible a siege brigade consisting of one heavy battery (four 9.45-inch howitzers) and two medium batteries, which were to be expanded to two batteries each and were to be equipped with 6-inch howitzers.[61] One medium battery was sent to France on 19 September. Two days later, HQ BEF was clamouring for further heavy batteries and a second siege brigade, consisting of two 6-inch batteries, was sent to France by the end of the month. A further brigade with sixteen 4.7-inch guns was sent out at the beginning of October. These guns, which were Boer War veterans, were of little value. Their accuracy was so in doubt that they were known as 'strict neutrality' for the tendency of their shells to land on friend and foe with equal impunity.[62] As for the 9.45-inch howitzers, these, too, had been developed during the Boer War, being modelled on an Austrian Skoda gun of much the same calibre. It was decided that these were unsuitable. Instead, the authorities looked to two 9.2-inch railway guns which had been built just before the outbreak of war.

The first of these was dismounted from its railway carriage and sent out on 11 October. It was accompanied by two 6-inch coastal guns and titled 6 Siege Battery RGA. The guns were towed by steam tractors and the ammunition carried on 5-ton Foden lorries used by the breweries, their drivers enlisted into the ASC(MT) at 6/9d (six shillings and nine pence) per day. The 9.2-inch was quickly named Mother and, guarded by infantry and an anti-aircraft section, fired its first shot in anger on 31 October.[63]

In the meantime, an Army Council Instruction (ACI) dated 22 October announced the formation of a siege train for service abroad. A Siege Committee was established under Major General H. P. Hickman to set it up. It reported in December. By this time approval had been given for the production of thirty-two 12-inch howitzers, thirty-two 9.2-inch howitzers, and twenty-four 8-inch howitzers. In addition, seventy-six 6-inch guns and the two 9.2-inch guns were already in existence. The idea was that the siege train itself would be a major general's command and would consist of twenty-one brigades, each of two batteries. Two brigades were to be formed each month and then undergo two months' training at Lydd in Kent. The first brigade was ready in December and deployed to Portsmouth prior to crossing to France. It was also recommended that the siege train include a sizeable engineer element – four railway companies, two works companies, ten fortress companies and a divisional signal company. But this never came to fruition since the siege train *per se* never operated as such, the siege artillery being distributed among the armies.[64]

More serious than the lack of heavy artillery was the realization that pre-war estimates of ammunition expenditure were wildly over-optimistic. Indeed, on 31 October Kitchener warned Sir John French: 'The supply of ammunition gives me great anxiety ... Do not think we are keeping munitions back. All we can gather is being sent, but at [the] present rate of expenditure we are certain before long to run short, and then to produce more than a small daily allowance per gun will be impossible.'[65] In the case of the 18-pounder gun, the work-horse of the Royal Field Artillery (RFA), by mid December 1914 there were stocks in France of only 648 rounds per gun, when there should have been 1,000. Sir John French stated that he needed fifty rounds per gun per day for December, but only six rounds per gun arrived, showing that Kitchener's gloomy forecast had been no idle warning. Furthermore, it was not until mid October that the 18-pounders had received their first high explosive rounds, far more effective than shrapnel in trench warfare, 'for trial and report'.[66] True, as early as 10 August the War Office had issued contracts for maintaining the BEF and equipping the first six divisions of the New Army with munitions, but, stripped of staff for the BEF, the MGO's department was facing an increasingly uphill struggle.

Part of the mobilization plans dealt with the establishment of base depots in France through which reinforcements for the BEF would flow. The officer responsible for organizing these depots was Major R. F. Pearson, a retired officer of the Buffs and veteran of Indian Frontier campaigns and the South African War, who was commanding the Cheltenham College OTC in August 1914. On mobilization he was ordered to Woolwich, where he was tasked with setting up six General (GBD) and six Infantry Base Depots (IBD). They crossed to France and even before the Battle of Mons was fought, the IBDs were established at Le Havre and the GBDs at Harfleur. The former were numbered 1 to 6 and each supported a particular division, with No. 1 reinforcing 1st Division, and so on. The GBDs supplied the remaining arms and services as follows: No. 1, RGA; No. 2, RHA, RFA; No. 3, RGA, ASC, RE; No. 4, RE; No. 5, RAMC and Cavalry; and No. 6, Corps Details. The first reinforcement, which was calculated at 10 per cent of a unit's war establishment, arrived on 22 August. In the case of No. 2 IBD this totalled fifteen officers and 1,147 other ranks, who were sent forward three days later, with the complete first reinforcement of some 6,000 men being concentrated at Amiens.[67] But with the BEF in retreat and its path taking it away from Amiens and towards Paris, there was no practicable way for these reinforcements to be delivered to their units. Consequently, they were sent back to Rouen. Here they came under the control of No. 2 Large Rest Camp.

Once they had fulfilled their function of passing troops up-country during the initial deployment of the BEF, the Large Rest Camps had experienced a lull. But now No. 2 Large Rest Camp had to cope with the first reinforcement. No sooner had it received it than the camp and the 6,000 men now under its control were ordered to move by train to Le Mans. Here, on 31 August, the first stragglers from the retreat from Mons also began to arrive. Within three days a total of 3,340 had been collected in addition to the first reinforcement, which was finally despatched on 3 September.[68] By now the retreat had come to an end and the units were finally able to receive it. John Lucy of the 2nd Royal Irish Rifles noted that they 'more than made up for the hundred we had lost'.[69] As far as the reinforcements were concerned, General F. S. Robb, the Inspector General of Communications, wrote to the CIGS in mid September that while pre-war training had emphasized the supply system anticipating wants, he now realized that the situation was governed 'by the ability of the unit to receive and not of the L of C to send up'.[70]

In the meantime, a second reinforcement had arrived in France, No. 2 IBD receiving twelve officers and 1,047 other ranks. But then, on 31 August, because of the threat posed to the existing lines of communication, the bases were moved by sea to Saint-Nazaire, where they remained until returning to Le Havre and Harfleur in November.[71] Meanwhile, the rest camps were grappling with the straggler problem. These were in three categories: parties or individuals who had become separated from their units and had been despatched from the railheads; sick and slightly wounded; and men who had temporarily lost their employment, i.e. cavalrymen without horses, gunners without guns and MT drivers without lorries. But lack of ordnance stores meant that the only way they could re-equip the stragglers was to take equipment from the unfit and give it to the fit, who were then sent back up the line. The rest camps remained at Le Mans until just before Christmas when they moved to Boulogne. Here their role changed to receiving individual reinforcements from England and then either despatching them to the base depots at Etaples, Harfleur and Rouen or forming them into units.[72]

For some left at home the period of mobilization was frustrating. Harry Davson was commanding G Battery RHA at Ipswich. This and its sister battery were earmarked as a Reserve brigade to maintain the RHA batteries already deployed to the Continent with reinforcements. It was therefore with some anguish that Davson began to send his men to Newbridge and his horses to Aldershot. In their place, on 6 August he received 150 reservists who had to be hurriedly armed as a precaution against German invasion. Three days later, the War Office changed its mind and Davson was ordered to mobilize his battery for war. Horses and more reservists arrived, but the former proved a problem: 'They were good horses, but were mostly hunters brought in from grass and totally lacking in condition.' They were also 'untrained for draught work'. Even so, by the 15th Davson had succeeded in bringing his battery up to strength, but five days later he found himself encumbered with 150 raw New Army recruits, followed by orders to move to Shorncliffe. It soon became clear that it was an impossible task to train the recruits and simultaneously prepare the battery for war. The recruits being looked after by Davson's brigade were therefore formed into six separate new batteries, to which he lost all his officers. Consequently, for a month he found himself training his battery on his own – a period which proved 'the most wearing of my career'. It was not until the beginning of October, when the battery was ordered to join the 8th Division, then forming in the Winchester area, that Davson got his officers back.[73]

Once they had processed the Regular reservists, the regimental depots had their hands full receiving recruits for Kitchener's rapidly expanding New Armies (*see Chapter 4*). Additionally, they were also handling members of the National Reserve. On 6 August 1914 the War Office had announced that National Reserve members would be accepted for enlistment up to the age of 42 if they had previous military experience, while those without would be taken if they were under 30. The age limits were raised to 45 and 35 respectively at the end of that month. Meanwhile, the initial supply of reinforcements to the BEF, as far as the infantry was concerned fell largely on the shoulders of the Reserve and Extra Reserve battalions. But the Special Reservists, in the eyes of some, were not of the same quality as the Regular reservists. John Lucy of the 2nd Royal Irish Rifles thought that they 'had not the smartness of the Regulars, and I could not take them rapidly to my heart. Their habits were unsoldierly and repellent to me.'[74] By early November, National Reservists were being sent to France, but their quality was even more doubtful. Henry Rawlinson complained to Kitchener that there were too many elderly reinforcements – 'men of over 40 years of age and sometimes 50 – They cannot stand the work in the trenches and crack up after the first 3 or 4 days'.[75] This was supported by the commandant of No. 3 IBD who noted that a number were medically unfit.[76]

Most of the Reserve and Extra Reserve battalions remained in Britain throughout the war and continued to be concerned primarily with training. There were exceptions, however. On 4 March 1915, the 4th King's (Liverpool) Battalion entrained at Edinburgh. Eight days later they were in the trenches at Neuve Chapelle as a much-needed reinforcement for the Sirhind Brigade in the Indian Lahore Division.[77] In the summer of 1916, three further Extra Reserve battalions (the 7th Royal Fusiliers, 4th Bedfords and what was formerly the 2nd (Reserve) Battalion the Royal Dublin Fusiliers) were sent to France to help form the 190th Brigade as part of 63rd (Royal Naval) Division (*see page 109*). The 4th Bedfords, who were based at Landguard, Felixstowe, seem to have had little warning, receiving orders to mobilize on 10 July and crossing to France fourteen days later. The 10th Royal Dublin Fusiliers, on the other hand, had been converted to a Service battalion in February 1916 and crossed from Dublin to England on 6 August. They were allowed a further twelve days to complete their mobilization at Pirbright in Surrey before being sent to France.[78] Finally, in October 1917, two further Extra Reserve battalions, the 4th South Staffordshires and the 4th North Staffordshires, both of which were stationed at Canterbury, were also deployed to France to join the 25th and 56th Divisions respectively.[79] Apart from the demands for replacement manpower by the BEF, the rationale of sending these battalions would appear to be that they already had a good number of trained Medical Category A men and that their contribution to the training role could be taken on by other units.

By early October 1914, several Regular units had arrived back in Britain from service overseas. The first to arrive were used to help form the 7th Division and the 3rd Cavalry Division,* which were sent to Belgium under Henry Rawlinson in a vain attempt to prevent the Germans from capturing Antwerp. The 7th Division included two battalions from Malta, two from Gibraltar, three from South Africa and one from Egypt, while the 3rd Cavalry had the two cavalry regiments which had been based in South Africa and that from Egypt. Indeed, the 3rd Dragoon Guards and 2nd Gordons arrived back from Egypt just five days before they set sail once more. Rawlinson noted that when the 7th Division first came under his command that it was 'still rather green – the men who have recently come

*The Cavalry Division itself had been reorganized into the 1st and 2nd Cavalry Divisions in early September.

home from abroad are not yet fit and do not therefore march well – the Discipline of the "services de l'arrière" is also bad for the units are mostly composed of recently embodied civilians who do not know what discipline means.'[80] While some of its support elements, including three out of the four ASC companies, had also returned from overseas, others were formed from Kitchener volunteers, including all three field ambulances. The next Regular division to be created was the 8th Division and this drew on the first battalions to arrive back from India, as well as others from Egypt, Malta, Aden and South Africa. Its supporting units were also a mixture of existing Regular and newly raised, with its three field ambulances coming from the Wessex Division, which had been sent to India (*see page 73*). The 8th Division also had little time to shake down, being sent out to France in early November when the fighting at Ypres was at its height.

The remaining Regular battalions came largely from India and the Far East. One or two had already had an interesting time. Some officers and men of the 2nd Duke of Cornwall's Light Infantry, which had been stationed in Hong Kong, had spent the early weeks of the war serving as marines on board the pre-Dreadnought battleship HMS *Triumph*. The 2nd South Wales Borderers had already seen action, cooperating with the Japanese in the successful capture of the German concession port of Tsingtao in China in September 1914. It was originally intended to use these battalions to train the New Armies, but the desperate fighting around Ypres during October and November caused a change of heart.[81] They were therefore used to form the 27th, 28th and 29th Divisions, which were so numbered because they were created after the first three batches of New Army divisions.

The 27th and 28th Divisions laboured under a number of problems. Their units arrived back in Britain from the tropics in the midst of winter and it took time for the men to acclimatize. Their support units were a mixture of New Army and Territorial Force and, for the 27th Division at least, there was little time for the division to shake down, since it found itself in France just before Christmas 1914. The 28th Division was allowed more time, but it had to suffer under canvas amid weather which moved the GOC, General Sir Edward Bulfin, to write a furious letter of complaint on 1 January 1915:

The condition of the Camps is deplorable ... [it] is to-day quite impossible to allow troops to remain in [them]. Owing to the continuous rain the tent bottoms in some cases are afloat. I have ordered 50% of the men to go on three days furlo' [leave] at once and the remainder to move to-day into billets in Winchester. In the case of the 85th Brigade the condition is not quite so bad, but it is still very bad indeed. To-day there is not a man with a dry suit of clothes on him and the Camp is one huge quagmire with men and horses wading about. I am putting this Brigade to-night into billets. I need not tell you the difficulties of mobilising are very great – blankets, clothing, saddlery – all are soaking wet ...[82]

Not surprisingly, this had a detrimental effect on training and both divisions' reputations suffered, especially that of the 28th. During its first tour of the trenches, in early February 1915, it was shelled out of them on more than one occasion.[83] Rawlinson wrote to Kitchener: 'They don't seem to be able to tumble to this trench warfare business and Sir John [French] is much displeased with them.'[84] Billy Congreve noted in his diary on 21 February: 'The 28th Division has come in on the left of the 27th Division and is of about the same type – hurriedly put together Regular battalions, given staffs made up in the same way and thrown out here. A most rotten arrangement.'[85] Sir John French took the drastic step of exchanging 28th Division's brigades with seasoned ones from the 3rd and 5th Divisions.[86] They were returned just before the Second Battle of Ypres in April 1915, when both the 27th and 28th Divisions suffered very heavy casualties. Eventually, in October 1915 the 28th Division was sent to Salonika, being followed by the 27th at the beginning of 1916. Both spent the remainder of the war there.

The penultimate Regular division, the 29th, was formed in the Midlands early in 1915 from battalions which had returned from the Far East. There were only eleven of these available and so the unusual step was taken of adding a Territorial battalion, the 1st/5th Royal Scots. All its support units were also Territorial, the majority coming from divisions which had been sent on garrison duties to India and Egypt. This division was sent to the Dardanelles, where it gained a high reputation, which it maintained on the battlefields of France and Flanders from mid 1916. Not all Regular units were brought back from overseas, however. One cavalry regiment (the 21st Lancers) and eight infantry battalions remained in India throughout the war, although they did provide drafts for Mesopotamia. The other British units stationed in India at the outbreak of war were part of formations which comprised the various Indian expeditionary forces which were sent to France, Mesopotamia and East Africa.

Finally, there was the formation of the Guards Division in August 1915. Up until this time there were eight battalions of Foot Guards serving in France in two dedicated brigades. In addition, the Grenadier, Coldstream and Scots Guards had each formed another battalion after the outbreak of war and in February 1915 the Welsh Guards had been created, initially as a single battalion. There was also one pre-war battalion, the 3rd Grenadier Guards, still in England. Thus, there were now thirteen Guards battalions in existence and it appears to have been King George V's own idea that they should be formed into a single Guards Division. But to the officer who would be appointed to command the new division it all came as a complete surprise.

In July 1915, the Earl of Cavan, himself a Grenadier, had just been given command of the 50th (Northumbrian) Division (TF) in France. His wife fell ill with diptheria and on the 17 July he returned to England on compassionate leave. As a matter of course, he called in at the Regimental Headquarters Grenadier Guards, where 'to my intense astonishment' he was shown a paper ordering the immediate preparation of the 3rd and 4th Grenadiers for service abroad as part of the Guards Division. It was the first he had heard of this new formation. Two days later, Cavan was summoned to Windsor, where the King invested him with the CB and then explained the concept behind the new division, indicating that Cavan had been selected to command it. He told Cavan to go and see Kitchener. The following day, he was summoned by the Adjutant General, who went through the proposed organization of the division. Cavan objected on two counts. First, he abhorred the breaking up of the 4th Guards Brigade, whose battalions had been together since the outbreak of war. He also objected to a brigade made up entirely of the Grenadier battalions on the grounds that, if it had heavy casualties, it would be very difficult to find sufficient officer replacements. His arguments were accepted.

On the evening of the same day, 20 July, Cavan saw Kitchener, who told him that the divisional cavalry squadron and cyclist company would be recruited from the Household Cavalry and the artillery, engineers, divisional train and field ambulances by the BEF in France. The Signal Company RE would be raised from the Foot Guards. Kitchener told Cavan to remain in England to select the men for the Signal Company, but Cavan pointed out that he was still commanding a division in France and could not just leave it. Kitchener relented and Cavan returned to France the following day. En route to the 50th Division, he called in to see the Military Secretary at GHQ who reassured him that he would find the staff for the new division, but added that the King wished the Prince of Wales to be appointed to it, but not as an ADC.

On 4 August Cavan was succeeded in command of the 50th Division by Major General P. Wilkinson. Cavan returned to England and carried out a hasty inspection of the Guards Division's supporting arms and services, the bulk of which had, after all, been selected from units in Britain. It proved impracticable to form the Signal Company from Guardsmen and the 16th (Irish) Division's Signal Company was transferred *en bloc*. Two weeks later, on 20 August 1915, the new division officially came into being at Saint Omer and fought its first action, at Loos, the following month.[87]

Turning back to 1914, as the BEF had its first experience of trench warfare on the Aisne and then took part in the so-called 'Race to the Sea', which would culminate in the grim battles around Ypres during the latter part of October and most of November, the Territorial Force began to take the field.

three

THE TERRITORIALS

The King's Proclamation at the outbreak of war was the signal for the Territorial Force (TF) to mobilize in order to fulfil its role of home defence, while the Expeditionary Force (BEF) crossed the Channel. This policy was confirmed by Kitchener, whose deep prejudice against amateur soldiers caused him to raise his New Army rather than build on the structure of the Territorial Force. Those Territorials already serving now had to serve an additional year. TF members who were not at camp at the time knew what they had to do. Bryan Latham of the London Rifle Brigade related that the mobilization orders

> told me that I should parade at headquarters in marching order; folded in the greatcoat and in its pockets and haversack I should have 1 pair of socks, a toothbrush, 1 pair of bootlaces; towel and soap, razor and case, shaving-brush, table knife, spoon and fork; clasp knife with tin-opener carried on person, and a housewife fitted with needles, thread, buttons. When the company commander had satisfied himself that I duly possessed all these articles, he would issue me with the sum of £5.10s which seems quite a liberal allowance in the value of money in those days.

But, before rations began to be issued, some two weeks after mobilization,

> I was only to receive 9d per day in lieu of rations. Even with a loaf of bread at 3d, tea at 2s a lb and sugar 2d a lb, this does not seem very adequate.[1]

The immediate task was to deploy the TF to its war stations to defend against a possible German invasion. The East Coast was seen as the most vulnerable and it was for this reason that the Central Force was formed under General Sir Ian Hamilton,* with headquarters in a London hotel. The Mounted Division of four Yeomanry brigades deployed to Suffolk, while the remainder of the TF formations allocated to the Central Force were organized in three 'armies', although they were, in fact, more like corps in size and their titles probably reflected the confusion over the term 'army corps'. The First Army had its HQ in Bedford and consisted of the Highland Mounted Brigade and Highland Division, which were based on Huntingdon and the Bedford area respectively. The Second Army (HQ Aldershot) had the 1st London Division in the Aldershot area, with the South-Eastern Mounted Brigade and Home Counties Division in Kent, while the Third Army (HQ Luton) controlled the North Midland Mounted Brigade (Bishop's Stortford), 2nd South-Western Mounted Brigade (Colchester), East Anglian Division (Brentwood), North Midland Division (Luton), South Midland Division (Leighton Buzzard), and 2nd London Division (St Albans).[2] In spite of the strain being put on the railways by the deployment of the Expeditionary Force to France, the movement of the TF divisions was achieved by the end of the fourteenth day of mobilization, something which Brigadier General H. O. Mance, who at the time was the Staff Captain for Railway Transport at the War Office, claimed that no one had believed possible.[3] There was also a plan to deploy the Welsh Border Mounted Brigade, and the West and East Lancashire Divisions to Ireland, but this was not carried out.[4] The East Lancashire Division was despatched overseas (see page 72), while the West Lancashires were scattered and the Welsh Border Mounted Brigade joined the Mounted Division. As for the other 1914 TF formations, they remained within their peacetime home commands for the time being, some being engaged, alongside Special Reserve units, in the defence of ports. But the Territorial Force as a whole now found itself being pulled in different directions.

* Hamilton had returned to England from Malta on 17 July 1914, his appointment as Inspector General Overseas Forces due to come to an end on 1 August. The idea was to combine this post with that of Inspector General Home Forces to ensure uniformity of training throughout the Empire. Hamilton hoped to be appointed, but was told on 29 July that he was to command the Home Army. In practice, C-in-C Home Army, which implied command of all troops in Britain, was not recognized as such and Hamilton was left to concentrate on the Central Force (Lee, *A Soldier's Life*, pp. 127–30).

On 10 August, Lord Kitchener had sent a memorandum to the Director-General of the Territorial Force, General Edward Bethune, asking him which units were prepared to volunteer for service abroad and which wanted to remain part of the Home Defence Force.[5] His thinking was driven by the need to replace the Regular units being brought back from overseas to strengthen the Expeditionary Force. Each unit then invited its men to sign the Imperial Service Obligation, which would enable them to serve overseas. A unit would be considered available for foreign service if 80 per cent of its strength volunteered* and it recruited additional men to make up the shortfall. Although sixty-nine battalions had made themselves available by 25 August, this figure was not easily achieved.[6] W. N. Nicholson, a Regular officer on the staff of the Highland Division, noted that its initial returns had often been made without consulting the rank and file.

There was also a view that the government had 'broken faith': 'We joined the Territorials for Home Service and now you want us to go abroad. Well, we won't.' Nicholson went on to record a conversation he had with a Territorial officer: 'The Territorial Force was a last resort, in his opinion; it was not meant to come into the war until all the Regulars had been killed; a Regular was not playing the game if he let a Territorial come and fight alongside him so early in the war as this.'[7]

Another view is given by the Hon. Walter Guinness. The Suffolk Yeomanry, of which he was second-in-command, had received an urgent telegram from the War Office in the early hours of the second day after it had mobilized at Ipswich, asking for the number of men willing to volunteer for overseas service. Apart from the difficulties of going round the regiment's scattered billets to see the men individually, the officers faced another problem.

> Being called for in such an urgent hurry, the men not unnaturally thought
> that it meant they were going to be sent over in a few days, and many of
> those who were ready enough to volunteer felt that, in view of the
> absurdly insufficient training done by the Territorial Force under peace
> conditions, they ought not to be asked to go overseas until they had had
> a much more thorough training.[8]

* At the end of 1914, the War Office reduced the requirement to 50 per cent [National Archives, Kew WO 32/18620].

Prior to being ordered to establish the number of men prepared to accept the obligation, the 4th Northamptons were addressed by both their brigade commander and commanding officer, who stressed that no one was to be coerced into volunteering, which was viewed by many as an invitation not to do so. Consequently, when the time came, only some 200 stepped forward. It took much persuasion by the company commanders that it was the men's duty to volunteer to raise the total to a respectable 800 out of 950.[9]

There was hesitation about taking the Imperial Service Obligation in the 5th Scottish Rifles, but for a different reason, as John Reith (later the BBC's first Director-General), one of its officers, explained. A letter from the Director-General Territorial Force dated 15 August had laid down that in cases where a unit did not achieve the 80 per cent take-up for foreign service, it could merge with another to produce one battalion for overseas and one for home service. Where the percentage of volunteers was very low a brigade could form a composite foreign service battalion. The latter applied to the Scottish Rifle Brigade, of which Reith's battalion was part. The intention was to form a composite unit commanded by Reith's CO. This did not go down well with the 5th Scottish Rifles: 'Our way was clear: we would volunteer for foreign service with the 5th, but we would not connive at its dispersion nor would we go abroad with a composite lot.'[10] Other battalions ignored this sentiment, however. The 4th Royal Scots took two companies from the regiment's 6th Battalion, while the 7th Royal Scots absorbed two companies of the 8th Highland Light Infantry; not that this got them abroad any quicker.[11] Indeed, both remained in Scotland on coast defence duties until joining the Lowland Division in April 1915 and subsequently sailing to the Mediterranean. In contrast, the members of the London Rifle Brigade, then in camp at Bisley, seem to have had little reservation over volunteering. 'The general opinion was that we should go to Gibraltar, Malta, or perhaps even India. The news from France was generally better, the Battle of the Marne had been fought and the war still seemed a long way away.'[12] All those who did volunteer had to undergo another medical examination, and some were found to be medically unfit for foreign service. In the case of the 4th Northamptons, the unfit and those who had not volunteered were formed into three small home service companies but remained part of the battalion for a few weeks. They 'were the subject of many nasty remarks from the Imperial Service Companies'.[13] Those battalions which had accepted the Imperial Service Obligation were then given formal permission to form second-line battalions from their home service men, and second-line TF divisions would soon begin to be formed to administer these battalions.

The units earmarked for overseas service were making earnest efforts to bring themselves up to strength. They were conscious that Kitchener's call for volunteers for his New Army was acting against them, and, indeed, he had specifically asked the County Associations, which were responsible for the administration of the TF, to give priority to recruits for the New Army, except for foreign service units, which were allowed to recruit over their war establishment.[14] In these cases, the TF was surprisingly successful in its campaign, which was operated at unit level. At the end of August, 2nd Lieutenant Stanley Goodland of the 5th Somersets was sent to Minehead to recruit more men. His target was forty, but he managed to recruit over double the number.[15] Indeed, such was the success of the campaign that, by the beginning of November 1914, the TF was nearly 20 per cent over establishment. This enabled them not only to offer their units for overseas service up to strength, but also to ensure that drafts would be available to reinforce them.

On 29 August, the War Office made the decision to send two TF battalions – the 7th and 8th Middlesex, which had volunteered for overseas service prior to August 1914 – to Gibraltar and the 1st London Infantry Brigade to Malta to replace the Regular garrisons which were to be used to help form the 7th and 8th Divisions. A complete TF division (East Lancashire) was to be sent to Egypt for the same reason. In France, the majority of Regular battalions designated lines of communication troops had been quickly drawn into the fray, forming the 19th Infantry Brigade. Further TF battalions would be needed to take their places. Therefore, on 12 September, the decision was made to send the London Scottish (14th Londons) to France. Three days later it was the turn of the Infantry Battalion Honourable Artillery Company (HAC) to be warned for imminent overseas service. Its CO told the War Office, however, that 500 of its men were not fully trained. In consequence, it was agreed that it could go to France a mere 800 men strong; that is, 20 per cent under war establishment. Seven days later the Oxfordshire Hussars were ordered to entrain immediately for Southampton and would be one of the first TF units to land in France, together with the HAC.[16] Before the end of the year, by which time the strength of the TF had been doubled, a total of twenty-two TF battalions had been sent to France. The original intention was that they would serve merely on the lines of communication, but once the Expeditionary Force came under pressure at Ypres they began to be used to bolster Regular divisions at the Front.

On 24 September, it was decided that the Wessex (later 43rd) Division TF would be sent to India. The day before, the divisional commander, Major General Colin Donald, had been summoned to see Kitchener at the War Office. Donald professed himself shocked when Kitchener asked him if his men were prepared to go to India. Having already ensured that his units were up to strength in terms of men who had undertaken the Imperial Service Obligation, Donald said that they had not really thought about India, but was sure his men would go. Just two weeks later the division was on its way. It would be five years before some of its members set foot in England again. One of those was Lieutenant Stanley Goodland of the 1st/5th Somersets. He wrote to his fiancée:

> Next to going to France Indian service is supposed to be the greatest honour the War Office can bestow upon on a regiment. Lord K said that after a while he would probably relieve us with other troops and send us to the Front, so we are likely to see some service after all. At any rate India will be a great experience for me.[27]

The 1st Home Counties Division (later 44th Division) went to India the same month. It was also intended to send the Welsh Division to India, but this formation was part of David Lloyd George's dream of a Welsh Army Corps and he objected to it being sidelined (*see page 100*). As a result, the War Office took the decision to send one of the recently formed second-line TF divisions, the 2nd Wessex (later the 45th Division) and this sailed in December. All three of the divisions bound for India left their supporting arms and services behind, except for their artillery.

The units of the TF divisions which replaced Regular units were scattered throughout India and Burma, but soon found themselves supplying drafts to replace casualties in Mesopotamia. In May 1915, Stanley

Goodland took a draft of 1st/5th Somersets to reinforce the 2nd Dorsets, who had suffered heavy casualties. He himself soon went down with typhoid and was evacuated back to India. He returned to Mesopotamia with a further draft at the end of 1915 and this time was attached to the 1st/5th Buffs, which had been part of the 44th (Home Counties) Division and had just arrived in the theatre. This time Goodland was slightly wounded, became adjutant, and won an MC for rescuing the wounded CO of the 37th Dogras under fire before once more being evacuated back to India, this time with jaundice. Of the battalions that formed the 43rd (Wessex) Division, six served in Mesopotamia, one in Aden, one in Aden and Palestine, two in Palestine alone (including Goodland's 1st/5th Somersets) and one in Egypt and France. Only the 1st/5th Hampshires remained in India throughout the war. The pattern was much the same for the other two divisions in India.

Some of the battalions in these divisions travelled widely, none more so than the 1st/4th King's Shropshire Light Infantry. It went to India with the Home Counties Division, arriving in Bombay on 1 December 1914. Two months later, it was deployed to Singapore, with a detachment on the Andaman Islands. In April 1915 the KSLI sent two companies to Hong Kong, which rejoined it two years later. The battalion spent a month in Colombo before sailing via Cape Town back to Britain, landing at Plymouth on 27 July 1917. There was no time for the men to enjoy the comforts of home after nearly three years away. Two days later they re-embarked at Southampton for France. On arrival, the battalion was given a special leave dispensation, in spite of the need to train in the New Warfare, and by the end of August a quarter of its strength were on furlough in Britain. Even so, on 11 September the 1st/4th began their first tour in the trenches as part of the 63rd (Royal Naval) Division.[18]

Those units which were sent overseas early were largely unprepared in many ways. Much of the problem lay in the fact that, unlike Regular units, the TF did not hold mobilization equipment in peacetime. The idea was that on mobilization the Ordnance Department would provide some, but the major part of the equipment needed was the responsibility of the TF County Associations, which had to obtain it by local purchase. A report on how the mobilization had gone observed: 'This system was unsatisfactory. In some districts suitable vehicles and equipment were not obtainable and in the case of a large number of units considerable delays occurred.'[19] Thus, the HAC, which received just forty-eight hours' warning of its departure for France, was lacking modern rifles and ammunition. Its transport was, like that of the TF as a whole, a miscellany, most of it impressed civilian vehicles. It received rifles and ammunition on the very eve of its departure, but many men had no chance to fire their weapons until they arrived at Saint Omer at the end of October, after spending six weeks split up into detachments at the French ports being used as British bases.[20] The 9th Londons (Queen Victoria's Rifles) did at least have the opportunity to fire a week's musketry course at Shoreham in mid October, but were then deployed to guard the railway between Winchester and Basingstoke. On the 28th of that month they received their orders for France. Each man was given twenty-four hours' embarkation leave and was issued with a new rifle – the Long Lee-Enfield adapted to take Mk VII ammunition, as used with the Regulars' SMLE.[21] Recognising that TF units about to embark overseas were deficient in equipment, a rest camp was established at Southampton in November 1914 for the specific task of completing the equipment of both TF units and reinforcement drafts prior to embarkation and continued to operate until mid 1916. As it was, much of the money expended by the County Associations on equipment subsequently found to be unsuitable for overseas service was totally wasted.

Another problem under which the TF units that went abroad early laboured was that of under-age soldiers. Because the minimum age for enlistment in the Territorials was 17, compared with that of 19 for the New Armies, it was inevitable that TF units would contain a significant proportion of youths. This and their poor standards of training resulted in a rap across the knuckles in the form of an Army Council Instruction of 23 December 1914:

> Complaints have been received that untrained and immature lads have been allowed to proceed overseas with certain TF units, notwithstanding the orders that have been issued that no one in a unit of the TF is to be allowed to proceed to join the EF [Expeditionary Force] unless he is medically fit, fully trained, and is 19 years of age or over.

In May 1915, in order to tighten up on the problem of under-age Territorials, the enlistment age bracket was altered from 17 to 35 to 19 to 38 (except for the Inns of Court and Artists' Rifles, which were seen as officer producing units).[22] Even so, the problem remained and was aggravated by the number of youths giving false ages when volunteering for both the Territorial Force and the New Armies. One of these was Victor Silvester, the future dance-band leader, who enlisted in the London Scottish in November 1914. He gave his age as 18¾, but was actually four years younger than this. He joined the 2nd Battalion and remained with them for the next sixteen months. In his autobiography he claimed that he was never included in a draft for the Front because his true age was suspected. This may be so, although a study of his service papers shows that in September 1915 he was found temporarily unfit for foreign service because of flat feet. He was also 'temporarily demobilized' for two months that November, possibly because of his feet, and rejoined the battalion in January 1916. The following month, however, his father, a vicar in Wembley, wrote to the CO of the 2nd London Scottish enclosing Victor's birth certificate and asking that he be posted to the 104th Provisional Battalion (*see page 85*) 'for home service or any other capacity in which he can serve his country.' In the event, because he was still under 16, Victor was discharged. His CO did, however, state that Victor was 'well up with required standard for 18½ years,' which implies that they did not realize that he was so young.* [23]

For the Territorials at home the requirement to guard railways was another distraction, and a task only properly identified after the outbreak of war. The country was divided into four regions: No. 1 Line of Communication (with its HQ at Waterloo Station, London), covered southerly lines; No. 2 westerly railways (HQ Paddington Station, London); No. 3 northerly

---

* Silvester claimed in his autobiography that he transferred to the 3rd Argylls, staying with them for seven months before reaching France, where he stayed for six months. Whilst there he witnessed an execution by firing squad before being sent back to the base as under-age, but then enrolled in the ambulance unit run by the historian G. M. Trevelyan, in Italy. He was apparently wounded and, like Ernest Hemingway, awarded an Italian decoration. According to his service papers, he did enlist in the Argylls in September 1916, but was almost immediately discharged, again because of his age. However, his Medal Index Card shows that he was entitled to the British War and Victory Medals for service with the British Red Cross and Order of St John of Jerusalem in Italy, which implies G. M. Trevelyan's ambulance, and commencing on 1 October 1916. There is no mention of any service in France. What is certain is that he was back in Britain by the end of 1917 and joined the Inns of Court at Berkhamsted for officer training in January 1918, a month before his 18th birthday. He was posted to No. 6 Officer Cadet Battalion in June, but then to the 2nd Artists' Rifles in September 1918 and was with them until the end of the war. This implies that he failed his officer training, although he claimed to have been commissioned just after the Armistice.

(HQ Carlisle Town Hall); and No. 4 easterly (HQ Liverpool Street Station, London). Railway lines were classified A and B, the former being those considered vital.[24] Among these were the lines leading to the ports of embarkation, which were given priority of protection. The London & South Western Railway Waterloo–Southampton line alone required 4,000 men to secure it. Initially, TF battalions were used in this role. Not only did this detract from training, it could also prove dangerous. The 1st/6th King's Liverpool (Liverpool Rifles) were made responsible for 60 miles of the London, Brighton and South Coast Railway: 'It called mainly for night patrols and constant vigilance. A false step meant death and during the seven weeks we performed these duties, eight riflemen were killed by trains.'[25] However, on 22 August the War Office authorized TF County Associations to enlist National Reserve Class II men into the home service units at Territorial depots within their local areas for the purpose of guarding vulnerable points.[26] Their tasks were soon enlarged to include guarding prisoner of war camps and munition factories as well, and Class III men began to be accepted as watchmen in civilian clothes. Then, in October 1914 the TF Associations were specifically ordered to form companies of National Reservists for railway protection so that the battalions occupied in this task could be relieved. These companies were to be affiliated to Territorial battalions.[27] Some, however, were already carrying out railway guards. John Reith was guarding a stretch of the Perth railway with a detachment of 5th Scottish Rifles in September 1914 and was relieved by 'the National Guard, a body of which we had not previously heard'. He described it as 'a body of middle-aged civilians carrying prehistoric rifles and with bayonets projecting from their pockets.'[28]

Back at home, in the midst of the distraction of an increasing number of its units being sent overseas and its home defence tasks, the Territorial Force needed much training to make it fit to fight. W. N. Nicholson noted that the members of the Highland Division tried very hard, but had not developed soldierly instincts. This was revealed especially among the officers, whose 'indecision was painful to see. They wanted to be the leading strings, and from the most senior to the most junior they looked round for someone to help them.' With many of the Regular adjutants having been posted, there was often no one available to do this. Consequently, the

Territorial officers suffered from loss of confidence. One symptom of this, as Nicholson noted, was that

> they were engrossed in their own affairs; they marched in silence at the head of their companies, putting on their mackintoshes when it rained; forgetful that their men had none. They had not been taught to carry the rifles of the weary, to encourage the footsore; they only spoke to them to give a perfunctory order. They did not know that the welfare of their command must always be their first consideration.[29]

In many cases, there was an initial lack of urgency about training, especially in those units that were not part of the Central Force. Linton Andrews, the 28-year-old bespectacled news editor of the *Dundee Advertiser*, enlisted in the ranks of the 4th Black Watch:

> Our main work was cleaning up the drill-hall, cleaning our eating utensils, and cleaning ourselves for going out. It was some weeks before we got rifles to carry. We marched out on those smiling August and September days on to country roads, halting where it pleased us best. When we bun-wallahs announced that it was time to clear the dust from our throats, a willing sergeant stopped the march and postponed training for half an hour.[30]

In the second-line battalions there was even less urgency. Aubrey Smith, who had joined the 2nd London Rifle Brigade on 1 September, did his initial training at the depot in London, but in November the battalion went into billets at Haywards Heath, Sussex.

> We lived as we might have done at home, having meals with our 'landlords', sleeping in proper beds and rising just in time for breakfast in the mornings. Our parade each day was at 9 o'clock and at 1.30 our training was over. We really had a most slack time and, instead of becoming hardened for the fray, we were like turkeys fattening up for Christmas.

Smith and his fellows did have a week on the ranges, but bad weather meant that he only fired twenty rounds, few of which hit the target. 'Officers and everybody considered this a huge joke and there did not seem to be any attempt to give any extra practice to the poorer marksmen.'[31]

Those units sent overseas also often appeared to have little idea of how to train for war. Arthur Behrend sailed to Egypt with the 4th East Lancashires. Once there,

> the one thing the battalion did learn was how to produce smart and well-drilled guards. In other branches of military art our progress seemed less satisfactory, I suppose it was too much of a case of the blind leading the blind.[32]

No wonder that Sir Charles Douglas expressed his concern to Kitchener at the end of September that 'considerations of home defence are being sacrificed to the idea of imperial service abroad in the near future.' He observed that while on paper the Territorial Force might appear reasonably strong, the splitting of battalions into foreign and home service, with priority being given to the former, frequent changes of unit locations and a lack of efficient officers and NCOs, as well as of modern rifles, meant that training was not at the standard that it should have reached.[33] The situation was further aggravated by the decision at the end of September 1914 to post a number of Regular NCOs serving with TF units to the New Armies as instructors.[34]

Those Territorial units which retained their Regular adjutants were lucky. The 1st/7th Royal Warwicks also had a Regular CO, but it was the adjutant who impressed Henry Ogle as

> a dynamic personality. He is responsible for instilling into a crowd of young men that *esprit de corps* that more than anything turns it into soldiers. He addresses an individual as 'Soldier' if he does not know his name, in which case he very soon gets to know it, and never forgets it. After a man has been addressed at any length by the Adjutant, he feels better for it, even if he has been reprimanded.[35]

Another in the same mould was George Hawes of the 1st/3rd Londons, now helping to garrison Malta.

> I have started most intensive training, beginning with the rudiments of barrack-square drill. I feel convinced that we shall go to war sooner or later, and I want to go there with a properly trained battalion. Some of the older officers think they know better, and that I am wasting their time, and they are making difficulties.

79

Luckily, Hawes had a former Brigade of Guards RSM and an ex-Regular orderly room clerk to help him.[36] He was also right in forecasting that it would not be long before the battalion was in action. The 1st London Brigade, of which it was part, moved from Malta to France in February 1915. The 1st/3rd Londons joined the Garwhal Brigade of the Meerut Division and were soon in the thick of the Battle of Neuve Chapelle. As for their performance, Hawes wrote: 'I can't say enough in my admiration for these Territorials. Officers and men, they are magnificent.'[37] The 4th East Lancashires in Egypt benefited from the attachment of four Regular sergeants in November 1914. They stayed for five months and did much to help prepare the battalion for the grim fighting in the Dardanelles.[38]

Much of the problem with the Territorials lay in their sometimes informal discipline, especially in the 'class corps', which regarded themselves as 'gentlemen's clubs', with all ranks paying an annual subscription for the privilege of being members. Frank Hawkings of the 9th Londons wrote that when the battalion marched from Pirbright to Crowborough in September 1914, they arrived at a camp of sodden tents in pouring rain.

> Practically everyone has gone into Crowborough to secure rooms for the night at the two hotels, the Beacon and the Crown. Twelve of the fourteen men in my tent have gone off ... I hear that as some officers were late getting into Crowborough, they found things rather crowded out by the men who got there first and booked the best rooms.[39]

This was behaviour that would have been unheard of in a Regular battalion. But many Territorials defended their more relaxed discipline. Writing of the London Rifle Brigade, Bryan Latham noted that 'the discipline of men who knew by their upbringing when discipline was necessary and to whom obedience was due. They did not need to have it drilled into them on the parade ground.'[40] Henry Ogle said of the 1st/7th Royal Warwicks:

> What they did they did because they wanted to, not because punishment loomed as a permanent background. Such extreme iron discipline, based on the blind, undeviating, inhuman inevitability of punishment is impossible with troops bound together by lifelong friendship and even kinship ...[41]

As for the Regular Army, Rory Macleod, who took over a Territorial battery in the 48th (South Midland) Division in April 1917, observed:

> The officers did not appear to take a grip of their sections, nor the sergeants of their subsections. Orders were given in a conversational tone, almost as if asking for a favour, and the men did not jump to them. When I checked an NCO for this and for seeming to be too familiar with some of his men, he said he had to be careful because one of the men in civil life was his foreman and the rest his work mates![42]

But not all Territorials were disdainful of the Regular Army's ideas on discipline. The 1st/4th Black Watch found itself brigaded with its own 2nd Regular Battalion when it arrived in France. Linton Andrews commented:

> The way they carried out their trade and made no fuss about it appealed immensely to our imagination. Our admiration for the 2nd Black Watch was boundless. Merely to watch them loading up rations for the trenches was a pleasure. Almost everything was done at the double and with the minimum of commands. Our men still shouted and argued too much.

So much was this admiration that when out of the trenches the Territorials got the 2nd Black Watch to help them bring the battalion closer to the Regular standards of smartness and discipline.[43] However, as the war wore on and the character of the Territorials became diluted, especially after conscription was introduced, their discipline did become much more akin to that of the Regulars.

Obsolete equipment also put the Territorials at a disadvantage. They went to war with the old Long Lee-Metford and Lee-Enfield, but with the chamber modified so that a charger could be used to reload using ammunition clips. These types were known as the CLLM and CLLE rifles, CL standing for 'charger-loading'. Before departing overseas, some units were given the Regular Army's rifle, the Short Magazine Lee-Enfield (SMLE) instead. But there were two types of SMLE. The older version took Mk VI blunt-nosed ammunition, which was also used by the CLLE, while the other used the higher velocity Mk VII sharp-nosed round. Unfortunately, some units were given the older version, but once in France were supplied with the Mk VII ammunition. The problem with this, as the London

Scottish discovered when they fought their epic battle at Messines on 31 October 1914, was that, if loaded from a clip, the rounds jammed in the chamber. The men were therefore reduced to loading single rounds, which radically reduced their rate of fire in the face of German mass attacks. The East Lancashire Division went to Egypt still armed with the CLLE rifle, but when it arrived on Gallipoli in May 1915 many men forsook these for SMLEs, a good number of which had been abandoned after their original owners had become casualties. But the division itself only had Mk VI ammunition. Although this could be fired from the SMLE, its performance was erratic. As Arthur Behrend described,

> there was always a sporting chance that you could pick up enough Mark VII to see you through, but it was unwise to rely on it. Hence a Divisional order was published recalling all short rifles, but since most of our long rifles had by then been scattered far and wide over the dusty fields of Gallipoli this order went the way of many more orders and was ignored.[44]

Artillery was another vexed subject for the Territorials. While the New Army divisions were equipped with the 18-pounder field gun, the TF divisions initially had to make do with the obsolete 15-pounder. This gun proved to be very ineffective. Indeed, General Ivor Maxse commented in the late summer of 1915 that it was 'absolutely worthless and cannot be put in the line at all!'[45] It was not until the winter of 1915–16 that the TF divisions were able to acquire 18-pounders.

Further pressure was placed on the TF when it was decided towards the end of September 1914 that six of its divisions would eventually be sent to France. The first of these, the North Midland, was warned on the 27th to hold itself in readiness.[46] However, at the end of October, because of the heavy casualties being incurred by some Regular battalions, it was decided to send additional individual Territorial units to relieve them. This would delay the equipping of the North Midland Division and so its move to France was put on hold.[47] A number of TF field companies RE were also despatched and not until the beginning of January 1915 was a decision taken on the order in which the TF divisions should move to France. The North Midland was to go first, followed by the South Midland, 2nd London, Welsh, Highland and West Riding. This changed twice, however, during the month and eventually it was agreed that the revised order should be North Midland, 2nd London, South Midland, West Lancashire, West Riding and Northumbrian.[48] Simultaneously, second-line formations of these divisions were to be formed and based on the 2nd Battalions of the infantry regiments involved.[49]

The North Midland and 2nd London Divisions duly crossed to France in early March 1915. The South Midland followed later that same month, and then West Riding and Northumbrian Divisions in April. However, the West Lancashire Division had by now lost nine of its original battalions, which had been sent individually to France. It was therefore decided that the Highland Division should go in its place. This, however, had itself already lost battalions to France and so had to borrow from the West Lancashire Division to bring it up to strength. That done, the Highland Division went to France in May 1915. The Dardanelles also beckoned. Apart from the East Lancashire Division, which went from Egypt in May 1915, the Lowland Division was deployed from Britain in the early summer. One of its brigades was delayed, however, by a disaster to two companies of the 1st/7th Royal Scots who were involved in a multiple train collision near Gretna Green on 22 May, just before they sailed. Of the 500 men on board their troop train, some 87 per cent were killed or injured in what is still Britain's worst rail disaster. The remainder of the battalion sailed from Liverpool two days later, but the two companies which had suffered so badly were quickly brought back up to strength and sent out. In July 1915, two further Territorial divisions – the Welsh and the East Anglian – also departed for the Dardanelles. This left just two first-line TF divisions in Britain, the West Lancashire and the 1st London, which like the former, had seen almost all of its units sent out to France individually or used to reinforce other formations. These two divisions would eventually be reformed in France in early 1916.

Across the English Channel, Rawlinson was impressed with the West Riding Division – 'certainly a fine lot of men' – but not with its staff; he had to loan the headquarters some of his own staff officers. The 51st (Highland) Division, on the other hand, he found to be very green, noting that the officers did not seem to know much about war.[50] At the lower level, Gerald Burgoyne reported:

> We came on the South Midland Division marching through Bailleul on its way to Nieppe (Armentières). A band of some Territorial Battalion in Bailleul played them through the Market Square. Splendid lot of men marching with such a swing. The men impressed me more favourably than the officers.[51]

In the meantime, the second-line Territorial divisions had formed, initially taking their titles from their equivalent first-line formations; thus the 2nd East Lancashire Division and, in the case of the two London divisions, 2nd/1st and 2nd/2nd London. Simultaneously, each TF infantry regiment formed a third battalion, which took on the responsibility for training recruits. However, in July 1915, so as to avoid confusion between the likes of the 2nd London Division with the Regular 2nd Division, it was decided that the TF divisions should be numbered. They were to take precedence after the 41st Division, which was the last of the New Army divisions formed at that time, and divisions would initially be numbered in the order they were sent overseas. Thus, the first to leave Britain, the East Lancashire Division, became the 42nd (East Lancashire) Division and those that had gone to India the 43rd (Wessex), the 44th (Home Counties), and the 45th (2nd Wessex), although, to all intents and purposes, they were no longer functioning as divisions. The remainder of the first-line divisions were numbered 46 to 56, again in the order that they went overseas. Apart from the 45th Division, the second-line divisions were numbered 57 to 69, each paired with a first-line division. Bringing the titles of the TF divisions more into line with the rest of the army marked one of many steps which increasingly blurred the unique character of the Territorial Force.

The second-line TF divisions were soon in difficulties. Although the intention was that they would eventually be sent overseas, they found themselves having to supply drafts to their first-line equivalents. Thus, the 60th (London) Division had to send reinforcements to the 47th (London) Division, while it sent its home service men to the third-line units. The result was that by the end of 1915 no battalion in the division was more than 400 men strong. It was only then that the War Office stepped in to lay down that these units be brought back up to strength through the supply of men from the third line.[52]

With the third-line Territorial battalions concentrating on the training of recruits, there were a significant number of Territorials who were not medically fit for service overseas or who were still refusing to take the Imperial Service Obligation, and were surplus to establishment. Therefore, during the summer of 1915 it was decided to form Provisional battalions from those refusing to serve overseas and others who were Medical Category C, which prevented them from doing so. Sixty were formed and were allocated numbers as follows:

1–12 Scottish Command
21–29 Northern Command
41–52 Western and Northern Commands
61–72 Eastern Command
81–86 Southern Command
100–108 London District

In most cases a single battalion was raised from the TF home service men of a regiment. Thus, the 72nd Provisional Battalion was made up of men of the Royal Sussex and the 11th from the Royal Scots Fusiliers. Some regiments had sufficient men to form more than one Provisional battalion. The Essex Regiment raised no less than three (Nos. 65 to 67), while the London Regiment provided all nine of those in London District. In contrast, the Somerset Light Infantry, Dorsets and Wiltshires formed just the 85th Provisional Battalion.[53] In July 1915, all-arms Provisional brigades were formed, each consisting of a Yeomanry squadron, a Cyclist company, four Infantry battalions, an RFA battery, field company RE, field ambulance, and an ASC company, and these were deployed largely to guard the East Coast.[54] In order to maintain the strength of the Provisional units, it was agreed in September 1915 that men aged 40–50 could be recruited and that they would not be expected to take the Imperial Service Obligation.[55]

At the same time as the formation of the Provisional battalions, efforts had also been made to tidy up the situation with regard to the National Reservists. In November 1914, all Class I and Class II men who had not come forward were ordered to present themselves for enlistment. At the end of the following month a further War Office instruction laid down that reserve TF units must have at least 50 per cent of men accepting the Imperial Service Obligation and that Class II reservists should join these units or the protection companies formed for guarding vulnerable points. However, the County Associations were already becoming swamped by Class II members. Prior to its departure for Egypt, the East Lancashire Division had taken advantage of this to incorporate a number in its ranks to make up the shortfall in establishment caused by those who had not volunteered for service overseas. In most cases, however, the associations had many on their hands for whom they could find no immediate employment and they were experiencing difficulty in raising further protection companies because of the lack of suitable officers. In January 1915, the War Office tried to ease the situation by laying down that no medically fit soldier under the age of 38 was to join the protection companies, even if he was merely home service. Some counties misunderstood these instructions. The Flintshire TF Association, for example, thought that no more home service men were being accepted and told some of those on its register of Class II men that they were liable for service overseas and ordered them to report for a medical. This resulted in letters of complaint to the War Office from some of the victims and it was forced to point out to Flintshire that such actions were in direct contravention of Territorials' right not to volunteer for foreign service. At the same time, it encouraged further protection companies to be formed, even though some of the officers were often over the maximum Class II age of 55. This was successful, and by March 1915 the Warwickshire TF Association had formed no less than eight such companies.[56] Finally, in March 1915 the protection companies were renamed Supernumerary TF companies, each being made an additional sub-unit to an existing TF battalion; thus, No. 2 Supernumerary Company, 8th Worcesters TF.[57]

Given the ever-increasing demands for manpower, in July 1915 the men of the Supernumerary companies underwent another medical to identify those who could be employed in a more active role. The authorities were looking for those capable of marching 10 miles with a rifle and 150 rounds of ammunition after 'reasonable training'. Nearly 15,000 men were so identified and concentrated at Halton Park Camp, Wendover. Those in Category A were posted to Service battalions, with the Category Cs joining Provisional battalions. The remainder, the Category B men fit enough for garrison duty abroad, were then organized in seven battalions, which became 18th to 24th Rifle Brigade TF. During December 1915 these battalions were shipped to Egypt (19th to 22nd) and India (18th, 23rd and 24th) to replace Territorial units which had been committed to the Dardanelles and Mesopotamia. Montie Carlisle, returning to the 8th Northumberland Fusiliers after being wounded at Suvla Bay the previous August, travelled out to Egypt with two of these battalions. He described them as 'a funny crowd' and considered their officers 'mostly very common and know very little about soldiering'.[58] Even so, they fulfilled a valuable, if unglamorous role.

The rump left behind in Britain, some 335 men, became the Provisional company of the 18th Rifle Brigade and were joined by a company of the 21st Rifle Brigade. They moved to billets in Reading and furnished working parties to the Ordnance Works at Didcot, for which the men were paid an extra eightpence a day. There were, however, only two officers, until a CSM was promoted lieutenant and quartermaster in April 1916. The Provisional company also found itself having to deal with sick men, which the battalions had left behind and medically unfit men sent back by them. To this end, its name was changed in March 1916 to the Depot Rifle Brigade TF. To increase the burdens placed on it, the Depot was warned by some of the Rifle Brigade TF battalions overseas that they would be requiring reinforcements. The matter was raised with the War Office, which told the Depot that it was unlikely that it would be called upon to supply drafts. Nevertheless, at the end of June 1916 it was ordered to supply 150 men for the 23rd and 24th Battalions in India, which it duly did. The stresses placed on the Depot were only finally lifted at the end of August when it was given a new role. It would now be designated the 25th (Reserve) Battalion the Rifle Brigade TF, with an establishment of 1,504 all ranks and stationed as a garrison unit at the Cornish port of Falmouth. A new depot would be formed in London to support both the new battalion and those in Egypt and India. Throughout its trials and tribulations the Depot Rifle Brigade TF had just one consolation; it had at least managed to retain the same cap-badge throughout.[59]

Throughout the first twenty months or so of the war there was no compunction on Territorials who had completed their term of service to remain in uniform. Those who became time-expired had two options. They could either re-enlist, in which case they were granted a month's leave and a bounty, or they could return to civilian life. A number took the second course and their attitude is summed up by a senior NCO in the 1st/6th Northumberland Fusiliers. He was conscious that 'there was still a large number of young men who had not yet enlisted. His view was that it was they, not he, who should be fighting.' The NCO duly obtained a job in a munitions factory, probably with considerably better pay than he had been receiving as a soldier.[60] However, the passing of the second Military Service Act in May 1916 removed the right of time-expired Territorials to return to civilian life. Instead, they found themselves automatically recalled to the Colours. Even so, some men serving in France preferred to allow themselves to be conscripted and join a strange unit, rather than remain with their chums, so that they could spend time back in Britain.*[61]

The Military Service Acts also finally removed the right of Territorials not to take the Imperial Service Obligation. The immediate result was a combing out of men fit for overseas service from the Provisional brigades. They were posted to the second-line 59th, 60th and 61st Divisions TF. Those who joined the first-named found themselves in Ireland, to where the 59th Division had been sent in the immediate aftermath of the 1916 Easter Rising. Apart from internal security duties, the division supplied drafts to its first-line sister division, the 46th (North Midland), and did not itself go to France until early 1917. In contrast, the 61st and 60th Divisions went to France in May and June 1916 respectively. At the same time, the third-line TF battalions were redesignated Reserve battalions and had their fractional numbers removed. Thus, the 3rd/4th and 3rd/5th Borders became the 4th and 5th (Reserve) Battalions the Border Regiment TF. The Reserve battalions were also organized in Reserve groups, each responsible for supplying drafts for a first-line Territorial division. Thus, the East Lancashire Reserve Group, which consisted of the two Border Regiment Reserve battalions, four from the Lancashire Fusiliers, two East Lancashire,

---

* This also applied to Regular soldiers whose term on the Reserve had expired, even though they, too, had served their extra year. Up until then, they had been entitled to discharge, although AO 252/15 of 22 June 1915 had given them the opportunity to extend their term of service until the end of the war. Those who had reached the age of 41 were also allowed to stay on, if they wished, and were entitled to a month's leave and a £20 bounty as an inducement.

and six Manchester Regiment Reserve battalions, supported the 42nd (East Lancashire) Division. In September 1916 there was a further change. The number of Reserve battalions was radically reduced and the Reserve groups became Reserve brigades TF. In the case of the East Lancashire Reserve Group, its title now was the East Lancashire Reserve Brigade TF and the number of battalions under its command was reduced to six – two Lancashire Fusiliers, one East Lancashire, one Border, and two Manchester. The surviving Reserve battalions absorbed the remainder, the 5th Manchesters taking in the 6th and 7th, and the 8th Reserve Battalion incorporating the 9th and 10th.

A further right of the Territorial was removed by the Military Service Acts, that of remaining with the unit in which he had enlisted, as enshrined in the 1907 Territorial and Reserve Force Act. In early 1915, the War Office, concerned over the high level of casualties among Regulars and conscious that the supply of reservists had all but dried up, approached the TF County Associations with a request that they invite men to transfer to the Army Reserve so that they could be posted to Regular units. It then investigated the possibility of amending the 1907 Act. A draft bill was prepared, but there was much political opposition to it and so it was dropped. Instead, in May 1915 an Army Order declared that the relevant paragraph in *Territorial Force Regulations* was now in abeyance and that henceforth Territorials would be transferred in the same way as Regulars. The following month, the Imperial Service Obligation was amended so that a man agreeing to it accepted that he might be posted to another unit. Not only new recruits, but serving TF members as well, were expected to sign this form. This was not a popular step and the Earl of Derby, the Director of Recruiting, went so far as to claim that it was 'murdering recruiting'. Consequently, the measure was dropped in early July 1915.[62] When the first Military Service Bill was being debated the following January, the Under-Secretary of State for War, H. J. Tennant, warned that TF soldiers could be attached, as opposed to posted, to Regular or other TF units and that this was not in contravention of the 1907 Act. In March, after the bill had become law, the Member for Inverness raised the question of the 1st/4th Cameron Highlanders in Parliament.

The battalion had been serving in France with the 7th and then the 8th

Division, and in January 1916 had been posted to the 51st (Highland) Division, then refitting behind the lines. This had gone to France with one of its brigades made up of West Lancashire battalions, the original units in the division having been sent to France early in 1915 to reinforce other divisions. It was decided that these should be sent back to their original division, the 55th (West Lancashire), and replaced by Highland battalions. The other battalions joining the 51st Highland at this time were the 1st/4th Seaforths, 1st/4th Black Watch and the 1st/5th Black Watch. At the time, the thirty-nine divisions comprising the BEF were some 75,000 men under strength and Douglas Haig, who had succeeded French as C-in-C in December 1915, had already pointed out the serious shortage of manpower in some battalions to Wully Robertson, who was now CIGS. Robertson replied in a letter dated 1 February that although second- and third-line TF units often had plenty of men, few of them were trained. There was therefore little early prospect of bringing their first-line equivalents up to strength. He was also conscious of the rule that forbade Territorials from being transferred to other units. Even so, Robertson pointed out that a number of brigades still had more than four battalions, a situation which had existed since the previous winter as a result of TF units reinforcing Regular formations piecemeal. He warned that this could not continue to be so.

As far as the 1st/4th Camerons were concerned, their CO, together with those of the 1st/4th and 1st/5th Black Watch, as well as the CO of the 1st/9th Argylls, which had already undergone a temporary amalgamation with the 1st/7th Argylls and was now part of VI Corps troops, were summoned to see Haig's adjutant general on 14 February. He informed them that the intention was to amalgamate the two Black Watch battalions and to make the other two draft-producing units for their Regular battalions. The COs apparently considered that their men would not object too strongly and the reorganization went ahead. However, in March 1916 the Member for Inverness asked in Parliament why it was that the 1st/4th Camerons were being absorbed by the Regular 1st Battalion, which was in the 1st Division, in contravention of the 1907 Act. The government's reply was that there was no intention of destroying the 1st/4th and that 'if it had been finally absorbed, it had been absorbed into a battalion so famous, it would be a fact about which nobody need grumble'. In fact, the 1st/4th was not absorbed *per se*, but sent to Etaples, where it provided drafts for all Cameron battalions in France, although the majority went to the 1st Battalion via No. 1 Entrenching Battalion (*see page 221*). In July 1916 the strength of the battalion was pegged at four officers and 100 other ranks and the surplus was posted to No. 19 Infantry Base Depot, which was also responsible for supplying the Camerons with men. Even so, the 1st/4th Camerons continued to process drafts until it was finally disbanded in February 1917. It would thus seem that the War Office had found a way of circumventing the 1907 Act, but Territorial sensitivities remained strong. Indeed, much the same situation occurred with the Provisional battalions, from where men objected to being posted to units other than those in which they had originally enlisted. In the event, clauses in the second Military Service Act of May 1916 removed the bar on the posting of Territorials.[63]

The May 1916 Act further curbed the Territorial Force's 'independence'. With the introduction of Lord Derby's scheme, the halfway house between the volunteer army and conscription which was introduced in autumn 1915 (*see page 131*), the War Office wanted to block direct enlistment into the TF. However, it hesitated to do so until conscription was introduced. When it was, all recruits were enlisted for general service and then allocated to units. Yet there were exceptions to the rule. These were the so-called 'class corps' – the HAC and various of the London TF regiments – traditionally containing a good deal of officer material within their ranks which was probably why they were exempted.* These exceptions were removed in May 1917, although the right of the Artists' Rifles, as well as that of the Inns of Court, to recruit directly was restored for a short time at the end of the year since they were both officer cadet units, or at least the 2nd Artists' Rifles was – the 1st Battalion was by then serving with 63rd (Royal Naval) Division.[64]

---

* Apart from the HAC, the regiments concerned were the 5th Londons (London Rifle Brigade), which had 409 men commissioned from those who served in France during 1914–15, the 14th Londons (London Scottish) (503 commissions), 15th Londons (Civil Service Rifles) (332 commissions), 16th Londons (Queen's Westminster Rifles) (297 commissions), and 28th Londons (Artists' Rifles), which was already training officers. The one anomaly was the 8th Londons (Post Office Rifles), which was not considered a class corps, since it did not levy an annual subscription from all ranks and had only thirty of its 1915 veterans commissioned. It may have been its close connection with the GPO which made it exempt.

Another development which affected the Territorial Force in the spring of 1916 was a review of home defence carried out by the newly appointed C-in-C Home Forces, Sir John French. The general view was that the Germans could assemble an invasion force of up to 160,000 men. This was not likely to attack Scotland, although French recommended an addition to the one mounted brigade and four Cyclist battalions already deployed there. Northern Command was also 'reasonably secure', with a series of garrisons covering the coast. In any event, the likely German objective in its sector would be the 'munitions centres' in Yorkshire and the North Midlands and these were well inland. Eastern Command remained the most vulnerable. Its defence was still largely in the hands of the Central Force, which continued to have three subordinate headquarters. These were now HQ Mounted Troops, and First and Second Armies, that of the Third Army having been dissolved. But the GOCs of the training centres, which looked after the New Armies (*see page 95*), were also involved and, in French's view, command and control were untidy. He therefore recommended that the Central Force be disbanded and the training centre commanders excluded from the chain of command. Instead, home defence should become the responsibility of the home commands, with Eastern Command taking control of the crucial East Anglian coast. Furthermore, the subordinate Central Force HQs should be reduced to two, with their line of demarcation running from Ipswich via Haverhill to Saffron Walden. As for the troops involved, there were seventeen New Army mixed brigades, thirteen second- and third-line TF divisions, ten Provisional brigades, twenty-three Cyclist battalions and nineteen independent Provisional battalions. French recommended that the last-named be disbanded and their manpower made available for garrison duties.[65] All these points were agreed to by the Military Members of the Army Council at a meeting held on 23 February 1916. While the Mounted Corps HQ was disbanded, the other two Central Force headquarters were retitled HQ Northern and HQ Southern Armies and placed directly under Eastern Command.

Sir John French made a further recommendation and this concerned the Supernumerary companies TF. He noted that they now had a total strength of 39,000 of whom 10,000 were guarding railways, assisted by the civil police. The remainder were involved in vulnerable point guards under the control of the home commands. However, their administration remained in the hands of home-based Territorial battalions and TF associations. French considered this to be untidy and recommended that they be formed into a separate body. The upshot of this was the creation of the Royal Defence Corps (RDC). Its role was local defence of Britain and, as such, it took over the Supernumerary companies TF, which were paired to form Protection companies RDC, with a strength of 250 men each, and lost their former regimental affiliations. Reserve companies were also formed in each home command to take in and train newly embodied conscripts and provide drafts for the Protection companies within that command. In addition, fourteen Observer companies were created to provide early warning of the approach of Zeppelins and hostile aircraft.*[66]

By summer 1916, the Territorial Force had lost a significant degree of integrity. Much of the cause for this had been manpower problems. The first was the restrictions over the posting of Territorials, which had resulted in a lack of flexibility in the distribution of manpower throughout the army as a whole. The second was that from the outset of war the TF had been engaged in a struggle for recruits with Kitchener's New Armies and many had been swayed into joining the latter because they believed that they would embark on active service more quickly.

---

* The Observer companies were distributed around the country and formed cordons of observation posts around critical areas – industrial and ports. The outer cordon was positioned 50–60 miles from the edge of the threatened area and the inner cordon 30 miles from it.

four

THE NEW ARMIES

On 2 August 1914, Lieutenant Colonel Charles à Court Repington, *The Times* Military Correspondent, wrote: 'If war breaks out we may see thousands of volunteers flocking to the Colours. But we need every man we can get for our general service army, and masses of untrained Volunteers in the Territorial Force will be rather an encumbrance than an aid.'[1] It was an opinion shared by Lord Kitchener, with his deep prejudice against 'amateur' soldiers. Furthermore, he did not agree with the popular view that the war would be over by Christmas and wanted to raise a large army capable of sustained action. He was also determined that it should be trained along Regular, rather than Territorial Force lines.

Accordingly, on 6 August, just after he had become Secretary of State for War, Kitchener decided to raise 100,000 Regulars from volunteers. They were to be trained at regimental depots, but their accommodation was to be separate and distinct from those troops undergoing mobilization.[2] The following day, the Prime Minister requested Parliament to sanction an additional half million men for the army, while the Press published Kitchener's call for an immediate 100,000 men aged 19 to 31, who would be enlisted for three years or the duration of the war. Kitchener also appealed to the TF County Associations for help in raising this new force. That same day, 7 August, the War Office instructed every Regular battalion to send forthwith to its regimental depot one captain, two subalterns and two serving sergeants, and a further thirteen other NCOs from among their reservists, to assist with the formation of Kitchener's new 'Regular Army'.[3] Three days later, a captain and subaltern from each infantry Special Reserve battalion were similarly detailed.[4]

On 9 August, an Army Council Military Members meeting confirmed that a 'New Expeditionary Force' was to be formed as battalions and administered by training centres, each a general's command. The force would eventually be sent abroad organized in six divisions, one from within each of the peacetime home commands. That raised by Southern Command would, however, be a light division, created from additional battalions of light infantry and rifle regiments. The new units were to be designated 'Service battalions' to distinguish them from Regular, Special Reserve, and TF battalions. Initially, one Service battalion was to be formed by each two-battalion line regiment and three by each four-battalion regiment. Training centres were to be established at Aldershot (8th and 9th Divisions) and Salisbury (13th Division), with a further one in Ireland (10th Division), and three for what was to be the Eastern Division (12th Division) at Shorn-cliffe, Colchester and Rainham. The training centres for 11th Division being raised in Northern Command were announced as Grantham, Leeds, and Sheffield a couple of days later.

The rapid expansion of the New Armies meant a recall to the Colours of numerous retired senior officers. Some were very quick to volunteer their services. General Sir Archibald Hunter, who was approaching 58 years old and was currently Governor General of Gibraltar, wrote to Kitchener on 9 August: 'I live in hopes of you giving me a command ... My French is quite good enough for all practical purposes. I am ready to go anywhere and do anything at a moment's notice.' He wrote again two days later and his perseverance was rewarded when Kitchener had him appointed to run the Aldershot Training Centre in place of Sir Horace Smith-Dorrien, who had been summoned to take over Grierson's corps in France after the death of its commander. Hunter had been a divisional commander in South Africa and was well known to Kitchener. He ran Aldershot Command for three years and then became a Conservative MP. Another senior South African veteran was Major General Robert Kekewich, who had made his name defending Kimberley against the Boers. He had been retired for ten years and was now aged 66. He was delighted to be given command of the

'13 Western Training Division' on Salisbury Plain. Writing to Kitchener on 21 August, he was honest enough to state: 'I am afraid I am a bit rusty, but you can rely on me doing my bit.'[5] The strain proved too much, however, and Kekewich committed suicide at the beginning of November 1914.

Recruiting for the New Armies rose steadily. Between 4 August and 8 August, just under 8,200 men had come forward. Over the following seven days 43,764 volunteers were attested. The next week the total was just under 50,000 and that ending Saturday 29 August netted 66,310. The weekly total peaked during the period 30 August – 5 September, with almost 175,000 volunteering, moved by the fact that the Expeditionary Force was in retreat. Thereafter the weekly total declined until, from the beginning of October, it was between 15,000 and 18,000. Probably motivated by the BEF's desperate struggle at Ypres, there was a small surge in November, with the weekly figure rising to over 36,000, but it declined once more, with only just over 10,300 signing in the last week of December. By then, nearly 806,000 men had been attested.[6] Such was the success of the initial recruiting drive, helped by Kitchener extending the upper age to 35 at the end of August and appealing to married men as well, that on 2 September the formation of a second New Army (K2), also comprising six divisions (numbered 14 to 19) was announced. However, because of the decision to create an 8th Regular Division, the numbering of the New Army divisions was altered, with K1 comprising the 9th to 14th Divisions and K2 the 15th to 20th Divisions. This was followed by K3 and K4 by the beginning of October. K4 itself was formed from men posted to Special Reserve battalions who were surplus to establishment.

The 11th King's Liverpool claimed on 25 August that it was fully recruited and was the first Service battalion to reach establishment.[7] Some of the battalions of the 14th Light Division attained a strength of 2,500 men, more than twice the official establishment. With the creation of K2, these battalions were paraded and company officers told to fall out half their men to create the new battalions. Captain C. E. Jesser-Davis

> … was drilling with D Company of the Eighth Battalion [Rifle Brigade] when I was sent to take command of C Company of the Eleventh Battalion. I found three hundred and twenty men and boys in every variety

of civilian attire, mostly rather shabby (although one man was in possession of a white collar) waiting in the road with their newspaper parcels under their arms, and had to get them into the very limited accommodation allotted to me – one barrack-room and two or three bell tents.[8]

In terms of the quality of recruit, Rory Baynes, adjutant of the 9th Scottish Rifles noted: 'The first lot … were a pretty rough crowd. The next lot were rather better. They'd had jobs and had given them up and joined the army. Then later a superior class came down. These were all very well dressed, with a couple of them carrying suitcases, and later on came an even smarter variety.'[9]

As well as the New Army units being formed strictly under War Office auspices, a new type of battalion also began to come into being. These were raised by individuals or municipalities, the aim being that friends and those with a common background or employment should be allowed to join up and fight together. The origins of these Pals or Locally Raised battalions, as they became known, were diverse and no one individual can really claim responsibility, although the earliest intimation was a letter from a Mr E. J. Gordon of the Services Insurance Agency Ltd to the War Office on 15 August 1914. Written on behalf of his Managing Director, James J. Mackay, it proposed 'that a Regiment be raised comprised entirely of old members of recognised public schools, of ages from 30 to 40, who do not come within the scope of any of the recently issued proclamations, and for whom no opportunity is open to offer their active services'. The War Office, under mounting pressure, made no immediate reply.[10] In the meantime, on 19 August a lunch took place at the Travellers' Club in London between General Henry Rawlinson, who had been made Director of Recruiting, and Major the Hon. Robert White, a veteran of the 1884–85 Sudan campaign and South African War who was now on the Reserve of Officers and had close connections with the City of London. Rawlinson told White that Kitchener wanted more men for the Royal Fusiliers in London and suggested that White raise a battalion from men who worked in the City. White was enthusiastic and immediately wrote letters to all the financial houses and, on 21 August, set up a recruiting office in

Throgmorton Street in the heart of the City. Six days later he had 1,600 men on his books and they were formed into the 10th (Stockbrokers Battalion) Royal Fusiliers. Meanwhile, the Bristol Citizens' Recruiting Committee proposed the raising of a battalion from the 'better class young men in Bristol'. The War Office sanctioned this on 30 August, but administrative delays meant that the committee was not notified for some days. Nevertheless, on 3 September it decided to go ahead with recruiting for what became the 10th Gloucesters.[11]

Another scheme, similar to that proposed by James Mackay, was triggered by a letter published in *The Times* on 26 August. Signed by 'Eight Unattached', who described themselves as 'between thirty and thirty-five, absolutely fit and game for active service', with OTC experience and qualified as marksmen, they complained that they had been rejected for commissions in the New Army as being too old and that their services as musketry instructors had been turned down on the grounds that they were too young. They concluded that the only answer was to enlist in the ranks. They invited 'all public school men of similar age and qualifications' to a meeting to be held the following day with a view to forming a 'Legion of Marksmen'. A Mr H. J. Boon drew up a scheme for enlisting 5,000 men aged between 21 and 35 throughout the country from schools mentioned in the *Public Schools Year Book*. He saw Kitchener's private secretary, Sir George Arthur, and through him obtained the War Minister's permission to raise the corps. By 12 September, 5,000 had been enlisted and there was a growing waiting list. Within a week the University and Public Schools' (UPS) Brigade was in training at Woodcote Park, Epsom, on ground loaned by the Royal Automobile Club.[12] It would form four battalions (18th to 21st) of the Royal Fusiliers. Meanwhile, James Mackay had finally received a reply from the War Office sanctioning the raising of his Public Schools battalion, which, he was informed, would become part of the Middlesex Regiment. Within two weeks of receiving the letter, Mackay already had half his battalion camped on Kempton Race Course and its official title was the Public Schools Battalion, The Middlesex Regiment, later the 16th Middlesex. Christopher Stone, a bespectacled 32-year-old novelist, was one of the founder members. His joining instructions came in the form of a telegram sent on 12 September. It read: 'Parade

Waterloo Station eleven o'clock Tuesday morning (15th). Bring enough kit for ten days and one blanket.'[13]

The Royal Fusiliers would also include two Sportsmen's battalions (23rd and 24th), which were raised by the then well-known sportswoman Mrs E. Cunliffe-Owen. The 1st Sportsmen's Battalion had a wide cross-section of background and experience. In one hut at the unit's first camp at Hornchurch

> the first bed was occupied by the brother of a peer. The second by the man who drove his car ... Other beds were occupied by a mechanical engineer, an old Blundell School boy, planters, a mine overseer from Scotland, a man in possession of a flying pilot's certificate secured in France, an old sea-dog who had rounded Cape Horn on no fewer than nine occasions, a man who had hunted seals, 'with more patches on his trousers than he could count', as he described it himself, and so on.[14]

The man who really put the Pals battalions on the map, however, was Lord Derby, chairman of the West Lancashire Territorial Association, whom Lloyd George would later call 'the most efficient recruiting sergeant in England'. On 24 August he lunched with Kitchener, who agreed to the formation of a battalion drawn from the business houses in Liverpool. Derby then summoned his brother, the Hon. Ferdinand Stanley DSO, a veteran of the Omdurman campaign and South African War who had been recalled to the Colours and was now serving as a captain in the 3rd Grenadiers, and invited him to command the battalion. Such was Derby's standing in Liverpool that 1,500 men responded to his call to attend the Drill Hall in St Anne's Street on the evening of 28 August. No attestations actually took place at the meeting, but a weekend's chance to reflect did not dampen the ardour, and on the following Monday 31 August the ranks of the new battalion were filled to establishment and well beyond. Cunard Line employees offering their names numbered 120, and 218 men volunteered from the Cotton Exchange. In all, there were sufficient recruits to form three City battalions, with a fourth being raised in mid October. They became the 17th–20th King's Liverpool Regiment and were formed into the 89th Brigade under Stanley's command.[15] Manchester and Birmingham quickly followed Liverpool's example. Hull raised four battalions of

Pals for the East Yorkshire Regiment: the Hull Commercials (10th Battalion), Hull Tradesmen (11th), Sportsmen and Athletes (12th), and, for want of a better name, T'others (13th). Tyneside was especially energetic when it came to raising Pals battalions. By the end of January 1915, the Northumberland Fusiliers contained one Newcastle City battalion (16th), one formed from members of the North East Railway (17th), two of Tyneside Pioneers (18th and 19th), four Tyneside Scottish (20th to 23rd) and four Tyneside Irish (24th to 27th). These were in addition to the seven Service and one Reserve battalions formed under War Office auspices. The Scottish Lowlands were also active, with the City of Glasgow raising three battalions of Highland Light Infantry in September 1914. In all, of the 557 Service and Reserve battalions raised up to June 1916, no less than 215, or 38 per cent, were locally raised.[16]

The concept of privately raised battalions proved especially attractive to a War Office already swamped by the rapid enlargement of the army, which saw it as a means of shifting the ever heavier administrative burden that it was carrying. A deal was therefore made that those responsible for raising these units would be initially responsible for providing accommodation, uniforms and rations, while the War Office would make over sums of money to cover the costs. It retained responsibility for the supply of weapons and transport, however.

Two other segments of the New Armies had a more political background. On 19 September 1914, David Lloyd George, then Chancellor of the Exchequer, made a speech at the Queen's Hall, London. He declared:

> I should like to see a Welsh Army in the Field. I should like to see the race that faced the Normans for hundreds of years in a struggle for freedom, the race that helped us win Crecy, the race that fought for a generation under Glyndwr against the greatest Captain in Europe – I should like to see that race give a good taste of their quality in this struggle in Europe; and they are going to do it.

Two days later, a group of prominent Welshmen met at Lloyd George's official residence, 11 Downing Street, and agreed to set up a scheme for a Welsh Army Corps of two divisions. It was launched in the Park Hall, Cardiff on 29 September and a National Executive Committee (NEC) was established to oversee the creation of the corps. The committee first met four days later. It recognized that the formation of a Welsh Army Corps was not going to be easy. For a start, 50,000 Welshmen had already enlisted in the armed forces, including several who had joined English, Scottish and Irish regiments. This represented nearly one-sixth of the total number of Welsh males aged between 20 and 35 according to the 1911 census. The committee also accepted the need to maintain the supply of manpower to the Regular battalions of the three Welsh infantry regiments via their third battalions, as well as that to the Welsh Division TF. Furthermore, a number of battalions were already committed to the New Armies: 8th Royal Welsh Fusiliers, 4th South Wales Borderers and 8th Welsh to K1; 9th Royal Welsh Fusiliers, 5th South Wales Borderers and 9th Welsh to K2; and 10th and 11th Royal Welsh Fusiliers, 6th, 7th and 8th South Wales Borderers and 10th and 11th Welsh to K3. In addition, the number of volunteers coming forward had already peaked. There was also suspicion over the seemingly political nature of the army corps on the part of the GOC-in-C Western Command, General Sir Henry Mackinnon, under whose authority Wales came.

Even so, the committee managed to raise 3,000 men by the end of October 1914, but these included the 10th Welsh, which the War Office had handed over. The committee agreed that the three brigades of the 1st Division should be based on Llandudno, Rhyl and Colwyn Bay. These were respectively the training centres for the Royal Welsh Fusiliers, Welsh Regiment and South Wales Borderer battalions formed for the Welsh Corps. Officers appointed to the Welsh Army Corps were to be selected by the Lords Lieutenant and County committees, but there is no doubt that Lloyd George took a personal hand in the selection of senior commanders. Appointed to command the 1st Brigade, after a personal request by Lloyd George to Kitchener, was Colonel Owen Thomas, a Welsh Liberal MP. Another Liberal MP (for Southampton) given a brigade command was 53-year-old Ivor Philipps, who had retired from the 5th Gurkha Rifles in 1903 after extensive active service in Burma and on the North-West Frontier of India, before winning a DSO in China in 1900. Thereafter he had commanded the Pembrokeshire Yeomanry and been appointed a GSO2 at the War Office after the outbreak of war. According to Lloyd George's personal secretary and mistress, Frances Stephenson, Lloyd George felt that he owed Philipps a favour. Some years before, when Lloyd George's political prospects did not look good and he was also suffering financial problems, he was offered a loan of £500 by Philipps's elder brother, Lord St Davids. Lloyd George declined, but clearly felt that he was in debt to the Philipps family. Two months after being promoted to brigadier general, Lloyd George engineered Ivor Philipps to command of the division, remarking to Miss Stephenson that he had 'never forgotten St Davids' generosity, and St. D will never ask him for anything in vain'. Significantly, Lloyd George also arranged for his younger son Gwilym to be Philipps's ADC. While both Thomas and Philipps were on the National Executive Committee, the third brigade commander, Colonel R. H. W. Dunn, a 'dug out' who had retired from the army in 1897 and had been brought back to command the 13th Royal Welsh Fusiliers, was not.[17]

By the end of 1914 the Welsh Army Corps had reached a strength of 10,000 men and the 1st Division, which would take its place as the 38th Division in the army, was taking shape, although it still lacked artillery. However, in March 1915 a row broke out between the National Executive Committee and the GOC-in-C Western Command over recruiting. The committee wanted to appoint an inspector general for recruiting to cover the whole of the principality and for all Welsh regiments, whether Regular, Territorial or New Army, to be regarded as the 'Welsh Contingent of HM's Army'. Mackinnon, fearing that the NEC would give priority to the Welsh Army Corps over maintaining the strength of the Regular and TF battalions, objected. The row simmered on throughout the summer and it was not until almost the end of October 1915 that the Army Council made a ruling. Recruiting in Wales was to concentrate on building up reserves rather than creating new units. It marked the death knell of the Welsh Army Corps, which had almost reached its original target of 50,000 men. The majority were with what was now the 38th (Welsh) Division and carrying out their final training on Salisbury Plain prior to going to France. Seven other battalions had been formed – four of Bantams (of which more later), which became a brigade in 40th Division, and three which became Reserve battalions.[18] Ivor Philipps was extracted by Lloyd George to be Parliamentary Secretary to the newly created Ministry of Munitions in the summer of 1915 and became Acting Director-General of Munitions Supply, but returned to the division in August, well before it left for France.[19] He was, however, removed from command during the fighting on the Somme in summer 1916, but was compensated by being made a KCB in 1917. Owen Thomas did not take his brigade to France and was given a training brigade instead. Dunn, too, was considered too old for active service.

The other 'political' formation was the Ulster Division. During the first half of 1914 Ireland had been in crisis. In January 1913 the third Home Rule Bill had passed its third reading in the House of Commons and looked set to become law. It was modest in its structure. While Ireland would be given its own parliament and a degree of autonomy, foreign and defence policy, as well as most taxation, would remain in the hands of Westminster. Even so, the largely Protestant north had been outraged from the outset and demanded that the nine counties of Ulster be excluded. It raised the paramilitary Ulster Volunteer Force (UVF), many of whose members were ex-soldiers. Asquith wavered and seemed to be about to placate the Unionists. In reaction, the Catholic south formed the Irish Volunteers. It was much weaker than the UVF and the British government was faced with the prospect of having to use force to ensure that the Act was put into effect.

In March 1914, Sir Arthur Paget, the GOC-in-C in Ireland, was told that should his troops have to move against Ulster, officers who lived there would be allowed to slip away and anyone else disobeying the order would be dismissed from the service. Paget then canvassed his officers and fifty of those in Hubert Gough's 3rd Cavalry Brigade declared that they would prefer to be dismissed. Haig, too, declared that Aldershot Command supported Gough's stance and Asquith felt forced to back down. The Curragh Mutiny, as it was called, led to the resignations of Jack Seely, the Secretary of State for War, and Sir John French, the CIGS.* Asquith now tried to amend the Act to the extent of excluding some of the Ulster counties, negotiations over which were continuing when Britain declared war against Germany. This took the heat out of the situation for the time being and hopes now were that Irishmen of both causes would rally to the flag.

* Seely, a keen Yeomanry soldier, had won the DSO in South Africa and would command the Canadian Cavalry Brigade with much dash during the war.

As early as 7 August 1914, Kitchener summoned Colonel T. E. Hickman MP, who was president of the British League for the Defence of Ulster, and told him that he wanted to incorporate the Ulster Volunteer Force in his New Army. He was particularly attracted by the fact that its members had a modicum of military training. Hickman advised consultation with the Ulster Unionist leader, Sir Edward Carson, who insisted that the UVF be incorporated as a distinct entity rather than its members being recruited individually. Kitchener also conceded that they could incorporate their UVF battalion titles and wear the Red Hand of Ulster as their emblem. But this was still not enough for Carson. He wanted the government to give an undertaking that the thorny Home Rule question be shelved until after the war. But this had to be balanced by the Nationalist stance that, unless a measure of Home Rule was assured, they could not support the recruiting campaign in Ireland. If this was the case, it would make the creation of the K1 formation 10th (Irish) Division that much more difficult, although some UVF men had already enlisted in it. Asquith decided to put the matter 'on hold' until some acceptable compromise could be worked out. That the 10th Division's recruiting was not going nearly as well as that in the other K1 divisions became clear to the War Office before the end of August. It noted that the Service battalions of the Inniskillings and the Royal Irish Regiment, which recruited in Ulster, were especially weak in strength. The view was that, unless the UVF and Irish Nationalists were persuaded to give active support for the war effort, the prospects of forming the K2 Irish Division were minimal.[20] However, the Battles of Mons and Le Cateau and the subsequent retreat by the BEF resulted not only in a surge in recruiting, but a change of heart on Carson's part. He declared that he would put the UVF at the disposal of the War Office with no strings attached. The Ulster Unionist Council, meeting in Belfast, gave its formal approval on 3 September. The Belfast battalions immediately enlisted en masse, followed by those in Londonderry and the rural areas. They formed battalions of the three Ulster-based regiments: Royal Inniskilling Fusiliers (two battalions), Royal Irish Rifles (nine) and Royal Irish Fusiliers (one).[21] They became the 36th (Ulster) Division at the end of October, but since the UVF had no artillery and the British government did not want the UVF to possess any after the war, the division's integral field batteries were provided by the mainland.

In the meantime, the struggles to bring the 10th and then the K2 16th (Irish) Divisions up to strength continued. The key to overcoming the problem was John Redmond, leader of the Irish Nationalists. While he had been moved by the plight of Belgium and viewed it as churlish not to support Britain when Home Rule seemed about to be granted, he was not prepared to support recruiting fully until he had had a firm assurance from the government that the Home Rule Bill would be placed on the statute book. Furthermore, he would only agree to encouraging the enlistment of the Irish Volunteers provided that they did not have to take the oath of allegiance to the King and that they would be used only for the defence of Ireland. Asquith, distracted by the numerous other issues that had developed as a result of the war, did nothing until mid September, when he intro-duced the bill and, in spite of the Conservative opposition walking out of the House of Commons in protest, it received royal assent on the 18th. Even though it was accompanied by an Act that ensured that it would not be put into force until after the end of the war, as well as another bill designed to resolve the problem of Ulster, there was much rejoicing in Irish Nationalist circles. Redmond threw himself into recruiting – indeed, in a speech made at Woodenbridge on 20 September, he declared that the Irish Volunteers would go 'wherever the firing line extends, in the defence of right, of freedom and of religion in this war', thus overturning his previous policy of refusing to countenance Irish Volunteers serving outside Ireland.[22] Asquith gave him further encouragement by talking about the formation of an Irish Army Corps. But while Kitchener was happy to accept the idea of a Welsh Army Corps, he was not prepared to grant the same to the Irish. Redmond's request that 'Irish Brigade' (in memory of the Irish who had fought for France in the eighteenth century) should be incorporated into the title of the 16th (Irish) Division was rejected, as was the adoption of a special Irish badge.[23] Even so, for the time being at least recruiting in Ireland kept pace with that on the mainland. By the end of April 1915 over 75,000 resident Irishmen had enlisted, although some 40 per cent came from the six largely Protestant counties in the north, and the future of the three Irish divisions was secured.[24] Like the Ulster Division, 16th (Irish) Division did not have its own integral artillery, and indeed did not receive its four artillery brigades, three of which came from London, until two months after it arrived in France. It also received its third brigade, which had been left behind under-strength in Britain, at the same time.[25]

A further element of the New Armies was the Bantams. At the outbreak of war, the minimum accepted height for recruits was 5 feet 3 inches. This was rigorously enforced and many volunteers under this height, who were otherwise fit and suitable, were turned down. One such case came to the attention of Alfred Bigland MP, who headed the Birkenhead Recruiting Committee. The man in question was a Durham coalminer who had hiked all the way to Birkenhead, calling at numerous recruiting offices en route in the hope of enlisting. Every time he tried, he was turned down because he was an inch below the minimum height. Finally, he crossed the Mersey and reached Chester. Rejected once more, he threatened to fight any man in the recruiting office and was only removed with difficulty. One of Bigland's committee had been present and told him of this. The upshot was that Bigland wrote direct to Kitchener to tell him of his committee's view that 'a very valuable contingent of his army could be raised of "Bantams", men of five feet to five feet three inches, provided they were strong, sturdy fellows' and suggested that by stipulating for an extra inch in the chest measurement over the regulation 33 inches, 'sickly weedy men with insufficient stamina would be excluded.'[26] Bigland did not receive a direct reply from Kitchener, but he was summoned to see Sir Henry Mackinnon, GOC-in-C Western Command, who told him that the Secretary of State for War was interested in the Bantam concept. He also gave Bigland details of the new locally raised battalions. Bigland took the hint and decided to form a Bantam battalion himself. He set about finding accommodation and earmarked the local agricultural show ground. He circulated details about his Bantam battalion to recruiting offices around the country. This was as well, since Bigland found that many of the potential Bantams from his local area failed their medicals because they could not expand their chest measurements to the required 34 inches and there was a danger that his idea would be still-born. The upshot was that numerous recruits arrived after having passed medicals at their local recruiting offices and been issued with railway warrants. Thus, on 18 November 1914 the 16th (Service) Battalion the Cheshire Regiment (1st Birkenhead) came into being. Bigland, however, soon had almost a thousand surplus recruits on his hands and was able to quickly raise a second Bantam battalion (17th Cheshires).

With the doctors concentrating on chest measurements, some Bantam recruits were accepted even though they were under the minimum height of 5 feet. Cyril Wright, a shipyard worker, recalled: 'I was exactly four foot ten inches when they accepted me. I turned up at the Town Hall office with very little hope of getting in, but as I was a strong healthy lad otherwise, they just said my heart was big enough to make up for height, and a soldier I became.' Others were able to slip through, even though they were under-age. Jeff Pritchard was just 14½, but keen to enlist.

> My mother was poorly in a county home and my father had six other mouths to feed. So one morning, I just walked away from my job as a cart-handler down the mine and went to the recruiting office. 'How old are you my lad?' the doctor said. I looked him in the eye and said 'Eighteen, sir.' 'Hmm,' he said, 'And what does your mother think of you going for a soldier?' I told him she was dying, and he just patted me on the shoulder and signed my acceptance without another word.[27]

But it was not just Bantams who evaded the minimum age for enlistment. The *Daily Mirror* of 16 September 1916 carried a picture of Private S. Lewis of the East Surreys who had reputedly joined his regiment at the age of 12 in August 1915 and fought for six weeks on the Somme before his true age was discovered.[28]

During the first part of 1915, with fewer volunteers for the New Armies coming forward, the Bantam movement grew in strength. A song was soon being sung in music halls throughout the country:

> Have you ever seen a Bantam in a fight?
> No other bird can stick it
> Like a Bantam, or can lick it.
> And you never saw a Bantam taking fright![29]

The Lord Provost and City of Glasgow raised a Bantam battalion in February 1915, which became the 18th Highland Light Infantry. The Lancashire Fusiliers had three battalions. Wales provided a complete brigade of four battalions of Bantams, which had originally been raised for the Welsh

Army Corps. In the end, sufficient battalions were formed, largely from the north of England and the Midlands, to create two complete Bantam divisions: the 35th and 40th. But the formation of the latter division indicated that the barrel was starting to run dry. Men were recruited who were clearly below the minimum medical standards. This was revealed when one battalion (13th Cameronians) was reduced to a mere 200 men after it had been subjected to a series of medical inspections after joining 40th Division at Aldershot. Three other battalions in the division (the 12th South Lancashires, 18th Sherwood Foresters and 21st Middlesex) also had to be disbanded during the winter of 1915–16 and replaced by non-Bantam battalions. Their men who passed the medicals were posted to other Bantam battalions within the brigade.

One final and unique formation should be mentioned at this stage. Although not a New Army division *per se*, the Royal Naval Division (RND) did have similar characteristics in that many of its men were volunteers. Prior to the outbreak of war, arrangements had been made for a brigade of Royal Marines, known as the Advanced Base Force, to be formed on mobilization. When war did come, the Admiralty realized that it had too many reservists for the number of ships available and so, at Winston Churchill's instigation, two brigades of bluejackets were formed. Some 40 per cent of them were volunteers, including some 600 miners from the north-east of England who were queuing to enlist in the Durham Light Infantry or Northumberland Fusiliers, but were diverted to the RND instead. The men were formed into eight battalions named after famous admirals. Churchill then offered the division to the army, on the proviso that it would continue to be administered by the Admiralty and enjoy naval pay rates. It was gratefully accepted by Kitchener. The Royal Marine Brigade was sent to secure Dunkirk, but then it was decided that the RND should be sent to Antwerp to bolster the Belgian defence of the port. It was in vain, with some 2,000 men of the two naval brigades being interned in Holland for the rest of the war. After being refitted, the division was sent to the Dardanelles. While it had engineers and supporting services supplied by the army, the division was totally lacking in artillery.

The RND suffered heavy casualties on Gallipoli and had to go through another reorganization. Worse, the Admiralty could not supply any more replacement manpower because of the wartime expansion of the Royal Navy, and 500 men from the division who had previous sea service were sent back to Britain. It meant that the strength of the RND was now so reduced that its future was in serious doubt. Furthermore, in the aftermath of the evacuation from Gallipoli in January 1916, the remainder were now garrisoning three islands in the Aegean and morale was low. After hurried negotiations between the War Office and the Admiralty, it was agreed that the division would be transferred to the army, although the Admiralty would continue to be responsible for pay and for supplying manpower. In accordance with this, it was formally placed under the Army Act on 16 April 1916. The following month, the division moved to France, where it underwent a further reorganization. The RN and RM battalions were placed in two brigades (the 188th and 189th) and a newly formed army brigade (the 190th) brought in. The division was retitled the 63rd (Royal Naval) Division and finally received its own artillery, which came from the newly disbanded 63rd (2nd Northumberland) Division TF, together with trench mortar batteries. Thereafter it fought with distinction on the Western Front.[30]

The experience of the BEF in the first months of the war made the authorities realize that the New Armies might well also suffer heavy casualties when they got to the Front. It was therefore important to establish a system for maintaining battalions at the Front with the necessary manpower. The regimental depots had been made responsible for providing drafts for the first three New Armies, while the Locally Raised battalions had been each ordered to form a depot company for the same purpose. Doubts grew as to whether the regimental depots could adequately maintain K1, 2 and 3. So, in April 1915, the seventy-five battalions of the Fourth New Army were designated 2nd Reserve battalions and formed into Reserve brigades. A new Fourth Army was created from the locally raised units and Bantams. The Fifth New Army was similarly constituted and included the 36th (Ulster) and 38th (Welsh) Divisions. The locally raised depot companies in each brigade were then concentrated into sixty-eight Local Reserve battalions. The problems of raising the New Armies paled into insignificance, however, compared to the difficulties of accommodating and equipping them.

The accommodation of troops was the pre-war responsibility of the War Office's Peace Distribution Committee. At the outbreak of war, its chairman was Major General G. K. Scott-Moncrieff, the Director of Fortifications and Works, and the members were the Director of Military Training, Director of Recruiting and Organisation, Director of Supplies and Quartering, the Assistant Director of Movements and the Principal of Works Finance. On 9 August 1914, the Army Council instructed the committee to produce plans for the housing of Kitchener's First New Army. It proposed that the new recruits should spend about a week in their regimental depots and then be moved to the training centre for their division, occupying the barracks of the Regular units which by then would have left for France. However, the depots themselves quickly became flooded with recruits. An officer serving at the depot of the Cameron Highlanders wrote: 'It sometimes happened that although we had practically cleared the barracks one evening there would be some 400 recruits on parade the following morning, these having come in during the night.'[31] The Reverend William Drury recorded the case of a group of young men from Cranleigh and neighbouring villages in Surrey who volunteered for their local county regiment, the Queen's. They were given a great send off by the local populace, but when they arrived at the regimental depot at Stoughton Barracks, Guildford, they discovered that there was no room for them and they were forced to return to their homes.[32] Those who did spend time in the regimental depots often found the catering arrangements to be basic in the extreme. Some existed on a diet of bully-beef sandwiches. Others did receive hot meals, but they had to eat these with their fingers as knives, forks and spoons were lacking.

It quickly became obvious that the available barracks would not be sufficient to house even the full complement of K1. Indeed, from the outset the Royal Engineers' depot at Chatham had been forced to resort to billeting, organizing the recruits into 'billeting companies', with serving sappers and bandsmen acting as NCOs, each taking charge of a group of 100 men.[33] The War Office therefore decided to erect tented camps until hutted camps could be built. One of the staff captains working in FW2, the branch within the Directorate of Fortifications and Works responsible for barrack design, had already been thinking about hutted camps.

Indeed, Major B. H. O. Armstrong had drawn up designs for battalion hutments which could be constructed in two days. Approval for these camps to go ahead was given by the Army Council on 17 August and within days contracts were being issued. But Scott-Moncrieff soon began to doubt whether the building programme would be completed before winter set in. He suggested that priority should be given to cookhouses, messes and recreation rooms. This would give the men somewhere warm to go, even if they still had to sleep in tents. He was overruled by Sir John Cowans, the Quartermaster General, who laid down that the camps must be completed in toto. When the influx of recruits rose sharply towards the end of August, the War Office decided that the existing barrack construction machinery could not cope. One of the QMG's directorates was that of Supplies and Quartering. In terms of barracks, the Directorate of Supplies and Quartering (DSQ) was responsible for appropriation and occupation, as well as the hire of buildings to supplement barracks. Cowans now decided that the DSQ should be split into separate directorates, but while the old director was a mere full colonel with the temporary rank of brigadier general, the new Director of Quartering, C. E. Heath, was a major general. R. G. Long, a former ASC officer who was the previous DSQ, now became Director of Supplies, but received no elevation in rank. Such was the importance now attached to resolving the New Army's accommodation problem. As for Scott-Moncrieff, he was summoned before the Army Council and told that the selection of sites for camps had been passed to Heath. 'When I asked that I might have some opportunity, on engineering grounds, to co-operate in the selection, I was refused with, I think, gratuitous rudeness. I therefore bowed and left the room.'[34]

The creation of K2 presented Heath with an immediate headache, but he managed to find locations for the six divisions, although two-thirds of their men had to make do with tented accommodation. No sooner had he done this than Kitchener announced the formation of K3. By now the six training centres had run out of available space and Heath had to find fresh sites. The situation was aggravated by the requirements of the Territorial Force, which had now deployed to its home defence stations and had many of its units in billets, as well as the needs of the newly created second-line TF units and, for that matter, the Special Reserve battalions on port defence duty. The only answer appeared to be to slow the influx of recruits temporarily, and on 11 September the minimum height was increased to 5 feet 6 inches, apart from ex-soldiers. This caused a slump in recruiting, from which Colonel Gosset, the AAG in charge of recruiting at the War Office, claimed it never recovered.[*][35] By the second half of September, contracts had been placed for the building of hutted camps sufficient to house nearly 500,000 men, but it was clear that this programme could not be completed until the end of November at the earliest. Heath's only consolation was that the specially raised battalions did not increase his burden, since their accommodation was the responsibility of those who created them.

Soon much of southern England was a swathe of tented camps, but the conditions in them were often grim, as they were in the now overcrowded barracks. An officer in the 15th (Scottish) Division at Aldershot wrote:

> The discomfort was appalling. Crowded into quarters far too small for them, with one blanket or piece of tweed apiece to cover them, without mattresses, or even the barest necessities of life, the men never grumbled; they knew that those in authority were doing their best, and were content. Luckily the weather was fine and no sickness broke out, but the first six weeks were anxious ones for the medical officers of the division.[36]

Even more aggravating was that the newly raised units were now thrown much more on their own devices. The quality of food and the way it was served may have been a culture shock to many of the volunteers, but now they had to find their own cooks and often had little in the way of kitchen paraphernalia. Some units subsisted on bread and cheese because they had no one with any knowledge of cookery, while others overcame the problem by enlisting civilian cooks at high rates of pay. In some cases they were forced to use bits of planking in lieu of plates. Those who did their initial training with Reserve and Extra Reserve battalions were luckier. Charlie Cook was with the 3rd East Surreys in a tented camp at Dover.

> The grub all along has been pretty fair. The dinners have mostly been stew or roast beef with potatoes and haricot beans or peas, and the last two days we have had cabbage. The breakfasts have been bacon, liver,

---

* The minimum height was soon progressively lowered again to 5ft 2ins (apart from Bantams) by the beginning of November 1914 and reached 5ft 1in in May 1915, although it was quickly restored to 5ft 2in.

cold bacon, tinned fish (this has now stopped though), and kippers. Tea is either jam or cheese with bread, and today we had some cake.[37]

In the tented camps, the early weeks of good weather were a particular blessing, especially since tentage was short and overcrowding rampant. George Coppard with the 7th East Surreys at Purfleet was unlucky to have his sleeping place by the entry flap.

This meant that I couldn't lie down until everyone was in the tent. There were forty-four feet built up in tangled layers converging in the general direction of the centre pole. Nights were a nightmare to me and I dreaded them. Outside the tent flap within a yard of my head stood a urinal tub, and throughout the night boozy types would stagger and lunge towards the tent flap in order to urinate. I got showered every time and worst of all, it became a joke.[38]

In mid October there came a prolonged spell of bad weather and conditions in the camps deteriorated still further. Private Alexander Thompson of the 9th Northumberland Fusiliers in camp at Bovington in Dorset wrote in early November: 'We have had continuous rain for over a fortnight and the last week has been far beyond a joke. Our tents will not stop the rain coming in and many nights were spent, with candles lit, in trying to stop the rain from soaking us.'[39] Morale plummeted and in some cases there was close to open mutiny. Lieutenant M. J. H. Drummond experienced such an incident with the 10th Lancashire Fusiliers at Wool, also in Dorset.

The men were in rags, they were too many to a tent, they had very few blankets, and after two days of solid rain the mud was appalling and the tents flooded out … They threatened to pull the officers' tents down. The RSM … being the worse for drink, called them 'Northern Cowards' which did not improve matters. However, my company commander, Major Scott, a dear old man, appeased them and promised improvements.[40]

Matters were not helped by the fact that the camp building programme was falling ever more behind schedule. This was in part caused by the bad weather, but also because of a shortage of carpenters, many having enlisted.

Unskilled labour was brought in to make good this shortfall, but this merely led to poor workmanship. A shortage of materials also played its part. To overcome a problem that was reaching crisis proportions, troops in tented camps were moved into half-finished hutments, but, with winter now arrived, the cold meant that they were just as uncomfortable as they had been in their tents. Consequently, at the beginning of December 1914 the War Office decided that the only answer was billeting.

During the winter of 1914–15 no fewer than 800,000 troops – Special Reserve, TF, and New Army – found themselves billeted in private houses. Cowans set up a system of Area Quartering Committees under a Permanent President. These were responsible for arranging billeting, including rent and damage assessment. The allowances given to householders were generous – ninepence per night's lodging for each soldier, and three shillings for an officer. Messing was done in one of three ways. The troops ate in their own cookhouses; their rations were handed over to the householder; or the householder was responsible for feeding them, in which case he or she was paid two shillings and sevenpence halfpenny a day. Stanley Casson of the 3rd East Lancashires, who were billeted in Plymouth, commented: 'What they [the soldiers] got was worth about five shillings [per week] , so the eagerness and patriotic fervour of the citizens of Plymouth knew no bounds.'[41]

Experiences of billeting varied. W. A. Tucker was with the 15th Royal Welsh Fusiliers, which was quartered in boarding houses and hotels in the North Wales resort of Llandudno. He recalled: 'The troops were received almost as holiday visitors. They occupied ordinary bedrooms and were catered for by the hotel waitresses and general staff.'[42] Men like Arthur Winstanley of the 2nd/5th Manchesters in Colchester were made part of the family. 'We lads never went out at night; after a day's work ... we thought of nothing, only getting into a light pair of slippers, and gathering together with the family in the drawing room.'[43] Others were less fortunate. One 'landlady' in Canterbury, who did not want soldiers billeted on her, managed to get rid of them by putting jam into the chambers of their rifles.[44] Some adopted a Scrooge-like attitude to ensure that they made the maximum profit from the billeting allowances. But on the whole, the troops welcomed billeting. Certainly, it was infinitely better than living in sodden tents or half-built huts. By spring 1915, however, the accommodation crisis was largely over and the troops were able to move into properly established camps.

Lack of suitable accommodation was not the only problem that the New Armies had to face during the first months of their existence. Uniforms, weapons and equipment were also woefully lacking. In terms of uniforms alone, by the time the Regular reservists and first-line Territorials had been clothed, the army had few stocks left. Consequently, the New Armies suffered. Some of the men of K1, like Henry Jourdain's 5th Connaught Rangers, were lucky enough to be fully clothed in khaki almost as soon as they formed as a battalion. This battalion was also fortunate in having a high proportion of former Regular members of the Connaught Rangers who had completed their statutory seven years in the Reserve. The majority of Kitchener's men, however, had to survive in the clothes in which they had reported to their depots. George Butterworth of the 6th Duke of Cornwall's Light Infantry, another K1 battalion, complained in mid September:

> This is the chief grievance; every recruit on enlisting was told that he would be provided with full kit immediately, and was consequently advised to bring next to nothing with him. As a fact, for many days nothing at all was supplied; underclothing and boots are now being gradually doled out, but no khaki or overcoats; hence the men have no protection from wet and no proper change of clothes, and every shower of rain means so many more on the sick list.[45]

True, on 8 September Kitchener had authorized a 'one off' payment of eight shillings and sixpence to each man who provided himself with a serviceable suit, boots and overcoat, raising it to ten shillings two days later. But this could not prevent civilian clothes from wearing out very quickly. Colonel C. R. Sylvester Bradley, RAMC, wrote of the autumn of 1914:

> The availability of shirts, boots and socks was not more than one per cent of the requirements, and it was a painful sight to see men walking about having worn their boots and socks through to their bare feet and with the tails of their shirts protruding through what should have been the seat of their trousers!

He also stated that the issue of bars of soap and towels was restricted to one each for every twelve men, and that underclothes and razors were unobtainable.[46]

To overcome the problem, the War Office took a number of initiatives. First, it managed to lay hands on half a million blue serge uniforms, some obtained from the Post Office. It also made available obsolete scarlet tunics and items of ceremonial uniform. It placed numerous contracts for khaki uniforms, including massive orders with firms in Canada and the United States. The Territorial County Associations were also made responsible for maintaining not just the uniforms of existing first-line TF units, as was the previous agreement, but for outfitting every new Territorial recruit. Likewise, the locally raised units were expected to procure their own uniforms. This, however, led to some confusion, with too many agencies chasing clothing contracts. As for the blue uniforms, there was no great enthusiasm for them, but at least some of the men felt a little more like soldiers. Unfortunately some units, like the 6th Camerons, found themselves with a miscellany of clothing: 'Who can recall them without a shudder? The startling reds of the tunics, the postmen's trousers with the red stripes, and the crowning absurdity – the cap comforter which we wore in lieu of better headgear.'[47] Rory Baynes of the Cameronians had been on leave from West Africa when war broke out. He was sent from his regimental depot to help raise the 9th Scottish Rifles, becoming adjutant:

> We had absolutely nothing in the way of uniform or equipment or anything else. In spite of that we started marching quite soon, as one of the first things to do was to get the men as fit as possible. I think that broomsticks, instead of rifles, were the first equipment we had to drill with. Then a certain amount of uniform started to arrive. This was old full dress uniform from every kind of unit, and you got a most extraordinary selection on parade. You'd see a man for instance in a rifle tunic and tartan trews, wearing a straw hat, next to somebody else in a red coat and some civilian trousers.[48]

Kitchener had already reminded officers in command of depots that they could make use of local purchase to make good deficiencies, but by no means all took advantage of this. One who did was Major General J.

M. Babington, commanding the 23rd Division in K3, who obtained clearance to spend £17,000 on clothing and sent two officers to the north of England to purchase boots and underclothes.[49] The Locally Raised battalions often fared better, especially if their creators were men of energy. Brigadier General Stanley had his wife to thank for obtaining uniforms in reasonable time for Lord Derby's City battalions of the King's Liverpool Regiment. She managed to place an initial contract for 1,000 on the day recruiting opened. It saved the men having to go round in 'that terrible blue uniform'.[50] Likewise, as soon as authority to raise the Ulster Division had been given, Captain James Craig, one of the leading figures on the Ulster Unionist Council, went straight to a company in London which had supplied the UVF with khaki uniforms and placed an order for 10,000 more. Some of the battalions which were intended to make up the Welsh Army Corps were clothed in *brethyn-llwyd*, a hard-wearing brownish-grey local cloth, which might have reinforced suspicions in some quarters that Lloyd George was intent on creating an army within an army.[51]

Webbing was another problem. The infantry went to war wearing the 1908 web equipment, but the reserves were only sufficient to maintain six Regular and the existing TF divisions. The manufacture of the webbing required special machines, which only two firms in the country possessed in August 1914. Because of the immediate difficulties in obtaining additional machines, the War Office decided to introduce a modified version of the 1908 pattern for issue to the New Armies and second-line Territorials. The 1914 Pattern Infantry Equipment consisted of a web large pack and haversack, but the ammunition pouches, belts, water-bottle holder and bayonet frog were made of leather. The problem with this material, which had been used prior to the introduction of the 1908 pattern, was that it tended to sweat and corrode cartridge cases. Nevertheless, it seemed to be the only solution and large orders were placed both in Britain and North America. In the meantime, units had to make do as best they could, some using beer bottles for water bottles and school satchels for haversacks. Locally Raised battalions, as they were able to do with uniforms and accommodation, were often able to steal a march on the War Office sponsored battalions and obtain webbing which was of better quality than the official issue. Some of the equipment initially issued dated back to 1882 and it was not until spring 1915 that the New Armies began to receive the 1914 pattern equipment in any quantity. This reflected a lag of some four months after the issue of khaki uniforms. Nevertheless, K1 was properly clothed by the end of October, K2 by the end of March 1915 and K3 very shortly afterwards. The Locally Raised battalions, who made up K4 and K5, were fully supplied by July.

As discussed in Chapter 1, the other major problem faced by the New Armies was weapons and ammunition. The Regular Army went to war with the Short Magazine Lee-Enfield (SMLE) Mk III, which had been resighted for use with the Mk VII 0.303-inch high velocity round, introduced in 1911. But there were still a significant number of SMLE Mk IIIs which had not been converted and still fired the Mk VI ammunition. Matters were further complicated by the fact that the earlier SMLE Mk I, which came into service in 1904, and differed from the Mk III in not having a charger bridge rather than guide to enable clips of rounds to be fed into the magazine and in lacking a magazine cut-off, was still in service. Furthermore, there were still even older models in service. These were based on the original Lee-Enfield, known as the Long Lee since it was 5 inches longer than the more modern SMLE. A large number of these had been converted to SMLE through the installation of shorter barrels. Others had had charger bridges installed and were known as Charger-Loading Lee-Enfields (CLLE) and, as we have seen, were issued to the Territorial Force.

In August 1914 the army's stock of rifles was just short of 800,000, of which some 55 per cent were modern SMLEs. Most of the existing rifles of all types were already issued and only 70,000 remained in reserve. This was insufficient to equip even K1, let alone second-line TF units. Since the average annual production of rifles sighted for Mk VII ammunition were less than 50,000, there was clearly a problem. When it came to equipping the New Armies, the situation was aggravated by the fact that supplying the newly forming 7th and 8th Divisions, together with the Indian Corps, three Colonial divisions, the Mounted Division and seven first-line TF divisions with the SMLE Mk III, took priority over the New Armies. Von Donop, the Master General of the Ordnance, placed orders for increased production by the existing manufacturers – the Royal Small Arms Factory at Enfield and the Birmingham Small Arms Company – and brought in two other companies (Vickers and the Standard Small Arms Company) to start rifle production. He realized that it would be some time before these steps had any significant effect on the situation and so also placed orders abroad, including one for 100,000 rifles from the Canadian Ross Rifle Company and then with Winchester and Remington in the United States. The Ross Rifles could be delivered quickly, but the American orders would not be met until summer 1915. Consequently, von Donop shopped around other countries. Neutral nations were unable to deliver because of German diplomatic pressure, but Japan delivered 130,000 rifles and India was able to furnish some as well.

The New Armies had to largely make do with the Ross and Japanese rifles for training. The Ross had a major problem in that the bolt could be inserted in two ways, one of which was incorrect and dangerous to the firer. It was also prone to jamming unless kept clean. Indeed, the Canadians themselves began to give the rifle up in favour of the SMLE after their experiences with it during the Second Battle of Ypres in April 1915. The Japanese model was even more unsuitable. As John Nettleton, who had experience of it, recalled: 'It took about five seconds to take the thing to pieces and about five hours to reassemble it – more if you had not taken the precaution to spread a towel or a piece of paper on the ground to catch the bits and pieces that sprang out. They were beautiful toys, but quite useless under war conditions.'[52] Many New Army battalions had to wait weeks before they received weapons of any sort. Some improvised with poles and broomsticks. Drill Purpose (DP) and wooden rifles were issued, but they hardly made the men feel like soldiers. The Liverpool City battalions of the King's obtained some DP rifles. As their brigade commander commented: 'Those poor old rifles! I was indeed sorry for them. They were never out of use, with being handed from one company to another, so that eventually, with such hard use, they got into a deplorably bad condition.'[53] Again, not until the spring of 1915 did the New Armies begin to become fully equipped with the SMLE Mk III.

Machine-gun issues were also slow in being realized. In August 1914, the Vickers was in the process of superseding the Maxim medium machine gun on the basis of two guns per battalion. One hundred and six Vickers guns had been delivered and during the remainder of the year a further

266 were manufactured. But the decision in November 1914 to increase the battalion allocation to four guns meant further delays in issuing the gun to both the New Armies and the Territorial Force. In addition, although additional orders were placed with Vickers to deliver 1,792 guns by 1 July 1915, the firm was able to produce only just over 1,000 by 10 July. The upshot was that battalion machine-gun sections had to make do with Maxims and wooden models of Vickers for several months and some did not receive real machine guns until just a few weeks before they left for the Front. The Lewis gun situation was much the same, especially since at the beginning of the war the weapon was still in development.

Artillery, too, produced major headaches for the New Armies. In August 1914 the army possessed a total of just 602 modern field guns (the 18-pounders), of which ninety-eight were in reserve. This excludes those in India and the Dominions. Again, the War Office placed large orders, but although 2,338 had been contracted to be delivered by 30 June 1915, only some 800 had been produced. After two months the K1 divisions each had an average of six 18-pounders out of an establishment of fifty-four and K2 only began to receive its first guns in February 1915, initially on the scale of one per battery. Given all these shortages, it is understandable that the training of the New Armies suffered.

The Director of Remounts at the War Office was soon wrestling with the problem of how to obtain a sufficient number of horses. He calculated that the creation of the New Armies meant an immediate requirement for 245,000 horses. He hoped to obtain 68,000 horses from Britain and 75,000 from Australia, as well as 70,000 mules from the United States, but was racking his brains as to how to make up the shortfall. He warned the QMG: 'The horse supply of the world is not what it was in the South African War, and we are not the only buyers. The supply will be exhausted if the war goes on for long. It is of importance therefore to replace horses as much as possible by mechanical traction and cycles.' In the meantime, he drastically restricted the New Armies, allocating a mere two horses to each training centre, one to each brigade HQ and two to each battalion (for the CO and adjutant). Only artillery officers were favourably treated, being allowed one horse each.[54]

An Army Order dated 21 August laid down a ten-week course for New

Army infantry recruits. It concentrated on drill, musketry, physical training, basic field training (including night work), route marching, bayonet fighting and entrenching. In comparison, prior to the outbreak of war Regular Army soldiers underwent six months' recruit training, as Special Reserve members. For the Royal Engineers, the Kitchener recruit training lasted three months and included fortifications and demolition work. In contrast, that for the Royal Artillery was a mere six weeks, including gun drills and, for the drivers, horsemastership. While the New Army infantry graduated to company and battalion training, the gunners went on to learn signalling and rangefinding, with mounted drill for the drivers. This was followed by battery and brigade training. The sappers progressed to bridge building and then combined training with infantry and artillery. It was hoped that a New Army division could be made ready for departure to a theatre of war in six months, the final month being spent on divisional collective training.[55] In view of the difficulties over equipping the New Armies, this was an optimistic target.

Matters were not helped by the quality of some of the officers and NCOs in the New Armies. Basil Liddell Hart, the future renowned military theorist, joined a Service battalion of the King's Own Yorkshire Light Infantry after attending an officer's course of instruction. While he was impressed with his first commanding officer,

> his successor was a depressing contrast – ludicrously fat, pompous and incompetent. The recently appointed second-in-command was a foul-mouthed bully, later sent to gaol for embezzling mess funds. Another fresh arrival was a major who greatly impressed us with his three rows of medal ribbons – an array then only matched by the veteran Commander-in-Chief in France – until we found out that he had never been in action, and had collected them by assiduously visiting base areas whenever and wherever minor campaigns happened to occur.[56]

The novelist Gilbert Frankau's battalion, the 9th East Surreys, suffered from what today would be called cronyism. Although he was coy about it in his autobiography, he relates the saga in some detail in his semi-autobiographical novel *Peter Jackson Cigar Merchant*. The commanding officer was weak, delegating to his adjutant, a Territorial who did not volunteer for overseas service. This individual brought in his friends and had them promoted over longer-serving officers like Frankau. Schisms grew and in the end Frankau transferred to the RFA.[57] Guy Chapman had an equally depressing experience with the 13th Royal Fusiliers, which he joined at the very end of 1914. 'It was not the men in shabby blue clothes and forage caps with their equipment girt about them with bits of string; it was the obvious incapacity and amateurishness of the whole outfit which depressed.' None of the three ex-Regulars were Royal Fusiliers and they knew nothing about the regimental traditions and history. Of the other officers,

> many displayed only too patently their intention of getting through the war as quietly, comfortably, and as profitably as they could manage. They effectively discouraged the juniors from demonstrations of excessive zeal, and by sheer negation tried to stifle our hunger for information. They failed, but nevertheless, the miasma of petty jealousy, bickering and foolish intrigue, which surrounded them, was the cause of much melancholy and profanity to us juniors.[58]

The age of many of the senior officers within units also counted against them. Ivor Maxse, who had been sent back from France to lick the 18th Division into shape, commented on his battalion and company commanders to Kitchener in February 1915:

> The severe winter weather had knocked out quite a large proportion of the officers who were too old for the work of training companies for eight hours a day in the winter months. They have done their very best, but some are already invalided, others are on the sick list, and more are unfit for strenuous duty.[59]

Another problem with training was the lack of experienced NCOs. The War Office looked initially to former Regular soldiers who had rejoined the Colours. Unit commanders were told that one ex-Regular could be promoted to sergeant for every twenty-five recruits and to corporal for every twenty. Three lance corporals were allowed for every fifty men.[60] To assist training further, each Special Reserve battalion was ordered to select twenty old soldiers for duty as drill instructors with the New Armies. There was also a call for ex-NCOs up to the age of 45, with those earmarked to be warrant officers allowed to be up to the age of 50. Police sergeants, too, were to be loaned as drill instructors.[61] Likewise, members of the National Rifle Association were taken on to teach musketry.[62] Some units used their own initiative to obtain decent NCOs. In September 1914, when it was agreed that members of the Ulster Volunteer Force could be enlisted, F. P. Crozier, a former Regular soldier and commander of the West Belfast Volunteers, was given leave to travel to London and select NCOs for what was to become the Ulster Division from among old soldiers who gathered each day on Horse Guards Parade. Those he chose were immediately sent by the nightly mail train to Ulster.[63]

Many of the lance corporals were selected from among the Kitchener recruits themselves. A. P. B. Irwin, who was on home leave from the 2nd East Surreys in India in August 1914 and found himself appointed adjutant to the 8th Battalion of his regiment, describes the selection process:

> We were given a dozen old Reservists, who were promptly made lance-corporal, much to their horror and indignation. Then the whole battalion was paraded and an appeal was made for anybody who had ever been in charge of anyone else, or who wanted to be. About forty men stepped forward, we tied white tape and made them lance-corporals too. A rough and ready system, but it worked well and nearly all of them made good.[64]

However, Donald Hankey, a former Regular officer in the Royal Garrison Artillery who joined up in the ranks of the 7th Rifle Brigade on 7 August 1914 and within two weeks was a sergeant, noted that those who volunteered to become NCOs were of two basic types – 'ambitious youngsters or blustering bullies'. The former 'thinks that as a lance-corporal he will find life easier and more flattering to his self-esteem. He soon finds his mistake. He annoys the sergeant-major by his incompetence and the men by his superior airs.' As for the bully, 'the men hate him; but he sometimes manages to bluff the officers and sergeants into thinking that he is a "smart NCO". Usually he comes to a bad end through drink or gambling.' Eventually, after many of the initial selections had been reduced to the ranks, 'comes the turn of the man who does not covet rank for its own sake, but accepts it because he thinks that it is "up to him" to do so. Generally he is a man of few words and much character.'[65] Many of the ex-Regular NCOs also had their shortcomings. The main problem was that the new drill brought about by the reorganization of the infantry battalion into four companies was unfamiliar to them.

Recognizing the NCO problem, an Army Council Instruction (ACI) dated 1 March 1915 laid down that two Regular sergeants and two corporals who had seen service in France should be posted to each battalion in the First New Army so as to ensure that each company had one combat experienced NCO. In fact, some New Army battalions had already received some Regular NCOs. Rory Baynes, with the 9th Scottish Rifles, recalled two arriving from the regiment's 1st Battalion in France:

> I was sitting in the orderly room and these two corporals came marching in, halted, turned right, and saluted. I saw immediately that our standard of NCOs and everything else was far below what it really should be. It was absolutely amazing the difference between two first-class, smart corporals like that and the rest of the NCOs.[66]

Another major problem thrown up by the creation of the New Armies was the volunteering of workers from vital war industries. Indeed, 10,000 skilled engineers had enlisted by the end of 1914, among them 16 per cent of those employed in the metal industries.[67] As early as September 1914, the Vickers armaments firm had proposed that men in reserved occupations should be allowed to wear a special lapel badge to protect them against pressure from recruiting officers and others to persuade them to enlist. The Admiralty accepted the scheme that December, but the War Office did not follow suit until the following March. In the meantime, War Office contractors, deluged with orders for ever more munitions, became vociferous in their protests over their workmen being persuaded into the army, and a reluctant Kitchener was forced to agree to the release of some men. In January 1915, the War Office sent a letter to Sir John French and the commanders-in-chief home commands listing the individuals who had been demanded back by their previous firms. They were to be summoned by their COs and told that they were to return to their places of work. They would, however, continue to be soldiers and be allowed to wear uniform 'when and where they like'.[68] But by the time the Ministry of Munitions had been established in the summer of 1915 to oversee war production, only some 3000 men had gone back into civilian life. The new ministry therefore established a Release from the Colours Department, to which employers were asked to submit the names of their men whom they knew had been recruited. They were then screened by both the department and the War Office. Provided they were still in Britain and had not undergone advanced training, these men were released from active service, though they remained soldiers and were still subject to military discipline. They could also be sent anywhere in the country to work and would be paid the local going rate or army pay and allowances, whichever was higher. Some 20,000 names were put forward, of which 14,000 were placed in the scheme. Yet the growth of the munitions industry was becoming rapid and ever more skilled men were needed for it.

Consequently, during July and August 1915 what was called a 'bulk scheme' was put into effect. Skilled men serving with units in Britain, which did not need their skills, were invited to put their names forward for release. Seven thousand did so and 2,100 were successful. This was immediately followed by the second bulk scheme. Ministry of Munitions representatives addressed a total of a million and a half soldiers over a four-week period beginning on 23 September. Eighty-seven thousand volunteered for work in the munitions industry and just over 40,000 were accepted. However, this trawl, wide as it was, could not make good a serious shortage in highly skilled trades involved in the metal industry – tool-makers, universal millers, coppersmiths, lead-burners and the like. Consequently, attention turned once more to the army in France.[69] A BEF GHQ order of 29 October 1915 called for men in these particular trades to volunteer for 'special service', the agreement being that up to 2,000 men would be transferred to industry. While the BEF went through the motions of doing what the Ministry of Munitions wanted, it is clear that it was not particularly willing to release the men. A letter from GHQ to the War Office dated 27 November stated that lists of potential tradesmen had been submitted by the armies but that some were earmarked for transfer to the Royal Flying Corps and Royal Artillery and possibly the Army Service Corps. It warned: 'It is hoped that no man will be taken unless his services at home are indispensable. The needs of the Army in the Field are a constant drain on the locally available resources of skilled metal workers.' Nevertheless, the scheme did proceed. Ministry of Munitions inspectors were sent to France and a test centre established at Le Havre. By the following spring 1,732 soldiers had passed the test, but only 1,542 had been cleared for release. The shortfall was explained by eighty-one Canadians, who could not be released because of financial complications, seventy-one ASC(MT) members who could not be spared and thirty-eight others whose skills were needed in France. A further 219 men had been provisionally selected for the tests, but had not sat them and the tests themselves had been suspended. The reason for this was that the Direct Application scheme, through which employers could demand back their men, was still in being. GHQ in France considered that the latter formed part of the 2,000-man ceiling and now that this had been reached it was not prepared to release more men.[70]

In spite of the serious difficulties which the New Armies faced, the first Kitchener division, the 9th Scottish, arrived in France in May 1915, some nine months after it had been formed. It was quickly followed by the 10th, 11th and 13th Divisions, which were sent to the Dardanelles, while the two remaining K1 divisions were in France by the end of June. Hot on their heels came the K2 and K3 divisions, which were all in France by the end of September. Thus, by the autumn of 1915 no less than eighteen New Army divisions were serving in war theatres, a remarkable achievement given the difficulties under which they had been raised and trained. As for what the Regular and Territorial troops thought of them, Kitchener was apparently initially disappointed by their performance. The cause of this, in Sir Charles Callwell's eyes, was that:

> The New Army troops had shown magnificent grit and zeal while preparing themselves in this country for the ordeal in the field, under the most discouraging conditions, and they had come on very fast in consequence. Their very experienced divisional commanders, many of whom had come conspicuously to the front in the early months of the war and had learnt in the best of schools what fighting meant under existing conditions, were therefore rather disposed to form unduly favourable estimates of what their divisions would be capable of as soon as they entered upon their great task in the war zone.[71]

But this self-confidence was also present in the ranks as well. After showing a New Army field company RE the front line in June 1915, V. F. Eberle concluded:

> They are full of enthusiasm, but I do not think they liked being showed the tricks of the trade by a Territorial unit. They are supremely confident that the 'New Army' will finish off the war, whereas we have been a stop-gap till they come out. This attitude is rather different from that of the Regular Army units. They have helped and treated us as if we were younger brothers.[72]

H. S. Clapham of the Honourable Artillery Company reported:

> We were relieved by a North Country battalion of Kitchener's New Army – the first I have seen. They were rather quaint birds. They talked as if the War would be over in no time, now that they were out, but as soon as they got into the trench, a lot of them jumped on the first-step, and started firing at our own line, just in front. We had to pull some of them down.[73]

Ernest Shephard, serving with the 1st Dorsets, was also critical:

> ... on the whole the troops I have met and had in the trenches with me seemed pretty good. They lack confidence, and at times seem very 'windy'. The latter might be expected in new troops, the former will wear off in time. The officers, however, are below standard in many cases, also the senior NCOs.

He did concede, however, that the New Army men could out-perform his battalion when it came to marching.[74] Jack Ashley's battalion, the 1st/7th Londons, had two companies of Gordons from 9th Division attached for trench familiarization in July 1915. He described them as a 'magnificent body of men – all Scot, and absolutely fit.'[75] John Lucy, who had been out since Mons, took a different view of the Kitchener volunteer:

> He was undersized. He slouched. He was bespectacled. He wore uniform in a careless way, and he had a deadly earnestness, which effectively took the place of our cold-willed *esprit de corps*. He saluted awkwardly, and was very clumsy with his weapons. His marching was a pain to look at,

and the talkative methods of his officers and NCOs made us blush. His childish admiration for what was left of the old army was very disarming.[76]

Arthur Osburn, another Old Contemptible, sums up the initial suspicion which the Regulars had for the New Armies:

In England there is not one but several nations, and our New Army comrades were mostly strangers with an outlook and ideas differing from our own; it was fashionable to think them inferior; class distinctions and educational snobbishness had created gulfs not easy to pass.[77]

The baptism of fire for the New Army divisions provided a stiff test. On Gallipoli, one brigade of the 10th (Irish) Division and the 13th (Western) Division took part in the Australian and New Zealand landings at Anzac Cove on 6 August, while the other two Irish brigades and the 11th (Northern) Division were involved in the Suvla Bay operations, which took place at the same time. All three divisions suffered heavily. In France, the New Armies' first battle was Loos at the end of September. The 9th (Scottish) Division covered itself in glory on the first day, but because Sir John French had insisted on the reserves being held too far back its successes could not be exploited in time and the division found itself under heavy counter-attack, with some of its units cut off. The reserves themselves included the 21st and 24th Divisions, which were flung into the attack on 26 September after a series of forced marches; both incurred heavy casualties, with nothing to show for their efforts. In the aftermath of the battle, GHQ decided that both divisions should be stiffened by the inclusion of Regular battalions, a fate that other New Army divisions, but by no means all, would suffer.

By the summer of 1915, with the army facing increasing competition for manpower and volunteers declining in number, the War Office realized that it was facing a growing problem. As a first step, it decided that the Medical Category B men in the New Armies should relieve TF units serving in overseas garrisons so that the latter could play a more active part in the war. These men were formed into twenty-eight Garrison battalions during the latter half of 1915. They were affiliated to regiments, but they had their own system of numbering, for example 1st (Garrison) Battalion the Cheshire Regiment. Often within weeks of forming, the Garrison battalions left Britain for India, the Dardanelles, Egypt, Malta and Gibraltar, and remained overseas for the rest of the war. By this time, however, the government had accepted that it would have to look at other ways than voluntary enlistment, to satisfy the army's ever-increasing demands for manpower.

five

CONSCRIPTION

Between August and December 1914, nearly 1.2 million men voluntarily enlisted in the army. Over the early months of 1915, recruitment was maintained at an average of 100,000 men per month, but it was clear that this could not be maintained under the existing maximum age limit. Therefore, this was raised to 40 at the end of May.[1] But the army also had to compete with the demands of the munitions industry and it became clear that a comprehensive manpower strategy needed to be drawn up. Consequently, at the end of June 1915 the National Registration Bill was introduced. With a view to calculating the manpower available for the armed forces and industry, all men and women aged between 15 and 65 who were not already in uniform were called upon to register their employment details and skills. This was done on 15 August. The details of every man aged between 18 and 41 were then transferred to a pink form, with those engaged in essential war work marked with a black star to signify that they were exempt from military service. These became known as 'starred' occupations. The exercise revealed that there were almost 5 million males of military age who were not in the armed forces, of whom 1.6 million were in starred occupations. The question was how to make use of the 3.4 million who were technically available for military service. The majority of Liberals had consistently opposed conscription and Asquith feared that if it were introduced, his coalition government would fall.

Even Kitchener was ambivalent, though this was partly because he, too, did not want to see Asquith removed. However, in a memorandum to the War Cabinet dated 8 October, he accepted that voluntary enlistments were beginning to dry up. July and August had each seen the totals fall to 95,000; during September it fell even more sharply to under 72,000. There were also the heavy casualties incurred during the Battle of Loos, fought that month, to take into account, as well as the continuing losses in Gallipoli. Kitchener stated that the army required 35,000 recruits every week to maintain its existing strength. He therefore proposed a scheme which would be a mixture of voluntary enlistment and conscription. Each district would be given a quota and, if this was not fulfilled through volunteers coming forward, the shortfall would have to be met by conscription. The Cabinet considered the scheme unworkable and, instead, appointed Lord Derby, who had been so successful in helping to raise the New Armies, as Director of Recruiting. He immediately drew up a plan which came to be known as the Lord Derby scheme. All men of military age, i.e. aged 18 to 40 inclusive, were invited to register voluntarily and would be called up for service in batches by age. Single men were categorized in Groups 1–23, each group made up of those of the same age, with Group 1 containing the 18-year-olds and Group 23 the 40-year-olds. Married men were similarly organized as Groups 24 to 46, the intention being to call up the single men first. The last day of registration was to be 15 December 1915. Eighteen-year-old Norman Gladden, a civil servant in the Post Office, attested at the recruiting office at Great Scotland Yard five days before the cut-off date and was placed on the reserve in Group 1. He was given a day's pay and

> a khaki armlet emblazoned with the royal crown which, worn on the sleeve, announced to the public one's special status and placed one outside the attentions of the recruiting sergeants, who still found plenty to do, for in fact the Derby scheme was only moderately successful, and there were those who still held back and might be winkled out by that sort of persuasion.[2]

Gladden was right about men holding back. Nearly 50 per cent of the 2 million single men and 40 per cent of the almost 3 million marrieds failed to attest. Of those in starred jobs, 45 per cent of the singles and 48 per cent of the marrieds attested, but when it came to the unstarred the percentages were 38 per cent and 54 per cent respectively. That more marrieds than singles had attested was largely because the former did not believe that they would be called up for a considerable time. During the period of the scheme, 103,000 single men actually enlisted, as did just over 112,000 marrieds, but the monthly recruiting figures did not improve and indeed dropped to 52,000 in December. Even though attestation was reopened on 10 January 1916, it was now more than clear that voluntary enlistment was fast drying up and the government had to accept that conscription was the only way in which the army's strength could be maintained. Consequently, the Military Service Bill was drawn up and the first draft considered by the Cabinet on 1 January 1916. All men who were unmarried on 2 November 1915, when Asquith had pledged that single men would be called up first, and aged between 18 and 41 on 15 August 1915, when National Registration had taken place, were deemed to have enlisted. Ireland, however, was excluded in recognition that conscription might inflame the already delicate political situation. Individuals could also be exempted if they were in essential war work, had people dependent on them (which included fathers of young children) or were medically unfit. The cabinet was initially split, with Sir John Simon, the Home Secretary, going so far as to resign. His fellow Liberals were, however, appeased to a degree by the insertion of a clause which allowed conscience as grounds for being exempted. Kitchener, General Nevil Macready, the newly appointed Adjutant General, and Brigadier General Wyndham Childs, the Director of Personal Services, wanted this to be restricted to religious grounds, but Asquith rejected this, although he refused to specify the other allowable forms of conscience. The bill was given its first reading on 5 January and was passed by 403 votes to 105, the latter including sixty Irish Nationalists, reinforcing the view that excluding Ireland was a sound decision. There were, however, 160 abstentions, mainly Liberals. The Trades Unions were also opposed, although at a conference held at the end of January they reaffirmed their support for the war. Nevertheless, the bill became law before the end of the month and was put into effect on 10 February. Single men aged 19 to 30 were called up on 2 March and were quickly followed by the remaining single groups. The Derbyites were called up in parallel with the conscripts, with Groups 2 to 5 being summoned to the Colours during the last two weeks of January, and Groups 6 to 13 by the end of February. The remaining single groups, apart from the 18-year-olds, were taken during March.

The percentage of 'Derby men' actually reporting for duty was disappointing. The CIGS told the Cabinet at the end of March that of the approximately 194,000 men so far called up, nearly 30 per cent had failed to appear. Part of the reason for this was that the National Register was found to be very inaccurate. Brigadier General Auckland Geddes, who succeeded Derby as Director of Recruiting, claimed in May 1916 that it had over a million errors. Yet the register was the only means of establishing who was liable for military service. The key to the system were the Area Recruiting Officers, who held details of the local men on the register. These were on white index cards and, apart from the inaccuracies in information, many were also stolen, making it difficult to track the individuals whose details they contained. It was a situation which did not change, even after the administration of conscription was passed from the War Office to the Ministry of National Service in August 1917.

The large number of men failing to present themselves as a result of the Military Service Act was of great concern to the War Office, especially with the Allies planning a major offensive on the Somme and committed to a new theatre of war in Salonika. Therefore, on 7 April the first of the married groups (Group 25) was called up and it was announced that all 18-year-olds, including the few that were married, would be ordered to report for military duty as soon as they reached their nineteenth birthday. But the main consequence of the disappointing response in terms of reporting for military duty came in May 1916 with the passing of the Second Military Service Act. All men aged 18 to 40 inclusive, single and married, were to be made liable for military service, although they would not be sent abroad until they had reached the age of 19. In addition, the 1907 Territorial and Reserve Forces Act was amended so that time-expired men could be recalled to the Colours for the duration of the war. The reaction at the Front was voiced by Rowland Fielding, temporarily attached to the Guards Entrenching Battalion in France, in a letter to his wife:

So we have conscription at last! It is about time, too. The Conscripts have not, of course, reached us as yet, but some Derby (commonly pronounced 'Durby') men have. It is funny how these latter are despised by the other men – more so than the conscripts, who are regarded as having at least shown the courage of their convictions. To be called or even thought of as a 'Durby man' is, in fact, an insult.[3]

The first conscripts began to arrive in France to replace the heavy casualties suffered during the opening days of the Somme offensive. The 2nd Royal Welsh Fusiliers received a mixed draft of 540 volunteers, Derbyites and conscripts at the end of July 1916 to replace their losses during the bitter fighting for High Wood. Captain Dunn, their MO, observed that while

the average physique was good enough … the total included an astonishing number of men whose narrow or misshapen chests, and other deformities or defects, unfitted them to stay the more exacting requirements of service in the field … Route-marching, not routine tours of duty, made recurring temporary casualties of these men.

A considerable number had received less than six weeks' training. 'They had fired only five rounds of ball cartridge; many of them did not know how to load and unload a rifle, to fix and unfix a bayonet.' Furthermore, many came from other regiments and resented having to change cap badges.[4]

The situation over medical fitness became particularly severe in the 35th (Bantam) Division, which was heavily embroiled in the fighting on the Somme during July and August 1916. Colonel H. M. Davson, whose artillery brigade was part of the division, claimed that 'any under-sized, degenerate man was at this time considered to be a Bantam and sent to the 35th Division; and this in the midst of the most appalling battle the world had known up to date and against the best troops in the German Army'. He considered that the main problem was accepting men with less than a 34-inch chest measurement.[5] The division itself was pulled out of the battle towards the end of August and sent north to the Arras sector. On the night of 26 November, the Germans launched three simultaneous raids against the division's trenches. Unfortunately, a gas attack had been arranged for earlier that night but was then repeatedly postponed. Many of those in the front-line trenches were wearing gasmasks as a precaution and this, together with the sudden German assaults, proved too much for some of the Bantams and they fled. Many of these were from the 19th Durham Light Infantry and seven, including a sergeant, were charged with 'shamefully casting away his arms in the presence of the enemy', in the case of the senior NCO, and 'shamefully abandoning their post' for the others. All were court martialled, found guilty and sentenced to death. For the corps commander, General Sir Aylmer Haldane, this was the last straw. He had already issued two orders to the division aimed at 'weeding out undesirables' and now took more drastic action. On 21 December he took a parade of the 16th Cheshires near his headquarters and personally weeded out any Bantam whom he considered physically unfit for front-line service. The other battalions in the division were also medically examined and a total of 2,784 men were posted out and returned to Britain. Their places were taken by drafts largely drawn from dismounted Yeomanry regiments. Thus, the Bantam Division began to lose its unique character. Lieutenant Colonel Harrison Johnston, CO of the 15th Cheshires, noted: 'A circular letter has just come round which states that we are not to be known as the Bantam Division any more and that our reinforcements will in future be normal-sized men. I'm sorry, as the little men have done so well ...' In contrast, Major General A. J. S. Landon, the GOC of the 35th Division, when commenting on the guilty findings resulting from the courts martial of the DLI men, commented on their 'mental and physical degeneracy', which applied to all the Bantams who had been weeded out. In the event, three of the seven had their death sentences upheld, the remainder being given terms of hard labour. As for the 35th Division, its final Bantam connection was cut in spring 1917, when its rooster divisional sign was replaced by one depicting seven fives in a circle. The Bantam experiment had ended in failure, but the portents had been clear with the weeding out that the 40th Division had to undergo in 1915. Sloppy medical examinations, brought about by the insatiable demand for manpower, had sealed their fate.[6]

Those who wished to apply for exemption, whether Derbyites or conscripts, had to appear before a local tribunal. This was made up of civilians, usually those involved in local government, Justices of the Peace and other dignitaries, although there was always a military representative present. Typical of the members was Ernest Read Cooper, Town Clerk of Southwold, who was appointed clerk to the local Derby Scheme Tribunal. It sat for the first time in mid February 1916. 'Not very many Southwold men applied but about 60 men from the 101st Provisional Battalion tried to get off but did not get much sympathy.'[7] These were clearly men who wanted exemption from service overseas, a right which had been removed from the Territorial Force as a result of the first Military Service Act. It also illustrates where the tribunal's sympathies lay. As John Rae has written:

> The local tribunals of the First World War were civilian, middle-class and public-minded. Their members represented above all the interests and attitudes of local government. Service on the tribunal was service for the country and there was no place for men who were not wholeheartedly behind the national cause.'[8]

Furthermore, no less than 750,000 men applied for exemption during the first half of 1916, which meant that the tribunals had very little time to consider each case. It is therefore hardly surprising that the majority of applicants who appeared before them had their appeals rejected. Sometimes, though, the tribunals had great difficulty in gauging what civil employment was considered essential to the war effort. In February 1917, a tribunal at Fareham in Hampshire was unable to decide whether local strawberry growers should be exempted from military service. The War Office ruled, however, that this activity did not count as food production and their appeal was turned down.[9]

One particular type of applicant for exemption was to cause many headaches – those who objected to military service on grounds of conscience. This was not least because of the failure of the Military Service Acts to define what these grounds were. During 1916–18, some 16,500 men registered as conscientious objectors (COs). Of these, 6,000 had their objections upheld and were totally exempted. Nearly 5,000 more were granted exemption from combatant service, while the remainder had their applications rejected. A further 2,425 conscientious objectors refused even to apply for exemption.

But for the purpose of employing those excused just combatant duties it was decided to form a new corps. They could have joined the RAMC, RE Labour battalions and ASC Labour companies, none of which bore arms, but it is likely that the authorities feared that these units might be contaminated by the pacifist views of the objectors. The new branch of the army was to be called the Non-Combatant Corps (NCC) and was created by Royal Warrant dated 10 March 1916. It was to be organized in companies, 100 men strong, for service in Britain and France. 'Companies of the NCC will be trained in squad drill and in the use of various forms of tools used in field engineering. The privates will be equipped as infantry except that they will not be armed or trained in arms of any description.' They were to be paid as infantry privates and their officers and NCOs were to be drawn from medically downgraded infantrymen.[10] However, until the NCC was properly formed, those bound for it were to be initially sent to regimental depots or Reserve battalions. In fact, this remained the practice throughout the remainder of the war, since a formal NCC depot was never established, although a headquarters was set up at the depot of the Royal Warwicks. The strength of the corps remained at just over 3,000 men for most of the war and eventually comprised thirty-two companies, eight of which served in France. They took their titles from the home commands in which they were formed – thus, No. 1 Northern Company, No. 3 Eastern Company, etc. Those in France were kept well away from anything directly connected with the fighting and spent most of their time quarrying and camp building. According to the Director of Labour, the NCC company commanders considered the work of their men satisfactory in every respect, but did comment that while 'the men are healthy and very strong physically, they are mostly men with some slight mental derangement'.[11]

The main problem was the hardcore of conscientious objectors, those who refused to even apply for exemption, and the others who refused to accept the findings of the tribunals. Indeed, the War Office had to set up a special branch – AG3(CO) – to deal with these. The COs were deemed to have enlisted and, if they failed to comply with Army Form W.3236, which summoned them to the Colours, they were arrested, charged as deserters and brought before a court of summary jurisdiction. If found guilty, they were fined and placed in military custody. It was now that the difficulties for the army really began, since the COs refused to undergo medical examinations, sign forms or wear uniform. Furthermore, they began to publicize complaints over their treatment by the army. This was done largely through the No Conscription Fellowship (NCF), which had been formed in 1914 by Fenner Brockway, Clifford Allen and C. H. Allen and whose membership was made up of pacifists and socialists. Many of the complaints that the fellowship received from COs who were attempting to resist the army's efforts to turn them into soldiers were viewed by the War Office as mere horseplay, used to jolly them into compliance. But the army was well aware that it was dealing with a sensitive issue and had to tread carefully. Indeed, *The Tribunal*, a publication supporting the COs, carried a letter from the NCF in its 4 May 1916 edition:

> We have to acknowledge a decided improvement in the treatment of con-
> scientious objectors by the military authorities. With some exceptions,
> notably three cases of brutal ill-treatment which we are investigating,
> our men are receiving a fair measure of consideration. In many cases we
> find officers and men expressing sympathy with their views and in most
> cases their sincerity is acknowledged.

The truth was that commanding officers who found themselves with con-scientious objectors foisted on them were puzzled as to how to handle them. This was even though AG3(CO) had laid down that if conscientious objectors refused to obey military orders, they should be punished by the commanding officer. In France this would take the form of Field Punish-ment No. 1, while the maximum punishment he could award in Britain was twenty-eight days' detention. If the man continued to refuse to obey orders, he was to be remanded for court martial, which could award him up to two years in a military prison or detention centre, although this was later reduced to 112 days. But some commanding officers were hesitant over taking even the initial steps to bring their COs to heel. George Suther-land, a master at Harrow School who had refused to apply for exemption, was arrested and sent to a camp at Shoreham:

> The colonel refuses to punish us; to avoid friction instructions are issued
> that we shall be given no military orders … The RSM is greatly distressed

about the whole business. He put us all into a large detention room together last night and says they will have to wire the War Office to put up a bigger one.[12]

Just after the NCF letter was published in *The Tribunal*, the first Non-Combatant Corps contingent arrived in France. It included a number of hardcore conscientious objectors who were resisting all military orders. Seventeen of them were immediately sentenced to twenty-eight days' detention in the Boulogne Field Detention Centre. A month later, in mid June 1916, several COs who were still refusing to obey orders were court martialled and, because they were in a war theatre, thirty-four were sentenced to death. However, the Cabinet had, in the meantime decided that no conscientious objector should suffer capital punishment. This was as a result of a letter from Macready to Kitchener of 13 May, which proposed that a civilian organization be set up to employ those conscientious objectors whom the army found unfit to be soldiers and that the work given to them should be 'under conditions as severe as those of soldiers at the front'. The upshot of this was the issue of AO 179 dated 25 May 1916, which stated that all conscientious objectors who were handed down military sentences of imprisonment should serve their time in civil jails. This meant that the prisoners would not be subject to military orders and could not therefore inflame the situation for the authorities. Consequently, those condemned to death at Boulogne had their sentences commuted to hard labour.

With regard to the genuine cases of inhuman treatment by the military authorities, General Childs viewed them with the greatest displeasure. In June 1916 he received a complaint from the NCF concerning Private James Brightmore, who was with the 3rd Manchesters at South Sea Lane Camp, Cleethorpes. He had been sentenced to solitary confinement in a pit dug within the camp. Childs ordered the GOC-in-C Northern Command to investigate and the latter sent one of his staff officers to the camp. This individual merely interviewed the adjutant of the 3rd Manchesters and reported back that there was no case to answer. Childs was not satisfied and a further investigation was mounted. This reported back that the NCF complaint was substantially true. Consequently, the camp commandant, a brigadier general, was relieved of his command, the Manchesters' commanding officer was forced to resign his commission and his adjutant discharged on medical grounds. Childs's efforts were appreciated by those who supported the conscientious objectors. John Graham, a Quaker minister and chairman of the Friends' Peace Committee, described him as 'an able man, and among the qualities which constituted his ability was an affable and courteous attitude towards the friends of the persecuted. He was always accessible, agreeable and reasonable'. Nevertheless, 'beneath the velvet glove was the iron hand, and with all the mutual courtesies there were many disappointments'.[13] As for Brightmore, his grounds for conscientious objection to military service were upheld and he was transferred to the Home Office. This was in line with a new scheme for dealing with conscientious objectors which was now coming into force.

On 21 June 1916, under the auspices of the Home Office, the Brace Committee was established to oversee the employment of conscientious objectors, the idea being that they should be employed in areas such as agriculture and forestry. A week later, Asquith overhauled the tribunal system. In future, every conscientious objector who was court martialled would have his case reviewed by a central tribunal. Those classified as genuine exemptions would be released from custody and handed over to the Brace Committee. The others would complete their sentences. The first sitting of the central tribunal was on 27 July 1916 and its last was not until May 1919. During this time it processed just under 6,000 cases, which it placed in five categories. Category A covered those having an objection to all forms of military service, while B represented cases with a question mark as to whether the subject's convictions were convincing enough to place him in Category A. Both categories were referred to the Brace Committee. Category C men were those with an objection to war in general but who were prepared to fight in one whose aim they approved, while D cases displayed no real conscientious objection to military service. Both these, and later Category B cases, were to complete their sentences. If they were court martialled again, the central tribunal would reconsider and usually recategorize them A. This left Category E, the so-called 'absolutists', who refused to have their cases considered by the tribunal after being court martialled a second time. By June 1917 there were some 600 of these men serving a second and subsequent prison sentence and neither the government nor the War Office could find any other means of dealing with them other than repeated courts martial and jail terms. For, although they served their terms in civilian jails, the objectors were handed back each time to the military authorities once they had completed their sentences and there appeared to be no way out of this vicious circle.

A typical recalcitrant conscientious objector was Corder Catchpool, a Quaker. In 1914 he had, however, volunteered to serve with the Friends Ambulance Unit (FAU) in Flanders and by the end of 1915 had risen to be its adjutant. Because of the selfless and courageous work the FAU was carrying out at the Front, its members were exempted from military service when conscription was introduced. But Catchpool and some of his fellows now viewed the FAU as a form of conscription in itself. They therefore resigned, which meant that they were liable to be called up. Catchpool himself was not conscripted until January 1917 but refused to report. He was therefore arrested, fined and taken to a Recruit Distribution Centre at Worcester. He declined to obey orders to put on uniform and a subsequent court martial sentenced him to 112 days' hard labour in Wormwood Scrubs, London. On release that May, he was taken to a unit serving in Devonport. Once again he would not obey orders and this time the subsequent court martial raised the sentence to two years' hard labour reduced to one year because of his FAU service. He served this in Exeter Gaol and was released in mid October 1917, having gained remission through good behaviour. By this time his battalion had moved to Harwich and so Catchpool was taken there under military escort. Six days later he was court martialled for a third time, receiving a further six months' hard labour, which he served in Ipswich prison. This time he completed the full term before being returned to his unit. Still refusing to wear uniform, Catchpool faced his fourth court martial. This time he wore the 1914 Star, to which he was entitled through his FAU service in Flanders, but this did not prevent him from being sent down for another two years' hard labour, although six months of this were remitted. Consequently, he was still in jail when the war ended. Thus, the situation between Catchpool and the army remained a stalemate throughout, as it did with the other absolutists.[14]

While the conscientious objectors caused headaches for both the government and the army, they represented a mere one-third of 1 per cent of those enlisted, voluntarily or compulsorily, during the duration of the war. As for the attitude of soldiers to the 'conchies', Dick Read came across them in the early summer of 1917 when he was at the depot of the Leicesters while awaiting posting to an Officer Cadet battalion. He commented:

> If hate is the word, I hated these figures of men just then, far more than any German. At least the Germans were worthy of respect as fighters, but when I thought of what my mates might possibly be enduring then, in front of Fontaine les Croiselles, while these long-haired apologies for men skulked at home and went to extremes to avoid what we deemed to be their clear responsibilities ...

He had to escort a number of them to Wormwood Scrubs after they had been court martialled and came across only one whose views he respected.[15]

Another class of conscript also caused some heart-searching during spring 1916. While enemy aliens had been interned, although many not until after the sinking of the *Lusitania* in May 1915, there were the naturalized British citizens of enemy parentage. Not to conscript them was likely to cause anger among the remainder of the population. On the other hand, the authorities had doubts over their loyalty and did not wish to allow them to serve in combatant units. Consequently, they issued ACI 1209 on 17 June 1916. This stated that all recruits of German, Austrian, Hungarian and Turkish parentage were to be sent to the Middlesex Regiment, which was to raise a special Works battalion for them. This came into being as the 30th Middlesex the following month and soon became known as the 'Kaiser's Own'. The ACI also laid down that all serving aliens of enemy parentage should be transferred to this battalion. It was soon over establishment and so, in September, the 31st (Works) Battalion was also formed. Typical of their members were Freddie Wiehl and his brother Carl, who were of German parentage. Freddie was a Durham policeman, who had enlisted as a volunteer in the 28th Northumberland Fusiliers in summer 1915 and become an NCO instructor. This impeccable record did not prevent him from being forcibly transferred to the 31st Middlesex. What he felt about this is not recorded, but he did rise to become a warrant officer.[16] Both battalions were initially home service units, but this would change (*see page 230*).

The one exception with regard to enemy aliens were the non-interned Czechs. Although subjects of the Austro-Hungarian Empire, they were generally unwilling members of it and there was a Czech Legion fighting alongside the Russians on the Eastern Front. For this reason, domiciled Czechs were allowed to enlist in any branch of the British Army. As for interned aliens, the War Office blanched at a Home Office suggestion that they should be enlisted into special Labour battalions, proposing that the Home Office form its own civil labour units.[17]

One class of friendly alien also caused a longstanding problem for the War Office. Many British Jews, keen to demonstrate their patriotism, had volunteered for military service before conscription was introduced. In some cases, however, recruiting officers rejected them. For example, the *Jewish Chronicle* of 14 October 1914 reported the difficulties that some had in trying to enlist in the 10th (Hackney) Battalion the London Regiment, which recruited from the East End, where many Jews resided. A belief grew up that Kitchener was opposed to Jews joining the army. In particular, Russian Jews who wanted to enlist were almost invariably rejected because of their foreign-sounding names. Besides which, many did not have British citizenship; they had fled their native country in recent years following the pogroms, although some were revolutionaries and regarded with suspicion by the authorities. Complaints from the Jewish community led to the War Office's agreeing to set up the Jewish War Services Committee under the chairmanship of Edmund Sebag-Montefiore and the establishment of a recruiting office in the East End. This did result in improvements, but Russian Jews were still excluded, especially those who did not hold British citizenship.

In December 1914, Vladimir Jabotinsky, an internationally respected Russian Jewish journalist, who was based in Egypt, and Joseph Trumpeldor, a veteran of the Russo-Japanese War who had settled in Palestine, proposed to the War Office that a force be raised in the Middle East from Russian Jews who, like Trumpeldor, had been expelled from Palestine for refusing to become Turkish citizens. They believed that unless the Jews themselves took an active part in driving the Turks out of Palestine, their claim to a Jewish homeland there would be weak. Because they were foreign nationals, the British were reluctant to enlist them, but eventually agreed to the formation of a transport unit, the Zion Mule Corps (ZMC), which came into being in March 1915 in Egypt. While Trumpeldor was prepared to go along with this compromise and, indeed became the unit's adjutant, Jabotinsky was not and continued to press in vain for a Jewish combatant unit.

The ZMC landed on Gallipoli on 29 April 1915, with 300 of its men supporting the 29th Division and 330 with the Anzacs.[18] Its role was to act as a supply link between wheeled transport and the front line and it did good work. That October, Jabotinsky wrote to the War Office proposing that the ZMC be converted to a combatant unit to assist in the liberation of Palestine. The response was that the unit was performing a useful job and there was no benefit to be gained by a change in role. By this time, however, the strength of the ZMC was declining, in spite of efforts to recruit more Russian Jews in Egypt. Indeed, by 10 December 1915 it had been reduced to 133 men and was moved back to Egypt at the end of that month.[19] Rather than formally disband it, the authorities in Egypt allowed it to waste away, and by May 1916 it had ceased to exist.

Back in Britain, Sebag-Montefiore wrote to the War Office in March 1916 requesting that the status of the Russian Jews be reconsidered. He was supported by a Mr Cyril Jackson, who pointed out that many East End Jews were now trying to evade conscription by claiming that they were exempted on the grounds that they were aliens and this was creating anti-Jewish feeling.[20] Finally, at the end of May, Major H. L. Nathan, serving with the 1st/1st Londons in France, also wrote to the War Office while he was home on leave. He had been much involved in charity work among his fellow Jews in the East End and on a recent visit to the area had been 'much struck …by the fact that a large number of men of eligible age and suitable physique are excluded from the Army, though themselves willing and anxious to serve, on the grounds that they are not British subjects.' In view of the army's demands for manpower, he considered the situation 'unfortunate' and offered to raise a battalion personally for general service from among these aliens.[21] With the days of Locally Raised battalions now long over, the War Office turned down his request, but it was finally facing up to the problem. On 6 June 1916, ACI 1156 was issued. It stated the enlistment of 'friendly aliens' was permissible up to a total of 2 per cent of the army's existing strength. The only rider was that before individuals could be embodied, their 'identity books' would have to be submitted to the War Office for checking. In the case of the Russian Jews, they were required to produce a certificate from the Jewish War Services Committee and 'if they so desire, may be posted in batches to serve together in the same unit'. Indeed, the Adjutant General was now working on the idea of raising Russian or non-European labour units to replace British Labour units in Britain and France so that their men could be released into civil life and replace young men working in starred occupations who in turn could be enlisted in the combatant arms.[22]

Meanwhile, Jabotinsky, now joined by Captain Trumpeldor, who had been wounded on Gallipoli, continued to bombard the authorities, including the Prime Minister, with pleas to form a combatant unit of Russian Jews. To demonstrate the intensity of his feelings, Jabotinsky himself enlisted in the ranks of the 20th (Reserve) Battalion the London Regiment, which was stationed at Winchester. Other Russian Jews from the Middle East joined him and one platoon in the battalion became totally Jewish. Jabotinsky proposed that this provide the nucleus of the 'Jewish Legion'. He also recommended Lieutenant Colonel J. H. Patterson DSO, who had commanded the Zion Mule Corps and become a good friend of Jabotinsky, as commanding officer. In a further letter to the Prime Minister dated 24 January 1917, he widened the scope of recruitment to include the Dominions, France and neutral countries. He claimed that 150 Russians recruited in Egypt were now in Britain, with most being trained by the 20th Londons. A second batch of 280 were still in Egypt, and there were also some 200 Russian Jews who had attested in Britain prior to 25 October 1916. However, a large number of these had joined the Buckinghamshire Battalion, part of the TF element of the Oxfordshire and Buckinghamshire Light Infantry. The British authorities were hesitant, however. What mainly concerned them was that once the Turks knew that such a unit was being formed for service in the Middle East the result would be wholesale massacres of Jews still resident in Turkish-occupied Palestine. They also feared that they might be accused of using the Russian Jews as cannon fodder.

April 1917 proved the decisive month for the Russian Jews. For a start, the US entry into the war brought the powerful American–Jewish lobby into play and the formation of a Jewish Legion was seen as a means of mobilizing the support of this and the Jews in Russia, who had been lukewarm in their support for the war, for the Allied cause. Lord Rhondda's Committee on Military Service Exemptions was also recommending the conscription of aliens of friendly countries. Furthermore, intelligence sources were reporting that the Turks were, indeed, murdering Russian Jews in Palestine. There was also continuing resentment in the East End of London that Russian Jews were not in uniform. On 16 April 1917, in a routine report, the Assistant Provost Marshal of London District observed in relation to a disturbance among Jewish soldiers in Whitechapel Road in London's East End that 'a great deal of feeling exists in that quarter over the enlistment of Russian Jews. Unless some steps are taken to enlist these men, further trouble will probably occur.' The authorities therefore decided that a Russian Jewish battalion should be raised, but hopes that it could be formed of volunteers from among the 31,000 Russian and Polish Jews resident in the country had already been dashed. Maurice Aaron, a prominent Jewish citizen, had spent a week in the East End at the beginning of April. In a letter to the War Office dated the 11th he reported that such was the attitude of the Russian Jews that very few were prepared to volunteer. Conscription was therefore the only solution, but at the time there was no legal basis for conscripting aliens. The only hope lay in the Military Service (Conventions with Allied States) Bill, which was being drafted. Through this, but only with the agreement of the ally concerned, the right was established to conscript friendly aliens domiciled in Britain and their only avenue of appeal would be to the ambassador of the relevant country. But until this became law and Russia signed the convention, nothing could be done to bring Jabotinsky's dream to reality. The bill did become law in July 1917 and the Russians duly signed the convention. Finally, the Jewish battalion could be formed, but there were still pitfalls to be overcome.

On 10 July, the War Office asked infantry record offices to forward names of Yiddish- or Russian-speaking warrant officers and NCOs for service with 'the Jewish Regiment of Infantry'. A month later the title 'the

Jewish Regiment' was agreed and home commands were informed. Simultaneously, Colonel John Patterson, Jabotinsky's original recommendation, was appointed to command the unit. But, to the War Office's surprise, there was an immediate outcry from Jews and non-Jews alike over the title of the regiment. They complained that it smacked of religious segregation and detracted from the efforts that British Jews serving elsewhere in the army were making to demonstrate their patriotism. The matter was considered by the War Cabinet on 3 September and it was decided to drop the title. Instead, the War Office made the unit a numbered battalion of the Royal Fusiliers, which was a London-based regiment. On 12 September 1917, ACI 1415 was issued. It announced the formation of battalions (the intention was to raise a total of four) for 'the reception of Friendly Alien Jews', although they were also open to British-born Jews. To this end, the 38th Royal Fusiliers was already forming at Plymouth. But the War Office's problems were not quite all over. It received letters from the editor of the *Jewish Chronicle* and the Jewish War Services Committee pointing out that the battalion's office stamp was inscribed '38th Royal Fusiliers (Jewish Regiment)', once again raising the accusation of segregation. The stamp had to be hastily destroyed and a new one made without the offending part of the title. By early December 1917 the battalion had reached a strength of 925 men, but with the men in different stages of training and of varying medical categories Patterson did not consider that it would be ready for overseas service until June 1918.[23]

The October 1917 Russian Revolution and the subsequent Russian armistice with Germany, which culminated in the Treaty of Brest-Litovsk in March 1918, created further problems over the Russian Jews in Britain. General Sir George Macdonogh, the Director of Intelligence, stated at a War Cabinet meeting held on 23 January that some 25,000 Russians of military age, most of them Jews, were in the country, of whom 3,000 had been conscripted. But the appointment of Maxim Litvinov as the Bolshevik representative to London had thrown in doubt the previous arrangement, whereby all applications to be exempted from military service were handled by the Russian ambassador, since it was likely, now that Russia was no longer in the war, that Litvinov would uphold all appeals for exemption. The fear was that this would create further unrest in London's East End, where the discontent over Russian Jews taking over the businesses of men who had been called up continued. From the counter-espionage point of view, Macdonogh believed that these Russians must either be conscripted, interned or deported to Russia. The majority of those who had been enlisted were with the 38th and 39th Royal Fusiliers at Plymouth and the Adjutant General reported that there had been some unrest in these two battalions, with some Russian Jews objecting to being in uniform now their country was no longer in the war. However, Colonel Patterson told them that they would be deported back to Russia if they refused to serve in the British Army. The Russians took the point and peace was restored. The Adjutant General believed that it was important that these two battalions were despatched early to the Middle East and Dr Chaim Weizmann, President of the English Zionist Federation and later Israel's first President, agreed. Consequently, the 38th Royal Fusiliers had received its mobiliza-tion orders on 11 January and left Britain for service in the Middle East on 5 February, with a strength of just over 1,000 all ranks. Those left at Plymouth, some 1,300 men, were formed into the 39th and 42nd (Reserve) Battalions the Royal Fusiliers.[24] As for the as yet unconscripted Russians, the War Cabinet agreed at the same meeting that those resisting being called up would be sent to 'concentration camps' prior to being shipped back to Russia. However, in February the War Cabinet had a change of heart. Litvinov was making furious objections to the continuing con-scription of Russians and it had become clear that there was no shipping available, nor likely to be for the foreseeable future, to take the recalci-trants back to their country of origin. In addition, there was the fear that their forcible detention would create further unrest. Consequently, the War Cabinet dropped the idea and, in view of Litvinov's opposition, decided not to recruit further Russians.[25] But this was not the end of the matter.

At the beginning of March 1918, a Russian called Kotchinsky took out a writ of habeas corpus against the CO of the 39th Royal Fusiliers, demanding the release from the army of the 1,600 of his fellow country-men still at Plymouth. He also made clear his intention of serving a similar writ on the Secretary of State. The War Cabinet decided that it would fight the action and the court found for the defendant, declaring that the recruiting convention with Russia still had legal force, even though the country had left the war. As a result, and with the grim situation in France caused by the German offensive at the forefront of their minds, the War Cabinet decided on 25 March 1918 to resume the conscription of Russians, but there would be a difference.[26] On 8 April, mindful that there had been more unrest among the members of the 38th Royal Fusiliers on its arrival in Egypt, a decision was made to send no more Russians to combatant units. Instead, they would be posted to two specially raised battalions of the Labour Corps (*see page 241*). In future, the Jewish battalions of the Royal Fusiliers would recruit from Jews of British nationality, including those serving in other units, as well as from the USA.[27] Palestinian Jews could also enlist and in July the 39th Battalion, which had arrived in Egypt at the end of April, received drafts of 673 Palestinians and local Jews, as well as 295 American Jews. Most of the latter were men who were not yet naturalized American citizens or were aged under 21 and not, at the time, liable for the draft, and had first been sent to Canada before crossing the Atlantic. Some, however, appear to have been diverted to other units, probably because of administrative mistakes. In March 1918 the CO of the 7th Northumberland Fusiliers received a draft which included seven Russians who had enlisted in Chicago and did not speak English. The fact that they had managed to get through their recruit training at Dover without any questions being asked does raise doubts on the effectiveness of the training system, at least at this camp. As it was, the CO managed to offload his Russians onto a nearby labour unit.[28] In July 1918, the 42nd Battalion was redesignated the 40th (Service) Royal Fusiliers and was sent to Egypt the following month, where it became a forward depot for the 38th and 39th, while the 1,700 men still at Plymouth became the Royal Fusiliers Depot (Jews).[29] Both the 38th and 39th Royal Fusiliers played their part in the final and decisive stages of the Palestine campaign, where they formed part of Chaytorforce, which, in September 1918, broke through on the British right flank at Megiddo, enveloping the Turkish Fourth Army. Jabotinsky's dream had finally come true, but the Jews would have to wait another thirty years before their own independent state in Palestine came to fruition.

Returning to the late summer and early autumn of 1916, the heavy casualties incurred in the Somme offensive aggravated the army's manpower problems. From July to November inclusive the BEF, excluding Dominion troops, suffered almost 415,000 men killed, wounded and missing. Some 8,000 casualties were incurred in other theatres. During that same period approximately 455,000 men joined the Colours, but a significant proportion of these were not fully medically fit and therefore only of limited use. From October 1916 they included men who had reached the age of 41, but who were now no longer exempted. The War Office was concerned that it was not obtaining its due share of manpower and it was at the suggestion of the Adjutant General that a Manpower Distribution Board was set up in September 1916 to consider the claims of the various departments of government. This was followed by the appointment of a Director-General of National Service (DGNS) in December and the following month he took over the responsibilities of the Manpower Distribution Board, which was wound up. But War Office hopes that the DGNS would have a unifying effect were dashed. In the Adjutant General's view, the existence of his department 'has done much to complicate an already difficult situation'.

In December 1916, Lieutenant General H. M. Lawson, the GOC-in-C Northern Command, was sent to France to investigate the numbers and medical categories of men serving in the base areas and on the lines of communication with a view to economizing on manpower so as to make the maximum number possible available for the BEF's fighting element. He began by looking at the base areas, where he found almost 3,000 officers and just over 126,000 other ranks, including those from overseas, permanently employed. They included four Yeomanry squadrons, which were used to guard German POWs on working parties, two Territorial and four Garrison battalions. General Lawson also identified units which contained a significant number of Category A men. Among them were the GHQ 3rd Echelon at Rouen, many of whose over 3,100 clerks were fit for general service. Some of the ASC Labour companies also had a good number of Category A men under the age of 40, as did the majority of Military Foot Police (MFP) in the base areas. By replacing these men with those of a lower medical category, Lawson believed that an additional 26,000 men could be made available for the fighting arms. He also strongly advocated the employment of women (*see chapter 8*).

As far as the more forward areas were concerned, Lawson noted the significant number of men required for the various army, corps and divisional schools, as well as at the technical workshops, divisional baths and laundries, canteens, cinemas and concert parties. While he accepted that much of this manpower was provided by Permanent Base (PB) men of low medical fitness, infantry battalions were on average supplying some 100 men each, and this excluded those away on courses. Lawson believed that the majority of these could be returned to their units if home service men were sent out. After all, he stated, Medical Category C restricted these men to home service because they were not fit enough to be sent just to tropical climates. Temperate France was no different to Britain and so there was no reason why they should not serve there. The War Office took on board most of Lawson's recommendations and a policy of combing out Category A men from the base and rear areas in France was instituted. Yet, it was to be ten months before the penny dropped over the anomaly surrounding Category C men.[30]

In the meantime, at the end of November 1916 the War Office had spelled out its monthly manpower requirements for 1917. For the first nine months of the year it needed a total of 800,000 Category A men and 140,000 of lower categories. Part of this, it was hoped, would be found by combing Category A men out of reserved occupations and replacing them with men of lower medical categories who had already been enlisted, except for those who had trades specifically required by the army. The soldiers sent to work in industry were termed Army Reserve Munition Workers (ARMW). In return, the War Cabinet agreed in January 1917 that 30,000 men engaged in agriculture, 20,000 miners and 50,000 semi-skilled and unskilled munition workers would be made available. In addition, men aged 18 to 22 who had been given exemption by government departments would also be released for military service. Twelve thousand railwaymen were also to be released by the end of January 1917. Reviewing the situation in June 1917, the Adjutant General painted a depressing picture. He had requested 570,000 Category A men for the period January–May, but only just under 310,000 had been made available. True, there had been an excess of 50,000 lower-category recruits, but these had been more than swallowed up in the massive overseas transportation expansion, which had not been foreseen the previous November, when he submitted his manpower requirements and had necessitated the raising of several Infantry Labour companies for service in France. Of those in reserved occupations, none of the January 1917 targets had been met and government departments appeared most unwilling to release employees whom they had originally exempted from military service. While the War Cabinet was unwilling to raise the maximum age of enlistment above 41, in May 1917 the Adjutant General obtained the Secretary of State for War's permission to recruit voluntarily up to the age of 50. This was announced in the Press on 12 May, but Macready was then told that it was not possible to issue posters and follow-up announcements. 'Even this chance of securing men for the auxiliary services and departmental corps is therefore closed to me', he complained. Lord Derby, in his covering note to Macready's depressing memorandum, concluded that the army appeared to be at the bottom of the pile when it came to satisfying the demands for manpower. 'Unless this policy is changed, the strength of the Army will continue rapidly to diminish, and, so far as military operations are concerned our chances of winning the war will be correspondingly reduced.'[31]

Yet, in spite of Macready's concerns, the total strength of the army did rise during 1917, from just over 3,347,000 to over 3,900,000, and this was taking the heavy casualties incurred, especially in Flanders, into account. In April, a further Military Service Act, the third, was enacted. This enabled more comb-outs from industry and also a re-examination of those who had previously been rejected on medical grounds. One who fell into this trap, and that of those aged 41 no longer being exempt, was Alfred Hale, a minor composer of independent means and a bachelor, who received his call-up notice just after the Third Military Service Act had been passed. He had duly registered under the Derby scheme and had been medically rejected in January 1916 when he attempted to enlist in the Royal Naval Division. Hale was now graded C2 – fit for home service labour units – at his medical examination and found himself in 5 Labour Company. He lacked physical coordination and found army life totally confusing. Very quickly a berth was found for him as batman to an RFC officer.[32]

Where there was a growing problem was in the proportion of combatant arms to the services that supported them. In France alone, on

1 September 1915 the services made up 17.64 per cent of the overall strength of the BEF. By 1 March 1918 this had grown to just over 32 per cent. As far as the combatant arms were concerned, as 1917 wore on, the reservoir of A1 men – those medically fit for general service and fully trained – in Britain fell steadily. In September 1916 there had been just under 400,000. The total fell month by month to 130,000 in December 1917. True, as a result of a War Cabinet decision in mid January 1917, the minimum age for conscription was lowered from 18 years and 7 months to 18, but the rule that no soldier could be sent abroad until he reached 19, even though he had completed his training, remained, at least theoretically, in force.[33] The most significant effect of this was on the infantry. This reached a peak wartime strength of just over 2 million in May 1917, but thereafter the total fell away and was down to 1,750,000 in January 1918. It meant that the infantry divisions in France and Italy (including Dominion formations, but excluding the divisional Pioneer battalions) were on average 15 per cent below establishment, but at a time when the British sector in France was being extended and Italy, of course, was a fresh commitment. The upshot was a serious decrease in the density of infantry holding the line at the very moment when Central Power offensives in both France and Italy were increasingly likely.

Another effect of the heavy casualties on the Somme was a major reorganization of the training system of the New Armies. The War Office was particularly conscious of the high losses in many of the Pals battalions and the effect that this was having on local communities. On the first day of the Somme alone, five of the eight Northumberland Fusilier battalions in the 102nd (Tyneside Scottish) and 103rd (Tyneside Irish) Brigades of the 34th Division incurred over 500 casualties each. Not only were these losses deeply felt by the Tyneside community, but the Reserve battalions of the Northumberland Fusiliers were very hard pressed to supply timely reinforcements to make good the shortfall. Consequently, on 1 September 1916 the 143 2nd Reserve and Local Reserve battalions were reduced to 112 and lost their regimental designations, becoming instead Training Reserve battalions, numbered consecutively from 1 to 112. These were then formed into twenty-four Training Reserve brigades made up of battalions which came from the same region. Thus, the 16th Training Reserve Brigade was made up of the 21st to 22nd King's Liverpool and the 25th to 27th Manchesters, which became 67th to 71st Training Reserve Battalions and absorbed the 13th South Lancashires. The one exception was the 15th Training Reserve Brigade. This was made up of battalions of the Royal Inniskilling Fusiliers, the Royal Irish Rifles and the Royal Irish Fusiliers, which retained their regimental titles and were dedicated to supplying drafts to the 36th (Ulster) Division. The draft supplying units of the 10th and 16th (Irish) Divisions also remained outside the scheme, being Reserve and Extra Reserve battalions.

Typical of the Training Reserve battalions was the 3rd TR Battalion. Formerly the 10th North Staffordshires, it now belonged to the 1st Training Reserve Brigade and was affiliated to the Durham Light Infantry. It was organized in six companies, of which three were dedicated to recruit training and two contained BEF veterans recovering from wounds or sickness. The sixth company was made up of medically unfit but otherwise employable men.[34] Infantry training remained at fourteen weeks, after which a soldier was ready for drafting to an active division.

The system, however, did have disadvantages, especially for men unwillingly conscripted. H. E. L. Mellersh was posted as an instructor to the 5th Training Reserve Brigade at Rugeley, Staffordshire in the summer of 1917, after being wounded in France: 'The men did not know each other nor have anything in common; neither did the officers,' he wrote. A major problem was that they lacked the loyalty and traditions engendered by being with a county regiment, which meant that 'one belonged to an entity. In belonging to the 5th TRB one belonged to nothing. The war was becoming impersonal.'[35] As for the finished product, it was notable that the older men, whether Derbyites or conscripts, generally displayed a better attitude than their juniors. Arthur Hanbury-Sparrow of the Royal Berkshires, taking part in the Somme fighting, noted:

> The battalion has a draft of Group 40 men under the Derby scheme. These are married men of 41, and their bodies simply can't stick this hardship. Yet their spirit is superb, and they shame the younger and stronger men into greater efforts. For they feel so terribly the shame of going sick.[36]

CQMS Linton Andrews of the 4th/5th Black Watch, a Territorial with two years service in France, felt sorry for the middle-aged conscripts they were receiving in early 1917: '... to be put straight into action, as many of them were, was beyond all question a far greater trial than we veterans had to begin with. Yet for the most part they made a good show.'[37] But not all looked favourably on the conscripts. Padre Drury, writing at the end of 1917, commented:

> I was much disgusted with the attitude of mind which I found shortly afterwards amongst some of our newer ranks. There were men who sneered at the volunteers of early days, saying that they were largely the most worthless part of the population, who had little to lose. The newcomers were the prosperous men who really matter![38]

Both the Derby scheme and conscription meant that many more men below Medical Category A were being enlisted. More Garrison battalions were therefore formed. Five were sent to France in the spring and early summer of 1916. One of these was the 4th (Garrison) Battalion the Royal Welsh Fusiliers, which was created on 11 May 1916 out of drafts from no less than thirty different units in Western Command. Just over three weeks later, it arrived in France and spent the next twenty-two months on guard duties at Le Havre. Another was the 4th (Garrison) Battalion the King's Own Yorkshire Light Infantry, which arrived in France in July 1916 and was immediately split up, with a company going to each of the four British armies to man traffic control posts. One of the Garrison Reserve battalions, the 1st (Garrison Reserve) Battalion of the Suffolks, also sent independent companies overseas. Two served on the lines of communication of the Mediterranean Expeditionary Force from September 1917 while a third went to France (*see page 240*).[39] Finally, Home Service Garrison units were introduced for those not considered fit enough to serve abroad. These were also created through drafts from various units. Thus, the 1st (Home Service) Garrison Battalion the Middlesex Regiment was formed from men recovering from wounds and sickness, as well as under-age soldiers, from drafts provided by the 3rd Queens, the 3rd Gloucesters, the 14th East Surreys, the 3rd Northamptons and the 5th Middlesex. It formed part of the Thames & Medway Estuary Reserve Brigade.[40] By the summer of 1917, there were forty-three Garrison battalions either overseas or shortly to be sent, twenty-three Home Service Garrisons, and six Garrison Reserve battalions in existence.

A further implication of the influx of lower medical category recruits was a combing out of Category A men from the supporting services at home. In November 1916 a scheme was instituted whereby Category A ASC men who were not skilled tradesmen were replaced by Category B and C men and transferred to the infantry, artillery, and Machine Gun Corps. The army was also looking for men below Category A in the infantry who had bakery, butchery or horse-drawn transport experience for transfer to the ASC; it was prepared to accept those up to 50 for these trades. Younger ASC officers were encouraged to volunteer for transfer to the 'teeth arms' and in May 1917 it was ruled that no officer under the age of 35 would be commissioned into the corps unless he was medically unfit or possessed particular technical qualifications. Similar programmes were instituted in the Army Ordnance Corps and Remount depots. Indeed, it was claimed that the non-commissioned personnel of the Army Veterinary Corps experienced a complete turnover three times during the war largely because of this.[41]

The last months of 1916 saw the beginnings of attempts to begin rationalizing the now somewhat fractured organization of the army at home. By this time, all the existing New Army divisions were abroad, the majority in France. Some of the second-line TF divisions had also left Britain and others would depart in early 1917. The 64th (2nd Highland) and 65th (2nd Lowland) had, however, been designated home defence divisions, and the 63rd (2nd Northumbrian) disbanded because it was unable to maintain its strength (its number was handed over to the Royal Naval Division). There were also the Provisional brigades TF involved in home defence, as were the Protection and Observer Companies of the Royal Defence Corps. In addition, there was the Territorial training organization in the shape of the Reserve brigades TF, and the New Army equivalent, the Training Reserve brigades. Furthermore, the Reserve and Extra Reserve battalions of the Special Reserve were continuing to train and supply drafts. In November 1916, three new divisions (71st to 73rd) were formed for home defence. Each initially consisted of nine battalions, with one brigade made up of

Provisional battalions TF, another of battalions from the disbanded 2nd Northumbrian Division and the third of two New Army Home Service battalions and one Provisional battalion. Thus, for the first time New Army and TF units were being mixed in the same formation.

The next step came on 1 January 1917 with the handing back of the Provisional battalions to their original regiments. Thus the 86th Provisional Battalion, which had been originally formed from medically low grade and home service Territorials of the Duke of Cornwall's Light Infantry and Devonshire Regiment, now became the 15th Devons TF and the 100th, 101st, 107th and 108th Provisional Battalions were retitled the 29th to 32nd (City of London) Battalions the London Regiment. Some Provisional battalions had fallen by the wayside, largely because of the removal of the right of the Territorial to opt for home service only, and there were now only thirty-nine in existence to receive their new titles.

On 31 May 1917, ACI 873 was published. This sought to introduce some rationalization to infantry recruit training. In future, there would be four streams. Soldiers of 18 years and 1 month of medical categories A4, B1 and C1 were to be sent to Young Soldiers battalions, which were in the process of being formed from Training Reserve units. Junior Training Reserve battalions would accept any of the above recruits whom the Young Soldiers battalions could not take, as well as B2, B3, C2 and C3 recruits under 18 years and 8 months. Reserve and Extra Reserve battalions, as well as TF Reserve battalions, would cater for those above 18 years and 8 months who were A2, while Senior Training Reserve battalions would train the Category B and C recruits of this age and above. This ACI was followed by another (925/17) in June, which laid down that a Young Soldiers battalion would provide four months' training and a Junior Training Reserve battalion six months. Those still under 19 after they had completed their training would now be sent in formed companies to a Graduated battalion for specialist training until they were old enough to be drafted. Those above 18 years and 8 months would continue to undergo the fourteen-week training package, including leave, after which they were available for posting overseas.

Of the existing 112 TR battalions, twenty-one became Young Soldiers battalions, retaining the numerical part of their existing titles, thus for example the 59th TR Battalion became the 59th Young Soldiers Battalion.

A further forty-one TR battalions became Graduated battalions. These were given random numbers between 201 and 286 and were officially titled Infantry battalions. They were soon joined by five newly raised TR battalions, which were also converted to this role. The Infantry battalions were gradually moved out of the TR brigades and joined the 64th, 65th, 67th, 68th and 69th Divisions, which were now the primary home defence formations. Some of these battalions were replaced in the TR brigades by newly created TR battalions, but other TR brigades were broken up. Inevitably, this reorganization created some turmoil.

An example is provided by the 1st Training Reserve Brigade, which consisted of the 1st to 5th TR Battalions. From the spring of 1917, the 2nd, 4th and 5th Battalions were tasked solely with the training of under 19-year-olds, while the other two battalions trained everyone else. That June, the 1st and 3rd Battalions were made a Senior and Junior TR unit respectively, although there was no change to their titles. The 4th TR Battalion was then designated a Graduated battalion and left the brigade in mid July, becoming the 258th Infantry Battalion. A month later, it was replaced by a new 4th TR Battalion. At the same time, the 2nd and 5th Battalions became Young Soldiers battalions, and the 3rd and the new 4th were made Graduated battalions. The latter two battalions left the brigade in September and October, becoming the 276th and the 273rd Infantry Battalions respectively. In their place the brigade received the 12th and 13th TR Battalions (Young Soldiers) from the recently disbanded 3rd TR Brigade. Finally, the 1st TR Battalion was disbanded at the end of November, presumably because of shortage of manpower.[42]

Bryan Latham had been posted to the 3rd/17th Londons in September 1916 after being wounded for a second time in France:

> There [sic] were the days of the notorious thirteen-week infantry training course which, plus four days' leave, saw a recruit transformed from a civilian into a fully trained soldier alleged – on a ship bound for France. Clearly the training was intense, every hour of the newly joined soldier's time had been carefully mapped out by experts at the War Office, and in view of the urgent demands of the Army in France for reinforcements, was all that could be done. The results, however, to some extent dictated

the infantry tactics on the Somme and the battles of 1917. There was no time to teach the rank and file initiative; they had to pick it up in France if they could survive long enough!

Up until spring 1917 he was training intakes 'largely composed of middle-aged men under the Derby scheme, many of whom were burdened with family ties and were not easily adaptable to the rough change from a civilian to a soldier's life'.[43] There were also clearly still imperfections in the training. Rory Macleod, with his field battery at Third Ypres in the late summer of 1917 wrote:

> Many of the men who had joined to replace casualties had hardly seen a gun before. As I was going round the battery during a shoot I noticed the layer at one gun having trouble with the dial sight. He said he had never seen one before and had only been a soldier for a fortnight! I could not be sure of some of the others, so had to go round and practically lay every gun myself.[44]

In terms of the quality of recruit, things did change. Bryan Latham noted that the 3rd/17th Londons began to receive drafts from Young Soldiers battalions. 'These young men were splendid material for training, active, physically fit, and keen.'[45] Typical of them was Frederick Hodges, who reported to the depot of the Northamptonshire Regiment on his eighteenth birthday in July 1917. Here he was kitted with uniform and sent to the 27th TR Battalion (formerly the 10th Bedfords) at Dovercourt near Harwich. He noted that each company consisted of recruits whose ages were within a few weeks of one another. At the end of September the battalion moved to Clipstone Camp, near Mansfield, Nottinghamshire. A month later it was retitled the 53rd (Young Soldiers) Battalion the Bedfordshire Regiment. Hodges now wore the Bedfords cap badge instead of the cloth '27' of the TR battalion, but also had new officers and NCOs, presumably from the Bedfords. He fired a full range course, went on several route marches, had one field day and was issued with a gas mask. At the end of November, his basic training completed, Hodges was given six days' leave and was posted to either the 51st or 52nd (Graduated) Battalion of the Bedfords at Colchester. He was selected for training as a signaller and spent the next four months at the brigade signal school learning morse and semaphore.[46]

The decision to give Infantry (Graduated) and Young Soldiers battalions regimental affiliations was made by the War Office in October 1917. The Infantry battalions now became the 51st and 52nd Battalions of twenty-three designated regiments, and the Young Soldiers the 53rd Battalion of the same regiments. Thus, the units in 1st Training Reserve Brigade were retitled as follows:

> 2nd TR Battalion – 53rd (YS) Battalion Durham Light Infantry
> 5th TR Battalion – 53rd (YS) Battalion Northumberland Fusiliers
> 12th TR Battalion – 53rd (YS) Battalion The Leicestershire Regiment
> 13th TR Battalion – 53rd (YS) Battalion Notts & Derby Regiment

It meant that some TR battalions were returned to their former regiments – the 2nd TR Battalion had originally been the 17th Durham Light Infantry. On the other hand, the 5th TR Battalion was formerly the 10th Leicesters and both the 12th and 13th TR Battalions had been Notts & Derby. Two additional YS battalions – the 53rd Welsh from the 62nd TR Battalion and 53rd Gordons from the 11th (Reserve) Battalion of that regiment – had to be formed to bring the total up to twenty-three. Apart from the 53rd Gordons and 53rd Highland Infantry, which were part of the Lowland Reserve Brigade TF, the YS battalions remained in their Training Reserve brigades. As for the Graduated battalions, the 273rd and 276th Infantry Battalions, which had been TR battalions in 1st TR Brigade prior to their change of title, now became the 52nd Durham Light Infantry and 52nd Northumberland Fusiliers. The new concept was that the YS battalions would now send their trained recruits in companies to the Graduated battalions of the same regiment.

Of the remaining TR battalions, in December 1917, six (the 7th, 24th, 25th, 36th, 49th and 79th) were designated Recruit Distribution battalions, retaining the numerical part of their titles, i.e. the 7th Recruit Battalion. They were allocated on the basis of one to each home command and their purpose was to take in and post B2 and B3 recruits. Simultaneously, they provided training for those who stood a reasonable chance of becoming B1 within three months.[47] Four others, 84th to 87th TR Battalions in the

20th TR Brigade, retained their existing titles and were now dedicated to providing basic training for recruits of the Machine Gun Corps (MGC). The same applied to the later raised 113rd to 116th TR Battalions.[48] However, the 84th, 85th and 87th TR Battalions were given regimental titles in early 1918, becoming the 29th and 30th Northumberland Fusiliers and the 21st Durham Light Infantry respectively, although they retained their MGC role. Once the MGC recruits had completed their basic infantry training, they were sent to the Machine Gun Training Centre, whose A, B and C Training Battalions provided special-to-arm training.

Training continued to become more intense. R. H. Kiernan joined a Training Reserve battalion at Catterick as a 17-year-old volunteer in autumn 1917. As young soldiers, he and his fellow recruits were given double rations to build them up. After two months he was posted to a Reserve battalion of a line regiment, where the training became much more concentrated. A typical day began with a 7 a.m. inspection followed at 8 by an hour's arms drill. Not until after this was it time for breakfast – 'an inch or two of bacon swimming in dirty grease, and a big mug of weak tea'. Four hours of musketry training took up the remainder of the morning. 'After dinner, black meat, again swimming in grease, and the pale yellow water of custard skins, we go to bayonet fighting and field exercises.' At 5 p.m. 'a mug of tea and some bread', followed sometimes by night exercises. Kiernan observed that the majority of his NCO instructors had not been to France and were brutal in their conduct, 'because they want their squads to be efficient lest they themselves should be put on a draft'. Those who had been on active service were mainly Kitchener men. 'They are much kinder and less soldierly than the others.' Officers he seldom saw.[49]

A further step towards rationalizing home defence also took place in August 1917, when eighteen Home Service Garrison battalions were transferred to the Royal Defence Corps (RDC). They were preserved as battalions, but numbered in order of regimental precedence. Therefore, the senior unit, the 2nd (Home Service) Garrison Battalion the Royal Scots, became the 1st Battalion Royal Defence Corps and the most junior, from the Camerons, was retitled the 18th Battalion RDC. In most cases, the new RDC battalions were formed largely from existing RDC companies, merely utilizing the headquarters element of the Garrison battalion which had operational control of them. For example, the 12th Battalion was created at Barrow-in-Furness from the HQ of the 5th (Home Service) Garrison Battalion the Royal Welsh Fusiliers and 305, 323, 325 and 326 Companies RDC. The new battalion was some 1,200 strong and consisted of B2 and C2 men over 41. It took over the Royal Welsh Fusiliers' guard duties in Barrow and Liverpool.[50] The 1st (Home Service) Garrison the Middlesex Regiment transferred all its C3 men to the Labour Corps. Many of the others were transferred to Cyclist units and to the 6th (Reserve) Battalion the Middlesex Regiment, with the balance joining 6, 8, 54, and 50 Protection companies to form the 17th Battalion RDC.[51] Of the five remaining Home Service Garrison battalions, two had been disbanded and the other three were in Ireland, which at the time was outside the RDC remit. By October 1917 the RDC had, besides its newly acquired battalions, sixty-eight independent protection and twelve Reserve companies. It also had an additional battalion, the 19th. This had an unusual role. It was scattered in small detachments of an NCO and between four to six men on airfields and landing grounds throughout the country to operate flare paths for aircraft flying at night.* However, in January 1918 the RDC's roles were revised. Its units were withdrawn from coastal defence and all guard duties, except for vulnerable points and prisoner of war camps. These were widely scattered, especially those camps where the prisoners of war were being used to assist with local agriculture, which were often in remote places. In these circumstances, battalion HQs found it difficult to control their companies, which were now dispersed over a wide area. Consequently, by the end of April 1918 the battalions were broken up and the RDC reverted to a company organization. At the same time, it was agreed that ten Protection and one Reserve companies should be deployed to Ireland in view of the worsening situation there. Of the 27,000 RDC men now actively engaged, 14,000 were guarding prisoner of war camps, 8,000 vulnerable points, 2,000 the munitions industry and the balance of 3,000 were in Ireland.[52] This excluded the Observer companies and the 19th Battalion.

Increasing reliance was being placed on another home defence force, the Volunteer Force, which was the equivalent of the Home Guard of the

---

* It is not clear where this battalion drew its manpower, but it is likely that it was from the Observer companies, which had been reduced from fourteen to seven companies.

Second World War. Its origins lay in a letter published in *The Times* of 6 August 1914. The author was Percy A. Harris, a London County Councillor and lawyer. He declared:

> Thousands of people desire to be of service to the State, but either because they belong to no Territorial unit or because of age and infirmities they can be of no military value. These potential energies are wasting themselves in crowding around and cheering at the Palace and Government offices, embarrassing the police, and in no way helping the defence of the country.

To channel their energies, Harris proposed the setting up 'in the [London] parks of an evening camps on the lines of the Irish Nationalists and Ulster Volunteers.' Old soldiers could be used as instructors and those eligible for military service, could, once they had been judged proficient, pass into the Territorial Force. County Hall could coordinate the camps while the City could provide the necessary finance. Various prominent citizens rallied behind Harris's call and the London Volunteer Defence Force held its first meeting on 10 August, electing Lord Desborough, a well-known sportsman whose three sons were leading lights of the younger generation, as president.* Much work was done during the next two weeks to set up the organization and raise the necessary funding. But, at the end of August the War Office declared that it was vetoing the concept. The hand of Kitchener was clearly behind this, since he was certain to see the volunteers as an impediment to raising his New Armies.

Harris, who had been appointed secretary of the central committee, was unabashed. He wrote to the Under-Secretary of State for War, H. J. Tennant, explaining that units were already 'springing into existence' and some businesses were initiating drills for their employees. He proposed that a deputation from his committee visit Tennant, who agreed to receive it. The upshot was that Kitchener relented and allowed the committee to organize drills and carry out musketry at miniature ranges, but 'it is not

---

* Of Desborough's sons, Julian Grenfell was a regular officer in the Royal Dragoons and won the DSO. He wrote the then celebrated poem *Into Battle* and was mortally wounded at the end of May 1915. His younger brother Billy joined the 8th Rifle Brigade in August 1914 and was killed at Hooge on 30 July 1915, within a mile of where his brother had fallen. The third and youngest brother, Ivo, survived the war, but was killed in a car crash in 1926.

desired that a Force should be raised for the defence of London'. Consequently, the title of the organization was changed to the Volunteer Training Corps (VTC). Units in other parts of the country asked to be affiliated and so Harris's committee renamed itself the Central Organization. Battalions and companies were formed, but, conscious of the stipulations in *King's Regulations*, the Central Organization had to tread warily when it came to uniforms and ranks and had to make do with a War Office authorized armlet in red with 'GR' inscribed on it, which soon gave the volunteers their nickname – the Gorgeous Wrecks. Ernest Read Cooper, the Town Clerk of Southwold and a former member of the old-style Volunteers became adjutant of the Lowestoft Volunteer Battalion. His unit carried out three evening drills each week, as well as miniature range practice. But much of their effort went into fund raising, since no public money was available for equipment.[53]

In November 1914, the War Office relented to the extent of allowing the VTC to wear uniform, provided that it was clearly distinguishable from that of the army and did not bear military rank badges. The corps therefore adopted a grey-green colour, with 'officers' wearing a jacket based on an officer's service dress tunic and other ranks either one akin to a Norfolk jacket or a Tommy's tunic. While non-commissioned members had ranks similar to those of the army, the officers had titles ranging from platoon commander to county commandant. All ranks wore specially designed rank insignia on the cuff. In addition, officers wore the Sam Browne belt with sword and pistol, while the others were armed with ancient Martini-Henry rifles and bayonets. Cap badges were those of the regiments to which each Volunteer unit was affiliated.[54]

During the first eighteen months of its existence, the VTC concentrated largely on preparing men for military service and organizing recruiting rallies. By the end of 1915 the VTC claimed to have passed one million men into the army, but still had 250,000 on its books. Yet, the Central Organization believed that, in order to justify its position, the VTC needed a more official military status. In particular, there were serious legal doubts as to whether it could be used to help repel a German invasion, should one occur. Accordingly, the Cabinet decided to revive the 1863 Volunteer Act. This came into force in May 1916. The two key measures were that the volunteers were now subject to military discipline and that the officers had the right to hold His Majesty's commission and bear military ranks. But even before this the VTC had been fulfilling some useful roles – digging trenches for home defence forces and guarding munition factories, to name but two. Another task was giving directions to soldiers returning from the Front at Victoria Station in London.

A further result of the revival of the Volunteer Act was that the VTC changed its name again, becoming the Volunteer Force. Though this was an indication that it was now more than just a training organization, there were still two unsatisfactory anomalies. First, any member could resign, provided he gave fourteen days' notice. In addition, men of the Volunteer Force continued to receive no official financial assistance. This was remedied in December 1916, with the passing of the Volunteer Act. This stipulated that, in return for allowances, volunteers had to sign a statement that they would remain in the force until the end of the war, attending a minimum number of drills per month. If they failed to fulfil this, they were subject to military law.[55] The Act also enabled the authorities to enlist compulsorily those in reserved occupations into the Volunteer Force. The War Office was, however, aware that the force still had some way to go before it could be considered in any way efficient. Early in 1917, it provided Regular adjutants and some NCOs to improve volunteer training. Captain Basil Liddell Hart, who had been gassed on the Somme, was appointed adjutant to a Gloucestershire Volunteer battalion that April: 'My first impression from a round of the companies and outlying detachments was one of dismay at the state of their training, which was reminiscent of the poorer Territorial or raw New Army battalions seen in 1914.' He initially had an uphill struggle, not helped by one of the NCOs who was a journalist and inserted items 'in the gossip columns of the local press conveying that the Volunteers did not want to be "regularized"'. Liddell Hart got this man onto his side and matters began to improve.[56]

While the bulk of the volunteers were infantry, units of other types were also formed. In February 1916, the GOC London District, Sir Francis Lloyd, approved the formation of a Motor Volunteer Corps (MVC) to transport soldiers arriving in London after midnight, when public transport had stopped running. A year later, the War Office gave authority for the

MVC to become a nationwide organization. It was used for transporting the Volunteer battalions, evacuating hospitals in the event of an emergency, assisting in the aftermath of air raids and for recruiting. Eventually, in July 1918, the MVC became part of the ASC and was retitled ASC Mechanical Transport (Volunteers).[57] Medical units were also formed, as was a Signalling Corps, which was organized in combination with the Telegraph Department of the Post Office. There were even some coastal artillery units.[58] As 1917 wore into 1918 and the army's demands for more manpower increased, the Volunteer Force became a significant element of home defence.

In terms of allocating the recruits to arms and services, an ACI detailing the numbers required was issued each month. Each home command was given a special allotment of the numbers required for arms and services other than infantry. These were subdivided by medical category and those required for overseas and home service. ACI 92 of 29 January 1918 stipulated that 2,000 men under 18 years and 8 months in Categories A and B1 were needed for the cavalry and 100 for RE Signals to train as wireless operators. The split of the latter between the various commands was: Scottish, ten men; Western and Northern, twenty each; Southern, fifteen; and Eastern, thirty-five. The remaining recruits in this age group were to be posted to the infantry, either to Young Soldiers battalions for those aged 18 years and one month or to Reserve, Extra Reserve, and TF Reserve battalions catering for A4s. Those over 18 years and 8 months who were Category A2 and A4 were needed primarily for the artillery, with 1,950 gunners and 1,300 drivers for the RHA and RFA and 6,175 and 550 for the RGA. In addition, the Irish Guards required 150 men, although it is not clear why they were singled out. All others were to be posted to Reserve, Extra Reserve or TF Reserve battalions. B1 men over 18 years and 8 months were specially allocated to the RFC (1,000 men, of whom 50 per cent were to become MT drivers); Yeomanry cyclists (1,000); RHA and RFA (1,000 gunners, 400 drivers); RGA (1,000 gunners); RE (500 horse transport drivers); ASC (1,500 horse transport drivers); RAMC (500); and AOC (150). The balance was to be posted to the Reserve Garrison battalions and any surplus to regimental reserves. The priority laid down for Category B2 and B3 men was posting to the Recruit Distribution battalions. B2s not sent to a Recruit Distribution battalion were to be allotted to arms and services as follows: RFC (1,000); ASC (1,500 horse transport drivers); RAMC (500, but a quarter could be B3); AOC (100); AVC (200). Any surplus was to be posted to the Labour Corps. As for the B3s, those not posted to a Recruit Distribution battalion were to be sent to the Employment companies of the Labour Corps for duty as 'storemen, batmen, cooks, orderlies, etc'.

The minimum acceptable height was now 5 feet, as laid down by ACI 1293 of June 1916, but there were variations among the separate corps. That for the Household Cavalry was 5 feet 9 inches, while line cavalry and cyclists had to be a minimum 5 feet 4 inches. Royal Artillery drivers could be as small as 5 feet, but RHA gunners had to be 5 feet 7 inches or above, the same minimum height as the Brigade of Guards. The one exception to the 5 feet rule was that recruits of good mental and physical standard could be accepted into the infantry for service in tanks once they had completed their basic training.* Age and medical category were also factors in selecting recruits for the different branches. They should not be posted to the cavalry if they were aged over 30 and could not ride, or if they suffered from varicose veins and hernias. The latter complaint also barred men from the artillery. Telegraph and wireless operators in the RE Signal Service needed knowledge of Morse code or wireless. Failing this, 'they must be men of good education not over 20 years old and possessing previous experience in office work'. ACI 92/18 warned: 'Labourers, whose arm muscles are set and hard, are not suitable for these trades.' Even so, a proportion of telegraph operators had to have the same fitness as the infantry, as they would be working with them in the trenches. Men for the RE Special Brigade (*see page 188*)had to be 'over eighteen years and eight months of age of superior intelligence, good education and preferably some training in chemical work'. They also needed to be of good physique in order to manhandle gas cylinders.

No one who was unlikely to achieve Category A or B1 after training was to be accepted for the infantry. Yet many physically and mentally deficient men were still slipping through the net and being posted to battalions at the Front. Basil Peacock of the 22nd Northumberland Fusiliers recorded that in March 1918: 'My platoon numbered twenty-two all ranks,

* This came into force in November 1916 [*Chronology of Events Connected with Army Administration, 1916*].

and in one of my sections the lance corporal was the only fit man – of the three privates one was deaf, one was almost blind and one mentally sub-normal.'[59] Much of the cause of the problem was that low medical category men were sent to France for duties at the base or on the lines of communication. Indeed, in October 1917 and in line with General Lawson's recommendation at the beginning of the year, the decision was finally made to do away with Medical Category C altogether, with those so labelled being recategorized in the corresponding Category B subdivision.[60] But the constant demand to weed out those who were capable of taking a more active part in the war put pressures on medical boards to upgrade them. Captain Dunn, the MO of the 2nd Royal Welsh Fusiliers, related that in June 1917 they received a man who had been invalided out of the Navy suffering from shock after being torpedoed four times. He was conscripted into the Army as C3, but then reclassified Category A. At the same time, the rule on under 19-year-olds not being sent overseas was clearly being ignored. The 2nd Royal Welsh Fusiliers received two drafts at the end of October and in early November 1917 totalling 270 men, of whom 'all but a score' were 18-year-olds.[61]

For the ASC(MT), B1 and B2 men were accepted up to the age of 50, with a minimum age of 18 years and 8 months. The ASC(HT) branch was also open to B1s and B2s, but the former had to be over 25 and the latter 30. The same applied to the Army Veterinary Corps (AVC). ASC clerks should be B2 and B3, with a maximum age of 50. RAMC recruits were to be of 'fair education and good intelligence'. B1s had to be 25 and B2s 20, while for the Army Ordnance Corps (AOC) the minimum ages were 30 for B1s and 25 for B2s. The Labour Corps was open to B2s, although B3s were accepted for the Employment companies.

> As a general rule, however, any man who is able to walk a distance of $2\frac{1}{2}$ miles to work and back, and who can see and hear sufficiently for ordinary purposes, may be posted to the Labour Corps provided he has no defect which renders it impossible for him to handle a pick or shovel or to perform the ordinary work of a labourer in civil life.

The army was also looking for a wide range of tradesmen. ACI 92 listed twenty-three general trades, ranging from draughtsmen to machinists of various types. Once they had reported to a reception depot or Recruit Distribution battalion, recruits who claimed to have such trades were sent to the army's Trade Test Centre at Charlton Park Camp, Woolwich. If they passed the tests, the centre was responsible for distributing them among the corps needing such trades. At the same time, within the home forces there was a monthly demand for transfers between arms and services of Category A and B men who were either surplus to the establishment of their units or were better suited, because of their medical category or qualifications, to another arm or service. ACI 93 of 29 January 1918 detailed demands for just over 21,000 men for various slots. One thousand B1 gunners were needed by the RGA, and 7,150 B1 and B2 MT drivers were required by the ASC and Royal Flying Corps. The RE Road and Quarry Troops demanded 500 B2 labourers and eleven B2 and B3 boilerwashers, while the Army Pay Corps (APC) wanted 450 B2 and B3 clerks. The restrictions on the employment of Category B men were being gradually relaxed, however. In early 1918, the War Office ruled that the 15,000 B1s sent to France during the last quarter of 1917 could be posted to Pioneer battalions or used on the tramways close to the front line.[62] But one reason why the army increasingly had to juggle with its new recruits was the growing number of new corps – and specialities within corps – which had grown up as a result of the new form of warfare that it was waging.

six

NEW WEAPONS, NEW ARMS

The so-called 'new warfare' being practised in France and Flanders from the end of 1914 not only produced demands for new weapons with which to conduct it, but also the realization that these new weapons would need specialist corps and branches to operate them. Yet the first of these new corps did not reflect a new weapon.

On 7 November 1914, the Army Cyclist Corps (ACC) came into being. It embraced all the divisional cyclist companies, which had now been increased by the formation of those in the 7th and 8th Divisions, thus bringing all these cyclists under one cap badge. The original companies had performed well during the opening weeks of the war, but once the fighting became static there was little scope for their reconnaissance role. During First Ypres they helped to hold the line, but after the fighting died down divisions began to see them as a source of manpower for the many humdrum tasks which needed to be carried out. Thus, the cyclists found themselves being used for patrols in the divisional rear areas, both to assist the military police and checking for spies. They were employed on digging and repairing trenches as well as burying signal cables. The 27th Divisional Cyclist Company was given a more interesting task in January 1915. A platoon's worth of its men received training in bombing and trench mortars and subsequently became the divisional bombing platoon. Later, in June, the company was used to help set up the division's bombing school, digging practice trenches and constructing bomb stores. The

8th Divisional Cyclist Company, on the other hand, was providing a team of snipers in January 1916.[1]

In spite of the absence of a clear role for the cyclists in France, it was decided that the Territorial and New Army divisions training in Britain should also form Cyclist companies. Gerald Brenan, who had been commissioned in the 1st/5th Gloucesters, was seconded to the South Midland Division Cyclist Company: 'I now found myself messing with eight young officers, all of them except our company commander under twenty-one, who for various reasons had made themselves disliked in their battalions'.[2] W. A. Tucker, with 1st London Welsh (15th Royal Welsh Fusiliers) remarked:

> Before long a battalion notice appeared inviting suitable volunteers to form a Divisional Cyclist Battalion. Preference would be given to those knowing something about maps and one or more foreign languages. As I had a rudimentary knowledge of German and an acquaintance with maps (I had been touring secretary of a cycling club) I was accepted for the new Cyclist unit.

He joined the 38th Division Cyclist Company.

> The bicycles, when they did eventually arrive, were incredibly heavy. They were made to fold with the idea of being portable. But the genius responsible for their construction must have imagined he was working for a tribe of Herculian [sic] cyclists because it was only by help from at least two other people that the folded machine could be hoisted and strapped to one's back. So in practice these crazy vehicles were replaced by cycles of standard design …[3]

Soon all divisions, including those dedicated to home defence and garrison duties abroad, had their Cyclist companies, although in the latter case they appear to have remained in Britain.

The thirteen TF Cyclist battalions which existed at the outbreak of war did not become part of the ACC and retained their regimental identity. They quickly spawned second- and third-line elements, apart from the 5th East Yorkshires, whose members refused to take the Imperial Service Obligation.[4] The majority of the first- and second-line battalions were committed to coastal defence throughout the war. Three of the first-line battalions were, however, converted to infantry at the end of 1915 and then sent to India, finally finishing the war in Vladivostok. All the third-line battalions were disbanded by the end of 1916. The formation of the Provisional brigades (*see page 85*) also included the creation of Provisional Cyclist companies.

In July 1916, the 1st and 4th Mounted Divisions were converted to the 1st and 2nd Cyclist Divisions, with the 3rd Mounted Division being retitled the 1st Mounted Division. The two Cyclist divisions consisted of a total of nine brigades, with a further five Cyclist brigades joining local forces in Northern and Southern Commands. No less than forty out of the forty-five Territorial Yeomanry regiments serving at home had to exchange their horses for bicycles. The Cyclist divisions had only a short existence, being broken up in November 1916 and the total number of Cyclist brigades was reduced to ten. One or two of the Yeomanry regiments were re-horsed, while others were amalgamated. A further change occurred in September 1917, when the 1st Mounted Division was renamed the Cyclist Division and took in three of the Cyclist brigades. In spring 1918, John Nettleton, on a break from France, served with the 2nd/1st Suffolk Yeomanry, which was at Ipswich and part of the 3rd Cyclist Brigade. He described the CO, adjutant and QM as elderly and that the remainder of the officers had either been wounded or, like Nettleton, were being rested after lengthy service at the Front. Many of the soldiers were 'under-age'. The CO and adjutant each had a car, while other officers had motorcycles as chargers. The regiment's machine guns and their ammunition were carried on a platform fixed between two bicycles.[5] In the spring of 1918 a number of the Cyclist brigades were sent to Ireland and the Cyclist Division itself was dissolved before the end of the war.

The divisional Cyclist companies continued to increase as each new division arrived. They also served in the Dardanelles and later in Salonika, but the static nature of the war meant that they remained largely employed on humdrum tasks. An ACC training centre and depot was established at Chiseldon in Wiltshire, but was dissolved in September 1917, the supply of drafts to the theatres of war being placed under the umbrella of the Cyclist Division.[6] In summer 1916, the decision was made to concentrate the companies into Corps Cyclist battalions. This was achieved by amalgamating the companies of the divisions within each corps at the time. Thus, XV Corps Cyclist Battalion was formed from the 7th, 21st and 39th Divisional Companies.[7] But this did not mean a change of role. XV Corps Cyclist Battalion appears to have spent much of its time cable burying and guarding German prisoners, while IV Corps's cyclists were tasked during the Battle of the Somme with working and maintaining the light railway running from Bray to the Front.[8] During the German withdrawal to the Hindenburg Line in March 1917, they did come briefly into their own, conducting follow-up patrols, although without their bicycles. Indeed, it was not really until the final weeks of the war that some, at least, of the Cyclist battalions saw mounted action again. The 1st/1st Yorkshire Dragoons had become the II Corps Cyclist Battalion after losing their horses as a result of the disbandment of the 4th (formerly 1st Indian) Cavalry Division in February 1918. During the final offensive in Flanders they were used for flank protection of the 9th Division as it advanced. James Jack, now commanding one of the brigades in the division noted:

> As soon as the environs of Deerlyck have been made good, the Yorkshire Dragoons (on pedal cycles, apart from punctures!) and No. 7 Motor Machine Gun Company, acting as 'Independent Cavalry', pass through our lines to seize the village of Vichte, and do what damage they can to the enemy. Dashingly handled and followed by the Cameronians together with the Fusiliers, they reach Belgiek, capturing a battery on the way; some of them get as far as the St Louis-Vichte road, 'mopping up' another battery, 40 prisoners, and some stores.[9]

More relevant to the new warfare was the formation, also in November 1914, of the Motor Machine Gun Service (MMGS). Equipped with motorcycle combinations, and organized in batteries of eighteen combinations, with six Vickers machine guns per battery, its role was to provide highly mobile machine-gun detachments which could be deployed to critical points on the battlefield. The first batteries were sent to France at the end of 1914 and in early 1915. The original plan was to provide one company for each division, but, because of the limited availability of equipment and manpower, this was soon changed to one battery per corps. A total of twenty-five batteries were eventually formed, including at least two in India, and some would subsequently serve in the Middle East and Italy. One who volunteered for the MMGS was Edmund Malone, a former Regular Royal Fusilier now in the Special Reserve. Apart from the attraction of getting to France quickly, 'I saw in the prospectus that the battery commanders got a car, so I volunteered at once. Fancy going to war in a car! Beyond one's wildest hopes'. He was, however, clearly not very mechanically minded: 'Some of the senior officers on this MMG show are not so bad, but the juniors are awful. All talking about pistons and sparking-plugs. Painfully different from the old Regular Army.'[10]

At the end of the First Battle of Ypres in November 1914, a machine-gun school was established at Camiers to train machine gunners to replace the many that had been lost in the recent fighting.* It was to be the first of many such schools established in France and other theatres of war. During the early part of 1915 the infantry battalion's two Maxim machine guns were replaced by four Vickers, which increased demands on Camiers. Then came the introduction of the Lewis light machine gun, initially on a scale of four per battalion. This, and the realization that machine guns needed co-ordination at a higher level to make their fire effective, resulted in the appointment of a brigade machine-gun officer to control the four Vickers sections within the infantry brigades. As the number of Lewis guns per battalion rose (the establishment was eventually sixteen), the decision was made to form a separate arm to operate medium machine guns. A further reason for this was that training machine gunners would be more effective if it was centralized. The Machine Gun Corps (MGC) was created by Royal Warrant on 11 October 1915. At the same time, the battalion Vickers were brigaded.

The MGC eventually consisted of three branches: MGC (Infantry); MGC (Cavalry); and MGC (Motors). The MGC (Infantry), as its title suggests, was integrated into the infantry divisions, with a sixteen-gun company attached to each brigade and, eventually, a fourth company, which became a divisional unit. Graham Seton Hutchison, who had been the brigade machine-gun officer in the 100th Brigade (33rd Division), was sent back to the newly formed MGC (Infantry) depot at Grantham, Lincolnshire,

---

* Many of the instructors were from the 1st Artists' Rifles, whose main responsibility was providing guards at GHQ.

to form 100 Machine Gun Company. He recalled that the camp was 'indescribable chaos, thousands of men tumbling over each other through the mud of Lord Bedford's park, while dull-minded officers, most of whom had never seen a shot fired, and were also in command of the camp, drove the Company Commanders, ripe with enthusiasm from France, almost to lunacy'. Hutchison was, however, given *carte blanche* to select the men for his company. But when he got back to France he faced a further problem. The battalion Vickers sections with the 100th Brigade were to be absorbed into his company, but

> there was a very natural opposition on the part of the Battalion Commanders to parting with the cream of their battalions; and, as the Captain of the Company, with the full support of my Brigadier, over and over again I returned men who were sent to me, on account of their inefficiency and lack of physique.[11]

These problems over manpower were, however, overcome and the MGC quickly settled down. At the beginning of 1918 it underwent a further change in organization, when the four MG companies within the division were formed into a battalion, which took the same number as its division. Thus, Hutchison took command of the 33rd Machine Gun Battalion in the 33rd Division, becoming the divisional MG adviser at the same time. The only infantry MG companies which remained outside the MGC were those in the Guards Division. They became the 4th Battalion the Machine Gun Guards and then, by Royal Warrant dated 8 May 1918, the Guards Machine Gun Regiment was formed, with Nos. 1 to 3 Battalions being provided by the Household Cavalry and No. 4 by the Guards Division.

The MGC (Cavalry) had a separate depot at Uckfield in Sussex and provided a machine-gun squadron for each cavalry brigade. The machine-gun sections of the cavalry regiments were brigaded just prior to the Somme, but it was not until after the offensive opened that the other ranks exchanged their cap badges for MGC ones. The officers, however, appear to have retained their regimental badges for a time.[12] The MGC (Motors) absorbed the MMGS, retaining its depot at Bisley. It also took over responsibility for armoured cars. These had originally been developed on an unofficial basis by the Royal Naval Air Service (RNAS) in the early weeks of the war. They owed their existence to one of the navy's pioneer aviators, Charles Rumney Samson, who took his RNAS squadron to the northern French port of Dunkirk in the first weeks of the war with the mission of attacking the Zeppelin sheds at Düsseldorf and Cologne. After a brush with Uhlans, Samson decided to armour some of his cars. Churchill, as First Lord of the Admiralty, became interested and within a short time the Royal Naval Armoured Car Division (RNACD) was formed, with its depot at Wormwood Scrubs, London. By summer 1915, the RNACD consisted of no less than eighteen squadrons, five of which consisted of motorcycle machine-gun combinations. The armoured car squadrons were mainly equipped with Rolls-Royces and Lanchesters, but some were designated heavy squadrons containing Seabrook armoured lorries fitted with a 3-pounder gun and Maxim machine gun. The RNACD squadrons were deployed in virtually every theatre of war. No. 1 Squadron served in South-West and then East Africa, while part of No. 4 Squadron was sent to Egypt. The remainder of this squadron, together with Nos. 3 and 9 to 12 (motor-cycle) Squadrons went to the Dardanelles. Apart from three squadrons retained in Britain for home defence, the remainder operated in France and Belgium.

The War Office did not initially show much interest in armoured cars. It did, however, allow one sub-unit to be formed. In February 1915, a Midlands industrialist, Sir John Willoughby, formed a battery of four cumbersome Leyland armoured cars, which he titled No. 1 Armoured Motor Battery (Willoughby's). Willoughby himself had taken part in the infamous 1895 Jameson Raid in South Africa and had been jailed for his part in it. But though deemed too old to fight in 1914, he remained keen to demonstrate his patriotism. He even had a special cap badge designed for the unit – a Leyland surrounded by laurel branches, with the King's crown on top, and 'Willoughby's' emblazoned at the base. The War Office allowed the battery to join the order of battle, but prosaically designated it 322 Company ASC on the basis that armoured cars were mechanical transport and therefore the province of the Army Service Corps. Even so, in March 1916 Willoughby's battery was sent to East Africa and served there for fifteen months before being finally disbanded. The bush proved too much of a challenge for the lumbering Leylands and it is surprising that they lasted as long as they did. The only other army units to possess armoured cars during the early part of the war were a few Yeomanry regiments, who built one or two cars privately, and some Cyclist battalions.*

Not until the beginning of 1916 did the army begin to take over the cars of the RNACD, but it was a protracted and complicated business. Those RNACD squadrons in France were withdrawn and their cars handed over to the MGC (Motors) at Bisley. Those which had served in the Dardanelles returned to Egypt and were handed over to the army there. There were two significant exceptions. First, an RNACD armoured car force had been sent to Russia at the end of 1915. It remained under Admiralty control until leaving the Eastern Front at the beginning of 1918, when it was sent to Persia to join Dunsterforce and became the Duncar Brigade. The other exception was No. 20 Squadron RNACD. This was formed in June 1915 as a tank trials unit and remained in being, albeit passing under the control of the Royal Marines at the end of 1917, until the end of the war. The designation of the army armoured car units was also complicated. They were initially called Armoured Motor Batteries (AMB), Light Armoured Batteries (LAB) or Light Armoured Car Batteries (LACB) and had a four-car establishment. Later in the war some would be converted to Light Armoured Motor Batteries (LAMB), each consisting of eight cars. Some initially served in France, but by early 1917 they were all in the Middle East. A further element of the MGC (Motors), which also came into being in Egypt in spring 1916, were the Light Car Patrols (LCP). Each consisted of five Ford Model-T cars and a stores tender and were used for reconnaissance. One curiosity about the MGC (Motors) was that the drivers were badged ASC, reflecting a rather 'trades union' policy that MT drivers were supplied by this corps alone. There was, however, an exception to this rule – tank drivers.

The Tank Corps (TC) was the only other new combat arm which became entitled to its own cap badge. The story of the development of the tank has been told many times and need not be repeated here.** Suffice to say that much of the early development work was undertaken by No.

---

* 1st/8th Cyclist Battalion the Essex Regiment, for instance, had two Rolls-Royce armoured cars during the winter of 1915–16.

** The classic account is probably Captain B. H. Liddell Hart *The Tanks: The History of the Royal Tank Regiment and its Predecessors Heavy Branch Machine-Gun Corps, Tank Corps and Royal Tank Corps, 1914–1945*, Vol. 1, Cassell, London, 1959. A more concise account is David Fletcher *Landships: British Tanks in the First World War*, HMSO, London, 1984.

20 Squadron RNACD at Wormwood Scrubs. The first model, 'Mother', was demonstrated to Lord Kitchener, David Lloyd George and others on 2 February 1916. Ten days later, the Army Council signed an order for 100 tanks and a Tank Supply Department was set up by the Ministry of Munitions. Appointed to command the Tank Detachment was Lieutenant Colonel E. D. Swinton RE, who had begun the war as an official correspondent, writing under the pen name of Eyewitness. He established his headquarters at the aptly named Siberia Camp, which was next door to the MMGS depot at Bisley. The name of the unit was then changed to the Armoured Car Section of the MMGS, which itself provided much of the early manpower, with some coming from No. 20 Squadron RNACD, although not as many as was hoped since these men were ranked as petty officers and were paid three times as much as an army private. Swinton's initial plan was to form fifteen companies organized in three battalions, but GHQ in France rejected this, stating that it wanted a company-based organization. Consequently, Swinton formed six companies, lettered A to F, each containing twenty-five tanks. In May 1916, however, the unit underwent another name change, becoming the Heavy Section of the MGC, which was adjusted that November to Heavy Branch, Machine Gun Corps (HBMGC).

The first tank companies began to cross to France on 13 August 1916 in response to an urgent demand for them from Haig. A month later, on 15 September, they were in action for the first time, at Flers-Courcelette. Haig was sufficiently impressed by their performance to request that a further 1,000 be built. The four companies in France were to be expanded into four battalions (lettered A to D) each of three companies, while the two remaining in England would provide the basis for a further five battalions. At the same time, a Heavy Branch headquarters was established at Bermicourt, near Saint Pol, where it would remain for the rest of the war. A new commander was appointed in France, Lieutenant Colonel H. J. Elles RE, who had been GHQ's liaison officer over the tanks since the beginning of the year; he was given a BM, DAA&QMG, staff captain, and intelligence officer. Close to Bermicourt, a Central Workshops was established at Erin, which was on the railway, the only method of transporting the tanks. In Britain, too, there were changes. The depot had moved from Bisley to

Elveden in Norfolk, for reasons of better security, in April 1916. It moved again, to Bovington Camp,* near Wool in Dorset, that November. Swinton, who had had much to do with the genesis of the tank, was posted to the War Cabinet Secretariat and his place taken by a former infantry brigade commander.

During the closing months of the Somme offensive the tanks saw little action. The expansion of the arm continued, however. In December 1916, Elles received a GSO2 to act as his chief of staff. This was Major J. F. C. Fuller, who would become one of the leading theorists of armoured warfare. In February 1917, C and D Battalions were formed into the 1st Tank Brigade commanded by Lieutenant Colonel C. d'A. B. S. Baker-Carr, one of the RAC gentleman chauffeurs of August 1914 (*see page 53*) and the first commandant of the machine-gun school at Camiers. The formation of the 2nd Tank Brigade (A and B Battalions) and the 3rd Tank Brigade soon followed. Elles wanted an emblem to distinguish those who were serving with tanks and in March 1917 approval was given for all ranks to wear a tank badge on the right upper arm, a practice continued by today's Royal Tank Regiment. At the beginning of July 1917, the King visited the Heavy Branch in France and on the 27th of the month it was retitled the Tank Corps by Royal Warrant and given its own cap badge. Earlier, the new corps had been given authority to expand to eighteen battalions.

The summer of 1917 was, however, a grim time for the Tank Corps as it struggled in the mud of Third Ypres, but in November 1917 it revealed what it could do when, without any preparatory artillery barrage, a massed tank attack took the Germans entirely by surprise at Cambrai. Early in 1918, the battalions of the Tank Corps changed their letters for numbers, with A Battalion becoming the 1st Battalion, and so on. By this time the BEF was on the defensive, preparing for the expected German offensive. There appeared to be no real role for the slow-moving tanks and, in view of the shortage of manpower, GHQ in France decided to reduce the target strength of the Tank Corps from 24,000 to 16,000 men. By the time the Germans struck, there were nine battalions with the Mk IV, three were being equipped with the new medium tank, the Whippet, while a thirteenth battalion had just arrived in France but had no tanks. The Tank

* Today it is the home of the Royal Armoured Corps.

Corps did perform useful work, especially the Whippets, which made some successful counter-attacks, but in mid April GHQ ordered a reduction to four brigades and for 2,600 men to be transferred to the infantry. Because it had other transportation priorities, GHQ also stopped the much improved Mk V tank from being sent to France. It seemed as though the Tank Corps might wither on the vine.

Led by 'Boney' Fuller, the Tank Corps fought for its preservation. In May, the Mk V finally began to arrive in France, enabling those battalions which had been involved in the recent fighting to re-equip. The battle was won, however, and by the end of July 1918 there were sixteen tank battalions in France, including the 17th Battalion, which was equipped with Austin armoured cars. The crowning moment for the corps came on 8 August 1918, when it achieved a spectacular breakthrough at Amiens. Two further battalions were sent to France before the Armistice and a further seven were in training in England. All this was in preparing to create a massive Allied tank force should the war have continued into 1919.

Another new weapon was the trench mortar. 'This trench warfare in which we are now engaged is causing a demand for all sorts of things which are not recognised by regulations', wrote Horace Smith-Dorrien to the Master General of the Ordnance (von Donop) on 7 December 1914. In particular, he cited the German *Minenwerfer* as 'horribly effective' and there were calls from his subordinate commanders for the BEF to be equipped with similar mortars to combat this new threat.[13] Yet as early as 20 October Sir John French had requested trench artillery.[14] There was, however, no branch of the War Office specifically tasked with the development of new weapons. The closest, especially within the context of trench warfare, was the Directorate of Fortifications and Works (DFW) and it was to this that all requests were passed. It so happened that the head of FW3, which dealt with fortifications, ranges, gun and electric light emplacements, as well as barracks and hospitals abroad, was a certain Colonel Louis Jackson. He had retired the previous year after being Chief Engineer London District but had been recalled on the outbreak of war. Jackson had not only been an instructor in fortification at the School of Military Engineering at Chatham, but had also made a special study of field defences and siege warfare. Von Donop therefore turned to him and he quickly became the focus for the development of all trench weapons, although this was in addition to his normal work.[15]

In the meantime, Smith-Dorrien managed to obtain a few old French mortars as a stopgap. This was largely thanks to the initiative of Henry Rawlinson's brother Toby, who had been attached to HQ IV Corps as a civilian chauffeur and made use of his French contacts to obtain some mid nineteenth-century models from their arsenals. These 6-inch weapons had to be modified to use smokeless, as opposed to black powder, and by the time that trials had been carried out and sufficient ammunition manufactured it was not until Aubers Ridge in May 1915 that Rawlinson had thirty-two mortars ready. They worked well, but many were destroyed by counter-battery fire and Rawlinson himself was laid low by concussion and sent back to England. He had unofficially been given the rank of colonel, but the War Office then reminded him that he was still only a civilian. Rawlinson therefore joined the Royal Naval Armoured Car Division in the rank of lieutenant commander.[16]

As a result of the demands from France, von Donop moved quickly and put tenders out to civilian firms to produce mortars. Most of these were adaptations of existing weapons. He sent a prototype trench 'howitzer' and 500 rounds of ammunition to the front at the beginning of December. Smith-Dorrien commented, however, that its 50lb bomb was too bulky and produced too much give-away smoke.[17] At the same time, some individuals used their own initiative to design and build crude mortars, using water pipes, some of which fired homemade bombs made from ration tins.[18] These, however, proved excessively dangerous to their users. In early March 1915 Rory Macleod was posted to an RHA battery supporting the 2nd Indian Cavalry Division in the Neuve Chapelle sector, but found it in 'low spirits'. It had been detailed to demonstrate a homemade mortar.

> The barrel looked like a bit of gas piping on a stand and it fired bombs consisting of jam tins filled with high explosive and nails. The Battery intended to practise first. They formed in a hollow square around the mortar. The first three bombs were fired successfully, Wingate-Guy, a subaltern, being the demonstrator and lighting the fuse. The fourth bomb exploded in the bore and killed the Major, who was my old friend Mark

Leigh Goldie, and 13 men and wounded about 40 others, including a subaltern, Purchas. Wingate-Grey, by some miracle, escaped injury.[19]

Even so, before the end of 1914 the Royal Engineers had established a makeshift factory at Le Havre and were producing 1,400 mortar bombs per month.[20]

The first standard mortar issued to the BEF was the 4-inch light mortar. This was made by boring out 6-inch naval shells and was the only rifled mortar to see service. By June 1915 there were forty in service, but they were phased out a year later after a total of 168 had been produced. While it had a range of some 900 yards, the accuracy of the 4-inch was poor.[21] A further light mortar, the 3.7-inch, was designed by the Indian Corps, using 95mm French piping. It was manufactured by the Decimals Ltd of Birmingham, who also produced grenades, and twenty were sent out to Gallipoli. The forces here were also given four Japanese mortars. According to Arthur Behrend, it took time to work out how to use them because the instructions were in Japanese.[22]

Medium mortars were also introduced in 1915. The Vickers 1.57-inch fired a bomb shaped like a toffee apple. This began to be deployed to France in March 1915, but at 260lbs it was very heavy and difficult to transport in the trenches. Simultaneously, a 2-inch weapon was developed by the Woolwich Arsenal. Again, this fired a 50lb toffee-apple bomb and was cumbersome, with a range of not more than 500 yards, as well as being inaccurate, with a slow rate of fire. In September 1915, the 9.45-inch mortar came into being. This was largely of French design and was manufactured under licence.

The British trench mortar was, however, revolutionized by Wilfrid Stokes. He was chairman and managing director of Ransomes & Rapier, an engineering company based at Ipswich. He was made aware of the army's urgent need for mortars towards the end of 1914, after a talk with H. A. Gwynne, the editor of the *Morning Post*, who had just returned from a visit to the Front. Stokes was a believer in simplicity in design and quickly submitted a proposal for a tube mounted on an adjustable bipod and firing a bomb. The War Office initially rejected it, but Stokes persevered, refining his design, and eventually, in March 1916, his 3-inch mortar was accepted.

It replaced the 4-inch mortar, which was handed over to the Special Brigade RE (*see page 188*), and by the end of the war over 11,400 had been produced. The Stokes design also led to the 6-inch medium mortar, which replaced the 2-inch in mid 1917. It was sometimes known as the Newton mortar, after Captain H. Newton, a Territorial officer in the 5th Sherwood Foresters and, in peacetime, a director of an engineering firm in Derby. He had already become interested while serving as a company commander in France. His expertise was officially recognized and he was appointed OC Second Army RE Workshops, where he built on the Stokes design to develop the new 6-inch model.[23]

In February 1915, Major General J. P. du Cane, the artillery adviser at GHQ in France, had recommended that trench mortars be made the responsibility of the Royal Engineers. In practice, when the first batteries were formed that April, they were drawn from the infantry, with each brigade being given one battery of four mortars manned by infantrymen from within the brigade.* Each army in France established its own trench mortar school and those selected for trench mortars attended a two-week course of instruction and then joined their brigade as a formed battery. The cumbersome 2-inch mortar was soon removed from the brigade batteries and placed directly under the control of the divisional artillery. Each division eventually consisted of three medium trench mortar batteries, designated X, Y and Z Batteries and manned by artillerymen. Rory Macleod, serving with an RHA brigade in France, recalled:

> GHQ sent down a letter stating that as the Horse Artillery had had such an easy (!) time, they expected subalterns to volunteer for the new trench mortar. Our Adjutant, Captain Alan Brooke (the late Field Marshal Lord Alanbrooke) replied that out of the nine original subalterns [in the brigade], 3 had been killed and 3 wounded, and if any more left it would affect the efficiency of their batteries. Nevertheless one officer of V Battery decided to go so we had only 2 subalterns left.[24]

* In September 1915, Winston Churchill proposed forming a Trench Mortar Corps. With the Dardanelles in mind, he suggested that a battalion be formed consisting of two companies, each with ninety-six Stokes 3-inch mortars, and a third company armed with forty-eight 2-inch mortars. His concept was to use all 250 mortars in a concentrated barrage. Although discussed by the War Committee, the idea was not taken further, presumably because of (a) the continuing clamour for mortars in France and (b) the ever more dismal situation on Gallipoli. [National Archives, Kew CAB 37/134/31, CAB 37/135/17]

Gunner officers coming to France for the first time and allocated to trench mortars appear to have had little previous knowledge of them. A. B. Scott arrived at the Front in July 1916 and was posted to the 32nd Division's artillery. 'We were posted to a unit which we had heard little of at home, and what little we had heard was bad – the Trench Mortars. On hearing our fate our spirits fell considerably as on the way up to the line we had been advised to steer clear of a trench mortar battery.'[25] Indeed, trench mortars became known as the Suicide Club,* because of the frequent and often effective *Minenwerfer* retaliation to their bombardments. These also made the trench mortar batteries unpopular with the infantry whom they were supporting. To coordinate the divisional batteries, a Divisional Trench Mortar Officer (DTMO) was created. One who was appointed to this position at the end of 1915 was R. T. Rees of the Loyals, who was offered it apparently on the grounds that he was a Cambridge MA in classics. He did a one-week course at a trench mortar school, followed by a week's attachment to the DTMO 9th Division prior to taking up his appointment with the 25th Division.[26]

The first heavy mortars were deployed in early 1916. Their batteries, which were also under divisional control, were designated 'V' and had two mortars each. Initially, they were formed from what manpower was available. Thus, the 32nd Division's V battery had an RFA officer and one from the Dorsets. The 32nd Division, like some others, also formed an additional heavy battery ('W'), with the men drawn from the artillery brigade and divisional ammunition columns within the division. These W batteries were, however, disbanded at the end of the Battle of the Somme.[27] Eventually, however, the heavy batteries were badged RGA. In February 1918 there was a reorganization, with the Z battery in each division being disbanded and the two other batteries increased to a strength of six mortars each. The 9.45-inch batteries were also reduced in number, with just one for each corps.

Another speciality which became officially recognized in early 1915 was tunnelling. Soon after the advent of trench warfare the Germans began mining operations. At 6 a.m. on 20 December 1914, they successfully exploded ten mines in the sector of the Indian Sirhind Brigade. By early

---

* It was a nickname also claimed by the Machine Gun Corps.

afternoon the Germans had driven the Indians back and captured the village of Givenchy. During the next two months the Germans exploded other mines on the British front. The only British unit which had any training in mining operations was 20 Fortress Company RE, but its skills were not up to dealing with the waterlogged trench systems. However, on 15 December 1914 John Norton-Griffiths MP had written to the War Office. Norton-Griffiths himself ran an engineering company, one of whose contracts was for a drainage system in Manchester. It involved tunnelling the clay subsoil, using the technique of 'clay kicking' in which the miner lay on his back with his feet towards the face of the tunnel and dug out the clay with a light spade. Norton-Griffiths proposed that some of his 'moles' as the clay-kickers called themselves, be sent to France.

The War Office passed a copy of the letter to GHQ BEF, but French, seeing no reason to remove responsibility for mining from the Royal Engineers, took little notice of it, as he did of pleas from Henry Rawlinson to form a special mining battalion. Norton-Griffiths heard nothing more until he received a personal summons from Kitchener on 12 February. The Secretary of State was instantly impressed by Norton-Griffiths's proposal and sent him forthwith to France to meet French's engineer-in-chief, Brigadier General George Fowke. Three days of frantic meetings and a tour of the Front followed, by the end of which Fowke and his staff, and indeed French himself, had been won over. On the 19th, Norton-Griffiths, still in France, received formal War Office approval to raise seven Tunnelling Companies RE (Nos. 170 to 176), each with an establishment of five officers and 269 men. The companies were to be commanded by Regular Royal Engineer officers and would be placed under the direct control of the two army HQs. Norton-Griffiths's own role was to act as the liaison officer between Fowke and the companies. But even before he had received formal authority, Norton-Griffiths had already stopped work on his Manchester sewer project and recruited twenty of the clay-kickers. He also began to recruit mining engineers and ex-miners from the New Army battalions: the 9th North Staffordshires, the 8th South Staffordshires, the 8th South Wales Borderers and the 11th Welsh were the first to provide recruits. Remarkably, the first batch of 'moles' went to France as early as 22 February and was sent to the infamous Hill 60, where it was joined by a large detachment from the 1st and 3rd Monmouths. The clay-kickers themselves were regarded as specialists and were paid six shillings a day, while their assistants received two shillings.

The tunnelling companies grew to twenty-five, together with three from Australia, one from Canada and one from New Zealand. Their crowning moment came at Messines on 7 June 1917 when they exploded nineteen massive mines underneath the German trenches. Norton-Griffiths was not, however, present to witness it. In March 1916 he resigned his post in order to attend to his private affairs. Later that year, he was sent on a special mission to destroy the oilfields and wheat in Romania, putting the wells out of action for two years. He was knighted in 1917 for his services.

After Messines, mining operations on the Western Front declined and the tunnelling companies were increasingly employed in the construction of dug-outs and subways. Indeed, during 1917 on the First Army front alone no less than 20 miles of subway were excavated. During the spring 1918 German offensives, many tunnelling companies found themselves fighting as infantry. They were also involved in demolition work. When the Allies began their ultimately victorious offensive in August 1918, the tunnelling companies were given another role – making safe enemy mines and booby traps. They were also used to help repair roads and bridges.

The Royal Engineers took on another specialist role after the German gas attack at Ypres in April 1915. The initial response concentrated on defensive measures. Responsibility for this was given to the RAMC and Lieutenant Colonel S. L. Cummins was appointed the gas adviser at GHQ in France. He also had a small team of assistants and a chemical laboratory under him. The latter concentrated on identifying the chemicals being used by the Germans. Gas advisers were also appointed to each army HQ. Cummins liaised closely with a newly established branch under the Director-General Army Medical Services (DGAMS) at the War Office, especially with regard to protection against chemical attack. The result was a series of steadily improving gasmasks. Initially, an *ad hoc* face-pad was issued. It was made of cotton waste soaked with hyposulphate (sodium thiosulphate) and sodium bicarbonate and enclosed in cotton netting, the ends of which were tied behind the head.[28] Frenchwomen were employed in their production.[29] Gas goggles were also provided to protect the eyes. Some who wore them were not impressed. Stanley Casson wrote:

> Whatever benign personage contrived these amiable death-traps I do not know. But anything more futile could never have been devised by the simplicity of man. On the whole we preferred to resort to the face-towels dipped in our own urine which an earlier order had suggested would be a temporary palliative.[30]

V. F. Eberle also mentions wooden boxes filled with gunpowder. 'These boxes were designed for anti-gas-cloud protection in the front line, to cause an upward current of air, to lift the gas over the trench.'[31] Another device was the Vermorel sprayer. This was a commercial piece of equipment used for spraying weedkiller or disinfectant. It consisted of a backpack copper container with a hand pump and sprayed sodium thiosulphate to neutralize the gas.

The next form of gas protection was issued in June 1915. This came in the form of a helmet made of flannelette with a celluloid eyepiece, the bottom of the helmet being tucked in under the jacket. Air was breathed in through the flannelette, which was impregnated with hyposulphite. A. D. Gillespie wrote that it had an advantage over the pad in that he could at least give oral orders when wearing it. But it also had its disadvantages. John Lucy recalled that 'it was most distressing trying to breathe in these, as they had no outlet valve of any kind', while Captain Hitchcock thought them 'very sticky, messy gadgets'.[32] A few months later came an improved version of the 'hypo' helmet known as the P helmet, with a mouthpiece and outlet valve. It also had glass eyepieces and was impregnated with phenol, as well as hydrosulphite, to protect against phosgene gas as well as chlorine. When the Germans actually began to use phosgene at the end of 1915, the P helmet was given additional protection in the form of hexamine and it was renamed the PH helmet. There was, however, recognition that the Germans might well employ new gases and to impregnate the PH helmet with additional chemicals would weaken the protection against chlorine and phosgene. Accordingly, a new type of mask was developed – the large box respirator. This had a canister, which contained charcoal and other chemicals. It was connected by means of a flexible tube to the face mask, which incorporated breathing valves. A major advantage of this system was that the contents of the canister could be adjusted to combat any new gas that the Germans employed. The large box respirator began to be issued in February 1916, but was considered too bulky to be carried by infantrymen and therefore only the supporting arms received them. A more manageable version, the small box respirator, was introduced six months later, with over a million being issued within three months. Captain Hitchcock thought them 'a vast improvement', while Brian Lawrence described it as 'a pretty toy'.[33] Certainly, they were infinitely more effective than anything that had gone before and provided the British Army with anti-gas protection for the remainder of the war.

As for the offensive use of gas, the government authorized this in May 1915. Major C. H. Foulkes DSO RE was appointed to coordinate gas operations at GHQ in France. Wully Robertson wrote to von Donop to explain the appointment: 'He [Foulkes] has no pretence to technical knowledge, as far as I know, and it is not considered that he need have very much. But he has had much experience at the front, and can best explain what we need and how we can perhaps best use it.'[34] At the War Office, Colonel Louis Jackson, who had been so closely involved with the development of the trench mortar, had already been in touch with scientists over the best means of discharging the gas and, indeed, what type should be used. The only gas immediately available in any quantity was chlorine and on 4 June a trial was carried out at a chemical works at Runcorn in Cheshire. The gas was discharged from cylinders and when the decision was made to use this method, urgent orders were placed in both Britain and the USA for their production. Meanwhile, in France, Foulkes set up a depot at Helfaut, close to GHQ at Saint Omer, where the officers and men to man this weapon could be trained. The new organization was titled the Special Brigade RE, which was a cover name, and initially four companies were formed. There was an urgency to the preparations since the plan was to use gas at the forthcoming attack at Loos. At one point, because of an officer shortage, Foulkes had to borrow a number from TF battalions at rest.

The British employment of gas for the first time on 25 September 1915 certainly took the Germans by surprise, but its effect was variable, because of the wind direction. Nevertheless, in the aftermath of Loos, the Special Brigade was expanded at the request of Sir Douglas Haig when he took over command of the BEF in December 1915. The original four companies were numbered 186 to 189, but under the new organization the brigade was organized in battalions. Four battalions each consisted of four cylinder companies, lettered A to Q. They also operated smoke candles. A further battalion of four companies, numbered 1 to 4, was equipped with 4-inch Stokes mortars for firing gas, thermite and smoke bombs. Finally, there was Z Company, which was formed on the eve of the Somme offensive in response to another new German weapon.

In the early hours of 30 July 1915, the Germans made a sudden attack using flame-throwers against elements of the 14th Division holding the Hooge sector. Although few of the defenders actually suffered burns, the use of flame-throwers did induce shock. The MGO's Trench Warfare Department was immediately tasked with developing a similar weapon. Several types of one-man flame-thrower were investigated, but GHQ in France was not convinced that they were the answer in the conditions that then existed, especially since the operator would be an easy target. At the end of 1915, a two-man semi-portable type was demonstrated. Although both the operator and the designer were burnt during the trial, and the equipment was too heavy to be carried except by truck, there was some interest in the concept. At the same trial, a heavy flame-thrower was also demonstrated. It consisted of four units, each made up of four 20-gallon fuel cylinders, which could be used as single units, in pairs or all together, when a flame duration of 45 to 50 seconds could be achieved. However, it weighed a massive 2,500lbs and was very bulky. One present at the demonstration was Captain W. H. Livens RE. He enlisted the help of his father at the firm of Rushton Proctor in Lincoln and they designed and built both a medium and heavy flame-thrower. The former was a two-man weapon with a 12-gallon fuel tank, the fuel being discharged by gas from a second tank. It was not really portable in action and had to be set up in a firing position. So, too, did Livens's heavy flame-thrower, which resembled, in one writer's words, a 'mechanical sea serpent',[35] with the nozzle representing its head, and seven sections of 9-inch diameter pipe in series and containing fuel and a reservoir tank as the body, and twelve gas cylinders as the tail. The idea was that it would be buried in a mine gallery running towards the German lines. The head, which could be elevated, would then rise above the surface and discharge flame.

Livens managed to persuade the authorities to allow him to try them out in France and in June 1916 he brought across twenty-four of his medium flame-throwers and six heavies. These were formed into Z Company of the Special Brigade. Four of the heavies were installed in time for the opening day of the Somme, one with the 7th Division and the other three with the 8th Division, but two were knocked out by shell-fire. The others enjoyed some success but had little influence on the overall outcome. The medium flame-throwers were also used, but to little effect. A further attempt was made in September with both the heavies and the mediums, after which they were put into storage in the open. One further use of them was made in October 1917 during Third Ypres and that was the end, apart from four heavy and several medium flame-throwers being on board HMS *Vindictive* during the famous Zeebrugge raid of St George's Day 1918. Their main problem was that they took too long to prepare and their effect was not worth the effort involved. Long before then, however, Livens had introduced a new method of dispensing flame. This was the Livens Projector, which had its battlefield debut at Pozières on 28 July 1916. In essence, it was a mortar which fired an incendiary bomb filled with oil. It consisted of two cans, an outer one which was the projector and the inner the oil can itself. It was fired by placing black powder in the outer can and had streamers of oil sacking to act as a fuse. These were ignited when the black powder was detonated. On landing, the bomb would burst and the oil set alight by the burning streamers. The Livens Projector went through a number of modifications and proved an effective means of delivering flammable substances. Z Company was equipped with it for the remainder of the war and Livens himself received the DSO and MC for his services.

The Special Brigade continued its operations, although gas warfare was increasingly waged by the artillery through the use of gas shells. At the higher level, Haig decided in April 1916 to combine offensive and defensive gas operations under one director, Brigadier General H. P. Thuillier, with Cummins appointed his assistant director and in charge of protection against gas, while Foulkes was responsible for the offensive side as commander of the Special Brigade. This remained under GHQ control, with its companies being temporarily attached to armies. Gas officers were deployed down to and including divisional level.

Bombing was initially an RE responsibility, since it was the sappers who produced the first homemade grenades, based on the ration jam tin. In March 1915 standardized types began to appear from Britain and each infantry brigade was ordered to form a bombing company and each battalion provided two NCOs and fourteen men per company to be trained in bombing, the training itself being carried out by the field companies RE within the division. The main problem was that there were too many different types of grenade produced. Billy Congreve recorded in his diary on 18 April 1915, during the desperate fighting on Hill 60 near Ypres:

> Our fellows are mostly untrained in bomb throwing, so it is rather an uneven contest – especially as we are issued with about six different patterns of grenades. If one man knows one sort, he probably doesn't know the others. It's months and months ago since the urgent need to a good hand-grenade was realised, and we haven't one yet![36]

In addition, many of the types were unsafe or too heavy to achieve much range. The 'good hand-grenade', the No. 5 Mills, made its appearance the following month. It was named after a marine engineer, William Mills, who also established the first aluminium foundry in Britain. His inspiration came from a Belgian engineer, whom he met in 1914 and who showed him a design for a grenade. What was revolutionary about it was that, unlike the other grenades, the Belgian design had an automatic fuse detonation and ignition system, which did away with the need to light a fuse, in itself the cause of many accidents. Mills radically refined the design and presented it to the Inventions Branch of the Directorate of Royal Artillery in late January 1915. It was well received and production began in the late spring of 1915. Manufacturing problems meant that the rate of production was initially slow, with only 16,000 out of a War Office order for 5 million being delivered by the beginning of July 1915. The Trench Warfare Department therefore took over the contracts side and soon over twenty contractors were involved in the manufacture of the grenade. By

October, 300,000 were being produced per week and this would rise by a further 100,000.

On 20 November 1915, the Army Council decided that the Mills grenade would now become the British Army's standard grenade. All outstanding contracts on other grenades were cancelled and the following month the local manufacture of grenades in France and elsewhere was also halted. The Mills Bomb, as it became commonly known, underwent modification during the war and ended up as the No. 36 Grenade, which remained the standard grenade not just throughout 1939–45 but for many years beyond.[37]

The importance of bombing was reflected in the growing plethora of schools. In Britain, a bombing school was initially established on Clapham Common in London, which also had a trench mortar school, and soon each home command had its own. In France, bombing schools existed down to brigade level and another was established at the Imperial School of Instruction at Zeitoun in Egypt. A further school was also found on Gallipoli. Initially, grenade throwers were called by the traditional term of 'grenadiers', but under a General Routine Order (GRO) issued by GHQ in France on 4 April 1916 the name was changed to 'bombers'. The previous October, those who had successfully attended a bombing course were entitled to wear a flaming grenade badge worn on the right sleeve just below the shoulder.[38] This in itself recognized a new infantry specialization, one of many. CSM Shephard of the 1st Dorsets complained in late August 1916:

> Every few hours I get a message asking for names of men for course of Lewis gunnery, trench mortar, Stokes gun, physical training, cooking, signalling, etc. We are already under strength a good deal, and this constant demand for men to be trained as specialists causes less strength now, and later when these men have finished their courses they are likely to be called for to fill vacancies caused by casualties in the various specialist units.[39]

R. B. Talbot Kelly observed at the end of 1916:

> By this date in the war the British infantryman had almost forgotten that

ABOVE The Regular Army deploys to France. Troops after detraining at Southampton Docks. (IWM Q33550)

BELOW 2nd/9th Londons (Queen Victoria's Rifles) on a lunch break, late 1914. The 1st/9th went to France in early November, and the 2nd/9th was left with a mixture of men – medically unfit for active service, those who had not taken the Imperial Service Obligation, youths too young to be sent overseas, and new recruits. (IWM Q53457)

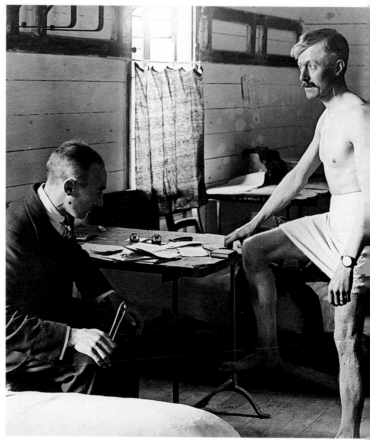

RIGHT A Kitchener recruit undergoing a medical inspection. Civilian doctors were paid a fee for each inspection they carried out, which might have tempted some to be less meticulous than they might have been. In the early months the deluge of volunteers also often meant that the medicals could be little more than cursory. The overall result was that several low medical grade men were accepted for the army. (IWM Q30062)

ABOVE The 6th (Service) Battalion the Lincolnshire Regiment parades in early September 1914. The few in uniform may have been those with some previous military experience. Being a K1 battalion, it has managed to obtain a few rifles and it would not be long before the whole battalion was in khaki. Later Kitchener formations would not be so fortunate and had to wait months before they were properly equipped. (IWM Q53285)

ABOVE Members of the University and Public Schools Brigade (18th–21st Royal Fusiliers) build their own hutted camp at Epsom, Surrey, October 1914. These were Locally Raised Kitchener units and responsible for obtaining much of their equipment. Not until July 1915 did the War Office formally take them over. Many members of the UPS Brigade were commissioned early on and three of the four battalions were disbanded in France in April 1916, most of their men being posted to Officer Cadet battalions. (IWM Q53362)

BELOW The 8th Welsh Regiment carrying out miniature range practice at Bournemouth, December 1914 – January 1915. The first of the regiment's Service battalions, it had been under canvas, but was now in billets. It became the Pioneer battalion of the 13th Division and sailed for the Dardanelles in June 1915. (IWM Q53565)

ABOVE The 16th Cheshires practise trench digging. This was the first of the Bantam battalions and was raised by Alfred Bigland MP. Eventually, two divisions of these 'small men' were formed. The idea was not a success, since too many men with inferior physique were enlisted. Furthermore, it encouraged under-age boys to join up, to which the army was prepared to turn a blind eye for some time, in spite of a vigorous campaign by Arthur Markham MP to have them weeded out. (IWM Q53723)

BELOW Palestinian volunteers for the 38th and 39th (Jewish) Battalions of the Royal Fusiliers, Jerusalem, summer 1918. They may also have included some Jews from the USA. While these battalions were originally largely formed from Russian Jews, the Russian exit from the war in March 1918 caused further Russian conscripts in Britain to be posted to two specially raised battalions of the Labour Corps. (IWM Q12671)

TOP 2nd/1st Kent Cyclists Battalion TF ground their mounts while on training, 1915. The majority of TF Cyclists battalions were home defence, although the 1st/1st Kent Cyclists, together with three other battalions, were converted to conventional infantry and sent to India in February 1916, ending up in Siberia in October 1918. The TF Cyclists remained separate from the Army Cyclist Corps, which was formed from the infantry division Cyclist Companies, although they did provide drafts for the ACC during the last year of the war. (IWM Q53661)

ABOVE The Royal Scots Greys in France, May 1918. They managed to maintain some of their traditional grey horses. While the Regular cavalry regiments did keep their role, many Yeomanry regiments were converted to infantry and, in Britain, to cyclists. In addition, a large number of cavalry recruits were transferred to the infantry and the number of Reserve cavalry regiments, which stood at seventeen on mobilization, eventually reduced to nine, which included three for the Household Cavalry. (IWM Q8952)

ABOVE Junior officers undergoing bayonet fighting instruction, Third Army School, Flixécourt, October 1916. The two instructors (in white) were members of the team brought across to France by Major Ronnie Campbell, the Bayonet King. The object of the schools in France was not just to bring officers and NCOs up to date on the latest tactics, but also to improve their instructional skills. (IWM Q1597)

BELOW Frenchwomen producing camouflage netting for concealing roads from the air, September 1918. By this stage, each army in France had its own camouflage factory, some of which were supervised by assistant administrators of Queen Mary's Army Auxiliary Corps. (IWM Q7091)

ABOVE Members of the staff of HQ XIV Corps at Meaulte, south of Albert, May 1917. Five of the six in the front are staff officers *per se*, distinguishable by the gorgets on their lapels. They are also wearing red–white–red brassards on their right arms, indicating a corps HQ. The other officers are either staff learners or holding non-staff positions. (IWM Q2166)

ABOVE Cadets at the Royal Military College Sandhurst, November 1917. At this stage in the war the course was nine months long and gave the cadet a Regular as opposed to Temporary commission. Only a small proportion of the latter transferred to Regular commissions during the war, largely because it meant losing all the seniority they had gained and starting again as brand new 2nd Lieutenants. One wonders how many of the young men in this picture survived the battles of 1918. (IWM Q54268)

TOP Members of No. 1 Cadet School RGA at Trowbridge, Wiltshire, carry out gun drills on an 8-inch howitzer, November 1917. The white bands on their hats distinguish them as officer cadets. A good proportion of them would have served in the ranks in France, quite possibly on this same type of gun. (IWM Q54254)

ABOVE Men of an Infantry Labour battalion on road repairs, Hamel, 1916. Thirty-three of these battalions were formed from Category B conscripts during summer 1916 to help overcome the growing labour crisis in France. They were absorbed into the Labour Corps on its formation in early 1917 and road maintenance remained their main task, often carried out under shellfire. (IWM Q1591) an infantryman's best friend is his rifle. In the trenches he lived at such close range to his enemy that a hand grenade was a more usual weapon than his rifle. Extraordinary examples of this were constantly occurring in which a man, with a full magazine, would never think to use it and shoot down his enemy at a distance, but would wait until he came within the thirty yards of a grenade, or still closer, when he could deal with him with a bayonet. The exceptional standard of musketry that was the base of the old regular army of 1914, and that was unique in its day (Continental Armies taking little trouble about training in musketry) had been forgotten by the New Armies, and the rushed training at home had not given the instructional staff time to produce first-class shots.'[40]

By spring 1917, the rifle platoon in France was organized as one Lewis gun section, one of bombers and two of riflemen and rifle grenadiers. But then came the order to form a battle patrol platoon of one officer and fifty-three other ranks. It would be held at battalion HQ and used to exploit success in an attack. Its members were to wear green armbands and were to march at the head of the battalion, presumably in recognition that they were an elite. James Jack, commanding the 2nd West Yorkshires disagreed with the concept on the grounds that exploitation was something the rifle companies did in any event and also that 'weak companies were therefore robbed of their best NCOs and men, whom they could not afford to lose, without any advantage'. He therefore resorted to subterfuge to placate his superiors and the idea was soon dropped. Even so, John Nettleton of the 2nd Rifle Brigade recorded that it and other battalions in the 8th Division did employ battle platoons during the German spring 1917 withdrawal to the Hindenburg Line.[41]

The cavalry did not change its shape to any significant extent as the war progressed and was under continual pressure to surrender manpower to the other arms. By the beginning of 1915, there were three British and two Indian cavalry divisions in France. There was also still a cavalry squadron attached to each Regular infantry division* while the Territorial divisions, which soon began to arrive in France, also had them, as did the New Army formations. With the onset of trench warfare, the prospects

---

* In April 1915, the 15th and 19th Hussars, which had provided the squadrons for the first six infantry divisions of the BEF, were replaced by Yeomanry squadrons, and helped to form the 9th Cavalry Brigade.

for mounted action were reduced to virtually zero and the cavalry found itself, as it had done during First Ypres, often acting as infantry in holding the line. Towards the end of 1915, a dismounted division was formed, with each of the three British cavalry divisions supplying a three-battalion brigade. But serving as infantrymen created problems, as Burgon Bicker-steth of the Royal Dragoons commented at the end of 1915:

> The truth is, the infantry are prepared for this sort of thing, but we are not. Our kit is cavalry, not infantry kit, and shorn of our horses we have poor means of carrying everything we should carry. We have had to decide what is the best method of carrying a pack. The pack itself is merely a mackintosh ground sheet wrapped round a coat, undercloth-ing, towel, etc. We have nothing provided in the way of a proper square infantry pack. The whole organisation of the regiment on infantry lines was novel too... We all got rather mixed up with platoons, companies, squadrons, troops.[42]

Hopes that the cavalry could be used to exploit a breakthrough at Loos and on the Somme were soon dashed, although on a couple of occasions during the Somme fighting there were small-scale cavalry actions. During May and June 1916, the divisional cavalry squadrons, which each New Army division also possessed, were withdrawn and formed into corps cavalry regiments. Thus, the three squadrons of the 1st/1st Yorkshire Dragoons, which had been with the 17th, 19th and 37th Divisions, became the II Corps Cavalry Regiment. Because the priority need was for infantry replacements, the winter of 1916–17 saw many cavalry recruits diverted to this arm, reducing the cavalry reserve from 15,000 men to below 3,000 and the fourteen Reserve cavalry regiments diminished to six. Further-more, many cavalry officers had been transferring to other arms because of the lack of opportunity for action. The Cavalry Corps' problems were aggravated, too, by the creation of cavalry Pioneer battalions for labouring tasks towards the end of 1916 (*see page 218*). There were some further minor cavalry actions during the German withdrawal to the Hindenburg Line and briefly at Arras. In the aftermath of the latter battle, the War Office demanded that Haig dismount one of his cavalry divisions in order to provide more infantry as well as to save on forage being shipped across from Britain, a problem exacerbated by the growing shortage of ships. Haig resisted and proposed dismounting some of the corps cavalry regiments instead.[43] During the late summer of 1917, three out of the six Special Reserve regiments, the 1st North Irish and the 1st and 2nd South Irish Horse, were dismounted, with the latter two regiments amalgamated and absorbed by the 9th Royal Irish Fusiliers and 7th Royal Irish Regiment respectively.* In addition, of the fifteen first-line Yeomanry regiments serving in France, the majority as corps cavalry, seven suffered a similar fate. The overall result was that just three corps were left with cavalry regiments and one of these, 1st/1st Yorkshire Dragoons was switched to the Cavalry Corps in October 1917.

The cavalry's one major chance of charging through what was known as the 'the "G" in Gap' came at Cambrai, but, largely because of the 'fog of war' caused by the perennial communications difficulties, the opportunity was lost, in spite of the brave efforts of a squadron of the Canadian Fort Garry Horse, which actually got through into the open country beyond the German defences. The cavalry's stock in the aftermath of the battle reached its nadir. One sapper officer at Third Army HQ noted: 'People are daily more annoyed with our cavalry'.[44] Winston Churchill, brought back into the government as Minister for Munitions, wrote in a memorandum on manpower for the War Cabinet:

> Are we really to keep in being at a time when every man is precious … 30,000 to 40,000 cavalry with their horses, when these admirable cavalrymen would supply the personnel for the greatest development of mechanical warfare both for offence and defence in tanks, in armoured cars … that has yet been conceived?[45]

It was a view strongly supported by Lloyd George. No wonder that Archibald Home, Chief of Staff of the Cavalry Corps, wrote in his diary on Christmas Day 1917:

> As regards the Cavalry – people at home ask 'They had a great chance at Cambrai – is it any use keeping them? They will never have such a chance again.' This is the crux of the whole matter – on this they may do anything

---

* A fourth, 2nd King Edward's Horse, was sent back to England and its personnel absorbed by the Tank Corps. This left just the 1st North Irish Horse and 1st King Edward's Horse still acting as corps cavalry.

– make the Cavalry into latrine caretakers. I shall be glad to have a rest – that is that.[46]

In early January 1918, Haig went over to London to defend the *arme blanche*. He argued that the cavalry should be regarded as 'resembling highly trained mobile infantry rather than the old cavalry arm', which better accorded to the defensive posture that he had now adopted in France. Furthermore, 'once the cavalry had been disbanded it would be difficult to build up again so highly trained and technical an arm, and it would be many months before the cavalry, once dissipated, could be re-created.'[47] Haig was successful in saving his cavalry, but there were sacrifices to be made. For a start, the two Indian cavalry formations, which had been retitled the 4th and 5th Cavalry Divisions in 1916, were broken up and the Indian regiments within them sent to Palestine, together with HQ 5th Cavalry Division.* The remaining Yeomanry regiments in France were also to be converted to Cyclist or Machine Gun battalions, as were the three Household Cavalry regiments. In addition, the three remaining divisions in the Cavalry Corps were reorganized. One brigade in each division was ordered to form a 'Pioneer battalion' of 400 men to assist with the preparation of defences in the Fifth Army's area. In the midst of this reorganization, the German March 1918 offensive struck. The Cavalry Corps was immediately ordered to form dismounted 'divisions', with each brigade providing a battalion of 400 to 550 men in four companies, together with a machine gun company. The Pioneer battalions were absorbed by these new formations. In spite of the chaos that this hasty reorganization clearly created, the dismounted cavalrymen did well. Archibald Home noted in his diary on 25 March: 'The Cavalry barometer stands very high again, it was very low a month ago.'[48]

Once the crisis had passed, the Cavalry Corps regained its horses, but the reorganisation had to be modified because of casualties. Four of the Yeomanry regiments were mounted again and dispersed by squadrons to the three cavalry divisions. One, 1st/1st Yorkshire Dragoons, became the II Corps Cyclist Battalion. Two, 1st/1st Northamptonshire Yeomanry and 1st/1st Northumberland Yeomanry, remained as corps cavalry regiments, while the 1st/1st Queen's Own Oxfordshire Hussars, the first Yeomanry

---

* The two divisions had consisted of five Indian cavalry brigades, each including one British regiment, and the Canadian Cavalry Brigade.

regiment to cross to France, remained as part of the 2nd Cavalry Division, as it had been since November 1914. The three Household Cavalry regiments became lorry-borne machine gunners in the summer of 1918 and came under the Cavalry Corps umbrella. The reorganized Cavalry Corps played its part in the attack at Amiens on 8 August, although there were problems over cooperating with tanks. On 1 September, the Cavalry Corps was withdrawn from the front line to retrain with other arms, notably lorry-borne infantry and the Royal Air Force. Thereafter, apart from two brigade-sized actions in October, the cavalry were primarily used in the reconnaissance role. By the time of the Armistice, the strength of the cavalry in France was little more than it had been at the beginning of September 1914 and its percentage strength to that of the combat arms as a whole had dropped from over 9 per cent to just over 1.5 per cent.

The scope for cavalry in other theatres also got off to an unpromising start. Three Yeomanry regiments were despatched to Egypt in September 1914 and formed the Yeomanry Brigade there in January 1915. At this time, Kitchener decreed that Egypt should be a base for operations in the Near and Middle East and among other troops sent out was the 2nd Mounted Division, as well as brigades from the 1st Mounted Division. These all found themselves operating as infantry on Gallipoli. When they were withdrawn back to Egypt at the end of 1915, they were reorganized into four mounted and four dismounted brigades. The latter were eventually merged into the 74th Division in February 1918. The mounted brigades took part in the campaign in Palestine. However, the demands for more men in France in the aftermath of the March 1918 offensive caused a break-up of these brigades. Some of their regiments joined the Indian cavalry regiments sent from France in the newly created 4th and 5th Cavalry Divisions and became part of the Desert Mounted Corps (DMC), which achieved spectacular results during the final phase of the campaign against the Turks during September–October 1918. The remainder were converted to five Machine Gun battalions, lettered B to F in April 1918. Two months later, they went to France, were retitled Nos. 100 to 104 MG Battalions, and served as army troops.

The cavalry finished the war with the sword, lance and rifle with which it entered it in August 1914 and went through no major technological change, although on the Western Front, at least, the addition of motorized machine gunners and infantry, as well as cooperation with aircraft, did point the way to the mobile warfare of the future. In contrast, the Royal Artillery not only took on new responsibilities but took great strides forward in the science of gunnery.

Apart from taking over responsibility for medium and heavy trench mortars, another Royal Artillery speciality was that of anti-aircraft defence. In August 1914, the army possessed a mere thirty anti-aircraft (AA) guns, of which twenty-five were 1-pounder pom-poms. They were deployed to protect vulnerable points, especially arsenals and key ports, and were the responsibility of the RGA. Because of this paucity, the BEF crossed to France with no AA guns. Recognition of the air threat gradually dawned and in October each of the eight infantry divisions then in theatre was allotted a 1-pounder pom-pom. These were very ineffective, and 13-pounder and 18-pounder field guns began to be converted to the AA role. Three sections, each of two 13-pounders mounted on the back of lorries, and a single horse-drawn 18-pounder were in France by the end of the year. Lieutenant Travis Hampson RAMC describes an early engagement at Ploegsteert:

> Thereabouts we heard our anti-aircraft guns firing at a German plane, so we went on half a mile or so and found their emplacements by a farm. There were two motor lorries with a 12 pounder [sic] mounted on each ... Over came a Taube, looking like a louse in the sky, and they opened up on it ... They got a string of bursts which looked very near, but the plane just went straight on.[49]

More sections arrived and in October 1915 they were grouped into four-gun batteries and controlled at army level, with AA staff officers being attached to Army HQ. Additionally, a small air raid by night near GHQ at Saint Omer in March 1915 prompted a request for searchlights to be sent out from England. These were manned by the Royal Engineers, and the first two sections, each of three searchlights and manned by a mixture of Regulars and London Electrical Engineers TF, arrived the following month. They found themselves carrying out a dual role, assisting in AA defence and being used to illuminate no-man's-land at night.

In Britain, the beginning of the Zeppelin raids in January 1915 caused major concern over the air defence of London. The army was unable to provide AA guns and searchlights, the majority of the latter being committed to coast defence, and so the Admiralty took the initiative, forming a unit armed with a variety of guns and supported by searchlights manned by part-time Royal Navy Volunteer Reserve personnel, many of whom were also special constables.* Input on the lay-out of the defences was also provided by the indefatigable Colonel Louis Jackson of the Directorate of Fortifications and Works at the War Office. As Toby Rawlinson commented:

> The armament of the force both was totally inadequate and unsuitable for the purpose for which it was intended, as not only was it quite impossible for it to inflict any injury upon Zeppelin airships, but it was equally impossible that these guns could be fired over London without causing considerable injury to the unfortunate people whom they were intended to protect.[50]

He himself had been commanding an RNACD squadron, but had also been involved in helping to organize the air defence of Paris during winter of 1914–15. For this reason, the Admiralty called for his services in autumn 1915 and sent him across to France to obtain mobile AA guns in the shape of the 75mm *auto-canon*, which could fire HE shells with a suitable time fuse. These were obtained and the defence of London was divided into two parts, one comprising fixed guns and searchlights and the other a mobile element under Rawlinson's command and manned by men of his RNACD squadron. The London defences had also improved in September 1915, with the deployment of 50 Field Searchlight Company RE.

The air defence of the remainder of the country remained the responsibility of the War Office. However, in February 1916, GHQ Home Forces took over this task, including London, although the personnel involved in the defence of the capital continued to be administered by the Admiralty. In May 1916, the first comprehensive plan for the defence of Britain was published, the idea being that no Zeppelin could pass over the coast without being engaged, either from the air or the ground. The country was divided into twenty-four AA commands, with London being covered by seven of

* Part-time policemen.

them. A total of fifty-six RGA companies were formed to man the guns, with additional RE searchlight companies, both fixed and mobile. An AA school was also established at Shoeburyness. In addition, the Observer companies of the Royal Defence Corps manned a system of early warning observation posts (*see page 93*). A further refinement came in September 1916, with the creation of the Ever Ready Zone covering the coasts, with the defences on permanent alert, and the Inner Zone, where the crew were at 15 minutes' readiness. For the protection of London itself, the Metropolitan Observation Service was established under Lieutenant Commander H. Paget RNVR, formerly the Indian Police Commissioner in Calcutta. This was a voluntary body consisting largely of special constables. Equipped with instruments to measure vertical and horizontal angles, they manned a total of twenty-six observation posts (OPs) situated on high buildings and were connected by telephone to a central control room at County Hall in Spring Gardens, close to Trafalgar Square. This, in turn, was connected by telephone to the AA Defence Commander (based at Horse Guards Parade), the Metropolitan Police at Scotland Yard, the London Fire Brigade, and the GPO trunk telephone manager. A subsidiary system of OPs was controlled by the Chief Constable of Hertfordshire, who relayed sightings to the County Hall control room.[51] The Metropolitan Observation Service was undoubtedly the predecessor to the Royal Observer Corps which provided such sterling service during the Second World War.

But while the air defence organization appeared impressive, in practice there were serious shortfalls. Sir Charles Petrie, commissioned into the RGA in late 1915 and posted to AA guns in early 1916, after a course at Shoeburyness, observed:

> The only time a Zeppelin came within range we had no ammunition and were constrained to admire her beauty in the moonlight. Perhaps, however, the lack of shells did not matter so much as we imagined at the time, for when they did arrive, they were filled only with salt. Indeed, the position of many gun stations seemed to be dictated by political, rather than military, considerations. Lack of ammunition was the rule, rather than the exception, but all the same, officers and men had to pretend that the guns were ready for action, presumably to impress the

civilian population, and each night we were compelled to stand by as if we were in a position to open fire. It was a sorry and rather demoralising piece of make-believe.[52]

Matters, however, did improve. In the late summer of 1917, the country was divided into two AA commands, Northern and Southern Areas. Brigadier General E. B. Ashmore was appointed to command the latter and did much to increase effectiveness.

In France the AA defences also improved. In November 1917, the idea of AA batteries was dropped and AA sections reintroduced. Better guns, notably the 3-inch (achieved by boring out the barrel of an 18-pounder field gun) and the 13-pounder 9cwt, and rangefinders and fuse indicators increased effectiveness. There was, however, a major debate over how air defence should be directed. A committee was established to consider the problem and concluded that it should be a General Staff responsibility, with the Royal Artillery providing technical input. Anti-Aircraft Defence Commanders (AADC) were to be appointed, with staffs, to each Army HQ and to the lines of communication, with a directorate at GHQ to oversee matters. Sir Noel Birch, the Major General Royal Artillery (MGRA) at GHQ, disagreed, however, arguing that air defence was essentially an artillery matter, but he was overruled and the new organization came into being at the beginning of 1918. Earlier, on 1 January 1917, an Inspector of Searchlights (IS) was appointed at GHQ. He came under the engineer-in-chief and was to deal with all matters concerning searchlights, including advising on searchlight tactics in conjunction with the MGRA. This was followed by an assistant inspector being established at each Army HQ and on the lines of communication.

For the first half of the war, personnel for AA defence were drawn from all three branches of the Royal Artillery, although those based in Britain were predominantly RGA. This was formalized at home on 1 January 1917, with the sailors still involved with AA also being transferred to the RGA. Not until the end of November 1917 was it laid down that AA personnel serving abroad* should all be RGA as well. Manpower became an increasing problem, though, and in France many medically downgraded

---

* AA guns were also deployed to Italy, Salonika, Egypt and Mesopotamia.

infantrymen had to be transferred. Even so, the demands for AA units were never fully met and this branch of the RGA was very much 'nobody's child' in the field, with little opportunity to bond with the formations that it was protecting.[53]

Apart from taking on new weapons, the greatest revolution experienced by the Royal Artillery during 1914–18 was in the accuracy of its fire. This, too, resulted in new specialities. To a large extent, the transformation was connected to improvements in the accuracy of maps, resulting from more precise survey methods. After the initial drama over the BEF's map coverage (*see page 49*) and the advance to the River Aisne during early September 1914, a period of static warfare, albeit temporary, ensued. It was during this period that the first improvements in mapping came. These were as a result of the first steps in developing the technique of controlling artillery fire from the air. To better identify targets, a pilot drew a grid on the relevant map and gave a copy to the battery whose fire he was directing. He could then pass a map reference of the target over his very primitive and unreliable wireless. But the gunners also needed more accurate maps if they were to locate enemy batteries precisely. This was initially tackled by producing larger-scale maps – converting 1:80,000 to 1:40,000 and, especially for the artillery, 1:20,000. At the same time, the 1st Ranging Section RE was formed in England. Consisting of one officer and four other ranks recruited from the Ordnance Survey at Southampton, and equipped with two theodolites, its task was to improve air-artillery cooperation. The idea was that the aircraft would drop a smoke bomb over the target and the theodolites would be used to take bearings on it, work out the position and pass this to the battery. After carrying out trials on Salisbury Plain with artillery and the RFC, the section crossed to France with the 8th Division in early November 1914. It then carried out further trials with the GHQ RFC squadron before rejoining the 8th Division. Poor weather during the next two months hampered additional trials to perfect the system. By this time, the RFC had received an improved wireless and the services of 1st Ranging Section were no longer needed. It was, however, soon given a new task.

The BEF's maps were based on French and Belgian originals. While the latter were of good quality, the former were by no means perfect and their use was creating difficulties in ensuring that artillery fire was accurate. This was particularly important given the severe shortage of artillery ammunition from which the BEF was now suffering. An early attempt to improve the situation was to get 1st Ranging Section, which had been reinforced by further Ordnance Survey experts, to survey in the heavy guns now arriving in France, notably the first of the 15-inch howitzers, which was deployed at the end of February 1915. Simultaneously, the section, which was still part of 8th Division, was tasked with surveying parts of the British sector. Supervision of this was at army level and it was clearly nonsensical for the section to remain part of a division. It was therefore transferred to GHQ in April 1915 and retitled 1st Ranging and Survey Section. Its area of responsibility stretched from the reserve trenches to the rear. Forward of this, mapping was based on maps produced under Napoleon over 100 years before, with updating done through the use of air photographs. This was scarcely satisfactory and it was not until early 1916 that survey work could be carried out in the forward area and accurate trench maps produced. Because of the vast amount of survey work that needed to be done, it was decided in July that each army* should be given its own Topographical Section, with the bulk of 1st Ranging and Survey Section providing that for the newly formed Third Army, which had recently taken over part of the Somme sector from the French. The Topographical Sections soon found themselves with responsibilities other than just survey work.

Counter-battery work, the engagement of enemy batteries, was becoming an ever-more important artillery role and was the province of the heavy guns. Before the end of 1914 attempts had been made to locate German guns by taking bearings of the muzzle flashes at the moment of firing. The inaccuracy of the existing maps meant, however, that this system was largely ineffective. Improved maps, at least in the Ypres sector, led to more accurate flash spotting, which became the province of the Heavy Artillery Reserve (later Groups) in which the heavy batteries were organized. The paucity of accurate maps in the Third Army's sector, however, led to its Topographical Section being authorized to raise an

---

* Each army had already been given its own maps officer, together with a section from the Printing Company RE, in March 1915. They did not, however, have any survey resources.

Artillery Survey Detachment. Made up of gunners and ghillies from the 51st (Highland) Division, this manned a series of OPs along the Front. These had the dual tasks of flash spotting and gathering general intelligence on enemy movements. The other armies followed suit. Simultaneously, another system of locating German batteries was being developed.

Sound ranging was first employed by the French and German armies. The principle was to establish a line of microphones in precisely surveyed positions. These would record the sound of a gun firing and, noting the time differences between each microphone and taking the speed of sound into account, the position of the gun could be plotted on a map. The Royal Engineers in France became interested, although the gunners were apparently not. Eventually, the latter agreed to detail an officer to investigate it. The job was given to Second Lieutenant Lawrence Bragg, who was serving with an RHA TF battery in England. His name may well have come to the War Office's attention because he and his father had just won the Nobel Prize for Physics for their work on crystallography. Bragg arrived in France at the end of August 1915, by which time an officer from the War Office had visited the French and looked at their three sound-ranging systems, selecting one devised by Lucien Bull. Bragg went to examine this and then travelled to Paris to collect the Bull apparatus ordered by the War Office. Not until October was it in his hands and he was then ordered to report to Colonel E. M. Jack, who had been in charge of maps at GHQ from the outset. Jack told him to select another technically minded officer and to set up a sound-ranging section to operate in the Dickebush–Kemmel sector. Once a microphone picked up the sound of a gun firing, an electrical signal was sent down a wire to the 'recording station'. The signal was reproduced by cinefilm as a jagged line, with a toothed wheel interrupting light 100 times per second to give time marks on the film.

The main problem during the early months was that the microphones could not separate artillery firing from the myriad noises of the Front. Nevertheless, Bragg persisted and by the end of 1915 was able to locate a gun to within 500 yards. This was encouraging enough for further sections to be formed. These, like the flash-spotting sections, were placed under the Topographical sections. Information on enemy batteries was also supplied by the RFC, air photographs, corps intelligence reports and artillery OPs. To coordinate it all, a Compilation Section was set up at each army HQ and daily maps showing the location of enemy batteries began to be issued.

In February 1916, the Second Army established a sound-ranging school, while Third Army did likewise for flash spotting. Simultaneously, the topographical sections became Field Survey Companies (FSC) RE, with one company allocated to each army in France. The sound-ranging sections were increased to eight, including Bragg's, which became an experimental section. They were lettered backwards from 'W'. Bragg, himself, was still wrestling with the problem that while his sound-ranging microphones could identify a howitzer, they were confused by the two sounds that a gun made on firing. The first was a crack, represented by the shell in the air, the second a dull boom, which was the moment of firing. This could not be detected by the microphones because the frequency was too low. Eventually, in June 1916, with the help of Corporal (later Major) W. S. Tucker, who had recently joined the section from Imperial College, London, the problem was overcome by passing an electric current through a heated wire. The current varied when cool air was blown on the wire and this enabled the low frequency sound of the firing gun to be differentiated from the shell wave. The resultant Tucker Microphone radically increased the effectiveness of sound ranging* and by autumn 1916 there were sufficient sections to furnish one per corps.

The Observation sections became groups at the end of 1916. While nominally under the Royal Engineers, they drew their personnel from all arms. Each group had an HQ of two officers and ten other ranks. These included technicians, who operated the plotting boards, clerks, a cook and two ASC drivers. A group provided four OPs, except for No. 1 Field Survey Company, which had seven, although these were later formed into two groups. The theodolite was soon replaced by an artillery director, and then by a French instrument, which had a revolving eyepiece with three different magnifications, and finally by what was called the 'Watkins instrument', which appears to have been a combination of the Watkins depression range-finder and depression position-finder, which had been developed for coast

---

* One early problem with the Tucker Microphone was that the hot wire attracted earwigs, consequently, the microphone had to be fitted with a grill. This was officially designated Protectors, Earwig Mk 1.

artillery in the 1880s. As for the men of the Observation groups, Captain John Innes, who became adjutant to No. 1 Field Survey Company noted:

> Nearly every regiment in the British Army must have been represented in the Groups and Sections at this time. They ranged from Life Guardsmen to Able-Bodied Seamen (RND), and a visit to an Observation Post would possibly have shown one a kilted Highlander sitting, cheek by jowl, with a breeched RAMC orderly, or, perhaps, with an 'Aussie' with shirt-tunic, 'wideawake' [the Australian bush hat] – and drawl.[54]

To indicate their role, from November 1916 just below the right shoulder they wore a dark-blue patch with FSC in red.[55] However, in January 1917 all personnel in the Field Survey companies were transferred to the Royal Engineers.

Later in 1917, the companies were formed into Field Survey battalions on the basis of one per army. By the time of the Armistice, in November 1918 these battalions controlled twenty-five sound-ranging sections (Bragg's original section was now called the Experimental Section and came under GHQ) and twenty-four Observation groups, apart from their survey and map production elements. In addition, there were Field Survey companies in Britain, Egypt, Italy and Salonika. As for mapping, a significant improvement in production came at the end of 1917, when the Overseas Branch of the Ordnance Survey was established in France. The male staff members were enlisted into the Royal Engineers and the females enrolled in the Women's Army Auxiliary Corps (WAAC). By the end of the war in France and Flanders, no less than 6,000 square miles of territory had been surveyed and published as 1:20,000 maps and the rate of issues worked out at some 20,000 maps per day.

Precise mapping and the ability to locate targets accurately did much to improve the effectiveness of artillery, but there was one other crucial element in the equation. In 1913, at a meeting of the Royal Artillery Institute, the suggestion that meteorological conditions could affect a shell in flight was greeted with derision. Even as late as 30 June 1915, when HQ RFC in France asked the Artillery Adviser at GHQ, General John du Cane, whether details of wind speeds taken at 10 each morning would be of use to the heavy artillery, they were told: 'We cannot make any use of this information'. Even so, the heavy and siege batteries* had already begun to recognize that such factors as barometric pressure and temperature could affect accuracy. They termed this phenomenon 'errors of the day', but did not really understand the implications. Prior to the Battle of Loos, however, a meteorological expert, Captain E. Gold RE, was appointed to HQ First Army in preparation for the first British offensive use of gas. After Loos, Gold was made meteorological officer at GHQ and began to investigate the effect of wind on shells in flight. He published his findings in March 1916. So convincing were they that GHQ issued instructions on 12 April that in future daily reports on wind speed and direction at 2,000 and 4,000 feet would be issued to the artillery. The frequency of these Meteor telegrams, as they were called, was gradually increased until by March 1917 they were being issued six times a day. To support Gold, a Meteorological Section RE was established at GHQ and other sections deployed to Egypt and Salonika. This, and the efforts to provide accurate maps and more precise ways of locating targets finally bore fruit at Cambrai on 20 November 1917, when the tanks were able to attack without a preliminary barrage or, more importantly, pre-registration of targets, which had so often resulted in loss of surprise in the past. The artillery was able to open fire at H-hour confident that it would hit its targets.[56]

One other speciality undertaken by the Royal Engineers is worth mentioning. Shortly after the outbreak of the war, Solomon J. Solomon RA, a well-known portrait painter, had the idea of concealing trenches from the air through the use of dyed butter muslin and other materials supported on poles. He demonstrated his concept to the War Office at Woolwich and details of his proposals were passed to Sir John French. The war, however, was still mobile at that stage and GHQ showed no interest. In February 1915, the French established a camouflage detachment at Amiens and began to specialize in the production of concealed OPs. It was not until the end of that year that the British became interested and Solomon was invited to France to advise on camouflage. He was asked to create an OP on the Yser Canal and, noting the trees in this sector, made a steel structure covered with bark from a decayed willow tree in

* In autumn 1914, the RGA designated its batteries other than Coast, Heavy and Siege. Heavy batteries were armed with 60-pounder guns, while Siege were equipped with the larger calibres, which ranged from 6-inch guns and howitzers to 14-inch railway guns and 15-inch howitzers, although the last named were taken over by the Heavy Howitzer Brigade, Royal Marine Artillery.

Windsor Great Park. The result was the formation of the Special Works Park RE at Saint Omer in March 1916. Captain F. J. C. Wyatt MC, a Regular sapper, was selected to command it and Solomon made technical adviser with the rank of lieutenant colonel. Apart from seven French camouflage experts, the personnel for the new unit were drawn from artists and those who had been in the theatrical business. A factory was established at Amiens for the production of camouflage materials, with local Frenchwomen being employed. One interesting task was the camouflaging of the first tanks before they went into action in September 1916; so important was this aspect that from March 1917 a dedicated camouflage section was attached to the Heavy Branch MGC. By mid 1917, the Special Works Park had an overall strength of forty officers, including camouflage advisers attached to each corps, and 400 other ranks. It was also employing over 1,000 Frenchwomen in two factories, at Aire near Hazebrouck to support the northern British armies, and Amiens, which covered the southern part of the British sector. The HQ remained at Saint Omer and had an experimental section. Before the end of the year, the experimental section was running courses in camouflage and a further school was set up at Hyde Park, London. Apart from constructing OPs and producing vast quantities of camouflage netting to conceal gun positions and ammunition dumps and the like, the Special Works Park also constructed plywood human figures for use in feint attacks. At one point it was asked by the Canadian Corps to produce dummy corpses to tempt the Germans into no-man's-land so that prisoners could be seized. But not all appreciated the work of the Special Works Park. R. B. Talbot Kelly complained: 'One day three camouflage experts arrived armed with a lorry-load of paint and brushes and repainted in jazz colours and patterns our beautiful green guns. They painted all over our polished leather work, ruining months of labour, and quite uselessly infuriated our major and our limber gunners.'[57]

Towards the end of 1917, a camouflage detachment was sent to Italy, although it returned to France in March 1918. In January 1918, three women artists, ranking as assistant administrators in the Women's Army Auxilliary Corps (WAAC), were sent from England to take charge of the camouflage factories. Geneste Penrose took over that at Aire and was later awarded the Military Medal for her work. The citation read: 'Although the Town was frequently shelled and bombed, the gallant example and coolness displayed by this lady at all times resulted in most of the workers remaining at their posts.'[58] The German spring offensives of 1918 caused a relocation of the factories and they were re-established with a base factory at Wimereux, on the Channel coast just north of Boulogne, and the others at Rouen and Le Pont d'Arbres, south-east of Calais. The April 1918 offensive left the Germans holding the dominant Mount Kemmel feature. To conceal road movement in the area, over 100 miles of 12-foot-high wire netting, interlaced with strips of canvas, were produced by the camouflage factories. In July 1918, the Special Works Park was retitled the Camouflage Park RE and a factory was set up for each army, with a camouflage detachment for each corps. One of the final challenges that the Camouflage Park successfully met was the camouflaging of Henry Rawlinson's advanced Fourth Army HQ – a railway train.[59]

The growth of specialist schools in France and elsewhere to disseminate the secrets of the new warfare was rapid. Likewise, every arm and service also ran its own schools in France. Thus, in 1915 each army established an artillery school. Infantry schools were found at both army and division level, while there were corps battle schools. The ASC had its own school in the Pas de Calais and there was even a chaplains' school at Saint Omer, referred to as the 'Padres' Bombing School'.[60] As Charles Carrington wrote:

> There was no end to one's military education. Schools of instruction in all technicalities and at all grades sprang up behind the front with a deal of rivalry between corps and armies as to the fare provided for students. Sergeants and 'young officers' (how I disliked that patronising phrase!) were much exposed to educational treatment and if they had the greatest share of danger in the line they enjoyed the prerequisite – now and then – of being 'sent on a course'. At least it would be safe and comfortable, at best it might be a mere holiday – a 'binge'.[61]

A. P. White in early 1917 remarked: 'Courses are all the rage just now. In every third-rate village behind the lines you see officers careering about with note-books on some course or other. Literally, half the battalion were away then.'[62] But, besides providing a welcome break from the trenches, these schools did fulfil a vital purpose in broadening military education. Graham Greenwell, at the Fifth Army infantry school, stated that the aim of his five-week course was 'primarily to make officers efficient instructors in drill, bayonet fighting, engineering and field-work, in all of which subjects we get very rusty in the line.'[63] But it was also vital that those in the trenches be kept abreast of the latest tactics and techniques. One corps commander who laid great emphasis on this was Ivor Maxse. Greenwell attended a three-day battle course at Maxse's corps school in early September 1917, together with eight officers from each battalion in the 48th Division, as well as trench mortar and machine-gun officers: 'We are to be immersed for three days in the battle atmosphere. We discuss future operations, have lectures on tanks, aeroplanes, artillery and other technical subjects, and try to produce ideas for dealing with the latest Bosche method of defence, which certainly is a puzzler.'*[64]

There was, however, one form of instruction which left a unique impression on those who served on the Western Front but that did not necessarily reflect the new warfare. One of the organizations which suffered at the outbreak of war was the Army Gymnastic Staff (AGS). It was based at Aldershot and came under the Inspector of Gymnasia, who at the outbreak of war was Brigadier General V. A. Couper, late of the Rifle Brigade. He and his staff were responsible for training garrison and unit instructors. On mobilization, however, a significant number of the AGS were posted, many returning to their own units. Couper himself was tasked with raising the 14th (Light) Division and one of his key staff, Captain R. (Ronnie) B. Campbell of the Gordons, who was Superintendent of Gymnasia at HQ Southern Command, went to France as a railway transport officer (RTO). With the grave shortage of experienced officers for the New Armies, Couper himself went on to arrange for many of the experienced AGS instructors to be commissioned into his division. Among them was CSM Mick Delaney of the Buffs who in August 1914 was on the staff of the Devonport Garrison Gymnasium. He was commissioned into

* This was the elastic defence perfected by General Fritz von Lossberg, which placed great emphasis on a mobile as opposed to static defence, with maximum use of immediate counter-attacks. It caused the British problems during Third Ypres. A good description of it is given in Martin Samuels, *Command or Control? Command, Training and Tactics in the British and German Armies, 1888–1918*, Frank Cass, London, 1995.

the 10th Durham Light Infantry in October 1914, going to France with the battalion in May 1915.[65] The realization that the New Armies would need physical training and bayonet-fighting instructors caused the Physical Training and Bayonet School at Aldershot to be re-formed, with Colonel W. C. Wright, formerly the Assistant Inspector of Gymnasia, appointed Inspector. Among those who rejoined the staff was Ronnie Campbell, who had been posted to the 1st Gordons, after much of the battalion had been forced to surrender at Le Cateau (*see page 458*), and had been wounded in mid October. He reassumed his post as Superintendent of Gymnasia Southern Command at the very end of 1914. The following October he was promoted to Assistant Inspector of Gymnasia.

In the meantime, in France the need for education and re-education of the troops now encompassed bayonet fighting, which was seen as a good way of inculcating offensive spirit. Accordingly, at the beginning of March 1916 Major Campbell took across a team of instructors to establish a system of physical and bayonet training throughout the BEF. He also managed to obtain one or two of the pre-war instructors, one of them being Captain Mick Delaney, who was detached from 10 DLI for this purpose. Initially, Campbell's team was on a two-month attachment. Some of his instructors were deployed to the base depots at Rouen, Le Havre and Etaples, while he himself, with the remaining instructors, was sent to the Third Army school at Flixiécourt. He established a bayonet-fighting school for unit instructors and soon began to make an impression. Both Allenby and Haig saw the value of his approach to training and his school became a permanent fixture, being eventually established at Saint Pol, 20 miles north-west of Arras.

Campbell concentrated primarily on improving the techniques of trench raiding. He accepted that 'the number of men killed by the bayonet on the Western Front was very small, but it was superb as a morale booster. Get the bayonet into the hands of despondent troops and you can make them tigers within hours.' His blood-curdling talks earned him the nickname 'Bloody Campbell', but there is no doubt that he inspired. Siegfried Sassoon heard him speak at the Third Army School in April 1916: 'There was a great brawny Highland Major here today, talking of the Bayonet. For close on an hour he talked, and all who listened caught fire from his enthusiasm.' It moved Sassoon to write his poem *The Kiss*.[66] One attraction for Campbell's audiences was that he managed to obtain the services of some of the leading British boxers of the day – Billy 'Bombardier' Wells, Jimmy Driscoll, Jimmy Wilde and Johnny Basham. They gave some of the demonstrations and also helped to develop techniques of unarmed combat, especially for use against the bayonet, knife, rifle butt and club. This was very applicable to trench warfare and training men to become proficient in unarmed combat acted as a boost to their confidence and made them more effective trench raiders. Campbell laid out a comprehensive training area at Saint Pol. It included assault courses and replica trenches, even a mock shell-damaged house rigged with booby traps. All this was to make the training as realistic as possible and was a forerunner to the battle schools of the Second World War. Campbell also insisted that his instructors take part in trench raids and helped plan and observe some himself. Each army in France had its superintendent of physical and bayonet training and one also accompanied the British force sent to Italy towards the end of 1917. As for the school, it came under repeated shelling and aerial bombing with the opening of the German offensive in March 1918 and was eventually forced to move to Hardelot-sur-Plage during the second half of April.[67] Campbell himself returned to Britain in bayonet training at Aldershot in place of Colonel Wright. His work during the war was rewarded with the DSO, five foreign decorations and a brevet lieutenant colonelcy. Almost as soon as Campbell left France, however, GHQ decided that it was illogical that bayonet training should be separated from musketry and it was decided to merge the two. Musketry instructors were therefore sent on bayonet-training courses, but by then the war was virtually at an end.[68]

While Ronnie Campbell was able to standardize bayonet training and unarmed combat throughout the BEF, this was not the case with the majority of schools in France and Flanders. Guy Dawnay, the deputy Chief of Staff at GHQ, commented:

> There is no doubt that our training system is neither perfectly co-ordinated nor evenly distributed through the armies. I am constantly being told by divisions moving from corps to corps and from army to army

that they are being taught different doctrines as they move from one command to another.[69]

It was probably for this reason that in June 1918 Haig decided to appoint an Inspector General of Training and selected Ivor Maxse for the post. He was soon travelling far and wide among the BEF preaching his gospel on training, which was essentially 'Explanation, Demonstration, Execution, Repetition'.[70] What effect he had on the BEF during the final months of the war is difficult to gauge, but there is no doubt that its ability to handle the 'all-arms' battle at every level demonstrated that the quality of training had risen markedly. It was a clear indication that the British Army had embraced the new warfare.

seven

LABOUR

The supply of manpower to meet the army's growing demands for labour, especially in France and Flanders, became a major preoccupation. Under pre-war planning, the French had agreed to supply the necessary labour to support the Expeditionary Force (BEF). Consequently, little or no thought was given to the fact that the British Army might have to supply its own, especially since for the past sixty years it had fought nothing but colonial wars in which local labour had been plentiful and easy to obtain. The realization that it might have provide its own labour for a European conflict began to dawn on the day that Britain declared war, when an Army Order announced the establishment of Nos. 1 and 2 Labour Companies ASC. Raised from hastily recruited labourers, with peacetime foremen and gangers acting as NCOs, they arrived in France before the end of August and were employed in the base supply depots at the three Channel ports being used by the BEF.

By the end of the year, another four companies had arrived, with one being attached to the Army Ordnance Department at Le Havre. In addition, in January 1915 No. 1 and, later, No. 2 Railway Labour Companies ASC were formed for work on the railways. They were recruited by the Railway Executive from railwaymen and worked at the railheads in France and Flanders.[1] Two further companies (Nos. 35 and 36 Naval Labour Companies) were raised from stevedores and dockers to unload ships in the French ports being used by the BEF. It was probably to these that Gerald Burgoyne, in the trenches with the Royal Irish Rifles, was referring in a diary entry towards the end of February 1915:

> A force I heard of today for the first time is 'Kitchener's labourers'. I hear they've been going for many months at Rouen and Havre. They were dockers from London, Liverpool etc, brought out for unloading work, not enlisted at all, paid 4/- [four shillings] a day; a lot of hardy ruffians who used to be escorted to and from their work by a military escort to prevent them running amok in the town.[2]

Although commanded by ASC officers, these two companies were under the direct control of the naval transport officers at the ports, who were responsible for the movement in and out of shipping. In consequence, they were eventually transferred to the Royal Marines.

As for the mainstream ASC Labour companies, there were thirty-four in existence by early 1916, the majority being in France, together with the two railway Labour companies. Three of the Labour companies served in Salonika and one was retained in London District.[3] Tom Eades, aged 45 and a shipping clerk in civilian life, enlisted in 27 Labour Company ASC at Aldershot at the beginning of October 1915. Its members, whom Eades described as 'mostly big men, fathers of large families as a rule', had just eighteen days' training before they were despatched to the Dardanelles. Eades commented: 'They look very rough, but the khaki and 18 days drill and regular baths and shaving each day has made them quite a smart lot.'[4] On arrival, they were tasked with unloading lighters on Anzac beach and constructing dug-outs. But nowhere on Gallipoli was free from shellfire and some men became casualties. After the evacuation of the peninsula in January 1916, the company was sent to Salonika.

The Royal Engineers, in particular, needed large amounts of labour. Once the situation had stabilized in France after the First Battle of Ypres, the RE field companies were soon overwhelmed by the effort required to maintain the trench systems and the lines of communication. They were therefore forced to call on the fighting troops for labour, which was clearly unsatisfactory. The base area was largely the responsibility of the Works Directorate. This initially consisted of a director, an assistant director, and thirty-five officers, many of whom were sent to replace casualties. Operating under the IGC, the Works Directorate was responsible for the construction of camps, store depots and port facilities, employing indigenous labour. But given the demands of their own armies, the French were unable to supply the labour needed. Hence 20 Fortress and 29 Works Companies RE were allocated to the works directorate, but the former company was soon deployed nearer the front and was replaced by 42 Fortress Company. Matters improved in March 1915 when six TF Fortress companies were deployed to France. Later that year these companies were retitled Army Troops Companies RE.[5] But a grave lack of unskilled labour remained.

The initiative for overcoming this was taken in Britain rather than in France. The War Office informed home commands in early December 1914 of the intention to add a Pioneer battalion to each New Army division. This was confirmed in January 1915. Divisional commanders were to encourage battalions to volunteer, stressing that they would not only remain fighting infantry, but would also provide 'organized intelligent labour' in support of the Royal Engineers. The range of the work was to be wide, from road making through entrenching work to demolitions. The original intention was to attach an RE officer and NCO to each Pioneer battalion, but this never proved possible.

The New Army Pioneer battalions were formed surprisingly quickly. Most came into being in January 1915 and by April all the K1, K2 and K3 divisions (9th–26th), apart from one, had their Pioneer battalions on establishment. The exception was the 10th (Irish) Division, which did not have one of its battalions, the 5th Royal Irish, converted to the role until June, shortly before it sailed for the Dardanelles. In this case, it seems that the battalion did not volunteer, but was selected for the pioneer role because of the high proportion of miners and artificers in its ranks. The K4 and K5 divisions had Pioneer battalions incorporated by the autumn. One attraction was that private soldiers in these battalions were granted an extra two pence per day.[6]

In France, the process went much more slowly and, as a result, the infantry in particular suffered. Typical of the impact of the lack of specialist labour troops was the experience of the 1st/7th Londons. On 18 June 1915, they were relieved in the trenches, but no sooner had they arrived at their rest billets than they were immediately 'hauled out' for fatigues. This was followed by five further days of fatigues and working parties. The men were then allowed one day for baths, including the march to and from them. The battalion went back into trenches for four days. When it came out, it faced a further six days' working parties, followed by two days' rest and five more days of working parties. Then, it was back into trenches once more.[7] With a regime like this, it was inevitable that training and administration would suffer, detracting from a battalion's combat fficiency.

Not until the beginning of July 1915, and under War Office pressure, did GHQ BEF in France decide that it would have to follow the example of the New Armies and provide an additional Pioneer battalion to each division. Since there were now a grand total of forty-eight TF battalions in France over and above the existing establishment of twelve infantry battalions per division it seemed logical to look to these. But many were not willing. HQ IV Corps writing to the Second Army noted: 'In the 6th Division there are only two Territorial Battalions, and neither of them are suitable for pioneer work, both being London recruited and consisting more of clerks and shop-keepers than of artisans.' II Corps made a similar comment on the TF battalions with the 5th Division, pointing out that 'none are accustomed to manual labour'.[8]

There was another factor to be taken into account: the policy that the majority of these TF battalions would rejoin their parent divisions once these arrived in France. GHQ BEF therefore decided that those TF battalions which were suitable pioneer material should serve with TF divisions and that the Regular divisions would use New Army Pioneer battalions. But there were exceptions to this rule. The 1st/5th Cheshires had joined the 5th Division at the Front as an ordinary line battalion in February 1915. As early as May one of their subalterns noted that the battalion had 'got a splendid name in the Division for digging work'.[9] It was for this reason that it was made the division's Pioneer battalion in November 1915, there being no New Army battalions available. It was not popular with the men. As Captain Thomas Heald succinctly put it, 'we did not join to dig for others'.[10] George McGovern, who had recently left the battalion and was learning to become a brigade signals officer, wrote gloomily: 'They will cease to exist as a fighting unit & become the scavengers of the brigade.'[11] There was nothing that the Cheshires could do about it and they remained pioneers for the remainder of the war, transferring to the 56th Division when it arrived in France in early 1916. On the other hand, the 1st/5th Black Watch, which was initially the 8th Division's pioneers, reverted to being an ordinary Infantry battalion with the 51st (Highland) Division. The reason for this was that the division, which had been in France since May 1915, already had its Pioneer battalion, albeit the Lowland 8th Royal Scots. The result of this policy was that the first-line TF divisions in France had Pioneer battalions by the time winter arrived and it was only the Regular divisions which largely remained without. Not until the eve of the Battle of the Somme would all the Regular infantry divisions have a Pioneer battalion in place.* This was helped by the decision at the beginning of 1916 that some of the New Army divisions be stiffened by exchanging one of their brigades for one from a Regular division.

The Cavalry Corps had been used in summer 1915 to construct defences in the rear of the combat zone in France. In November 1916, cavalry divisions also formed some Pioneer battalions for work in army areas. Each consisted of eight officers and 260 men.[12] The 1st Cavalry Division raised such a unit from platoons drawn from the 11th Hussars and 2nd and 5th Dragoon Guards. It was later titled the 1st Cavalry Division Digging Party. During summer 1917 it was brigaded with two other cavalry Pioneer battalions, formed from elements of the 2nd and 9th Cavalry Brigades, but no trace of any exists after the end of 1917.[13] The majority found themselves involved in rail and road construction, but as an 11th Hussars officer commented: 'Nothing could have been devised to damp the spirit of cavalrymen more than to use them as Labour battalions on work about which there was no danger.'[14] For the Battle of Cambrai in November 1917 the Cavalry Track Battalion, comprising twenty British officers and 500 Indian cavalrymen, was temporarily formed. It would follow the initial attack, 'tear away the wire, bridge or level the trenches, fill up the shell-holes, and thus carve a broad track through the German lines to the country where the mounted branch could come into its own.'

---

* The 5th Division did not receive a pioneer replacement for the Cheshires until the 1st/6th Argylls arrived in June 1916.

The Pioneer battalions of the infantry divisions taking part in the attack also assisted in this.[15]

The tasks undertaken by the Pioneer battalions were many and varied. They normally worked under the direction of the CRE at division and when in the trenches much of the work entailed improving communication trenches, constructing strongpoints and road and light railway maintenance work. When an attack was taking place, pioneers were often called upon to repair captured trenches and dig fresh communication trenches forward to these. While the division was at rest, the pioneers would also be kept busy improving billets, repairing roads, even, at times, helping the local farmers with their harvest. One of their most agreeable tasks was forestry. C. P. Blacker, who served as an officer for two and a half years with the 4th Coldstream, the Guards Division's Pioneer battalion and won a well-deserved MC on the Somme, recalled an idyllic three months in spring 1916 when he commanded detachments from various Guards battalions in Clairmarais Forest, near Saint Omer. Trees had to be felled by axe and they were taught the art by the *Gardes Forestiers*. Once a tree was down, its branches were lopped off and made into fascines, bundles of long sticks used for a variety of construction purposes. After wintering in the trenches, 'the forest seemed to provide a protective canopy under which we all felt at home and it prompted one of the new arrivals in my party to remark that we had come to a good place for out-of-door work in this sort of weather [snow flurries]. I heard no grumbling and less bad language than usual.' By the end of the three months the guardsmen were experts at axemanship.[16] Blacker himself eventually developed a conscience that he was not putting himself at risk as he felt was his duty. Part of the reason was that his younger brother had been killed at Loos in September 1915 while serving with the 1st Coldstream, and Blacker had remained for so long in the 4th Battalion to placate his parents, as their one remaining child. In June 1918 he transferred to the 2nd Battalion, dropping in rank from captain to do so. He was wounded on the Canal du Nord that September, but recovered in time to rejoin his battalion before the Armistice.

Yet while Pioneer battalions generally experienced less risk than the conventional infantry battalions, there were times when they did see their fair share of actual fighting, especially at times of crisis like the German drives of March and April 1918, and suffered accordingly. The 5th South Wales Borderers was the 19th Division's Pioneer battalion throughout its time on the Western Front and suffered no less than 442 killed. Much of the work of the Pioneer battalions was also tedious and frustrating, and life was often just as uncomfortable as it was for the line battalions. The pioneers often had less opportunity for rest. Yet the vast majority learned to take pride in what they were doing and took comfort in their superior skill at carrying out such mundane tasks as revetting trenches and filling sandbags. Some battalions gained a name for themselves through specializing, especially in the laying of light railway track. The 17th Royal Northumberland Fusiliers was a Pals battalion, raised from employees of the North Eastern Railway. It became the 32nd Division's Pioneer battalion, but was detached to GHQ as railway construction troops in October 1916. Haig was warned by the War Office that they could not provide another Pioneer battalion to replace the Northumberlands in the 32nd Division, and so the division had to do without. GHQ France also had its eye on the 16th Royal Irish Rifles, which again contained a number of railwaymen, but did not transfer it.[17] So proficient did the 17th Royal Northumberland Fusiliers become during the eleven months that it was employed on railway work that rumours began to go around that it was about to be converted to a Labour battalion, which caused much resentment among its ranks. It was termed a Railway Pioneer battalion, but was released back to the 32nd Division in September 1917, only to revert to its former role two months later. Eventually, at the end of May 1918 it became an ordinary Pioneer battalion once more, this time in the 52nd Division.

During 1915, the divisions in France also formed Salvage and Convalescent companies. They were not catered for on the divisional establishment and were manned by the temporarily unfit and those under-age within the division. The companies carried out fatigues, provided guards for the headquarters and undertook salvage work, as well as burials. No allowance had been made for salvage in pre-war planning, but the need to recover weapons and equipment soon became apparent during the retreat from Mons, especially when shortages at home were being aggravated by a rapidly expanding army. The first initiative was to ensure that the personal equipment of those wounded or sick was recovered. Rifles were a constant concern and the lack of them for the New Armies caused von Donop, the MGO, to write to Smith-Dorrien, commanding II Corps in France, on 6 December 1914: 'May I suggest to you that you might ask all your subordinate commanders to use their utmost endeavours to see that rifles and bayonets [sic] from killed and wounded men are sent down to the base, as every rifle is worth its weight in gold.'[18] There was also an enormous wastage of small arms ammunition. As Gerald Burgoyne noted at the end of January 1915, each infantryman carried 150 rounds in his pouches, but also took an additional bandolier of 100 rounds into the trenches. This was left on relief and consequently the trenches were littered with surplus ammunition.[19] It was realization of this waste which brought about the formation of the Salvage companies, but since it was only one of their roles, they could not devote all their time to it. Much of their time was spent in clearing billets of abandoned equipment after units had vacated them. They began the battlefield salvage with Loos in September 1915. Even so, salvage was to remain largely a unit responsibility until 1917.[20] As for the divisional Salvage companies themselves, they were retitled Employment companies in 1916, taking on additional responsibilities, including running the divisional baths and laundry, as well as operating Foden disinfectors which were used for delousing clothing.[21]

Another measure taken in France to overcome the labour shortage was the forming of Entrenching battalions. These fulfilled two purposes. They provided a 'halfway house' for reinforcements en route from the infantry base depots (IBDs) to their units, thus avoiding overcrowding at the depots, and were a place where they could be held until the units were ready to receive them. In addition, in order to keep the men occupied, they were employed on trench digging and repair within the combat zone, although not in the front line. This enabled the drafts new to France to be gently broken into trench warfare and lifted a little of the labour burden from infantry battalions at rest. Ten Entrenching battalions were formed in July 1915 from drafts at the infantry base depots. Each had an establishment of twenty officers and 1,000 men and they were controlled by the DAG 3rd Echelon.[22] Thus, No. 2 Entrenching Battalion was made up of details from the 27th and 46th (North Midland) IBDs, while No. 6 drew on Nos. 3 and 5 IBDs.[23] Some of the battalions were based on divisional reinforcement camps, but others were under corps control. One of those formed was the Guards Entrenching Battalion, which came into being in December 1915 to support the Guards Division and was based on the Somme. Within the division it was known as 'the Diggers'. In certainly at least one case an Entrenching battalion came into being as a result of amalgamations of Infantry battalions. No. 11 Entrenching Battalion the Gordon Highlanders (also known as the 11th Provisional Battalion Gordons) was created from the surplus manpower thrown up by the amalgamation of three pairs of battalions in the 15th (Scottish) Division. The Entrenching battalions were found not just in France. In early 1917, two were formed in Salonika: No. 5 from elements of No. 27 IBD and No. 9 from the 60th Division IBD. But while they fulfilled a useful purpose, the Royal Engineers who employed them often found it frustrating. They frequently never knew how many men the Entrenching battalions had available because their strength fluctuated so much. For example, during the Battle of the Somme No. 11 Entrenching Battalion was down to a mere two officers and twenty-five men at the end of July, but at the beginning of October could boast twenty-one officers and 895 men.[24] The other main problem was succinctly put by the CRE of the 37th Division. The men of the two Entrenching battalions working for him at one point 'changed almost daily, neither the officers nor men have time to arouse the slightest interest in their work'.[25] Entrenching battalions remained in France until the summer of 1917, by which time the majority were concentrated in the Second and Third Army areas, each army providing a group HQ to control them. At the beginning of August it was decided to break up all of them, bar four and one group HQ, presumably because the heavy casualties accompanying the opening of Third Ypres meant that it was becoming impossible to maintain them at reasonable strength.[26] The remainder vanished before the year was out. In Salonika, while No. 9 Entrenching Battalion had a short life, being raised in March 1917 and broken up that July, No. 5 survived from January 1917 until June 1918.[27]

A further partial solution to the problem of shortage of manpower to support engineering operations was the formation of Labour battalions RE in August 1915. These were created at very short notice and drew on labourers in Britain, who were recruited through the labour exchanges.

The exchanges even identified the foremen, or 'gangers', for appointment as warrant officers and senior NCOs. The men were paid three shillings a day as an inducement.[28] The battalions were formed in camps at Southampton, the early ones with lightning speed. The 3rd Labour Battalion was first established on 18 August and just one week later crossed to France.[29] The 5th Labour Battalion had its problems, however. The officer appointed adjutant arrived at Southampton on 19 August. He located his men, 800 of them aged 35 to 50, at a recently pitched tented camp. They were in civilian clothes, had come from all over the country and, not knowing the gangers who had been included in their number, were totally leaderless. Apart from their tents, they had neither uniforms nor equipment; nor did they have any food. The adjutant managed to feed them with iron rations of bully beef and biscuits and began to attempt to get them in some sort of order. During the next couple of days the commanding officer and quartermaster arrived, and uniforms for the men were made available. More and more men also reported, until there were 1,200 – 150 men over establishment. Luckily, the weather remained fine. On 25 August, nine other officers arrived – recently gazetted civil engineers, who had to be sent to obtain uniforms for themselves. Not until the following day did the battalion begin to receive its equipment, but it was a desperate race against time since it was due to embark for France on the afternoon of the 28th. Before this took place, many men had to be dragged out of public houses and guards placed on them. The battalion then spent two days at Le Havre, before facing a twenty-two-hour train journey to Belgium. Nevertheless, in a little over two weeks since its inception the battalion was carrying out its first tasks behind the Front – road repairs and constructing concrete machine-gun posts.[30] The 11th Battalion was one of the last to form and began to do so on 22 September. There was a problem in that 128 men had to be medically discharged, an indication that the supply of suitable manpower was drying up. Perhaps because of this, the battalion did not cross to France until the end of the following month.[31] In all, twelve Labour battalions RE were raised, of which one (12th Battalion) went to Salonika and the remainder to France. The latter worked both under the various armies and on the lines of communication. Rifleman Aubrey Smith saw some on the Somme in June 1916, just prior to the opening of the offensive.

They were returning to their camp 'with picks and shovels ... they might have been making up either the road or a new light railway under construction in the vicinity. Many of the old boys were between 40 and 50 years old, and they looked as though they were dying for a pint of bitter at the end of their day's toil.'[32] Thirteen Labour companies RE were also sent to Mesopotamia during the second half of 1916, while 260 Labour Company RE served in Salonika.[33]

There was also a demand for specialized labour. One aspect had already been recognized before the war and in August 1914 there were two Regular railway companies RE, together with three Special Reserve companies of the Royal Monmouth and Royal Anglesey RE. But because the French had undertaken to maintain the railways used by the BEF, just one Railway company was initially sent across the Channel, only to find itself without any work to do. After the Battle of the Marne, however, the French railway repair resources became overstretched, and 8 Railway Company was finally deployed, its first task being the repair of a railway bridge. The second Regular company and the three Royal Monmouth and Royal Anglesey RE companies went to France in November 1914, although the latter were diverted to work on the defences in the Ypres sector and did not begin to practise their proper role until March 1915. By this time, the Railway companies were working under the direction of the Chief Railway Construction Engineer (CRCE), Lieutenant Colonel (later Brigadier General Sir William) W. D. Waghorn, who had been acting General Manager of the Indian North-West Railway and had been on leave in England when war broke out.

New Army Railway companies were also raised and by the end of the war there were thirty-two serving in France, together with Canadian Railway Construction battalions. Five further companies were in Egypt and three in Salonika. The companies themselves usually operated in groups of two or three under a Railway Construction Engineer (RCE). The railway construction troops also needed the support of unskilled labour. This was initially fulfilled by the two ASC Railway Labour companies. A Labour battalion RE was then allocated and, by the end of 1916, six Infantry Labour battalions (*see page 226*) were also dedicated to the role, as were some of the Cavalry Pioneer battalions.[34]

In the low-lying terrain of Flanders there was a constant problem with flooded trenches. In an attempt to overcome this, two Land Drainage companies RE were raised in September 1915. They drew their manpower from the fens of Lincolnshire, Cambridgeshire and Norfolk, where there were men who were well used to dealing with flooding. They were enlisted at a rate of three shillings per day, but were unarmed and received little military training. The two companies, Nos. 196 and 197, went to France that November.[35] Then at the end of December 1915 the Home Office wrote to the War Office stating that, apart from those companies engaged in government contracts, the quarrying industry was very slack in Britain. It was suggested that quarrymen might be recruited to work the quarries in the British sector in France. An officer from the Directorate of Fortifications and Works visited GHQ and the upshot was a letter from the QMG in France requesting the formation of a Quarrying Corps RE so that the quarries in the Boulogne area could be enlarged to provide the necessary materials for maintaining the roads in the British sector. The Army Council initially rejected the proposal on the grounds that additional labour, including Prisoner of War companies, was already being provided and any additions could only be at the expense of the BEF's fighting strength. GHQ France persisted in its demand and in July 1916 the Army Council eventually relented. Two Quarrying Companies RE (Nos. 198 and 199) were initially formed. Each consisted of 263 men, but only the officer commanding and senior NCOs were expected to have previous military experience. Like those in the Land Drainage companies, the quarrymen were paid above the normal rates. These two companies went to France in August 1916. A year later the number of Quarrying companies had grown to ten and there were thirteen working French quarries by the time of the Armistice. During 1918 they supplied no less than 2.8 million tons of stone.[36]

Unskilled labour remained a problem though, in spite of the introduction of Pioneer battalions and Labour battalions RE. Consequently, the ordinary infantry battalions were still called upon to do a considerable amount of labouring work, especially when in reserve. Guy Chapman, with the 13th Royal Fusiliers in 37th Division, records one spell in reserve just prior to the Battle of Loos. 'We were overwhelmed by working parties. One day was spent in the support lines at Hannescamps or Bienvillers, eight hours' digging, ten miles' marching; the next on a strong-point four miles westward ... There were parties to cut the brushwood beyond Pas, which frequently ended in the laying waste of some promising copse and a quarrel with the sappers, or an injury to a soldier who had been trimming the branches of a tree while his comrades were at work on the trunk'.[37]

The burden placed on the shoulders of the infantry was even heavier when it came to the enormous amount of preparatory work that needed to be done prior to launching the Allied offensive on the Somme. Rawlinson's Fourth Army, which was to mount the initial assault in the British sector, was allotted five RE Labour battalions, but they proved to be woefully inadequate, given the enormity of the task. Besides the construction of new camps, roads, dumps and light railways, the Fourth Army needed to bury no less than 7,000 miles of cable in the forward area and lay another 43,000 miles worth to the rear. Rawlinson had hoped that his infantry could concentrate on training for the attack, but inevitably much of their time out of the line was spent in labouring tasks. Ivor Maxse complained that as far as his 18th Division was concerned 'manual labour was being required day and night, whenever battalions were out of the trenches. Railways were built, roads created and repaired, tram lines laid, water pipes were put underground, cables were buried six feet deep. No rest and no training for the infantry, except during the 1 week.'[38]

To provide more military labour, the War Office decided in March 1916 to form Infantry Labour battalions. Thanks to the Military Service Act, there was now plenty of manpower below Medical Category A available to make this possible. The first of these units, 33rd (Labour) Battalion the Royal Fusiliers, was formed on the 3rd of the same month and was sent to France in June, albeit too late to relieve much of the pressure on the overworked infantry preparing for the assault on the Somme. In order to meet the demand more quickly, some drafts were sent out to France with the idea of forming them into Labour battalions once they arrived. Unfortunately, too few officers and NCOs were sent with them and so this could not be done. Instead, the drafts were used as reinforcements for the ASC Labour companies.[39] In all, thirty-three Infantry Labour battalions were created during 1916 and all went to France, except for the 17th and 18th Queens, which remained in Britain, and the 14th Queens which served in

Salonika. They were employed mainly on road maintenance, but sometimes suffered frustration in that too much was expected from them. On 8 November 1916, after complaints about its performance in repairing roads in the Guillemont sector of the Somme, the CO of 12 DCLI noted bitterly in the War Diary:

> Infantry Labour battalions were thrown together haphazard [sic]. The only qualification for the men was that they should have some physical disability. For the officers even this qualification was not insisted on. Of the 8 original company officers only one [sic] had had any experience of handling labour. Two were old soldiers and very valuable as such. The others had no special qualifications for the work and had been ordered to the battalion by chance. The NCOs were chosen from the men available, but those with any special qualifications were rare.[40]

Some men from these Labour battalions were posted to the divisional Employment companies, which now swelled to some 200 men strong.[41]

At the end of 1915, Infantry Works and Labour companies were formed for the provision of working and fatigue parties at home. The Works companies were initially established on the scale of one per home command and concentrated on road and hut repairs in and around the camps. These types of company were usually affiliated to local Special Reserve battalions and some were incorporated in Labour battalions. Thus, the 19th (Labour) Battalion of the Royal Scots was created from two Works companies (Royal Scots and Royal Scots Fusiliers) and two Labour companies (KOSB and Argylls), while the 10th (Labour) Battalion the Royal Berkshire Regiment was formed from four Wiltshire and five Royal Berkshire Labour companies.[42] During the summer of 1916 the remaining companies were reorganized into nine Infantry Works battalions for home service only. The 25th Durham Light Infantry, for instance, formed a Labour depot for Northern Command. Its men were unarmed and received minimal military training. Indeed, every home command now had a Labour depot.

More specialist among the Labour units at home was the 1st (Dock) Battalion the King's Liverpool Regiment. This was raised in April 1915 to ensure that the Liverpool docks kept working in the face of industrial unrest on the part of the dockers. There was no medical examination or age limit. The men lived at home, but had uniforms and were subject to military law. They also had to be members of the National Union of Dock Labourers. Should they resign their membership, they were discharged. In May 1918 the battalion was split into two, forming the 1st and 2nd Dock Battalions.[43] The docks concept was further developed with the formation of the 16th (Transport Workers) Battalion the York and Lancaster Regiment in March 1916. It was stipulated that, if engaged in civil labour, its members would be paid at civilian rates, although they would have to pay for their own billets. Indeed, although they were taught basic drill, they operated on trades union lines, with union officials as many of the NCOs. The battalion initially consisted of just three companies with a total strength of eleven officers and 212 men, but by the end of 1916 it had expanded to nine companies and a strength of nearly 2,000 men.[44] Nine more of these battalions were formed during the winter of 1916–17, with one, the 17th South Lancashires, concentrating on canal work. A further expansion in the manpower of these battalions came at the end of April 1918, when their total strength rose from 10,000 to 15,000 men. By now they were also being employed on the railways and in steel works, but were primarily seen as a form of mobile labour, which could be quickly deployed to ports which were under pressure.[45]

A further source of labour in France also began to be tapped in summer 1916 – prisoners of war. Up until then the majority had been sent back to Britain, but towards the end of June five POW companies were formed in France, primarily for repairing roads. They were each 425 strong, with an initial establishment of two British officers and sixty-one other ranks to guard and administer the POWs. With an increasing number of German troops being captured during the fighting on the Somme, the number of these companies rose rapidly and there were twenty-seven in existence by the end of September.[46] The POWs in England also began to be used for agricultural and forestry work.

At the same time, it was decided to draw on the resources of the Empire. Already local labour was being used extensively in the Middle East and East Africa and, after a request from the IGC Mediterranean Expeditionary Force (MEF), a contingent of Maltese served in the Dardanelles from September 1915 to the end of the campaign as stevedores and in road maintenance and other tasks. The first overseas contingent to sail for Europe, however, was the Cape Coloured Labour Battalion from South Africa in August 1916. It was followed two months later by the first element of the South African Native Labour Corps (SANLC), which eventually reached a strength of 21,000 men. Unlike the Cape Coloured Labour Battalion, whose men had been enlisted in the army for the duration of the war, members of the SANLC were technically civilians, although under military law, and were on one-year contracts. The British West Indies Regiment (formed in 1915) also began to send across Labour battalions to Europe and a contingent of the Bermuda Militia Artillery was also deployed. This was officially part of the RGA and was generally known as the Bermuda RGA. Both contingents had been trained as fighting soldiers, but the British authorities did not consider it ethical that they should be so employed against a European enemy, although this policy did not apply to Indian troops. Apparently at the suggestion of the British military attaché to China, Lieutenant Colonel D. S. Robertson, a Chinese Labour Corps (CLC) was established.[47] The hardy peasants of Shantung province in the north of the country were targeted, partly because they had displayed their ability to operate under adverse conditions when working in the South African gold fields, but also because the British had a small coastal concession in the province at Wei-hai-Wei, which could be used as a recruiting base. Because of the language problem, a key element was the Chinese gangers, thirty-two of whom were appointed in each company of 500 men. Also vitally important was the company interpreter clerk through whom the British officers and NCOs, few of whom were conversant with the language, communicated with the men. The contract was for three years and the men received some rudimentary military training before leaving Wei-hai-Wei. The first contingent departed in January 1917 and faced a four-month journey, which included crossing Canada. The Chinese labourers were paid one franc a day, but their families back in China also received £1 per month, paid in Mexican dollars.[48]

By late November 1916, there was a wide miscellany of labour units in France: eleven RE Labour battalions; thirty Infantry Labour battalions; the Cape Coloured Labour Battalion; two SANLC battalions; eight Non-Combatant Corps companies (*see page 137*); twenty-nine ASC Labour companies; two ASC Naval Labour companies; one Canadian Forestry company; two battalions of the British West Indies Regiment; the Bermuda RGA; and forty-seven prisoner of war companies. The time had come to establish a central agency, which could look after their disparate interests and coordinate their efforts. Hence, Lieutenant Colonel Evan Gibb CMG DSO ASC was appointed Director of Labour at GHQ. Originally commissioned into the West India Regiment, he had transferred to the ASC on the eve of the South African War, during which he won his DSO. He had so far spent the war at GHQ, as a DAQMG, Assistant Director of Transport (ADTn) and AQMG, and so had the right experience to fight his corner success-fully. Acknowledgement of the importance of labour was recognized in his rapid promotion to brigadier general, which was as well, since his empire continued to expand.[49]

The last months of 1916 also brought about a revolution in trans-portation in the British sector of the Western Front. The post of Inspector General of Communications (IGC) was abolished. In his place, Sir Eric Geddes was appointed Director-General of Transportation (DGT), with overall responsibility for the passage of supplies within theatre. During that winter, which was one of the coldest on record, road and rail com-munications in France were severely disrupted and additional labour became urgently needed to repair and maintain those in the British sector. In addition, Belgian and French civil labour was largely withdrawn. Accord-ingly, at the beginning of 1917 there was a trawl of the Training Reserve s for men who were medically below Category A. These were formed into Infantry Labour companies, each approximately 500 strong. Thus, 7 Labour Company Durham Light Infantry drew its manpower from the 1st and 2nd Training Reserve Battalions (formerly 16 and 17 DLI) at Rugeley Camp, Staffordshire. The first to arrive in France was 1 Infantry Labour Company of the Queen's Royal West Surreys on 17 January and two more companies from the same regiment arrived before the month was out. Eventually, by the end of April there were no less than 123 of these units in France, including four companies made up of men of enemy alien parentage from the 30th and 31st Middlesex (*see page 143*). There were also five additional companies which had no regimental affiliation and were formed from men serving in the base areas who were medically categorized Permanent Base.[50] The Infantry Labour companies were employed not just for maintenance work on the roads and railways, but also in unloading railway wagons.

Simultaneously, a number of Agricultural companies were formed in Britain to assist farmers. They were controlled by the Ministry of Agriculture. One formed at Rugeley Camp was No. 1 Agricultural Company Durham Light Infantry.[51] In effect, this formalized a system instituted early in 1915, whereby troops at home could volunteer to help with the local harvest.[52] At the same time, the War Office had announced its intention of forming special farmers' battalions after the harvest had been gathered, suggesting that they might carry 'Yeomen' in their titles. In fact, only one was formed, the 21st King's Royal Rifle Corps (Yeoman Rifles). This was raised in Yorkshire and Durham by Lord Feversham and one of its founding officers was 18-year-old future Prime Minister, Anthony Eden. The government clearly realized that allowing such units for general service was a mistake, since it served to aggravate the difficulties faced by wartime agriculture. Consequently, during the summer of 1916 there were further calls for troops to help with the harvest and that December it was decreed that no one could be called up from agriculture unless he found a substitute to take his place. This was followed by the formation of Agricultural companies early in 1917 from those below Category A. In addition, in March 1917 a large number of ploughmen serving with the home forces were returned to civil employment and soldiers who had been ploughmen even brought back from France to help with the spring ploughing.[53] The same happened at the end of the year, when the War Office asked for 4,000 former ploughmen to be returned from France.[54]

Recognizing that there were now a plethora of cap badges involved in labour, and conscious of the need for better coordination, the War Office decided in February 1917 to create one umbrella organization – the Labour Corps. Its object, as stated in the Royal Warrant for its creation, was 'to obtain more fluidity in utilising the services of men in Infantry Labour and Works units, and to simplify administration'. To this end, the majority of Infantry Labour battalions and companies were to be formed into Labour companies, with battalions each forming two Labour companies. Battalion HQs were to be converted to Labour Group headquarters, which would control a variable number of companies. The Infantry Works companies would become Home Service Labour Companies. In all, the aim was to produce 203 Labour companies, 42 Labour Group HQs, 54 Home Service Labour Companies, and 10 Depot Labour companies. In addition, seven of the nine Infantry Works battalions in Britain became Labour battalions.[55] The 17th and 18th Labour Battalions the Queen's Regiment, which had remained in Britain, formed the Eastern Command Labour Centre. The only infantry elements which were not transferred to the Labour Corps were the Infantry Labour companies which had been provided by the 30th and 31st (Works) Battalions the Middlesex Regiment (Aliens). While there was no objection from GHQ in France to them being absorbed by the Labour Corps, the War Office thought differently. The fact that the parentage of their members was from enemy countries loomed large. Indeed, severe strictures were laid down on the employment of these units. They were not to be employed in places where they could gain information which might be of value to the enemy, which meant deploying them to sparsely populated areas. They were not allowed near ammunition or prisoners of war. Consequently, their employment was limited to building hutted camps and in stores and workshops in the army rear areas.[56] As for the vast majority of the Infantry Labour units, there was resentment at having to exchange their regimental cap badges for the anonymous General Service Corps badge, with which the new corps had been issued. Not until autumn 1918 was the Labour Corps finally granted its own cap badge consisting of a rifle, pick and shovel bound together within a laurel leaf with the motto *Labor Omnia Vincit* ('Labour Conquers All').

As for those who found themselves in the new corps, Corporal J. Cumming Morgan was typical. A schoolmaster by profession, he had enlisted under the Derby scheme, but was graded B2 because of poor eyesight. In July 1916 he was finally called up and found himself in the 9th (Labour) Battalion Cameron Highlanders. He went to France, where his battalion was involved in work in the rear area. With the transfer of the battalion to the Labour Corps he became a member of 8 Labour Company, which was immediately deployed to the Ypres sector and went through the gruelling offensive that opened at the end of July. Any ideas that the Labour Corps only operated away from the fighting were soon dispelled. The company's main role was repairing roads damaged by shellfire, a frequent occurrence:

> As soon as the traffic was halted as a consequence, the cry went up 'Forward the Labour Corps'. A squad of men is quickly on the spot with pick and shovel, and the hole is filled up with any mortal thing that can be found – stones, beams, bricks, railway lines, sleepers, bits of cars or lorries, wheels, cases of bully, tombstones, dead horses – anything that will occupy space, and in a few minutes the traffic moves on once more, and the War goes on!

The company's dedication was recognized by the awards of one MC, one DCM and eight MMs.[57]

But this was only the first phase in the creation of the Labour Corps. In May 1917 it embraced the Employment companies – divisional, Area, Home Service, and Depot – as well as the Agricultural companies. The Depot Labour and Employment companies were then renamed Reserve Labour and Reserve Employment companies, while the Home Service Labour companies became Home Service Works companies. Then, in June, it was decided that the RE Labour battalions and ASC Labour companies serving overseas should also be transferred to the Labour Corps. The only exceptions to this were those units allotted permanently to the transportation services. The two ASC Railway Labour companies (now numbered 33 and 34) were absorbed into the DGT Stores companies, with the officers becoming RTOs and the NCOs and men clerks, checkers and pioneers.[58] The 30th Labour Battalion RE was converted into three Railway Construction companies and a Wagon Erecting company, while 271 Labour Company RE formed an additional railway construction company. The remainder formed additional Labour companies for the new corps. During summer 1917 Nos. 11, 12 and 13 Civilian Platelayer Companies of the Labour Corps also served in France. Their role was to provide professional expertise in the massive expansion of broad and narrow gauge railways in the British sector.[59] The Labour Corps also took over responsibility for the Graves Registration Units (GRU) (*see page 431*), at least in France. But ordinary Labour companies also became involved in grave digging and it is probable that Employment and Area employment companies did as well.

Another type of Labour Corps unit formed during summer 1917 were the Area Employment (Garrison Guard) Companies which guarded base areas and prisoners of war as well as military prisons.[60] In terms of the divisional Employment companies, their responsibilities were now enlarged. Thus, 47 Divisional Employment Company was now renumbered 241 Divisional Employment Company and took on additional tasks, including the administration of divisional and brigade staffs, as well as that of the division's concert party.[61] For the first time, the Employment companies formed dedicated salvage sections. At divisional level each consisted of one officer and fifty men, while the area employment companies provided one officer and forty-four men to each corps HQ. They were also supposed to supply an additional eleven men to each division within the corps and a further nineteen men to army HQ. No arrangements were made to provide dedicated salvage teams on the lines of communication, but two ordnance officers were deployed to advise units.[62]

The salvage itself was taken back to the base area and handled by the arm or service to which it pertained. Much effort was made to recycle the salvage in theatre. Colonel W. N. Nicholson visited the salvage depot at Le Havre in July 1917:

All the salvage from the battlefields of two armies came down to this depot. In one place rose a mountain of ammunition boxes and shell cases, which German prisoners were busy loading on deck. Further up the river many thousands of empty ammunition boxes lay in long lines. Ship succeeded ship as fast as she could be loaded; as soon as filled another empty one moored alongside. The disposal of all other sorts of salvage, from cast-iron fragments to equipment, interested me particularly. Here, in some twenty long sheds, 1,200 French women under two British Ordnance officers were employed cleaning leather equipment, water bottles, rifles, bayonets; everything except clothing, which went to Rouen. The salvage came down from the battle area indescribably dirty, old and broken, and practically everything was made use of; empty cartridge cases found a purchaser in the French Government. Unfired SAA had first to be cleaned then sent home for reboxing. Equipment was brushed, polished and made up into new; so that for the previous six months no unused equipment had been required from home. When the equipment was too old, the brass straps were cut off. Very little appeared to be too old. Everything found a niche. Leather that could be made up in the workshops was sold by weight to the French. At the time of my visit sixty truck loads a day came from the two armies this base served.[63]

The salvage taken back to Britain was mainly sent to the port of Richborough, near Sandwich in Kent. A depot was also established here for handling the salvage.

There was still more to be done. In November 1917, Andrew Weir, the Surveyor General of Supply (SGS), visited both France and Richborough and recommended the establishment of an Army Salvage Board to co-ordinate operations. This was duly set up, with the QMG as chairman. At the same time an Army Salvage Branch was set up under the Controller of Salvage, a major general. This was followed by the appointment of staff captains for salvage duties to each army and corps HQ, as well as to that of the lines of communication. Finally, in the autumn of 1918 the Labour Corps formed dedicated salvage sections, which, although still administered by the employment companies, operated under the Controller of Salvage and could not have their men switched to other duties, as had previously been the case. Such was the growing success of the salvage operations in France that by September 1918 it was producing a saving of £4m sterling per month.[64] There was also the salvage of captured enemy equipment. One offshoot of this was the appointment in December 1917 of Major General C. G. Donald CB, the former commander of the 43rd (Wessex) Division, as the Inspector of War Trophies. His brief was to gather exhibits for the planned National War Museum, today's Imperial War Museum.

With regard to specialist labour, at the end of 1916 the Royal Engineers in France set up a system akin to the Entrenching battalions. They established a number of Reinforcement companies RE, which were initially formed from drafts at the RE base depot. The companies were deployed to armies, being under the direct control of the Chief Engineer (CE). They had an establishment of two officers and two senior NCOs and were to hold 200 to 250 men at any one time. These were largely tradesmen – carpenters, joiners, ironworkers, bricklayers, masons, clerks and drivers and the like. While they were waiting to replace casualties, they were employed on various jobs, including the construction of camps and workshops. Two companies, Nos. 5 and 9, made a significant contribution to the building of the Tank Corps central workshops at Erin. But like the Entrenching battalions, they were largely disbanded by the end of 1917, although No. 5 Reinforcement Company RE was still in existence, but with the new title of No. 5 RE Reinforcement Party and a strength of a mere twenty-five men.[65]

Another specialized form of labour also came into being in 1917 – forestry. Pioneer battalions had been employed on this work in France, although during the winter of 1915–16 a small RE unit was formed to exploit the timber resources of the forest of Nieppe. Much of the timber used by the BEF was, however, imported from Canada, Russia and Sweden, but heavy shipping losses in 1916 forced Britain to turn almost entirely to France and under an agreement which came into effect in November of that year the British Army was allowed to exploit French timber on a wide scale. During 1916 the number of units dedicated to forestry work rose to five RE companies and three and a half Labour battalions. Recognizing the vital importance of maintaining supplies of timber, in March 1917 GHQ in France established a separate Directorate of Forestry under Lord Lovat, father of the famous commando leader of the Second World War. The Royal Engineers' contribution increased by the end of the war to eleven Forestry companies, but the bulk of the work was carried out by the Canadian Forestry Corps. The first Canadian Forestry battalion arrived in England in April 1916, and the Forestry Corps itself was established that October. It expanded rapidly and was soon supplying timber both in Britain and to Allied armies in France. Indeed, the arrangement was that ten Forestry Corps companies worked in forests paid for by the British government, while the other forty-six companies in France operated in forests at no cost to the British but supplied both armies with timber. Canadian Forestry Corps companies also operated in Cyprus in support of the Egyptian Expeditionary Force (EEF).[66]

1917 also saw a massive expansion in overseas labour. The Chinese contribution in France eventually grew to 95,000 and proved to be the most adaptable of all. Many were employed at the various workshops and one company (25 Company CLC) was permanently attached to the camouflage school. John Nettleton did a course there in the late summer of 1917 when he was the 2nd Rifle Brigade's intelligence officer: 'As you walked about, grinning Chinks would pop out of unsuspecting holes in the ground or from dummy trees and they loved doing it. It was like playing hide-and-seek with kids.'[67] Captain Travis Hampson MC, the MO to 40 Group Labour Corps, was surprised, however, when he visited a CLC unit to deal with an outbreak of mumps and discovered a number of women in its ranks.[68]

In April 1917, elements of the Egyptian Labour Corps (ELC) were also sent to France. They numbered 15,000 men and were on a six months' contract, returning to Egypt at the end of the year. They were followed in May by 100 Fijian volunteers, whose services were offered by the Governor of Fiji. They eventually arrived in France in early July, after crossing Canada, like the Chinese. The Fijians proved to be excellent dockers and the quality of their work was rewarded on 1 July 1918 by the official formation of the Fijian Labour Corps (FLC). In recognition of this a representative group crossed to England in August to be inspected by the King. But like the other units from tropical climes, they suffered in the European winter, and in January 1918 were moved to Marseilles.[69] Other contingents came from Mauritius and the Seychelles. The British West Indies Regiment expanded to a strength of nine battalions, serving not just in France, but in Italy and Egypt as well. It is noteworthy that the 1st and 2nd Battalions of the BWIR, which were sent to Egypt, reverted to their original role as infantry and fought as part of Chaytorforce in the final campaign in Palestine. An Indian Labour Corps was also formed for service in France, each company being made up of a different race. In the view of the AAG of AG1 at the War Office, which handled Labour Corps personnel matters, the Indian labour companies were 'as whole somewhat disappointing', but conceded that 'certain companies such as Burmans and Chins are good at Forestry work.' In all, over 190,000 men from overseas served in France and Italy on labour work during the war, making a significant contribution. Sadly, though, their treatment often left much to be desired. In line with the attitudes of the day towards race, they were often segregated and not allowed to mix with the troops of other nations, let alone the French and Italian populations at large. This resulted in a lowering of morale and a good deal of discontent.

In the other theatres of war, indigenous labour continued to be exploited. Over 70,000 Egyptians were recruited, while in Mesopotamia 46,000 locals were employed. East Africa drew 137,000 natives, many being used as porters. Apart from the RE, ASC and Infantry Labour units, all of which were transferred to the Labour Corps, no less than twenty-five battalions of the Macedonian Labour Corps were formed for service in Salonika. In addition, there was also a Serbian Labour battalion. Its origins lay with Serbians serving in the Macedonian Labour Corps. They were found to make very effective guards and watchmen and by May 1918 over 500 of them were serving in this capacity and so it was decided to form a separate unit of them. Unlike the Macedonians, they were provided with British uniforms and recruited from the Serbian invalid depot and refugee camp, as well as permanent base men on sick leave or furlough. In addition, in the late summer of 1917 two further Maltese Labour battalions were formed on the island. They were officered largely by members of the King's Own Malta Regiment of Militia. Both officers and men were volunteers, with the latter paid two shillings and six pence (2/6d) per day and receiving underwear and boots but no uniform. They were initially on a six months' contract, but could extend this by three months at a time. No. 1 Battalion went to Salonika in September and No. 2 that December.[70]

By September 1917 the strength of the Labour Corps in France was approaching 100,000 men.[71] The overseas labour contingents and employment of prisoners of war was also increasing. Yet the burden on the long-suffering infantry appears to have hardly decreased from the previous year. Arthur Asquith, commanding the Hood Battalion in the 63rd (Royal Naval) Division, wrote to his brigade commander on 9 October 1917 complaining that the employment of his men on road-making duties in the Saint Julien area was preventing any training from taking place. He pointed out that the longest period of training his battalion had undergone since the beginning of the year had been ten days in March. He feared that this would drag on to the detriment of offensive operations in which the battalion was likely to be engaged in November. This brought about a sharp rap across the knuckles from his brigadier: 'As I told you the other day, the work on the roads is most important, and I should be sorry to think that there is a danger of the work suffering by the fact that you seem to think that someone else should be doing it.' As it happened, the 63rd Division learnt on 19 October that it would mount an attack on the 26th and Asquith's battalion was relieved from its labouring duties. Even so, he remained worried that his men were insufficiently trained and told his brigade commander so. In fact, the Hoods performed extremely well, successfully repulsing a German counter-attack, and Asquith won a second bar to his DSO.[72]

In February 1918, Entrenching battalions were reintroduced on the Western Front. In order to mop up the surplus manpower thrown up by the amalgamations of the infantry battalions resulting from the reorganization of brigades into three battalions, no less than twenty-five Entrenching battalions, numbered 1 to 25, were created. Every effort was made to form them from at least units in the same division, but the number contributing to each battalion varied considerably. No. 22 Entrenching Battalion was raised from just the 11th/13th Royal Irish Rifles, itself an amalgamation from November 1917. In contrast, No. 3 Entrenching Battalion contained elements of no less seventeen battalions, not all disbanded ones, drawn from five divisions. GHQ laid down strict guidelines on their use. They were to be used for work on the defences only, and then not in front of the rearward zone, and were to be retained under army or corps control. In no circumstances were they to be split up or attached to 'fighting units' and were to be prepared to provide drafts on orders of the DAG 3rd Echelon.[73] The life of this new batch of Entrenching battalions was short, however. Most found themselves caught up in the efforts to stem the tide during the German March 1918 offensive. Thus, No. 20 Entrenching Battalion was building a light railway north of Péronne when the German drive opened. Five days later, on 26 March, it was broken up to provide reinforcements for the 16th Division. No. 19 Entrenching Battalion, which had been formed from elements of the 10th Royal Dublins and 7th Leinsters, was engaged in railway work in the Amiens area. It came under the command of the 24th Division on the second day of the offensive. On 3 April it was ordered to disband and to pass its surviving men over to the 24th Division. In this case the CO objected, saying that his men would prefer to be posted to an Irish division. GHQ relented and they were absorbed by the 16th (Irish) Division from which they had originally come. Those Entrenching battalions which escaped the March 1918 offensive were caught up in the German attack on the Lys in April and suffered a similar fate. Indeed, by the end of that month all had been disbanded to help make good losses and no more were ever formed.[74] A body of Italian labour, which had been sent to help the French Army, was also employed on the Fifth Army defences in the early months of 1918, but after the March offensive was returned to the French sector.

The crisis of March 1918 also forced a reorganization of some of the Area Employment companies and a change of role for them. On 6 April, VII Corps, which was part of the Third Army, formed the 199th (Garrison) Brigade. It consisted of the 1st to 5th Provisional Garrison Guard Battalions, each consisting of four Area Employment companies, apart from the 5th Provisional Garrison Guard Battalion which had three of these companies and the one company of the 1st (Reserve) Garrison Battalion the Suffolk Regiment which had been sent to France in 1916 to carry out police duties.[75] The brigade was joined on 19 April by the 4th (Garrison) Battalion the Royal Welsh Fusiliers, which had been on guard duties at Le Havre and had to hastily exchange its Long Lee-Enfield rifles for SMLEs.[76] This Garrison brigade was given the task of holding defences in depth. At the end of May it was decided that these Provisional Garrison Guard battalions should be given regimental titles and they were used to re-form the 40th and 59th Divisions and were thus lost to the Labour Corps for good.[77] The only exception was the Suffolk company, which returned to its duties on the lines of communication. Simultaneously, Category B1 Labour Corps men who had seen service as infantrymen were formed into garrison companies, which themselves were made into six Garrison Guard battalions, numbered 6 to 11. They, too, were to be used to hold quiet sectors of the line and were also removed from Labour Corps control (*see page 280*).[78] Two other Infantry battalions were also formed from Area Employment companies. In May 1918, the 43rd Royal Fusiliers came into existence. Its role was to provide guards for the five army HQs in France and for this purpose it had a total of eleven detached companies. Four months later, the 44th Royal Fusiliers was formed. This had an entirely different task, namely to provide air defence for vulnerable point targets, like army HQs, and was equipped with Lewis guns on anti-aircraft mountings. At the same time the remaining Garrison Guard companies were transferred to the 43rd Royal Fusiliers, whose strength rose to no less than forty-nine companies.

Following the decision not to enlist any more Russian Jews into the Royal Fusiliers (*see page 149*), the Director of Labour in France was informed that all Russians and other aliens whom 'it was not desirable to retain with fighting units' were to be sent to the Middlesex Regiment base depot at Etaples. Apart from the Russians, they were to be posted to the Middlesex Infantry Labour Companies, while the former would be sent to a separate labour unit. None were to be employed in the forward area, at ports, bases, important depots or near Tank Corps installations, which left limited employment possibilities. This enabled three more Middlesex Labour companies to be formed. The Director of Labour proposed that the Russians be sent to No.1 Scottish Company NCC or, for some reason, to 160 Labour Company and the QMG at GHQ agreed, although he preferred the NCC company since this worked well out of range of shelling. This did not work, however, because of the severe restrictions placed on where the Russians were allowed to work. They and Romanians, who had also been combed out of units as 'undesirable aliens', therefore formed a new Labour company (No. 991) in July.[79]

Simultaneously, ACI 414 of April 1918 called for the formation of two Russian Labour battalions in Britain. The 8th Labour Battalion formed up at Sevenoaks in Kent, while the 9th Labour Battalion drew from Northern, Western and Scottish Commands and was based at Fort Scoveston in south Wales. The ACI made it plain that men of these battalions were not to be transferred to other arms and services without War Office permission and that within the Labour Corps they were not allowed to serve with other units. The intention was to keep the units segregated, although this did not happen in practice. During the summer of 1918 the two battalions sent three Labour companies (Nos. 1001, 1002 and 1021) across to France. A fourth company (No. 1022) arrived in December.[80]

Although the overall strength of the Labour Corps rose steadily from nearly 110,000 men in June 1917 to a peak strength of over 395,000 in January 1919, manpower was a constant problem, especially during the last year of the war. Indeed, from the outset the Labour Corps was subjected to regular comb-outs of fitter men. The War Diary of No. 40 Group records monthly medical boards during the summer of 1917 of officers under the age of 35 and all other ranks. In July, three officers and forty-four men were judged fit for general service and were posted to the combatant arms. A further eighty-one men were similarly deposed of in August.[81] No wonder did the AAG of AG1 complain in his report dated 31 December 1918 that 'our best men were taken from us and we received a large number of quite useless men both recruits on the one hand and casts off from units on the other. This resulted in Labour Centres becoming congested with men awaiting discharge.' Matters were made worse with the decision in the late summer of 1918 to send battalions of Category B men to France. 'This resulted in a somewhat serious slump in Labour Corps drafts which we were never able to make good.' Indeed, the corps found itself with the very scrapings of the manpower barrel, much of which was 'only fit for sedentary work for whom we could not find any employment'.[82]

Yet in spite of the frustrations experienced by those administering the Labour Corps and the often humdrum nature of the work its members carried out, its contribution and that of the overseas labour contingents was invaluable. In particular, tribute should be paid to those of the labour companies who worked, armed only with shovels, for weeks at a time under shellfire in the combat zone. Many were formerly fighting troops who had been medically downgraded because of wounds. The courage of the Labour Corps was recognized by the award of some 500 Military Medals and its dedication to duty earned some 1,260 Meritorious Service Medals.[83] But perhaps its most challenging task would come after the war was over – the clearance of the battlefields in France and Flanders and the reburial of those who had fallen.

eight

WOMEN IN KHAKI

The War Office was slow to recognize that women could offer a partial solution to the manpower problem. British women in 1914 still did not have the vote, in spite of the efforts of the suffrage movement. Even so, just under 6 million of them did have occupations, a third of them in industry. With regard to the army, the only avenue open to women was nursing. The Queen Alexandra's Imperial Military Nursing Service (QAIMNS) supported the Regular Army and had 463 trained nurses in August 1914. There was also the Territorial Force Nursing Service (TFNS), with a strength of 2,783. In addition, there were three voluntary organizations. In 1907, the First Aid Nursing Yeomanry (FANY) had been founded on the concept of women galloping on to the field of battle to recover wounded and take them to field hospitals. The same year saw the establishment of the Women's Sick and Wounded Convoy Corps by Mrs St Clair Stobart. This again was medical in connotation, with training along RAMC lines and members taught to pitch camps, dig trenches and generally live rough at their annual camp. A report on that held near Swanage in 1910 described them as being 'dressed in a very service-like blue-grey uniform and [carrying] haversacks and water-bottles. Their kit consisted of a divided skirt, Norfolk jacket, and helmet.'[1] Mrs St Clair Stobart herself went out to the Balkans to provide humanitarian aid during the wars of 1912–13. Finally, in 1909, the War Office drew up a scheme open to both sexes for providing 'voluntary aid to the sick and wounded'.

This became known as the Voluntary Aid Detachments (VAD), which were formed under the auspices of the TF County Associations, but were managed by the British Red Cross Society (BRCS) and St John's Ambulance. Each detachment had a strength of twenty-three and in practice some two-thirds were women, of whom there were 26,000 by early 1912. Its main object was to provide medical support in the event of an invasion of Britain and the *Herne Bay Press* devoted much coverage to a camp held by the Kent VADs in the local area in June 1914. The climax was a field day, with the scenario of an enemy landing in the Herne Bay area and driving the defenders back towards Canterbury. Cadets from RMC Sandhurst played the part of attackers and defenders and simulated casualties. These were treated by the VADs and passed back along the evacuation chain to a stationary hospital. There is no doubt that these organizations did much to prepare women, physically and psychologically, for a European war that appeared increasingly likely.

On the declaration of war, members of the QAIMNS crossed to France to help man the stationary hospitals. Although the VADs were theoretically home service only, on 16 October 1914 Katharine Furse took a detachment to France. They initially went to Paris, but were returned to Boulogne, where they established a rest station at the railway station. This catered for wounded in transit, the VADs changing their dressings and supplying them with food and drink. They even performed emergency operations. Similar canteens, with first-aid facilities, were set up by Lady Angela Forbes at the Gare Maritime in Boulogne in November and by Lady Mabelle Egerton at Rouen the following month. Kitchener became concerned over the number of women in the base area, however, and wanted them cleared out. He was particularly worried over rumours of scandal and that wives of officers serving in France had managed to get themselves there in contravention of the regulations. The IGC wrote to Jack Cowans, the QMG, in April 1915, reassuring him that there was no truth in the rumours, but pointing out that he was powerless to control the influx of visitors to the base areas, since these remained under the authority of the French. There was therefore nothing he could do about women setting up canteens,[2] this despite the Army Council, in February 1915, ordering the Director of Supplies and Transport at the War Office to establish a military organization to run canteens, which were placed under the ASC umbrella as Expeditionary Force Canteens (EFC).

Meanwhile, the outbreak of war had produced a flurry of volunteers for the VADs among women in Britain who wished to 'do their bit'. At the same time, further voluntary organizations were established. The Women's Emergency Corps was founded on 6 August 1914 by the actresses (and sisters) Decima and Eva Moore, along with Lena Ashwell, who later established her concert parties in the war theatres, and the Hon. Evelina Haverfield. This offered a variety of women to fill jobs ranging from doctors and nurses to domestics and canteen workers and even included motorcycle messengers. It also provided refugee relief and assistance to women thrown out of work by the dislocation of industry caused by the war. An offshoot of this was the Women's Volunteer Reserve, which was established before the end of 1914 by the Hon. Evelina Haverfield, with the Marchioness of Londonderry as honorary colonel. This was much more militaristic in character and its formation was prompted by fears of a German invasion, fuelled by tales of atrocities brought to Britain by Belgian refugees. Its object was 'to provide a disciplined and trained body of women ready to assist the State in any capacity.' Unlike the Women's Emergency Corps, its members wore khaki uniform, which they had to purchase themselves, and were taught military drill. They also made use of a shooting range in the basement of Harrod's in London on the premise that members had to be prepared to defend their honour. A similar organization was the Women's Defence Relief Corps. One young volunteer for this recalled: 'We were trained by an elderly Segt [sic] in the Cheshire Regt: ie:, Voice drill, military and Swedish drill, semaphore signalling and shooting. I won my cross guns.'* [3]

There were, too, a number of specifically medical organizations. Doctors Flora Murray and Louisa Garrett Anderson, who had both been militant suffragettes, formed the Women's Hospital Corps (WHC), which went to France and established a hospital for the French Army in the Hotel Claridge in Paris. Because of their records as suffragettes, they did not bother to approach the British government and went straight to the French embassy to offer their services. At the end of October a WHC detachment

* Marksmanship badge.

went to Wimereux, where it was accepted by the British Army and became the WHC hospital. Although it had ninety-five beds, by January 1915 only a third were occupied at any one time. Consequently, it was merged with the Rawalpindi General Hospital and No. 5 BRCS Hospital and lost its individual identity.[4] Doctor Elsie Inglis, founder of the Scottish Women's Hospitals, did approach the War Office only to be disparagingly turned down and so she deployed her hospitals in support of the Belgian, French and Serbian Armies. Indeed, with the official attitude early in the war that the British Army did not need any outside assistance, it dawned only slowly that women could play a valuable role in releasing men for more active roles.

One of the first of the voluntary organizations to receive official blessing was the Almeric Paget Massage Corps, which had been set up by Mr and Mrs Almeric Paget in August 1914 to provide masseurs and masseuses for military hospitals in Britain. The Pagets paid for the first fifty masseurs to be so deployed out of their own pockets. They also established a Massage and Electrical Out-Patient Clinic in Portland Place, London for treating wounded. So impressed was Sir Alfred Keogh, the Director-General, Army Military Services (DGAMS), that it was laid down in early 1915 that all those engaged in massage at military hospitals should belong to the corps. At the end of 1916 it became the Almeric Paget Military Massage Corps (APMMC) and in January 1917 deployed some of its members to hospitals in France and later Italy.

The majority of the women's organizations formed during the first part of the war were overwhelmingly upper- and middle-class in character, with members usually being expected to pay a subscription and purchase their uniforms. With this in mind, in July 1915 Lady Londonderry founded the Women's Legion, which drew on a much wider spectrum of society. Unlike the other women's organizations, it offered paid work, which was attractive to the lower classes. She had considerable political influence and in July 1915 was able to persuade Sir John Cowans, the Quartermaster General, to employ cooks of the Women's Legion at convalescent hospitals. At the beginning of the following month the first detachment was sent to one at Dartford, Kent and proved so successful that the Women's Legion Military Cookery Section soon came under the control of the Inspector of Army Catering.[5] The activities of the section spread to command depots, rest camps and officer cadet units, with over 4,000 cooks and waitresses replacing men, but hospitals remained the province of the VADs. Conscription caused the call-up of a number of male drivers in government service and Sir John Cowans persuaded Lady Londonderry to establish an MT section under Christobel Ellis, who had served in Serbia as a Red Cross ambulance driver. In April 1916 the ASC took on twenty Women's Legion drivers on probation. They were attached to 606 MT Company and soon proved their worth. The company was then detached to the Ministry of Munitions and largely made up of Women's Legion personnel. They wore the ASC badge and were paid by the army.[6]

By this time a few members of the FANY were driving ambulances in France. In July 1914, Surgeon General H. R. Whitehead CB, the Deputy Director Medical Services (DDMS) Eastern Command, had inspected the FANY at their annual camp. So impressed was he that he told Grace Ashley-Smith (later Mrs McDougall), the head of the FANY, to approach the DGAMS for official War Office recognition. Yet when war was declared it was not forthcoming; nor would the BRCS recognize FANY. Grace Ashley-Smith herself was en route to South Africa to see her sister, but immediately returned to Britain. While on board ship, she met the Belgian Minister for the Colonies who suggested that the FANY help his country. The eventual upshot was that at the end of October 1914 the first FANY convoy consisted of six 'Fannies', three nurses, two orderlies and Ashley-Smith's brother Bill.* Together with one ambulance, they crossed to Belgium and set up a hospital in a convent school. This was gradually reinforced with further personnel and ambulances, as well as a motorized kitchen and bath unit. In July 1915, Mrs McDougall, as she had now become, asked the War Office to reconsider. Again, she met with refusal. By this time the convoy supporting the Belgians had deployed partly to Calais, which was now a British base. There was a shortage of ambulances and soon the RAMC were using the FANY convoy, although its priority remained the Belgians. As it happened, Surgeon General Whitehead, who had formed such a high opinion of the corps just before the war, was the DMS of the base area. He asked the convoy what it would like as a reward for its help and the reply was to work

---

* He was later commissioned into the KOYLI, but was killed in early 1916.

for the British. He is supposed to have replied: 'I feared you would say that! Now how are we going to manage it? You're not BRCS. You're not St John's. I know, alas, that you are not army … you're neither fish, flesh nor fowl, but you're damned good red herrings.'[7] The upshot was that on 1 January 1916 the FANY formed the Calais Convoy. They took over ambulances which had been operated by the BRCS, although the latter continued to provide funds to maintain the vehicles. The army, however, merely supplied rations, although during the first few months the convoy had to find its own. Also, unlike the Women's Legion MT Section, FANY members were unpaid volunteers, who had to provide their own uniforms and pay their travel expenses, a policy that remained in being throughout the war. The Calais Convoy proved so successful that similar FANY convoys were established to support the French Army, in addition to that they were giving to the Belgians.

Some women used their own individual initiative. In August 1914, Dr Hector Munro, a socialist and supporter of feminism (as well as founder of Britain's first nudist camp), set up the Munro Corps with the object of establishing a field ambulance in Belgium. Four women were included in his party and the ambulance was initially deployed to Antwerp. They rescued wounded from under fire and, when the city fell, withdrew to Furnes on the Belgian coast. The Munro Corps was now absorbed by the Scottish Women's Hospital, but Elsie Knocker, a trained nurse and midwife, who was also a pioneering lady motorcyclist, and 18-year-old Mairi Chisholm had other ideas. They established a first-aid post in a cellar in the ruined village of Pervyse. Here they treated sick and wounded and soon won the respect of both the Belgian and British Armies, who allowed them to stay where they were. Elsie Knocker married a Belgian aviator, the Baron de T'Serclaes, and the Women of Pervyse, as they were known, remained in the village until early 1918, when they were gassed during an artillery bombardment. For their services they were each awarded the Order of the Crown of Leopold, the British Military Medal and the Order of St John of Jerusalem.[8]

Very much less altruistic and a good deal stranger was the case of Dorothy Lawrence, which caused the British authorities in France much embarrassment. After trying without success to get to the Front as a war correspondent, Lawrence managed to get to Paris in the summer of 1915. There, still determined to get to the Front, she disguised herself as a soldier, persuading two privates of the Leicesters to obtain her a uniform and getting a military policeman to cut her hair. She forged a pass and obtained a French permit allowing her to travel to Calais via Amiens and Bethune. She reached Amiens by train and, wearing her own clothes, continued her journey by bicycle. She arrived in Albert, having been given wrong directions to Bethune, and found herself among the 51st (Highland) Division. She was arrested and spent the night at divisional HQ. Told that she must leave the area, she wondered off and met a sapper, who obtained an RE cap badge for her, and found a ruined cottage where she changed into the uniform she had brought from Paris. She spent some days mingling with troops in Albert and hiding up in her cottage. Thanks to her sapper friend, who was in a tunnelling company, she was able to smuggle herself on to nightly RE working parties in the trenches. After ten nights of this she became worried about implications for others if she was caught, killed or wounded. She therefore told a sergeant her secret and he arrested her. She was taken to a Highland battalion, where she was entertained by the bemused CO and his officers. Next day, she was taken off by two Intelligence officers, who, deeply suspicious that she might be a spy, subjected her to a series of cross-examinations. Eventually she reached HQ Third Army, where she was brought before the army commander, Sir Charles Monro, and other generals and staff officers:

> At this moment, when Allied forces were hoping that a great victory might result from the first battle of Loos, I, a foolishly unimportant English girl, occupied the undivided attention of six famous Generals, together with, approximately, twenty staff officers and other officials. Though that fact suggested what was laughable, I felt, as an Englishwoman, that there seemed singular gravity in the situation; our Higher Command surely lacked imagination and proper perspective, otherwise this trivial escapade never could have assumed such proportions nor claimed this vast attention.

She did, however, finally receive female clothing and was put in the charge of a captain, who was a friend of a friend. He took Dorothy to GHQ at

Saint Omer, where she was housed in a convent for two weeks prior to being ordered home by Sir John French. She travelled back on the same boat as Mrs Pankhurst, the leading suffragette, who was most interested in her story and wanted Dorothy to speak at a forthcoming recruiting meeting. Dorothy, however, had been warned that any public utterance about her escapade would be contrary to the Defence of the Realm Acts. On arrival at Folkestone, she was again interviewed and warned not to divulge any information. Not until she had reported to Scotland Yard for a police interview was she finally released. She subsequently joined the Women's Land Army, but wasted little time in bringing out an account of her adventure once hostilities had ended.[9]

There was also Isabella Lady St John, wife of a diplomat, who in late 1915 heard at a London tea party that her son was a casualty in France. Obtaining no satisfaction from the Officers' Casualty Inquiry Office, Whitehall, but warned that no unauthorized persons were allowed at the Front, she set off on her own to Bethune. After crossing to Calais, she persuaded a French booking clerk to sell her a railway ticket to Hazebrouck. A carter took her on and, after his cart broke down, handed her over to a British officer who took her to the village where her son was in billets. He was aghast and, to her deep disappointment, asked her to leave. She was allowed to stay in the village for two days, although neither her son nor anyone else would have anything to do with her. She tried to persuade a general to allow her to become a nursing orderly, but to no avail. She therefore returned sadder but wiser to England, arriving back at her house in Chelsea just five days after she had left it.* [10]

After Katharine Furse's pioneering efforts with the VADs at Boulogne shortly after the outbreak of war, increasing numbers of VADs did slowly cross to France to work in the base hospitals, while members of the QAIMNS and TF Nursing Service were gradually allowed as far forward as casualty clearing stations (CCS). Some, however, were keen to go further forward. John Charteris recorded in his diary on 5 August 1916:

> Yesterday I was motoring up towards a Divisional Headquarters, when
> I overtook two young women on foot going the same way. I asked them

* Lady St John's untimely visit to her son did not do him any harm professionally. He served in the Royal Scots and won the DSO and MC and was three times mentioned in despatches.

what their destination was, and they said they wanted to walk to a unit in the front line to see what it was like to be under fire. I put them in a car going the other way and told them not to be naughty. They were both nurses at one of the casualty clearing stations having their day off. One of them was under twenty and said she was at school in August, 1914.[11]

The rule that women were not to be allowed within 3 miles of the trenches was still being upheld.

However, as 1916 wore on and the army's manpower problems began to increase, more and more thought was given to using women more actively to replace men. Katharine Furse herself wrote in September: 'Personally I have been convinced the last 6 months that if the war continues we shall require some form of Conscription or Enlistment to supply sufficient suitable women for the needs of the Government in various spheres of work.' She began to draw up schemes for a women's military corps, as did the Women's Land Service Corps, which had recently been formed to assist agriculture.[12] At much the same time, the Expeditionary Force Canteens organization (EFC) was intending to start officers' clubs in France. Since ASC men staffed the canteens, the QMG's department proposed that these clubs be run by the Women's Legion. Accordingly, Mrs Burleigh Leach, who was in charge of the Women's Legion Cookery Section, went over to France at the beginning of December 1916 to see for herself.[13] Simultaneously, the Adjutant General was also beginning to consider the possibility of using women in some military roles and wrote to seek Sir Douglas Haig's views on 4 December, the very same day that Mrs Leach left for France. Then, on the 16th of the month, Lieutenant General H. M. Lawson crossed to France to examine the employment of manpower (*see page 150*), the same day that GHQ wrote to the War Office accepting in principle the substitution of male clerks by females in 'certain offices' at GHQ and on the lines of communication. Lawson himself aired the subject at all the headquarters he visited and this triggered further GHQ letters, dated 12 and 15 January 1917, to the War Office, stating that the Paymaster-in-Chief in France was willing to employ 500 women in his offices and that women could also be employed as telegraphists and telephone switchboard operators. Meanwhile, Sir Eric Geddes, the Director-General of Transportation, had written to the Chief of Staff at GHQ on 18 December, stating that he was also prepared to accept women, but he did add a rider. His experience with female clerks in civil life had convinced him that 'roughly speaking, it takes 10 to 12 per cent more women to do the work of male clerks. They cannot stand the long hours which men will work, nor can they stand times of extreme pressure extending over a period of weeks. Further, the proportion of them who are off work for minor complaints is greater than is the case with men.' He would therefore need an increase in establishment to allow for all this.[14]

Lawson submitted the first part of his report on 16 January 1917. In his preamble, he pointed out that both GHQ and France had already accepted in principle the employment of women as clerks. In addition, there were numerous jobs being done by men in France that in Britain were normally done by women: 'It does not look well, nor is it fair on the men themselves to have quantities of men in khaki doing work which all over England is being done by the other sex.' In the body of the report, he observed: 'In the last year or more in England the employment of women has developed to an immense extent through lack of men and has been attended with remarkable success.' In particular, the army at home had benefited and 'the sex difficulty has not been anything like what some have predicted. The women have been hard at work and felt that they were out for the job and the men have respected them ...' As for the type of job that they could do in France, Lawson identified not just clerking, but drivers, orderlies, storekeepers, cooks, charwomen and waitresses, among others. However, 'those who work with their heads will naturally be chosen from the better and educated classes.' He believed that over 12,000 soldiers in France could be replaced by women. The War Office itself was in two minds, fearing that the women might be influenced by the Trades Unions or the suffragettes. If they were to be employed, it would have to be as soldiers rather than civilians. Lawson, however, recommended that the women be organized under their own officers, who would be responsible for their administration and welfare, and recognized that it might take time to organize their accommodation and conditions of service. It was on these lines that Sir Nevil Macready, the Adjutant General, proceeded.

It was decided that the new organization should be raised under the auspices of the Director-General of National Service, with the Director of Recruiting, Brigadier General Auckland Geddes (the brother of Eric), the War Office representative on its committee. While it realized that several women's organizations were providing labour for a variety of military branches at home, the War Office had very little idea of what pay and conditions they were operating under. Mrs Leach did advise on the Women's Legion, but it soon became clear that the way this operated was not in accord with other organizations. Macready was inclined to make the new organization a collection of separate branches, each with its own head, but Miss Rachel Crowdy, in charge of the VADs in France and whom he consulted on the matter, strongly disagreed, arguing for full integration as one body. Macready accepted her view and a template for this new body was drawn up on the basis that its rank-structure mirror that of the army, with officers and NCOs. Pay should also equate to that of soldiers, with the proviso that an equal number of women could not take over from the same number of men on a particular job. Discipline, too, was to be subject to military law. But a debate now arose as to whether the women should be treated as per military or civilian practice, especially over pay, where there were queries as to whether officer positions, as the War Office saw them, equated to the civilian view of rank structure, where the boundary between management and workers was often blurred.[15]

At this point General Geddes turned to his sister, Mrs Chalmers Watson, a distinguished Edinburgh doctor who had a reputation for getting things done. She attended a meeting at the War Office on 6 February 1917 presided over by Lord Derby. Also present were Mrs Leach and Mrs Margaret Tennant, the latter head of the newly formed women's section of the Directorate of National Service, together with her deputy. The heads of the proposed drivers' and clerks' sections under the Macready plan also attended. With the debate over pay and conditions continuing, Lord Derby was unable to come up with any cast-iron proposals. He merely stated that the new corps would be uniformed and housed in military accommodation. The only decision made by the meeting was that the corps should be unified under one head, rather than be a loose conglomerate of specialist sections, which was in line with Miss Crowdy's view. Appointed to control what was about to become the Women's Army Auxiliary Corps (WAAC)* was Mrs Chalmers Watson. She was given the title Chief Controller, while Mrs Leach became Controller of Cooks and began to select members of her Women's Legion for posting to France. The titles granted to Mrs Chalmers Watson and Mrs Leach reflected the decision not to bestow military ranks on the WAAC.

The WAAC headquarters was co-located with that of the VADs in Devonshire House, London, and a new branch of the AG's department (AG11) was established to administer the corps. Two days after the War Office meeting, Mrs Leach went to France again, this time to investigate the employment of female pay clerks. At the same time, it was realized that someone would be needed to head the WAAC in France. Among the names suggested was that of Helen Gwynne-Vaughan. She was head of the Department of Botany at Birkbeck College, University of London, and had been recently widowed. She had also just qualified in bacteriology and was hoping for a post in an RAMC hospital or mobile laboratory. She and the Chief Controller met and immediately established a rapport. Gwynne-Vaughan was interviewed by Macready on 13 February and a week later was made Overseas Controller of the WAAC. On the same day, the announcement of the formation of the WAAC was published in the newspapers. On 25 February, Mrs Gwynne-Vaughan accompanied Mrs Watson on a further visit to France. Mrs Watson met her other brother, Eric, the Director-General of Transportation, who gave her numerous ideas to ponder over, while Helen Gwynne-Vaughan toured the base areas. Her main concern was accommodation, which had to be less spartan than that of the men's. She opted for Tarrant and Nissen huts, both of which could be easily erected and moved, but then had to establish such basic requirements as the number of lavatories, baths and cooking facilities to be provided and how many women could be decently accommodated in a hut.

Back in Britain, there was a flood of volunteers to join the WAAC. They were subjected to a medical examination, but could not be enrolled until Mrs Gwynne-Vaughan had returned from France. At the same time,

---

* The original proposal was that it should be called the Women's Auxiliary Army Force. [National Archives, Kew, WO 32/5250]

Mrs Leach was picking volunteers from the Women's Legion. A WAAC depot was established at Ingram House, Stockwell, but this soon became full and additional premises were found at the Connaught Club in London, whose members were forced to leave. The first draft was soon ready to leave for France, but nothing further could be done until the ACI officially promulgating the WAAC was published. This took place on 28 March and it was only then that the women could be formally enrolled in the WAAC, although ACI 537/17 stipulated that no woman under 20 or over 40 could join.* For the fifteen members of the first draft, there was a flurry of activity before they departed on 31 March 1917, their task to establish an officers' club at Abbeville.[16]

One of the actions that had to be taken was obtaining passports for the WAACs to travel to France. This was an indication that their status was more civilian than military, but their precise status was not resolved until the publication of ACI 1069 on 7 July 1917. The oath was done away with, and it was confirmed that the WAACs would be enrolled, rather than enlisted, and would sign a document which was, to all intents and purposes, a civil contract. The WAACs in Britain were made subject to the Defence of the Realm Acts, which meant that they could be hauled up in front of a civil court for serious transgressions. Those in France were regarded as camp followers under Section 184 of the Army Act, which made them liable to court martial, although this would only be for crimes that endangered the army. In practice, the most severe punishment that could be awarded was to return a woman to Britain, but this could only be done if she had been four times previously found guilty of offences and, once back in Britain, she could only be prosecuted if she offended again. The rank system, too, was different. Under the controllers, who equated to lieutenant colonels, the other 'officer' ranks in descending order of seniority were unit, deputy and assistant administrators. The term 'officer' was not, however, used formally, 'official' being the correct designation; and officials were not entitled to salutes by soldiers. The WAAC equivalents to the NCO were forewoman and assistant forewoman, with the rank and file being designated workers. It was also laid down that WAACs could only have social dealings with soldiers of equivalent rank. They were forbidden to smoke in public

---

* The minimum age was later lowered to 18, but no one under the age of 21 could be sent overseas.

places and were not allowed to drink alcohol, except under medical supervision.

Besides helping to run the officers' clubs in France, the WAACs were also employed as clerks at GHQ at Montreuil, the GHQ 2nd Echelon at Hesdin, and the 3rd Echelon at Rouen. Others fulfilled the same role with HQ of the Director-General of Transportation at Wailly, as well as the Army Pay Department (APD) at Wimereux. In addition, they provided telegraphists and telephone operators who wore the same blue-and-white brassard as the RE Signal Service. In the base areas they also worked in MT and ordnance depots, base depots and bakeries. In August 1917, WAAC gardeners were sent to France to tend the war cemeteries. Frank Fox was full of praise for those who worked at the officers' club at Montreuil: 'It is difficult to imagine what a touch of "England, Home and Beauty" those deft young women gave after experience of soldier orderlies as waiters.'[17] Others were not so sure. Brigadier General John Charteris, Haig's intelligence chief, commented in a diary entry of 10 May 1917: 'I am afraid that my lady clerks are not altogether a success. One of them wants to get married at once; another is engaged; and a third has lost her mother. So I am trying to send them all back and have recourse to the less amorous male.'[18]

Under ACI 1069/17, issued on 7 July, the aim of the WAAC was re-emphasized as 'to effect substitution of women for soldiers in certain employments throughout units, formations and offices administered by the Army Council (other than the War Office, Hospitals, and those administered by the Finance Member) at Home, and at the Bases, and on the Lines of Communication overseas.' The ACI also stated, echoing Sir Eric Geddes's views on female versus male clerks, that four of the former were equivalent to three of the latter, with the same ratio applying to 'technical' jobs in the RFC and ASC. In addition, the WAAC was to gradually absorb the cookery and MT sections of the Women's Legion. It succeeded with the cooks but, largely thanks to Sir John Cowans, the MT section remained outside. The QMG argued that, since its members drove ASC vehicles, they should be under the control of that corps.

Another organization which was not absorbed by the WAAC was the Women's Forage Corps. In July 1915, the War Office enrolled women supervisors to oversee the transport of hay from farms to railway stations.

Then, in March 1917, as part of the policy of substituting female for male labour, the Women's Forage Corps was created under Brigadier General H. G. Morgan CB DSO, a retired officer who had been put back into harness at the beginning of the war and had been the administrative member of the Forage Committee since January 1915. Mrs Athole Stewart was appointed superintendent of the corps and some 4,200 members were enrolled. They had their own rank structure of administrators, officials and industrial workers and wore a khaki and green uniform with ASC badges and 'FC' shoulder titles. They operated throughout Britain and each area had its own Forage Corps Area Administrator who oversaw a number of districts, each of which was headed by an assistant administrator and a purchasing officer. As there was rivalry among government ministries over manpower, so there was over womanpower. To this end, the Women's Land Army attempted to take over the Women's Forage Corps. The former had been created under the patronage of the Board of Agriculture in early 1917 and had agricultural, timber cutting and forage sections. To complicate matters still further there was also a Women's Forestry Service, which had been established under the Board of Trade in summer 1917. From early 1918, all three organizations were enrolled through a joint system, but the War Office seems to have been so concerned that the Women's Forage Corps might lose its unique identity that in late October it issued an ACI stating that it was independent from the Women's Land Army and was to continue to be administered by the QMG's department.[19] The WAAC did, however, absorb some VADs working in France, in particular those who were supervising French female labour at the smoke helmet repair depot, although at the time, with the small box respirator having replaced the PH helmet, it was soon to be wound up.

The VADs themselves were not just employed in hospitals, but also elsewhere. This itself became a matter for debate. There was a threat to absorb them in the WAAC, one that was bitterly resisted by Katharine Furse, who argued that VADs should concentrate on hospital work so as to maintain a difference in role with that of the WAAC. On the other hand, and reflecting the fact that the HQs of both were in Devonshire House, she pursued a policy of close cooperation with the WAAC. The VADs themselves came under the umbrella of the BRCS and the Order of St John of Jerusalem and many were individual members of one of these two organizations. As such, they were regarded as non-combatants under the Geneva Convention, while the WAAC did not qualify for this status. This argument enabled the VADs to maintain their independence. Supervising the VADs was the task of the Central Joint VAD Committee under Sir John Slattery, which was all-male until well into 1916. When, in 1915, the War Office began to look to the VADs to help in military hospitals, it paid them direct. This ran across the tenets of the Red Cross and so the military authorities began to enlist members of the Women's Legion, kitting them out in VAD uniforms, to the chagrin of Mrs Furse. Even so, by September 1916, some 8,000 VADs were working in military hospitals, but not just as nurses. Under what was called the VAD General Service scheme, which had come into effect that June, they could be employed in all manner of jobs, from cooking to storekeeping. In truth, although some became hospital dispensers and technical assistants, this meant that the VADs became mere skivvies, who were looked down upon by professional nurses. In any event, they often viewed nursing VADs as semi-trained amateurs. Mrs Furse was conscious of this and was irritated that the welfare of the VADs was in the hands of the War Office, something which the Red Cross and Sir John Slattery seemed happy to accept.

In October 1917 a medical section of the WAACs was established to enable the corps to be self-sufficient for medical support. While female doctors had been active in the Women's Hospital Corps (WHC) and the Scottish Women's Hospitals from the outset, the War Office was, for a long time, resistant to their being employed in military hospitals *per se*. But the demands for doctors had forced it to accept women doctors in hospitals at home. They were employed as Civil Medical Practitioners (CMP), had no rank or uniform and were not entitled to rations or travel allowances. Sir Alfred Keogh, the DGAMS, admired their efforts, but would not countenance female doctors serving in a theatre of war. Indeed, in March 1915 he persuaded the WHC hospital at Wimereux to move to London to a new military hospital in Endell Street. The WHC doctors were given no rank, but were graded for pay and allowance purposes according to military ranks. In 1916, the demand for military doctors grew even greater and the War Office felt that it had no choice but to invite female doctors to volunteer for military service. They were deployed not just to hospitals at home, but to Egypt, India, Malta and Salonika. However, they were merely attached to the RAMC and, like the CMPs and those in the WHC, were given no rank. This put them in an impossible position since, unlike the WHC and Scottish Women's Hospitals, they were working in a largely male environment. Their pay seldom exceeded that of a captain RAMC and they found themselves junior to every male doctor in uniform. Even worse, while VADs working in hospitals were entitled to travel first-class in trains, the doctors attached to the RAMC had to go third-class with the rank and file. The Medical Women's Federation, founded in February 1917 to champion the interests of female medical workers, took up the cause of the doctors working with the army. It was able to improve their financial situation by obtaining Treasury agreement that they be taxed at the service rate rather than as civilians, but was not so successful over their status. The dispute over uniforms was of particular concern to those serving overseas for, if captured in civilian clothes, there was no guarantee that they would not be treated as spies. As for rank, the president of the Medical Women's Federation wrote to General Thomas Goodwin, the DDGAMS, in March 1918:

> We are constantly receiving letters of complaint describing the annoyance our women are suffering from because of their lack of rank and status ... Nothing will satisfy most of them except equal terms for equal work with men, and as they truly say men in the ASC have rank and so have the Chaplains and if they have there is no earthly reason why women should not have it too.[20]

In the meantime, those women doctors working directly for the RAMC were given the right to wear uniform, which in fact was that of the WAAC but with RAMC badges. Heading the medical section were the President of the Medical Boards in Britain and the Medical Controller in France. It was agreed that both should have the equivalent rank to an RAMC lieutenant colonel, but when it came to equivalent pay the Finance Department of the War Office refused to award them more than 60 per cent of the basic pay of the latter. Dr Laura Sandeman, who had been selected as the Medical Controller, refused to take up the appointment, especially since she had been earning well in excess of the amount to which she felt entitled. Mrs Chalmers Watson remonstrated with the War Office, only to be told that others with sufficient patriotism would be content to do the work for less pay than the men. Dr Sandeman therefore continued to refuse the appointment. Lord Derby, the Secretary of State, was intensely irritated by this:

> I am between the devil and the deep blue sea. On the one hand I consider it outrageous that no woman will accept an appointment under £700 a year. On the other hand I cannot obtain a Medical Service for the WAAC in France and I am therefore obliged to agree this salary, but I strongly recommend that neither of the two ladies in question be given the appointment.[21]

As it happened, Laura Sandeman did take the job in France, while Dr Isabel Cameron had occupied the post of President of the Medical Boards at home, in spite of the relatively low level of pay, until Lord Derby made his reluctant decision. Their medical officers also received WAAC ranks and pay equivalent to their male counterparts. This gave them higher rates than their equivalents in the regular WAAC, but they were not entitled to official accommodation. As for those women who were working as civilian doctors attached to the RAMC overseas, the authorities continued to refuse to recognize their difficulties in having no formal rank and status.

If the War Office was making life difficult for women doctors working with the army, it also created problems for the FANY. In conjunction with the BRCS, it decided to abolish the ambulance convoys in France, apart from that at Calais. A BRCS party arrived to disband the convoy working with the Belgians, but its members had already alerted the Belgian authorities and the BRCS delegation was met by a Belgian general and his staff. The general pointed out that the Red Cross members were on Belgian soil and that, as far as he was concerned, the convoy was part of the Belgian Army. The BRCS delegation withdrew and thereafter the Belgian and French armies took direct control of these convoys. In January 1918, however, a FANY convoy was established at Saint Omer, but it did not have enough drivers and so VADs were co-opted. The latter were by this time running their own convoys based on the British bases in France. The new convoy was officered by Fannies and initially there were some problems because the VAD code of discipline was different from that of the FANY. The latter permitted its girls to attend dances; the former did not. The convoy commander appealed to the VAD controller, who relented to the extent that the VAD drivers would be allowed to dance in their own mess.[22]

Saint Omer also saw the WAAC active in new areas. Six assistant administrators, all excellent linguists, were attached to the intelligence branch, where their services were in demand for the cracking of German coded messages. They were euphemistically known as the 'Hushwaacs'. In November, when the Overseas Branch of the Ordnance Survey was established at Saint Omer (see page 206), the women employees were enrolled in the WAAC and were hastily taught drill by a sapper sergeant-major before departing for France. WAACs also provided catering staff for the army schools. The First Army commander, Sir Henry Horne, was so impressed with the staff at his school that he insisted that the administrators wore the same brassard as the instructors and the others the First Army patch. The women also established their own concert party at this school, the 'Waacsworks'. There were also the three assistant administrators posted to the Special Works Park RE to supervise the manufacture of camouflage materials by Frenchwomen (see page 208).

At the end of December 1917, ACI 1874/17 laid down that the WAAC was to be split into two branches – mobile and immobile. Those in the mobile branch could be posted anywhere in Britain or to France and received additional pay, while the remainder were guaranteed permanent employment in one place, something which was attractive to those who had home commitments.

Although the uniformed women in France soon proved their worth, rumours began to circulate about the morals of the WAAC, the bulk of whom came from working-class backgrounds, unlike the VADs. On 24 January 1918, the *Daily Sketch* noted: 'One hears wild and varying stories about the relations between the rank and file of the WAACs and the regular army.' Some asserted that literally hundreds of WAACs had been sent home pregnant. This had a drastic effect on recruiting, with parents unwilling to allow their daughters to enrol. The authorities appeared to believe that many of the rumours were started by pacifists and even enlisted the help of the Archbishop of Canterbury to quash the stories. The Chief Controller,

Mrs Watson, had to go to the extent of swearing an affidavit that none of her women had been 'requisitioned or sent to France for an immoral purpose whatever'. Unfortunately, at the very height of the controversy she resigned, although it was solely for personal reasons in that she had a very sick son. Mrs Florence Leach, the Controller of Inspection, succeeded her. In the meantime, the Ministry of Labour had appointed a commission of six women to go to France to investigate the charges of immorality. They carried out their tour of inspection in early March and reported on their return: 'The general impression left upon us by the Corps is that of a healthy, cheerful, self-respecting body of hard-working women, conscious of their position as links in the great chain of the Nation's purpose, and zealous in its service.' Indeed, statistics on those women returned to Britain from France revealed that during the period March 1917 to February 1918 only fifteen cases were on the grounds of pregnancy and that they had all been so before leaving for France. Those prosecuting malicious rumours about the WAAC began to be charged under the Defence of the Realm Acts. A primitive Methodist minister was fined £40 and a socialist leader in the Rhondda Valley a total of £50. In the meantime, the WAAC in France had been caught up in the March 1918 retreat. Many had to be evacuated in a hurry to the base areas, but their conduct won them high praise. In recognition of this, on 9 April the Queen, who was a stalwart supporter of the corps, declared that from henceforth it should be known as Queen Mary's Army Auxiliary Corps (QMAAC) and that she would be its Commandant-in-Chief. This silenced many of the critics, although accusations of immorality continued.

By this time, those women serving in France were coming under fire from attacks by German night bombers, which carried out a number of raids on the rear areas. In April 1918 the Saint Omer convoy particularly distinguished itself during a raid on the town, with six FANY and five VAD ambulance drivers being awarded the Military Medal for their bravery under fire. On 29 May German aircraft attacked a camp at Abbeville. A bomb struck a trench in which members of the QMAAC were sheltering. Eight were killed outright, one died of wounds and a further six were wounded. Three officials and a forewoman were awarded the Military Medal for their part in restoring order and attending to the wounded.

Indeed, even though they were never allowed near the actual Front, eight officials and seventy-five members of the QMAAC were killed or died in war theatres. The nurses, who operated further forward than the other women's organizations, also won their share of MMs, ninety-one all told. They and VADs also lost their lives, a total of fifty-one being killed or drowned through enemy action and a further ninety dying abroad.[23]

In April 1918, in parallel with the formation of the Royal Air Force, the Women's Royal Air Force (WRAF) was formed. This took over WAACs who had been serving with the Royal Flying Corps and those of the Women's Royal Naval Service (WRNS)* who had been supporting the Royal Naval Air Service. Mrs Gwynne-Vaughan, who had been such a tower of strength as the WAAC controller in France, became head of the WRAF in September 1918 after the incumbent, the Hon. Violet Douglas-Pennant, had been found wanting.** In the summer of 1918, 500 members of the QMAAC were detached to work for the American Expeditionary Force (AEF). To reduce shipping space, the AEF had crossed to Europe with the minimum of administrative staff and the QMAAC were used largely to run its record office at Bourges. Up until now the QMAAC base depot in France had been at Le Havre, but the additional influx caused by the AEF contingent resulted in a new base depot being established at Harfleur. At the same time, the QMAAC was becoming ever more military. Officials were now being referred to by their ranks rather than as Miss or Mrs and saluting was commonplace. A new purpose-built depot was opened at Bostall Heath, Essex. QMAAC police patrols were also established both to deter crime and to guard morals. In terms of the latter, romances in France inevitably flourished and not infrequently led to marriage. The rule that a husband and wife could not be in the same theatre of war remained, however, and the policy was that it was the wife who would be immediately shipped back to Britain. The QMAAC authorities were none the less

---

* This had been formed at the end of November 1917 under Dame Katharine Furse.

** There were faults on both sides. Violet Douglas-Pennant was accused of being high-handed and meddlesome, while she complained of lack of support from the Air Ministry. The affair eventually culminated in a House of Lords Select Committee of Inquiry in October 1919. This upheld her dismissal, but during the inquiry she accused the male commanding officer of the WRAF Motor Transport Pool of improper relations with Gwenda Glubb, daughter of a distinguished sapper general and brother of the future Glubb Pasha. Miss Glubb, who had been an ambulance driver with the Scottish Women's Hospital in Serbia, was forced to produce medical evidence to prove that she was still a virgin.

sympathetic to their new brides, especially since, in at least one case, the new wife immediately went absent in France on the night of her wedding. The solution was 'honeymoon cottages', villas and cottages whose owners were told that they might let rooms to newly-weds whose marriage had been sanctioned by the authorities. If the husband had been successful in obtaining local leave, the QMAAC delayed the paperwork necessary for sending his bride back home.

By November 1918, the QAIMNS had a strength of just over 7,700 trained nurses, over half of whom were serving abroad in every theatre of war, while the Territorial Force Nursing Service had some 5,000. In addition, there were approximately 90,000 female and 30,000 male VADs. The QMAAC grew to a strength of some 40,000. The War Office had been slow to realize the value of women, especially in their ability to release men for more active roles. Much of this had to do with the social attitudes of the day and even when they were officially put into uniform there were wide but mainly unfounded suspicions that they were corrupting the men. The truth was that the vast majority made a significant contribution to the war effort, often in very humdrum roles. The women also demonstrated that they were not lacking in physical and moral courage.

nine

MANPOWER AT THE FRONT AND THE CRISIS OF 1918

Formed units arriving in a theatre of war were first sent to rest camps, used continuously since August 1914 to allow them to re-form after their voyage and until transport could be arranged to take them forward. Drafts of re-inforcements, on the other hand, were processed through the base depots. In most cases, as every infantry division arrived in France, it established an infantry base depot (IBD). Thus, when the 9th and 14th Divisions were sent across in May 1915 they established Nos. 9 and 14 IBDs respectively. In one or two cases, divisions formed their IBDs from ones already in existence. One of these was the 46th (North Midland) Division, which took over No. 6 General Base Depot (GBD) when it arrived in-theatre in March 1915.[1] By June 1916 there were thirty-nine IBDs in France, together with one for the Guards Division. Five general base depots now existed: No. 1 handling RGA drafts; No. 2, RHA and RFA; No. 3, Canadian troops; No. 4, Royal Engineers (except for TF field and army troops companies); and No. 5 catering for cavalry and Regular RAMC. In addition, there were two Territorial base depots, which looked after TF personnel other than infantry, two Australian base depots, an Indian base depot and one for the Machine Gun Corps.[2] When the Indian Corps arrived in France in autumn 1914, it established base depots at Marseilles. The 22nd, 27th and 28th Divisions also moved their IBDs there in preparation for deployment to Salonika and these moved with the divisions to the new theatre. In Egypt, on the other hand, base depots were formed for each arm and service, with no individual IBDs for each division.

Within each divisional IBD, there were lines for each individual regiment within the division and initially every effort was made to post reinforcements to a battalion of their own regiment. The depots were responsible not just for processing the men, but for giving them a final spell of training, including introducing them to new tactical techniques and completing their equipment. Once gas warfare had made its appearance on the Western Front in April 1915, the base depots also ensured that troops had effective gasmasks by putting them through a gas chamber test. If the emphasis was on making the men realize that they were now in a theatre of war, there was also a realization that the training that they had received in Britain was often incomplete.

The conditions at the IBDs in the early days were often grim. George Ashurst was at one at Le Havre in November 1914:

> The camp was under canvas and six inches deep in mud. Food was rotten and insufficient, Woodbine cigarettes were sixpence a packet, and one had to queue up for a packet even when they were to be got at all. Only one blanket per man was issued, and we had to keep warm at night by sharing each other's blankets and sleeping in our uniforms. Life was just terrible, the route marches were almost killing, and one was delighted to see one's name on the list of a draft for the front line.[3]

The majority of IBDs came to be concentrated at Etaples, where a large training area, known as the Bull Ring, was established.

Conditions did improve, but those who passed through the IBDs and the Bull Ring continued to have mixed reactions. Norman Gladden found himself in No. 32 IBD in summer 1916. The food, served in a large dining hall, was adequate, but the plates and bowls were poorly washed, and 'the tables were usually covered with filth from previous sittings, and the whole atmosphere stank of stale food and crowded humanity. It was not a place to dally in'. The Bull Ring itself:

comprised a series of training grounds, more or less naturally separated by space and higher dunes, amidst which the most up-to-date training impedimenta had been set up. There was an immense levelled parade ground, numerous drill enclosures, bayonet courses, and practice grounds for bombing throwing, rifle marksmanship, Lewis gun practice and the rest. The situation was pleasant enough and from the parade grounds by the seashore the scene over the estuary across the sandy ridge had a beauty all of its own.

In Gladden's eyes, the Bull Ring had two main drawbacks. First, that the sand made 'the simplest military evolution ... an act of great labour'. The other was the instructors, known as 'canaries', from the yellow armbands they wore: 'Most of them had come from the front, a fact that they treated without modesty. Their manner, with few exceptions, was immoderate and irascible; their aim no doubt was to break us in the shortest possible time.' Yet, 'taking it all round, our training ... seemed effective'.[4] Young officers, like Alan Thomas, also found it a depressing experience:

> The trouble about Etaples was the feeling of loose-endishness it gave you. There you were, doing parades which couldn't interest you because you knew you were only doing them to fill in time. For the rest you wandered about, knowing that at any hour of the day or night you might be ordered away. More than ever you felt at the mercy of a huge, impersonal machine which might pick you up at any moment or might forget all about you and leave you lying around for weeks, sometimes for months. There was nothing you could do either to hasten or delay things. The only thing left was to pray for your name to be called.[5]

In mid July 1916 there was a change in policy over which drafts the IBDs handled. The heavy casualties incurred by divisions initially involved in the Somme offensive meant that the IBDs to which they were connected were unable to supply sufficient reinforcements to bring them back up to strength quickly. In contrast, other IBDs had drafts for which their divisions, which had not taken part in the early phases of the battle, had no room. Consequently, it was decided that, with certain exceptions, each IBD would lose its divisional affiliation and would instead supply particular regiments which recruited in the same geographical area. Thus, No. 38 IBD, which had been supporting the Welsh Division, now found itself providing drafts for the East and West Surreys and the Buffs, and No. 47 IBD, while it continued to supply drafts for the London Regiment, whose battalions made up the 47th Division, was also made responsible for the KRRC and Rifle Brigade. This was logical, since many of the London Regiment battalions had affiliations to these regiments. Among the exceptions were No. 36 IBD, which continued to supply the Ulster Division, the Guards Division Depot and No. 63 IBD. The last, originally No. 61 IBD, had been set up to supply the 61st (2nd South Midland) Division, which had crossed to France in May 1916. However, when the 63rd (Royal Naval) Division arrived from the Mediterranean a month later, it switched to supporting this formation.[6]

Sergeant Frank Warren KRRC was at No. 1 IBD in October 1916 and spent just over two weeks there. From his daily programme, the life at Etaples does not seem to have been too arduous. On Day 1, which was wet, there was a medical inspection and one by the commandant. The next two days were spent in training – bayonet fighting, work in the miniature trench system which had been laid out and wiring. Day 4 was a Sunday and so there was no work, and not much was done on the Monday, which was wet, the day being spent on what the army euphemistically called 'interior economy', which meant little more than fatigues around the camp. Day 6 covered bombing and sniping, and also included a lecture on trench warfare. The next day saw further lectures – on bombing and 'Modern Methods in the Attack' – followed by bombing practice. Day 8, by way of contrast, saw the men transferring bales of sandbags from ships to trains in Le Havre. Day 9 was devoted to gas training. Another Sunday came round, again with no work, and the second Monday was also devoted to interior economy. Day 12 was another wet one and was occupied in indoor lectures, while Day 13 was devoted to collecting large pebbles on the beach for use in road making. Days 14 and 15 were spent in dug-out construction and musketry, with Warren leaving to help conduct a draft to the 17th KRRC on the following day.[7] Norman Gladden returned to the Bull Ring in May 1917, after a spell in England resulting from a bad case of trench foot. He noted that conditions had improved, with less discipline and improved amenities.[8] Rifleman Aubrey Smith was at No. 47 IBD in July, following leave in England after hospitalization in France. He was not so impressed:

> Breakfast was at 5.45 a.m., and at 7 or 7.30 those eligible for infantry drill were fallen in and marched to the Pimple, a vast training ground where everything from platoon work to open order skirmishing and bayonet fighting was practised daily in the blazing heat by thousands and thousands of men. Two biscuits and a piece of cheese were carried by each man, this being the sole nourishment afforded him until 5.30 or 6 o'clock at night, when he returned.

As a convalescent, he was expected to spend three weeks at the Bull Ring before being sent to a unit.[9]

On 21 October 1916, Lieutenant Colonel James Jack, commanding the 2nd West Yorkshires, which was preparing for the assault at Le Transloy on the Somme, wrote in his diary:

> In accordance with Army Orders, the second-in-command, 2 captains, 5 subalterns, Regimental-Sergeant-Major, 2 Company-Sergeants-Major, and 10 others per company are to be left at the transport lines as a reserve in case of too serious casualties. This practice has resulted from the crippling losses generally sustained in trench attacks on the Somme; losses which have left battalions with insufficient personnel to reorganize them on coming out of action.

The 'battle surplus', as it was called, thus provided a framework on which the battalion could be rebuilt, not just physically, but spiritually as well, in that it preserved the character of the unit. This was even more important since reinforcement drafts were often not of the same cap badge. Thus, when the 2nd West Yorkshires came out of the Battle of Le Transloy:

> A draft of 200 men had joined us. Circumstances permitting reinforcements from the Base are sent to their own regiments; but the battles of the Somme have imposed an exceptional drain on personnel, and this draft consists largely of Northumbrian and Durham miners, with a sprinkling of Midland lads and cavalry, besides some of our own corps. We

hope that the strangers will soon settle down, as I have done,* to be West Yorkshiremen while with the Regiment.[10]

For those infantrymen who were found to be medically unfit by the IBDs, what was called the Permanent Base Battalion was established at Etaples in November 1916. This had an initial establishment of 4,300 men. A number were retained for work in the Etaples area, while the remainder were posted to units on the lines of communication, some to replace Category A men who could then be re-employed at the Front and others to the rapidly increasing number of Prisoner of War companies. Some of the early arrivals were Bantam rejects from the 35th Division (*see page 135*) and the CO was impressed by them, noting that they performed well in ordnance and supply depots, as well as in humping ammunition for the anti-aircraft units.

By January 1917, the PB Battalion was receiving some 200 men daily from the IBDs and the Details Camp, which supplied local labour and was just over 1,100 strong, of whom 39 per cent were in their 20s, 25 per cent were aged 30 to 40, 31 per cent were in their 40s, and 5 per cent were over 50. (Although no under-20s are mentioned, this gives a relatively accurate representation of the overall age make-up of the BEF at this time.)

By April 1917 the CO had drawn up an employment classification. Category 1 were suitable for employment as batmen; 2 as cycle orderlies; 3 for digging duty with the Graves Registration Unit (GRU); 4 were 'light fatigues'; 5 were suitable as POW escorts; 6 as stretcher bearers; and 7 for heavy fatigues. But, by the end of May he was complaining that the camp was 'choked with PB men classified 1, 2, and 4', noting that some had been at Etaples for over a year. These categories were the most difficult to find worthwhile employment for and the following month a medical board was established to identify the 'weakly' PB men so that they could be sent back to Britain. In September 1917 the PB Battalion was retitled the Employment Base Depot Etaples.[11] Similar depots were established in other French ports in the British zone and in March 1918 they underwent another change of title, becoming Nos. 1 (Havre), 2 (Rouen), 3 (Etaples), and 4 (Calais) Employment Base Depots.[12]

* Jack's parent regiment was the Scottish Rifles (Cameronians).

Efforts were also made during 1916 and 1917 to weed out under-age soldiers in France and get them returned to Britain. ACI 1186 of June 1916 laid down that parents could reclaim their sons if they were aged under 18. This meant that they were returned from France and then discharged. Those between 18 and 19 years old were to be retained and, if in France, would be sent to training units in the base area. The 1st Artists' Rifles, among its many other roles, acted as a holding unit for these youngsters and arranged for them to be sent back to the base. In April 1917, there appears to have been a change of policy. The boys in France were to be retained at the base until they attained the age of 18, when they would be returned to their units. They were formed into a special unit under the command of Major H. Cardinal-Harford and this was taken under the wing of No. 29 Infantry Base Depot at Etaples. Cardinal-Harford was 'given a free hand with regard to the selection of the staff to be formed from Base details, and gather together a really fine set of NCOs, all of whom had been wounded and were unfit for the Front'. The boys themselves were formed into five companies – Scottish, Northern, Southern, Midland, and one of Irish, Welsh and South Africans. In addition, Cardinal-Harford also received a number of Immatures, 19- and 20-year-olds who had undeveloped bodies, some of them doubtless former Bantams. In due course, he had some 1,200 under-age and immature soldiers under his command. Training, good food, and plenty of opportunities for sport were used to both keep them active and improve their physique. In January 1918, after the reorganization of the IBDs, the unit moved to Cayeux at the mouth of the River Somme, where it came under the umbrella of No. 5 Convalescent Camp. The influx of under-age soldiers eventually just about dried up, but the problem of the Immatures remained and in September 1918 they were formed into Nos. 1 and 2 Young Soldiers Battalions, with a third such battalion being raised the following month.[13]

Private John Dewar was an under-age volunteer, but he was not combed out. He enlisted as a Bantam in the 18th Highland Light Infantry and arrived in France in February 1916, aged 16. When the battalion ceased to be designated a Bantam unit and was amalgamated with elements of the Glasgow Yeomanry, which had been dismounted, Dewar was transferred to 10/11 HLI. He was wounded at Arras in April 1917 and again at Laventie a year later. During this time he had had one home leave, in July 1917. He was due for another when the German March 1918 offensive broke. After recovering from his wound in France, he was posted to 2 HLI. He survived two tours in the trenches before reporting sick with dysentery, but apparently the MO did not think that there was anything wrong with him and he was punished, presumably for malingering, with ten days CB. It was the final straw for young Dewar. He went absent and found himself near Calais, where he fell in with another absentee, Private J. Flanagan of the 1st King's Liverpool. Flanagan had a revolver and the two eventually found themselves in Saint Omer, where they disguised themselves as an RE sergeant major and sergeant. A military police sergeant attempted to arrest them but was shot dead. Eventually, they were apprehended and were court-martialled in December 1918. Both were given the death sentence, although this was commuted to several years of penal servitude.[14] One can only presume that Dewar never did come clean about his age and by April 1918 it was too late.

In mid December 1917, the IBDs underwent further major changes, partially as a result of the Etaples mutiny (*see page 403*). They were radically reduced in number and were given letter titles running from A to M. Thus, No. 29 IBD now became D Infantry Base Depot. While it was largely supplying battalions of the Royal Warwicks before the change, its remit was now broadened and it found itself providing drafts for nine regiments, including the Royal Warwicks, the Somerset Light Infantry, the Hampshires, the Wiltshires and the Newfoundland Regiment.* By this time three of the IBDs (K, L and M) were based at Calais, with M supplying drafts for Scottish regiments and L supporting the 16th (Irish) Division.[15] The Guards Division depot retained its title, and as far as the other infantry depots went, there was one dedicated to Garrison battalions and others to Australian and Canadian infantry. The other base depots remained dedicated to particular arms and services, with the cavalry base depot incorporating military police drafts. There was also an RHA/RFA base depot, an RGA base depot and a separate depot for the Royal Marine Artillery. The Royal Engineers

---

* Because Newfoundland had Dominion status in its own right (it did not become a province of Canada until 1949), the regiment served with the British Army, rather than the Canadian Expeditionary Force. It was granted the 'Royal' prefix for its performance at Cambrai in November 1917.

had a general depot as well as one dedicated to the Signal Service. There were Tank Corps and Machine Gun Corps depots, and one for the Cyclist Corps, which also included RAMC personnel. The QMAAC had its own depot, as did the New Zealanders, the Australians and the Canadians. The ASC had one depot to cover horse transport and supply and another for its mechanical transport branch. The Army Veterinary Corps incorporated its depot with No. 2 Veterinary Hospital, while the transportation troops also had their own depot. There were three Indian depots: one for Royal Artillery ammunition column personnel,* a general depot and a third for the Indian Labour Corps. While the Labour Corps itself had its own depot, there were special depots for the British West Indies Regiment and for Chinese labourers. There were also the four base employment depots.

Drafts proceeding up the line in France did so by rail. Once close to the line, if the unit they were going to was out of the trenches, the drafts would go directly to it, either by lorry or on foot. If not, there were a number of options. During 1915–17 they could be sent to an Entrenching battalion (*see page 221*) or to a divisional or corps reinforcement camp. However, with the major reorganization of the IBDs in late 1917, the 'top up' training of drafts was handed over to the corps reinforcement camps.

The reduction in the number of IBDs in France was also indicative of the growing manpower problem which the army was facing, especially with regard to infantry. On 6 December 1917, the War Cabinet decided to establish a committee headed by Lord Derby and General Sir Nevil Macready, the Adjutant General, to investigate the matter. According to Maurice Hankey, Chief of the War Cabinet Secretariat, Derby and Macready did not make a convincing case. On the one hand, at the same time that Haig was claiming that Third Ypres had drained the German divisions, they were pleading a shortage of manpower in France. 'The fact is, however, that the War Office figures and statements are utterly unreliable, and their facts are twisted to support their arguments' wrote Hankey. 'If they want men they make out that their can hardly hold the line … If they want to do an offensive they make out that the enemy is exhausted and demoralised, and that they have lots of men.'[16] On the other hand, Allenby was

---

* Indians replaced British artillerymen in many of the divisional ammunition columns as another means of reallocating manpower. A number of junior cavalry officers were also seconded to the DACs.

clamouring for more divisions to be sent to Palestine so that he could finish off the Turks. He was supported in this by the War Cabinet, especially Lloyd George, who believed that a speedy defeat of Turkey would make troops available for other theatres. Four divisions were also en route from France to Italy to prop up the Italians after the Central Powers' break-through at Caporetto, and Plumer, who was commanding the British con-tingent, had been promised two more. In addition, Russia was now to all intents and purposes out of the war, enabling the Germans to reinforce their armies in the west to a significant degree. Hopes that the Americans might place some of their troops under British command in France were also soon to be dashed by Pershing's determination that the American Expeditionary Force (AEF) should fight as a distinct entity and not allow itself to be dissipated piecemeal among the Allies. Furthermore, the BEF had agreed to extend its sector southwards, taking over an additional 30 miles of front from the French.

The War Office calculated that 600,000 Category A men would need to be called up during 1918 to maintain its existing strength overseas. Given that in October 1917 only just over 37,000 recruits of all medical categories had been received and that in December 1917, when the estimate was drawn up, this total fell to 25,000, this was a very optimistic demand. It could only be satisfied by radically reducing the quotas for the Royal Navy, industry and agriculture. Neither the Manpower Committee nor the War Cabinet were prepared to do this, especially since denying industry might well bring about economic collapse. Lloyd George himself, horrified by the casual-ties incurred during Third Ypres, had no wish to provide Haig with more cannon fodder for another offensive. Indeed, the War Cabinet believed that the Allies should remain on the defensive in France throughout 1918 to enable the Americans to build up their strength. Consequently, the Manpower Committee was not prepared to allocate more than 100,000 men to the army.[17] As the DMO, General Sir Frederick Maurice, gloomily noted in his diary on 5 January: 'Got copy of Cabinet Committee on manpower. Most depressing. Navy – Air Service – food – ship-building – timber felling all given precedence of the Army. We shall get little or nothing.'[18] As it was, three home service divisions, the 71st, 72nd and 73rd, had to be broken up in early 1918 and the number of Category A and B men available for posting fell by nearly 44 per cent between January and February 1918.[19]

In the light of the manpower shortage and the fact that the average infantry battalion in the BEF was the equivalent of a company's worth of men under strength, Haig accepted that he could not maintain the forty-eight British infantry divisions that he had in France on their existing thirteen-battalion organization. He himself wanted to disband divisions, but the War Cabinet advocated reducing the number of battalions in each, something that other armies, especially the French, had already done. Consequently, Haig decided to reduce each brigade by one battalion. This was to be done by amalgamating battalions or disbanding them and sending their men to other battalions with the same cap badge. The policy was that no Regular or first-line Territorial battalion should be disbanded and that second- and third-line TF units and the later-formed Service battalions would be given priority for disbandment.[20] Pioneer battalions were exempted. The reorganization took place during late January and February 1918. A total of 147 battalions were affected. Of these, twenty-two pairs of TF battalions were amalgamated and twenty-one TF battalions disbanded, together with eighty-four Service battalions. Usually, second-line TF battalions were amalgamated with first line. The principle of disbanding the more junior Service battalions was not, however, strictly adhered to. There was also not an even spread among the regiments. Thus, all three Service battalions of the Northamptons survived, although one was a Pioneer battalion, while the Royal Irish Rifles lost five battalions. This was partly because those who were the most under strength tended to 'go to the wall' and, in the case of the Irish regiments, replacement manpower was always a problem because there was no conscription in Ireland. Indeed, during 1916 only 19,000 Irish recruits had come forward and this total fell to 14,000 in 1917 and had already caused amalgamations among some of the Irish battalions.[21] The early 1918 disbandments initially affected only the divisions in France and Flanders, but the 41st Division, which had been sent to Italy, returned to France in mid March 1918 and immediately lost three of its battalions. In contrast, the 5th Division, which came back from Italy the following month, maintained its thirteen-battalion structure until October 1918.

The majority of men from the disbanded battalions were sent to other battalions in the same regiment, but there was a surplus of some 20,000, who were formed into Entrenching battalions (*see page 239*). A number of the surviving battalions were also moved to different brigades, sometimes to different divisions. Three battalions of the Guards Division were formed into the 4th Guards Brigade and moved to the 31st Division to replace one of its brigades which had been broken up. Guy Chapman, with the 13th Royal Fusiliers, which was posted to another brigade within the 37th Division, received a large draft from the disbanded 20th Royal Fusiliers:

> The main problem at present was the absorption of the new officers, NCOs, and men. The newcomers were nearly as strong as ourselves, and though they were willing enough to conform to our tenets and customs, they were naturally reluctant to part with those of their disbanded battalion. All tried honestly to achieve a common basis, but at first the process was slow. Some things we did they considered silly; some they believed in we thought rank heresy.[22]

But there was little time for the reshaped battalions to settle down before the German March 1918 offensive struck.

On 23 March, two days after the German attack opened, General Maurice noted in his diary: 'All our drafts in France are already exhausted and by stripping England of men we can just about replace our casualties.'[23] But to do this, the authorities felt forced to break the under-19 rule and send out soldiers aged 18$\frac{1}{2}$ and over, who had had six months training, to France.[24] This 'practically denuded' the battalions of 1st Training Reserve Brigade.[25] But all Graduated battalions felt the strain. The 52nd Notts & Derby had four companies at the time. A Company had recently arrived from the 53rd (Young Soldiers) Battalion, but C, D and E were trained. There was no time to allow draft leave for the men of C and D Companies and they went to France on 28 March and were in the firing line within two weeks. E Company had a little more time and its men did receive four days' leave before crossing the Channel on 14 April. During those hectic days, the young reinforcements, who became known as A4 Boys, were seldom posted to battalions of the regiment in which they had trained. Frederick Hodges had been in a Graduated battalion of the Bedfords and arrived in Calais, wearing their cap badge, in April 1918. He and his fellows appear to have been earmarked as reinforcements for 17th (Northern) Division:

> ... we were lined up in a very long single row. We were then counted off into groups destined for different battalions. Friends who stood in line next to one another were parted by a hand and an order, and marched off to different Regimental Base Headquarters. These were bell tents in a long line, where our particulars were taken, and to our surprise, new regimental numbers were given to us. My number was changed from 44243 to 57043. In this peremptory way, I and about 300 others suddenly became Lancashire Fusiliers, while some of our friends became Manchesters or Duke of Wellingtons or East Yorkshires.[26]

Eighteen-year-old Jimmy Taylor had done his training with the 3rd/19th Londons (St. Pancras), but on arrival in France was rebadged 2nd Worcesters: 'As I had never developed any particular loyalty for the London Regiment, into which I had been unceremoniously thrust a few months previously, and no one had taken time or trouble to tell us anything about the traditions or battle honours of the regiment, it was not difficult to transfer to a new regiment equally unknown.'[27] On the other hand, and unusually, the whole of E Company 52nd Notts & Derby was sent to reinforce the 10th Lincolns.[28]

On 7 April, Sir Sam Fay wrote in his diary that over 200,000 men had been sent to France in the past ten days.[29] But the total BEF casualties in France during March and April were over 281,000 and the overall strength of the British contribution, excluding Labour units, fell by 53,500.[30] Two days later, as the Germans launched their next offensive on the Lys, Lloyd George, who had been attempting to blame the debacle of March 1918 on Haig, told Parliament that the British Army in France had been stronger in January 1918 than it had been twelve months earlier. This was true in that it had risen from 1,591,745 to 1,828,616 men, including Dominion and other troops. But what Lloyd George failed to admit was the steep rise in the percentage of non-combatant troops, from 15.51 per cent in September 1916 to 32.27 per cent in March 1918.[31] Indeed, it was the reduction in the number of combatant troops, especially infantry, which had forced Haig to reorganize his infantry divisions. At bottom, there was a widely held suspicion in military circles that Lloyd George had been purposely holding back Category A troops in Britain so as to prevent Haig carrying out his plan of a further offensive in Flanders, something which he had proposed.* Furthermore, Lloyd George also claimed that Allenby's forces in Palestine contained a mere three 'white' divisions, when the true total was seven.

Sir Frederick Maurice, who had been DMO since the end of 1915, crossed to France on 14 April. It was his farewell visit to the BEF in post, since Sir Henry Wilson, who had succeeded Robertson as CIGS, wanted to replace him with someone who had more recent experience of the Front. Maurice noted in his diary the following day: 'People here are very dissatisfied with LG's speech of 9 April.' He appears, however, to have initially taken little notice of the newspaper reports on the speech, for on 20 April he wrote in his diary: 'Went through LG's speech again. Pity I didn't read it before. It is clearly an attempt to shovel off responsibility on to the soldiers while trying to treat them generously.'[32] On the same day, Maurice handed over to General Percy Radcliffe, who had been BGGS to the Canadian Corps for the past two years.

Maurice continued to mull over the Lloyd George speech in his mind. Finally, on 30 April, he wrote to the CIGS telling him of the bad effect it had had on the army in France, producing 'a feeling of Distrust & lack of confidence … You probably know this already but although I have ceased to be your DMO I think it right to make certain that you are aware of it.' Wilson left a written comment on the letter, to which he did not reply: 'Maurice never mentioned this when he was DMO.' He did, however, show it to Lord Milner, who had taken over from Derby as the Secretary of State for War. He commented: 'Similar representations have been made to me. There is, of course, something in them.'[33] Receiving no response from Wilson, Maurice decided to take the bull by the horns and wrote to the Press, accusing the government of lying. His letter was published in four newspapers on 7 May and was, as the *Star* called it, a 'bombshell'. There was a clamour for Lloyd George to answer Maurice's allegations and for an official inquiry into them. At this juncture, the Adjutant General's department produced revised figures for the British strengths in France on

---

* This was not so. In January 1917 the number of Category A1 men (ready for posting overseas) was 321,139 all ranks. By January 1918 the total had fallen to 125,470. [*Statistics of the Military Effort* pp. 112, 115]

1 January 1917 and 1 January 1918. The flaw with the original figures, which Lloyd George had used in his original speech and which had been prepared by Maurice's deputy, was that they included 86,000 troops which had been sent to Italy towards the end of 1917. When Lloyd George got up in the House of Commons on 9 May, he chose to ignore these revised figures, and launched an attack on Maurice, stating that the original figures had come from his, Maurice's, own department. He concluded by stating that he had just returned from France, where the generals had warned him that the Germans were preparing 'perhaps the biggest offensive of the war'. The generals wanted 'certain help' and Lloyd George had 'brought home a list of the things they wanted done, and I wished to attend to them'. He concluded: 'I really beg and implore, for our common country, the fate of which is in the balance now and in the next few weeks, that there should be an end to this sniping.'[34] It was a masterly performance and won him a majority of 187 votes against the setting up of a select committee to investigate Maurice's allegations. Maurice himself was left with no option but to resign his commission. As Haig commented in his diary on 7 May: 'No one can be both a soldier and a politician at the same time.'[35] The whole affair illustrated the passions aroused by the army's manpower crisis.

In the meantime, the Military Service (No. 2) Act was brought into effect. This raised the age ceiling for conscription to 50 (55 for the RAMC), although boys of 17 and men aged 51 to 55 could be accepted as volunteers. It could not, however, help overcome the immediate manpower shortage in France. Not only would these men need to be first trained before they could be of any use, but 17-year-olds could still not be sent to the Front while those above 40 were most unlikely to be fit enough to be fighting troops and could only be used to replace Category A men serving in the rear areas or at home. Nevertheless, the monthly recruiting figures were increased from barely 30,000 men in March 1918 to over 88,000 in June, although they thereafter fell away again.[36] But further comb-outs were already taking place in France. The cause of this was the decimation of no less than ten divisions as a result of the German March and April offensives.

The Labour Corps was particularly hard hit, with many of its fitter men being formed into Garrison Guard and Provisional Garrison Guard battalions for holding quiet sectors of the line (*see page 240*). A request from GHQ in France for more B1 men to be sent out to France resulted in eight battalions being sent out from Britain in May 1918. They were made up of seven TF battalions (25th King's Liverpool, 23rd Cheshires, 15th Essex, 2nd/6th Durham Light Infantry, 11th Royal Scots Fusiliers, 11th Somerset Light Infantry, 36th Northumberland Fusiliers) and the 2nd (Home Service) Garrison Battalion the Royal Irish Regiment. On arrival, they were all designated Garrison Guard battalions and all bar the Cheshire and Royal Irish Battalions were taken over by the 59th Division, which had been badly mauled during the recent fighting on both the Somme and the Lys. The division also took over the five Provisional Garrison Guard battalions, together with the 4th (Garrison Guard) Battalion the Royal Welsh Fusiliers, which had been in France since May 1916. On 25 May all these battalions were given new titles. Thus, the 1st Provisional Garrison Guard Battalion became the 17th (Garrison) Battalion Worcesters, while the Royal Welsh Fusiliers battalion dropped 'Guard' from its title.[37]

Another formation which had suffered heavy casualties was the 40th Division. During the first half of June its losses were made good by addition of the 6th to 11th Garrison Guard Battalions of the Labour Corps, and four of the battalions sent out from Britain, two of these being transferred from the 59th Division. The Garrison Guard battalions were now also given regimental titles.[38] The understanding was that, because the men of these battalions were Medical Category B, they would be used for line holding only.* Some within the two divisions had other ideas. F. P. Crozier, a brigade commander in the 40th Division, had three of these battalions: the 13th East Lancashires (formerly the 8th Garrison Guard Battalion); the 13th Royal Inniskilling Fusiliers (formerly the 7th Garrison Guard Battalion); and the 12th North Staffordshires (formerly the 12th Garrison Guard Battalion).

> I see the regimental doctors and tell them what I want. They comb out
> about fifty per cent of the old fellows whom they consider beyond hope

---

*The War Office view of how these men should be used is amplified by an Army Council discussion, probably on 3 July, over the sending of two complete Category B divisions to France. Sir Sam Fay was present at it and recorded that they should have a fortnight's training in Lewis gun and rifle shooting. 'Thereafter, they might be sent to a very quiet part of the front if necessary, they are unable to march more than a few miles, and that without packs and *very slowly* [sic], and will be provided with sufficient transport to enable them to move a short distance.' [Fay, *War Office at War*, p. 181] of physical redemption. After repeating this performance with fresh drafts, we at length have three battalions and a trench-mortar battery which I consider will be capable of being mesmerised out of themselves. 'It is great to forget one is ill: it is fine to be fit', became our slogan.[39]

The battalions were designated Service battalions in July and were soon operating as such. Indeed, the 13th Royal Inniskilling Fusiliers won a DSO, four MCs and eleven MMs as a result of its first significant action at the end of August.[40]

Two other Garrison battalions were sent to France from Britain in July 1918. The 1st Garrison Battalion KOYLI became the 16th (Garrison) Battalion KOYLI and deployed a company to each of the four armies, where they were employed on manning traffic and examining posts, thus relieving the military police of some of their burdens.[41] The North Staffords' 1st Garrison Battalion became the 13th (Garrison) Battalion North Staffords and was employed on the lines of communication.

The 40th and 59th Divisions were resurrected in time to take part in the final Allied offensives, but others were not so fortunate. The 39th Division was reduced to a cadre. It lost all but two Infantry battalions, its trench mortars and machine guns, and was used largely to train American troops. Its artillery was also removed for a time to become army field artillery brigades. The 66th (East Lancashire) Division was another formation which suffered heavily in March 1918. All its battalions were reduced to cadres and it lost its artillery and machine guns. It spent the summer reorganizing and being used as a training cadre. During this time, five of its original ten battalions were disbanded and three posted to other divisions. In their place, it received new battalions, including three Irish ones from the 10th (Irish) Division, which was in Palestine. At the same time, the division had pass through it no less than twenty-four other battalions, most of them at cadre strength, for which it acted as a foster-mother while their future was determined. Some were posted to other divisions and others disbanded or absorbed. Eventually, on 23 September 1918, the division received a fresh formation, the South African Brigade from the 63rd (Royal Naval) Division and said farewell to its 197th Brigade. During

October it was in action at Cambrai and in the battles around the River Selle, but it did not receive a Machine Gun battalion until the middle of that month and its integral artillery was not returned until three days before the armistice. As for the 197th Brigade, it retained ten of the battalion cadres and its trench mortar battery and was used to train young soldiers on the lines of communication in France, with no less than 10,000 men passing through its hands in October alone. The 34th Division was also reduced to a cadre for a time and used to train US troops. It was, however, reconstituted in June 1918, but by then its original character had been totally transformed. Two of its brigades had originally been made up of Royal Northumberland Fusiliers, but one, the 103rd (Tyneside) Irish, had had all its original battalions disbanded during the February 1918 reorganization. Now the other lost its Fusilier battalions and the division as a whole was transformed from being New Army to one consisting of TF battalions with a stiffening of Regulars.

Three other badly mauled divisions – the 14th, 16th and 25th – went back to Britain to re-form. The 14th (Light) Division lost all its rifle and light infantry battalions and was re-formed largely from newly raised Service battalions, spending just three weeks in England before returning to France. The new Service battalions themselves were all formed in June 1918 and consisted largely of men combed out of home service units, with the balance made up of newly trained 18- and 19-year-olds, although these were from Special Reserve rather than Graduated battalions. Research on those who were later killed while serving with these battalions reveals that a number had had previous service in France but had presumably been sent home wounded or sick.[42] Twenty-three of these battalions were created and all bar four were sent to France. Some were absorbed by the battalion cadres which had returned from France, while others took over the cadres themselves. Every effort was made to ensure that these mergers involved battalions of the same regiment or from the same part of the country, although this did not always work in practice. Thus, the newly formed 25th Welsh Regiment was taken over by the 18th Welsh cadre, while the 18th York and Lancaster absorbed the cadre of the 2nd/7th West Yorkshires.

One of the new battalions, the 29th Durham Light Infantry, formed on 19 June at Brookwood in Surrey, initially consisted of just the cadre of the 2nd/7th Duke of Wellington's, which had arrived from France and was a mere nine officers (including the CO) and fifty other ranks strong. That same day it received a draft of 103 men from the West Riding Reserve Brigade TF, followed late on the same night by a further 800 men from no less than eight northern regiments. All were Medical Category B1 and B2. It was soon noted that their training was 'very backward', but the priority was equipping them for overseas service. Matters were not helped by the fact that no further officers were posted in until 27 June, although a few were loaned by two of the other new battalions, the 33rd Londons TF and the 18th York and Lancasters. There was also an awareness that a significant number of men were unlikely to be fit for foreign service. Indeed, over 250 potentially unfit men were identified by 24 June. The following day, a Travelling Medical Board (TMB) found forty-two men to be totally unfit and categorized a further 100 as B3, meaning that they could be posted overseas but employed only in sedentary jobs. However, this was partly compensated for by the arrival of another draft of 100 men from the 27th Durhams. In spite of all, the men were able to fire on the open range and carry out some training, including testing their gasmasks. This was just as well since, on the last day of June, 29 DLI received orders to proceed overseas. The transport and baggage entrained on the following day, when another TMB found an additional 227 men to be unfit for foreign service. On the night 2/3 July the main body left for France, just two weeks after the battalion's formation.[43]

The experience of the 33rd Londons was slightly different. It was formed at Clacton on 7 June as the 33rd London Regiment (Royal Fusiliers) but was to be administered by the 29th Londons, who were also at Clacton. The first drafts of both officers and men came from other battalions of the London Regiment, but these were followed by sizeable numbers of men from the 17th Gloucesters and the 2nd/8th Essex, both being TF training units, and 28 DLI, a Home Service battalion. The 2nd/1st Denbighshire Yeomanry also supplied eighty-six men. On 13 June, the battalion was finally given a commanding officer, Lieutenant Colonel J. W. Stackpoole of the Royal Munster Fusiliers. Drafts continued to trickle in. Then, on 18 June, the battalion moved to Pirbright, where it was joined by the 'training staff' of the 7th Rifle Brigade, which was actually its cadre. Initially, it was thought that 7 RB would merely train and administer the battalion, but on the following day the cadre took control. The battalion was retitled the 33rd London Regiment (Rifle Brigade) and the CO of the cadre took over command, Colonel Stackpoole being posted back to his own regiment. Like 29 DLI, it crossed to France at the beginning of July, though not before 141 men had been classified as unfit for overseas service and posted to the 225th Mixed Brigade.*[44] The merging of TF and Service battalions was itself a further indication of the blurring that was taking place between the Territorial Force and the remainder of the army.

The 25th Division spent somewhat longer in England – some six weeks. It lost its 75th Brigade, which was renamed the 236th and earmarked for north Russia, but the original brigade was reconstituted. The original intention may have been to bring the division back up to strength by incorporating some of the new Service battalions, but there were not enough available. In any event, it was the three divisions in Italy – the 7th, 23rd and 48th – which provided the solution. They were finally put on the ten-battalion organization in September 1918 and the nine battalions made surplus were sent back to France and joined the newly returned 25th Division.

The 16th (Irish) Division faced the problem of a shortage of recruits from Ireland. The question of introducing conscription had been reconsidered by the War Cabinet as a result of the huge losses resulting from the March 1918 offensive. The April 1918 Military Service Act did authorize its introduction by proclamation, but the outcry against it from nationalist elements and, indeed, also from loyalists, who objected to the promises of Home Rule on a partition basis which accompanied the measure, caused the government not to put it into practice. Consequently, the 16th Division was left with just one Irish battalion, the 5th Royal Irish Fusiliers, which had come from the 10th (Irish) Division in Palestine and had then absorbed the regiment's 11th Battalion, which itself had incorporated the cadre of the 7th Royal Dublin Fusiliers. The remaining new battalions in the division were either newly formed Service battalions or existing cadres which had absorbed these new battalions. They represented English, Scots and Welsh

---

* Mixed brigades were formed in autumn 1917 from existing home service infantry brigades. Each consisted of four TF battalions, an RFA battery, a field company RE, an ASC company and a field ambulance. Some had a heavy battery RGA attached. They were numbered 221 to 227.

regiments. Only the divisional Pioneer battalion, the 11th Hampshires, remained of its original infantry units. The 10th (Irish) Division in Palestine also lost its national character. True, it kept the three Regular Irish battalions which had joined it in Salonika in November 1916, but all its Service battalions, including the pioneers, returned to Europe and their places were taken by Indian battalions. As a result, it lost its 'Irish' title.

This policy of Indianization affected other divisions in Egypt and Palestine and was part of a deliberate policy to release British troops so that they could also be used to make good the strength of the armies in France. Both the 53rd (Welsh) and 60th (London) Divisions underwent the same process in summer 1918, each retaining just three British battalions. The 75th Division, which had begun to form in April 1917, was essentially made up of Territorial battalions from India. It sent three battalions to France in May 1918, two joining the 62nd Division and one the 34th Division. These were replaced by Indian battalions. A further three battalions were disbanded that August. Two other divisions were sent to France complete. The 52nd (Lowland) Division was redeployed at the end of March and, to bring it down to the ten-battalion organization, in June it passed three of its battalions to 34th Division. The other division to move complete was the 74th (Yeomanry) Division. This had been formed in March 1917 from dismounted Yeomanry brigades which had been manning defences on the Suez Canal. It took part in the Palestine campaign from the second Battle of Gaza in April 1917 onwards and moved to France a year later. It was given a Pioneer battalion, the 1st/12th Loyal North Lancashires TF, previously part of the 60th Division, just before it left Egypt, but lost three of its thirteen battalions to the 31st Division in June 1918. The result of these redeployments was that just one purely British infantry division was left in Palestine. The 54th (East Anglian) Division had fought in Gallipoli between August and December 1915 and had then moved to Egypt. It was the only division in the army to retain four-battalion brigades, although it never had a Pioneer battalion. The four divisions in Salonika – the 22nd, 26th, 27th and 28th – also contributed to the forces in France. Each lost three battalions during June and July 1918, with five going to the 50th Division, six to the 66th Division and one to the lines of communication.

The German amphibious threat against Britain had receded, but there was still the possibility of a major raid. Thus, though the home defence forces were reduced they remained in place. By October 1918, East Anglia, the most threatened area, was protected by XXIII Corps, based on the 64th, 67th and 68th Divisions. Both the 64th and 68th Divisions were entirely made up of Graduated battalions, while the 67th had eight of these battalions and what was called the 214th Special Brigade, which had two infantry and two Cyclist battalions. There was also Kent Force (formerly Independent Force), with its HQ at Canterbury and consisting largely of cyclist troops. Additionally, a number of local defence commands covered the East Coast from Lincolnshire up to and including the Firth of Forth. The Volunteer Force also played an active part. In June 1918, Special Service companies were formed from among the Volunteers, presumably to make good the reduction in manpower created by the formation of the new Service battalions. Ernest Cooper, the Town Clerk of Southwold commanded one: 'We understood we were to hold the coast until the troops in the depots and camps were rushed up in case of attack but we have good reason to believe that most of the available men from the camps had already gone and no doubt the situation was critical in the extreme.'[45]

By August 1918, with the Germans having finally shot their bolt in the west and the Allies poised to go over to the offensive, the BEF in France stood at just under 1.43 million, an increase in strength of 15,000 men over the total on 1 March. But significantly, in spite of the massive effort to make good the infantry losses during the past few months, the infantry's strength had fallen from nearly 515,000 on 1 March to just over 496,000 men. In contrast, the strength of the ASC had risen by 11,000 men and the Labour Corps by almost 5,000.[46] It reflected the army's continuing struggle to obtain sufficient Category A men. Indeed, on 1 August Sir Henry Wilson, the CIGS, commented to General John du Cane, the British representative to the Allied supremo, Ferdinand Foch:

> The more we look into the question of our manpower the uglier it seems
> to be. Agriculture, Vital industries for ourselves and our Allies, Coal,
> Shipbuilding, Aeroplane & Tank Construction – & personnel – & so on &
> so forth all show such formidable demands that little remains for the

fighting services. The Cabinet therefore are anxious about the future. They do not want to end the war in an absolutely exhausted condition.[47]

It was for this reason that the Cabinet was unwilling to share Haig's growing optimism after his success at Amiens on 8 August, when the Germans were driven back up to 7 miles in one day, that the war could be won before the end of 1918. Indeed, Lloyd George and others seriously believed that victory would not be achieved until 1920, once the US strength in France had become overwhelming, and wanted to reduce the British forces in France and Italy to a mere thirty-six divisions as a means of deterring Haig from any more costly offensives.[48] At the end of the month, as Haig began to approach the Hindenburg Line, Lloyd George ordered Wilson to send Haig a telegram cautioning him over his assault on it, and ending 'I know the War Cabinet would become anxious if we received heavy punishment in attacking the Hindenburg Line without success.' Haig was furious, seeing it as a ploy by Lloyd George to provide himself with an umbrella, should the attack fail. He wrote an irritable reply to Wilson, who, in turn, tried to placate Haig: 'No, it is not want of confidence in you so much as the feeling that, when the end comes, we must still possess a formidable army. My wire therefore was only intended to convey a sort of distant warning & nothing more.' Haig was not convinced and dashed across to London to see Lord Milner in order to instil some optimism.[49] Even so, the politicians remained anxious.

Between August 1918 and the Armistice, the British Army in France suffered just under 280,000 killed, wounded and missing, but it managed to maintain its overall strength at just over 2 million men. While the strength of the combatant arms, which bore the brunt of the casualties, fell by 60,000 men over the same period, there is no doubt that the reinforcement system was now sufficiently robust to sustain the BEF. If it had not been, it is doubtful whether Haig's men would have been so at the forefront of the successive Allied victories which eventually forced the Germans to seek an armistice. The same is also true of the victories in Italy, Salonika, Palestine and Mesopotamia. By this time, the four strands that now represented the British Army – Regular, Territorial, Kitchener volunteer and conscript – had been firmly welded into one.

ten

OFFICER SELECTION AND TRAINING

The 1914 Regular Army relied primarily on the Royal Military College Sandhurst and Royal Military Academy Woolwich for the supply of young officers. The latter trained officers for the 'scientific arms' – the Royal Artillery and Royal Engineers – while Sandhurst catered for the Cavalry, Infantry and Army Service Corps, as well as the Indian Army. Candidates had to sit an entrance exam and paid fees to attend. The course at Sandhurst lasted for eighteen months and was broken down into three terms, while that at Woolwich was of two years' duration. Woolwich supplied no less than 99 per cent of the Regular gunner and sapper officers, but Sandhurst provided only two-thirds of those in the other arms and services. Approximately 15 per cent of Regular officers came from the universities, having undergone training in the senior division of the Officers' Training Corps (OTC) at university and gained Certificate B.* Others came from the Special Reserve, which was regarded as the 'back door' to a Regular commission since no exam was involved and the candidate merely required suitable personal recommendations. Just 2 per cent, outside quartermasters and riding masters, who were on a separate roll, were commissioned from the

---

* This was another Haldane innovation. He also established the junior division of the OTC for schools, with cadets working towards Certificate A. The overall aim was to produce a pool of potential officers in time of general war. In November 1914, under War Office Instruction No. 22, examinations for Certificates A and B were suspended for the duration of the war.

ranks. Territorial Force officers also required Certificate B, but could also undergo an officers' training course at the Inns of Court. Some did transfer to the Regular Army.[1]

At the outbreak of war, the courses at the RMA Woolwich and RMC Sandhurst were reduced to six months and three months respectively and fees were suspended. The senior term at each institution had been commissioned shortly before the outbreak of war. The next most senior term at Woolwich was commissioned immediately, after the commandant had approved each case. The same applied to some who had been in what had been the junior term, the others staying on for a further two months before receiving their commissions. Thus, John Wedderburn-Maxwell, who had been at Woolwich for six months, was commissioned into the RFA on 12 August and ordered to report to 45 Brigade RFA in Leeds. He went to France at the beginning of November with the 8th Division.[2] Much the same happened at Sandhurst, although those of the previous junior term were first given a four-week refresher course in tactics. The September entry faced the new abbreviated course, which would continue to result in Regular commissions, though the cadets found themselves having to cram a lot into their days. Francis Law, who was to serve in the Irish Guards, attended the first wartime course at Sandhurst:

> We were worked very hard as was only to be expected, for casualties in France had been heavy and a steady flow of trained young officers was required to replace those lost in battle. Our days started early and there was little time for games, though when there was we played vigorously. It was a tough but healthy life and being strong and fit I certainly enjoyed it, though a few broke down under the strain. Our training apart from drill was simple but strenuous and severely practical. The aim was to teach us speedily all that was thought necessary for a young platoon commander to know, that he might lead and inspire men in battle, and look to their welfare at all times. We took part in simple tactical exercises, map-reading, compass work by night, patrolling and shooting on the range. On the whole those of us who survived the first two months, and most of us did, learnt a lot, were reasonably competent and had gained an increased self-confidence.[3]

At Woolwich, after two weeks of basic training, the gunners and the sappers pursued separate courses of instruction. R. B. Talbot Kelly decided on a Regular commission in the gunners and returned to school for the autumn term 1914 to sit 'a curiously adapted exam' – the Civil Service entry exam which potential cadets for both the RMA and RMC continued to sit in order to gain entry.

> On a Saturday afternoon in October, at half time in a House match, a telegram was handed to me ordering me to report to the RMA Woolwich on the coming Monday. I was at the 'Shop'* from October 1914 until March 1915. The life was incredibly harsh and exacting. By the weekends we were utterly exhausted, mentally and physically. The exertions of the war itself were mild in comparison. Yet out of it, unnoticed by any of us, was bred self-confidence and a physical fitness undreamed of before. Quickness of eye and hand and brain were ruthlessly driven into us, and a standard of cleanliness, smartness and alertness demanded that gave us a lead to follow and maintain throughout our service. No excuses for failure in anything were taken, and soon never offered. But it was all for our good, and we left to join the Sappers or Gunners, unconsciously fitted to carry on their great tradition of service.[4]

By the end of the year there were 323 cadets at Woolwich and 960 at Sandhurst. But the latter included newly commissioned officers from the New Armies undergoing courses of instruction. Yet this was only a fraction of those aspiring to commissions or granted them and both groups urgently needed training.

Apart from the university OTCs, the only other officer producing unit in August 1914 was the Inns of Court, which largely trained officers for London TF regiments. It had gone to Perham Down on the edge of Salisbury Plain for its annual camp on 2 August, but was ordered to return to London in the early hours of the following morning. Lieutenant Colonel Errington, the commanding officer, expected to be deluged with new recruits but in fact only six reported to the headquarters in Lincoln's Inn during the 3rd. Errington therefore immediately wrote a letter to the news-

*The nickname for RMA Woolwich, from the fact that when founded in 1841 it was housed in a converted workshop in the Woolwich Arsenal.

papers. The effect was instantaneous, with no less than 213 men being enlisted during the next two days. Former members of the Inns of Court also returned to the Colours. Training was soon in full swing, part of it carried out on Wimbledon Common and in Richmond Park. On 10 August, however, Lord Kitchener published an appeal in *The Times* for 2,000 men between 18 and 31, who were of 'good education' and were 'cadets or ex-cadets of OTCs', to come forward to take temporary commissions in the New Armies. Errington immediately dashed up to the War Office and asked why the Inns of Court had not been approached. He was told that the unit had been overlooked, but the War Office promised that Inns of Court applications for commissions would be given priority. As it was, the majority of the early commissions granted to Inns of Court members were in the Special Reserve and it was not until the beginning of September that Errington was asked to supply officers for the New Armies.[5] Those men considered ready to take commissions were prepared by the adjutant, who ran a special instruction course, since the Director of Military Training had stressed that, because of the lack of experienced NCOs in the Kitchener battalions, officers were needed who were capable of training men without the help of non-commissioned instructors.

Yet the Inns of Court OTC could satisfy only a fraction of the demand for officers during the first few months of the war. The vast majority were commissioned direct, usually on the basis of school and/or university OTC experience. Those who had service with the senior division of the OTC merely had to present themselves at a university board and the names of those found suitable were sent to the War Office, which granted them commissions without further formality. Applicants who possessed only junior division service had to take the additional step of obtaining a commanding officer's recommendation. The poet Robert Graves had just left Charterhouse, having won a scholarship to Oxford, and was one of these. He was holidaying in north Wales when war broke out. He decided to join up and, thanks to a recommendation from the secretary of a local golf club, obtained a Special Reserve commission in the Royal Welsh Fusiliers. He reported to the regimental depot at Wrexham on 11 August and was gazetted four days later.

Most of the other applicants for commissions were boys who had failed to get into the Royal Military College at Sandhurst, and were now trying to get into the regular army at the old militia back-door – re-named the Special Reserve. Only one or two fellows had come, like myself, for the sake of the war, and not for the sake of a career.

Graves and his fellow second-lieutenants 'learned regimental history, drill, musketry, Boer War field-tactics, military law and organisation, how to recognise bugle calls, how to work out a machine-gun, and how to conduct ourselves on formal occasions.'[6] Those with Special Reserve commissions were soon being sent out to France to replace casualties in the Regular battalions.

Arthur Behrend, a trainee with the London & North Western Railway and former member of Sedbergh OTC, telegrammed the adjutant of the 4th East Lancashires TF, a family friend, on 6 August and received a reply the following day: 'Come tomorrow prepared to stay bring all necessary kit.' He spent his first few days in civilian clothes, but was soon kitted out at cost of £14 7s 6d with a service dress jacket with collar badges, one pair of breeches, one pair of slacks, two ties, one cap plus badge, Sam Browne belt with holster, one pair of puttees, one water bottle, one whistle and lanyard, greatcoat with stars and brass 'Ts' to denote Territorial Force and a greatcoat carrier. He was also supposed to be equipped with a sword, for which the outfit allowance of £50 granted to each newly commissioned officer was more than adequate. But because of the ever rising flood of applications being received by the War Office, Behrend's commission was not gazetted until 5 September.[7]

Neville Lytton's entry was even more informal. He was aged 36 and hence over-age when the war broke out. He was of independent means, married with a family and lived in Sussex. Despite having no military experience, he was moved to answer the call. He

noticed that Colonel Claude Lowther had obtained leave from Lord Kitchener to raise a battalion of Sussex men, and I determined to go to him and put myself at his disposition. He received me most amiably, and I told him that I was willing to be a private in his battalion; he asked me whether I had any influence in the county and whether I thought I could raise him some men. I said that I had a certain amount, and that I would do my best, so he gave me a big parcel of attestation papers and sent me off. The next day I hired a car and started on a tour of my part of the county; some days I got a doctor to come with me and, being a JP [Justice of the Peace] myself, we examined and swore in the men then and there as we went from house to house ... After about a fortnight's work I had got together the best part of a company, which was not so bad.

During his spare time Lytton received coaching from a drill sergeant and practised the words of command on his family, but 'found it difficult at that stage of my military career to get a squad composed of my two daughters and a governess to form fours satisfactorily.'[8] Lowther's battalion became the 11th (1st South Down) Battalion the Royal Sussex Regiment with Lytton, in spite of his lack of military experience, one of its company commanders.[*]

However, those without a public school education were often refused commissions in the early days, as R. C. Sherriff, the author of the play *Journey's End* and who had attended a very reputable grammar school, found out when he presented himself at the depot of his local county regiment.[9] A study of those who had been members of school OTCs and had been granted commissions up to March 1915 reveals that the bias against grammar schools was much more pronounced in southern England than in the rest of the country. Dartford Grammar School had a mere twenty-two old boys commissioned, while 121 were serving in the ranks. Maidstone Grammar School had much the same figures, with seventeen commissioned and 120 in the ranks. In contrast, Manchester Grammar School recorded thirty commissioned and ten other ranks, while Leeds Grammar had twenty-one officers and twenty-five in the ranks, and the Royal Grammar School Newcastle-upon-Tyne eleven and fourteen respectively.[10] The probable reason for this was the predominance of Pals battalions in the Midlands and North of England, with the managerial classes being selected for commissions regardless of their school education. But whether public school or not, it remained the case throughout the war that those commissioned into the New Armies were granted only temporary

[*] Lowther raised two further battalions of the Royal Sussex (the 12th and 13th). Their subsidiary titles were the 2nd and 3rd South Down, but the three battalions were known collectively as Lowther's Lambs.

commissions. After conscription was introduced in early 1916, this applied to all commissions, apart from those granted to cadets at Sandhurst and Woolwich and for officers transferring to Regular commissions. Those who held temporary commissions were disparagingly called 'temporary gentlemen' by the old Regular Army.

OTC experience was often not of much help to those who took commissions in the technical arms. Julian Tyndale-Biscoe was posted to C Battery RHA after being commissioned in mid September 1914. He met his battery commander, who said: 'Here is the Battery – I would like you to train these men.' When Tyndale-Biscoe told him that he had no artillery training, the reply was: 'Oh, that does not matter, you just watch the others do it, and then do it yourself.' The young subaltern then spent 'three or four miserable days watching the men being marched everlastingly around the barrack square, feeling as sorry for them as I was myself'. Becoming desperate, he managed to persuade his major to send him to an eight-week course at Woolwich, which he described 'as most interesting and pretty strenuous', the day beginning with stables at 6 a.m. and ending at 7 p.m., after an hour in the riding school. After dinner the students were required to study their manuals. But the course stood him in good stead and he returned to his battery with much greater confidence.[11] Not until 1915 did the Royal Artillery formally establish training schools for young officers.

In contrast, sapper officers fared better over technical training. Those commissioned from the 'Shop' were immediately sent on a young officers' course at Chatham. In peacetime this had been two years, but was now reduced to six months. With the exception of those with particular specialities, candidates for Special Reserve and temporary commissions had to have proven engineering knowledge. They could be recommended by the President of the Institute of Civil Engineers and/or have attended the senior division of the OTC, have a degree in engineering and a recommendation from their university OTC. Those from abroad had to have practical engineering experience and have passed an interview with AG7, the War Office branch that looked after RE personnel matters. Once commissioned, they attended a course in drill, riding and military engineering at a Reserve Training Centre (RTC). Initially, this lasted seven weeks and took place at Chatham, but during 1915 two further RTCs were opened, at Newark and Deganwy, and the course extended to eleven weeks.[12]

A shortage of ASC officers was identified early on and an ACI of 17 August 1914 instructed home commands to recruit 'capable local gentlemen aged, say, from 22–40, with a knowledge of business matters.' But not all had this background. Monk Gibbon left school in summer 1915. He had toyed with the idea of joining the Royal Naval Division, but his father dissuaded him on account of his small and slight stature. He had, however, won a history exhibition to Keble College, Oxford, and took up his place that October. He enrolled in the OTC, stating on the entry form that he wished to take a commission in the ASC, although he was warned that they were accepting few officers at his young age. Nevertheless, he applied and was promptly turned down. However, the wife of his family doctor happened to be the sister of General Sidney Long, the Director of Supplies and Transport at the War Office. Long sent his sister the necessary recommendation with a brief covering note: 'If young Gibbon sends the enclosed back to his Adjutant OTC together with a fresh application there should be no difficulty.' Just over two weeks later Gibbon had attained his goal and was ordered to report to No. 2 Reserve Horse Transport Depot at Blackheath, London. Training was concentrated on horsemanship and horsemastership, including learning to drive wagons, limbers and carts. He also attended a more demanding three-week course on the same subjects at the ASC Training Establishment at Aldershot. After being caught up in the 1916 Easter Rising in Dublin, where he was temporarily attached to a battalion of the Royal Irish Rifles in the city as their transport officer, he was in France early that summer.[13]

Some men quickly became impatient over the delays in granting their commissions. A. D. Gillespie, who was reading for the Bar, was a member of the cavalry squadron of the Inns of Court and attended the abortive camp at Perham Down. He wrote home on 2 August: 'I have just sent my name through the Colonel for a Commission in the Special Reserve of Officers.' He trained with the Inns of Court throughout August, but became frustrated by the non-appearance of his commission. He therefore joined the 4th Argyll and Sutherland Highlanders TF as a private soldier and obtained a commission in the regiment that October. Gillespie went to

France in February 1915 and was killed at Loos the following September. Cecil Slack tried first for a Regular commission and then offered himself for a Territorial commission. In the meantime, he joined the ranks of the 10th (Hull Commercials) Battalion of the East Yorkshires to gain some military experience. In due course, he was granted a commission in the 4th East Yorkshires. He therefore wrote to the CO of the 10th East Yorkshires to tell him that he was leaving.

> This apparently was not the correct procedure, and, shortly afterwards, whilst serving with the Territorials then stationed in Darlington, I received from my father a letter saying that a squad of soldiers had called at home to arrest me for desertion. In time the matter was cleared up and I received back-pay for the period of my 'desertion' as well as pay as a second lieutenant.[14]

Other men believed that enlisting as private soldiers would get them to France more quickly than if they applied for commissions. Among these were Christopher Stone and several of his friends who enlisted in the Public Schools Battalion of the Middlesex Regiment. It was only pressure from his wife that eventually made Stone apply for a commission, but he was twice turned down by his commanding officer, probably because of his short-sightedness.[15] The War Office viewed the Public Schools Battalion as a rich vein of potential officers and, by the end of 1914, 350 of its men had received commissions. In January 1915 the War Office demanded another 150 of its men, and it was probably as a result of this that Stone received his commission in the 22nd Royal Fusiliers. He rose to be second-in-command of his battalion before serving on the staff; he finished the war with the DSO and MC. The result of the 16th Middlesex giving up so many men (over 900 had been commissioned by July 1915) was that it soon lost its social character. Its commanding officer was also continually having to asked permission to recruit over the establishment figure of 1,100 men in order to maintain the battalion's effective strength. The same applied to the four battalions of Royal Fusiliers raised by the Public Schools and University Men's Force at Epsom in mid September 1914, as it also did to King Edward's Horse, which was formed from high quality volunteers from the Empire. Sir Ralph Furse, who served with the regiment, noted: 'We had to hand over most of our other ranks for promotion to commissioned rank (in the end over 500 men from the regiment got commissions) and train a new lot.'[16]

There is no doubt that the forming of New Army battalions such as the Public Schools, manned entirely by the middle and upper classes, aggravated the problem of finding sufficient officers for what was a rapidly expanding army. So, too, did the maintenance of some of the more prestigious Territorial Force regiments, or 'class corps', as fighting units. Indeed, commanding officers were dissuaded from encouraging wholesale applications for commissions by their men for fear that it would reduce their battalions to mere skeletons. That battalions like the Honourable Artillery Company (HAC), the London Scottish and the London Rifle Brigade were sent out to France early did not help, since the heavy casualties suffered by the BEF meant that these units were desperately needed to help hold the line. As the CO of the London Rifle Brigade reputedly pointed out in his reply to a request from the War Office to recommend some of his men for commissions, 95 per cent of them were suitable, but as this would mean the LRB becoming an OTC he did not wish to recommend any.[17]

The BEF had suffered heavy officer casualties in France during the opening weeks. As early as 19 September 1914, General Hubert Hamilton, commanding the 3rd Division and destined to be killed the following month, wrote personally to Kitchener pointing out that in one of his brigades the four battalions each had no more than five, six, seven and nine company officers respectively. 'The great pressing need is for officers. Without them the reinforcements are practically wasted.' Sir John French himself echoed this concern, pointing out to Kitchener five days later that such officer replacements as were being sent out were often 'young and almost untrained'. He warned: 'The proportion of reliable leaders to the men they have to direct and lead is becoming most serious throughout the Whole Force.' A statement giving the reinforcements sent to the 3rd Division on 23 September bore out his and Hamilton's claims. While each battalion in the division received some 160 men, the allocation of officers was only two per battalion and, apart from a couple of senior subalterns, they were all raw second lieutenants.[18]

The War Office laid down five measures to make good the losses. First, it turned its eye on the K1 battalions, laying down that one of the two

Regular captains and one or both of the Regular subalterns who had been ordered to join them were to be posted to France. The same applied to officers on leave from India and those who had been on the Reserve of Officers. Special Reserve battalions were also to be raided. Battalions at the Front were to promote from the ranks and to be prepared to accept officers of a different cap badge.[19] The units in France responded quickly to this. In a General Routine Order dated 1 October 1914, the commissioning of no less than 105 warrant officers and NCOs was announced. They were each given £150 outfit allowance, three times that for the normal newly commissioned officer. The 2nd Royal Welsh Fusiliers commissioned three of its senior ranks – the RSM, the RQMS and a CSM – at the end of October. Former RSM (now Second Lieutenant) Murphy bewailed his fate: 'There was I, a thousand men at my control, the Commanding Officer was my personal friend, the Adjutant consulted me, the Subalterns feared me, and now I am only a bum-wart and have to hold my tongue in Mess.'[20] Even so, many of these promotions did extremely well. Former CSM W. H. Stanway of the 2nd Royal Welsh Fusiliers was commanding a Service battalion of the Cheshires within two years of being commissioned and finished the war with a DSO and MC. The RQMS, P. B. Welton, also rose to command a battalion of South Wales Borderers and won a Military Cross. Equally distinguished was J. F. Plunkett of the Royal Irish Rifles. Recommended for a Victoria Cross as a warrant officer in 1914, he, too, was commanding a battalion by early 1917. His brigade commander, F. P. Crozier, recommended him for the VC for a second time, again unsuccessfully, for his performance during the Battle of Cambrai in November 1917. After this Plunkett was invalided home with a strained heart, but managed to get back to France in time for the final offensive in 1918. By the end of the war he was one of the most decorated officers in the army, with three DSOs, an MC, a DCM and the French *Croix de Guerre*.[21] Sergeant W. J. Cranston of the Greys, a Boer War veteran, was commissioned into the Royal Scots Fusiliers in July 1915. When the war ended he was the holder of the DSO, was a brevet lieutenant colonel, had commanded a Machine Gun battalion and had been recommended for command of a brigade.[22]

As for posting in officers from other regiments, the Regular battalions, whose officers regarded themselves as a close-knit family, did not at first relish this measure, but were forced to accept it. Indeed, some battalions soon became almost unrecognizable. When Robert Graves, much against his will, was posted to the 2nd Welsh Regiment in May 1915 instead of to one of the two Regular battalions of his own Royal Welsh Fusiliers, he found that

> all the company officers, with the exception of two boys recently posted from Sandhurst and one Special Reserve captain, came from other regiments. There were six Royal Welch Fusiliers, two South Wales Borderers, two East Surreys, two Wiltshires, one from the Border Regiment, one from the King's Own Yorkshire Light Infantry. Even the quartermaster was an alien from the Connaught Rangers.[23]

An idea put forward by Lord Kitchener was that the Post Office should scan all envelopes, noting those addressed to anyone with a military rank and passing details to the War Office. At the same time, lists of all who had served as Regular Army officers were to be drawn up.[24] Many Regular TF adjutants were also extracted, but as W. N. Nicholson, then DAA&QMG to the Highland Division commented, it 'was a blow from which the Territorial divisions did not recover for many months; for perhaps the whole of the course of the war'.[25] Indeed, like others of these emergency measures, it was a question of 'robbing Peter to pay Paul', but they were not enough to solve the BEF's immediate problem, which was further aggravated by the desperate fighting around Ypres in October and November, as the Germans made their final attempts to break through the Allied line and bring the war in the west to an early conclusion.

Given the ever grimmer situation, Sir John French took drastic action. He inspected the 1st/28th London Regiment (Artists' Rifles), which had been in France for less than three weeks and was under GHQ Troops, and decided to award immediate battlefield commissions. On 12 and 13 November 1914, a total of ninety-two of its members became second lieutenants and were posted to Regular battalions, initially wearing their Tommy's uniforms with the addition of pips worn on their shoulder straps.[26] It worked. Henry Rawlinson, whose 7th Division took the first fifty to be given immediate commissions, wrote to Kitchener: 'The young officers we have recently taken out of the ranks of the Artists are doing first class

[sic] with the regular battalions and the cry is "give us more"'.[27] Some were killed, however, before they could be gazetted. As a result of this successful experiment, Major H. N. R. Cowie DSO of the Dorsets, who had been serving as a company commander at RMC Sandhurst, was attached to the Artists on 27 November for the purpose of training officers. He set up a school, which operated in parallel with the Artists' main role of providing GHQ guards.* At the end of 1914 the establishment was formally titled the Cadet School and students attending the commissioning course were to be paid as second lieutenants.[28] Duncan Bell from the London Rifle Brigade was at the school in March 1915 and described it as 'a large white house in the Rue de Musée, Bailleul. We have to parade as spotless as in peacetime, no easy job with an equipment fresh from a winter in the trenches. This is a four-weeks' course of drill, field work, map-reading, M.G. work, elementary surveying, billeting, trench-fighting, etc.' The instruction also included a 48-hour attachment to a battalion in the trenches, on which the students had to submit a written report, and time spent in an artillery observation post. At the end of the course, Bell was given five days' leave in England to kit himself out as an officer before joining a Regular battalion of a Highland regiment back at the Front.[29] The 2nd Royal Welsh Fusiliers received their first products from the Artists in January 1915. All three made good and played a significant part in the battalion's history during the years that followed. Initially, the Artists' Rifles cadet school turned out seventy-five officers per month, a figure that soon increased to 100.

In one case, the initiative for obtaining instant officers was taken at a much lower level. The 1st Battalion HAC was serving in the 3rd Division as part of the 7th Brigade. In early January 1915, the brigade commander, Brigadier General C. R. Ballard, asked the HAC to furnish him with twenty-three men to make good the shortfall in junior officers among his four Regular battalions. Colonel Treffry, the CO, could not spare any NCOs, since he had already lost a number through commissioning. He therefore called for volunteers from among the privates. These were interviewed by their prospective commanding officers and those selected were immediately transferred wearing, like the early commissioned Artists' riflemen,

---

* Cowie did not stay long at Bailleul. He was called upon to take command of the 1st Battalion of his regiment at the end of March 1915, only to die of wounds received on Hill 60 that May.

their existing uniforms with just the addition of second lieutenant's stars. However, unlike those potential officers attending the Artists' Rifles school at Bailleul, they were to continue to be paid as privates until they were gazetted. It was also laid down that this would not happen until they had attended the Artists' school. Indeed, the battalions to which they were sent regarded them very much as 'probationary officers'. Colonel Treffry considered this grossly unfair and went so far as to raise the matter with the army commander, Horace Smith-Dorrien. He won his case and the proposal to send them to the Artists' school was dropped. Also, when they were finally gazetted at the end of March, their commissions were backdated to the day on which they had joined their new battalions. As with the early Artists' battlefield commissions, by that time some had been killed and others badly wounded.[30]

Others among the Territorial units in France applied for commissions after they had returned home sick or wounded. Typical was the author Henry Williamson of the London Rifle Brigade (LRB), who was sent home sick and on recovery obtained a commission in the Bedfordshire Regiment after receiving the necessary recommendation from the CO of the 3rd/5th Londons. Indeed, in spite of their commanding officer's initial objections, some 50 per cent of the men of the LRB who went to France in November 1914 were commissioned during the next twelve months.[31] Many used contacts at home to obtain the necessary recommendations from commanding officers so as to circumvent the CO of the LRB's reluctance to make them. However, Rifleman Aubrey Smith considered that 'the great attraction was not the star on our shoulders but the prospect of an unlimited period of training in England', which would get them away from the endless fatigues in which the battalion, on the lines of communication after suffering heavy casualties during Second Ypres, was now engaged. Smith himself did try to apply to the commanding officers of various London regiments when he was home on three days' leave in June 1915, but was unable to obtain an interview. When he got back to France he wrote to one or two COs, who replied that he should come for interview next time he was on home leave. At the same time, Colonel Bates, commanding 1 LRB, allowed those who had been unable to obtain commissions on recommendation of COs in Britain to attend the Artists' Rifles school in France, but the mere five days' commissioning leave defeated the object of those who wanted to get back to England for a long spell. Eventually, Smith himself became well ensconced in 1 LRB's transport section and gave up all thoughts of a commission. 'I had made fast friends and was absolutely attached to the LRB and could see quite well that I should not strike in any officers' mess a better set of companions than I had about me in the transport section.'[32] Norman Ellison, serving with 1st/6th King's Liverpool in France, also tried in vain to obtain a commission in autumn 1915. He obtained a recommendation from his company commander, but heard nothing further and eventually gave up the idea. 'We heard that Officer's Commissions [in the New Armies] were being granted to inexperienced youths almost straight from school, whereas men at the Front, eminently more suitable because of their experience, found every approach to HM Commission blocked.'[33] The main problem was the need to have confirmation from a CO that he would accept the candidate in his battalion, and in both Smith's and Ellison's cases their families lacked the right connections. Yet some serving at the Front in 1915 talked of applying for commissions but felt guilty about leaving their battalions. As Linton Andrews of the 1st/4th Black Watch put it, 'it would seem like giving in'.[34]

The War Office had quickly realized that many newly commissioned officers had only limited military knowledge. Temporary schools of instruction were therefore hastily set up at Oxford, Cambridge, Dublin, Edinburgh and London universities. These offered a one-month elementary training course in recruit drill, musketry regulations, the infantry training manual, *Field Service Regulations (Part 1)* and basic military law, as well as providing 'detailed knowledge for both peace and war of the organisation, administration, equipment, establishment, terms of service and pay of infantry'. The courses were a 'one off' and ran from 26 August 1914, after which the schools were then closed because of the new university year. Montie Carlisle attended the course run by Cambridge UOTC. His first week was spent entirely on the drill square, after which the course moved to a tented camp at Royston. At the end of it, Carlisle was commissioned into the Northumberland Fusiliers.[35] Later, in mid November 1914, each TF brigade HQ was ordered to form a school capable of taking twenty-five young officers at a time. The idea was that they should attend a six-weeks' course before joining their battalions. The syllabus was very much the same as that of the university courses, but significant additions were sanitation and first aid, sniping, and what was called 'Notes from the Front'. The authorities accepted that some officers attending these courses might have had front-line experience while in the ranks and stressed that the purpose of the course was to teach the theory, with which they were probably not totally *au fait*. If there was a danger of these officers considering the course a waste of time, they should be used to assist in the instruction and, if need be, understudy the adjutant of a local TF battalion.[36] The Staff College at Camberley, which had ceased fulfilling its normal role at the outbreak of war, also offered short courses, which were run by Sandhurst. In November 1914, Ivone Kirkpatrick was commissioned into the 8th Royal Inniskilling Fusiliers but was told to report first to Camberley for a month's course. He was one of 200 officer students: 'We were kept hard at work. First parade was at 6.30am and no respite was given until 10pm, when we all went cheerfully to bed. Most of us picked up a great deal of knowledge at Camberley and I shudder to think what we should have been without the course.'[37] Guy Chapman was probably on the same course, which he termed 'strenuous' and attended after three months at the Inns of Court OTC.[38] The courses at the Staff College continued until April 1916, when it was taken over for Sandhurst cadets.

Others, however, used their own initiative when it came to officer training. Lord Derby, who had recently raised New Army battalions for the King's Liverpool Regiment, organized a tutor from London to be brought in to teach 'officers' work' to candidates for commissions.[39] So successful was Derby's school that it also trained officers from the Service battalions of the Manchester Regiment and those from locally raised artillery units.[40] However, in the summer of 1915 Brigadier General F. C. Stanley, Lord Derby's brother, who was commanding the 89th Brigade, which contained the battalions of the King's Liverpool Regiment raised by Derby himself, apparently conceded that the Inns of Court could do the task much more efficiently. Those recommended by the battalion commanders were interviewed by the Inns of Court and the men selected underwent training at Berkhamsted, where the Inns of Court was now stationed, and were then commissioned back into their battalions.[41]

General Sir Lawrence Parsons, GOC 16th (Irish) Division, also set up his own officer training school. On the formation of the division, he had received a flood of applications for commissions, many of them on the recommendation of John Redmond, the Irish Nationalist leader. These he looked at in terms of 'suitable gentlemen who have been associated with the National Volunteers and are likely to induce them to enlist'. He was not prepared to allow religion or political belief to bar applicants from obtaining commissions. This paid dividends. John Wray, an officer in the Enniskillen Volunteers, was granted a commission in the 6th Connaught Rangers at Parsons' behest and brought in 200 of his men as recruits. Another officer of the Louth Volunteers was similarly rewarded for recruiting seventy-five of his men, even though he was 50 years old. At the same time, the War Office was also supplying him with officers and soon Parsons had his full establishment. Yet the applications continued to arrive on his desk. Some, he complained to the War Office at the end of November 1914, were 'from all sorts of impossible people as officers who write their applications in red or green ink on a blank bill-head of a village shop'. But although he was a snob when it came to considering officer material, Parsons did not want to turn off the tap for fear of 'hurting susceptibilities and possibly adversely affecting recruiting'. He had therefore set up an officer cadet company in the 7th Leinsters. Every future applicant would be interviewed by the GOC in person and, if found acceptable by him, would have to spend time in it prior to being commissioned. One of the early cadets was John Staniforth. He had come down from Oxford in summer 1914 and enlisted in the 6th Connaughts in mid October, but soon found life in the ranks not to his liking. His fellows were 'indescribable villains', while living conditions in the barracks at Fermoy were grim. He therefore applied for a commission and joined C (Officer Cadet) Company 7th Leinsters on 12 November. He was one of fifteen cadets, but their training, unlike that of the other officer training institutions, was strictly 'hands on'. Each cadet found himself responsible for a squad of twenty recruits, which he was expected to train. While they lived in barrack rooms, the cadets were also initiated into the ways of the officers' mess. 'Mess in the evening is a parade, and as such is compulsory. Clean white collars, black ties, khaki trousers and pumps is the attire, with the ordinary khaki tunic.' They attended all lectures given to the officers by Parsons and his staff and were allowed to keep their lights on in the barrack room until 10.30 p.m. so that they could study. Staniforth himself was commissioned into the 7th Leinsters and the cadet company had trained no less than 161 officers by the time the division went to France at the end of 1915.[42]

Meanwhile the Inns of Court OTC, still the only official officer cadet unit in Britain outside Sandhurst and Woolwich, was going from strength to strength. By mid 1915 it was turning out eighty officers per week. It eventually established no less than 22,000 'voluntary information agencies' both at home and overseas to inform potential candidates of the existence of the Inns of Court and to encourage them to put their names forward. Typical of its public relations effort was a letter written by Major J. A. Hay, commanding the depot, to clergymen overseas in July 1915. He asserted:

> What is happening today is that many men, unfitted to be British officers and leaders of men, are applying to take up commissions without the necessary training, while others admirably suited to become officers are joining the ranks, where many experience difficulty in obtaining permission to accept commissions or be transferred to an Officers' Training Unit.

The Inns of Court provided the solution for the aspiring officer candidate and Hay believed that clergymen 'by reason of their official position and acquaintance with local conditions, can greatly assist us by acting as Advisory and Information Bureaux for this Corps'. However, this attempt to use the Church as an unofficial recruiter in the Empire backfired. A copy of the letter was shown to Lord Liverpool, the Governor of New Zealand. He wrote to the War Office, implying that the Inns of Court was attempting to poach potential officers from the Dominion's own forces, and stated that they needed every such man themselves. The War Office accepted the point and the Inns of Court were forbidden to send further such letters overseas.[43] But the impression that Colonel Errington was attempting to create a form of monopoly over officer training was in time to lead to a rift between him and the War Office.

Those who did apply to the Inns of Court appeared before selection boards, which were made up of a mixture of military and civilian members and sat in London, Scotland, Wales, Ireland and the West Country. During the course of the war they interviewed an estimated 130,000 men of whom roughly one-tenth were accepted for training. Colonel Errington freely admitted that in the early days of the war the Inns of Court only accepted men who had been to major public schools, but then the War Office had made it plain that it was the public schools from which officers should be drawn. Complaints about the restrictive practice reached his ears and so he went to the War Office to obtain a definition of 'public school'. He was told that it was 'a school open to the public'. Hence, with the agreement of the Director of Military Training, Errington dropped the school criterion from the selection process. Instead, 'our principle of selection should be the possession by the candidate of such qualifications as we thought necessary for his training as an officer'. These, however, certainly included participation in sport, as William Carr from Scotland found to his cost when he was interviewed at Lincoln's Inn in January 1916. Having not played games at school his application was rejected.[44] Successful candidates first joined the Depot Company, which continued to be based at Lincoln's Inn until July 1916, when it moved to Berkhamsted.

One part of the depot was the 'unattested contingent', which accepted men who wanted some training without going through the complete programme. Examples were those destined to be officers in the RE Tunnelling companies and RFC balloon observers.[45] Seventeen-year-old H. E. L. Mellersh joined the unattested contingent in the spring of 1915 with a view to obtaining a commission in the Special Reserve. 'Its trainees comprised men of the legal profession, men for instance who had been abroad and so had not joined up earlier, together with a few youngsters like myself who had at least school OTC training behind them'. Because of the lack of accommodation, Mellersh commuted by train daily from home. His days were spent mainly drilling, with some weapons training. On Saturdays they marched to Hampstead Heath, where 'we practised "open order" drill and mock attacks, advancing in "sectional rushes" and throwing ourselves down whilst the other half covered us from imaginary enemy fire with rifles equally imaginary'. Mellersh was frustrated by fact he had been a sergeant in his school OTC and had Certificate A and felt that he knew it all. 'No doubt I did dimly realise that, Certificate A or no Certificate

A, I was a callow youngster amongst these men of greater age and much greater standing, and that my disgust and chagrin were ridiculous.' He was commissioned into the 3rd East Lancashires in June 1915 aged just over 18.[46]

Another callow youth who joined the Inns of Court, this time in September 1915, was the novelist Alec Waugh (brother of Evelyn). He intended to do the complete course, aiming to obtain an early commission, but was thwarted when the minimum age for commissioning was raised to 18½. Furthermore, and an indication of how the net for officer material was widening beyond the confines of the public schools, 'I found myself with a group of men much older than myself, with backgrounds that were unfamiliar to me, whom I found uncongenial.' To pass the time, Waugh wrote his first novel, *Loom of Youth*, which caused a major stir for its revelations of homosexuality in public schools and resulted in Waugh himself being struck off the register of Sherborne Old Boys. Waugh then went to Sandhurst, where the course had been lengthened to nine months, to fill in time. In contrast to the Inns of Court, 'the training was interesting. There was a day-to-day eventfulness about the progress one made; there was an urgency about everything one did – a need to get one's commission quickly, to get out to France as soon as possible.' He was eventually commissioned in May 1917 into the Dorsets, but was seconded to the Machine Gun Corps and captured during the March 1918 retreat.[47]

Those who had not already been commissioned from the Inns of Court Depot Company were then posted to one of the infantry companies or the cavalry squadron at Berkhamsted. 'The quality ultimately aimed at was leadership, to be built up on a solid foundation of drill and discipline, with a superstructure of knowledge and practice in command, and with full emphasis on the moral qualities needed in those who have to lead men in the field.' Drill gave the cadet his first experience of commanding others and was given much emphasis at the Inns of Court. Musketry was also taught, but suffered under severe disadvantages. There was a lack of live firing facilities and of weapons capable of being fired in safety. Furthermore, for a long time the Inns of Court had only one Lewis gun, which it managed to obtain on its own initiative. Entrenching was taught, with the emphasis on the design and siting of trenches, but little time was spent in teaching the mechanics of trench warfare, since 'a week in France or up the [Ypres] Salient taught more than months of playing at it at home could do'. The one major exception was bombing, which was introduced at the beginning of 1916, after the commanding officer visited the Second Army bombing school at Cassel. Indeed, the Inns of Court largely taught open warfare, including night operations, because this gave much more opportunity to develop initiative. Map reading and marching, especially march discipline, played an important part in field training. During the early part of the war, physical training was restricted to morning runs and only later was this subject put on a more formal basis, with PT instructors joining the instructional staff. Bayonet fighting, too, was only introduced during the last part of the war. Lectures also played their part: the majority were on tactics, but military law, discipline and sanitation were also included. During the last month of the course, the potential officers attended the adjutant's special instruction class and when he judged that they were ready for commissioning he earmarked them for units which were requesting officers from the Inns of Court. The relevant commanding officer then interviewed the man and, if he accepted him, applied to the War Office for his commission. It was a system that generally worked well, with little external interference.

Officers commissioned from the Inns of Court were not expected to attend subsequent young officers' training courses, which were now set up by the training brigades and garrisons of the New Armies in addition to those run by the TF brigades. The aim of these Young Officers companies, as they were often called, was to take in officers who could not be satisfactorily trained by the Reserve battalions of the former Fourth New Army.[48] But many proved unsatisfactory. Rory Baynes, a Regular officer who had been badly wounded at Festubert in May 1915, was sent to instruct at one of these schools at Catterick. The commandant was an Oxford Professor of Zoology, who was 'pleased to see somebody who he knew had some practical training'. There were some thirty to forty officers undergoing training.

> They were, all round, a very good lot though varied and discipline wasn't
> all that good. They were rather off-hand in many cases, and the first

job that I was put on to was officer in charge of discipline: a curious appointment which should not have been necessary at any establishment at which normal discipline existed.

Young Charles Carrington, who had served for six months in the ranks of the 14th Royal Warwicks before being commissioned into the 9th York and Lancaster, was sent to such a company in August 1915 after being left behind in England because his battalion was over strength in officers when it went to France. He spent ten weeks 'in utter dejection'. The staff 'were themselves second-class soldiers, the dregs of the senior ranks as we were the dregs of the junior ... Most of us were smarting under the slur of dismissal by the regiments to which we were devoted, and were indignant at our reduction to the status of officer cadets.' To escape, Carrington used the good offices of his uncle, who was with the 1st/5th Royal Warwicks in France, to get him transferred to the 2nd/5th Royal Warwicks and he was out in France before end of 1915.[49] In most cases, however, officers attended these courses immediately on commissioning and were then sent to a Training battalion to await drafting to one of the active war theatres.

Yet even once the training organization for the expanded army had been properly established, the newly commissioned officer, unless he had attended Sandhurst, Woolwich, the Inns of Court or the Artists' Rifles, still suffered a grave shortfall in his training. In an attempt to improve the standard, two measures were introduced in October 1915. First, it was laid down that all young officers were to be examined by a board consisting of a brigade or garrison commander and two commanding officers before being declared ready for drafting overseas. Second, all infantry young officers were to attend an abbreviated Sandhurst course lasting for one month at a military school prior to going to Reserve battalions for drilling with recruits. These schools were in addition to the Young Officers companies, which would continue. There is, however, little evidence, certainly from personal accounts of the war, that these new regulations were put into practice to any extent.[50] There were, however, anomalies. Jack Morten of the 1st/7th Manchesters had applied for a commission in early 1915 when his battalion was in Sudan. It went to Gallipoli in May; in late August, Morten heard that his commission had been granted, backdated to March 1915. He served as a platoon commander until he was invalided with a poisoned hand and found himself back in England in time for Christmas 1915. He was sent to the 3rd/7th Manchesters, who were at Codford St Mary in Wiltshire, and was put on a junior officers' course.

> ... We are doing exactly the same things that we learned in Khartum. We are going through the course as though we were raw recruits, we might never have been in the army before. So long as we do not get too much of it, it will do us no harm as there are little details in drill which one is apt to forget when one has spent six months in the trenches where there is no such thing as drill.[51]

He did not escape until May 1916, when he returned to his battalion, which was now back in Egypt.

During the early days of the New Armies, the young officer largely learned 'on the job' how to command his platoon. Many gained their military knowledge from the study of military manuals and books like Brigadier General R. C. B. Haking's *Company Training*, which had been published just before the war and had become an instant bestseller.* This self-learning worked very effectively, as General Ivor Maxse, who had been sent back from France to take command of 18th Division, commented:

> They [his subalterns] spend eight hours a day with their platoons and identify themselves with the men's interests both on and off parade. Their keenness to learn the work of training men makes some think that after six months service they will be as good platoon commanders as the average subaltern of the Old Army. This is also the opinion of several commanding officers.[52]

Major Neil Fraser-Tytler, a pre-war Territorial who was commanding a 4.5-inch battery in the 30th Division, supported this view in a letter home from France in December 1915:

> The regular brigade takes life pretty easily, and in their smooth running batteries the officers have but little detail work to do. The result is that many of their subalterns who have joined straight from the 'Shop' know

---

* Haking was commanding the 5th Infantry Brigade, which he took to France in August 1914. By the end of 1915 he was commanding a corps.

very little about the interior economy of their batteries. They step into the machine and glide along with a first-class BSM and QMS behind them. Personally I would rather have my own older New Army subalterns, who went through the ranks of the early divisions, and having seen their battery grow up from the first days of wooden guns and twenty horses per battery, know every detail of the equipment and requirements of a battery and have quite a sound knowledge of gunnery too.[53]

Once the training organization was properly set up, the scope for the young officer to get used to commanding men was drastically reduced. H. E. L. Mellersh, who had obtained a Special Reserve commission in the East Lancashires through the Inns of Court Unattested Contingent at the age of 18 in June 1915, attended a worthwhile month's young officers' course at Worcester College, Oxford, before reporting to the 3rd (Reserve) Battalion of his regiment. 'To my utter disgust, I found myself drilling and being drilled yet again: an officers' squad taken by a regular sergeant.' He was also taught ceremonial sword drill under the personal supervision of the commanding officer. But the squad ended abruptly when the sergeant committed suicide.

> We, the members of the class, were at a loose end. It was probably true that we were as unwanted as surplus baggage; for the training of the men was adequately in the hands of NCOs returned from the front or held back from the two regular battalions, and there was almost nothing for us to do but watch these NCOs at their job and pretend to be in charge.

He was taught to ride under the supervision of the adjutant and then attended musketry course on Hayling Island and became assistant musketry officer. But the only chance he had to develop his powers of leadership was when for a time he ran a twelve-man cyclist squad. Mellersh was only saved in early 1916 by the relaxation of the ban on subalterns going to France before they reached the age of 19.[54] This lack of leadership experience among junior officers was much remarked upon when they joined units at the Front. Indeed, in the spring of 1916, 47th (London) Division felt forced to institute classes for young officers, which were run by battalion seconds-in-command.[55]

Better officer training was conducted by the 2nd Artists' Rifles, which had been supplying drafts for the 1st Battalion, as well as officers for the Territorial Force. In May 1915, it was also ordered to set up a school for newly commissioned Territorial officers on the same lines as the cadet school in France. Bryan Latham attended the 2nd Artists' school in the autumn of 1915, after being commissioned into the 17th Londons from the London Rifle Brigade.

> This was in hutments near Romford, and trained a hundred officers at a time. It was extraordinarily well run and every effort was made to convey to those attending the conditions they were likely to find awaiting them in France and to train them in these eventualities. Each course lasted six or seven weeks and consisted of lectures and field exercises. Many of the lecturers were officers who had returned wounded from the front, so that they knew what they were talking about. The educational foundation of the course was a book issued by the Artists Rifles headquarters which I still have, entitled 'Notes of Training' and running to some 170 pages. It was divided into three parts: part 1 – Open fighting: part 2 – and by far the most useful – Trench warfare: and part 3 – Machine-gun tactics, which again was extremely practicable and built up from first-hand experience in France. The book was well illustrated with plans and diagrams.

During the summer of 1915, but apparently unofficially, the 2nd Artists also began to train its own men for commissions. Francis Foster had joined the battalion in Richmond Park in May 1915:

> We had to sleep on bare ground or hard floors; our rations were of poor quality and badly cooked by amateurs; leave was rarely granted; training was rigorous and intensive. But once my body became inured to these hardships, I welcomed the long hours of work and general discomfort because they staved off the dreadful anticipation of eventually going into the firing line.

In November, Foster and five others were paraded in front of a visiting lieutenant colonel and he and one other were selected for commissions and he found himself in the East Lancashires.[56] However, in that same month of November 1915 the 2nd Artists were merged with the 1st Battalion in France, while the 3rd Battalion officially became the 2nd Artists' OTC.[57]

The general lack of training among the new officers was not the only thing that concerned the Regulars. James Jack of the Cameronians, dining with a friend in London in March 1915, reported: 'We were both shocked at the unsoldierly appearance and manners of many of the new officers.' Edmund Malone, appointed to command a Reserve battalion of the West Riding Regiment (Duke of Wellington's) the following year, found it

> a very new experience indeed. It made me feel very shy at first. Whenever I entered the Mess every officer stood to attention till I told them to sit down. This was more than I could bear, so I sent for them all to the Orderly Room and told them they need only stand up when I entered before dinner. I also told them to desist from saying, 'Please pass the mustard, *Mister* Jones'. None of them play any games. I think they spend their time in pubs in Nottingham. I find it very difficult to understand these chaps. I have nothing in common with them.

Padre Victor Tanner writing from France in 1916, noted:

> One thing that depresses me more than any other is the change in the character and attitude of the new officers. When I first came we had a wonderful lot, very friendly and helpful in every way. These new chaps are quite different. Many of them are not merely indifferent to religion but openly anti-religious.[58]

In an attempt to encourage the 'temporary gentlemen' to conform, a number of pamphlets were published to advise them on how to conduct themselves. Captain A. H. Trapman in *Straight Tips for Subs* warned young officers against such sins as addressing captains by their rank alone ('only tradesmen ... do that') and standing rounds of drinks on entering the Mess. He also laid down how a new subaltern should address his brother officers in the Mess. The commanding officer should be addressed as 'Sir', majors as 'Major', and the remainder by their surnames. 'CN's' *The Making of an Officer* came down hard on the subaltern who spent his leisure time 'motor-cycling with females' or became a 'Kinema creeper, bookworm, or bar-loafer'.[59] But although the advice was meant to be helpful, many of the new class of officer found it alien and difficult to swallow. Where a New Army battalion had an effective commanding officer and adjutant, the young officers could be broken in gently; in those where these were lacking the problem remained. The lack of 'gentlemanly conduct' among the new officers was something which the Regulars would bewail throughout the war. This was particularly so in the cavalry, many of whose best officers transferred to other arms after the onset of trench warfare in France. Captain J. A. T. Price of the 5th Lancers, writing to his parents in September 1917, remarked:

> Some of the 'temporarys' who appear are rather terrible and we rather want to get hold of some nice regulars if possible. So if you do meet anyone of that description you will doubtless suggest to them that you have a very nice son in a likewise regiment and that they should send their sons here.[60]

The introduction of Lord Derby's scheme and the passing of the Military Service Acts put a new complexion on officer training. The reservoir of those who had OTC experience had all but dried up, apart from young men leaving school, and many now being considered as officer material were lacking any form of military experience. In February 1916, the War Office therefore decided that in future no man was to be commissioned without undergoing basic training in the ranks, although OTC experience would be accepted in lieu. Simultaneously, and in an effort to standardize training, Officer Cadet battalions were established in Britain, with twelve in existence by June 1916. These ran a four months' course. One immediate effect of this in France was the disbandment of three of the four Public Schools battalions of the Royal Fusiliers (18th, 19th and 21st). They were withdrawn from the line in February 1916 and immediately began to supply drafts for the OC battalions. This so denuded their strength that they were dissolved at the end of April, with the balance of their men being posted to other battalions of the Royal Fusiliers.[61]

The Inns of Court OTC also underwent some reorganization. Underlying this was the appointment of Sir William Robertson as CIGS in autumn 1915. As part of his reorganization of the War Office, he was determined to bring the Inns of Court under tighter control. The first indication of this came in November 1915. A number of officer candidates had already been selected by commanding officers and were awaiting their commissions, when the War Office ordered Colonel Errington to present them for interview. 'To our surprise ten were rejected, and were declared not fit for commissions.' Errington complained to the Director of Military Training, especially since this action cast doubt on the Inns of Court selection and training methods, and the rejected candidates did eventually receive their commissions. But worse was to follow almost immediately. The Inns of Court were suddenly told that no new commissions were for the moment to be granted. No reason was given. Errington was thrown into a dilemma. Roughly one hundred men a week were entering the Inns of Court to replace those who had been commissioned.

> The recruiting tap, however, could not be regulated: it was impossible to turn it on or off strictly according to requirements. If a large number of men appeared in one week, they had to be taken, they would not wait. To turn off the tap altogether would have been suicidal. The fact of our having closed recruiting was certain to spread like wildfire, and no amount of explanation that it was purely a temporary measure would have been of the slightest avail. It is very doubtful whether we should have ever been able to catch up again.

Consequently, Errington decided to continue to allow recruits to enter the Inns of Court and, with the commissioning embargo remaining in force for two months, its strength swelled to over 4,000 men.

In February 1916, the War Office offered Errington the choice of training men for the new Cadet battalions or incorporating Cadet companies within the Inns of Court. He chose the latter course and four Cadet companies were formed in addition to the existing six companies. Those who had no previous military experience would be trained in the original companies before graduating to the Cadet companies, which would also take in serving soldiers recommended for commissions and former schoolboys with OTC experience. But the Inns of Court was grossly overstrength and Errington's proposal that its establishment be increased to cater for this was rejected. Furthermore, he was now told to halt recruiting until he was back down to strength. As a means of achieving this, the War Office asked Errington how many of his men were prepared to take commissions in the artillery. One hundred and seventy-eight men volunteered, and two officers from the War Office came down to interview them. No interview lasted more than a couple of minutes and was devoted entirely to school, occupation and parental background. A large number were rejected and Errington was ordered to transfer them as privates to other units. Once again, the Inns of Court selection techniques had been thrown into question. Errington raised the matter with several Members of Parliament and questions were asked in the House. Eventually, the order to transfer the men was rescinded. Equally inexplicable was another War Office order to transfer 139 men aged under 18 to the 101st Provisional Battalion, albeit without endangering their chances of gaining commissions. 'It proved, however, a mistake to mix up boys of that age with the ordinary private, and eventually they were re-transferred to the Corps.'[63]

Other members of the Inns of Court were transferred to the new Officer Cadet battalions. Alan Worden, a qualified solicitor, had enlisted in the ranks of the King's Liverpool Regiment in September 1914. After twice being refused permission by his company commander to apply for a commission, he eventually joined the Inns of Court in September 1915. In late February 1916, 'after some months' intensive training I succeeded in passing the very high standard of efficiency required and was awaiting notification of my gazettement.' Instead, he was ordered to report to No. 3 Officer Cadet Battalion at Bristol, which meant a further four months' training before he could be commissioned.

> It is not difficult to imagine my feeling of frustration as I was anxious to contribute my little bit towards the common effort without delay. However, I was subsequently more than grateful for the extra training and for the constant reiteration that it entailed, for it is only by constant repetition and going over the same ground that the tenets of war can be instilled into the soldier's blood-stream and so become part of himself. Let no one labour under the delusion that a few months' training is all that is necessary; it take years to turn out a really efficient soldier.

Worden was eventually commissioned into the Lancashire Fusiliers in July 1916.[64]

One effect of the establishment of Officer Cadet battalions was to take some of the pressure off Sandhurst and Woolwich. The course at the latter was extended to nine months and in January 1917 this was further increased to one year. But there were an increasing number of cadets whose lack of academic ability meant that they either had to be removed or made to repeat a term. By spring 1918 this figure had risen to 20 per cent of an intake. Yet for the gunner cadets at least, the lengthening of the course did have one bonus. They were now able to carry out a week's firing practice at Larkhill, which stood them in good stead when they went to join their batteries. At Sandhurst, too, the course was gradually extended, becoming nine months in 1917. The training, however, was as rigorous as ever. A cadet who joined in January 1918 remembered:

> We were drilled and drilled and had lots of riding, gym and rifle instruction, together with elementary tactics … We were taught law up to courts martial and administration up to battalion level. We started at 6 a.m. and worked all day, and with lectures after mess, this took us up to 11 p.m.[65]

Finally, in May 1918 it was announced that the courses for both Sandhurst and Woolwich would each revert to eighteen months from 1919, with entries in June and December.[66] In all, during the war Woolwich produced 1,928 officers and Sandhurst 5,013, but this represented a mere 3 per cent of the total combatant commissions.

The War Office continued to exert pressure on the Inns of Court. The senior officer in charge of the Cadet companies was a Regular Army major. He asked Errington for permission to apply for the rank of temporary lieutenant colonel on the grounds of the increased pay and allowances. Errington told him that this would make matters difficult if there were two lieutenant colonels in the Inns of Court, but his objections were overruled and the officer was duly promoted. At much the same time, the Lincoln's Inn depot was closed for training by the War Office and became merely a reception centre. Errington began to sense that there were moves to force him to give up command of the Inns of Court. He was right. On 15 August 1916 he received a personal letter from General Sir Edward Bethune, Director-General of the Territorial Force, who had handed over control of the Inns of Court to the General Staff at the War Office. He wrote that Errington ought to have the opportunity to go to France and offered him the post of commandant of No. 58 Infantry Base Depot, adding that the War Office wanted someone to take charge of the Inns of Court who had been in France. Errington reflected: 'I was rapidly drifting into an impossible position, having either to accept a cramped form of training in which I disbelieved, or to risk the future of the Corps by putting up a fight over what would soon be made to appear to be my personal position.' He therefore accepted the post in France.[67] The cadet companies became ever more independent of the remainder of the Inns of Court and in September 1916 became No. 14 Officer Cadet Battalion and eventually, in January 1918, moved to Catterick. In its place a school of instruction for officers of OC battalions was established at Berkhamsted, where the remainder of the Inns of Court stayed until the end of the war. By that time it had supplied nearly 11,500 officers.

The 2nd Artists' Rifles underwent a similar reorganization to the Inns of Court. In March 1916 four cadet companies were formed in addition to the four training companies already in existence. Once a man had completed his initial training, he passed from the latter to the former. That August, the cadet companies became No. 15 Officer Cadet Battalion under their own commanding officer, thus becoming virtually divorced from the 2nd Artists, although the battalion continued to provide some of the instructors. Furthermore, potential officers who carried out their initial basic training with the Artists could be sent to any Officer Cadet battalion, while No. 15 also trained men from other units besides the Artists.

In France, the Artists' cadet school had been moved in April 1915 from Bailleul to the village of Blendecques, 4 kilometres south of Saint Omer. It became known as the GHQ Cadet School, divorcing it from the battalion. However, the Artists ran their own training of potential officers before they attended the cadet school in what was known as the 'colonel's class'. So seemingly successful was this that in July 1916 GHQ agreed that any Artist recommended by the CO for a commission would be granted one without having to attend the Cadet School. John Nettleton was one of these. He had been posted to 1st Artists' Rifles in August 1915 and, in order to avoid the tedium of guards at GHQ, he joined the Signals Section. The following summer there was a drive to encourage men in the Artists to apply for commissions. Nettleton was persuaded and, after an interview with a brigadier general, joined the colonel's class. He found the training largely limited to close order drill under the RSM, with the cadets

> taking it in turns to command platoons and companies. A platoon was represented by a length of rope held by a man at each end. After weeks of this, we could, all of us, take a battalion and turn it upside down and inside out and get it into its original formation with speed and precision, but we had no inkling of an officer's other duties.

At the end of August, Nettleton carried out a three-week attachment to the Royal Naval Division in the trenches. For most of the time he carried out normal private soldier's duties, but was appointed platoon commander's runner for the last week. Then it was back to close order drill, apart from one week at Bull Ring at Camiers, near Etaples, where the cadets were badged as sergeants. Nettleton was eventually commissioned into a Regular battalion, the 2nd Rifle Brigade, in November 1916, but he 'did not feel in any way competent to take a commission'. He was allowed just one day to obtain kit from the officer's shop at Saint Omer before reporting to his battalion, which had few temporary officers. Nettleton took a long time to settle in, making several mistakes – the battalion, luckily, being at rest – and felt very uncomfortable in the officers' mess.[68]

In contrast, the training at the cadet school itself was apparently much more focused. CSM Ernest Shephard of the 1st Dorsets was originally nominated to attend a course beginning in November 1916, but because of heavy officer casualties on the Somme the current class was commissioned early, and he was ordered to report to Blendecques on 12 September. Shephard and his fellow cadets were arriving straight from the trenches and were first sent to a convalescent camp so that they could have baths and their uniforms laundered. They were then directed to the school's probationers' camp, where they were ordered to remove their badges of rank and replace them with a red armlet with 'CSIC' (Cadet School Infantry Company) on it. Shephard discovered that the school was organized in three 'houses' – Somerset, Marlborough and Beresford – each with its own probationary section. The idea was that candidates spent four to six weeks as probationers* before being recommended for the cadet schools proper,

---

*A similar but smaller 'preparatory class' (seventy as opposed to up to 250 students) was established at Etaples.

where the course was of six weeks' duration. Shephard's first day consisted of a lecture on military terms, an inspection by the Military Secretary at GHQ and then musketry, apart from cavalrymen on his course, who were taught infantry drill. The next couple of weeks were taken up with drill, fatigues and lectures. These included one by Professor Adkins of Cambridge University, who was lecturing under the auspices of YMCA. His topic was the causes of the war and Shephard found it 'extremely interesting and instructive'. Shephard was duly recommended and on 4 October he moved to Marlborough House and began his officer training in earnest. Much of it was taken up with tactical schemes, in which the cadets filled command positions from company commander downwards. Others acted as 'critics' to the cadet company and platoon commanders and reviewed their actions during the debriefs. Shephard also had a two-day attachment to the 1st Cheshires in the trenches. Unlike Nettleton, he was given a particular task, 'to note all details, sketch and report on return' and was attached to a company commander for this purpose. A week before commissioning, cadets put in for a particular regiment (Shephard naturally chose the Dorsets) and indented for officers' kit. Their instructors wrote confidential reports on them, which, if adverse, would result in the man being returned to his unit. Shephard was commissioned on 17 November and posted to the 1st/5th Dorsets. Next day, he collected his officers kit from 7 Army Ordnance Depot and departed for his new battalion on the 19th. Unlike Nettleton, Shephard experienced no problems in settling in as an officer. Indeed, he found himself having to guide his company commander, who had not yet been under fire. But then he had the advantage of having considerable front-line experience as a warrant officer, while Nettleton had been a mere rifleman with little or no opportunity to shoulder responsibility.[69] Sadly, though, Ernest Shephard's promise as an officer was cut short when he was killed while taking part in a local attack near Beaumont Hamel in January 1917.

Back in Britain, the Officer Cadet battalions got off to an uncertain start. Arthur Graeme West was sent to No. 9 or No. 10 OC Battalion at Gailes in Ayrshire in March 1916, after four months' service with the 16th Middlesex (Public Schools) in France. The emphasis appeared to be on drill and fatigues, with musketry taught by a sergeant who was unfamiliar with the SMLE rifle. In the belief that discipline in the army at home was declining, the commanding officer was determined to teach his cadets to be 'smart officers' who, as the 'first products of new methods', would put things right. West, who was an intellectual, found it a depressing experience, not helped by the poor standard of food, and very nearly became a conscientious objector. Norman Collins, who had enlisted in the Seaforths at the age of just 18 in June 1915 and had risen to the rank of lance sergeant, joined No. 8 OC Battalion at Lichfield at much the same time. He was similarly unimpressed:

> We are always scrubbing floors, forming fours etc, doing 160 paces per minute on the square, brushing boots every hour from 5 a.m. until 7.30 p.m. when we are free to write up our notes until 9.30 p.m. [We] are called miscellaneous names by Sergeants etc who know nothing, it's a dog's life and several cadets from the firing line want to go back.[70]

But the quality of training at the Cadet battalions did improve. Dick Read, who had spent almost two years in France with the 8th Leicesters and had risen to the rank of sergeant, attended No. 8 OC Battalion a year later:

> There was no doubt that we received splendid instruction here for undertaking the responsibilities of commissioned rank – principally training for ruthless war as junior leaders. For me it was four months of absolute physical fitness; striving for all I was worth to attain the end marked out by our instructors.

Basil Peacock trained with No. 2 OC Battalion, which was based at Pembroke College, Cambridge, and recalled that 'a great deal of instruction was directed to turning us into instructors'. Certainly, life for the cadets was civilized in those battalions based in Oxford and Cambridge. L. P. Hartley attended the Garrison (later No. 22) Officer Cadet Battalion at Cambridge and was accommodated in Sidney Sussex College. 'There we slept four to a room instead of 30, as at Catterick, and 250, as in my first camp.' But the key to improving the quality of the instruction was the instructors themselves. Henry Ogle, with No. 19 OC Battalion at Pirbright in spring 1917 after service in the ranks of the 1st/7th Royal Warwicks in

France, noted that his mentors were 'seasoned officers and NCOs who had been given these jobs as a reward after arduous services. They were indeed very good. They did not try to make themselves popular with the cadets but earned our respect and willing obedience.' He also relates that the commanding officer's aim was to turn them into 'Officers and *Gentlemen*' and to this end a certain number of cadets dined with the officers each day. The only aspect of the course which did not impress Ogle was the field training exercises, complete with blank ammunition to aid realism: '… they were most unrealistic, especially when the major's wife and children appeared in the woods with a picnic basket and the war was stopped for lunch'.[71]

Every applicant for a commission had to complete form MT.393A. Among the many questions it asked was whether the candidate was of 'pure European descent'. Prior to 1914, both the British Army and the Royal Navy had a policy that no one would be granted a commission if they were coloured or of mixed race. But, while the Admiralty made this plain in its regulations, the War Office was somewhat coy and merely made it a factor in the entrance medical that each young man had to attend. Most cases concerned British fathers and non-British mothers and were all turned down for commissions. In 1910, the War Office did finally make the restriction clear, stating in the *Manual of Military Law* that 'any Negro or person of colour' was able to enlist in the army, but could 'not be capable of holding higher rank in His Majesty's Forces than that of warrant officer or non-commissioned officer'.[72] This remained the situation until well into the war. But then questions began to be raised, initially concerning the contingents from the West Indies, where mixed marriages were by no means uncommon. In December 1915, the Army Council rejected the notion of mixed blood officers in the Jamaica contingent. The following autumn the point was made that it was unjust to enlist coloured men in the ranks if commissions were to be barred to them, but the Army Council would not accept this. However, the policy did change.

In November 1916, an Anglo-Indian was admitted to Woolwich, and the following April the War Office conceded that temporary commissions might be granted to 'slightly coloured gentlemen' in the West Indies contingents, which by now were making a sizeable contribution to the labour forces in France. The precedent had been set by Reginald Emmanuel

Collins, a civil servant in the West Indies who had enlisted in the Royal Fusiliers in August 1915. He successfully applied for a commission and was posted to No. 6 OC Battalion. Its CO was unhappy about this, however, baldly asserting that Collins was 'not suitable to be an officer owing to his colour.' A debate followed over whether he should be discharged from the army and sent back to the West Indies or returned to the Royal Fusiliers. In the end, Collins was granted a commission in the British West Indies Regiment at the end of March 1917.[73] Three months later, the Army Council agreed that any candidate 'not of pure European descent' could put himself forward for a temporary commission if recommended by his CO 'after serving with credit in the ranks of an Expeditionary Force'. One who took advantage of this was Walter Tull. His father was West Indian and the family had come across to Britain, where Walter had been born. He was educated in Northampton and played professional football for the town. He enlisted in the 17th Middlesex in December 1914 and clearly showed promise as a soldier, rising to lance sergeant by early July 1915. He went to France with his battalion that November, but was invalided back to England early the following May suffering from shell shock. Recovered, Sergeant Tull returned to France at the beginning of November 1916. A month later, he applied for a commission and was recommended by both his CO and brigade commander. Tull joined No. 10 OC Battalion at Gailes and was commissioned into the 5th (Reserve) Battalion Middlesex Regiment at the end of May 1917. He returned to the 23rd Middlesex in France, but was killed on 25 March 1918.[74]

When it came to Regular commissions, Sandhurst and Woolwich appear to have continued to drag their feet. As late as May 1918, a boy whose mother was Burmese was barred from sitting the entrance exam. But the Army Council now had to think again, because of a War Cabinet decision to allow ten places each year at Sandhurst to natives of India, as well as the granting of the permanent King's Commission to twenty deserving Indian officers on Viceroy commissions and temporary commissions to a further 200 Indians. In view of this, Sandhurst was now prepared to accept candidates of mixed blood on the assumption that they would be commissioned in the Indian Army. However, Woolwich was not open to Indian Army candidates and the son of a British judge in Burma and a Burmese lady was initially debarred from entering Woolwich, which appears to have ignored the precedent of W. O'C. Evans, the Eurasian who was accepted in November 1916 and commissioned into the Royal Artillery.* Eventually, however, the Army Council saw sense and the man was admitted.[75]

By the end of 1916 there were no less then twenty-one Infantry Officer Cadet battalions, together with one for the Household Brigade and another for Garrison officers. In addition, other arms and services had their own Cadet battalions. Two cavalry cadet squadrons were formed, at Netheravon on Salisbury Plain and at Kildare in Ireland, while the Royal Artillery had two RFA cadet schools – one at St John's Wood, London, where it made use of Lord's cricket ground, with some cadets being housed in the pavilion, and the other at Exeter. In addition, the RGA had a school at Trowbridge. In February 1917, the gunners dramatically enlarged their officer-training organization. Two more RFA schools were formed, at Weedon and Brighton, while the RGA established others at Bournemouth and Weymouth, although the former was disbanded that October and No. 3 Cadet School at Weymouth moved to Golden Hill on the Isle of Wight.[76] There was an RFC Cadet Battalion, one for the MGC and another for the ASC. In 1918 a Tank Corps Cadet Battalion was also formed. Because of its numerous specialities, the Corps of Royal Engineers developed a network of cadet schools. They were established at the School of Military Engineering at Chatham and at its training centres at Newark and Deganwy. In May 1917 the three were amalgamated as the RE Officer Cadet Battalion, which was based at Newark.[77] The RE Signal Service Training Centre at Bletchley had a cadet school, as did the Wireless Training Centre at Worcester. As for the Young Officer companies, these were finally broken up in June 1916, four months after the initial establishment of the Cadet battalions.

Unlike the other arms and services, the Machine Gun Corps operated a filter system for its potential officers. The reason for this was that when the corps was originally formed it found itself landed with a significant number of low-grade officers, whom battalions had offloaded on the new corps. Therefore, officer candidates had to report first to the MGC Training Centre

---

* Evans was wounded in action, but survived the war.

at Grantham for a 'weeding out' course. Acting RQMS Harbottle of the 6th Northumberland Fusiliers was persuaded by his commanding officer to take a commission in the MGC in early 1917. On arrival at Grantham, he and his fellow students were ordered to remove all rank badges, in line with all officer cadet units. Harbottle recalled that the initial phase of the training consisted largely of intensive squad drill and musketry, together with rigorous hut and kit inspections. During the final week the cadets had to drill squads. Eight out of Harbottle's course of fifty failed to make the grade and were returned to their units, while the remainder, after a week's leave, reported to the MGC OC Battalion at Bisley.

> Conditions were very much better than Grantham both in treatment and location. The huts were for 20 and one end was for sleeping with decent iron beds and that nearer the door contained tables and chairs, where we were expected to study for our ultimate examinations. Also we were now clothed in officer uniforms without rank indications and with the white cadet band round our caps ... Life as a cadet was interesting with a lot of tactical exercises, musketry instruction, visual training and a fair amount of arms drill thrown in. Bisley with its wealth of rifle ranges enabled us to get a good amount of rifle firing. We had a degree of leisure for football or cricket, according to the season and were also supposed to do work on drill books, Infantry Training and trench warfare.

Halfway through the four-month course, which also included a riding course, the cadets were granted a long weekend leave. After successfully completing the course and gaining his commission, Harbottle then returned to Grantham to do his machine-gun course. However, from 1 October 1917 the MGC adopted a new policy. It would only accept officers on secondment, rather than being directly commissioned into the corps, and these officers had to have at least three months' commissioned service. In consequence, the MGC Cadet Battalion was converted into an infantry unit, moving to Catterick and becoming No. 23 Officer Cadet Battalion.

The emphasis on sport was common to all cadet units. Robert Graves was an instructor at No. 4 OC Battalion at Oxford during the summer of 1917: 'Our final selection was made by watching the candidates play games, principally rugger and soccer. Those who played rough, but not dirty, and had quick reactions, were the sort needed, and we spent most of our spare time playing games with them.' But the cadets did not have to play ball games. Frank Hawkings was a cadet in Graves's OC battalion. He spent his two sports afternoons per week on the river and was elected captain of the rowing club. It was therefore perhaps logical that he should take a commission as a sub lieutenant in the Royal Naval Division.[79]

If J. B. Scrivenor is to be believed, the attitude in the specialist Royal Engineer cadet schools was somewhat different to the mainstream training organization. Aged 40 and a scientist in the Malayan Civil Service, he had arrived in Britain at the end of 1916 and enrolled in the Inns of Court, but with a Medical Category of B1, which meant garrison service only. He joined the staff of the Cadet battalion at Berkhamsted and rose to the rank of lance sergeant, before electing to obtain a commission in the RE Signal Service in June 1917. Wearing a cadet's white cap band, he was immediately put into a signals class made up of two captains, a number of subalterns and two cadets. He was not happy:

> The depot was not comfortable. The cadets' mess was overcrowded, no less than a hundred cadets being there for training. The procedure also in the depot was, to my strict ideas, odd. Parades were sloppy, and labourmen who waited in the mess also appeared on guard at the gate ... In the infantry cadet schools at Berkhamsted, the cadets were encouraged to regard themselves as officers as soon as they entered the school and were treated as such. In the signal service the cadets were told bluntly that until they had passed their examination and 'learned their trade' they were not considered as even the equals of pioneers.*[80]

The high level of casualties among junior officers on the Somme in 1916 created a crisis in that there not enough men voluntarily offering themselves for commissions. Almost all the officer material in the Territorial Force had already been drawn in, but there were still possibilities, especially in the HAC. The 1st Battalion had spent a stint as GHQ troops from October 1915 until July 1916, when it became part of the 63rd (Royal Naval) Division, and had been supplying some thirty potential officers per month.

---

* The lowest rank in the Royal Engineers and held by those who had not yet gained a trade.

In September 1916, the 2nd Battalion was preparing to go out to France and was addressed by the Director-General of the Territorial Force. He pleaded for men to put themselves forward for commissions and nearly 300 did so, which must have caused considerable disruption, even though their places were immediately filled by a large draft from the 3rd Battalion, which itself was ordered to supply twenty-five candidates for commissions per month.[81] But the HAC's contribution was a mere drop in the ocean compared with the numbers required. By 1917, 10,000 new officers were needed annually. In January 1917, the 17th Division, for its part, was ordered to provide fifty candidates for commissions per month. As a general rule, no one under the rank of full corporal was allowed to be put forward, except for commissions in the ASC. But as W. N. Nicholson, 17th Division's AA&QMG, pointed out:

> To obtain these we depended on the recommendations of unit commanders. But only the best unit commanders were prepared to lose their best NCOs for they did not necessarily come back to them as officers. Moreover many of these NCOs declined to leave the home they knew; so that our fifty candidates did not necessarily represent the pick of the bunch.

James Jack, now commanding the 2nd West Yorkshires, had to submit the names of five men per month. He adopted the policy of selecting his best warrant officers to fill vacancies in his own battalion, while submitting 'others of high quality' for commissions in other regiments. But battalions were often unable to provide such a number of suitable candidates every month. Some tried to circumvent the rank rule by promoting private soldiers to the rank of acting unpaid corporal before their names were submitted. At one point, the CO of the 4th East Yorkshires, under pressure from his brigadier to put forward names, nominated two Boer War veterans who were battalion sanitary men. The brigadier was initially indignant, but was eventually forced to accept the situation.[82]

At the receiving end, Robert Graves noted that two-thirds of the entry to his OC battalion were recommendations from France, with the remainder being boys fresh out of public schools, with OTC experience. Approximately one-sixth of a course would fail. They were 'sometimes public-school boys without the necessary toughness, but usually men from France, recommended on compassionate grounds – rather stupid platoon-sergeants and machine-gun corporals who had been out too long and needed a rest.' That was the penalty that had to be paid for forcing commanding officers to meet a monthly quota. Yet, from the outset the OC battalions did not shirk from returning cadets who did not match up to their units. Norman Collins, three-quarters of the way through his course with No. 8 OC Battalion, commented:

> About 20 per cent of the cadet battalion have gone or are going back to their units. Three weeks ago we were on parade and a list of names was read out of men to go back. The funny part is that the majority of them have obtained splendid marks in the exams and have good conduct sheets, done well in practical work and yet are told that they are not the class of men wanted. The following are the only 'reasons' given. No. personality, too much personality, would probably be too familiar with NCO[s]. Social position has nothing to do with it …[83]

By early 1918, however, candidates for commissions from France were not necessarily being sent direct to Cadet battalions. Finally persuaded to undergo officer training, 1914 volunteer CQMS Linton Andrews of the Black Watch was sent first to the 5th (Reserve) Battalion Highland Light Infantry at Bridge of Allan. He spent nearly two months here, the training largely consisting of drill and route marches. It was hardly arduous, with work normally finishing by 4 p.m. each day, but the prospective officer cadets were still warned that they would be returned to their units if they failed to match up. Not until he arrived at Gailes in early May 1918 was he permitted to wear an officer cadet's uniform. Conditions, though, seem to have improved dramatically since Arthur West's sorry experiences of spring 1916. He was pleasantly surprised by his first meal: 'WAAC waitresses, table-cloths, soup-plates (just think of it, soup-plates), flowers on the table …' The cadets were kept busy, but 'there appeared to be little risk of anyone failing to get his commission, the standard being pretty low. The officers and instructors were men of fighting experience who were home for a rest. They had no motive for pressing us too hard.' Even so, when it came to the mid course exams, some of the failures were returned to their units. Andrews gained the impression, however, that the shortage of officers was not what it had been. He was still at Gailes when the war ended and only learned that he had been commissioned when he was demobilized in January 1919. Sergeant Harry Morgan of the Royal Warwicks, who had been in France since October 1914, was selected for officer training and was sent in February 1918 to the Reserve battalion of the London Scottish at Chiseldon Camp, Wiltshire. The training here seems to have been more comprehensive than that which Linton Andrews experienced with the HLI, and included musketry, map reading and general education. After passing the course, Morgan was kept in limbo for some weeks, awaiting posting to an Officer Cadet battalion. A senior officer told him and his fellow potential officers that too many men from France had been selected for officer training and they would all now be posted to Training battalions in Britain in their current ranks. His disappointment 'extreme', Sergeant Morgan spent the remainder of the war with the 5th (Reserve) Battalion of the Royal Warwicks.[84] Perhaps with this in mind, in July 1918 the War Office set up two Reception battalions, at Larkhill and Ripon, to receive and train candidates for infantry commissions prior to admission to a Cadet battalion.[85] Similarly, No. 4 RFA Cadet School was converted in November 1917 to an artillery reception brigade.[86]

At the end of June 1917, the 1st Battalion Honourable Artillery Company was withdrawn from the line and became GHQ troops once more, this time relieving the Artists' Rifles in its role of providing guards for GHQ. The Artists, after their long stint behind the lines, now had the opportunity to take a more active part in the war and took the HAC's place in the 63rd Division. But the primary reason why the HAC was withdrawn was because it was considered that it still contained much officer material in its ranks which was in danger of being frittered away. However, with the plethora of Cadet battalions in Britain, it was decided that the GHQ Cadet School should be wound up. Instead, the HAC would, besides its guard duties, provide candidates for the Cadet battalions and demonstration platoons for attachment to the various schools of instruction in France. By the summer of 1918 it was sending potential officers home in batches, with 100 going in June and another fifty in early July.

Where senior ranks were put forward for commissions in their own battalions, it is clear from what Jack writes that they could still be granted commissions in the field, as they had in the early days, without going through the four-month cadet school course, although no Army Council Instruction or Army Order was promulgated to this effect. However, a footnote in form MT.393A did state that 'soldiers serving in the Regular Army on a 12 years' engagement or re-engaged are not eligible for admission to an Officer Cadet Unit.' This certainly applied to John Lucy, a pre-war Regular and Old Contemptible of the Royal Irish Rifles. He was now a sergeant at his regimental depot and recovering from wounds. In May 1917 he was persuaded to apply for a commission and was summoned in front of a general for an interview.

> He asked me why I enlisted. I didn't know. Did I find the life rough? Yes, sir, rather rough, but many others found the same. Would I like a commission? I should. Why? Mainly from the comforts point of view. I had been at Mons? Yes, and I remembered his regiment there. I looked pretty fit. Was I all right now? Yes, quite all right thanks. Well, he'd see about it. He shook hands with me, I saluted and left.

Lucy was commissioned into the Royal Irish Rifles the following month and was formally 'dined in' in the officers' mess.

> My reception was openly warm. Men who had officered me in peace and war rose to meet me and bring me in. My late title of sergeant evaporated in the first breath of an atmosphere easier and more congenial, though not perhaps as openly intimate as that of the troops. 'Come on, old John. Here you are at last. The first one's on me.' Someone said: 'No. On the mess.' They drank my health in sherry. They each recommended their own tailors – good tailors, who would let you run a long account. I was given the choice of four good batmen and the offer of the loan of any article of Kit or equipment I temporarily lacked.[88]

However, in the late summer of 1918 it was laid down that there would be no more direct commissions and that every candidate would have to attend cadet school.[89] In general, though, the genuine ex-ranker officers (as opposed to those who could have been officers from the outset but chose to serve a spell in the ranks) continued to use their considerable experience to become excellent commanders in battle. But the men they led were sometimes ambivalent in their attitude towards them. Alan Thomas stated that there were several ranker officers in the 6th Royal West Kents, but 'all of them unpopular with the men – mainly because they knew their job and there was no chance of "swinging it over them"'.[90]

Arthur Hanbury-Sparrow, the 25-year-old CO of the 2nd Royal Berkshires, noted that by the late summer of 1917 gentleman officers had become 'a very rare thing'. He observed:

> Many seniors used to grumble heavily about the class the cadet schools were passing out. Indeed, the problem of dealing with the somewhat uncouth, but very willing officer reinforcements was not easy. But why blame the schools you used to argue. They could only treat the material they received, and it was obvious the supply of gentlemen was on the verge of exhaustion.

R. T. Rees, himself a public school master and serving with a Service battalion of the Loyals, agreed with the lack of 'the public school type' among the new officers joining his battalion during Third Ypres. He commented that

> though they often made good, it took them rather longer to acquire the sense of responsibility and the faculty of leadership which the Public Schools are supposed to foster, and which, as a matter of fact, they generally do foster. We had some anxious moments with them at first because of the lack of these qualities.[91]

Yet more may have been expected of the public-school men than they could give. Some had had a very sheltered upbringing and were naïve when it came to the world at large. One who suffered from this was P. J. Campbell, who went to France in May 1917 as a 19-year-old gunner subaltern and was initially posted to a divisional ammunition column: 'I was lonely and had no friends; I was inexperienced and ignorant of an officer's duties; I never knew what mistake I should make next or who would have to pay for it.' It was this feeling of insecurity which prompted a number to decline the prospect of a commission. A. Stuart Dolden, who in 1914 had been an assistant solicitor in the Great Eastern Railway's legal department, was serving as a cook in the London Scottish on the Somme. In October 1916 he was invited to take a commission on the staff of the Railway Communications headquarters in Paris:

> The offer was very tempting and I gave it a great deal of thought as to whether I should accept it or not. I came to the conclusion, however, that to transfer from the Somme to a post possibly in Paris would require great strength of character if I was not to be undermined morally. After weighing up the pros and cons, therefore, I decided to refuse the commission.[92]

He stayed as a company cook for the rest of the war.

Brigade and battalion commanders remained critical of the officer training given back in Britain. Brigadier General Crozier, writing about 1917, noted: 'It became increasingly difficult, as time went on, to obtain correct reports from officer patrols, as regards information about the enemy line on which to base plans for raids. This was due to the lack of training at home of young officers.' James Jack complained a year later: 'The thorough and prompt attention to orders, formerly the rule in the Regiment, is now notably absent. This is not due to unwillingness, but to the present officers (save those from the Royal Military College), not having been well grounded at Home in their duties.' Basil Peacock conceded that 'we were not particularly well trained'. The fault, however, lay not so much in the Cadet battalions, which aimed to turn out platoon commanders who would be effective in battle, but in the continuation training offered by the Reserve and Training battalions to which newly commissioned officers were posted prior to being sent to a theatre of war. As had been the case earlier in the war, there was little opportunity for them to develop their leadership skills by being given platoons to command and train. Instead, they found themselves put into young officers' schools or 'wings', which, according to Henry Ogle, who joined one when posted to the 4th (Reserve) Battalion of the King's Own Lancaster Regiment, no one took seriously. 'We drilled each other in squads to practise words of command, voice-carrying and that sort of thing; if it did nothing useful it may have been a better way of spending time than merely hanging about camp.' V. F. Eberle, a sapper who commanded a Pioneer battalion in France during the last part of the war, identified the nub of the problem:

> From our experience of the later replacements, most of them had been given little opportunity for regular command or control of even a small body of men. It was understandable that much of what now seemed to us elementary principles were new and strange to them under active-service conditions. In their home training schools it had been mainly a case of each man for himself. They might have been lectured on the duties and relationships of an officer to his men, but they had not the experience of putting them into effect.[93]

Consequently, when the new officers arrived at the Front and found themselves pitchforked into commanding platoons, often without an experienced platoon sergeant to back them up, many were bewildered and it took them time to settle in. It is true that the quality of material did decline from the point of view of traditional officer qualities, but, as Robert Graves argued, 'greater efficiency in action', as developed in the new breed of officer by the Cadet battalions, 'more than compensated for their deficiency in manners.'[94] Cadet battalions themselves were responsible for 48 per cent of the 229,316 combatant commissions granted in the British Army during 1914–18 and the fortunes of its officer corps rested on their shoulders for the last two years of the war. That the army was able to endure the frustrations of 1917 and, on the Western Front, the near disasters of early 1918, and then go on to achieve victory on every front shows that the products of the Cadet battalions were not as deficient in officer qualities as some made out and that the training given by them was on the right lines.

There is no doubt that the character of the officer corps did change during the war, reflecting the fact that by 1918 the British Army was a largely civilian force. No precise statistics exist for the social background of those granted commissions during the war, but some indication can be gained from a War Office survey of just over 144,000 officers demobilized between 11 November 1918 and 12 May 1920. The survey categorizes them by civil employment and it is noticeable that nearly 60 per cent came from what can be viewed as middle-class occupations: 'commercial and clerical', 'students and teachers' and 'professional men'. Of the balance, a significant number came from backgrounds that can only be described as lower-middle- or working-class: 'carters', 'seamen and fishermen', 'leather tanners', 'coal and shale miners' and 'warehousemen and porters', to name but a few.[95] Indeed, Graham Seton Hutchison revealed that his 33rd Machine Gun Battalion had as company commanders in the final months of the war the son of a Scottish miner, holder of two MCs and a DCM, a former Regular sergeant in the Scots Guards (MC, DCM), a wool salesman (MC and bar) and a medical student with a DSO and MC. None had attended a public school, and nor had his adjutant, the son of a land agent and also the holder of two MCs.[96] It was a very different officer corps to that of 1914, but, once demobilization had taken place, its character would largely revert to that of the pre-war army.

eleven

THE STAFF

'One can understand that those people at Army and Corps headquarters behind the line some thirty miles, with nice chateaus [sic] in which to live, are in no hurry to end the war.' So wrote Captain Harry Yoxall MC at the end of 1916.[1] The vast gulf that appeared to exist between the staff and the front-line soldier, especially in France and Flanders, is one of the dominant themes of the British Army in the Great War and Yoxall's comment is typical of the attitude of those in the trenches. But, as the army expanded and the war became more complex so there was an increasing demand for competent men to become staff officers.

At the outbreak of war, the British Army was unable to fill all the posts which required qualified staff officers, those who had *psc* or *qs** after their names in the Army List. The total number required was 245. This was made up of twenty-two staff officers for the HQ of the Expeditionary Force bound for France and nine each for the three army corps HQs which made up its immediate subordinate headquarters. Each of the six infantry divisions earmarked for France required nine staff officers, including the three brigade majors for each of the brigades that a division controlled. The two cavalry divisions and their brigades also needed a total of sixteen. And then there was the Territorial Force, whose fourteen infantry divisions and fourteen cavalry brigades required a total of 126 staff officers. In

---

* *psc* meant that the holder had successfully passed the staff course at Camberley or its Indian Army equivalent at Quetta. *qs* reflected an officer who had qualified for the staff by virtue of successfully completing a tour as a staff officer, rather than attend Camberley or Quetta.

addition, the War Office required its quota, as did the higher headquarters responsible for home defence. In August 1914, there were a total of 937 qualified staff officers, but this included those required for the Indian Army as well. Furthermore, many were serving in command appointments. The upshot was that there was a shortage and positions had to be filled by officers with little or no experience of staff work. The fact, too, that Army Staff College was closed down at the outbreak of war did not help.[2]

The War Office, as we have already seen, was subject to much turbulence at the outbreak of war, with many of its key staff removed to take up positions with the Expeditionary Force and their places largely taken by Reserve officers who were not *au fait* with the current situation or, in some cases, how the War Office functioned. Matters were not helped by Kitchener's autocratic approach, combined with an ailing CIGS, Sir Charles Douglas, who lacked the will to stand up to him. Consequently, Kitchener, as the Secretary of State, was prone to take decisions without consultation.

A classic example of this during the early days was over the despatch of the 7th Division and the 3rd Cavalry Division to Belgium in early October 1914. Charles Callwell, who as DMO should have been involved from the outset, did not learn of Kitchener's decision until after the orders had been sent out. He realized that no thought had been given to organizing a base and lines of communication for the force and had to sort it out on his own initiative.[3] Sir Charles Douglas himself died from overwork that same month and was replaced as CIGS by Sir James Wolfe Murray, who had been the Commander-in-Chief in South Africa. He, too, was unable to stand up to Kitchener, and, according to Maurice Hankey, was nicknamed 'Sheep' Murray by Winston Churchill. In the same diary entry, dated 23 September 1915, and covering discussions over whether to commit British troops to Salonika, Hankey described Kitchener's method of working with the General Staff: 'He sits at the head of the table and talks a lot, and bludgeons everyone into agreeing with him ... Then K. proceeds to dictate, and it is dished up next day as a Memo. by the General Staff.'[4] General Sir William (Wully) Robertson, Sir John French's chief of staff, put his finger on what was wrong in a letter to Lord Stamfordham, the King's private secretary:

The Govt must receive the best military advice at home … The S. of S. for War has not the time to study matters & formulate advice, in addition to his other work. The General Staff, with a trusted & competent head, should be allowed to function & do the work for which it was designed, & which it alone can do.[5]

The Cabinet, too, were becoming frustrated by Kitchener's autocratic manner. On 22 September, the day before the Salonika discussion described by Hankey above, Asquith took advantage of Kitchener's absence from a Cabinet meeting to obtain agreement from the members that the Secretary of State organize an effective General Staff 'to guide and advise the cabinet, and its committees, in matters of strategy'. Asquith wrote to Kitchener the following day asking him to replace Wolfe Murray with his deputy, Sir Archibald Murray, who, unlike his namesake, had first-hand experience of the war as chief of staff to the BEF. He was also to select a few high-class staff officers from the theatres of war to assist the new CIGS and to arrange that 'there be drawn up once in every week a considered appreciation by the General Staff here, of the military situation, actual and prospective'. Kitchener acted fast and Sir Archibald became CIGS on 26 September.[6]

Some members of the Cabinet, notably Bonar Law and Lloyd George, still wanted to get rid of Kitchener, but Asquith, realizing his continuing value as a recruiting figurehead, continued to stand by him. Yet it was becoming clear that Kitchener's view of strategy was becoming increasingly warped, especially over the Dardanelles and Salonika. With opposition to him growing in the Cabinet, Asquith arranged at the beginning of November 1915 for Kitchener to be sent on a fact-finding tour of the Mediterranean theatre of operations. In the meantime, he himself would act as the War Minister. He also established a new system for the overall direction of the war. At the outbreak, the Committee of Imperial Defence (CID) had been placed in suspended animation and in November 1914 Asquith established the War Council. This was superseded in June 1915 by the Dardanelles Committee, but both this and its predecessor proved too unwieldy. Consequently, in November 1915 Asquith created the War Committee, an inner cabal of ministers, with the First Sea Lord and CIGS available to offer advice.* Robertson, however, continued to bombard the government with his views on the conduct of the war. On 6 November he sent Asquith a paper arguing that the war could only be won in France and Flanders. He concluded:

> We are now conducting four distinct campaigns, and we hold in England large disposable reserves. It is essential in these circumstances that there should be one military authority responsible for advising His Majesty's Government regarding military policy in all theatres ... Experience has shown that in a war of the magnitude of the present one it is undesirable to combine in one person the functions of supreme military adviser and of War Minister.[7]

This appears to have made a deep impression on the Prime Minister and, by early December, he had made up his mind to appoint Robertson as CIGS. In the meantime, Kitchener returned to Britain at the end of November. Conscious of his unpopularity in government circles, he tended his resignation to Asquith, who refused it. He did, however, tell Kitchener that in future the CIGS, and not him, was to be the government's principal military adviser. Nevertheless, Asquith persuaded him that, in view of his national standing, it was Kitchener's duty to remain in office. The Prime Minister then proposed Robertson, who happened to be in London, as CIGS and Kitchener invited him to dinner. The upshot was that Robertson wrote to Kitchener stating that he would accept the post, but only under certain conditions. Apart from being recognized as the government's prime military adviser, Robertson laid down that it was he who should issue all orders to theatre commanders and have direct contact with them, without being required to seek the sanction of the Army Council. This would leave the Secretary of State with merely the responsibility of administering the army.

Kitchener accepted Robertson's terms and on 23 December 1915 Robertson duly became CIGS, with Murray appointed to command the forces in Egypt. Some, like Hankey, wondered why Murray had been replaced.[8] Charles Callwell provided the answer. While he considered Murray 'an excellent administrator' and a charming character, as well as having a good knowledge of the conduct of war,

* In December 1916, Lloyd George changed it to the War Cabinet.

he was not disposed by instinct to address himself in the broader aspects of strategy and of military policy. His bent was to concern himself with the details. Somewhat cautious, nay diffident, by nature, he moreover shrank from pressing his views, worthy of all respect as they were, on others, and he was always guarded in expressing them even when invited to do so.[9]

The CIGS's new powers were enshrined in an Order in Council dated 27 January 1916 and the only concession that Robertson allowed Kitchener was the right to put his signature on orders to theatre commanders. Robertson stamped his blunt personality on proceedings from the outset. One of his first acts was to recommend strongly to the War Committee that Gallipoli be totally evacuated and this was done. For the next two years he would ensure that the view that the war could only be won on the Western Front would dominate strategic thinking. Even when Lloyd George, the most ardent of the 'easterners', took over the War Office after Kitchener had fallen victim to a mine when en route to Russia aboard the cruiser HMS *Hampshire* in late May 1916, he was unable to exert much influence. Lloyd George placed himself in a stronger position when he became Prime Minister in early December 1916. Even so, he was aware that much of Fleet Street and the Conservatives within his coalition continued to support the 'westerners'. On Robertson's recommendation, Lord Derby succeeded as War Minister: 'He knows the ropes of the office.* The country believes in him as a good honest man. The Army likes him.'[10] He and Robertson formed a good team, but Lloyd George remained determined to reduce Robertson's influence. His opportunity came with the Allies' agreement at Rapallo on 7 November 1917 to establish a Supreme War Council at Versailles to direct strategy. Lloyd George had Sir Henry Wilson, renowned in the army as an arch schemer, appointed as the British representative. The Prime Minister then began to work through him, largely bypassing Robertson. There then followed the question of who was to control the Allied general reserve which was to be created. Lloyd George managed to engineer the Executive War Board to do this, with Ferdinand Foch as its chairman, but Robertson pointed out that this meant British

* Derby was the Under-Secretary of State for War at the time.

troops being commanded by a foreign general and that the correct chain of command for the British contribution to it lay through the CIGS. A furious debate followed, during which Lloyd George tried to arrange for Wilson and Robertson to swap places. It finally forced Robertson's resignation in February 1918.

Henry Wilson was duly appointed CIGS in Robertson's place, but with a reduction in powers, while Derby, who had disagreed with Robertson over the Allied general reserve, remained in office until that April. He was succeeded by a Lloyd George ally, Lord Milner. One who mourned the passing of Derby and Robertson was Sir Sam Fay, who had been appointed Director-General Movements and Railways in March 1918, having previously served as Director of Movements at the War Office: 'When Derby and Robertson were in control there was a sense of stability, of confidence, of knowledge that law and order prevailed. With their departure an uncertainty, a looseness and a lack of confidence became general. Everybody felt uneasy and worried.' Fay recorded a conversation he had with Sir Nevil Macready, the Adjutant General, in early July 1918:

> AG [Macready] told me afterwards on some question he and I wanted settling by SofS [Milner] not available, except for the equivalent of one day a week. That he, SofS, did not try to learn the job. He listens to outside talk and appears to pay more attention to those who have opinions, but no knowledge, than to those who are doing the work and have the experience and knowledge of the particular subject.[11]

Yet, in spite of this, and the pressures under which Haig, especially, was put, the British armies did play the major part in gaining victory before the end of 1918.

As for the War Office itself, it inevitably went through a number of reorganizations as the war progressed. On the G side, which was directly answerable to the CIGS, a Director of Home Forces was created in December 1914, but this post was abolished when Sir John French became C-in-C Home Forces a year later. Sir John's headquarters also took over many of the training functions of the Director of Military Training and this post was also removed, the balance of its work being taken over by the Director of Staff Duties. More significant, once Robertson took over as CIGS, was his decision to separate intelligence from the Director of Military Operations (DMO) by creating a new Directorate of Military Intelligence (DMI), thus finally recognizing that this activity was too important to be submerged in another branch, even though operations and intelligence do go hand-in-hand to a significant degree. Likewise, the Press Bureau, which had been run in conjunction with the Admiralty to regulate censorship, was passed over to the Home Office soon after the outbreak of war. On the other hand, the need for military censorship remained. This was placed under DMI, with its head titled Director of Special Intelligence (DSI), although this was changed to Deputy Director of Military Intelligence (DDMI) in March 1918. The creation, too, of a Deputy Chief of the General Staff in December 1915 helped to lift some of the burden from the CIGS's shoulders.

The Adjutant General's branch also spawned new directorates. The Directorate of Recruiting and Organization (DRO) was split into two. The recruiting crisis of autumn 1915 saw Lord Derby appointed as Director-General of Recruiting, but two years later all recruiting matters and manpower as a whole was passed over to the Ministry of National Service. The Directorate of Mobilization (DM) was dissolved soon after the outbreak of war, but was reconstituted in 1917 to deal with demobilization plans and those matters previous dealt with by the Recruiting Directorate which were not taken over by the Ministry of National Service. A prisoner of war information section had been established, in accordance with the Geneva Conventions, in August 1914 to provide information on enemy prisoners of war and internees. This became a fully fledged directorate in February 1915. In May 1916, a Directorate of Graves Registration and Enquiries (DGR&E) was established under the Adjutant General, absorbing the Graves Registration Commission (GRC) which had been set up in France the previous July (*see page 431*). The QMG's empire remained largely as it was at the outbreak of war, apart from the splitting of the Directorate of Supplies and Quartering (*see page 111*). The principal change to the MGO's department was the creation of the Ministry of Munitions in June 1915, which by degrees took away many of the MGO's procurement duties.

Under the Civil Member, who was represented by the Under-Secretary of State, there was a significant erosion in the independence of the Territorial Force. Some aspects which had common ground with the Regular

Army and Special Reserve were transferred to other branches at the outbreak of war. Medical aspects were removed from the Director-General of the Territorial Force (DGTF) in April 1916 and passed to the Director-General, Army Medical Services (DGAMS). Then, in April 1917, following the transfer of further duties to the Military Secretary and Director of Mobilization, together with the War Office embracing the Volunteer Force, the Director-General was retitled Director-General of the Territorial and Volunteer Forces. The Civil Member also took over all questions relating to the acquisition of land for not just the War Office but for the armed forces as a whole and for the Ministry of Munitions in January 1917. The Finance Member's department witnessed a massive increase in the work of the Directorate of Army Contracts.

Eventually, in March 1917, Andrew Weir, a shipping magnate, was asked to investigate the army's supply branches with a view to improving the efficiency of the system. As a result of his report, he was appointed Surveyor General of Supply (SGS), with responsibility for coordinating the army's needs for supplies, stores and work services and to oversee all contracts. In this respect, the Directorate of Contracts was made subordinate to him. Another new director-general in autumn 1916 came as a result of Sir Eric Geddes' investigation into transport arrangements for the BEF. This was the Director-General of Movements and Railways (DGMR).

This rapid expansion of the War Office resulted in its staff increasing from less than 2,000 at the outbreak of war to 22,279 on 11 November 1918, with many women being taken on.[12] Given the massive enlargement of the army, this was inevitable.

The various staff branches of the army in the field reflected the organization of the War Office. Thus, the General Staff or 'G staff' dealt with operations, intelligence, organization, training and press matters, while the A (Adjutant General's) branch was responsible for personnel matters, and the Q (Quartermaster General's) branch covered supplies, quartering, transportation and postal services.

At the lowest level, that of infantry battalion and equivalent, the commanding officer's principal staff officer was his adjutant, who dealt with G and A matters. It was a demanding job. Nineteen year-old Charles

Carrington was made acting adjutant of the 1st/5th Royal Warwicks shortly before the opening of the offensive on the Somme:

> It was my business to run an office – a line of activity in which I had no experience – to cope with confidential and secret correspondence, to issue daily routine orders and occasional operation orders, to receive the instructions and enquiries from brigade behind our backs, to anticipate the needs of the companies in front, to stall off minor troubles from the colonel if I could deal with them myself, to be on duty for twenty-four hours a day, and to answer a hundred questions from high and low.[13]

During the course of the war, the adjutant was provided with some help in the form of an assistant adjutant and an intelligence officer, that is if the unit had sufficient officers available. But he continued to carry a heavy burden, even when out of the line, as Stormont Gibbs, the adjutant of the 1st/4th Suffolks, makes plain:

> … he could not rest like the others, for he had to start at once organising drafts to replace casualties, writing reports, seeing people, talking on the telephone, dictating to typewriters, arranging billets, huts, tents, supplies, perhaps even attending courts martial. So he might have several nights in the line with nearly no sleep and then come back to full days of office work, training and parades and more interrupted nights with phone calls from Brigade about the next move.[14]

Training was usually the responsibility of the second-in-command, while the quartermaster largely looked after the Q side.

But at battalion level, these individuals were not considered as staff officers *per se*. The lowest level at which the genuine article was found was brigade headquarters. At the outbreak of war a brigade commander had a brigade major and a staff captain to assist him. The former looked after G matters, while the latter was responsible for A and Q. Almost all who served on the staff are generally agreed that a brigade major's job was the most satisfying. The future field marshal, Bernard Montgomery, termed it 'the most interesting of all Staff jobs'.[15] Twenty-year-old Anthony Eden was made brigade major of the 198th Brigade in summer 1918 and welcomed it as a job I had always coveted, whether seen from below as an adjutant or from the, for me, less congenial remoteness of divisional headquarters. The brigade and its staff seemed of exactly the right size and scope for individual efforts to be rewarding, while the contacts with the units were close enough to have a human interest.[16]

At the end of March 1916 Eric Gore-Browne was attached to HQ 140th Brigade from the 1st/8th Londons, where he had been second-in-command, to understudy both the brigade major and staff captain so that he could fill in for them when they went on leave. In a letter home dated 1 April he wrote:

> I am beginning to get a little the hang of this business and I will try and tell you how it goes. The first thing is that one officer always has to be here … There appear to be three busy times during the day, one just after breakfast when the General goes through all the papers etc that have come during the night; the BM has to know all about these and say what steps he has taken in each case, and the same ritual takes place at 2 and at 6pm. I find that the Staff Captain does all the Q matters, eg rations, ammunition, bombs, motor lorries, horses etc and the Brigade Major all the G branch, ie operations, working parties, reliefs, etc and there is no doubt that at first sight the BM's job is vastly the more interesting as the Staff Captain is largely a Quartermaster's clerk, while the BM does the exciting part including intelligence … The BM's side of the business seems to be mostly very careful thinking and care of detail and the test of good orders seems to be not to have any telegrams sent from Battn asking questions about them … Hours are very strict here. Breakfast sharp at 8 and dinner at 7.30 bed at 10pm.'[17]

Others also echoed Gore-Browne's comments on the staff captain's job. J. B. Scrivenor, who was a brigade signals officer, observed:

> One of the most trying tasks in the army must have been that of a staff captain. It entailed an enormous amount of work in obtaining a steady service of supplies with no excitement to enlighten it, but plenty of complaints if the least thing went wrong; no jolly times at advanced brigade headquarters when in the line, but dull office-work behind.[18]

Indeed, the normal practice was that the BM accompanied the brigade commander into the trenches, while the staff captain remained behind in the wagon lines.

As did other levels of headquarters, the brigade staff expanded as the war progressed. Intelligence officers were introduced. D. V. Kelly explains the rationale behind this:

> It came to be accepted as a general rule that in battle all touch with units, whether in one's own line or on the flanks, had to be personal, and though runners could carry messages, reliable information could only be obtained by personal contact with the officers in the different areas. This was the primary reason for the attachment to all Brigade and Battalion head-quarters of 'Intelligence Officers', though in normal trench warfare we were expected to make ourselves useful in a variety of other ways, especially in organising a systematic service of observation, sniping, and the provision of up-to-date maps.[19]

As one of the initial steps towards creating the Machine Gun Corps, a brigade machine-gun officer was appointed in 1915, to coordinate the battalion MG sections. During the latter stages of the war some brigades had assistant brigade majors and, at times, there was also a brigade gas officer. The brigade transport and signals officers also helped to swell the strength of brigade HQ and some ran two separate messes as a result, but an efficient brigade HQ did rely on its members getting on with one another. Sidney Rogerson recalled, with deep affection, the staff of the 23rd Brigade on the Aisne in May 1918. The brigade commander, W. G. St. G. Grogan, was holder of the VC, CB, CMG, DSO and bar. The BM was also highly decorated, with the DSO, two MCs and the *Croix de Guerre*, while the staff captain wore the MC and bar, and the IO and Rogerson, who called himself the 'dogsbody', were also MC winners. It was, he recalled, 'a happy and youthful family'.[20]

Divisional level saw a much larger staff than that at brigade. The G side was looked after by three officers: the GSO1 (a lieutenant colonel); the GSO2 (usually a major); and the GSO3 (a major or captain). Bernard Montgomery was appointed GSO2 to 33rd Division in January 1917 after serving as BM 104th Brigade. He described his new post as 'an interesting one', but not such hard work as being a BM, where he also had to supervise the staff captain, who was an inexperienced New Army officer. While the GSO3 was responsible for intelligence, he explained, 'the GSO1 and myself divide the work between us and I am responsible that it is done and nothing is forgotten. There is a lot to be done, but one has more time to do it than a brigade has.'[21] On the AQ side, the senior staff officer, and before the outbreak of war the only one, was the Assistant Adjutant and Quartermaster General (AA&QMG) who ranked as a lieutenant colonel. He had two majors under him – the Deputy Assistant Adjutant General (DAAG) who dealt with A matters; and the Deputy Assistant Quartermaster General (DAQMG), who looked after Q aspects.

The division was the lowest formation in which the supporting arms and services had direct representation at the headquarters. Both the Royal Artillery and Royal Engineers had HQ staffs there, headed by the Commander Royal Artillery and Commanding Royal Engineer (CRA, CRE). The CRA was a brigadier general (a full colonel in cavalry divisions) and the CRE a lieutenant colonel and they acted as advisers to the divisional commander and also controlled all artillery and engineer units within the division. They were, however, officially only attached to the divisional HQ. There were also representatives of the RAMC, the Army Veterinary Corps and the Ordnance Department, as well as a Deputy Assistant Provost Marshal (DAPM). During the early days of the war there were also Assistant Directors of Transport and Supply at divisional HQ, but their duties were soon taken over by the commander of the divisional column and his supply officer. The divisional HQ also had various specialists, like the divisional gas and MG officers, attached at various times during the war.

The divisional commander was usually the highest-ranking officer with whom the ordinary front-line soldier came in contact. A major reason for this was that while the units within a division did not change very often, divisions themselves were often placed under the command of different corps, especially in France and Flanders. Indeed, on the Western Front corps HQs were essentially static organizations, which enabled them to get to know their sectors of the Front very well. Their organization was basically the same as that of a division, but larger and with the department heads of higher rank. Thus, the G staff was headed by a Brigadier General General Staff (BGGS) and by the end of the war consisted largely of GSO2s.

The A and Q sides were also in charge of a brigadier general, the Deputy Adjutant and Quartermaster General (DA&QMG). Because it was largely static, the corps HQ had control over matters like light railways and camouflage in its sector and had advisers on these. Under the Labour Commandant, corps also controlled the labour units within its area.

Corps headquarters seemed remote places to regimental officers and the like. J. F. C. Fuller, later an eminent military theorist, joined VII Corps as a GSO3 in July 1915. It was situated in a chateau in the village of Marieux, south-east of Doullens. The building itself

> was of the normal one-room-deep type, and being surrounded by a high wall, in appearance it resembled a fortified house. It was some ten miles from the front, and the only signs of war were an occasional hostile aeroplane, the distant bombing of a gun, and at night-time the reflection of the gun and Very light flashes on the skies.[22]

It was this separation from the war that irritated the fighting troops. Charles Carrington said that when mistakes were made

> the remoteness and anonymity of corps headquarters were such that the Corps Commander, inevitably, was blamed. Heaven knows, we grumbled and joked about brigade and division, but within reason. Knowing them, we made allowance. Corps we did not know and, since battles in France were mostly disastrous, the Corps Commander was rarely popular.[23]

Oliver Lyttelton, later Viscount Chandos, saw both regimental service and spent time on the staff: 'Corps commanders settled into their chateaux like householders, not temporary tenants: their staff with them: the paperwork grew comfortably under the military version of Parkinson's Law. No *esprit de corps* could be built up: none of the troops knew to which corps they belonged. Furthermore, this static bureaucracy got out of touch with the troops and the conditions under which they lived, fought and died. In all my time I only saw one corps commander further up than Brigade HQ: he was Sir Julian Byng.'[24] Guy Chapman, who served as a staff learner at a corps headquarters during the early months of 1917, also noted the wide gulf that existed between division and corps:

A Corps staff which had been well dug-in for a year on a quiet front, resembled nothing so much as the menial hierarchy of a ducal palace – with the duke away. Never having had a division on their hands for more than a month or so they had come to regard them as persons to be employed but not encouraged. Their interest lay in the smooth airs which caressed Army and GHQ. They were in constant touch with the higher aspect of war, shown to them by visitors, delicious information about what Foch thought, how the French wanted a single command under Nivelle, how old So-and-So was at last about to be sent home, what Lloyd George had promised the Italians, and how his lavish promises did not suit the French. In short, it was a rare atmosphere, which the fears and anxieties of troops in the line never poisoned'.[25]

A further complaint came from Archibald Home, when he was the GSO1 of the 46th Division in April 1916: 'I hate changing corps because they generally run things a little differently and one has to get into new ways.'[26]

Army HQ was even more rarified, but the army commanders were better known to the men than those commanding corps. To a junior officer the atmosphere was daunting. Captain Thomas Heald of the Cheshires did a two-week attachment at HQ First Army in January 1918: 'I feel quite lost here. Everybody is either a General or a Colonel and the place is stiff with red tabs. However, I have got a very comfortable billet with a real bed and sheets.'[27] The senior staff officer was a major general and by the end of the war had nine G staff officers under him. Significantly, the A and Q sides were headed, like that at corps HQ, by a DA&QMG, but he also had nine officers working for him. Transportation was a significant element, with a relatively large staff to look over the light railways within the army area, and a sub-branch dealing with roads. By the end of the war there was even an Agricultural Production Officer at each army HQ in France, reflecting the policy of creating a degree of self-sufficiency for the BEF (*see page 449*).

The ultimate level was the theatre headquarters. That in France grew rapidly. In August 1914 the GHQ of the Expeditionary Force numbered thirty-six officers. By the end of the war it had grown to over 300. This reflected the fact that in four years the BEF had expanded from seven divisions to sixty-six (including ten Dominion and two Portuguese) organized in five armies and the increasing complexities of modern warfare. A theatre HQ had a chief of staff and in France the G side was broken down into four branches. The Operations branch was headed by a Major General General Staff (MGGS), with a BGGS as his deputy. The Staff Duties (SD) branch, which was responsible for organization, training, and other matters not directly connected with operations, had a similar set-up. The third branch covered censorship and the press (CP) and was headed by a Colonel General Staff. It looked after journalists, both British and foreign, and visiting military attaches, as well as the issue of communiqués. Finally, there was the intelligence branch, which in 1914 had embraced CP, and was headed by a BGGS. The Adjutant General had a deputy and three brigadier generals, who looked after personal services, organization and mobilization. He also had a DAG at the base, who was known as the DAG 3rd Echelon and was responsible for processing all returns on personnel, including casualties and prisoners of war, as well as notifying the War Office of in-theatre requirements on personnel. The BEF's Quartermaster General had an empire which grew to two deputies, five brigadier generals and twenty-eight other officers.

In terms of supporting arms and services, the senior artillery officers at corps, army and GHQ were initially described as 'advisers' and exercised no command function. Indeed, artillery operational planning was largely carried out by the G staff, and the artillery representatives at the higher HQs merely advised on technical matters. In May 1916 Major General J. F. N. Birch took over as the artillery adviser at GHQ in France and gradually began to press for further responsibility. By December 1917 it was agreed that the Major General Royal Artillery (MGRA), as he was now titled, would be responsible to the General Staff for estimating artillery requirements in terms of the numbers and types of guns and mortars and their ammunition and recommending the deployment of guns and mortars in line with operational plans, as well as the adoption of new equipment and changes in artillery organization and policy. However, because GHQ in France itself directly controlled no artillery units, apart from the Anti-Aircraft (AA) School of Gunnery and two AA sections, the MGRA could still not be called a commander, unlike his subordinates at army and corps who did indeed have considerable numbers of guns under their direct command. Nevertheless, the MGRA was now involved more closely in operational planning and to this end a GSO1 was appointed to his staff for the purpose of coordinating the artillery of neighbouring armies. The titles of artillery staff officers also provoked problems during the middle part of the war. There was a strong school of thought that considered that they should not be regarded as General Staff officers since few were graduates of the Staff College. In July 1916 it was decided to rank them as DAAGs, which made little sense since most of their work involved operations rather than administration. Not until over a year later did the War Office finally relent and agree that they should be graded as mainstream staff officers.[28] But not all those who served on artillery staffs were gunners. Francis Law of the Irish Guards served a two-month attachment to HQ IX Corps in summer 1916 as an artillery IO. He was tasked with plotting German battery positions, and 'despite my ignorance of artillery I was given every facility and a completely free hand.'[29]

The Royal Engineers also initially suffered problems. In 1914 neither *Field Service Regulations I* nor *II* made any reference to the duties of the chief engineers at corps or army or for what was termed the Brigadier General RE at GHQ. Indeed, the artillery adviser to the original Expeditionary Force is supposed to have remarked to Brigadier General G. H. Fowke, the BGRE, 'I don't suppose that you will have much to do in this war!' The fact that these two officers were provided with just a single staff car – and the solitary clerk alloted them with just a bicycle – did not bode well for either. Indeed, when GHQ settled down at Saint Omer during First Ypres they were allotted just one room. By this time both had managed to obtain assistants and these shared a table. However, the growing engineer demands brought about by the advent of trench warfare made it clear that Fowke needed to be given executive powers in order to make the best use of RE resources. Consequently, after the BEF was organized into the First and Second Armies at the end of 1914 Fowke was elevated to the title of Chief Engineer BEF. Simultaneously, one of his assistants was made Deputy Director of Works, with responsibility for coordinating work on road communications and accommodation within the army areas. The Chief Engineer's empire continued to grow, especially with the introduction of mining operations and gas warfare and the development work on trench mortars and other new weapons. As a result, in July 1915 Fowke was made the Engineer-in-Chief (EinC) BEF. To enable him to delegate some of his now wide responsibilities, Chief Engineers were appointed at army and corps. By the end of the war, the EinC's staff had grown to over twenty-five officers dealing with everything from bridging to electrical engineering, this in spite of a significant portion of his empire having been hived off to the Director-General of Transportation. Unlike the artillery staff, RE staff officers were not given formal General Staff status, largely because they tended to be specialists.[30] This, however, did not prevent several Sapper officers, like gunners, from serving on the General Staff.

The Machine Gun Corps also had a representative at GHQ in the form of a BGGS, assisted by a GSO2. The Tank Corps, the other new teeth arm developed during the war, did not, since it had its own headquarters. The same applied to the Royal Flying Corps. The position of the directors of the various services changed as the war went on. *FSR II* laid down that the Director of Army Signals was directly answerable to the G staff, even though it was a branch of the Royal Engineers, while the Director of Medical Services and the Deputy Judge Advocate's and the Chaplain's departments came under the Adjutant General at GHQ. The other directors were nominally under the QMG, but those of railways, remounts, works, veterinary services, postal and ordnance services in fact came under the Inspector General of Communications.

In general terms, the staff advised the commander and put the flesh on the bones of his plan. Much of their work involved paper since, so that there could be no misunderstandings, orders were generally in writing. These became ever more complex as the war progressed, with new weapons systems being introduced into the order of battle. General Tom Bridges, who commanded the 19th Division at Messines in June 1917 recalled:

> Divisional operation orders for this attack covered innumerable sheets
> of foolscap. Compared with those of 1914 they were whole volumes. For
> the staging of a battle in 1917 required an extraordinary amount of

thought and care. Every unit had its place in the scheme, various objectives had to be attacked in different ways, artillery barrage maps made and orders for the gunners, signallers, machine-gunners, Royal Engineers, Pioneers, Field Ambulances and all the administrative services carefully worked out. Nothing could be left to chance in the original plan, though much had to be left to initiative once battle was joined. No doubt the Germans had to do the same, for the science of killing each other had become a very complicated business entailing much paper and ink and hard work into the night for the General and his staff. I never saw a game of bridge played in a divisional headquarters throughout the war except occasionally when back in rest billets and even then we were generally busy with schemes of training or plans for some future devilry.[31]

The chief of staff of the Cavalry Corps, Archibald Home, preparing for the assault at Cambrai in November 1918, wrote: 'Our preparations for the attack are nearing completion. It is always a bad time for the Staff Officer – all work is capable of improvement – yet so great is the military machine and so complicated its cogs and wires that it is seldom the Staff can say "Now I have finished – let the thing rip."'[32] At GHQ in France, which moved from Saint Omer to Montreuil, with its better communications, at the end of March 1916, the situation was much the same. Indeed, Frank Fox, who served on the Q staff, referred to the 'Monks of Montreuil'. He stated:

> … in my time, in my branch, no officer who wished to stay was later than 9am at his desk; most of the eager men were at work before then. We left at 10.30pm, if possible, more often later. On Saturday and Sunday exactly the same hours were kept. 'An hour for exercise' in the afternoon was supposed to be reserved, in addition to meal-hours, but it was not by means always possible.[33]

Logistics, too, had to be deployed to support the operational plan and became increasingly complicated. But even when major operations were not taking place, the armies had to be housed, fed and trained. There was also the constant need for information on the enemy so that future operational plans could be formulated. This meant that the staff at all levels had to keep its finger on the pulse of the army and this was done to a large extent by regular reports in the form of returns. Arthur Asquith, serving as a company commander in the Hood Battalion of 63rd (Royal Naval) Division in July 1916 noted that he had to submit daily to battalion HQ situation reports as at 2.30 a.m. and 2.30 p.m., an indent for RE stores at 7.30 a.m., and a strength return at 9 p.m. In addition, he had to send an intelligence report and a casualty return at 3.30 p.m. Each week he had to submit a statement recording the amount of small arms ammunition his company held and a certificate stating that each man had his iron ration intact. Finally, each month he had to send certificates confirming orders received, that no fires had been lit in the billets (a frequent cause of expensive French claims for damage to buildings) and that no private cameras were possessed by the company.[34] There were, too, constant requests for additional information from higher HQs. These might be in the form of a trawl for men with experience of a particular trade, or surveys on the quality of rations or clothing. Sometimes these could appear at unfortunate times. Guy Chapman records an incident during Third Ypres when the remnants of his battalion were grimly hanging on after a failed attack and waiting to be relieved:

> About three o'clock a runner from brigade came staggering in. I tore open the brown envelope, which a glance assured me did not contain relief orders. 'On visiting your horse lines today, I found the grease-traps were not in good condition. For information and necessary action, please. AB Area Sanitary Officer.' It was too grim and too old-fashioned a jest. The brigade runner was thirstily swallowing a mug of tea. 'What time did you start?' I asked him. 'Ten o'clock, sir. I've had to lie up several times on the way.' He had spent five hours crossing two miles of country to carry this triviality.'[35]

At battalion level there was often a sense of being deluged in paper, especially prior to a major offensive. James Jack's diary in June 1916 notes:

> While the battle storm blows up in front we have to ride out a gale of paper at our backs. There are sheaves of orders, amendments, counter-orders, returns and reports to be dealt with. But, by the Grace of God, we may be able to overcome all our enemies, the Germans in front, the Staff in rear.

A year later, while preparing for Third Ypres, he commented: 'In the Line and out of it, the volume of correspondence is astounding, between operations, training, administration and routine. Seldom are pen, paper and map laid down until bed-time.'[36] Others considered that it was during the quiet times that the paper predominated. Hal Siepmann writing home in October 1917 noted: 'The less fighting there is, the more paper you get from any kind of superior authority. In a battle, paper nearly ceases altogether. But in "peace warfare" it becomes almost impossible to cope with.'[37] It continued right up to the end of the war. James Jack, now a brigade commander, wrote two days before the Armistice: 'When battles are to the fore, the General Staff branch keeps us busy with papers; the moment operations finish, the Quartermaster-General's branch takes up the running. So, between "G" and "Q" less exalted headquarters get no peace at all.'[38]

There was, however, a noticeable divide between the G and the A and the Q staffs. W. N. Nicholson, who served on the administrative side at all levels of command from division upwards after graduating from Camberley in 1912, noted that 'the best of our staff officers were on the general staff' and that they 'never troubled to learn what the administrative staff did, never realised that unless they themselves had a practical knowledge of administration they could never be capable staff officers'. One indication of this was the HQ mess system. Nicholson describes how when the 51st (Highland) Division went to France in 1915, the headquarters operated three messes. One consisted of the divisional commander and the G staff, while No. 2 Mess contained himself as AA&QMG and the remainder of the administrative staff officers, and the third consisted of the attached services. Nicholson considered this 'most unwise', pointing out that 'good combination and good understanding can only be assured if the heads of the staff and services live together and their juniors pair off in the remaining messes'.[39] R. H. Mottram, attached to HQ 6th Division in spring 1916 to deal with damage claims by the local inhabitants, was placed in G Mess, with the veterinary and medical officers and the French and Belgian interpreters.[40] Matters did improve, however. In summer 1918 the Hon. William Fraser, then GSO2 of the 66th Division, shared a mess with his general, his two ADCs, the GSO1 and, significantly, the AA&QMG.[41] The separation of the staff branches was a topic considered by a committee which was established under General Sir Walter Braithwaite at the end of the war. It noted that there was a tendency to 'keep a man at the work that he knows best' and that this had led to too much specialization. The committee was very much against the idea of separate G, A and Q messes and recommended that the sentence in *FSR II* that stated 'The Staff is organised in three branches' should be amended and the principle of 'one staff' stressed.[42]

The Braithwaite Committee did, however, recommend the retention of the staff's distinctive distinctions, notably the red tabs or gorgets worn on lapels and the red hat bands. Initially, these were restricted to G, A and Q staffs down to and including brigade majors and staff captains. ADCs were also entitled to gorgets, although the Braithwaite Committee did acknowledge that this had irritated the troops and recommended their removal.[43] This policy was gradually broadened. Thus, in October 1914 directors, assistant directors and deputy assistant directors of War Office directorates also became entitled.[44] By early 1916 the entitlement had broadened still further. Blue gorgets were introduced for the likes of paymasters, munitions department staff officers, veterinary officers, camp commandants and works and postal officers, while district barrack officers, recruiting officers, musketry advisers, hygiene and catering officers and intelligence officers serving in Britain were entitled to green gorgets.[45] Another means of identifying a staff officer was the brassard worn on his right upper arm. These, too, proliferated. The basic brassards were to identify which level of HQ the officer belonged to. They were red and blue for GHQ; red/black/red for army; red/white/red for corps; red for division (with 'CD' in black letters for cavalry divisions); and blue for brigade (with 'CB' in black for cavalry brigades). Those working on the lines of communication wore a red brassard, with 'L of C' in black letters. Provost marshals wore a black brassard with 'PM' emblazoned on it in red, and town majors the same with 'Town Major' in red. Railhead officers had bright green brassards and RTOs white, with 'RTO' in black. Not just staff officers wore brassards – all medical personnel and military policemen did, too. Train conductors wore brown canvas armbands with 'Train Condr' in black letters, while cadets at the GHQ cadet school wore green with 'Cadet School' in silver letters. Even the servants of press correspondents and foreign military attaches were given brassards – green for the former, yellow for the latter.[46] Though the intention was to enable everyone to immediately identify the individual, these embellishments also made the fighting men feel that the staff was remote and had little in common with them.

In France, the staff enjoyed the privilege of their own leave boat, which left Boulogne four hours before that for the ordinary troops. On return from leave, the normal train left Victoria Station, London, for Folkestone at 7.30 a.m., while that for the staff leave boat departed from Charing Cross at the much more civilized time of 12.30 p.m.[47] While on the French side, the ordinary officer and soldier had to endure many hours of discomfort in a train and then walk or hitch a lift back to his unit, the staff officer could normally be assured of a car to meet him at Boulogne. Sometimes villages and towns close to higher headquarters were placed out of bounds to the majority of troops. D. A. Foulis, who served with a Service battalion of the Scottish Rifles, recalled that after a tough battle in which his battalion had suffered heavy casualties, he

> was detailed to ride back to Corps HQ to get pay for the troops from the Field Cashier. Having got the money we were informed by the MP [Military Police] that this beautiful untouched town was out of bounds for anyone not on the corps staff. We were not allowed to even get a cup of tea although the tea shops and cafes that abounded were full of staff officers and their clerks. We were all but put under arrest.[48]

The attitude of the staff could also irritate. Norman King-Wilson of the RAMC had some stinging comments to make about Sir Ian Hamilton's headquarters ship during the Gallipoli campaign, which was anchored at Mudros

> at a cost of £6,000 per month rental as a comfortable summer home for the General Staff who directed the Gamble. Why they were not housed ashore and the valuable transport released for more worthwhile service, God knows, but, while I do not usually grouse, the very name of *Aragon* stank. Officers reporting for duty or orders to the *Aragon* were kept waiting hour after hour, and it was with difficulty that they could buy a

meal. Why officers reporting should have to buy sustenance passes comprehension but this was the fact and just part and parcel of the treatment meted out to any poor mortal who had to report there.[49]

Indeed, the comparative comfort in which the staff lived was the cause of much grousing. At the end of November 1916, when the fighting on the Somme finally closed down, young Norman Collins of the 6th Seaforths was ordered to take out a party to bury the remains of those who had fallen on 1 July, the opening day. On completion, he reported to brigade HQ to hand over the personal effects that he and his men had found:

> I was in a deep dugout in the chalk, and I stood there amazed by the luxury of the officers who were down there. I was asked very politely to have a cup of tea, and they handed me some cakes, which I ate. It was incredible. I was glad then to get up. I couldn't really face it … the officers down in this dugout all had red tabs on and they were all spick and span, polished boots and Sam Browne belts. And there I was dirty, and probably lousy, wearing just a tommy's uniform. I've never forgotten that and rather resented it.[50]

On the other hand, while Boney Fuller accepted that 'life on the Staff … was too comfortable to be an example to the entrenched front', he made the point that 'to have organised discomfort, as one or two Generals attempted to do, in no way popularises the Staff and ends in making it discontented'.[51] In other words, unnecessary discomfort would have a detrimental effect on the quality of staff work.

Even so, the contrast between the conditions under which the staff lived and those in the trenches did encourage remoteness, especially at the higher headquarter level. W. N. Nicholson: 'For a brief spell, when transferred from Division to Corps, Army or General Headquarters we brought back with us the atmosphere of the front. But this was quickly lost. The vital importance of a real liaison from front to rear was never appreciated by those who could have ensured it.'[52] This comment has echoes of 1914, when John Charteris, then Haig's intelligence chief at I Corps, complained at the height of the First Battle of Ypres that, while Sir John French often visited divisional HQs, 'very few of [his] staff officers ever seem to come as far forward even as [sic] Corps HQ'.[53] Others echoed this. Gerald Burgoyne stated that during the winter of 1914–15,

> I never once saw any of our Brigade or Divisional staff come up to the trenches, and the ground around is to all the staff a terra incognita. I have heard so many other troops in other divisions say the same thing. In the whole five months I was in the trenches, I only once saw one of our Brigade Staff visit us, and not once did any of the Divisional Staff come near us.[54]

George Hawes was posted to GHQ in France to learn the Q aspects of staff duties: 'Some of the men here are fearfully out of touch with the realities of the situation, have never seen a trench, and do nothing but think in terms of rounds and rations. Most of them have the very highest opinions of themselves and their capabilities.'[55] At the lower level the situation was different. Writing in May 1915, V. F. Eberle, serving with the sappers of the 48th (North Midland) Division, noted: 'To give them their due, our Divisional Commander and Brigadiers and CRE set us a fine example by regular personal contact with the men, and viewing the conditions in the trenches. Our view of the higher-up commands is not so complimentary.'[56] Certainly, Bernard Montgomery daily visited the trenches, usually with his commander, when he was BM to the 104th Brigade, and J. F. C. Fuller was actually ordered to do so when he was a GSO3 at HQ VII Corps during the latter half of 1916.[57]

Two and a half years later, Charteris, now head of intelligence at GHQ, had somewhat changed his tune over higher staffs visiting the trenches:

> One of the great difficulties of everyone at GHQ is to get away from their office often and long enough to get in close touch with the front. Few can ever get much farther forward than the HQ of the armies … Forward at Army Head-quarters, one is nearer the fighting, but even they are now mostly in towns and villages several miles behind the front line. Farther forward still are the Corps Head-quarters [which] are now pretty big organisations and are almost always in a village. In front of the Corps Head-quarters the Divisions are mostly in farmhouses, but well in the fighting line. One can almost always get one's car up. But this is about the limit, and visits forward of them consequently take up a good deal of time.[58]

Guy Chapman saw 'the failure on the Somme' as breeding 'a wry distrust of the staff' and put it down to the fact that

> the Old Army could not grasp that the New Army cared nothing for sol-
> diering as a trade; thought of it only as a job to be done, and the more
> expeditiously the better. The man in the line wanted practical help; but in
> its place he too often received theory based on the type of warfare which
> had passed away with the Old Army before the end of 1914.[59]

This is specifically illustrated by Brian Lawrence of the 1st Grenadiers, who were dug in on the edge of Vaux Wood in March 1917. It was a wet night and in the early hours of the morning he was telephoned by the adjutant and told to dig a support line 250 yards to the rear and a reserve line a further 250 yards back:

> As the wood was very thick, and it was pitch dark and raining hard this did
> not sound inviting. I pointed out that it would take about 100 men four
> days, with axes and saws, to make the proper clearings in the wood for
> the required trenches, and as we had no tools except our entrenching
> tools, and as it was pitch dark, and the men tired out, and we were moving
> next day, the whole idea seemed futile. The Adjutant said he expected it
> was, but those were the orders. That is the army system all over. The
> Divisional General looked in his field training manual and saw that in an
> outpost position you should have support and reserve lines. He issued a
> general order to his brigadiers, who in their turn looked up in the training
> manuals and passed on a specific order to their battalion commanders,
> who gave the detailed order to their companies (a sort of house that Jack
> built). Of course we never made any attempt to dig the trenches, and no-
> one ever worried any more about them. But the Divisional General had
> issued the correct orders, and every subordinate had faithfully passed
> them on in strict accordance with the custom of the service, and everyone
> rested content with a sense of duty well done.[60]

It was this planning off the map which provoked General Neill Malcolm, the ruthless chief of staff of Gough's Fifth Army, into an outburst when visiting HQ XIX Corps during the grim fighting around Saint Julien in early September 1917. He asked whether any of the corps or divisional staff had been out to look at the ground which was being fought over. When told that they had not, Malcolm is supposed to have replied: 'Try it. It makes it much easier to plan an operation if you've seen the ground from a company OP. Don't worry about being hit. It encourages the fighting soldiers no end if a staff officer or two is killed off.'[61]

Yet GHQ in France was conscious that staff officers needed an awareness of the problems faced by the troops in the front line. Sir Ronald Maxwell, the QMG in France, wrote a letter to Sir John Cowans in early November 1915 on the question of finding additional Q staff officers: 'The opinion out here is that Staff Captains of Brigades are the best source from which to obtain young staff officers. They have been in close touch and sympathy with the men in the trenches and know their needs and difficulties, a most valuable qualification for a staff officer.'[62] At divisional level, in 17th Division at least, a system was introduced whereby battalion adjutants did a short attachment with the A and Q staff at division. As a result 'there was a good deal we learnt from each other. Best of all we parted excellent friends, aware of each other's difficulties.'[63] It was, however, easy to establish close relations within a division, since its subordinate units seldom changed. At corps level, it was a different matter, since it was largely a static organization through which divisions passed, seldom staying under its command for more than a couple of months. Even so, Plumer, the Second Army commander for much of the war, developed a scheme of attaching liaison officers to each corps, with instructions to get to know each Infantry battalion in it, spending at least two nights per week in the trenches.[64] Major General 'Tim' Harrington, chief of staff to the Second Army, was one who was very conscious of the gulf that existed between the staff and the regimental officer, as he revealed in a lecture given to potential commanding officers at the Senior Officers School, Aldershot, in February 1917. He considered that the main reasons for it were lack of training, too much paperwork and COs not being told enough, especially about the 'big picture'. The training aspect affected both sides. Harrington pointed out that there were only two *psc* officers at army HQ and one at corps. While the short staff courses being run helped, they did not provide the in-depth training that Camberley had before the war. Likewise, COs were not taking sufficient advantage of the numerous schools in France and elsewhere to broaden the military education of their officers. But, apart from often not having the officers to spare, the COs had not been told enough about the benefits of the schools. The nub of the problem was that 'in many cases the Staff do not know enough of the actual conditions in the trenches and the trench life, and the Commanding Officers feel that they do not know the Staff sufficiently as friends, and think that the latter come down to criticise'. Harrington had instituted a system at every level of command within Second Army, whereby staff officers made frequent visits to subordinate HQs. He believed that this personal contact could save 'seventy-five per cent of the writing in the Army'. Another measure he had instituted was to get a dozen COs at a time to spend a week at army HQ so that they could get a better understanding of the problems of the staff and vice versa.[65]

The Senior Officers School itself had been established very much along the lines of the Harrington philosophy. The idea originated with Lieutenant Colonel R. J. Kentish, when he was running the Third Army School at Flixécourt. He conceived the idea of taking some thirty COs and senior majors out of the trenches and putting them through a week's 'conference' at which they would be given free rein to vent their views. As it happened, in April 1916 he was promoted to command a brigade and J. F. C. Fuller, now GSO2 of the 37th Division, was ordered, at short notice, to run the course. He recalled:

> The Conferences were a huge success. Every evil, real and imaginary, concerning red tape, red tabs and reddest of red Higher Commands was ventilated in the most insubordinate way. Hot air was blown off in gusts and gales, and this blowing-off alone, I am sure, did a lot of good. I reported our suggestions fairly fully to Third Army Headquarters, because I considered that it was not a bad thing for the Higher Command to realise what the front line thought of them.

Indeed, such was the value of these 'conferences' that in the autumn of 1916 it was decided to move the course back to England. It was renamed the Senior Officers School and Kentish was brought back from France to run it. The course was extended to two and a half months, with 120 officers recommended for battalion command on each. Later, it also ran courses for instructors at army schools. R. T. Rees attended the school in January

1918: 'It was an excellent course, thoroughly up-to-date and covering all the ground necessary to fit one to command a battalion.'[66]

The shortage of trained staff officers was largely solved by recruiting 'staff learners' from battalions at the front. The idea was that they should do two months' probation at various headquarters in order to broaden their military knowledge before being appointed to a staff post. One of these was P. D. Ravenscroft, the Lewis gun officer of the 2nd KRRC, who had filled in as adjutant from time to time and had been training as an accountant before he joined the army. His battalion was in the 1st Division, and Ravenscroft began his staff training on 1 February 1917 by being attached to one of its brigades, where he understudied the staff captain. He found his duties many and varied. They included settling civilian claims for damages to property, taking samples of white calico, which was to be made into night shirts for patrolling in the snow, around the battalions and organizing band performances and billeting. After five weeks, Ravenscroft was sent to one of the field artillery brigades for two weeks and then to one of the division's three field companies RE for a further two weeks. Thereafter he was attached to the division's Q staff where his duties appear to have been mainly concerned with billeting, as the division was about to enter a period of rest. Once it had settled down in the Mericourt area near the River Somme, Ravenscroft found that he had nothing to do but answer the telephone, which quickly bored him. A request to the AA&QMG for permission to attend a concert being given by his battalion was met with the retort: 'You are always wanting to go to your Battalion. Have you nothing to learn here?' He was then told by the GSO1 that he could rejoin the KRRC and that once the division returned to the line he might continue his training with an attachment to the G Staff. As it happened, 1st Division was selected for a projected landing on the Belgian coast – part of Haig's plan for his summer offensive in the Ypres sector – and moved to the coast to begin training for it. Ravenscroft never did complete his staff attachment.[67]

The Hon. William Fraser of the Gordons was initially attached to the 8th Brigade in July 1915 to coordinate the training of specialists after two months' convalescence resulting from a wound as a company commander during fighting in the Hill 60 area. He carried out the staff captain's duties while the latter was on leave, but considered that it had 'too much Quartermaster work to suit me'. He wanted to become a brigade major, but feared that, as a substantive lieutenant with five years' seniority, he was still too junior. In October he was posted to HQ 76th Brigade, which both the 1st and 4th Gordons had just joined, in the belief that he was to be appointed brigade major, but there was no job for him and so for a month he kicked his heels. At the end of November he was made staff captain to the 27th Brigade. He did not enjoy it much, but recognized that the experience was worthwhile. An added interest was that Winston Churchill arrived in early January 1916 to command the 6th Royal Scots Fusiliers, one of the battalions in the brigade. Fraser visited him shortly after his arrival and was favourably impressed: 'he seemed to grasp the situation and was quite intelligent generally'.[68] In April, Fraser finally achieved his ambition and became BM to the 151st Brigade, but lasted only two months before his horse threw him and he suffered concussion and two broken ribs. Another who experienced life as a staff learner was Neville Lytton with HQ 116th Brigade during the Somme offensive. His main tasks were training the brigade's snipers and observers. He claims that there were 'eight or nine' staff learners at brigade HQ.[69]

Guy Chapman was sent to the 63rd Brigade as a G staff learner in the autumn of 1916 because he had been superseded as a company commander by a more senior officer who had recently arrived from Britain. HQ consisted of the brigade commander and brigade major, both Highland Light Infantry, the staff captain and 'the brigade bombing-cum-intelligence-cum-bottle-washing officer', plus the French interpreter. Chapman's duties – and this was during the last attacks on the Somme – were

> a mixture of scullion and aide-de-camp. To run with messages, to accompany the general on his visits to battalions in whose headquarters he would talk in his quiet impersonal way, as if the attacks were a matter of going down to the club for a drink and game of bridge, to sit up at night beside Brodie [brigade major, who had won the VC during First Ypres and would be killed in August 1918] and protect him from unimportant messages, to bully the servants into filling in the crater of an 8-inch shell in the roof of the dugout.[70]

Sometimes, staff learners found themselves thrown in at the deep end. Wyn Griffith was attached to a brigade of the 38th Division. In July 1916 the brigade was involved in the attacks on Mametz Wood and both the brigade major and staff captain were wounded. Griffith had just taken over from the latter: 'Now I was to be both brigade major and staff captain to a Brigadier-General in the middle of a battle. I consoled myself with the thought that if I could originate nothing, I could do what I was told to do.'[71]

Staff schools were established in France by the beginning of 1916. Certainly, Archibald Home records lecturing to the 'Staff course at GHQ' on 7 January.[72] Towards the end of the Battle of the Somme, however, the BEF established a six-week course for staff officers at Hesdin. The Senior Staff School took twenty students at a time and prepared them primarily for appointments as GSO1s and AA&QMGs. The Junior Staff School had fifty students, which it prepared for Grade 2 appointments.[73] One of the first students on the junior course was the Hon. Walter Guinness. The course was split into five syndicates, each of ten officers, who messed together. Guinness's fellow students

> were most of them Brigade Majors, the others Staff Captains or GSO3s and one learnt as much from discussing matters with them as from the lectures and exercises. In the morning we generally had certain actual operation orders of either Armies or Corps given to us and proceeded from them to work out our orders in syndicates in which we daily changed places and filled different posts. In the afternoons we had conferences and criticisms of our own and the Instructors' productions and the evenings were generally spent at a lecture by some expert from outside … We did a good deal of practical work in the open air, writing out of doors, after having ridden to examine the ground. We also visited various salvage, supply, ammunition and other depots to see the systems in force and also descended on the unfortunate Division who happened to be holding the line at Arras, so as to pick the brains of the various staffs and to write attack and relief orders and various other exercises based on the actual position there.

The commandant of the Junior Staff School, Lieutenant Colonel R. A. M. Currie of the Somerset Light Infantry, was a *psc*, who had been Brigade Major to the 13th Infantry Brigade at the outbreak of war.[74] At the end of the course Guinness returned to being second-in-command of the 11th

Cheshires, but in mid February 1917 was appointed Brigade Major of the 74th Brigade, although he spent a few days understudying his predecessor before taking over. His brigade commander, Keppel Bethell, was not an easy man to work for, being excitable and impatient, but was a first-class fighting soldier. Nevertheless, Guinness remained with him for a year, taking part in Third Ypres and the German offensive in March 1918 and, on Bethell's recommendation, winning the DSO and bar. Bethell was then promoted to command the 66th Division and managed, after a time, to get Guinness sent to him as GSO2. In the meantime, Guinness served briefly as BM 198th Brigade, being replaced by the 20-year-old Anthony Eden, who became the youngest brigade major in the British Army. Eden had already served as adjutant of his battalion of the KRRC and done tours as a GSO3 at HQ Second Army and the 58th (London) Division.

A similar staff school to that at Hesdin was established in Cambridge and the Staff College at Camberley also ran short courses from October 1917, although a year later it was converted into a senior officers' tactics school. Grade 1 and 2 staff officers were appointed by GHQ, but GSO3s and brigade majors were selected at army level. In April 1916, the qualifications for employment as a staff officer were laid down as either being *psc*, or to have held a staff appointment or to have successfully attended a staff course, which included one month's service as a staff learner prior to the course. Two months later, however, the attendance at a staff course by candidates for staff posts in Britain was waived, although they still had to do one month as a staff learner. This relaxation also applied, from September 1917, to those being considered for Grade 3 posts in an overseas theatre.[75]

But by no means all regimental officers recommended for the staff took up the offer. John Nettleton of the 2nd Rifle Brigade, perhaps embittered by the fact that during the grim fighting for Passchendaele in November 1917 he saw no staff officer above brigade visit the trenches, rejected the opportunity to become a staff learner, going against the advice of his colonel. His reason was that

> the young and fit men that one saw about as soon as one got well beyond
> the range of shell fire were looked down upon with scorn as gilded
> popinjays and quite beneath contempt. In the battalion, I had established

position and some reputation – a cock on a very small dunghill perhaps, but still my own dunghill and I could not give this up to become a gilded popinjay … Also, there was a tremendously strong feeling of loyalty to one's own battalion.[76]

Another who refused to join the staff, even though his services were requested on more than one occasion, was J. C. Mann, who served as adjutant to the 2nd Royal Welsh Fusiliers for almost two years until he was killed in late September 1917.

There is no doubt that some of the staff work during the first half of the war was found wanting. A major reason for this was the lack of trained staff officers and the increasing complexity of the new warfare. The quality, however, did improve once the need for staff training was recognized and by the end of the war much of the staff work was of high quality and made a significant contribution to the ultimate victories on every front. While the divide between the staff and those in the front line was never fully bridged, relations undoubtedly became better as the war progressed and both camps began to appreciate the other's perspectives.

twelve

DISCIPLINE

In 1914 military discipline was governed by the Army Act, as it is today, and which was and is reviewed annually by Parliament. Crimes went through several levels of investigation. All were first considered by the company commander or equivalent. For minor crimes he could award the man seven days' confinement to barracks or camp, as well as extra guards and picquets for offences in connection with these two duties. Where a man had been absent without leave for seven days or less, he would forfeit his pay for the period he was absent. In the case of junior NCOs the only award he could make was admonishment or reprimand, while, for sergeants and above the company commander could only dismiss the case or, if he considered it merited punishment beyond his powers, remand it for the commanding officer. The CO himself had a wider range of options: twenty-eight days' detention in a military gaol or guardroom; deductions from pay to make good losses of or damage to military equipment; fines for drunkenness; twenty-eight days' Field Punishment, deprivation of pay to a maximum of twenty-eight days. He could also remove acting or lance rank and award deductions of pay to NCOs. If the CO considered the charge to be too serious for him to deal with, he would refer the matter to higher authority, usually brigade, for possible court martial. A soldier, too, could elect for trial by court martial if the CO was proposing to award other than a minor punishment or a forfeiture of pay.

There were three types of court martial. The District Court Martial

(DCM) had to have a minimum of three members, with a field officer (major and above) as president, although a captain could fulfil this role if no field officer was available. It could award a maximum of imprisonment with hard labour (IHL), reduce an NCO to the ranks or discharge a man from the army. For the most serious offences of all a General Court Martial (GCM) would be convened. In Britain, India, Malta and Gibraltar it had to have a minimum of nine members, and five elsewhere, with the president a full colonel if possible. The GCM had the power to sentence a man to death, award penal servitude or any lesser punishment. Finally, there was the Field General Court Martial (FGCM) which was employed in the forward areas of a theatre of war. It had the same powers of sentence as a GCM. In exceptional circumstances it could consist of just two members, although they could not pass a death sentence. However, three was usually the minimum, with a field officer as president.

As for the types of offence committed by British soldiers in the theatres of war, many were considered petty in military eyes. Typical ones are revealed in the War Diary of the Town Major of Poperinghe, who noted in March 1916 that his military police made 162 arrests, the vast majority for drunkenness, absent without leave from billets or being in out-of-bounds areas, usually *estaminets* which had been placed off limits.[1] The majority of these crimes would have been dealt with at unit level, but inevitably some would have gone to court martial, especially if it was a repeat offence. In terms of overall discipline, some 5,700,000 men served in the British Army during 1914–18. During the period from 4 August 1914 to 31 March 1920 (the end date for the official statistics on the war effort) there was a total of 304,262 court martials, of which just over 89 per cent resulted in a conviction. The most common offence for both officers and men was absence without leave, which resulted in almost 30 per cent of the courts martial. Other significant offences were drunkenness (13.7 per cent), insubordination (just under 10 per cent) and desertion (12.7 per cent).[2]

The death sentence could be awarded for a number of crimes – murder, cowardice in the face of the enemy, mutiny, desertion, wilful disobedience, striking a superior officer, sleeping on post and quitting it and casting away arms in the face of the enemy – but more of this later. Penal servitude, which was served in a civil institution, was the next most severe punishment and a GCM could award a life sentence and a minimum sentence of three years. Imprisonment with hard labour was served in a military gaol with a maximum of two years. There was also straightforward imprisonment and detention. In France two military prisons, both on ships, were quickly established at Rouen and Le Havre, with the inmates spending their days unloading ships. Imprisoning fighting troops was, however, seen to be inappropriate since, as James Jack succinctly commented, it meant that 'the guilty one escapes battle risks'.[3] It was for this reason that a Parliamentary Act was passed in 1915 allowing prison sentences to be deferred until the end of the war. The upshot was a significant reduction in the number of men held in military prisons in France, from 5.1 per thousand in February 1915, when suspended sentences were introduced, to 0.7 per thousand that August. These figures were cited by Douglas Haig in his diary entry for 3 March 1918, though he mistakenly used them as a measure of the 'quite wonderful' discipline in his armies.[4] Even so, imprisonment was still used for those serving in the rear areas and the number of military prisons in France eventually grew to ten, although this reflected the rapid rise in the number of troops not serving in the combat zone rather than a proportionate increase in crime.

Rowland Fielding, a battalion commander, commented that suspension of sentences had a double advantage. First,

> the bad soldier had a sort of sword of Damocles ever poised above his head, and secondly, the better man, whose trouble had come from some momentary lapse (as ever-present a possibility in war, as in peace), had the chance of atoning for his delinquency, and often, by good behaviour or gallant act on the battlefield, he earned a complete reprieve.[5]

Indeed, there are numerous examples in first-hand accounts of soldiers having their sentences cancelled because of their bravery. R. B. A. Talbot Kelly mentioned an incident when a Royal Scots subaltern and private soldier in the 27th Brigade repulsed a German raid. The officer was awarded the MC while the private had his three-year penal servitude sentence washed out.[6] G. E. Hitchcock was also awarded an MC for leading a successful raid in January 1917: 'Besides the awards, several men who had heavy terms of imprisonment hanging over them, and were working them off in the trenches, were recommended by me, with a view to their sentences being remitted by the GOC. Without exception, all of these sentences were wiped out.'[7] On the other hand, as Fielding also pointed out, there was also a tendency to award Field Punishment No. 1 in lieu of a suspended sentence. This happened to some of the 'bad hats' in Fielding's battalion in spring 1917. 'The result is that instead of having got rid of these men they remain with the battalion, and are a constant source of annoyance', he complained. This was especially since Field Punishment No. 1 'falls so flat that that the hardened offender cares nothing for it.'[8]

Field Punishment itself was designed as a substitute for detention at unit level in the field, which was often impossible because of the lack of facilities. Under Field Punishment No. 1 the offender could be kept in irons and made to undergo labouring tasks. He could also be attached to a fixed object, using straps, irons or ropes, for a period not exceeding two hours in any one day. He was not to undergo this last for more than three days out of four or for more than twenty-one days in all. Field Punishment No. 2 was a slightly milder form in that the attachment of a soldier to a fixed object was not permitted. This could be awarded in Britain, but Field Punishment No. 1 was only carried out abroad. In both cases the soldier forfeited his pay for the duration of the punishment and was forbidden cigarettes and other canteen comforts. It was not carried out when in the trenches. John Lucy came across it for the first time in August 1914 when he was detailed guard commander while his battalion was in billets. 'I had in my charge four soldiers who were being punished for drunkenness and one of them was an old war veteran and ex-corporal. They were tied up daily to a tree or wagon wheel in public for a fixed period, and they loathed it.'[9] Arthur Osburn observed: 'This mediaeval and rather barbarous form of punishment aroused the pity, not to say the indignation, of the French peasantry.'[10] On the other hand, John Nettleton, who served in the ranks in France before being commissioned, commented:

> A lot of hot air has been talked about the iniquity of this, but I cannot see that it was so terrible. You were not lashed tightly to the wagon wheel; you were never kept there for more than an hour at a time; you were

loosed if it got too hot or too cold or if it rained, so there was little physical discomfort. Presumably, it was the moral effect that was supposed to be the deterrent.[11]

The views of the high command were equally mixed.

On 22 October 1916 an item appeared in the Robert Blatchford column of the *Illustrated Sunday Herald*. It was based on a letter from a reader who quoted a friend of his who knew a woman whose son had been serving in France. Apparently, he and five others had been crimed for losing their gas helmets in a marsh. 'They were tied by the neck, waist, hands and feet to cart wheels for one hour; when released her son was dead: Mrs S— says: "They murdered my son; the indignity would kill him."' Blatchford himself was an old soldier, who had served in the Victorian army and written a book on his experiences, *My Life in the Army*. He expressed his horror at this form of punishment and demanded its immediate abolition. The revelation produced a public outcry, with several readers writing to the Prime Minister while numerous trades union branches and other organizations passed resolutions condemning the barbarity of Field Punishment No. 1. Questions were tabled in Parliament and it was clear that the War Office needed to act, and quickly. A letter was sent to all overseas theatres asking if any man had lost his life as a result of undergoing this punishment and requesting views on its retention. None of the commanders had any knowledge of fatalities caused by it, but their opinions on Field Punishment No. 1 varied. The Commander-in-Chief India was strongly in favour of abolition, but if it was to be retained a standard method of securing the culprit would have to be drawn up. C-in-C Mesopotamia also voted for abolition, suggesting a new punishment of eight to ten hours of fatigues per day, although the soldier could be kept in irons, straps or ropes 'for the purpose of safe custody'. In contrast, both Egypt and Salonika wanted the punishment retained, although the former agreed with C-in-C India that a standard method of attaching victims to a fixed object should be drawn up and this part of the punishment limited to one hour at a time.

The War Office took most note of Douglas Haig's reply. He had canvassed his army commanders and all save one considered that Field Punishment No. 1 should be retained. The dissenter was Edmund Allenby of the Third Army, who likened it to 'the stocks or pillory', a view dismissed by Haig on the grounds that the offender 'is not exposed to the view of civilians', although this was not always so. Haig concluded that there were three major reasons for maintaining the punishment. First, there was no 'adequate substitute'. Imprisonment removed men from the front line and cut across the 1915 Suspension of Sentences Act. It was also difficult to make conditions in the military prisons in the field harsher than those found in the trenches without sacrificing humanity. Furthermore, there was the need for a punishment 'for the purpose of arresting incipient deterioration in a soldier's behaviour' which was less severe than imprisonment. Second, Haig argued, Field Punishment No. 1 was effective as demonstrated by the

> high standard of discipline in the firing line ... attained by British Troops with a short period of training, and that this result has been attained without bullying on the part of non-commissioned officers and with a percentage of capital sentences which would, I think, compare favourably with that of other armies.

Furthermore, abolishing the punishment, especially that part involving tying the soldier to a fixed object, would mean that a 'far larger percentage of those men whose moral fibre requires bracing by the daily fear of adequate punishment would give way in moments of stress, and the recourse to the death penalty would have to become more frequent'. Finally, 'it is suggested that descriptions and possibly drawings of men tied up with their arms extended may have aroused prejudice owing to the unfortunate use of the term "crucifixion" as a simile in this connection, and I therefore, think the definition be such as to exclude this position'. Haig suggested that the offender be attached with his feet 'not more than 12 inches apart, and it must be possible for him to move each foot at least three inches. Likewise, his arms should be secured to his sides or behind his back and that there must be six inches play between them'. In line with the pre-war regulations, he reiterated that a soldier should not endure this punishment for longer than two hours and not more than in three out of four consecutive days, or for longer than a period of twenty-one days. The War Office agreed with Haig and accepted his recommendations on how a man should be secured. Field Punishment No. 1 would therefore remain in being for the rest of the war.[12] Indeed, it was the main type of punishment meted out by courts martial abroad.

While Field Punishment may appear barbaric to modern eyes, there is no doubt that it did provide a means of dealing with serious crimes without inflicting a more draconian sentence, thus giving the soldier another chance. Another way of doing this was through unofficial punishment. Gerald Burgoyne, commanding a company of the 2nd Royal Irish Rifles in the trenches during the winter of 1914–15, had no hesitation in punching his men for indiscipline: 'All men like an officer who compels obedience, and it's no use punishing a man on Active Service as one does in peacetime; the only thing is to hit him at once and hard.'[13] In August 1917, Cecil Slack wanted to charge three of his men with cowardice during a German raid. They were paraded in front of the brigade commander who, rather than initiate court martial proceedings, ordered them to undertake nightly patrols of no-man's-land, which Slack considered 'a realistic and effective decision'.[14]

On occasion, an officer was faced with the grimmer prospect of shooting his own men. There are hearsay accounts of this taking place during an attack when men were hanging back, but nothing that can be substantiated. However, Alan Thomas, then a 21-year-old company commander in the 6th Royal West Kents, did on one occasion find himself close to having to do this. It was summer 1917 and he was ordered to take a load of railway sleepers by night from one mile behind the reserve trenches to the support line. The ground had been badly chewed up by shellfire and, after difficulties in finding the dump from where the sleepers were to be collected, it began to rain. After struggling with their loads, his men decided that they had had enough and refused to go a step further. Thomas exhorted them to further effort, but to no avail. In desperation, he reminded them that they were on active service and that he had a loaded revolver. He told them that after fifteen seconds he would shoot any man who did not obey his order to move on.

> I spoke as though I meant it. The effect was immediate. Muttering curses the men picked up their sleepers and moved on. I do not look back on

this incident with pride … If my bluff had been called I might have caved in … I learnt my lesson – to think twice before giving a fatal order of that kind again.[15]

Occasionally, units with a high crime rate were moved to a different formation. When the 36th (Ulster) Division landed in France in October 1915, its 107th Brigade suffered a bout of severe indiscipline, including numerous incidents of looting and four senior ranks of the 9th Royal Irish Rifles court martialled for drunkenness. The divisional commander therefore arranged for the brigade to be banished to the 4th Division for three months, receiving the 12th Brigade in its place.[16]

In modern eyes, however, it is the handing down of death sentences by courts martial which provokes the fiercest debate. It is, however, worth pointing out before going any further that capital punishment was still enshrined in both English and Scottish law and practised during 1914–18. It would not be finally repealed until 1969, although it was suspended four years earlier. In the British armed forces, capital punishment remained legal for certain offences until as late as 1999, although the last military execution was carried out in 1942.

Much criticism by those who believe that some, if not all of those soldiers whose death sentences were confirmed during the Great War, should be pardoned is levelled at the court martial system itself, on the grounds that the accused was not given the full facilities for an adequate defence. The first step was made by the soldier's unit, which was responsible for applying for a court martial. In its application, the unit included a summary of evidence, largely statements by witnesses of the crime, the proposed charges and a certified true copy of the soldier's conduct sheet, on which were listed all his previous offences and the punishments he had received. Once the court martial had been convened, the same rules of evidence applied as in a civilian court. Thus, the accused was presumed innocent until it was proved that he was guilty, hearsay evidence was inadmissible and opinion and belief, other than by experts, was not accepted as evidence. It was stressed that the president of the court was to ensure that the accused had a fair trial and that he was not obstructed in his defence. In the early years of the war the accused did not have a defending officer, but the prosecutor was instructed to be impartial and to ensure that all evidence, both for and against the accused, was brought out in court. From 1916 onwards, however, there was an increasing incidence of an 'accused's friend' or 'prisoner's friend', who had a right to cross-examine witnesses. Where the death sentence might be handed down, every effort was made to obtain an officer with legal training as prisoner's friend. It was also clearly laid down that the president must establish that the accused understood the charge. All evidence on oath was to be taken down in 'narrative form'. Where the accused made a plea on medical grounds, a medical witness had to be called. Once the evidence had been heard, the court closed to consider the verdict. If 'not guilty', the accused was released forthwith. Otherwise, the court would hear evidence of the accused's character and any pleas of mitigation. Only then did the court consider the sentence, which, if death, had to have the unanimous agreement of the court.

Notes for Commanding Officers suggested a simple method of gauging the seriousness of the offence. 'With premeditation, without provocation' was the most serious; 'without premeditation, with provocation' the least. However, the prisoner was not informed of the sentence because it had not been confirmed. This was done by the confirming officer, usually the officer who convened the court martial – the brigade or divisional commander. The proceedings, together with the defendant's conduct sheet and his CO's comments on the man's character, were forwarded to the confirming officer, who would then confirm or reduce the sentence and return the proceedings to the CO, who would then inform the prisoner, who had no right of appeal. In the case of the death sentence for all ranks, and imprisonment, penal servitude, cashiering and dismissal for officers, the proceedings were passed up the chain of command, with commanders at every level adding their comments, to the highest level – GHQ. Here the case was considered by the Judge Advocate General (JAG). He would make his recommendation to the commander-in-chief, who was the ultimate arbiter. All these instructions were clearly laid out in Rules of Procedure, the 'bible' on the conduct of courts martial and contained in the *Manual of Military Law*.

In general, officers did not enjoy being members of a court martial. While all had received rudimentary instruction in military law, their inexperience, especially among junior officers, often did not help the course of good justice. Guy Chapman recalled his first court martial, that of an elderly King's Royal Rifle Corps pioneer sergeant accused of being drunk in the trenches. He was found guilty and the court retired to consider the sentence. 'I hurriedly turned the pages of the *Manual of Military Law,* and found to my horror that the punishment was death, *tout court.*' When the president asked Chapman, as the junior member, for his view on the sentence, he replied:

> 'Oh death, sir, I suppose.' Major Keppel blenched and turned to my opposite number, Gwinnell. Gwinnell, who was as young and unlearned in expedience as myself, answered, as I had 'Death, I suppose.' Our good president looked at us from the top of his six feet and groaned: 'But, my boys, my boys, you can't do it.' 'But, sir,' we protested in unison, anxious to justify ourselves, 'it says so here.' It was only after a moving appeal by the president that we allowed ourselves to be overborne and to punish the old ruffian by reduction to the rank of corporal in the place of executing him; but we both somehow felt that Major Keppel had somehow failed in his duty.[17]

Matters began to improve when forty-three Court Martial Officers (CMO) were appointed in Home Forces in September 1916. They were men who had belonged to the legal profession before joining up and their task was to sit as members of courts martial and advise the president on matters of law and procedure. Early in 1917, CMOs were introduced in France on the establishment of one per corps. They were stretched a little thin to be present at every court martial, but there is no doubt that their presence significantly improved the quality of justice, as borne by the view of Gerald Hurst, himself a CMO in France:

> No one who has often taken part in courts martial cases will question the fairness, courtesy, and patience which characterize trials. An accused is given the benefit of any doubt. If the proportion of acquittals is comparatively low, it is due to the care which is usually taken not to convene courts martial in the absence of a real prima facie case against the accused.[18]

John Nettleton, who sat as a member on a number of courts martial in 1918, echoes this:

> I was impressed with the general fairness of the court martial procedure. The commander of an army in the field has to be given wide powers to deal with a variety of offences, but in the actual trial a great effort is made to give the prisoner every possible assistance and he is given the benefit of any possible doubt. In fact, everyone leans over backwards to make sure that the prisoner's case is not prejudiced.[19]

In contrast, Bernard Martin, who served as a junior officer with the North Staffords in France during 1916–17, regarded courts martial as a 'mere formality' since, at least in desertion cases, 'the verdict was certain, the punishment already determined'.[20]

Padre Bickersteth observed: 'A man will overstay his leave at home by a day or several days and will only get a few days CB [Confined to Barracks] as a punishment. He comes out here [France] and if absent from his unit for an hour without leave is liable to be shot.'[21] This was a slight exaggeration, but it does reflect the fact that punishments in a theatre of war were more severe than those in Britain. At home there were 141,115 courts martial of officers and soldiers during the period from 4 August 1914 to 31 March 1920 compared to 163,147 abroad. No death sentences were handed down at home and just one soldier was given penal servitude for life. In contrast, 346 death sentences were confirmed abroad and, among the other sentences, 143 soldiers were sentenced to life penal servitude.[22] In terms of the death sentences, from the outbreak of war until the end of 1918, less than one-tenth were confirmed and the sentence duly carried out. By far the most common charge was desertion. A total of 1,990 officers and men were found guilty of this charge, but in only just over 12 per cent of cases was the sentence confirmed. The next most common offence was sentries sleeping at their post, which accounted for 449 courts martial, though in only two cases was the death sentence carried out. Cowardice was the third most prevalent offence attracting a capital sentence, with just under 8 per cent of the 213 men found guilty of this charge facing the firing squad.

The very first death sentence to be carried out was on 19-year-old Private Thomas James Highgate of the Royal West Kents, who was found guilty by a Field General Court Martial of desertion on 6 September 1914 and was executed two days later. He had been apprehended by Baron Edouard de Rothschild's gamekeeper on his estate at Tournan by the River Marne. Highgate's error was to be found in civilian clothes, although his uniform was in the barn where he was caught. He made matters worse for himself through being unable to come up with an explanation of why he had changed his clothes. Given the deep concern that the high command in France had at the time that the BEF was in danger of disintegration as a result of the retreat from Mons, with literally thousands of stragglers, it is not surprising that the authorities felt that an example needed to be made. The result of Highgate's court martial and his subsequent execution were announced in GHQ France's Routine Orders of 10 September. All troops were made aware of it, and this remained the policy throughout the war *pour encourager les autres*.

But to demonstrate that strict discipline applied to all ranks, Routine Orders of four days later recorded the court martial of two commanding officers of infantry battalions. J. F. Elkington of the 1st Royal Warwicks, the battalion in which the young Bernard Montgomery was serving, and A. E. Mainwaring, commanding the 2nd Royal Dublin Fusiliers, found themselves with small bodies from their battalions at the tail end of the retreat from Le Cateau. They entered Saint Quentin in the hope that there might be trains available to evacuate them and their exhausted men. The last had left, however, and so the two commanding officers asked the mayor for help in obtaining one, but he said that none was available. He did, however, offer to produce food for the men. At that moment the mayor received a message that the Germans were about to enter the town. He pleaded with the two colonels to surrender so as to save the town from wanton destruction. Elkington and Mainwaring agreed and wrote out a surrender document which they handed to the mayor. Shortly afterwards, the British rearguard, two cavalry squadrons of the 4th Dragoon Guards under Major Tom Bridges, arrived. He began to get the stragglers organized, finding carts for the wounded and those incapable of marching. Bridges did not speak directly to the two commanding officers, since 'I knew one of the colonels well and had met the other, and they were, of course, both senior to me'. Instead, he used a subaltern of the 4th Hussars, who was acting as his interpreter, as an intermediary. This officer established the existence of the surrender document and retrieved it from the mayor. Then, after obtaining some toy instruments from a shop and organizing a makeshift band, Bridges got the column on the move. It eventually linked up with elements of the 3rd Division.

Bridges's feat in saving the Saint Quentin stragglers from the Germans was commemorated in a poem by Sir Henry Newbolt. The two commanding officers concerned suffered a very different fate. On 5 September 1914, the commander of III Corps ordered GOC 4th Division to convene a General Court Martial. The two colonels were charged with 'behaving in a scandalous manner unbecoming the character of an officer and gentleman' and the court convened at Chouy on the evening of the 11th, once the retreat had finished and the advance to the Aisne had begun. The president was one of the other brigade commanders in the 4th Division, A. G. Hunter-Weston. After two hours, the trial was adjourned and the court reconvened at 5 a.m. the following morning, a verdict being reached by lunchtime.[23] The defence was that Elkington and Mainwaring had acted so as to avoid unnecessary loss of civilian lives, but the court did not accept this and both were found guilty and sentenced to be cashiered. Mainwaring, who was aged 50, disappeared into obscurity, but Elkington enlisted as a private soldier in the French Foreign Legion. He saw much action during the spring and summer of 1915 and was badly wounded in September. He was invalided back to England after being awarded the *Medaille Militaire* and *Croix de Guerre*. Hunter-Weston, now a corps commander, came to hear of Elkington's gallant conduct and interceded with the Adjutant General. The result was that not only was Elkington officially pardoned and restored to his former rank, he was personally decorated with the DSO by the King.[24] Mainwaring was also pardoned.

Arthur Osburn was the 4th Royal Dragoon Guards MO and a witness to what happened in Saint Quentin. His sympathies lay with Elkington and Mainwaring.

> Without Staff, without maps or orders, without food, without ammunition, without support from artillery or cavalry, what *could* the remnants of broken infantry do before the advance of a victorious army, whose

cavalry could have mopped them up in an hour? Probably, looking back on it now, the two colonels did almost the only thing feasible and the brave thing. Middle-aged men, both of them looked. From their appearance they were suffering severely from the sun; that alone might account for their not having thought of making use of the Mayor as a collector of country carts.[25]

This is a charitable view, but given the dire circumstances in which the BEF found itself, and the likelihood that the incident would soon become common knowledge, it would have been foolish, in terms of morale and discipline, if the two COs had not been brought to book.

During the same time, a number of men were caught sleeping at their posts. They, too, were court martialled, but their death sentences were commuted, usually to two years hard labour. Indeed, of the eighty-five death sentences handed down by courts martial during the five months of war in 1914, only four were carried out, three for desertion and one for cowardice.[26] This was hardly extreme, and probably reflected the normal incidence of capital punishment at the time in Britain as a whole. Nevertheless, the Army Council was concerned enough to issue two instructions early in 1915. The first was an attempt to clarify cowardice and desertion. It made the point that the former was 'not limited in its application to behaviour on the actual field of battle, but applies equally to any behaviour of a soldier when on active service in the field who shows an undue regard for his own safety.' In other words, the soldier did not have to be in the front line to display cowardice. As for desertion, the normal peacetime interpretation was that a deserter was a man who had no intention of returning to military duty as opposed to an absentee who did return or intended to do so. The definition was now expanded to embrace a soldier who absented himself in order to avoid 'any special or dangerous duty', even if he then voluntarily returned to his unit after it had completed its mission. The Army Council reiterated that 'there must be sufficient evidence to satisfy the Court that the accused was in fact guilty of the offence charged'. The instruction went on:

A Court is bound to assume that an accused intended the natural and probable consequences of his actions: and before coming to a decision as to his guilt, must carefully consider the circumstances in which he absented himself, the length of time during which he remained absent, and the probability of that absence leading to the avoidance of any special or dangerous duty.

That such an absence did result in the avoidance of such duty 'raises the presumption that the accused absented himself with that object in view; and the Court is entitled to act on that presumption unless the accused can prove that it is not well founded'.[27] This appeared to imply that the defendant was assumed to be guilty unless he could prove otherwise, which is against the basic tenet of English law. In practice, the way in which the court should treat this matter is clearly explained in *Notes for Commanding Officers*. This emphasized that it had to be proved that the accused knew with 'reasonable certainty' that he was avoiding such a duty. This could only be done if it was established that the soldier was warned off directly for the duty, that he had been present when his unit was so warned or 'that according to the usual custom of reliefs [for trench duty] the accused must have known that the turn of the Company was imminent'. Failing any of these criteria, evidence must be produced to show that 'the period of absence was so long that the accused must have known for certain that he would miss active operations in consequence'.[28] In these circumstances the presumption that the man went absent to avoid the duty appears reasonable.

The Army Council was also concerned over the soldier who pleaded guilty to an offence which carried the death sentence. If he should do so, the basic facts of the case were merely laid out by the prosecution and the sentence passed without considering any evidence for the defence. The soldier, too, might not be aware of the ultimate implication of a guilty plea. Accordingly, GHQ France GRO 601 of 4 February 1915 laid down that in future the courts were not to accept a plea of guilty. One of 'not guilty' was to be entered, and the court was to 'thoroughly ascertain and record all the facts of the case'.

During the next three years the number of death sentences increased: there were 591 in 1915, 856 in 1916 and 904 in 1917. The percentage of those sentences which were confirmed also rose, from 8.96 per cent in

1915 to 11.17 per cent in 1917. In 1918 the number of death sentences fell to 515 and the confirmations to 6.99 per cent.[29] This can be explained in part by the fact that the army overseas expanded during 1915–17, from just over 330,000 at the beginning of 1915 to over 2.7 million at the end of 1917. It peaked at just over 2.8 million at the end of February 1918, but fell to under 2.7 million by that November.[30] The effect of the grim battles of the Somme and Third Ypres on morale were another factor. Indeed, there was a dramatic increase in the number of men recorded as being absent from their units. GHQ periodically issued lists of absentees and as at 8 December 1916 the list comprised 236 names. By the end of June 1917 the total had risen sharply to well over 1,300.[31] In contrast, the last half of 1918 saw the prospects of ultimate victory grow ever brighter and a consequent raising of morale.

In terms of the men who actually faced the firing squad, 291, including three officers, were from the British Army, thirty-one were from Dominion contingents (twenty-five Canadians, five New Zealanders, one South African), five were members of Colonial forces, ten were members of the Chinese Labour Corps, four were Coloured labourers, and five were camp followers.[32] The only Dominion which refused to introduce the death sentence for its troops was Australia. But their discipline when out of action left much to be desired and Haig noted in his diary entry of 3 March 1918 that one in every hundred Australians in France was in prison.

Gerard Oram has made the case in *Worthless Men*, published in 1998, that the authorities had a bias against Irishmen, members of the Dominion and Colonial forces, and ethnic colonial labourers. His arguments are not, however, convincing. The vast majority of the last category, including all the Chinese and three Cape Coloured labourers, were convicted on the crime of murder, which, of course, was a capital offence in civil society as well as in the army.[33] During the period from 1914 to 1920, soldiers in Irish regiments received 239 death sentences (8 per cent of the total) of which twenty-five were confirmed, which represents 8.6 per cent of the total executions in the British Army. True, this percentage is out of proportion to the less than 3 per cent contribution that Irishmen made to the overall strength of the army, but it should be borne in mind that political events in Ireland proved frequently destabilizing. It was this which was behind the mutiny of the 1st Connaught Rangers in India in the summer of 1920 and which resulted in sixty-nine of its members being court martialled, with fourteen receiving death sentences, although only one was confirmed. As for the Dominion troops, the proportion of Canadians who were executed to the total number who served overseas is 0.005 per cent, and those for New Zealand and South Africa are 0.004 per cent and 0.001 per cent respectively.[34] No precise figure exists for the number of British soldiers sent overseas during the war, but taking into account the peak strength overseas of 2.8 million, and the facts that 704,803 lost their lives and that 36 per cent of the 2,272,998 wounded did not return to full duty, a very rough figure of four million can be arrived at. The 291 confirmed death sentences thus work out at 0.007 per cent of the whole, which certainly does not indicate any bias against Dominion troops. As for the Colonial forces (East and West African troops, Caribbean contributions, etc) the overall total of those who served in theatres of war is difficult to establish. Taking 100,000 as a conservative estimate, the five capital sentences carried out gives a proportion of 0.005 per cent, the same as for the Canadian contingent, again demonstrating that there was no official bias against these men.

Where Oram's thesis does bear closer examination is his claim of the bias against what he calls 'worthless men'. The term comes from a comment that Douglas Haig made when he was commanding the First Army. It concerned the court martial of Private O. W. Hodgetts of the 1st Worcesters, who had gone missing on the eve of Festubert in May 1915, having already done the same during Neuve Chapelle, and just prior to this battle had been awarded ninety days Field Punishment No. 1. Supporting the death sentence handed down by the court, Haig wrote: 'This man is worthless as a fighting soldier.'[35] Indeed, the comments by those up the chain of command on the court martial proceedings of men who had been sentenced to death generally covered two aspects: whether the man was a good fighting soldier; and the state of discipline in his unit. The CO also had to add his personal opinion on whether 'the offence was deliberately committed with the sole object of avoiding the particular service specified'. In summary, the aim was 'to prevent a good fighting man from being shot for absence resulting from simple absence or a drunken spree'.[36] The implication was that those who did not possess the necessary fighting spirit could 'go to the wall'. The court martial proceedings of those soldiers who were sentenced to death but were reprieved no longer exist. A survey of those in which the death sentence was confirmed shows that 30 per cent were Regulars or reservists, 40 per cent were Kitchener volunteers, 19 per cent were Irish and Dominion soldiers, 3 per cent were pre-war Territorials and 9 per cent conscripts.[37] What this reveals is that the very soldiers that one would expect to be the most likely to turn out to be 'worthless men' – the conscripts – were in a clear minority. Whether this was because greater allowances were made for them cannot be established in the absence of the proceedings in which the death sentence was not confirmed. In contrast, the comparatively high percentage of Regulars and reservists who were shot probably reflects the fact that the army had traditionally recruited from those on the fringes of society and always had a number of 'bad hats' in its ranks, who regarded crime as a challenge. As for the Kitchener volunteers having the highest percentage, this undoubtedly reflects the pressure to find men for the New Armies. Lax initial medical inspections by doctors working under extreme pressure undoubtedly let in those who were in poor physical shape, as witness the sorry saga of the Bantams (*see page 134*), and recruiting officers allowed in men who were mentally and morally deficient, as well as those who were under-age. The massive recruiting campaign during 1914–15 also put social pressures on the male population to join up, the frequent handing out of white feathers being just one example of this.

The survey also shows that 40 per cent of those who were executed had been previously charged with serious crimes but had been allowed further chances to make good.[38] Harold Dearden relates the case of a man in his Guards battalion who had deserted before an attack and had been picked up behind the lines. Dearden considered him 'a pitiful degenerate, has drunk a lot in his time, and is no use to anyone'. The man persuaded Dearden, who was the MO, to speak on his behalf at his court martial. Dearden told the court that the soldier 'had always been a man of highly nervous disposition whose self-control was practically nil, and that I considered he was much below the standard of the ordinary [soldier] in every way mentally'. The man was acquitted and Dearden counselled him to pull himself together and make a fresh start.

ABOVE South African Native Labour Corps, France, February 1917. One of the many overseas labour contingents that served in France, they were technically civilians, in spite of wearing uniform and being subject to military law, and were on one-year contracts. Because of this, they were not permitted to work within 10 miles of the front line. They were also kept totally segregated. (IWM Q7835)

BELOW Bringing back salvaged rifles, La Boisselle, Somme, July 1916. The importance of retrieving weapons and equipment from the battlefield was recognized as early as September 1914. It would not, however, be until summer 1917 that dedicated salvage units of the Labour Corps were established, although divisions did form companies from among their less fit men in 1915 to carry out salvage as well as other general tasks. (IWM Q3994)

ABOVE Members of the Calais Convoy of the First Aid Nursing Yeomanry (FANY) in early 1918, with 'the Boss', Lillian Franklin, on the left and wearing three service stripes above the rank badge on her right cuff, indicating service overseas from 1915. The FANY ambulances first operated with the Belgians, but on 1 January 1916 began to support the BEF. Its members were not paid and the army merely supplied their rations, while the British Red Cross Society paid for the maintenance of the ambulances. (IWM Q7950)

BELOW QMAAC Camp No. 4, Rouen, probably autumn 1918. Rouen, being one of the main BEF bases in France, provided a wide range of work for the women, from clerking in the registry of GHQ 3rd Echelon to the various cookhouses. The Nissen huts provided ideal accommodation, since their interiors could be laid out to suit the wishes of the QMAAC. The photograph also gives a good idea of the uniforms worn, from administrators (the two ladies on the extreme left), to working and walking out dress. (IWM Q8120)

LEFT 9th (Scottish) Division walking wounded at a battalion aid post, Meteren, 18 August 1918. Their wounds dressed, they are now about to make their way to the Walking Wounded Collecting Station, prior to being taken to the Casualty Clearing Station, the furthest forward point at which surgery would be carried out. (IWM Q6953)

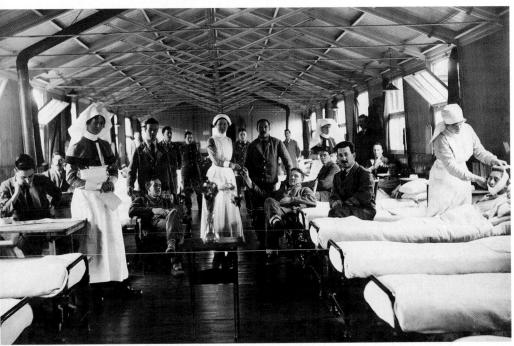

ABOVE A ward in No. 32 Stationary Hospital, Wimereux, also known as the Australian Voluntary Hospital. The patients are dressed in 'hospital blue'. Some will be evacuated back to Britain, while the others will be sent to a convalescent camp in France prior to rejoining their units. They are being cared for by QAIMNS sisters (with the mini-capes) and VADs. (IWM Q8002)

RIGHT Francis Derwent Wood, one of the leading sculptors of his day, measuring a badly disfigured soldier for a face mask. With plastic surgery very much in its infancy, Derwent Wood became concerned over the plight of those who had suffered severe facial wounds. Many feared going about in public and some even committed suicide. His solution was moulded and painted silver-covered electroplate masks, using pre-injury photographs of the victim as a guide. (IWM Q30456)

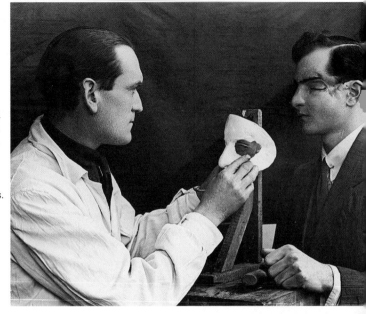

BELOW A returning supply column passes graves at Bernafay Wood on the Somme, September 1916. Although the War Graves Commission had come into being twelve months before, graves registration was still in its infancy. Much of the problem lay in the fact that the dead, once their identity discs and paybooks had been removed, were left with just a label, which soon became illegible, to identify them. Matters were improved after it was laid down in August 1916 that each man would wear two identity disks around his neck, with the second being left with the body. (IWM Q1541)

TOP Wounded horses and mules arriving at No. 5 Veterinary Hospital, Abbeville, April 1918. The Army Veterinary Corps had learnt much from the South African War, when some two-thirds of the horses perished, many from starvation or disease, largely because of ignorance. In contrast, during 1914–18 the AVC treated some 2.5 million animals, 80 per cent of whom were able to return to duty. (IWM Q10295)

ABOVE Incoming mail being sorted at Dernancourt, near Albert, September 1916. Addresses merely included name, rank, number, unit and theatre of war and were largely sorted in London. The mail has probably just been unloaded at the railhead and is being sorted prior to being distributed among the divisions. The efficient operation of the Army Postal Service was undoubtedly one of the administrative triumphs of 1914–18. (IWM Q4108)

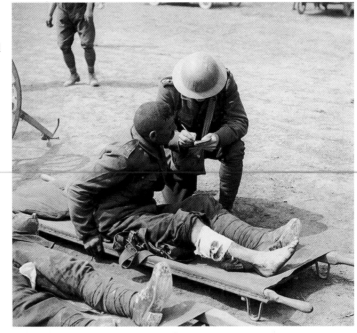

LEFT Bread production in the
ASC Field Bakery at Calais, March
1917. It was policy that, whenever
possible, troops should be supplied
with fresh bread on the daily scale
of 1.25lbs per man. By November
1918 there were fifteen of these
bakeries in France, together with
a further ten supporting the
Dominion troops. (IWM Q4792)

BELOW The arrival of the leave
train at Charing Cross, London.
Troops fresh from France queue
to exchange their francs. The
bearded figure in the foreground
is a member of the Volunteer
Force, sometimes known as the
National Guard, one of whose
duties was to give guidance and
help to leave men at the London
termini. (IWM Q30517)

ABOVE A padre takes down the personal details of a wounded German
soldier at an Advanced Dressing Station near Carnoy, 30 July 1916.
Chaplains not only looked after the spiritual welfare of their men, but
also provided practical assistance, including helping out at ADSs and
CCSs during battles, running unit canteens, and organizing entertain-
ments. (IWM Q4056)

BELOW A Church Army canteen at Saint Omer. It is not just the lure of
a proper cup of tea, as opposed to army 'char' in a tin mug, but also a
chance to talk to British girls. Some of the canteens were deployed well
forward, within range of shellfire, but did much for the morale of those
coming in and out of the trenches. (IWM Q7967)

ABOVE The Diamonds, 29th Division's concert party. The Columbine and Pierrot dress of the performers was adopted by most concert parties and was especially popular in seaside music hall, its origins lying in sixteenth- and seventeenth-century comic Italian theatre. Concert party members were found from within the division and drew on men who had pre-war theatre experience, whether on or back stage. Songs and topical sketches were the basis of their shows. (IWM Q58091)

RIGHT The commander of the 56th Brigade (19th Division) presenting medals to his men. These were probably immediate awards of the MC and MM, which could be approved within 48 hours of the recommendation being submitted. There was much anguish over the policy of awards and decorations, but the institution of immediate awards was a significant step in recognizing those who had shown outstanding bravery. (IWM Q233)

He promised he would, and asked if he might come and talk to me sometimes, for the other men in the company didn't understand and would scarcely speak to him. Of course, I said he could; but it will be an infernal nuisance, and in any case he'll never make anything, and will probably bolt again the first chance he gets. They tell me he'll probably get shot by his own mates the next time we go over the top, so it's a bright look-out anyway, poor devil!

Dearden was right. The day before the battalion was due to return to the trenches, the man went absent. He was apprehended once more and, as Dearden commented, he was 'a dead certainty to be shot this time'. He remarked further: 'One can't help hating a condition of affairs which makes cowardice a crime, and forces one already poor specimen of manhood into something too horribly near a beast. After all, cowardice ought not to be a crime, and yet one has seen so many splendid fellows lay down their lives so bravely that one can find no pity for such as he.'[39]

Padre Bickersteth relates the case of a man who was posted into the London Rangers (1st/12th Londons) in January 1917 under close arrest as a deserter and then absented himself four more times before being sentenced to death. This was probably Rifleman Walter Yeoman, who had been given a suspended sentence of fifteen years' penal servitude the first time he deserted and was eventually shot at the beginning of July 1917. Bickersteth added:

> there were not a few who said that he was mad, or at least there was something wrong with his brain, but our doctor was unable to certify that he was in any way not responsible for his actions, and certainly he was quite intelligent in a good many ways. He could read and write well.[40]

A similar case concerned Private B. A. Hart of the 1st/4th Suffolks at the end of 1916. He had been with his battalion in France for ten months and had already been in trouble. In early May he was awarded twenty-eight days Field Punishment No. 1 for 'not complying with an order' and then went absent when ordered to parade with a working party while carrying out this punishment. The result was a further twenty-eight days FP No. 1. Then, in August 1916 he was tried for desertion and found guilty of attempting to desert. For this he was sentenced to five years penal servitude, although this was suspended. Stormont Gibbs, the adjutant, later stated that he made Hart his servant, keeping him in the wagon lines when the battalion went into the trenches. This clearly did not happen, for Hart was warned off for the trenches, but was missing from his platoon when it arrived. He turned up again two days later, when the 1st/4th Suffolks came out of the line. At his court martial Hart claimed that ever since being buried by a shell in March 1916 he could not face shellfire and had tried to report sick, but without success. The court found him guilty and recommended the death sentence. His CO in his comments considered him a 'bad character' as a fighting soldier and 'indifferent' in his general behaviour. He went on: 'In my opinion the crime was deliberately committed with the sole object of avoiding the particular service involved, ie the tour of duty in the trenches.' The brigade commander concurred, claiming that Hart was one of three men 'who have been constantly setting a bad example to the remainder of the battalion by deserting themselves from tours of duty in the trenches'. The divisional commander also supported the death sentence, pointing out that Hart had 'escaped the extreme penalty before owing to insufficient evidence'. But General du Cane, commanding XV Corps, was not prepared to rubber stamp the sentence. He wanted confirmation that Hart had been earlier buried by a shell and for medical evidence of shell shock. There was therefore a month's pause while these matters were investigated. Two witnesses from the Suffolks came forward and stated that Hart had indeed been buried to such an extent that only his boots were showing above the ground. They had helped to dig him out. Hart was then put under four days' observation by the Fourth Army's neurologist, but he could find 'no evidence of feeble mindedness or other mental defects.' The death sentence was therefore confirmed, but there was one more twist to the tale.

It was the usual practice for the condemned man's battalion to provide the firing party, but it was arranged so that only two or three rifles were loaded with live ammunition, the remainder having blanks. In this way, no one outside the firing party would know who fired the fatal shots. In the case of Private Hart, there was an exception to this rule. Stormont Gibbs:

sent a chit to OC Companies to supply a few men each – wondering what would happen. As I expected, everyone refused to do it and I wasn't going to press the company commanders on the subject. I rang Brigade and had a rather heated conversation about it and finally the poor chap was shot by someone else … I had to write to the man's mother.[41]

Private Hart himself was almost certainly suffering from shell shock, as was 22-year-old Sergeant John Wall of the 3rd Worcesters. He had landed in France with his battalion in August 1914 and had been present at all its major actions. In August 1917, the 3rd Worcesters were engaged in operations in the Bellewarde Ridge sector. While moving up to occupy forward trenches, they came under heavy artillery fire and Sergeant Wall and several men took shelter in a concrete dug-out. The battalion then moved on, but Wall remained where he was and did not rejoin until two days later. The only excuse he could offer was that he had lost his way. He was described as a very good soldier, but no effort appears to have been made to find out why he had cracked. Wall faced a firing squad at Poperinghe on 6 September 1917.[42] As Lord Moran, who served in France as an RAMC doctor and was later Winston Churchill's personal physician during the Second World War, commented: 'Courage is will-power, whereof no man has an unlimited stock; and when in war it is used up, he is finished.'[43] This only began to be appreciated during the last year of the war, when men who had served for two years or more at the Front started to be posted home for a spell. Judge Anthony Babington cites the case of a lance corporal, whose CSM had said was an excellent soldier. In December 1915 a shell had burst close to him, killing a comrade, whose brains were spattered into the lance corporal's face. He apparently never recovered from this, reporting sick several times before going absent in May 1916.[44] This bears the hallmarks of shell shock, but the battalion MO seems not to have taken any positive action, perhaps because of his lack of knowledge.

Indeed ignorance on neurosis among unit MOs and officers sitting on courts martial during the middle part of the war was a factor which might well have caused injustices to be done. Captain L. Gameson was an expert witness at a number of courts martial while serving as MO to an RFA brigade. He believed that at least in one case his evidence on a man's mental instability saved him from the death sentence, but

> I felt that the machinery for dealing with such cases was inadequate. As an ordinary MO, with no experience whatever outside hospital, I was inexpert in both the thorny matter of mental states, and the technique of presenting a case. In theory at any rate, it was the Court's job to dig out the truth. Where the truth was handed to it intelligently the job was made easier. No other medical evidence but mine was offered and I am almost certain that I had had to shove myself into the picture, as I did later in one similar case.[45]

As for the death sentences themselves, some certainly changed their views during the war and after. M. St Helier Evans commented in September 1916:

> Officially this nauseating butchery is to be applauded, but I have quite changed my ideas. There are no two ways. A man either can or cannot stand up to the environment; with some the limit for breaking up is reached sooner than for others. The human being can only stand so much. Surely when a man becomes so afflicted it is a case for the medicals than for the Provost Marshal.[46]

Bernard Martin acted as a prosecuting officer at FGCMs on a number of occasions and had a similar change of heart. Reflecting many years later:

> As a general observation I'd say we PBI [poor bloody infantry] at the front had no contempt for Deserters such as we felt for Scrimshankers and Base-Wallahs. Deserters had volunteered to serve King and Country, but when they came out found that war was unlike what they supposed and they just couldn't take it ... Others may have overcome fear at first with courage but their courage had worn thin, as courage always does in time: they'd gradually crack up, and tried to get away without plan or hope. They deserved pity, not contempt.[47]

The case has also been made that officers received preferential treatment when it came to crimes attracting the death sentence. Five were given the death sentence during the war but only three were executed –

two for cowardice and one for murder. This was out of ten courts martial for cowardice, forty-six for desertion and twenty for quitting post (those for murder are not specified).[48] This was a tiny percentage of officers' courts martial, a third of which were for drunkenness. There is, however, evidence that a number of other officers committed capital military offences, which never came to court martial. F. P. Crozier tells of an incident in the summer of 1916, when he was commanding the 9th Royal Irish Rifles. He had two simultaneous cases of desertion on his hands. One was an officer who had fled the trenches during a *Minenwerfer* bombardment and the other was a rifleman. Both were found guilty at their subsequent courts martial and sentenced to death. Crozier was subsequently informed the officer's sentence had been quashed on technical grounds and was pressured to take him back, but Crozier refused to accept him. In contrast, the rifleman, who was also named Crozier, had his sentence confirmed. Although Colonel Crozier made no plea for clemency in his comments on the court martial proceedings, he personally ensured that the victim had a bottle of whisky on the night before he was to be shot so that he was virtually insensible when his execution took place.[49] Guy Chapman stated that during Third Ypres the CO of his Royal Fusiliers battalion reported two of his company commanders, one for malingering, the other for incompetence. Certainly, the former could have been court martialled. Instead, the divisional commander submitted an adverse report on both, which resulted in their having their commissions removed. Their fate, as was the case with all officers who were cashiered after the introduction of conscription, was to be re-enlisted as private soldiers.[50] In contrast, Hal Siepmann had a Regular subaltern in his RFA battery during the latter half of 1917 who was found drunk on duty no less than seven times. Rather than cashier him, the authorities merely posted him to another RFA brigade. Indeed, Siepmann was unlucky in his subalterns during this period. Another ended up in a VD hospital, and a third 'upset too many applecarts and then was put under arrest and cleared out'.[51] As for the officers who were court martialled and convicted, over half merely received a reprimand, which for a private soldier was as good as escaping punishment, but for an officer was a blot on his record which could hold up promotion.

In all, 377 officers were cashiered and a further 1,085 were dismissed the service during the war. Stormont Gibbs recalled what happened to one officer in his battalion who was sentenced to be cashiered for cowardice or desertion during Third Ypres:

> It is one of my most unpleasant memories. The ceremony is as follows. All officers are collected – in this case in a large room. The CO walks in followed by the Adjutant [Gibbs]. The officer to be cashiered is marched in by a guard for he is under arrest. The Adjutant is then supposed to read out a lengthy document about the sins of the unfortunate officer and the sentences of the court. He then advances to the officer and cuts off his badges of rank whereupon the Sergeant of the Guard says, 'Pte X – About turn – Quick march' – and it is over. I refused to read the stuff and the CO had to – I didn't see why I should always do the dirty work. But I had to cut the poor fellow's pips off – and they wouldn't come off – it was rotten for us both.[52]

Norman Collins of the 4th Seaforths recalled a similar case in summer 1917, but in this case the officer concerned was paraded in front of the whole battalion to have his rank badges removed.[53] Those officers who were dismissed were forced to resign without going through this indignity. But after the introduction of conscription, they, too, were also automatically re-enlisted in the ranks.

That officers, however distinguished their fighting records, could be treated just as harshly as other ranks, is illustrated by the sad case of 2nd Lieutenant Adam Stewart of the Machine Gun Corps (Motors). A pre-war Territorial with the 5th Scottish Rifles, he went to France as a sergeant with his battalion in early November 1914. He was wounded the following February and evacuated back to England, where he was discharged, having completed his term of service. He immediately re-enlisted and was appointed sergeant major to an MMGS battery. He was awarded an MC for bravery on the Somme and was subsequently commissioned. He won a bar to his MC, but in the closing days of the war was court martialled for issuing forged cheques in France. Found guilty on seven out of nine counts, Stewart was ordered to forfeit his commission and was sentenced to three years' hard labour, which he began to serve in Maidstone gaol. He also had to surrender his medals. Stewart lodged several petitions to be given another chance in the army, especially since he had a wife and two young children, who were receiving no allowances. Eventually, the Army Council relented and in May 1919 he was discharged from jail and allowed to re-enlist. Stewart went to Russia as a corporal in the 45th Royal Fusiliers. He distinguished himself on numerous occasions and, as a result, was granted back his medals. But in spite of his pleas, the Army Council refused to award Stewart a war gratuity for his service as an officer. Furthermore, when he re-enlisted as a Territorial in early 1922 it was made clear to him that he could not be considered for a commission.[54]

The first officer to be actually executed was 30-year-old 2nd Lieutenant Eric Poole of the 11th West Yorkshires. During fighting on the Somme in early July 1916 he was knocked unconscious by an exploding shell and evacuated to a base hospital as a shell-shock case. After seventeen days, he was sent to a convalescent home at Dieppe, where a consultant concluded that he was unfit for front-line service and should be temporarily employed on base duties. A week later, a medical board classified him fully fit and he returned to his battalion, which was refitting. On 5 October, the 11th West Yorkshires were told off for the trenches again that night. Poole apparently informed a brother officer that he was feeling unwell and was thinking of seeing a doctor. Once the battalion had completed its relief, Poole was discovered to be absent. He did, however, see the MO of another battalion the following morning and asked for tablets for his rheumatism. He was not seen again until two days later, when a military policeman arrested him some way to the rear and in a dazed state. On that same day, the 11th West Yorkshires made a successful attack north of Le Sars, but suffered eight officers and 217 other ranks as casualties. The CO organized a court of inquiry, which recommended that Poole be charged with desertion, and referred the matter to his brigade commander, Brigadier General T. S. Lambert. On 17 October, Lambert wrote to the divisional commander, Major General J. M. Babington, recommending that disciplinary action be dropped and that Poole should be given a home posting. 'He is of a nervous temperament, useless in action, and dangerous as an example to the men.' Babington tasked the ADMS of his division to arrange a medical examination. This found that Poole was 'of a highly strung and nervous temperament' and 'that it is possible that excitement may bring on a condition of mental aberration which would make him not responsible for his actions at the time'. Even though this supported Lambert's plea, General Sir Herbert Plumer, the army commander, insisted that Poole be charged with desertion. The preparations for the court martial therefore went ahead and it took place on 21 November 1916. Poole told the court that the shell shock he had suffered had been causing him fits of mental confusion and the 11th West Yorkshires MO supported him. It was not, however, enough and the court sentenced him to death. Even then, his CO, brigade, divisional and corps commanders all recommended that his sentence be commuted. Not so Plumer. He recommended that the sentence be confirmed. But before it was, a medical board examined Poole on 3 December. Its members concluded that, while his mental powers were below average, he was of sound mind and capable of appreciating the gravity of his crime. Three days later the court martial proceedings were placed before Douglas Haig. He recorded in his diary:

> After careful consideration I confirmed the proceedings. This is the first
> sentence of death on an officer to be put into execution since I became
> CinC. Such a crime is more serious in the case of an officer than of a
> man, and it is also highly important that all ranks should realise that the
> law is the same for an officer as a private.

Poole accordingly faced the firing squad on the morning of 10 December.[55] While Haig's attitude is understandable, what the Poole case does reveal are the conflicting views on shell shock held by the RAMC at the time and that the overriding authority lay with the medical boards, none of whose members would necessarily have a background in psychiatry. As a result, the evidence of Poole's shell shock was ultimately ignored.

The second case of an officer being court martialled for cowardice was better known at the time, thanks first to Horatio Bottomley's support for him in *John Bull*, and also to A. P. Herbert's thinly disguised 1919 novel about the case, *The Secret Battle*. There has also been much written since on Sub Lieutenant Edwin Dyett of the Nelson Battalion in the 63rd (Royal Naval) Division. Suffice to say that during the grim fighting on the Ancre in November 1916 Dyett was ordered to take reinforcements up to the front line, but vanished only to reappear in his battalion's billets when it came out of the trenches two days later.

He was charged with desertion and the Field General Court Martial convened on Boxing Day 1916. The president was a brigadier general and there were five members, including a CMO to advise on points of law. The fact that Dyett had turned up at the billets certainly did not indicate that he intended to absent himself permanently from his battalion, but he fell victim to the guidance on avoiding potentially dangerous duty given in January 1915. The prosecuting officer was from the Nelson Battalion and Dyett had an RNVR officer who had been a lawyer in civilian life as prisoner's friend. In his cross-examination, Dyett's defending officer established that the accused was prone to neurosis and was unfit to serve in the trenches. Yet Dyett declined to make a statement in his own defence. Given the damning prosecution evidence, the court felt it had no option but to find Dyett guilty as charged and to sentence him to death. But it also added a mercy rider on two grounds. First, Dyett was very young and had no experience of 'active operations of this nature', and also 'the circumstances, recently growing darkness, heavy shelling and the fact that the men were returning in considerable numbers, were likely to affect seriously a youth, unless he had a strong character'. That there were numerous officers in France who were younger than the 21-year-old Dyett and who had successfully come through equally difficult and similar situations does not seem to have weighed in the court's judgement or, if it did, it confirmed that someone like Dyett should never have been put in command of troops in action. General Shute, GOC 63rd Division, echoed the court's reservation and also recommended mercy, but apart from Dyett being 'very young and inexperienced', he knew 'of no reason why the extreme penalty should not be executed', which was a contradiction in terms. Not surprisingly, General Claude Jacob, commanding II Corps, who reviewed the proceedings on the same day, 30 December, recommended that the sentence should stand. Likewise, the army commander, Hubert Gough, also supported the sentence, adding, in line with Haig's view of the Poole case: 'If a private behaved as he did in such circumstances, it is highly probable that he would have been shot.' Haig confirmed the sentence on 2 January.

During the interval between the court martial and the review of the proceedings, Dyett had remained in ignorance of what had transpired and appeared to believe that the worst that could happen was that he would lose his commission. It therefore must have come as a shock when he was informed on the evening of 4 January that he was to be shot the following morning. On 23 February 1917, the weekly magazine *John Bull* carried a two-page account of the case, although Dyett, of course, was not mentioned by name. Horatio Bottomley, the magazine's proprietor, claimed that there had been a grave miscarriage of justice. Questions were asked in the House of Commons, but the government denied that Dyett had had little chance to prepare his defence. This did not deter Bottomley from continuing to rant against what he saw as the injustices in the court martial system.[56] Further questions were raised in the House in autumn 1917, notably by the Labour MP Philip Snowden. He began by asking whether the Army Act could be amended to provide for military trials presided over by a judge, with a jury of soldiers. Relatives of executed soldiers should be allowed to examine the proceedings with a view to appealing against the sentence; he argued, too, that the death sentence for soldiers be abolished. The Under-Secretary of State for War, Ian Macpherson, rejected all three proposals out of hand. Snowden and others then raised a number of individual cases in which they claimed injustices had been done, particularly in relation to those who claimed they were suffering from shell shock. In many incidents, the versions described were inaccurate, but Snowden was right in claiming that few of those claiming to be suffering from shell shock were given any form of medical examination to verify this. Indeed, Anthony Babington states that out of thirty-two soldiers executed during July to October 1917 only three were subjected to any form of medical investigation and that in all three cases they were found to be medically fit.[57]

Inadequate officers like Poole and Dyett should never have been placed in the position that they were and, likewise, there is no doubt that some of the other ranks who were executed did have a medical condition which was ignored. Yet all this must be balanced against the vast majority of officers and men who overcame their fears and neuroses and continued to do their duty. Furthermore, the fact that nine out of ten death sentences were commuted shows that the military authorities were not as heartless as some make out and that efforts were made to ensure that justice was done. That some errors were made is hardly surprising, given the continual pressures that commanders at all levels were under and the lack of specialist medical knowledge among unit doctors. These injustices are to be regretted, but there is no doubt that in the majority of cases those involved were guilty as charged and that they knew that the offences they committed would incur capital punishment.

A footnote to the carrying-out of capital sentences was the question of how the next of kin of the victim should be told of his death. As with other fatal casualties, they were informed by the relevant Army Record Office. The official letter read: 'It is with very great regret that I have to tell you that [Number, Rank, Name, Regiment] was sentenced after trial by Court Martial to be shot for [desertion, cowardice, or whatever the crime was] and the sentence was duly executed on [date].' This was obviously upsetting for the recipient of the letter, as the clerk to the War Pensions Committee at Widnes, Lancashire, pointed out to Lord Derby on 13 March 1917. He stated that his committee had recently received complaints relating to three such cases. Describing these letters as 'unnecessarily harsh', the clerk suggested that

> it might be sufficient to convey to the relations a simple intimation of the death of the soldier, without adding to their sorrow the indignity that must naturally be felt (and which feeling, no doubt, they will communicate to their friends) of knowing that their relations have suffered an ignominious death.

The War Office rejected the proposal on the grounds that it had to be made clear that the dependents of those executed were not on the same footing with regard to financial allowances as those whose loved ones had fallen in action. But as 1917 wore on, the War Cabinet began to have second thoughts and decided towards the end of the year that dependants of soldiers executed should be entitled to the same pension rights as anyone else. Furthermore, the official letter was amended to read: 'It is with great regret that I have to inform you that [Name, etc] has died on service on [date].' In addition, unlike the normal letter to next of kin, it was not accompanied by a message of sympathy from their majesties. Even so, the Army Council objected on the grounds that the softer approach was bad for discipline. The War Cabinet was, however, insistent.[58]

Apart from desertion or claiming to be shell shocked, there were a number of other methods that soldiers used to try to get themselves away from the trenches. Self-inflicted wounds (SIW) were not uncommon, They were usually gun shot wounds to the hand or toes. The policy was to keep SIW cases in the theatre of war and in France there was a special hospital for them at Mont des Cats.[59] Once they had recovered, they were usually court martialled. Henry Ogle relates the case of a man in the 1st/7th Royal Warwicks who shot his hand. He was sentenced to Field Punishment No. 1, returned to his unit and became a company cook, which at least kept him out of the front-line trenches.[60] In all twelve officers and 3,882 soldiers were court martialled for this crime during the war.

Some also tried venereal disease as an excuse. Again, VD treatment centres were set up within the theatres of war and anyone who contracted the disease was put to the bottom of the leave roster. Arthur Osburn of the RAMC described another method. This was to

> accuse a comrade, officer or man, of a crime of morality in which perhaps you were yourself implicated. This probably meant a court martial for both of you. Court-martials of this form of misdemeanour were often held at Havre or some other base far from the front line. If the scheme was successful, one or both of those implicated in the alleged offence would rely on getting two years imprisonment for 'indecency' to be spent in Wormwood Scrubs or some other English prison.[61]

He was, of course, referring to homosexual acts, which in those days were against the law of the land. From the outbreak of war to 31 March 1920, a total of twenty-three officers and 293 other ranks were court martialled for this offence, which was termed 'indecency'. Other soldiers were tried in civilian courts. There is virtually nothing remaining of the courts martial of other ranks, but some of those concerning officers are preserved in their personal files held at the National Archives, Kew. The majority of the alleged offences appear to have taken place in Britain and peaked, as F. W. Harvey has observed,[62] during the twelve months ending 30 September 1916. Indeed, almost a fifth of the officers court martialled during this period were charged with indecency or scandalous conduct, which usually involved issuing dud cheques. One contributory factor may well have been the fact that the quality of temporary officer commissioned before the Office Cadet battalions were instituted had been falling.

Officers convicted of indecency were cashiered. Those sentenced to terms of imprisonment were usually re-enlisted as private soldiers on their release. But there appears to have been no question of their terms being reduced in return for immediate enlistment and despatch to a war theatre. Two former officers who applied to do this had their petitions turned down. The army could also have a long arm when it came to tracking down culprits. An RFC officer was arrested and convicted of five counts of indecency at the Old Bailey. Among his papers was a letter from a young subaltern in the King's Royal Rifle Corps, in which he described the conquest of a young soldier in leave: 'His legs my dear, were too wonderful and I am feeling very tired to-day.' The subaltern himself was serving in the trenches in France and, although his conduct was exemplary in the eyes of his CO, he was brought back from France and court martialled at the Guildhall, Westminster, on the charges of indecency and 'behaving in a scandalous manner unbecoming the character of an officer and gentleman'. Acquitted on the first charge, he was found guilty of the second in that he had written the letter in question and was cashiered.

In other cases, officers managed to escape being charged with homosexual offences. Lieutenant Graham Seton Hutchison of the Argylls was serving with the 2nd Battalion in France during the winter of 1914–15. He formed a close relationship with his batman, even to the extent of arranging for him to accompany Hutchison on five days' home leave. Hutchison openly admitted this in his biography *Footslogger*, but he was also accused of pretending that the batman was his brother. The man was killed at the beginning of March 1915, but a few weeks later Hutchison sent a note to one of the sergeants in the battalion arranging an assignation: 'I will give you a bath in Armentiers [sic] at a new house I've got. We will go to the Follies – a new show, very good.' The sergeant was to wear a mackintosh, presumably to conceal his stripes. The letter got into the hands of the authorities and, although there was insufficient evidence to justify a court martial, Sir John French personally commented that he was 'strongly of the opinion that Lieut. Hutchison is not the class of officer whose services it is desirable to retain'. Hutchison was posted back to the 3rd Argylls in Scotland and the Director of Personal Services decreed that he was not to be sent back to France.

Hutchison, however, was undeterred. He had become interested in machine guns (he had been the 2nd Argylls MG officer) and designed one or two modifications to improve their effectiveness. He received a letter of thanks from the War Office. Encouraged by this, he applied for a recommendation for promotion – he had already been passed over three times – and for release from the 3rd Argylls. After some opposition, Hutchison managed to get himself posted as brigade MG officer to the 100th Brigade in 33rd Division, which was carrying out its final training on Salisbury Plain.[63] He never looked back, rising to command the 33rd Machine Gun Battalion and winning both the DSO and MC.

Understandably, homosexuality is not a subject which is much mentioned in trench memoirs, but two cases of officers approaching young soldiers in France are revealed in accounts by private soldiers. In September 1918, Jimmy Taylor of the 2nd Worcesters went on a sniping course at Port Mahon. His officer instructor was a colonial and

> began to treat me like an individual, quite a new experience for me. He made friendly advances and more and more towards the end of the second week, would confide in me his personal troubles. He appeared to be indescribably lonely, and in sharp contrast with his amazing vitality displayed during our work. He told me he had recently lost his only brother and was in need, so he said, of some understanding companionship.

The officer eventually invited Taylor 'to sample for the night the comfort of his room'. Taylor agreed.

> With a pair of his pyjamas and a bed with clean sheets, the first for over a year, I was prepared to enjoy this unusual but blissful experience. As he joined me he put his arm round me which made me feel somewhat uncomfortable, but when he began to explore my body I got a shock, and suddenly realised that I had behaved like an utter fool in my innocence.

Taylor then fled.[64] In August 1918, 18-year-old R. H. Kiernan was an officer's servant and was approached by an 'oldish' 2nd lieutenant in billets in France. The officer put his arms around Kiernan's waist, but he managed to slip away. He talked to another batman about it, but was warned not to report it as it would only be his word against the officer's.[65] This partly explains why more cases were not drawn to the attention of the authorities. Another reason was the understandable shame felt by the victim. Even so, it should not be concluded that the British Army of 1914–18 was riddled with homosexuality; it was no more so than the population at large.

Perhaps, however, the main measure of the discipline and morale of an army are the incidents of mutiny. During the period from 4 August 1914 to 31 March 1920, a total of 1,807 British soldiers were convicted of mutiny, almost two-thirds of them abroad. The first soldiers court martialled for mutiny were thirteen privates of the 3rd Leicesters at Portsmouth. The details are not known, but each received a sentence of one year's hard labour.[66] Much of the unrest at home was caused by poor accommodation and food, the result of the rapid expansion of the army. In some units the trouble was snuffed out before knowledge of it reached higher command. Typical was the incident in 152 Field Company RE, which was in the 37th Division. In March 1915 the company was stationed at Tidworth and its catering was carried out by a civilian contractor. The men noticed that the quality of food, especially the sausages, was deteriorating. After one breakfast at which these were served, they took their sausages and plates and laid them on top of their bedding in the barrack rooms. The officers carried out an inspection and the company was then summoned by bugle call to parade outside. The men stood at the edge of the parade ground and refused to fall in. The company commander appears to have left the matter to his senior NCOs, who established the cause and the men were assured that their complaints would be dealt with. They went back to work and the food improved. There was no further trouble.[67]

The overwhelming majority of mutiny cases abroad during the war itself involved only a few men, but there were incidents in which there was more widescale disruption within a unit. Unfortunately, the details of most of the mutiny courts martial no longer exist and unit war diaries, for understandable reasons, seldom make mention of these incidents. One serious case concerned the 1st (Garrison) Battalion the Sherwood Foresters at Kantara in Egypt in the early summer of 1917. No less than sixty-four men, all private soldiers, out of a detachment of two officers and 119 men, which had just been sent to Kantara, were charged and each sentenced to two years' hard labour. No mention of it is made in the battalion War Diary and the only incident recorded which might have had some bearing was that the Sherwood Foresters had been ordered to exchange their SMLEs for the notorious Ross rifle, but as this took place on 3 June and the court martial was two days later, the weapons exchange may well have taken place after the mutiny itself.[68] There is a little more light shed on the nineteen men of the 12th South Wales Borderers who were tried by FGCM in France at the beginning of December 1916. They all came from the battalion's A Company and had apparently refused to fall in for a defaulters parade. One, Private A. W. Leather, was charged with inciting mutiny and with the lesser offence of disobedience. He was sentenced to seven years' penal servitude. The remainder were charged with mutiny and disobedience. Two were found not guilty, one was awarded two years' hard labour, and the remainder eighteen months' hard labour. When the findings were promulgated, the CO paraded the battalion and read out Sections 4–44 of the Army Act, presumably to remind his men of the penalties of committing crime.[69]

Another significant mutiny took place in the 9th East Lancashires in Salonika, with twenty-four privates each being sentenced to one year's hard labour, but no mention of it is made in the battalion War Diary.[70] There was also the court martial on 15 April 1918 of no less than 117 members of the 49th Brigade in the 16th (Irish) Division. This had suffered very heavily during the fighting in March and casualties had been so heavy that the brigade was reduced to one composite battalion, which was formed the day before the court martial. Again, no clues are given in the War Diary, though battle exhaustion may have had something to do with it. As it was, the majority were found guilty and awarded five years' penal servitude, which was suspended.[71]

One case of mass mutiny did actually take place in the line and concerned the 1st Australian Infantry Battalion. The circumstances were clearly explained by the CO in a report which he sent to the 1st Australian

Brigade. It was September 1918, with the final Allied offensive in France getting into full swing. The battalion had spent much of September at rest, but on the 18th was back in action and during this and the following day achieved its objectives with the loss of forty-eight casualties, including one officer killed and four others wounded. It was due to be relieved on the night of the 20th/21st, but during the 20th was told that it was to make another attack on the 21st and that the relief was cancelled. The battalion duly attacked, but there was trouble. D Company was in support, but soon lost both its officers wounded. The other three companies captured their objective and D was ordered to reinforce them, but its men refused to do so. 'The whole coy then marched out.' The trouble spread to other companies: ' ... about 40 men of C Coy and smaller numbers from A & B having apparently just picked up their gear, including Lewis Guns, & walked away.' It left a mere eighty men to hold the newly captured positions. Lieutenant Colonel B. V. Stacy, the CO, went up and spoke to those who were left. Clearly they were disgruntled at the cancellation of the relief, 'the feeling existed that they were "not getting a fair deal" & "were doing other people's work".' Stacy commented: 'The men have not had a hard time as we have known hard times in the past but shelling had been fairly constant near their dugouts & their nerves seem on edge & they made themselves believe they were not fit to take part in an attack.' His conclusion was that the ringleaders were men with bad records, including one under suspended sentence. He also criticized the NCOs for not appreciating where their responsibilities lay and for siding with 'the men in the wrong'. He requested that the battalion be relieved that night, which was duly done. In summary, Colonel Stacy recommended that 'the severest punishment be meted out to those involved' and that 'I consider the lightness & suspension of sentences in the past for desertion as greatly responsible for the trouble'. He did, however, point out that at no time had the men shown disrespect to their officers. The upshot of this affair was that no less than 122 junior NCOs and men were court martialled for mutiny and desertion on 15 October 1918. The vast majority were found guilty of desertion, with just eleven acquitted. The guilty ones were sentenced to penal servitude, the terms ranging from ten years to three years, with most of the corporals receiving the heaviest sentences.[72]

The aftermath of the overthrow of the Tsar in February 1917 saw extremist elements within Britain clamouring for a similar revolution. In early June, a convention of socialists and pacifists meeting at Leeds called for the establishment of Soldiers & Workmen's Councils on the Bolshevik model. There appears to have been just one attempt to form one, when representatives of the Reserve battalions of the Buffs, the Royal West Kents and the Royal Sussex from the Home Counties Reserve Brigade met at Tunbridge Wells on 24 June. They drew up a list of demands, which the authorities considered remarkably moderate. They included an increase in dependant and separation allowances in line with that of food prices, for wounded not to be sent back to the Front without examination by a civilian doctor and for relaxation of the Defence of the Realm Acts and censorship. In addition 'the general treatment of soldiers be brought into line with the spirit of the Officers and men in daily contact. As things stand, the Army Council continually issue orders which have the effect of reducing the organisation to a cross between a reformatory and a lunatic asylum.' The council also asked for 'more generous treatment of younger officers who, out of a daily casualty list of over 4,000 suffer the heaviest proportionate burden.' This was hardly the stuff of revolution, although there were demands for the government to state the terms under which it was prepared to enter peace negotiations with the enemy and for those soldiers employed in civilian work to be discharged from the army and 'only called up in the ordinary way as though a civilian. The using of soldiers as Blacklegs revolts the instinct of every decent man'. In this respect, the War Office was worried about the involvement of the Army Reserve Munition Workers (ARMW) in strikes and asked firms experiencing industrial action to report on this. From those reports which survive, it would appear that most ARMWs were able to stay out of it and that the civilian work force understood their position. As for the Soldiers & Workmen's Council, Home Counties & Training Reserve Branch, the authorities moved quickly by arranging for the ringleaders to be dispersed through posting to other units. Thus, fears that the situation in Russia would precipitate widescale military unrest proved to be largely groundless.[73]

Nevertheless, the French Army mutinies in the summer of 1917 and the serious unrest in a Russian brigade serving with the French clearly influenced the British military authorities when it came to dealing with the aftermath of the so-called Etaples mutiny of that September. This has been recounted many times before, but in essence it was triggered by the arrest by military police of a New Zealand soldier who had overstayed his local leave in the town. This attracted a crowd of some 2,000 soldiers from the base depots, who demanded his release. Feeling threatened, one of the MPs fired a warning shot from his revolver. Unfortunately, the round hit a Scottish corporal. This infuriated the crowd, who chased the MPs into the town, knocking two about in the process. By 9 p.m. peace had been restored and next day training took place as usual. But once it was completed, another crowd gathered at the main exit from the camps and forced their way into the town, where many became drunk. Brigadier General Andrew Thompson, the commandant of Etaples Base, and his staff personally intervened and managed to persuade the men to return to their camps. He was, however, worried enough that the trouble might spread to arrange for 100 men from the Machine Gun School at Le Touquet to be sent to protect the nearby resort of Paris-Plage. On the third day, 11 September, the pattern was as before, but by now officer's patrols were stationed on the bridges over the River Canche. The crowds of soldiers approached these and at one the picquet was commanded by Captain E. F. Wilkinson of the West Yorkshires. The men began to push the picquet aside. Wilkinson ordered his subordinate officers to rally their men and then began to reorganize them. At this juncture a Corporal Jesse Short of the Northumberland Fusiliers told the picquet to ignore Wilkinson and throw him in the river. He then moved away and Wilkinson detailed an NCO and four men to arrest him if he returned. This Short did and was promptly arrested.

In view of the continuing unrest, General Thompson moved with great swiftness. Short was arraigned before an FGCM on the following day. In his evidence, Captain Wilkinson stated that he had been approached by 'about 70 or 80 men with notice boards torn up from the camps and waving flags which were handkerchiefs of all colours including red attached to sticks'. Other witnesses echoed this statement and the fact that Short had used abusive language to Wilkinson. Short's defence – that he had been drunk at the time – was dismissed, especially since witnesses intimated otherwise. The court accordingly found Short guilty of 'endeavouring to persuade persons in His Majesty's Forces to join in a mutiny' and sentenced him to death. His court martial did not, however, bring an end to the unrest. On the day of his court martial there was a further break-out from the camps at the end of the day's training and the pattern was repeated on the following day. Two battalions were now sent to Etaples from the Front and by 15 September order had been restored.

Besides Short, three other men were charged with mutiny: a 17-year-old Royal Scots Fusilier, an Australian machine gunner and a member of the Canadian Light Horse. All three were sentenced to ten years' penal servitude, although in the case of the Canadian this was reduced to two years' hard labour. As for Short, the proceedings of his court martial went up the command chain and the sentence was confirmed.[74] That some of the men had been waving red flags was, however, already known by Haig. On 12 September he noted in his dairy that his Adjutant General had told him about the Etaples disturbances and that they were 'due to some men of new drafts with revolutionary ideas who had produced red flags and refused to obey orders'. Eleven days later, he was briefed by General Asser, commanding the lines of communication, who again mentioned the red flags. It was therefore probably inevitable that he would confirm Short's death sentence as a means of snuffing out further dissent. Furthermore: 'I decided to carry out the training [of the newly arrived drafts] in future at Corps Schools, of which we have 17 for 20 Corps. This will keep drafts away from the dockers at the Bases. These are said to be very Republican.'[75] What the incident did illustrate was the nervousness of the high command over the possibility of a Bolshevik-inspired mutiny which would put the BEF in the same position that the French Army had been earlier in the year.

Yet whatever the incidents of unrest and imperfections in the military justice system, the British Army maintained its discipline throughout the war and, in spite of the use of the death sentence, it was reasonably humane by the standards of the day. It should also be remembered that military discipline is inevitably harsher than that in civilian life for the simple reason that without strict discipline lives will be needlessly lost.

thirteen

MEDICINE

At the outbreak of war the Royal Army Medical Corps (RAMC) had a strength of 1,509 officers and 16,331 other ranks. This included both Regulars and Territorials. Its tasks, as laid out in *Field Service Regulations Part II*, were 'the preservation of the health of the troops; the professional treatment and care of sick and wounded; the replenishing of medical and surgical equipment; and the collection and evacuation of sick and wounded from the theatre of operations.' In the field the RAMC aimed to achieve, above all else, 'rapid evacuation of sick and wounded'. To this end, it divided its operations into three 'zones'. The forward area was called the collecting zone and incorporated unit medical sections and the divisional field ambulances. Each cavalry regiment, infantry battalion, and artillery brigade had a medical section, which consisted of a Medical Officer (MO) and a party of stretcher bearers. Their tasks were to recover and administer first aid to the sick and wounded. The field ambulances were allotted one to each infantry or cavalry brigade and were controlled by the Assistant Director of Medical Services (ADMS) at divisional HQ. They were organized into bearer sections, which collected the wounded from unit aid posts, and tent sections, which provided Advanced Dressing Stations (ADS) where emergency operations could be carried out and patients' wounds re-dressed. There was also a divisional collecting station, to which walking wounded were directed. The wounded were then taken to Clearing hospitals, which, together with ambulance trains, formed the evacuating zone. The allocation was one clearing hospital per division and they carried out much the same duties as the ADSs but on a larger scale. From here the casualties were taken to the nearest railhead, often using empty vehicles from returning supply columns or requisitioned transport. Ambulance trains were also allocated on a scale of one per division. They transported the casualties into the distributing zone. Those expected to recover in a reasonably short time went to the Stationary hospitals, which were also on the lines of communication, while the more serious cases were sent to General hospitals, which were situated both at the base and in Britain. Hospital ships, also on the scale of one per division, were used to take casualties back to Britain or elsewhere outside the theatre of operations. That was how the system operated in theory.

Units were usually assigned MOs at the outbreak of war. Thus, Captain Arthur Osburn, a South African War veteran, knew that on mobilization he was to report to a cavalry regiment at Tidworth, but not until 6 August was he informed that this was to be the 4th Royal Dragoon Guards.[1] But there were insufficient Regular officers to fill these slots and all those at field ambulances and the hospitals. Consequently, the RAMC was heavily reliant on officers on the Reserve, as well as specially enrolled civilians. Sir Wilmot Herringham, who served as Consultant Physician in France, noted: 'At the front hardly any of the Field Ambulances or Clearing Stations had more than two Regular officers, and latterly they usually had only the CO.'[2] But finding the numbers needed for a rapidly expanding army was a continuing struggle. Matters were not helped by the fact that the initial maximum age for enlistment of 31 was also applied to doctors and many willing to offer their services were turned down on the ground that they were too old. Others found difficulties in finding locums for their practices. Those who did enlist did so for one year or the duration of the war, whichever was shorter, and this would in time increase wastage and cause resentment. Travis Hampson noted three doctors from his field ambulance in France relinquishing their commissions in August 1915, having completed their year's service. Two of them had 'only been a short time in the forward area'. He himself was a Special Reservist and had another cause for resentment. Civilian doctors who volunteered were were paid 24 shillings per diem from the outset, while a Special Reserve RAMC lieutenant received a mere 14 shillings. What rankled was that 'many of them were youngsters only just qualified, and none of them had given three valuable months as we had to in the Special Reserve, training in the Depot for a commission'.[3] Many medical students, too, abandoned their studies and joined other arms and services, thus denying the RAMC a further source of officers. D Company of the 4th Gordons, which was made up entirely of Aberdeen University graduates and students, had no less than twenty-eight men in its ranks who were studying medicine. Many of these were killed serving as private soldiers during 1915.[4]

In Herringham's view, the army also had a tendency to believe that the ordinary MO could turn his hand to anything and did not recognize the need for specialists. 'In consequence hospitals were sent out whose personnel were of regulation strength, but frequently contained no surgeon of any experience whatever.' This was one reason why Herringham was sent out to France in October 1914 as Consultant Physician, joining Sir Anthony Bowlby, who was Consulting Surgeon. They could help ensure that doctors were given appointments which reflected their expertise.[5] Casualties to medical staff during the early weeks of fighting in France exacerbated the situation. Colonel Arthur Lee, in a report to Kitchener in late October 1914, described the situation at the Clearing hospitals in France: '… apart from the fact that cases coming into the Clearing Hospitals have to wait unnecessarily long before their wounds are dressed, I have frequently seen Medical Officers who have been working for such prolonged periods, without sleep or proper food, that they are not in a fit condition to attend serious cases.' With insufficient staff to provide them with reliefs, it was clear that the establishments of medical units needed to be increased.[6]

It was not until March 1915 that Sir Alfred Keogh, the Director-General of Army Medical Services (DGAMS), took action over the growing shortfall in medical officers. He issued an appeal for more medical men to come forward, but, to retain the confidence of the British Medical Association (BMA), he stressed that he had no wish 'to denude the country of civil practitioners'. He then met with the BMA's Special Committee of Chairmen of Standing Committees to discuss how they could help. He explained that he had decided to relax the age restrictions and that in future doctors under 40 could be sent abroad while those over this age would be home service only. Those whose commitments made it impossible for them to enlist would be asked to help out through part-time work in military hospitals, attending to the troops' dependents and the like.

The BMA now worked closely with the army and by as early as July 1915 a quarter of the medical profession had joined up. The main agencies for recruiting doctors were the Central Medical War Committee in England and Wales and the Scottish Medical Service Emergency Committee. Every doctor under the age of 45 was expected to enrol with one of these committees and this system continued even after the introduction of conscription, since it was recognized that if every doctor of military age was called up civil health care would suffer. But increasing demands by an ever-expanding army, now committed in four major theatres of war, forced the authorities to increase the upper age limit for doctors in mid 1916. Now those aged 45 to 55 would be recruited for full-time service at home, thereby releasing younger men for foreign service. At the same time, medical students in the combatant arms were encouraged to return to Britain to complete their studies so that they could transfer to the RAMC. Nine of the surviving students of D Company 4th Gordons opted to do this.

But there was still a shortfall of doctors. Apart from casualties – some 400 RAMC officers became casualties during the 1916 Somme battles alone – the one-year contract remained in force and aggravated the wastage. Between August and October 1916 no less than 142 MOs in France refused to renew their contracts. Yet it was not until the end of 1917 that the rules were changed and henceforth those completing their contract would automatically be called up for the duration of the war. There was a right of appeal, but the reasons would have to be very good. In the meantime, soon after the US declaration of war a mission under Arthur Balfour was sent to America. General Tom Bridges was a member of it and was asked by Lord Derby to appeal for US volunteers to work with the RAMC. The United States made an immediate offer of 1,000 doctors and 500 nurses for service in Britain or France.* The agreement was that they would wear American uniform and be paid by the US government.[7] By 1918 several

* They were not, however, the first US doctors and nurses to be so employed. The Chicago Medical Unit arrived in France in June 1915 and took over the running of No. 23 General Hospital at Camiers. Its nurses were on six-month contracts, but the unit was broken up at the end of August 1916. The Harvard Medical Unit was also deployed to France at much the same time. [National Archives, Kew WO 222/2132]

unit MOs were American, and they generally performed extremely well, a number being awarded MCs. One or two American surgeons, like head specialist Harvey Cushing, also served with the British Army. He himself was insistent on maintaining the US Army's rule of not drinking alcohol on active service, to which many of his British colleagues reacted with surprise.[8]

One factor undoubtedly discouraged some doctors from volunteering for military service. This was the belief that unit MOs were generally very under-employed. An anonymous regimental MO in a letter published in the *British Medical Journal* in early 1917 stated:

> Even with the best intentions and the greatest keenness – sanitation, lectures to men and officers – it is difficult to spin the work out for more than an hour or two each day. Loafing about and trying to be amused is our usual lot day after day. Only during a push for the short time that one's own regiment is engaged does our work ever approach the amount done by an average general practitioner in busy practice every day.

Sir Wilmot Herringham's comment on views like this was: 'I have no hesitation in saying that such officers did not know their duty.'[9] Indeed, within a battalion the MO's duties were varied. Primarily, he was responsible to the CO for the health of the unit. To this end he was in charge of all sanitary arrangements. He was expected to attend all bathing parades and to assist the second-in-command in organizing baths when out of the line. He was to help in instruction on gas duties to all ranks and was to pay particular attention to the men's feet to ward off soreness and trench foot (*see page 414*). The training of the stretcher bearers and sanitary men was also his responsibility. When the battalion was in the line he was expected to visit the trenches at least once a day and to take measures 'to alleviate the evils resulting from exposure'. Finally, and perhaps most time-consuming of all, 'he must make himself acquainted with the characteristics and idiosyncracies of all ranks'.[10] Indeed, a good MO, like J. C. Dunn DSO MC of the 2nd Royal Welsh Fusiliers, could contribute much to the well-being and morale of a unit.

In terms of the treatment of wounds, the RAMC's experience was based on the South African War. But the type of wound which it came up against during the first few weeks of fighting in France was different. Sir Geoffrey Keynes, then a house surgeon at St. Bartholomew's in London, volunteered his services on the outbreak of war and found himself in France with a base hospital within two weeks of joining the army. After being evacuated by sea from Rouen to Saint Nazaire during the retreat from Mons, his hospital re-established itself at the Hotel Trianon Palace, Versailles, and received its first wounded. The policy at the time was not to interfere with 'clean bullet wounds' and allow them to heal on their own.

> We soon learned, however, of the differences between wounds sustained on the clean South African veldt and those contaminated by European mud. Anaerobic bacteria lurking in the soil were responsible for the gas gangrene which proved to be one of the chief causes of death among those who reached a base hospital alive.[11]

Arthur Osburn commented that the smell of it was such that 'even the Sisters and nursing orderlies would vomit after handling these poor wretches in their living death'.[12] Surgical practice was therefore revised and the emphasis now was on removing all dead and damaged tissue surrounding the wound and allowing air to get in to heal it. Where a limb was affected, immediate amputation was the order of the day. But as Sister Luard, who worked in Casualty Clearing Stations for much of the war on the Western Front, recorded, it was a constant struggle and it was only if gas gangrene was present 'in the superficial tissues' that 'you can floor it'.[13] Though the medical profession managed to reduce the incidence of gas gangrene in wounds from around 10 to 12 per cent during 1914–15 to 1 per cent by 1918, the threat remained.[14]

Tetanus was another danger from wounds, although, unlike gas gangrene, it had been known about for some time. The organism which causes it lives in the intestine of domestic animals and usually enters the wound through manured soil. For this reason, it was largely a phenomenon of the Western Front. As early as December 1914 James Jack of the 2nd Scottish Rifles was noting his diary: 'Tetanus is a great danger in this highly cultivated land. All casualties, however slight, are now immediately inoculated against it.'[15] A special anti-tetanus serum was used and the casualty marked with a 'T' on his forehead. If considered likely to be infected by it, he would be given repeated injections, but if these were not administered in good time death could take place quickly. R. B. Talbot Kelly recalls an FOO who was hit by a shell splinter in the fleshy part of the buttocks in November 1916. 'He stopped at our battery dugout for a drink where everybody gave him messages for those at home. He left us waving cheerily and walking easily; some 35 hours later he was dead of tetanus.'[16] As with gas gangrene, the mortality rate was reduced as the war went on – from 63.5 per cent fatalities to those inflicted with tetanus in 1914 to 37.9 per cent in 1918. Furthermore, the actual incidence of it was not as high as many supposed. The RAMC recorded just 2,569 cases during the period 1916–20.[17]

Shock, too, often accompanied being wounded and resulted from loss of blood and other fluids. The first line of defence against it, and to provide pain relief, was morphine. This was either administered by the unit MO or, at least during the early days, by an officer. Gerald Burgoyne, writing in Flanders in January 1915, observed: 'Every company commander is supplied with a tube of 1/4 grain tablets of Morphia; 1 to ease pain; 2 (or 1/2 grain) to cause semi-sensibility; and 3 to give complete insensibility until death comes.'[18] Once back at a dressing station, the patient was put on a saline drip. In 1914, blood transfusion was scarcely known about, but it was gradually introduced and had become relatively commonplace by 1917; by the beginning of 1918 blood transfusions were taking place as far forward as ADSs. Initially, blood was taken from the lightly wounded and sick and the reward of two weeks' leave meant that there was no shortage of volunteers. Later, blood banks were instituted.[19]

Early experiences on the Western Front gradually transformed the policy of speedy evacuation of wounded to the rear areas in favour of more treatment in the forward areas. During the winter of 1914–15 one field ambulance in each division formed a rest station for the treatment of the sick, who previously had been sent down the lines of communication. Typical treatment was three days' rest and treatment, three days' of light duties and a second week of physical exercise, including route marches and sport. The 3rd Division appears to have pioneered the concept and Billy Congreve claimed that, as a result, the division's sick rate was 'much the lowest in the whole army'. He wrote in his dairy: 'They [the men] stay in the home a week or ten days and are provided with games, books, sweets, tobacco and, in fact, are made as happy as can be.'[20] The field ambulances also provided baths and laundries, although this would change. It was Travis Hampson, serving with the 19th Field Ambulance in the Armentières sector, who claims to have initiated the practice of providing baths. He used a local brewery to provide these for his men at the end of November 1914. The 19th Brigade, which they were supporting, quickly got to hear of it and began sending battalions at rest to take advantage of this facility.[21] The provision of baths and laundry facilities reflected the RAMC's responsibility for hygiene and certainly in France and Flanders it faced a number of challenges.

In South Africa enteric fever, later renamed typhoid, had been a major problem. Personal hygiene was one means of keeping it at bay, but anti-typhoid inoculations had also been developed in the years leading up to 1914. Yet inoculation was not compulsory in the army, although Lord Kitchener was much in favour of it. This reflected the situation in civilian life, and was not helped by a virulent campaign mounted by the British Union for the Abolition of Vivisection against inoculation in the army. The consequences of the War Office's reluctance to introduce compulsory inoculation were brought into focus early on. A November 1914 survey of the number of typhoid cases in the 1st, 2nd and 5th Divisions in France revealed a total of seventy-one, of whom only two had been inoculated. Even so, and in spite of agitation from the medical profession, the army maintained its policy of voluntary inoculation throughout the war. But largely thanks to the persuasive efforts of MOs and unit officers, 90 per cent of the army was inoculated and the incidence of typhoid was a mere 2 per cent of that of the Boer War.[22] The key weapon in the fight against typhoid and other diseases was the mobile laboratory. The first of these deployed to France before the end of 1914, and was followed by two others, together with a Canadian laboratory, in spring 1915. One of their early successes occurred when the BEF took over the sector north of Ypres. There was an epidemic of typhoid among the local population. A Society of Friends hospital unit was treating some of the sufferers in a hospital at Poperinghe and the BEF medical authorities, having identified the source, worked with the Society of Friends and set up their own hospital for the Belgian patients, together with a convalescent hospital. The outbreak was therefore contained and eradicated, significantly reducing the number of typhoid cases in the BEF.[23]

Another ailment which challenged the mobile laboratories was first recognized in the early summer of 1915 in France. Sir Wilmot Herringham: 'It began like influenza, and the temperature fell to normal in three or four days; but, unlike influenza, a fresh attack began about the sixth or seventh day, and this process was sometimes repeated several times. It was, indeed, a relapsing fever with a cycle of about five days.'[24] Attempting to establish the cause of what became quickly known as 'trench fever' would concentrate minds, especially those of the RAMC's bacteriologists, for three years. Eventually, in October 1917 the Allies set up a Trench Fever Committee and a series of experiments were conducted at Saint Pol, using 150 soldiers as guinea pigs. These went a long way to establishing that lice were the most likely cause.[25] This was finally confirmed in March 1918, but the German counter-offensives intervened and delayed investigations into effective preventive measures. The answer was more rigorous disinfecting of clothing and equipment and in May 1918 'delousing pits' were introduced. These were simply pits, with brick stoves in them. When clothes were hung in them the resultant heat killed the lice. This simple device enabled delousing of clothes to take place in the unit, rather than having to rely on laundries. More frequent baths for the men were also laid down. The more mobile warfare of the last nine months of the war also played its part. Certainly, there was a significant decrease in cases of trench fever, although by this time the BEF was beginning to suffer from the Spanish influenza epidemic which was sweeping Europe and it was difficult to separate the two in terms of statistics.[26] To prevent trench fever and other diseases spreading to Britain, a new policy was adopted in the autumn of 1917 for men going home on leave from France, as Rowland Fielding noted: 'They are cleaned up and fitted out with good clothes before they leave, so that they do not arrive at Victoria covered with the mud of the trenches. Each man, too, has to have a certificate that he is free from vermin.'[27] To prevent those on leave in Britain from catching diseases and infecting their fellow soldiers, they were banned from areas where epidemics were raging. BEF General Routine Orders contained numerous such announcements. Thus, those for 12 March 1918 declared that part of

Stepney in East London was out of bounds to men on leave because of a smallpox epidemic, as was the whole of Leeds on account of measles. In the case of the former outbreak, the Bryant & May match factory was situated in Stepney and, according to A. Stuart Dolden, the smallpox outbreak prompted an order in France for all troops to hand in their matches for fear that those possessing them might fall victim to the disease.[28]

Trench foot made its presence quickly felt during winter 1914–15 on the Western Front; those who fought on Gallipoli during the following winter and on the Salonika front also suffered from it. As early as 20 December 1914, Gerald Burgoyne was noting that seventy men of his 2nd Royal Irish Rifles company were sick, 'most of them with swollen feet from standing in icy cold mud and water'.[29] Captain Kennedy of the 2nd Scottish Rifles recalled that 'at times it was agony to keep on one's boots. To take them off, however, to gain relief would have been fatal, as it would have been impossible to put them on again.'[30] The cause of trench foot, however, was not just long immersion of the feet in cold water. It was the combination of this and restricted circulation to the feet caused by closely bound puttees and tightly laced boots. In its secondary form gangrene would set in, almost inevitably resulting in amputation. GHQ's immediate solution came in the form of instructions issued in January 1915. Whale oil was issued for rubbing into the feet prior to going into the trenches. Puttees and boots were not to be too tightly bound and laced. Each man was to take a pair of dry socks into the front line to change into, and the men were to wash and dry their feet thoroughly on coming out of the trenches.[31] This certainly went a long way towards keeping trench foot at bay, but, unless closely overseen by the company officers, many men would not bother to take these essential precautions and would suffer the consequence. The grim winter of 1916–17 proved a particularly severe test. At one point the 6th King's Shropshire Light Infantry had no less than 200 men in hospital, the majority with trench foot.[32] Graham Greenwell, with the 4th Ox & Bucks wrote:

> Trench feet [sic] is going strong and the authorities are yelling themselves hoarse with bloodthirsty threats. Each man in my company has to be responsible for the feet of another … If B goes to hospital with trench

feet A is crimed and brought before the CO. Good idea. We wash and powder and change socks at every turn; unfortunately in the trenches, where the trouble starts, this is almost impossible.[33]

Even the institution of divisional 'dry sock factories', which were run by the Employment companies, did not help much. Yet the incidence of trench foot was used as a measure of the efficiency of a battalion and, indeed, of the divisions. Probably with this in mind, the 66th Division issued an order in 1918 that company officers would have to account personally for all cases of trench foot among their men. However, the 1st/7th Lancashire Fusiliers circumvented this by diagnosing trench foot as other forms of medical complaint.[34]

In early January 1915 clearing hospitals were renamed Casualty Clearing Stations (CCS).[35] Much of the reason for this was that the term 'hospital' gave the impression that casualties would be given comprehensive treatment rather than acting as a clearing house to ensure their safe and speedy evacuation to the rear. CCSs were placed under corps control, but still looked to the field ambulances to carry out emergency surgery, especially on abdominal and head cases. However, once the incidence of gas gangrene had been identified and the need for immediate surgery recognized, the field ambulances found that they lacked the facilities to do this or those to allow the patient the necessary post-surgery recuperative time. Sir Anthony Bowlby soon became convinced that CCSs should be used for this purpose instead, but they, too, initially lacked the necessary facilities and were also located too far from the front line. Gradually, he got his way and by spring 1916 the CCS had become the hub of the medical system in the field.[36] A typical CCS was tented and continued to receive casualties through the evacuation chain of unit aid post, advanced dressing station, and main and walking wounded dressing stations. Casualties were first taken to a reception tent, where they were examined and sent to other tents according to their needs. The surgery complex had a preparation tent and operating theatre in which an average of three surgical teams would be at work simultaneously. Other tents included two dressing tents (one for serious and the other for less serious wounds), a tent for chest wounds, one for septic cases, and evacuation tents for those fit to travel. In addition, there was a mortuary tent and, saddest of all, the moribund ward, also called Ward X and later the rescuscitation ward, for those not expected to pull through.[37] Every CCS also had a burial ground attached to it. Sister Luard provides a graphic description of a CCS at work during the Battle of Arras in 1917:

> The three CCSs filled up in turn and then each filled up again, without any break in the Convoys: we take in and evacuate at the same time. The Theatre, Dressing Hut, Preparation Hut and Wards and Tents are all humming – the kitchen goes on cooking, with a Day Staff and a Night Staff, and the stretcher-bearers go on stretcher-bearing, and the Mortuary Corporal goes on sewing up corpses in canvas. The Colonel carries the lame walking-cases on his broad back, and I look after the moribunds in every spare second from the Preparation Hut, which is (during take-in) the stiffest corner of all, and the Sisters, MOs, NCOs, Orderlies, Convalescent Men, and Permanent Base men all peg into it ... We meet for snatching meals and five-minute snacks of rest and begin again. All are doing 16 hours on and 8 off and some of us 18 on and 6 off. [38]

The growing importance of the CCS was reflected in the number of operations they carried out. During 1915 they operated on 15 per cent of all admissions during quiet times and just 5 per cent during heavy fighting. In 1916, the percentages increased to 25 and 10 per cent; in 1917 to 50 and 30 per cent. In mid 1917 Bowlby toured the base hospitals in France in the aftermath of the Battle of Messines and established from them that of 5,271 casualties received, only fifty-eight had died and just twenty-two had serious gas gangrene. The base hospital surgeons were emphatic that 'early operation was responsible for excellent condition of wounded'.[39] Abdominal wounds were regarded as the most critical and to ensure as early operation as possible an Advanced Abdominal Centre was set up for the opening of the Third Battle of Ypres at Brandhoek, well within German artillery range. The authorities became concerned about the safety of the twenty-nine sisters working at it and on 27 July ordered them to join two Canadian CCSs 6 miles to the rear. But recognizing that they were crucial to the centre, three days later, on the eve of the opening of the offensive, the order was rescinded. Sister Luard recorded that it received its first patients between 4 a.m. and 5 a.m. on 31 July and that 'in spite of the awful conditions, a remarkable percentage, especially of the first ones who came in early and dry, are doing brilliantly'. On 22 August, shellfire and air attacks, which caused casualties among the sisters, forced a temporary withdrawal to Saint Omer for seventy-two hours, but thereafter the centre continued its good work until finally withdrawn on 5 September.[40] Other CCSs were dedicated to gas casualties.

Transportation of the wounded relied on stretcher bearers as far as the ADS. Thereafter, horse-drawn and motor ambulances, as well as light railways, took them to the CCS. Wherever possible, this was close to a railhead, since the ambulance train was the main means of conveying them to the base area. While the BEF had an allowance of one such train to each division when it crossed to France in 1914, it took none with it and looked to the French to provide them. This proved unsatisfactory. The first three such trains were made up of converted goods wagons, using what was known as the Brechot apparatus, which enabled three stretchers to be fitted, one above the other, with twelve stretcher cases being carried in each wagon. There were a number of serious drawbacks. First, there were no interconnecting doors to enable the nursing staff to pass from one wagon to another while the train was moving. Loose couplings meant a very jerky ride, especially when the brakes were applied, and the wagons themselves came from seven different railway companies and had different lubrication, lighting, heating and brake systems. Finally, there was no allowance for sitting casualties. The standardization problem was overcome by ensuring that each train had wagons from the same source. These first three trains were also adapted to take a proportion of sitting cases. Thus Train No. 1 was converted from 396 lying cases to 198 lying and 330 sitting.[41] Even so, travel as a casualty on them was not a pleasant experience. Arthur Osburn experienced it after being wounded at First Ypres:

> The journey on the train was simply ghastly and seemed endless. The jolting was so bad that both I and a subaltern who was lying on the seat opposite me, his knee joint badly shattered, were twice jerked off on to the floor. Each time he lay and screamed in pain. It seemed ages before worn-out, pale-faced orderlies arrived to lift us back again.[42]

In the meantime, in September 1914 the British Red Cross Society (BRCS) commissioned two ambulance trains from the Wagons-Lit Company. These were certainly more comfortable, but each only carried eighty patients and the French raised objections to what they saw as civilian trains using their railways. The IGC therefore laid down that all trains provided by voluntary associations must be approved by the Director of Medical Services (DMS) and commanded by an RAMC officer. The coaches of these two trains were given to existing regular trains and the BRCS ordered another for itself. Simultaneously, ambulance trains began to be built in Britain, the first being sent to France in October 1914. A total of thirty were deployed. Temporary ambulance trains (TATs) using unaltered passenger coaches were also employed for major battles, fourteen being used on the Somme in 1916. For the medical staff of the ambulance trains, life on them was often like being in a time capsule. Sir Geoffrey Keynes worked on one during the first part of 1915: 'Headquarters were at Boulogne, but we had to be ready to move at a moment's notice to any part of the front in France or Flanders. Often orders came during the night, and the first question on waking in the morning was: "Where are we?"'[43] Ambulance trains provided an effective means of transporting wounded and caring for them en route, but, because of the quality of the track on which they ran, the problem of providing a smooth ride remained until the end of the war. Indeed, for the most serious casualties, like abdominals, ambulance barges were used wherever possible, even though they were considerably slower.

Once at the base, the casualty was taken to a Stationary or General hospital. The former had originally been intended to act as an intermediary between the forward medical units and the base and had been in the evacuation zone, but with the transformation of the CCS they became indistinguishable from the General hospitals. They were designed to treat both sick and wounded and either discharged their patients to a convalescent camp or held them until they could be taken by hospital ship out of the theatre of war. A. Stuart Dolden of the London Scottish spent a month in No. 26 General Hospital at Etaples at the end of 1916. He thought the food excellent, but found the 4.30 a.m. reveille a little tedious. Once out of bed, he was issued with a blue hospital uniform, which he exchanged for his fumigated khakis on discharge.[44] More glamorous was the Duchess of Westminster's hospital at Le Touquet. Private Norman Ellison of the 1st/6th Kings was a patient there in April 1915:

> A nurse's uniform suited Constance, Duchess of Westminster, as indeed it suits every woman. In her bosom she wore a red cross, fashioned out of rubies. She was petite, vivacious and charming. Every morning she made a tour of the wards with cigarettes and a cheery word for each patient.[45]

The hospital was staffed by society girls enrolled as VADs, and Bryan Latham claimed that 'many young officers completed their cure there rather than be evacuated to England'.[46] Another private hospital was the Duchess of Sutherland's at Calais. Equally celebrated back in England was No. 15 Canadian Hospital at Cliveden on the Thames, the home of the Astors. The American surgeon Harvey Cushing visited it in March 1918:

> We were at the far end of the pavilion gathered round a bed when Nancy Astor in her riding habit popped in the other end of the ward and began to vigorously abuse one of the Tommies – a huge Yorkshireman – sitting forlornly beside his bed. 'Get up', she said – 'you haven't any guts'. He does – and she belabours him with her crop. He roars with delight and the others join in. She is doubtless the best psychotherapist in the establishment; they all adore her.[47]

Life in a base hospital could be just as hectic as in a CCS during a major attack. Gwen Ware, a VAD at No. 11 General Hospital at Camiers, after the opening of the Battle of Arras in April 1917, recorded:

> The Great Push began on 10th and casualties poured down upon us. 11th and 12th were one continual convoy and evacuation. The men came in walking or hobbling rather, by the 100 ... It was one continual stream all down the roads. All the C. lines [for medical cases] became surgical on the spot, every atom of space was used up, even the floor of the Church tent was covered with stretchers and the tents took in appallingly bad cases. Huts were full and everywhere was understaffed: 1 SN [staff nurse] and 1 VAD and two orderlies for 52 beds.[48]

Life, too, in the base hospitals in France took on another grim dimension in the early autumn of 1917, when German bombers began to carry out night raids on the rear areas, hitting some hospitals.

Those who were discharged from a base hospital in France were sent to a convalescent camp to complete their recovery. Sir Wilmot Herringham described one near Rouen:

> On one side of the road were the dormitory huts, the mess-rooms, kitchens, parade-ground, and gymnasium. The morning was given up to spells of various training exercises. These included dancing, for which there was a band, and several of the games which have taken the place of the Swedish physical exercises, and are a great improvement on them. In the afternoons there were cricket or football matches and cross-country runs. In the evening concerts, plays, lectures, and boxing competitions … The Camp also farmed fifty acres of land, which to many of the men was an interesting form of exercise.[49]

But not all the convalescent establishments had the holiday camp atmosphere of this one. Henry Ogle spent a week at such a camp in the autumn of 1915, after being in hospital with a gunshot wound to the foot. '[It] must have been designed to make soldiers desire fervently to get away from it, even back to the very line itself … The routine consisted of camp chores without end. The NCOs were the typical "Base Wallah" type who bawled all day for fatigue parties.'[50] Aubrey Smith had a few days at another in summer 1917. Route marches, PT and children's games occupied his day, but he found the food totally inadequate and detailed a typical day's menu as breakfast – one slice of bread and jam, with a knob of cheese; dinner – bully beef and Maconachie, followed by a 'filthy concoction of soppy biscuits and dates'; tea – one slice of bread and jam.[51] They did improve. F. E. Noakes spent time at two convalescent camps after being wounded during the March 1918 fighting. He found the camp routine 'easy'. There were also excellent recreational facilities, including a cinema and theatre. The only drawback was compulsory country dancing: ' … we solemnly clumped, in our Army boots, through the complicated manoeuvres of several Old-English Country Dances, under the direction of some (no doubt, well-meaning) elderly ladies and accompanied by a tinkling piano, much to the amusement of the onlookers and our own embarrassed discomfort.'[52] Once the patients were deemed fully fit they were discharged to the base depots for drafting back to their units.

Those who were gravely wounded were treated at the base hospitals in France until they were fit enough to cross the Channel to England. Where the prognosis was bad and it was not expected that they would pull through, close relations were allowed to visit them in France. But often many more lightly wounded obtained the 'Blighty ticket' about which every soldier in France dreamed. A man who had been relatively lightly wounded close to the launch of a major attack might well be sent back to England so as to empty the hospitals as much as possible for the inevitable influx of wounded once it got underway. The same happened to those wounded during the battle. Once landed back in England, ambulance trains would take the casualties to a General hospital. Efforts were made to send the patient for treatment in the same area as his kith and kin. But this did not always work. Julian Tyndale-Biscoe was wounded on the Somme and arrived at Southampton, where

> some officious staff officer came round asking where we would like to be sent. I heard one say 'London', whereupon he was told he would be sent to Liverpool. I said 'Guildford', whereupon he said I would go to Oxford. I was just as pleased with this [he had relations there], but was careful not to show my pleasure, in case he sent me somewhere else.[53]

Padre Drury suffered a similar fate in summer 1917 after being wounded by a 5.9-inch shell. Asked by a doctor on the boat whether he wanted to go to a hospital in northern or southern England, he requested the latter. He ended up in Manchester.[54] But in spite of frustrations like this, the evacuation system could work remarkably quickly. George Ashurst of the 1st Lancashire Fusiliers was wounded in the leg on the Somme in 1916. Within forty-eight hours he was in bed in a Manchester hospital.[55] Once discharged from hospital in the UK, the soldier went to a convalescent hospital, which were allocated on the basis of one per home command. Officers were often sent to convalescent homes, many of them country houses lent by their owners for the duration of the war. Thereafter came the medical board, which judged the man's fitness and categorized him accordingly. Those likely to be fully fit for service within six months were made Category D;

those likely still to be unfit after six months were made Category E, though many of the latter would be invalided out of the army. Of the former, most would be granted a period of light duties at home prior to being sent back to a theatre of war. To this end, command depots were established early in 1916 to provide rehabilitation training.

According to Sir Wilmot Herringham, dentistry was 'one of the great blots on our medical arrangements'. The root of the problem lay in the fact that in peacetime the army had no dentists in uniform and relied on civilian dentists. No dentists accompanied the BEF to France in 1914 under the mistaken assumption that unit MOs would be capable of carrying out any essential dental work. Indeed, unlike doctors, dentists were not considered non-combatants. Not until November 1914 did the first dentists join the BEF, one being appointed to each clearing hospital.[56] However, the army dentists then often found themselves working under junior RAMC officers with little knowledge of dental practice. Herringham also stated that none was promoted beyond the rank of captain apart from two majors 'who had no registrable English qualification'. For most of the war there were still too few dentists, especially compared to other armies. Whereas the Canadians and Americans had one dentist for every 1,000 men, in the British Army it was one to every 10,000. While the Australians adopted a policy of having a dental unit within each field ambulance, the British dentists were further back, usually in the base hospitals, and very overloaded with work. As one told Herringham, 'he had an average of forty to fifty patients every morning. He could do nothing whatever but pull their teeth out. If he had tried to stop them, each would take three-quarters of an hour, which meant thirty hours' work in the twenty-four.' No wonder that army dentists tended to have a bad name, even though they were doing their best and, indeed, performed especially valuable work in helping to rebuild shattered faces. Herringham also stated that there was a severe shortage of dental mechanics, 'though there were several in the fighting ranks and Labour battalions'. Not until 1918 did matters begin to improve. An Advisory Dental Officer was appointed to the staff of the Director-General Army Medical Services in March to represent the dentists' interests. Simultaneously, dental tribunals, working closely with the Ministry of National Service, were set up in England and Scotland to select suitable dentists for military service.[57]

Shell shock was an aspect which caused much agonizing among the military authorities, both medical and lay.[58] While there were numerous historical precedents, notably from the American Civil War and Russo-Japanese War, the RAMC went to war in virtual ignorance of the fact that the stresses of battle could cause psychiatric casualties. The same was the case in the French and German Armies. Yet as early as the fighting on the Aisne in September 1914 Arthur Osburn, MO to the 4th Dragoon Guards, began to notice the growing effect of what he called 'nerves'.[59] Indeed, in that same month the first such casualties began to be evacuated back to Britain, but, under the assumption that their brains had been damaged by the blast of exploding shells, they were placed in normal hospitals. Growing concern was reflected in an editorial in *The Lancet* of 12 December 1914, which noted the 'frequency with which hysteria, traumatic and otherwise, is showing itself'. Charles Myers, an RAMC doctor who had seen such cases at Boulogne, first termed the condition 'Shell-shock', believing that artillery fire was the cause. In January 1915, the War Office ordered Lieutenant Colonel W. A. Turner, a consultant neurologist, to investigate shell shock cases and recommend the best treatment for them. He noted that many of the patients he saw in France were still in a state of 'hysterical stupor' and haunted by the horrific experiences they had been through. Significantly, though, the milder cases frequently made a full recovery after a short rest. To cater for those with more serious symptoms, neurological wards were established at two hospitals in Britain, the Royal Victoria Hospital, Netley, and No. 4 London General Hospital. Here a variety of treatments were developed. Those suffering from loss of speech were given electric shock treatment or an anaesthetic. Hypnotism was also used, especially for those with memory loss. From here they were sent to hospitals which special-ized in nervous diseases. These included former lunatic asylums, which made both patients and relatives fear that they would be branded insane, so much so that the government had to introduce the Mental Health Bill 1915, which laid down that anyone suffering from a 'mental disorder' as a result of the war could be treated for six months in one of these institu-tions without being declared insane. Lord Knutsford, a leading hospital reformer, also established four such hospitals for officers during 1915.

Yet doctors still continued to be misled by the term 'shell shock' and most continued to believe that it was the result of concussion induced by high explosive. They still did not recognize that war neurosis could be brought about by other causes, especially battle fatigue. There was also another puzzlement, spelled out by Neil Fraser-Tytler, who was a battery commander on the Somme in July 1916:

> This shell shock is a funny business: no one can quite explain why it affects some and not others. I would describe the feeling as a severe 'knock out' blow on both sides of the head at once, and, having been twice during the last few days half buried by 5.9s bursting on the parapet, I can claim practical knowledge of it.[60]

Unit MOs tended to play safe and hesitated to brand a man as a mental case, preferring to diagnose him 'shell shock (wound)' and to get him evacuated as soon as possible for fear that his condition might spread to others. This contravened Colonel Turner's finding of early 1915 that the milder cases could be successfully treated in the forward areas. As it was, the ever increasing number of neurosis sufferers being sent to the base area caused a backlash from the authorities. Arthur Osburn, now commanding a field ambulance in the 20th Division reported:

> Fierce and rather relentless mental specialists arrived from England to see that we did not malinger in the trenches. I was ordered to attend a conference of doctors; it degenerated into a lecture of a mental specialist who had 'visited' the trenches at least twice. Shell-shock, he sharply told us, was a fable, neurasthenia a myth. His ruthless contempt for a doctor who let any man down to the Base before he was actually mutilated was superb'.[61]

That the military authorities felt that MOs were 'soft' on shell shock cases is well illustrated by the affair of the MO of the 11th Border Regiment. The battalion had suffered very heavy casualties on the first day of the Somme, losing all its officers, including the CO, who was killed. The battalion, now some 250 strong and commanded by a captain from the one Regular battalion in the brigade, 2 KOYLI, remained in the line and on 9 July was ordered by its brigade commander to carry out a bombing attack that night. That evening, one of the two subalterns who was to lead the attack informed the acting CO that one-third of those due to take part had applied to see the MO on the grounds that their nerves were in tatters. The CO insisted that the attack go ahead, but, after further complaints from the men, ordered the MO, Lieutenant G. N. Kirkwood, to examine them. He stated in writing: 'I must hereby testify to their unfitness for such an operation as few, if any, are not suffering from some degree of shell-shock.' Kirkwood later told the court of enquiry set up to investigate the incident that the effect on morale of the heavy casualties suffered on 1 July, combined with the subsequent arduous time in the trenches under continuous shellfire, and with little sleep, had totally sapped the men. The CO immediately passed the MO's findings to the brigade commander, who ordered the attack to be mounted. By now time was getting on and there were further delays in getting to the start line, largely because the party, which had one subaltern at its head and the other at the rear, kept losing its way in the trenches. Realizing that the attack would not take place on time and that there was a 'great lack of offensive spirit', the subaltern in charge cancelled the attack. The brigadier's reaction was to place the four sergeants taking part in the attack under arrest for 'failing in their duty' and initiate an inquiry. In his written comments to the court of enquiry, the brigade commander, Brigadier General J. B. Jardine, stated that he had not realized that the 11th Borders were in such a low state of morale, pleading in part that he had been laid low with fever at the time. He did, however, make a revealing point, one that many Regulars held. Jardine stated that Lieutenant Colonel P. W. Machell, the previous CO, who had been killed on 1 July, had raised the battalion and from the outset had run it on the theory that 'you cannot in the new formations make NCOs of the kind you want as readily as you can officers.' Consequently, the officers did all the work and the NCOs had little responsibility. He accepted that after 1 July the battalion had received just three junior officers to make good its casualties, but denied knowledge of the fact that Lieutenant Kirkwood had previously sent down shell-shock casualties. He blamed the failure to carry out the bombing attack on the four sergeants involved and had them placed under arrest with a view to having them court martialled.

Major General W. H. Rycroft, commanding the 32nd Division, of which the battalion was part, criticized the brigadier for detailing the 11th Borders, making the point that its previous fighting record had been good, and also stated that the Judge Advocate's department had advised him that, with regard to the four sergeants, there was no case to answer. 'This I regret.' Rycroft placed the blame fully on Kirkwood's shoulders and relieved him from his post. 'Sympathy for sick or wounded men under medical treatment is a good attribute for a doctor, but it is not for a Medical Officer to inform a Commanding Officer that his men are not in a fit state to carry out an operation.' The corps commander, Lieutenant General Sir Thomas Morland also recognized the battalion's previous good record and regretted that the NCOs involved could not be disciplined. He made no mention of Kirkwood. In contrast, General Sir Hubert Gough, commanding the Reserve Army on the Somme, was scathing in his comments on the luckless MO: 'Conduct on the part of Lieutenant G N Kirkwood RAMC ... shows him to be totally unfitted to hold a commission in the Army, or to exercise any military responsibility.' He went on to state:

> Immediate steps must be taken to remove Lieutenant Kirkwood from the service. The 'certificate' which he signed and the reasons given by him in support of it conclusively prove that he has no conception of the duties and responsibilities of a Regimental MO and that so long as he is allowed to remain in the Service he will be a source of danger to it.

The fact that the ADMS of 32nd Division pleaded that Kirkwood had been with the battalion since October 1915 and had done good work was to no avail. Gough was adamant. But he was not yet finished. He also blamed the acting CO, Captain G. H. C. Palmer, for being 'largely responsible for the failure of the operations'. His action in asking for the MO's opinion was 'tantamount to questioning the orders received by him and was calculated to encourage the spirit of indiscipline and cowardice already shewn'. Jardine, too, was criticized for failing to send a staff officer to assist the young officer in charge of the attack. As for the 11th Borders as a whole, Gough ordered General Rycroft to parade the battalion without arms,

> in the presence of the remaining units of the Brigade (under arms) and should inform the Battalion that the Army Commander considers the conduct on the part of those who failed to do their duty on this occasion

has not only brought disgrace on themselves but also on the whole Battalion to which they belong.

This was duly done. Haig, however, disagreed with some of Gough's hotheaded comments. He considered that Palmer should not have asked Kirkwood the question in the first place, 'for though it is the duty of a Regimental Medical Officer to inspect individual cases, it is most improper to require him to give a general opinion on the physical fitness of 100 men in the circumstances set out in this correspondence'. Haig laid the blame primarily on Palmer's shoulders, but also reprimanded Jardine for his failure to take positive action. The final comment on the file was by Sir Arthur Sloggett, the Director-General of Army Medical Services. He made the point that Kirkwood had been asked to give his opinion and had done so only to be ignored. 'The whole case is deplorable. The MO appears to have been made the scapegoat.' Kirkwood himself was allowed to retain his commission and was found a job at base. The blot on Jardine's record prevented him from rising any higher. Palmer had already been removed from command after the inquiry. He was put before a medical board, which found that he was suffering from malaria and shell shock. He was recommended for command of a prisoner of war camp.[62]

Yet some MOs were beginning to recognize that the continual stress in the trenches could cause a man to break down. John Lucy, who went to France in August 1914, was given home leave in Ireland at the end of 1915 because of battle fatigue:

> My sleep was broken and full of voices and the noises of war. The voices were those of officers and men who were dead. One morning I was discovered standing up in bed facing a wall ready to repel an imaginary attack ... I had a real physical pain in my heart, and there was no lustre in my eyes. I had loved many men and lost them. My womenfolk cherished me, but they stood outside my great grief, and their warm sympathy tragically failed to alleviate a pain they had not shared.

Eventually, Lucy's family called a doctor and he was put into hospital as a neurasthenia patient. Good food and a peaceful rural existence cured him and he was soon posted back to his regimental depot on light duties.[63]

Lucy's case was undoubtedly genuine, but the authorities were concerned that malingerers might be slipping through the net. There was also the fact that once wound stripes were introduced (*see p. 492*), shell-shock casualties were being granted them under ACI 2075/16. The numbers so entitled in France rose from 1,387 throughout 1915 to 16,138 during the latter half of 1916.[64] GHQ therefore issued instructions that in future every case would be sent to a special centre (one was located in each army area) for diagnosis and that he must be accompanied by a statement from the man's CO verifying the circumstances. But as Sir Wilmot Herringham commented, 'the COs varied greatly in the care with which they certified their cases. Some certified every case, while others made real enquiry and certified few.' Then, in June 1917, unit MOs were told to categorize such cases as Not Yet Diagnosed Nervous (NYDN). The special centres would then complete Army Form W3436, describing his symptoms and the supposed cause of his stress. This would then be sent to the man's CO, who would make a report, stating whether the man had been subjected to exceptional stress. He would return this to the centre and only then would the man be categorized as sick or wounded. These steps certainly reduced the numbers reported as battle casualties, which in France fell to just over 7,000 during 1917. But there was still disquiet over those who were awarded wound stripes. As one anonymous medical officer put it: 'It is an awful strain on a man's nervous system to stick in a trench which is being heavily crumped, and there is really no reason why whole battalions should not go down "shell-shocked" once you admit the right of any man to do it.' He also warned: 'The term "shell-shock" has come to have an ominous meaning, and to a number of people it is synonymous with "cold feet".' This was cited by Haig's Adjutant General in a letter dated 13 April 1918. He went on to say:

> I think that in the vast majority of instances the question whether a man's nervous system sustains a permanent injury owing to his being buried, or blown in the air, depends on the quality of the nervous system with which he was naturally endowed. However much sympathy one may feel with the man whose nervous system has succumbed under the strain, it is not, I think, logical to decorate him with a badge in

contrast to the man whose nervous system has successfully resisted a similar experience.[65]

Indeed, the official view in France was that all shell-shock casualties should be classified as sick rather than battle casualties, but the Army Council was not so sure. For a start, bearing in mind that wound stripes had been awarded, it would create a sense of injustice among those neurosis cases who subsequently fulfilled the qualification for them. Furthermore, there was a feeling that a man who broke down under the strain of a long period at the Front or had been buried for a time as a result of a shell explosion was just as deserving of a wound stripe as one who had received a minor flesh wound.

The other side of the coin was that once conscription got underway, enlistment medicals and medical boards appear to have become much less stringent on medical gradings. Numerous complaints about the quality of drafts exist. The CO of the 1st/5th Royal Warwicks submitted a report to his brigade commander in mid July 1916 after a group of forty of his men holding a recently captured trench had very nearly been overwhelmed by a small German bombing party. He identified a total of 100 men in his battalion who were lacking in fighting spirit 'and I would prefer to be without them'. The brigade commander supported this request, noting that they were also physically weak. GOC 48th Division concurred, recommending that the men be transferred to a Labour battalion. The corps commander went even further, recommending that they be sent to a Docks battalion back in Britain: 'These men are degenerates. They are a source of danger to their comrades, their battalion, and the brigade.'[66] It was men like these who were most prone to shell shock. In other cases, battalions were unable to offload men who were simply not up to being front-line soldiers. John Nettleton records that in early 1917 the 2nd Rifle Brigade had a man who was physically and mentally deficient. Three times he was sent down to base, was boarded and returned to the battalion graded A1. He was only got rid after he shot his own finger off.[67] Some of these men who did remain with their units were among those who found themselves being court martialled for such offences as desertion and cowardice.

Lieutenant Colonel Charles Myers, who was now the Consulting

Psychologist to the BEF in France, made a visit to the French Army in June 1917. He noted that their policy was to treat neurosis patients as far forward as possible. Indeed, the French neurological centres were no further than 15 miles from the front line. He tried to establish a similar system in the British armies, but only one put it into practice, setting up a forward sorting centre, but was then ordered by GHQ to close it down. Nevertheless, by this time the British were at least aiming to treat as many shell-shock patients as possible in France, sometimes using convalescent camps in the process. But while it was now being recognized that for those suffering from straightforward battle fatigue rest and good food normally meant a full recovery in a matter of weeks, there was continuing pressure from GHQ to ensure that as many neurosis patients as possible were returned to their units quickly because of the increasing manpower problem. Only some 10 per cent of all shell-shock cases in France were evacuated to Britain, where, by the end of 1917 there were some twenty special hospitals in existence. The initial policy of trying to encourage the patient to block out the horrific events which had brought about his condition and of concentrating on removing the physical symptoms had also begun to change. Led by Dr W. H. R. Rivers, who was working at a neurological hospital for officers (the Craiglockhart War Hospital outside Edinburgh), the new school believed that successful treatment lay in getting the patient to confront his anxieties and learning to live with them. This proved to be a much more promising approach, but shell shock continued to worry the authorities until the very end of the war and was the subject of a committee of inquiry in 1922, which paved the way for the more effective methods of treatment in the Second World War.

The reporting and recording of fatal casualties also underwent major changes. Every soldier went to war in 1914 with an identity disc, of either metal or red fibre, which he wore round his neck. On it were recorded his name, number, unit and religion. *FSR II* laid down that 'anyone involved in burying a soldier, or finding a body after an action, will remove the identity disc and pay book ... and will note the number of the equipment and rifle, or anything else likely to assist in identification'. These items and any other information were to be passed to the nearest commander who was to forward them to the DAG 3rd Echelon at the base. While units took every care to make sure that graves were properly marked, there were inevitably occasions when they were destroyed by shellfire, often making subsequent identification of the soldier's remains very difficult, since they no longer bore his identity disc. There was also no system for registering graves. Initially, such work was carried by the Joint War Committee of the British Red Cross Society and Order of St John of Jerusalem. However, because of their other responsibilities, they were unable to devote much effort to this. In September 1914, at Kitchener's suggestion, the BRCS sent out a mobile unit to France to search the line of retreat of the BEF in August and its subsequent advance to the Aisne. Fabian Ware, former editor of *The Morning Post*, commanded the unit, which was subsequently attached to French formations in the Ypres area to assist with their wounded, but he continued to locate and mark British graves wherever he found them. The Adjutant General in France at the time, Sir Nevil Macready, recognized the immense value of the work that Ware was doing, and persuaded Sir John French to incorporate his unit in the BEF.[68] This happened in September 1915 and Ware's unit became the War Graves Commission. Ware was granted a commission as a temporary major and the commission organized as a headquarters with a section for each army and one responsible for the lines of communication. The initial total strength was twenty-four officers and 100 other ranks, with a burial officer attached to each corps.[69] Neil Fraser-Tytler, who had one living with his battery for ten days during Third Ypres, said that he was nicknamed the 'Body Snatcher' and 'Cold Meat Specialist'.[70]

At the time that Ware moved to GHQ, the general custom, at least in France and Flanders, was to use local civil cemeteries as the final resting place of British soldiers. It was clear, however, that these would not be sufficient and so, on Macready's instructions, Ware was to negotiate the purchase of land for British war cemeteries with the French government. There were fears that this might prove difficult, but, in a display of touching generosity, both French chambers approved a law on 29 December which stated that the French state would pay for all lands required as British and French war cemeteries. This law provided the model for agreements drawn up with Belgium and countries in other theatres of war.[71] The only proviso was that no permanent memorials would be erected while the war was still in progress. Then, in January 1916 the National Committee for the Care of Soldiers' Graves was established, with the Prince of Wales as chairman, and the following month Ware arranged for an 'expert gardener' from Kew to visit France and advise on the upkeep of cemeteries.[72]

The task of burying the dead was usually the responsibility of the chaplains. Padre Julian Bickersteth found himself doing this on the first day of the Somme. 'We removed all personal property and placed it on a sack, and identified the body by identification disc or paybook, and then marked it carefully by writing details on a label and tying the label to the coat and tunic and then passed on to the next.' Meanwhile the divisional Assistant Provost Marshal (APM) had organized a party to dig a large burial trench.[73] The system of using labels was clearly unsatisfactory since they were liable to perish or became illegible, making subsequent identification difficult for the Graves Registration Units (GRU). Consequently, Army Order 287, issued on 24 August 1916, stipulated that in future each soldier would wear two identity discs, one red, the other green. The former would remain with the body, while the latter was sent to DAG 3rd Echelon together with a burial report. Even so, there were clearly several instances of both discs being forwarded and GHQ in France had to issue a General Routine Order on 7 April 1917 to remind everyone of the correct procedure. By the time of Third Ypres much more care was being taken. Padre Murray Maurice wrote:

> The place [burial site] was marked on the map and correct map references made afterwards in reserve. The manner of marking such graves is either to place the man's tin hat on a reversed rifle or to put his name on a piece of paper in an empty bottle, neck down and corked with something ... Later, when the area becomes 'quiet', the GRU will come and put up their official crosses with the man's name, number, unit and date of death, or date of burial if the later was not ascertainable, on a strip of zinc stamped in capital letters just as you stamp your name in the penny-in-the-slot machines at home.[74]

The GRUs themselves operated in every theatre of war and were meticulous in their work. One copy of the original burial report was always sent to the GRU concerned. But no action was taken until the copy sent to the

3rd Echelon had been forwarded to the relevant record office so that the man's particulars could be checked for accuracy and then returned to the GRU, which then compared the reports and amended its own copy as necessary. An officer was now sent out to verify the grave and all details then sent to the Directorate of Graves Administration & Enquiries at the War Office, which had been established, with Fabian Ware at its head, in May 1916 to reflect the fact that graves registration was now operating in all theatres of war and not just France. The selection of cemetery locations was the responsibility of the Q staff and their locations were passed to every unit in the area. Every effort was made to ensure that all burials were in recognized cemeteries, jokingly referred to as 'rest camps' by the men,[75] and not haphazardly in out-of-the-way places. With the assistance of RE surveyors, the GRU drew up detailed plans of each cemetery, showing the location of every plot. Likewise, wherever possible RE photographers attached to the GRUs took photographs of each grave, the expenses being defrayed from a private fund administered by Fabian Ware himself.[76] Further recognition of the vital role that the War Graves Commission was playing came in May 1917, with the setting up of the Imperial War Graves Commission. The Prince of Wales was made its president and Ware, who rose to the rank of major general and was knighted for his services, its vice chairman, a post which he would hold until his death in 1948. The commission's main purpose was the care and maintenance of the war cemeteries, wherever they were located, after the war ended, a mission which the Commonwealth War Graves Commission continues today in exemplary fashion.

The treatment of sick and wounded animals was the responsibility of the Army Veterinary Corps. Every cavalry regiment, artillery and infantry brigade, divisional ammunition column and train had a veterinary officer attached. His duties were to treat sickness and injury and to oversee the care of the animals. Overseeing veterinary matters at divisional HQ was the Assistant Director of Veterinary Services (ADVS). He also controlled the Mobile Veterinary Sections (MVS), which were allocated on the scale of one per cavalry brigade and infantry division. These were the equivalent of the field ambulance and their main role was the collection and evacuation of sick and wounded animals from the battle zone. During periods of static warfare they also established hospitals to treat the less serious casualties. Animals were evacuated to the rear by train wherever possible, but horse ambulances were also used. They were categorized in four types of casualty, each indicated by a coloured label attached to the animal: medical cases (white); surgical cases (green); specific diseases (red); non-veterinary cases (blue). The animals were taken to veterinary hospitals in the base area, where they were given the necessary treatment. V. C. Leckie commanded the Indian Veterinary Hospital at Rouen for much of the war. It was situated on the outskirts of the town and was based on a large field, which provided plenty of grazing.

> Blocks of wood and corrugated-iron stabling, each holding a hundred horses were put up, so that two thousand five hundred horses could be housed at one time. There were also many other wooden buildings, such as operating theatre, pharmacy, surgery, various forges, forage barns, besides hutments for the men, dining-rooms, Messes and the Orderly Room and Office. There was also a light railway to the huge manure dump. So it may be considered rather as a factory for turning out fit horses from those who came down to us from the front, the sick, the lame, wounded, some with skin disease, some even burnt with mustard gas, the debilitated and the war-weary.[77]

Once on the road to recovery, the animals moved to veterinary convalescent depots, which also took in tired and worn-out animals in need of a rest. When fit, they passed into the hands of the remount services for reissue to units. Individual veterinary officers had the sad task of deciding whether a horse or mule had reasonable prospects of recovery. Those that did not were invariably shot. In France, the winter of 1916–17 proved the most arduous for the animals, with the monthly wastage rate rising to 7 per cent. Much of the reason for this was the clipping of coats, which the veterinary authorities had insisted on for fear of mange. This, combined with lack of shelter, left them hopelessly exposed to the elements. So concerned was Jack Cowans that he personally visited France in May 1917 to investigate the problem. The result was that clipping, when it did take place, was limited to trace high and Cowans provided more resources for shelters. Thereafter the loss rate fell. Apart from East Africa, where tetse fly was the main cause of an 89.5 per cent loss during 1916, the standard of horsemastership in the British Army had come a long way from the appalling 93 per cent wastage rate during the South African War.[78]

Maintaining the supply of veterinary officers was a constant struggle, however. Yet, it was not until September 1918 that a Veterinary Tribunal was formed. The Army Veterinary Corps was also given much support by the RSPCA. Many of its inspectors joined the corps and the society also provided material for hospitals and horse ambulances.[79] Medicine, both human and animal, made vast strides forward during 1914–18. Many challenges were faced and largely overcome and the RAMC, the nursing services and the AVC could be justifiably proud of their achievements.

fourteen

WELFARE AND MORALE

Mail, leave and food were the main factors which influenced the morale of the British soldier of 1914–18. In February 1913, the Royal Engineers (Special Reserve) Postal Section (REPS) was established. Colonel W. Price CMG VD was appointed Director of Army Postal Services and the initial establishment of the postal section was ten officers and 290 other ranks, sufficient to support an expeditionary force of six divisions. They carried out fifteen days training per year under the auspices of the GPO. According to *FSR II*, the postal section was to establish a base post office through which all mail for the troops would flow. Field Post Offices (FPO) would be attached to each supply train and Branch Post Offices to GHQ, and divisional and brigade HQs. Advanced Base and Stationary Post Offices would be set up as required. Each FPO had its own stores box, which represented its mobilization stores. Private mail sent by the troops was expected to be paid by them, with the FPOs holding stocks of stamps. If it was not possible to obtain stamps in the field, the recipient would have to pay the postage. In the event, postage on soldiers' ordinary mail from a theatre of war was waived.

All private mail was subject to censorship. *FSR II* laid down that no reference was to be made

> to plans of future operations whether rumoured, surmised or known;
> to organisation, numbers, and movements of troops; to the armament

of troops or fortresses; to defensive works; to the moral or physical condition of the troops; to casualties previous to the publication of official lists; to the service of maintenance; or in case the writer is one of the garrison of a besieged fortress, to the effects of hostile fire. Criticism of operations is forbidden, as are statements calculated to bring the army or individuals into disrepute.

The troops were encouraged to use a specially designed printed post card (AF A2042), which contained such statements as 'I am quite well', 'I have been admitted to hospital sick/wounded', or 'I have received your letter/telegram/parcel'. The sender merely struck out the phrases which did not apply and then signed and dated it. The major advantage of these cards was that censorship was not required and hence they would not be subject to delay. Other mail – ordinary postcards, letters and parcels – would be opened and checked at the base. The one exception was letters of an urgent nature, which could be censored by the man's commanding officer. These would be placed in a special red envelope (AF A2043), which would be sealed in the writer's presence and countersigned by him. Mail sent from Britain was to be addressed to the recipient, giving his number, rank, and name, unit and title of the expeditionary force and the country in which it was operating.[1]

The advance parties for the Base and Advanced Post Offices crossed to France on 11 August and the main bodies four days later, the subsidiary post offices travelling with their affiliated formations. The Base Post Office was established at Le Havre, the Advanced Base PO at Amiens and the Stationary offices, to help cover troops on the lines of communication, at Rouen and Boulogne. Assisted by the home depot reserve of the REPS, a mere thirty men, the GPO in London received all mail for the BEF and sorted it into unit bundles which they sent to Le Havre. Here they were again sorted and bagged according to unit and FPO and then sent by rail to Amiens. The Advanced Post Office then saw the mail to the railheads, where it was collected by the FPOs, which were based at the supply refilling points, and unit post orderlies then distributed it. The Base Post Office also liaised closely with DAG 3rd Echelon over changes of address and casualties so that mail could be redirected. But as with the supply system as a whole, the retreat from Mons placed enormous strains on the postal service. It soon became almost impossible to keep track of units, let alone individuals, and much mail had to be returned undelivered. The move of the main bases to Nantes and Saint Nazaire and the forward base to Le Mans aggravated matters further and it was not until November that the system finally settled down. No sooner had it done so, than it was faced with Christmas. This saw a 90 per cent increase in letters and 345 per cent in parcels. With admirable foresight, the REPS had drafted in extra staff over the period and deliveries worked remarkably well.[2] Gerald Burgoyne writing in the trenches on 30 December noted: 'I got three letters posted in Ireland on the 26th, and in England on the 28th, this afternoon, so letters are reaching us as quickly as if there were no war. It's really rather wonderful.'[3]

Adjustments were made in early spring 1915 to the type of mail which a soldier at the front could send, largely to reduce the burden on the censors. The red urgent envelope had not been much used and hence was abolished. In its place came a green envelope (AF A3078), with the writer signing a declaration on the front that it contained nothing secret. Each soldier was allowed one or two per week, but they were liable to opening by the base censor. Normal mail was now censored by the unit's officers, something to which most men do not seem to have objected. The field postcard continued to be used widely, usually when the man had no time to write at length or had been wounded.[4]

As the army expanded, so did the REPS. In September 1914 a Territorial Force branch of the postal section was established. Mails in Britain were now handled by the inland section. So as to avoid duplication in sorting letters and parcels, this was largely done in London, and the mails bagged here. By the end of the war the postal section in London had two army letter offices – one covering the BEF in France and all registered letters; and the other for other theatres of war and the Indian and South African contingents with the BEF – a Dominions army letter office for the New Zealand and Canadian forces, an army parcel office, an Australian Army post office, and an army returned letter and parcel office. Parcels were always the main headache. In April 1917 the number being handled per day rose to 125,000, placing heavy strains on sea and land transport. Luckily, the number of parcels then declined to 54,800 per day in June 1918. Two factors caused this. The growth of canteens in the war theatres reduced demands from soldiers to their kith and kin and, latterly, the imposition of rationing in Britain meant that people at home could not obtain spare items of food to send out. During major actions, when it was impossible for units to receive parcels, temporary divisional dumps were set up, thus preventing a backlog further up the chain.[5] There was one significant change in the handling of parcels which began to take place in mid 1916. Up until that time food parcels arriving for men who had become casualties were usually shared by their comrades. There were, however, an increasing number of complaints from relatives and, eventually, by February 1918 all undelivered parcels were returned to sender.[6] However, it was still often the case that a parcel arrived for a man before he had been officially noted as a casualty, and so the practice of sharing its contents continued. As for the personal effects of casualties, those of officers were sent via the army post office to the army agent – Messrs Cox & Co in London – while those for other ranks went to the DAG 3rd Echelon at base. Both agencies were then responsible for returning them to the individual or his next of kin.

The one theatre in which the postal system did not work well was the Dardanelles. Two Base Post Offices were set up: at Alexandria (which later became that for the Egyptian Expeditionary Force) and at Mudros. Lack of FPOs meant that some had to be improvised, notably for the Royal Naval and 42nd (East Lancashire) Divisions, and Beach Landing offices took the place of Stationary Post Offices. Matters were not made easier by the fact that these were often under fire. The lack of postal personnel, shipping and information on units and individuals meant lost mail and severe delays. In particular, trying to track down the sick and wounded was a nightmare because they were evacuated to various places – Mudros, Malta, Egypt, even back to Britain.[7] In Mesopotamia there were also long delays. Padre Drury noted in 1918 that outgoing mails went 'only rarely' and that they were often without letters from home for up to six weeks.[8] The problem here, however, was very long lines of communication which became ever more stretched the further the British advanced. In addition, this theatre, like East Africa, was the postal responsibility of the government of India and all mails from home were sent via Bombay.

But the root of the postal system lay in the FPO, which was, in effect, its stores box, as a piece in the *Daily Mail* of 22 September 1918 described:

> A Field Post Office is primarily an iron box – not a building, a black, heavy box, under the care of a Corporal and two sappers. The box holds postal orders, stamps, cash, lead seals for mails [sic] bags, rule books, and scores of other items – not forgetting the red-and-white flag of office. This box may be lodged anywhere – in an open field, a barn, a stable, a tent, cellar, dug-out, or a chateau; but wherever it is dropped there is the Field Post Office.

Leave was always a contentious issue. In France there was no home leave granted until after the end of First Ypres in late November 1914.[9] It was short to begin with, a mere four or five days away from the unit, although it later increased to a week and then ten days. Few, too, could be allowed away at any one time. Priority was in theory given to the Regulars who had been out from the start, yet John Lucy did not receive his leave until April and then he spent a large part of it travelling to Cork and back. The Territorials, some of whom had been out since September 1914, felt that this was unjust. H. S. Clapham, who had been with the HAC in France since January 1915, wrote in early July:

> The latest grievance is our leave. Very few of our men have had any so far, but most of the Regulars have had one leave at least. I spoke to one man to-day. He was just back, but had only come out in March. Every noncombatant who drives a motor-lorry seems to get leave every few months, but our own Division [3rd] has had less than any other in the Army, and our own battalion less than any other in the Division.

Clapham eventually got his first leave in late October, while Alfred Pollard, who went to France with 1 HAC in September 1914, had to wait until July 1915 for his first home leave. CQMS Harbottle of the 6th Northumberland Fusiliers was luckier and got home for three days in July 1915 after three months in France.[10] Indeed, three months appears to have been the time that a unit had to be in-theatre before it was allowed to begin sending men home on leave.[11]

Lieutenant Graham Greenwell, with the 1st/4th Ox & Bucks, noted in mid August 1915: 'Five officers are going on leave within the next few days, the Colonel, two captains and two subalterns. Leave only goes on when we are actually out of the trenches and stops for the eight days which we are in.' It was also stopped prior to a major operation and sometimes when shipping was needed for other tasks. Officers received home leave more frequently than the men. Greenwell had his first leave in late October 1915, the second at the end of January 1916, another spell in mid May 1916 and, after being hospitalized at the end of 1916, more leave in May 1917 and a final leave in mid September of that year. In contrast, Private A. Stuart Dolden did not receive a home leave until November 1916, after seventeen months in France. His second leave came in December 1917 and a third spell a year later, after the war was over. This was not unusual. Greenwell recorded in August 1917: 'A poor woman wrote to me to-night begging me to send her husband on leave: she hasn't seen him for fourteen months; but I had to write and tell her there are many who haven't been home for sixteen and eighteen months!'[12] Indeed, in mid summer 1917 there were over 100,000 in France who had not had home leave for eighteen months and in excess of 400,000 who had not received any for a year.[13]

The Royal Naval Division was particularly hard done by. It arrived in France in June 1916 direct from the Mediterranean, where it been through the Gallipoli campaign. Arthur Asquith, commanding the 2nd Hood Battalion, applied for an increased leave entitlement for his men. He stated that a third had not been home for over a year and had noticed 'symptoms of a spirit of discontent and lack of keenness among the men ... directly due to ... the small amount of leave they have received in comparison with other troops in France'. But with the Somme offensive just about to open, his plea fell on deaf ears. On average, as Charles Carrington stated, officers went on leave twice as often as other ranks.[21] They also had an advantage in being able to have leave in Paris as well. Indeed, in June 1918 Joseph Brotherton of the 1st Cameronians was able to get married in Paris, at the Scottish Church, and spend his honeymoon in the city.[14] The equivalent for other ranks was a spell in a rest camp.

Compassionate leave was also possible. Private Norman Ellison of the 1st/6th King's Liverpool had his first leave in December 1915, but his mother died suddenly the following month and, since his father was ill, he was given a further four days' leave. In July 1916 Rowland Fielding tried to obtain compassionate leave for a man in his battalion, whose elder daughter had been killed by a motor car. 'There are so many hard cases, and the Higher Authorities are likely to argue, in this one, that, since the child is dead, the father can do no good by going home; which is logical, if brutal.'[15]

By the end of the Battle of Cambrai in early December 1917, the British Army in France was tired, as Haig told Pétain on the 17th.[16] Two days later the Military Members of the Army Council considered Haig's request for more leave for his troops. He pointed out that on average they had only had fourteen days over the past fifteen months. In contrast, and as a result of Pétain's reforms in the wake of the spring 1917 mutinies, the French *poilu* got leave every four months.[17] Thereafter the situation did improve in the BEF and by mid 1918 every man was getting home leave after six months in France. Matters were also helped by a policy initiated in the summer of 1917 whereby officers and warrant officers who had served two years in France would be given the opportunity of serving for six months at home. This was extended to junior ranks in January 1918, with priority given to those who were noticeably feeling the strain or had compassionate grounds for going home.[18]

Food was also a primary factor in maintaining morale. The British Army subsisted on three meals a day – breakfast, the main meal at lunchtime (known as dinner) and tea. The officers, however, had four meals – breakfast, lunch, tea and dinner – but this merely reflected the civilian world of the day. The basic ration consisted of meat (fresh, frozen or, more usually at the front, tinned), bread and/or biscuits, bacon, vegetables (fresh or dry), cheese (usually Canadian cheddar), tea, condensed milk and jam. A small army school of cookery had been been established by the ASC at Aldershot in 1907, but the majority of regimental cooks learnt on the job. A messing adviser was also appointed in 1911, a retired ASC officer who held the post until after the end of the war.[19] The *Field Service Pocket Book* did give some hints on how to set up a kitchen in the field with the camp kettle or Dixie being the main cooking pot, although mess tins could be used as well. It gave definitions for boiling, stewing and frying and one or two recipes, including Irish stew, sea pie and rice pudding. Shortly before the war, horse-drawn travelling cookers were introduced on the scale of one per company. These were a great boon, since it enabled meals to be prepared while a unit was on the march.

The QMG's policy from the outbreak of war was to rely largely on frozen meat for the forces abroad, with bully beef being kept as a reserve, although until spring 1915 the troops in France subsisted largely on the latter. To ensure supplies, Cowans arranged for meat to be transported in refrigerating ships from North and South America, Canada, South Africa, Australia and New Zealand. To save on handling, it was taken direct to the base ports. Initially the meat was held on these ships until required, but losses to U-boats brought about the construction of cold stores at the ports. To ensure the quality of preserved meat from abroad, inspectors were deployed to check it before it was tinned. Fresh bread was provided by the ASC bakeries, which were situated at each base port. On Gallipoli, one operated at Cape Helles just 4 miles from the Turkish guns. Cheese initially came from Holland, but when this source was cut off, the authorities turned to Canada, Australia and New Zealand. Potatoes proved a major problem at one point, mainly because of the shortage of agricultural labour, but this was overcome by ordering large quantities from Ireland, France and Italy. In more far-flung theatres, like Egypt and Salonika, seed potatoes were despatched and cultivated locally.[20]

In terms of the ration itself, in France some formations had carried out surveys among the units under their command soon after the end of First Ypres to establish how the rations could be improved. Robertson, the QMG of the BEF, was not impressed. He wrote to Cowans that some of the recommendations had included 'kippered herrings, findon [finnan] haddocks, kippered mackerel, chestnuts, pork for Christmas, treacle, and last but not least bullseyes'. The last-named was 'the last straw'. He felt that 'the state of mind gradually growing in the army seems to be much more concerned with luxury and personal comfort than with killing the enemy'. Robertson went on to say:

> the absurd demands which have recently poured in – including officers' mess carts for all units, hanging lamps for the Divisional Trains, thermometers for the trenches, galoshes, etc. etc. – are becoming

intolerable. I suppose sedentary work, and very little of that, will always produce the same objectionable results, but they are there all the same, and a bad job it is so.[21]

Once trench warfare took hold, the initial policy was that the men carried out their own cooking. Norman Ellison of the 1st/6th Lancashire Fusiliers:

> There were no organised cooking arrangements in the front line. Each man had his raw rations – biscuits, bully beef, cheese, jam, bacon, tea and sugar – and he had to make shift as best he could. There were iron braziers and wet coke to be had, but these were of little use. The British Army lived on tea, all hours of the day or night, and bacon cooked over candles or weird lamps made of rag soaked in bacon fat.

Gerald Burgoyne was full of praise for the rations provided: 'The way we are fed is wonderful, packets of pea soup and cubes of Oxo are issued as rations. Machonocie [sic] tinned meat and vegetables. "Home & Colonial" margarine and very good too, and so much jam, cheese, bacon and bully beef …' He further remarked: 'The wastage in rations is terrible. Going round the place this morning. I saw enough good tins of Bully thrown away, or simply left in their boxes, to feed a battalion.' In contrast, H. S. Clapham of the HAC, writing of the same time (January 1915), complained that 'biscuits, jam, and bully beef were about all the rations we received'. He did accept, however, that there was a significant improvement in the rations during the next few months.[22]

Bully beef remained the staple throughout the war. Maconochie, a meat and vegetable stew, was also widespread, and was generally liked. Tinned pork and beans was introduced, but was not so popular. Julian Tyndale-Biscoe noted:

> The men complained the other day about their rations – tins of pork and beans had been issued in place of bully. It was not enough and no pork was visible. I reported this, and the reply came back that the complaint was not understood since the food value was the same as the bully and the pork was absorbed in the beans!

According to A. M. Beatson, an ASC officer, a railhead supply officer responded:

> In view of the rapacious appetite of the beans now being issued as rations of pork and beans, it would be advisable that, though a meat ration, the latter be not sent up from the Base in the same truck of the supply train as the fresh British meat, for fear of the devouring tendency of the once homely bean.

Jam was also tinned and the most common variety, with which the troops soon became bored, was plum and apple. In Egypt and Palestine the butter and jam came from Australia and, in Cecil Sommers' words, were 'very good'. But otherwise the rations were more limited than in France, with bully beef and biscuits the main staples. At the end of 1917, Julian Tyndale-Biscoe, now with a battery in Egypt, noted that there was nothing available except frozen Australian rabbit, and, with the salvage campaign in full force, 'we have strict orders to return the skins which are made into jerkins and are on issue to all ranks as may be required'. When the troops were first deployed to Italy in November 1917, the rations were initially just bully beef and biscuit, but were then supplemented by Italian rations. Norman Gladden: 'Not that we were as grateful as we should have been. The butter and bacon were putrid; the meat, we declared, must have been old bullock killed by overwork. Only the closely-woven and somewhat dry Italian army bread was both plentiful and edible.'[23] In every theatre of war, when all else failed, the soldier could fall back on his iron ration, although it was a breach of military discipline to open it without the authority of his CO. It consisted of a 1lb tin of bully beef, twelve ounces of biscuit, tea, sugar, salt, a small portion of cheese and two cubes of meat extract and was sufficient to keep the soldier going for twenty-four hours.

The ration itself remained much the same until 1917. Then, in view of a world shortage of foodstuffs, which was aggravated by the U-boat campaign, Cowans decided to reduce the daily rations of those on the lines of communication in France by four ounces of meat, one ounce of bacon, an eighth of an ounce of tea and one ounce of sugar, with one ounce of margarine instead of two ounces of butter. This did not make much noticeable difference, since those in the rear areas always seemed to feed better than those further forward. In November 1915, the 1st/6th King's was carrying out duties at HQ Third Army. Private Norman Ellison recounted that he was in a mess of fifteen men and he and one other did the cooking. 'Every morning we open the ball with porridge, bacon and fried bread, honey or jam and tea. Luncheon mid-day: steak and onions or mutton chops. Dinner 6.30pm: soup, roast beef or mutton, potatoes and another vegetable, milk pudding and jam, coffee and cigarettes.' Numerous *estaminets* in the town supplied British Bass beer to drink. Aubrey Smith experienced similar generous rations at HQ Third Army in March 1916. He commented: 'Was it not significant that when we were behind the line, serving not as an infantry battalion but as "army troops" we invariably had too much food, whereas in an infantry division rations were, as often as not, insufficient?'[24] Much the same happened in other theatres, but the climate also played its part. Thus, during the summer the cheese ration in Salonika and the Middle East was discontinued.[25]

At home, Cowans substituted a money allowance for part of the ration to enable units to take advantage of local produce and to add variety to the diet. In 1917, beginning at Kimnel Park Camp in Western Command, he also set up a system of centralized cooking at large camps, which led to significant savings. As for the cooks themselves, a cookery school was established by each home command. These ran a six-week course and trained some 65,000 cooks during the war. Others were trained by the London County Council and Scottish local authorities.[26] Similar schools were established in the overseas theatres, but in slower time. Some formation commanders set them up on their own initiative. Wyn Griffith of the 38th Division was deputed by his brigade HQ to run a cookery course during the winter of 1915–16 in France. He knew nothing about the subject, but got his battalion master-cook involved. One cook from each company in the brigade attended and they were taught how to make boiled puddings and rissoles out of bully beef and biscuits as well as to roast meat in field ovens.[27] At the higher level by January 1917 there was still only one school of cookery in France, which had been set up by the Fifth Army.[28] A school was established in Salonika in July 1917, which ran courses for officers, officers mess cooks and men's cooks.[29]

Cowans also set up a team of inspectors at home to report directly

to him on food matters, accommodation and recreation. They were officially titled Inspectors of Administrative Services and graded as DAQMGs,
with the rank of major. One was attached to each command and they
submitted their reports to the War Office with copies to the relevant
GOC-in-C. It was clearly a job which needed considerable tact if the
commands were not to regard them as 'spies' and those selected for these
positions needed to be of high quality. A number of Members of Parliament became inspectors, including the future Viscount Astor, as did
members of the aristocracy. Food waste became one of their priorities
and they soon identified the fact that considerable amounts of fat were
being wasted when this could be recycled, especially for the manufacture
of glycerine. It was calculated that 10lbs of glycerine could be produced
from every 100lbs of fat and that the army produced sufficient to provide
the fillings for 28 million 18-pounder shells. To manage this operation, the
army set up its own company, Army Waste Products Ltd, which was later
absorbed by National Waste Products, which operated under the umbrella
of the National Salvage Council.[30] Degreasing plants were established at
all the major camps in the United Kingdom and the bases in France. One
was also set up at Kantara in Egypt.[31] Julian Tyndale-Biscoe, on light duties
in Ireland in early 1917 after being wounded in France, was appointed
messing officer to an artillery brigade:

> Not a crumb must be thrown away. All the bones after the goodness has
> been boiled out of them are sent to certain firms who pay us for them,
> while every scrap of fat is collected and turned into dripping. Even the
> water that greasy plates are washed in is skimmed and the scum put into
> the dripping tins. All of it is then sent to the munition factories which
> pay well for it. In this way, with care, one can build up quite large funds for
> buying extra things to supplement the rations.[32]

The value of the Inspectors of Administrative Services was recognized
when in July 1916 Cowans sent the inspector of Northern Command to
report on how the system could be implemented on the lines of communication in France. The result was that an inspector was attached to the
HQ of the IGC. The organization grew until it had a staff of thirty officers
who were now attached to GHQ. At end of 1916 Cowans also appointed

full-time messing officers to units in Britain to relieve COs and their seconds-in-command of some of their administrative burdens.[33]

The officers did eat better than the men, although they paid for the extras out of their own pockets. Yet the other ranks do not seem to have expressed too much jealousy. Bernard Martin overheard his batman, who was 'cooking some tinned concoction from a shop still open in a derelict village', reply to a new draft who was grumbling about officers getting better rations: 'This stuff is not much more than a flavour. Officers have the same rations as you and me and anyway my officer is used to better grub at home than us ... it's hard for them to miss what they've always had.'[34] Brigadier General Kentish, commanding the Senior Officers School at Aldershot, made plain his views in an address to potential commanding officers in summer 1917: 'If our Officers are insufficiently fed and are living under depressing conditions, their health will certainly suffer, and with loss of health comes irritation, loss of temper, and weak Moral, and when this state of things prevails we all know that the men frequently suffer.' He went on:

> Listen to this: – Bully beef, Biscuit, Cheese, and Butter, washed down with Tea, as opposed to Soup, Saumon Mayonnaise, Filet de Boeuf aux Champignons, Pêche Melba, Sardines au Croûte, washed down with Heidsiek (Triple sec), 1906, followed by a cup of Coffee, a glass of old Brandy, and a 'Bon Cigare'. You can picture the two types of Messes, and you can almost scent the air of depression in the one, and hear the laughter in the other, with its Commanding Officer and his Officers all full of life and 'bonnes histoires'. Take my advice, gentlemen, and have nothing to do with the 'Bully beef' set![35]

Much depended on the officers mess cook. The 2nd Royal Welsh Fusiliers were lucky to acquire Private Parry, 'a Paris-trained cook from a first-class London restaurant', in June 1916.[36] His ability to serve up elaborate dinners under the most trying circumstances was often remarked and he certainly kept the officers at battalion HQ well fed. Brian Lawrence was also full of praise for what the officers' servants of his company of the 1st Grenadier Guards could produce in the trenches in the front on Trones Wood on the Somme in November 1916:

When we had seen the men started on their work, and the reliefs of sentries and working parties told off, we went down to our dugouts for some dinner. This was a quite wonderful performance consisting of soup, stew with vegetables, stewed fruit and sardines on toast, and drinks and coffee. It is quite amazing how well, and what a quantity of courses, our servants manage to cook on a coke brazier, in a dugout in which there is hardly room to turn around.

As Charles Douie, dining with brother officers in Italy on Armistice night, commented: 'How like this dinner was to a thousand other dinners, in which the tradition, handed down by generations of army cooks, that an officer must have a four-course meal in the evening in any circumstances, had been faithfully observed.' But not all officers in the line were able to follow this regimen. Charles Carrington in the Foncquevillers sector earlier in the year described a typical company officers' dinner as bully beef stew, followed by tinned apricots and washed down with weak whiskey and water. Lieutenant Joseph Maclean in the trenches with the 1st Cameronians near Messines in October 1917 wrote:

> I got my rations nightly, usually in a filthy wet sandbag and in general consisting of one excessively filthy loaf, tin of sausages or bully, COLD (business of shuddering), some jam or cheese, and a candle. My only implement was my pocket clasp knife. For drink we had the rum issue and we got water once; I also had a flask of whisky.[37]

Another method of offsetting the growing shortage of foodstuffs was for the army to cultivate its own. This was slow to get under way, although tentative efforts were made in Britain as early as 1915. It was not until late 1917 that the Army Agricultural Committee was established for overseeing military agriculture at home, and by the Armistice there were 6,500 acres under cultivation. In France efforts were made in 1917 to start growing food. Aubrey Smith, with the London Rifle Brigade in the Cambrai sector in September 1917 commented: 'Fortunately for us the Army has at last realised that we needed vegetables. Not only did they grant a small sum daily for the purchase of them, but they started a collection of vegetable gardens where we dug and planted cabbages and potatoes under Brigade orders.'³⁸ It was, however, difficult to maintain these gardens at the lower level, with divisions constantly shifting. A Director of Agricultural Production was therefore appointed in January 1918 at GHQ to coordinate cultivation at the highest level. A highly successful operation was also established in Mesopotamia, enabling the army to become self-sufficient in vegetables and the native population in grain.³⁹ Salonika, too, saw over 7,000 acres under cultivation by the spring of 1918.⁴⁰

Pay was not a major factor in maintaining morale, although as an article in the *Evening News* of 20 June 1917 pointed out: 'Tommy resents, and rightly resents, any holding up of allowances which are his just due, and he will grouse so that all the world can hear if there is any interruption in the flow to him of the none too handsome pay which he earns so gallantly.' Pay was the responsibility of two organizations. The Army Pay Department (APD) was staffed by officers, who were titled paymasters; with chief paymasters ranked as colonels, staff paymasters as lieutenant colonels and majors, and paymasters as captains and lieutenants. The clerks that supported them belonged to the Army Pay Corps (APC).* In 1912 a committee under Colonel John Clayton, the Command Paymaster Scottish Command, evolved a new pay system. Regimental officers were to be responsible for actually paying the men, recording the amount paid in each soldier's paybook (AB64), while the paymasters maintained the accounts at what were known as Fixed Centre Pay Offices (FCPO). These were established in the United Kingdom, with each infantry regiment having an FCPO attached to its record office, and the other arms and services having dedicated FCPOs. Thus, that dealing with Dragoon and Lancer regiments was at Canterbury, while the Royal Horse and Field Artillery were administered by an FCPO at Woolwich. The FCPOs maintained records of what each soldier should be paid and what he actually received. Copies of unit Part II orders, which gave details of every individual's change of circumstances, enabled the FCPOs to calculate the former, while the acquittance rolls, listing what each soldier had been paid, satisfied the latter requirement. In the field, pay offices were established at each base and money for paying the troops was obtained from field cashiers, who were deployed

---

* A similar organization pertained to the Ordance Corps. The officers belonged to the Army Ordnance Department (AOD), while the remainder were in the Army Ordnance Corps (AOC).

one to each division and on the lines of communication. Officers had their pay sent direct to their bank accounts, but could also cash cheques at field cashiers.

In 1914, the basic daily pay of a private or equivalent ranged from one shilling (1/-) for an infantryman to one shilling and ninepence (1/9d) for a Household Cavalry trooper. Proficiency pay could increase it by up to sixpence (6d). There was also corps pay to which trained men in the Royal Engineers, ASC, RAMC, AOC and AVC were entitled. In comparison, a senior warrant officer in the infantry was paid five shillings (5/-) per diem. Abroad, soldiers were paid in the currency of the country. In France the exchange rate was around 25 francs to the pound and a private soldier would usually receive the order of 10 francs per week, which allowed for stoppages of pay, etc. Soldiers were also given a separation allowance to be paid to wives and dependants and could make automatic additional allotments out of their pay to their families.

Prior to the outbreak of war, those invalided out of the army through wounds or sickness and were unable to work were provided with pensions, as were those with twenty-one years' service with the Colours. A former private could expect a disability pension of up to 2/6d per day. The widows of those junior ranks who died while on service were not, however, entitled to pensions, merely receiving a gratuity equal to one month's pay. Warrant officers' widows were considerably better off, receiving a pension of £20 per annum, with an additional £5 for each child. Matters were greatly improved when the Ministry of Pensions was established at the end of 1916, taking responsibility for all pensions, civil and military. A totally disabled private soldier, who had not been in civil employment prior to the war, now received £71.6s 0d per annum while those who had had civilian jobs had their pensions adjusted to reflect their previous earnings. Pensions, too, were now provided for the widows of junior ranks and their children. Another worthwhile responsibility that the Ministry of Pensions took on was the rehabilitation of disabled servicemen into civilian life. The plight of the amputees, of whom there were over 41,000 as a result of the war was particularly acute. The leading establishment was Queen Mary's Convalescent Auxiliary Hospital at Roehampton on the outskirts of London. Established in 1915, it provided artifical limbs for over 26,000 men; the others being catered for by similar centres set up in each home command, which also had workshops where they could learn a trade.

There was only one pay rise for the army during the course of the war. This came at the end of 1917. The pay of the infantry private rose to 1/6d per diem. He was now also receiving an additional penny per day for each year he was overseas. The only people who did not benefit were the privates of the Non-Combatant Corps, whose pay remained at one shilling.

While mail, leave and food were tangible methods which could be used to maintain morale, the army chaplain was a means of assisting it on the spiritual side. At the outbreak of the war, the army had 117 chaplains on its books. Their role according to *FSR II* was the 'spiritual administration and welfare of the Army'. They were officially ranked in classes. Ordinary chaplains were ranked as 4th class and equated to captains, while the senior chaplain in a division was 3rd class. At each corps HQ there was a Deputy Assistant Chaplain General (DACG)(2nd class) to represent the Church of England, which was by far the largest denomination in the army, as it was in Britain, and a Deputy Assistant Principal Chaplain (DAPC) to represent the other denominations. The senior chaplain in an army was ranked as an Assistant Chaplain General (ACG)(1st class), with non-Church of England denominations looked after by an Assistant Principal Chaplain (ACP). Because the BEF grew to five armies, there was a Deputy Chaplain General at GHQ, who was Bishop Gwynne. At the War Office the Chaplain General had overall responsibility for the Army Chaplains' Department (Church of England), while chaplains of other denominations were looked after by a civil servant. By the Armistice in November 1918, the number of chaplains in the army had grown to 3,475, of which 1,985 were Church of England, 649 Roman Catholic, 303 Presbyterian, 256 Wesleyan, 251 United Board (Baptists, Congregationalists, Methodists), 16 Jewish, 10 Welsh Calvinists and 5 Salvation Army.[41] The establishment of chaplains per infantry division was eventually established at seventeen, with one appointed to each Infantry battalion and to each of the two RFA brigades. Another chaplain was usually attached to one of the field ambulances. The denominational balance among chaplains depended on the nature of the division. By the middle of the war in France, English divisions had nine Church of England, four Roman Catholic and four Presbyterian or Nonconformist chaplains, while Scottish divisions were allocated nine Presbyterian, four Church of England and four Roman Catholic chaplains. The 16th (Irish) Division had nine Roman Catholic, four Church of England, and four Presbyterian. The 38th (Welsh) Division had the same balance as the Scottish divisions, with Nonconformists included in the nine Presbyterians. The make-up of chaplains of the other ethnically unique division, the 36th Ulster, was not specified, but was probably the same as an English division.[42] There was also a Church Army commissioner attached to each army in France.

For much of the war the various denominations tended to go their separate ways as much as they could, reflecting the separate governing structures for the established church and the other denominations. Padre Drury, who was Church of England, observed:

> The unity of the Allied cause threw into relief the deplorable divisions of the Christian force. At Wardan [Egypt] I actually had to sign a paper, sent by the General commanding the area, in which I promised never to hold united services with ministers of other demonitions. We were to be held apart like fighting dogs.[43]

Unofficially, they did intermingle. Haig, on a visit to the Third Army at the end of March 1916, noted in his diary: 'On the way I saw three parsons of different persuasions standing together, a Roman Catholic, a Wesleyan, and another; all most friendly!' But he went on to rail against the way in which the high and low elements of the Church of England were at each other's throats. 'It seems to me to be most disgraceful at the time like the present, that the National Church should be divided against itself, instead of giving us a noble example of unity and good fellowship.'[44] David Lloyd George, as Secretary of State for War, did set up an interdenominational committee at the War Office in August 1916 to consider questions relating to the ministration of the troops. All the significant churches in Britain sent representatives, but the Jewish religion was not included and when Edmund Sebag-Montefiore, chairman of the Jewish Recruiting Committee, asked if a Jewish representative could attend, he was told that this was not possible since the ministration of Jewish soldiers was 'of a unique nature'.[45] No records of the committee's deliberations remain, but the impression is that it did little to bring the churches in uniform closer to one another.

The policy up to the spring of 1915 was that chaplains should not go into the front line, but as one padre later pointed out:

> It militated against the influence of the chaplain if he did not share the dangers of the men and confined his activities to times when they were out of the line. In addition, the presence of the chaplain in the line was a source of inspiration and good cheer. The troops were able to talk to him in a way in which they were not able to talk even to their own officers, and some of the best work done by chaplains in the last war they were able to do in the front line.[46]

Indeed, Padre Julian Bickersteth stated that 'that padre is appreciated by the men so far as he busies himself with the recreational and comfort, and respected if he visits the front line and shares their dangers. When he does both, he is loved.'[47] Those that ignored this policy from the outset were almost invariably priests with the southern Irish battalions – men like Father Gleeson of the 2nd Munsters, who led the battalion out of action after all the officers had become casualties during First Ypres. Another in the same mould was Father William Doyle. He went to France with the 8th Royal Irish Fusiliers and was gassed and recommended for the MC at Loos. After going through the grim battles on the Somme, he was transferred to the 8th Royal Dublin Fusiliers and was finally awarded the MC in January 1917. He saw his most important role as giving absolution to the dying and was constantly in the forefront of the battle. He was unsuccessfully recommended for the DSO after Messines in June 1917 and was killed on Frezenberg Ridge in August 1917. Many believed that he should have been awarded a posthumous Victoria Cross. An Ulster rifleman paid this tribute to him: 'Father Doyle was a good deal among us. We couldn't possibly agree with his religious opinions, but we simply worshipped him for other things. He didn't know the meaning of fear, and he didn't know what bigotry was.'[48]

But chaplains of other denominations displayed equal courage. The Reverend Harold Spooner was present at the siege of Kut el Amara and during Holy Week in 1916 took voluntary services in the trenches under fire, with eighty-five men attending on one occasion and eighty on another. One senior officer told him that seeing a padre in the trenches was 'as water in a thirsty land'.[49] Geoffrey Studdert Kennedy MC, known affectionately as Woodbine Willie from his habit of handing out cigarettes in the trenches, was another. There was also 54-year-old Theodore Hardy, who, in quick succession in the first part of 1918, won the DSO for rescuing men stuck in the mud and wounded (despite a broken wrist), an MC and then the VC for repeated acts of rescuing wounded under fire during the bitter defensive fighting of that April. Sadly, he died of wounds before the end of the war. While chaplains, like doctors, were classed as non-combatants, there was the odd occasion when they appear to have forgotten this. Padre Victor Tanner was with the MO of the 2nd Worcesters at the battalion aid post, which was in a pillbox, during the Battle of Gheluvelt in late September 1917. The Germans launched a counter-attack.

> The Doc and I gravely discussed what we should do if the Boche reached the pillbox. I said we ought to fight until they actually entered it and then we should surrender. He had a revolver, which contrary to regulations, he always carried, and I had a rifle which one of the two wounded had left behind.

Luckily this eventuality did not occur, and Spooner went on to win two Military Crosses.[50]

Yet many wartime chaplains were soon disillusioned when they arrived in a theatre of war. Those who wanted to don uniform applied to their bishop and were given a one-year contract, which they could extend. But when they arrived at the Front they were often shocked. Julian Bickersteth went to France in February 1916 and, after reporting to the Deputy Chaplain General, Bishop Gwynne, was posted to the 56th (London) Division: 'Never has the failure of the Church of England been more apparent than it has been to the chaplains at the front: man after man to whom religion is simply a name has never been brought into contact with any sacramental teaching of any kind.' Oswin Creighton was the padre to an RFA brigade in the Arras sector in spring 1917. On the orders of the brigade commander, he set up a canteen, where he also used to hold evening services: 'The men filed out before it began, and were back again for cocoa when it was over ... I felt furious last time. What is the use of feeding men if they deliberately set themselves against any attempt to teach or help them see the truth?'

It was for this reason that some did not extend their contracts. The Reverend John Walker served with a casualty clearing station throughout the Battle of the Somme, but returned to Britain at the end of 1916:

> No, it is not worth staying out here whilst one has children at home. Tommy does not want religion, I don't persuade him. I give out a service and offer to conduct it and out of 500 [patients], 200 of whom can walk, about a dozen come to Matins and the same to Evensong. They would come as a favour to me If I pressed them, at least some would, but what is the use. They don't kneel when they come unless I ask them.

But other chaplains strongly disapproved of those who merely served for the year. Padre David Railton, who was with the 47th (London) Division, roundly condemned a fellow chaplain for doing this in April 1916: 'It is simply scandalous that all officers out here have to stick it for the duration of the war – and then a chaplain who has got to know the men well goes off as he has had enough of it – and as his year is up.'[51]

Part of the problem was that those coming from cosy rural parishes found it difficult to adjust to the rawness of life in the army, especially on active service. As Major Arthur Osburn DSO RAMC somewhat cynically observed:

> Chaplains more than other folk seemed to ignore the necessary effect of the War on men's general morality ... When one has to creep out and stab or strangle or otherwise do to death a fellow human being in the darkness of no-man's-land, one is bound to feel less seriously about the other forms of morality, including dishonesty, cruelty and sex indulgence.

Frederick Hodges recorded: 'The subject of religion rarely cropped up in the trenches, but the ever-present nearness of death occasionally raised the question of what happens afterwards.'[52] Those chaplains who preached hell and damnation to the enemy were also questioned, especially on the Western Front, where every German soldier had *Gott Mit Uns* inscribed on his belt buckle. Chaplains, too, could be unthinking. H. M. Davson recalls that during a 1917 Arras battle a padre held a service close to his battery positions dressed in a white surplice and using a red altar – a clear giveaway to any enemy aircraft or observation balloon.[53] John Nettleton writes of another who joined the 2nd Rifle Brigade in summer 1918 and complained about the battalion HQ dug-out, 'which was relatively well appointed, although a certain amount of "hot bedding" was inevitable. He said he needed somewhere separate to "meditate."' It was this sort of attitude which gave Lieutenant Joseph Maclean of the 1st Cameronians a very jaundiced view of chaplains, as he wrote in a letter to his brother in December 1917, after being forced to surrender his billet to a padre: 'Most chaplains out here are nothing but a nuisance, occupying good billets and drinking our drinks, and doing nothing noticeable for the spiritual welfare of the troops. As a class they are cordially disliked, with few exceptions.' Later he commented: 'My experience is that the padre who comes into the danger zone is a "rara avis"'.[54]

But a good chaplain, and there were many of them, could do much to maintain the morale of the men, even if he could not get them to come voluntarily to his services. Harold Thomas, a curate who chose to enlist in the RAMC, remembered a Church of England padre on Gallipoli:

> He was young, energetic, and merry-eyed, altogether just the person, or parson, for the job. He was always welcome in the tents and rarely left without cheering up the individual or the group with whom he had been talking. He exuded an atmosphere of genuine cheeriness which was far removed from that most depressing cloak of insensitive and assumed jocularity which is donned by a certain type of Divine.[55]

Because the padre was not part of the ordinary officer corps, the men could talk to him confidentially knowing that what they said would not be passed on to those in authority. A padre who could engage the men in conversation could do much for them. He could also help in more practical ways.

Many padres were deployed to casualty clearing stations or advanced dressing stations during an attack, where they performed valuable work. Padre Julian Bickersteth was with a 56th Division ADS on 1 July 1916 on the Somme:

> I was being given different jobs to do by the doctor in charge, first to get away the walking cases, then to superintend the loading of the

[ambulance] cars, then to see that the worst cases had 'Oxo' or hot tea
to prevent collapse, then to clear out a couple of dug-outs which in the
rush had been filled with wounded and being rather out of the way ran
the risk of being neglected, being out of sight.

That evening he led a stretcher party up to one of the battalion aid posts
to collect more wounded.[56] There was, too, the writing of letters and field
post cards for the badly wounded and giving words of comfort. Indeed,
the chaplain found himself being used as a 'jack of all trades'. His grimmest
task was giving solace to the dying and conducting burials. The latter were
particularly important. A dead soldier's comrades felt better if they knew
that he had been given a proper burial. There was, too, the very important
role that chaplains played in graves registration (*see pages 432*). On a more
mundane level, many ran unit canteens, which operated when out of the
line.

When the BEF went to France in August 1914, no allowance was made
for canteens. Kitchener had stated in August 1914 that the war would be
'no picnic', the implication being that troops' comforts had no place in it.[57]
The soldiers therefore relied on the local *estaminets* and shops. The first
canteen set up for the troops was that established for the wounded in the
Gare Maritime at Boulogne by Lady Angela Forbes on 4 November 1914
(*see page 244*). She then went on to open a canteen hut at Etaples, where
she had a house.[58] Not until February 1915 did the Army Council finally
recognize the need for canteens in the field. The Director of Supplies and
Transport, Major General R. G. Long, was tasked with setting up an organization to run them and set up the Canteen and Mess Co-operative Society,
using £27,000 accumulated by the canteens of the Boer War and which
had remained in being. A branch of the society was established in France
and soon Expeditionary Force Canteens (EFC) began to spring up. In July
they were absorbed by the ASC, becoming the Expeditionary Force
Canteens Section ASC. Those who worked in the EFCs wore uniform and
were subject to military law and by the end of the war some 5,000 ASC
men and 700 members of the QMAAC were so employed. In addition,
both the YMCA and Church Army set up canteens, many of them well
forward so that troops near the front line could take advantage of them.

They did not serve alcohol, but the hot drinks, cigarettes and chocolate were more than welcome. Others were run by the Salvation Army, British Red Cross Society, YWCA, Scottish Churches Huts, United Army & Navy Board, the Soldiers' Christian Association and the Wesleyan Soldiers' Institute.* In June 1917 Rowland Fielding noted a YMCA canteen in a pill-box and run by a Nonconformist minister on Wyschaete Ridge in the immediate aftermath of the Battle of Messines, while Norman Gladden recalled another at Lake Zillebeke at much the same time. Indeed, as ex-Guardsman Noakes of the Coldstream wrote: 'It might well be said that wherever there were troops, there was also the YMCA, with its canteen, its cheerfulness and its never-ending effort to bring some at least of the comforts of civilisation into our existence.'[59] The EFCs did not operate on the Gallipoli peninsula, but there was a canteen run by some Greeks, who ferried their supplies each day from Lemnos.[60] EFCs were, however, active in the Middle East.

During 1915 there were concerns over the canteens other than EFCs. Soup kitchens were set up under the auspices of the Red Cross. The DGMS pointed out that this was in breach of the Geneva Conventions if they served healthy troops.[61] There was also the question of women crossing from Britain to help run them. Kitchener himself had made it plain that he did not approve of their being in France and there was a strict rule that the wives of officers serving with the BEF were not allowed to be on the lines of communication. This created problems. In one instance, an officer's wife had a coffee stall in Rouen. Her husband was then posted as an AMLO to the same place. Sir John Cowans concluded that unless special permission could be granted for both to remain at Rouen, either the coffee stall would have to go or the husband found another post.[62]

In Britain, canteens were initially largely run by civilian contractors on a no-profit basis. Early in the war a Board of Control of Regimental Institutes was set up as an advisory body, especially for the purchase of canteen goods. In July 1916 this was superseded by the Army Canteen Committee. Later that year, the Royal Navy joined in to help form the Navy and Army Canteen Board (NACB), which was the forerunner of today's NAAFI.[63]

Before unit canteens began to come into being, some commanding

* Lady Forbes' Canteen at Boulogne became an EFC and her hut at Etaples was taken over by the Salvation Army.

officers used their own initiative. In May 1915, the 1st/4th Ox & Bucks were in the trenches at Ploegsteert and the CO arranged for 'a penny ration of beer per man' to be sent up, paying for it himself. It was a practice that continued. James Jack's quartermaster in the 2nd West Yorkshires often delivered beer to the men in the trenches during the early part of 1917.[64] Otherwise, in the front line the only alcohol available to the soldier was the daily tot of rum, which was introduced in October 1914, initially just for those in the trenches.[65] But even this came under threat at times. In the early months of 1915 the temperance movement in Britain was loud in its condemnation of drink. Gerald Burgoyne commented from the trenches:

> ... if instead of writing from the comforts of a nice cosy room, they'd put a few days in the trenches I am sure they'd change their mind. We don't want rum in the cold or for the cold; but we want it just as a 'pick me up' when we are 'done to the wide'.[66]

Some formations even went so far as to ban it for a time. A. E. Hodgkin of the 1st/5th Cheshires noted on 12 March: 'Today the rum ration stops under orders from Corps HQ! We all think the teetotal brigade in the House of Commons must have won a victory.'[67] His suspicion appeared to be reinforced when Lloyd George, addressing a trades union conference five days later, stated: 'Drink is doing us more harm in this war than all the German submarines.' To be fair, his remark was aimed at drunkenness among munition workers and this was largely overcome by the Defence of the Realm Acts, which by November 1915 had reduced the opening hours of public houses in Britain from 5 a.m. for a continuous nineteen and a half hours to noon–2.30 p.m. and 6.30–9.30 p.m. There was, too, the Royal Family's decision in early April 1915 to give up alcohol for the duration of the war. The rum ration was, however, saved, much to the relief of the troops. As Father Steuart put it:

> I think that those at home who opposed the issue of the rum-ration can hardly have tried to realise what it meant to the troops at 'stand to', in the chill before the dawn, when one's whole being, moral and physical, stood at its lowest coefficient after a night of broken sleep, cold, damp,

and wholly miserable. The rum-ration set the torpid blood coursing again, brightened heavy eyes, straightened humped backs, and recast the whole mis-en-scene. [In any event, the issue was] hardly more than a tablespoonful.[68]

The unit canteens themselves proved very beneficial. Neil Fraser-Tytler's battery set up a canteen during the second half of the Battle of the Somme. He obtained supplies from the nearest EFC and opened it for two hours a day. Anyone could use it and it was soon taking 2,000 – 3,000 francs daily, with all profits going to the battery fund. This enabled every man to have free coffee, biscuits and rum (in addition to the official issue) on most nights, and helped to maintain the battery's harness in 'top-hole order', as well as supplying gum boots and oilskins for the stable picquets and line orderlies so as to keep trench foot at bay. In May 1917 the battery held a two-day sports meeting when out of the line and the fund was able to supply 1,100 francs worth of prizes, 'free drinks, and so on'. The 6th Northumberland Fusiliers used their canteen to provide fresh vegetables and additional meat for the men. Another advantage of the canteens was that they kept the men out of the *estaminets*, where they were more likely to get into trouble. In October 1917 Rowland Fielding's battalion was in camp near Ervillers on the Somme. The devastation caused by the fighting of the previous year meant that there were no *estaminets* selling 'poison ... under the name of "wine"' and the battalion canteen restricted itself to weak French beer, with the result that there was virtually no crime.[69]

While no official wholesale ban was ever put on the *estaminets* themselves, efforts were made to control them, although this had to be done with the cooperation of the French authorities. In early 1915 they were forbidden to sell spirits to British troops. There were also restrictions placed on the opening hours for soldiers. Thus, a GHQ GRO dated 6 May 1918 laid down that opening hours for *estaminets* in army and GHQ areas were to be 10.30 a.m.–1.30 p.m. and 5.30–9.30 p.m., while on the lines of communication they were 12–2 p.m. and 6–8 p.m. No reason was given why those on the LOC should be more restricted. The army also did its best to ensure that the beer sold in the *estaminets* was drinkable. In June 1916, after the foulness of the beer in Poperinghe had come to the attention of DMS Second Army, the officer commanding No. 4 Mobile Hygiene Laboratory, whose main role was testing water quality, was made responsible for checking the brewing process in the breweries in the Poperinghe area and advising their managers on correct practice.[70] In 1918 Cowans went so far as to organize the brewing of British beer in France, sending out hops and malt from Britain.[71]

Some of the *estaminets* were also brothels – blue lamp for officers and red lamp for other ranks. This was especially so in the base areas in France. The army adopted an ambivalent attitude to the brothels. In Britain itself the military authorities could prevent known prostitutes from loitering at the entrances to barracks and camps, but otherwise they had to rely on the police. Action was taken, with the tacit approval of the War Office, by the National Union of Women Workers of Great Britain and Ireland, which established patrols at the gates of military camps in order to rid them of 'disorderly women'. The aim, however, was not to protect the soldiers but to safeguard young girls from 'seduction and ultimate prostitution'.[72] Apart from lectures by unit MOs and inspections, little was done by the authorities. Some COs did take unilateral action. When the 36th Division moved from Ireland to Sussex in July 1915, F. P. Crozier adopted a liberal policy: 'I was able, by arrangement with a medical officer, to ensure that every officer, NCO and rifleman was instructed and had access to disinfectants after indulgence in sexual intercourse, and that many of the girls and women had opportunities afforded them of similar facilities, free of charge.'[73] This echoed the policy in India, where MOs regularly inspected brothels for disease and hygiene.

In France, all brothels in the British sector, even those in the forward areas, were initially under the control of the French civil authorities. George Ashurst was out at rest at Armentières with the 2nd Lancashire Fusiliers in early 1915:

> We were allowed in the town in the evening and the boys were out to have the best possible time. Drink flowed freely in the *estaminets* and cafes, and as the music and singing went on the boys danced with the mademoiselles in the flimsiest of dresses, or flirted with them at the tables,

using the most vulgar expressions. All the evening Tommies could be seen either going to or from the girls' rooms upstairs, queues actually forming on the stairs leading to those rooms.

The proceedings were broken up one night by the padre and battalion provost sergeant, after which the CO addressed the battalion and laid down that in future leave passes would be issued to only a quarter of the men at any one time and would be limited to two hours in duration. The BEF did gain more control over the forward areas and was able to close down most of the brothels. Even so, the problem could not be entirely stamped out. In summer 1916 John Wedderburn-Maxwell's battery was at Givenchy, 'where our newest subaltern from Skye, Jimmy R got a "dose" from a snappy little tart who somehow landed in our billeting area.'[74]

The base areas were a different problem, since the French civil authorities remained firmly in control. As the brothels were not confined to a particular 'red light' district at each base, it was considered impossible to put them out of bounds to troops since it would involve too much manpower to police. The official line was to divert officers and men 'to pleasing and health-giving recreation huts, fields of sport and places of health-giving amusement during their off-duty hours.'[75] This did little to alleviate the problem and Padre Mellersh 'found it desirable to go down with the drafts and help men out of the *estaminets* and shepherd them to the train and at least save them from the women and men who fattened on the British soldier and robbed him of his money, health and honour.'[76] These measures were not enough to stop the high incidence of venereal disease, which accounted for over a quarter of the admissions of soldiers to hospital for disease during the war. Stoppages of pay for those infected and losing your place in the leave roster were similarly ineffective.[77] The military authorities, in conjunction with the local French civil authorities, therefore instituted what were called *maisons tolerées*. These were approved brothels, which were regularly inspected and were open to British troops at set hours. This certainly helped to reduce the incidence of VD: that at Rouen served no less than 171,000 British soldiers during its first year of operation, but only 243 VD cases were recorded.[78] At home, however, there was a growing outcry over the army's liberal attitude to the brothels. Matters came to a head in March 1918, when the War Cabinet felt forced to consider the matter. Lord Derby in a memorandum dated the 15th stated: 'My opinion is that unless we take some steps, the outburst of indignation will continue to increase and might have a far reaching effect upon the good-will of the most respectable part of the community towards the Government and the National cause.' He believed that there were two options. If the *maisons tolerées* were placed totally out of bounds, it would require a significant number of men to enforce the ban; further, it would merely lead to an increase in VD. On the other hand, Derby pointed out that Lord Sydenham, Chairman of the Royal Commission on Venereal Disease, did not believe that the *maisons tolerées* acted as much as a safeguard, 'and particularly so at the present time when medical authorities have not the time to inspect them daily and hourly as they should do to prevent contamination.' Alternatively, those establishments about which the local French population had protested could be placed off limits, but there were no confirmed incidents of such protests. Attached to Derby's submission was a table showing the number of VD admissions worldwide to military hospitals for the week ended 2 March 1918. Nearly 60 per cent of first time admissions were in Britain itself, indicating the difficulty that the military authorities had in controlling the problem at home. There was only one case in India and none in the Middle East, where the army regulated brothels. There were ten cases in the Colonies while the remainder had occurred in France, with Paris and Amiens having significantly higher totals than other places.

The War Cabinet did not hesitate. On 18 March it considered the subject. The Adjutant General warned that closing the approved brothels would result in an increase and not a decline in VD, pointing out that some 8,000 men in France were currently infected – the equivalent to putting a complete division out of action. But J. L. Macpherson stated that it was a national and not just a military matter and to maintain the status quo would not be defendable in Parliament. Consequently, the War Cabinet decided that the *maisons tolerées* in France should be placed out of bounds and that the French and Canadian systems for dealing with VD should be investigated. GHQ issued a GRO to this effect on 27 April, but Haig was not happy. On 4 June he wrote to the War Office stating that the War Cabinet decision had been promulgated, but expressing his reservations. He reiterated the need for military police to picket the *maisons tolerées*, stating that 350–400 additional men were needed, and these had to be of good physique, which meant drawing them from 'the ranks of those fit for active military duties.' Secondly, there was strong evidence that 'the women who used to belong to the *maisons tolerées*' were becoming 'women *en carte* [registered prostitutes] on the streets'. The result 'will be that instead of facilities being to some extent localised, men will be subjected to still more frequent temptation in whatever direction they may go, when perhaps at the time they have no intentions of this nature.' This was certain to increase radically the incidence of VD and he supported this claim with figures on infected prostitutes in Paris for the year 1917. Only 1.4 per cent of those in *maisons tolerées* were affected, compared with 19.8 per cent of registered street prostitutes and 36.3 per cent of 'clandestine prostitutes'. Haig also implied that the situation at home was a good deal worse than in France, stating that VD cases among his men originating in France over the period January–May 1918 was 6,767, while those caused in Britain were 8,395. 'These figures are very striking when it is borne in mind how rare, comparatively speaking, are the occasions on which men go home on leave,' he commented, although his case was slightly spoilt by ignoring the fact that a number of the home-based cases were likely to have occurred among drafts newly arrived in France. Haig ended his letter by regretting that his views had not been sought prior to the War Cabinet decision.[79] In summary, the War Cabinet allowed itself to be swayed by righteous indignation at home over military pragmatism in France.

There were also recreation rooms, both at home and abroad, the first in France being opened by the Church Army in February 1915. Norman Gladden frequented a Soldiers' Home at Newmarket in summer 1916. It provided 'light refreshments at nominal charges, had a reading and writing room with plenty of magazines, also a lecture hall fitted up with a stage'. Padre Julian Bickersteth ran a recreation room for the 56th Division in France at much the same time: 'We take forty or fifty francs a day by selling 1d cups of tea and 1d pieces of cake. The library is made use of to the full. We have nearly 300 volumes, and 150 are always "out".' Padre Grice-Hutchinson ran a similar institution for the divisional ammunition column of the 32nd Division. This was thanks to 'a very nice lending library sent out from home'.[80] The most famous of these institutions was undoubtedly Talbot House in Poperinghe, which can still be seen today, and was established by the Reverend Tubby Clayton MC at the end of 1915. Known as Toc H, from the signallers' phonetic alphabet, this provided a veritable haven of peace and quiet for those fighting in the Ypres salient.

A further source of entertainment were the divisional concert parties, which were based on the music halls. The first of these, the '2nd Division Follies', was apparently set up at the end of 1914.[81] A. D. Gillespie wrote in March 1915 that the Follies gave daily performances,

> with two French girls to help them. They are really very good, songs and stories, step-dancing and so go on for a couple of hours. The male performers are of course soldiers, but I think they are struck off their other duties, and certainly they deserve to be, for they do good work in keeping everybody cheerful.

The two French girls themselves lived in Armentières, and seem to have performed with whichever division was stationed in the area. In January 1915 they appeared with the '4th Division Follies' under the stage names Glycerine and Vaseline. That autumn they were with the 50th Division's 'Jesmond Jesters', though Glycerine had by now changed her name to Lanoline. When Julian Bickersteth became the senior chaplain of the 56th Division, he found that one of his duties was acting as treasurer to the division's concert party, the 'Bow Bells': 'It really is a "slap-up" affair. All the men are professionals; they never go into the trenches, but practise continually, and their job is to amuse the men. Their leave they use for visiting music halls, picking up tips.' Such was the demand that the 58th Division's 'Goods' performed no less than 250 shows during its first year.[82] While there were established theatres in which the concert parties performed, they sometimes found themselves appearing at some very makeshift venues. A member of the 47th Division's 'Follies' stated that they appeared in 'sundry corps schools, barns, aeroplane-hangars, farmyards, hospitals, concentration-camps, fields, middens, and other rubbish heaps, by electric light, gaslight, candle light, acetylene, daylight, and in the dark.' In March 1918, probably because of the manpower crisis, the strength of the 47th Division's 'Follies' was decreased and three times during that year it was temporarily disbanded, its members being attached to field ambulances.[83]

There were also professional entertainment groups. These originated with the formation of the Ladies' Auxiliary Committee of the YMCA under Princess Helena Victoria in December 1914, with a view to providing recreation huts and sending out concert parties to France. The latter was organized by the actress and theatre manager Lena Ashwell and the first performance was given at Harfleur on 8 February 1915. At their peak, there were no less than twenty-five Lena Ashwell travelling concert parties in France, giving 14,000 performances per year. There were also twelve permanent concert parties at the bases and six theatrical groups. In addition, two concert parties were sent to Malta and another to Egypt.[84]

It is revealing to see what was being taught in spring 1917 to potential commanding officers at the Senior Officers School, Aldershot, about how to keep their men entertained when enjoying a brief spell out of the line. The initial priorities were supplies of rum, Oxo and tea to greet the men when they arrived in their billets. It was suggested that regimental funds could be used to this end. Baths and pay had to be taken care of on the first day out of the trenches, although the students were warned that the field cashier only paid money on certain days. The battalion second-in-command and the padre were tasked with laying on a performance by the divisional concert party and for a performance by the divisional band. Battalions did not take their full bands to war with them, taking merely some drums and bugles and, in the case of Scottish and Irish regiments, pipes. However, drummers, buglers and pipers also had other tasks within the unit and their music was secondary. In 1915, however, it was authorized for each division to have a band and the regiments within the formation took it in turns to furnish their band, which was based at the regimental depot. It performed for units, at drumhead services, horse shows, sports meetings and parades. In the case of our notional battalion, the CO's idea was that it would play for the men and then stay on to accompany dinner in the officers mess. Arrangements were to be made for it to receive refreshments afterwards. Apart from the divisional concert party, the second-in-command and padre were also told to lay on a battalion concert, akin to the Follies but more intimate. The second-in-command was additionally charged with establishing whether there was a divisional or brigade canteen close by and ensuring that it was well stocked. If the canteen situation was unsatisfactory, the padre was to establish a regimental canteen. The CO also laid down that the local *estaminets* must be stocked with beer. If they had none, the second-in-command was to arrange for stocks to be obtained. Finally, enquiries were to be made of division via brigade HQ 'with regard to giving leave to deserving Officers to such places as Paris, and to a percentage of all ranks to visit Amiens, St Omer, etc.' A knock-out five-a-side football competition was also to be laid on.[85] This was the ideal to which COs should aspire, but it could seldom be met in practice. Training requirements, including absorbing new drafts and the likelihood that the battalion would be required to furnish working parties, lack of available transport and other factors would serve to confound the best-laid plans.

Divisional horse shows and, in the Middle East, race meetings, also helped to pass the time when at rest. In France a few units even managed to play polo during the first year of the war. Another pastime for some cavalry regiments was hunting, with both foxhounds and beagles, but after French complaints that the British were not taking the war seriously enough this was stopped.

A further form of entertainment, which became increasingly popular, was the cinema. In France the organization of this also came under the ASC's Expeditionary Force Canteen section. Billie Nevill of the 8th East Surreys refers to going to a performance at the 'divisional cinema' in October 1915. An ASC 'convoy of about twenty cars' took members of the battalion from their billets and returned them after 'a really fairly good show'. By the winter of 1916–17 Armentières could boast two cinemas. Padre Grice-Hutchinson, stopping off at a rest camp at Etaples on the way back from a chaplain's course at Saint Omer in April 1917 went to 'an enormous hut, where we saw a capital cinematograph. It was absolutely crammed, and the man told us that more than a quarter of a million soldiers had been in since it opened.'[86] At the same time, the Fourth Army alone could boast twenty-five cinemas, attracting 40,000 troops per week.[87] The EFC organization also supplied at least one mobile cinema in France.[88] The cinema reached the other theatres of war as well. A Cinema Company RE was established in Mesopotamia in July 1917 and based in Baghdad. It had an establishment of one officer and fifty-one other ranks, which operated in six detachments deployed throughout the region. They showed feature films and material issued by the War Office and by early March 1918 had laid on over 800 cinema shows, attracting a total audience of over one million.[89]

During the first year of the war the troops in France were also the benefactors of much charity from home. It was initiated by the Royal Family for Christmas 1914. An ACI issued on 10 December announced that every man serving with the BEF on Christmas Eve, as well as those who had returned to Britain and the next of kin of the dead, would receive a gift box containing a Christmas card, a photograph of Princess Mary, a packet of cigarettes and an ounce of pipe tobacco. Non-smokers received a writing case in lieu of tobacco. Two days later, a further ACI stated that the King and Queen would give a personal Christmas card to every man serving in France and Flanders and who was sick or wounded at home as a result of service with the BEF.[90] The Christmas cards were distributed remarkably quickly. III Corps noted the receipt of 45,100 on 20 December, together with 200 special cards for the sick and wounded.[91] The distribution of the Princess Mary gift boxes did not go so smoothly, but they were nevertheless much appreciated.

Other organizations did their bit to ensure that Christmas in the trenches would be as festive as the circumstances allowed. The *Daily Mail* organized a supply of Christmas puddings and the proprietors of a number of newspapers arranged free deliveries to France. A wide variety of items was supplied. The National Egg Society provided over 44 million eggs to hospitals during the war. Lady Roberts' (wife of the Field Marshal) Field Glass Fund supplied 300 pairs of binoculars per month, while Miss Gladys Story's Bovril Fund sent out jars of this beef extract to all theatres. During the first year of the war alone some £5 million of comforts were supplied to the army and the navy.[92]

The War Office did, however, become discomfited by the appeals for additional clothing for the men in the trenches, since these implied the supply system was inefficient. Sir John Cowans was unhappy about a report carried by the *Daily Chronicle* on 2 February 1915. It stated that Lady French (wife of Sir John), who had established a fund to provide winter clothing, had observed that there had been a significant drop in contributions from the public, which was under the mistaken impression that the troops at the Front were adequately clothed. Lady French claimed she was

> constantly receiving letters from commanding officers of units at the front asking for comforts. Clothing wears out very quickly under such trying conditions, and it is essential that there should be a continuous supply of such things as shirts, socks, underclothing, woollen caps and gloves, etc, to make good this wastage.

Cowans checked with his Director of Equipment and Ordnance Stores (DEOS), who denied that any clothing shortages existed. Cowans then spoke to one of French's daughters, who supported what her mother had said, although she did concede that the report of constant requests from COs was 'incorrect', but that two, those of the 1st and 2nd Argylls, *had* written to Lady French. She commented: 'It is difficult to know what to do to be right, as one day one is told that comforts are very badly wanted, and the next that they are an encumbrance.' Cowans therefore decided to let sleeping dogs lie.[93] In June 1915, however, an ACI was published forbidding officers 'to advertise their personal wants or to make any such appeal to public charity on behalf of the troops.' But the matter resurfaced the following winter. Cowans received a letter which had been submitted to the *Daily Mail* for publication and had been passed to him by the editor. The author was the wife of an officer in a Service battalion of the West Yorkshires. She wrote that her husband had told her that 'the plight of some of his poor men is pitiable. They are most of them without socks at all, many without shirts, and their boots are in a terrible condition'. She went on to plead for the public to send clothing parcels to France. Cowans sent details of this to General Sir Ronald Maxwell, the QMG in France, asking him to investigate the matter, commenting that 'it is a very curious thing, which we cannot make out, that we are having constant complaints about the want of shirts and socks particularly … the issues to France seem absolutely adequate'. Brigadier General Harold Tagart, the DA&QMG of the Third Army, investigated this and similar complaints. He wrote to Maxwell on 21 December 1915 that he could identify no shortages. He went on:

What I think is not realized at home by the people who write, and even by the QMG, that although there is no shortage, the man who is in the trenches and exposed to this awful weather will always say he wants more socks, and more shirts, and as long as he only has 2 shirts allowed him and 3 pairs socks he will continue to want more. So should I in his place, but that can't be helped.[94]

The War Office did not, however, want to ban or to discourage comforts and in September 1915 established the department of the Director-General of Voluntary Organisations (DGVO) under Sir Edward Ward to coordinate voluntary aid. It covered both gifts to war theatres and to hospitals. Some organizations did, however, retain their independence. These were Queen Mary's Needlework Guild, which supplied over 15.5 million items during the war, and the Joint War Committee, which oversaw the activities of the Red Cross and St John of Jerusalem. Regimental associations were also exempt. The DGVO established a 'comforts pool', which was responsible for the distribution of goods, in every theatre of war. Apart from handmade items, his department distributed cigarettes (just under 233 million), tobacco and games. Books, magazines and even false teeth also came under his remit.[95]

The British soldier has always had a fondness for animals and 1914–18 was no exception. Father Steuart:

We picked up dogs as children pick up measles. They joined us from every village on the march. They appeared hopefully, with ingratiating waggles, in the most unlikely desert places, and were always welcomed … Some few of them were faithful to the end; but the majority moved on, when the fancy took them, to any other unit that they might chance to meet.

One of the faithful few was Windy, a large black mongrel dog, who was adopted by the 1st Lincolns and served with them on Gallipoli, earning two wound stripes which he wore on his collar. Wounded again, with his master, early on 17 August at Third Ypres, they passed through the evacuation chain together, both ending up at No. 3 Canadian Hospital outside Boulogne. His master was then evacuated to England, brokenhearted that

Windy was not allowed to go with him because of quarantine laws. The dog remained behind, looked after by the head doctor at the hospital, but, once his fractured leg was well on the mend he became bored. Having been used only to soldiers he began to attack French civilians and was eventually poisoned by one.[96]

Another veteran was a cat called Dublin. He was originally acquired by 5 Battery RFA as a kitten from a public house in Leeds shortly after the outbreak of war. The battery, including Dublin, joined the 8th Division and crossed to France with it. Sidney Rogerson described him as

> large, black, and plebeian, and what he did not know about trench warfare was not worth knowing. Could he not tell which way a shell was coming, and to watch him was to have a shrewd idea of whether it was likely to burst close by or not. If he did not move there was no need to worry.

Dublin survived until the end and was taken back to Ireland by one of the division's veterinary officers.[97]

Other units, especially if they were serving in other theatres, were able to acquire more exotic pets. The Lincolnshire Yeomanry collected a large menagerie in Egypt during the winter of 1915–16. It included several pidogs, a desert fox and even a mongoose, all of whom helped to break the monotony.[98] But the prize for the most exotic pet must go to the 19th Division in France. In the spring of 1916 General Tom Bridges, the GOC, managed to acquire a lion cub in Paris, whom he called Poilu. He later recalled:

> Poilu soon made himself at home, for he was an amiable beast, and never showed his temper and he stayed with us, running loose, until September 1917 when I was wounded ... He helped to amuse the men and the legend grew that he was being trained to go over the top when he was big enough. He was not difficult to feed and it was one aide-de-camp's job to see that he did not go hungry and this officer could be heard sometimes telephoning, 'Anybody got a dead horse this morning? All right, I'll send a car down for a haunch.'

M. St Helier Evans, who was in the division, remembered seeing Bridges driving his staff car with Poilu in the back. 'Now we can say we have saluted a lion', he commented. Poilu himself then went to a private zoo in England and lived until the age of 19.[99]

Much of life in the British Army of 1914–18 was tedious and uncomfortable. The authorities were, however, very conscious of the fact that attention to soldiers' welfare was essential for maintaining morale. They also recognized that inactivity meant a disgruntled soldier and that every effort had to be made to keep the men occupied. In the war theatres, especially France and Flanders, time out of the line was often largely occupied in training and labouring tasks, as well as personal administration. But in between times there was a surprising range of leisure activities available, although it was inevitable that those in the rear areas would benefit more from them than the fighting troops. It must also be remembered that before the days of radio and television, people were used to providing their own entertainment and the ordinary soldier often obtained just as much pleasure from an impromptu singsong, sometimes accompanied by a mouth organ, as he did from more organized recreations. As for the staples of mail, food and leave, the first named was undoubtedly one of the success stories of the war. Food, while often monotonous, was usually substantial and better than many at the lower levels of society were used to in civilian life. Home leave was probably the most contentious subject and it is clear that many in France obtained it too infrequently. On the other hand, some of those in more far-flung theatres, especially the Territorial divisions sent overseas in 1914, did not see their homes for over four years.

fifteen

HONOURS AND AWARDS

On 13 August 1915, CSM Ernest Shephard of the 1st Dorsets noted in his diary:

> I read where a baker in the ASC is granted 'The Distinguished Conduct Medal' *for turning out* the maximum amount of *bread*. Ye Gods, what an insult to a *fighting soldier*, who risks life daily. What are the authorities thinking about to award medals in this way and bring contempt on what should be a prized honour? When will the man who washes the steps at the War Office get this medal? He deserves it as much as the ASC baker.[1]

His bitterness reflected the feelings of many front-line soldiers during the middle part of the war and the thorny question of awards and decorations was one that took time to evolve a reasonably equitable answer.

At the beginning of the war the only distinctions open to the army were the Victoria Cross, the Order of the Bath, the Distinguished Service Order (DSO), the Distinguished Conduct Medal (DCM) and the Meritorious Service Medal (MSM). The VC was open to all ranks and was specifically for bravery under fire, while the Order of the Bath, with its three classes of commander, knight commander and grand commander, was for officers of the rank of major and above. The order also had a civil branch, which during the war was awarded to officers who did not see active service. Thus, Sir John Cowans, the Quartermaster General throughout the war, was awarded the civil version of the CB during the war, but was advanced in 1919 to GCB

(Military).[2] The DSO, which had been instituted in 1886, was essentially aimed at officers below the rank of full colonel and was for meritorious or distinguished conduct in time of war. The DCM, which had originally been established to recognize meritorious service by sergeants only when it was introduced in 1845, was from the Crimean War onwards opened up to all non-commissioned ranks for 'distinguished conduct in the field'. It also attracted a gratuity of £20 on retirement or an addition to a recipient's pension of sixpence per day. The MSM was for senior NCOs and warrant officers. It could be awarded on two grounds. One was for long and meritorious service and this, too, attracted an annuity of £20, though each arm and service had a fixed total. Thus, the cavalry was allowed £780, representing thirty-nine serving or retired men. Only when one died could another MSM award be made to a cavalryman. The other reason for awarding this medal was for valuable and meritorious service in a campaign which had earned the recipient a Mention in Despatches. In these cases the soldier was granted an annuity if discharged and qualifying for a pension, and otherwise a straight gratuity. One final award was that of the Royal Red Cross (RRC), which was open to nurses and to the administrative services connected with military and auxiliary hospitals. Officers of field rank could also receive brevet promotions.

At the outbreak of war the Commander-in-Chief of the BEF in France was allotted five DSOs and an unlimited number of DCMs per month which he could personally award. Recommendations in addition to these had to be referred to the War Office. Sir John French announced the first awards list from his allocation in the Expeditionary Force General Routine Orders of 23 September. Five DSOs and twenty-two DCMs were awarded for 'gallantry and devotion to duty in the field'. The first awards list in the *London Gazette* appeared on 22 October 1914 and contained just the DCM winners announced by French a month earlier. A further list appeared on 8 November. This showed sixteen DSO recipients – six subalterns, eight captains and two majors – and a further twenty-three DCMs. Again, all were for acts of bravery on the battlefield. There was, however, a growing feeling that some form of distinction should be drawn between acts of gallantry by junior officers and those of field rank. Battalion commanders and their equivalents often displayed courage in a different form to the young lieutenant leading his platoon. In consequence, and apparently on the initiative of Kitchener, a new award was initiated at the end of December 1914, the Military Cross. It was originally open to officers below the rank of major and to warrant officers, but was extended in June 1917 to cover acting and temporary majors, as well as chaplains 3rd class. Following the practice of the time, the recipient was not entitled to put the initials MC after his name; this privilege was only accorded to VC holders and members of orders of chivalry, which included the DSO, as a means of establishing the order of precedence on formal occasions. Furthermore, as with the DSO, but not the DCM, an officer or warrant officer could not be awarded the MC more than once, a regulation that was to prove increasingly frustrating when it came to acknowledging repeated acts of bravery. The first MC list was published in the *London Gazette* on 1 January 1915. It contained the names of sixty-three British officers, five Indian native officers and twenty-seven warrant officers. Among them was Lieutenant J. H. S. Dimmer KRRC, who had already been awarded the Victoria Cross during First Ypres.

The next development came in January 1915 when the Order of St Michael and St George, open only to the Colonial Service, was extended to the armed forces to cover 'services during the present war'. As with the Order of the Bath, the lowest rank, that of commander, could not be conferred on officers below the rank of major. Thus another award was now available to more senior officers for actions not directly connected to the battlefield. Even so, it began to become general practice that officers on the staff and on the lines of communication, especially those below field rank, were awarded DSOs and MCs, to the fury of the front-line troops. Guy Chapman, when a staff learner at a corps headquarters in early 1917, recalls one of the ADCs, who had been wounded in the stomach at Loos, saying to him one day:

> The old man has just offered me the MC for the fourth time. I've refused again. Damn it, if I couldn't pick one up with the Brigade of Guards I'm not going to pick it up this way. He's given one to that little squirt he's just taken on. It isn't decent.[3]

In the autumn of 1915, D. H. Pratt, a sapper officer, developed a new trench mortar fuse, which he successfully demonstrated at the Second Army Trench

Mortar School in front of a galaxy of British and French generals. That evening the school received a telegram from Army HQ: 'To the Commandant of the Trench Mortar School – Congratulations. DSO and Military Cross.' These were for the commandant and adjutant.

> One subaltern cried out 'but it's your fuse.' I was not disturbed. If the Army Commander had received such enthusiastic reports as to send out decorations wholesale within six hours of the demonstration, I was amply rewarded ... In this case it went round all the trench mortar batteries that all officers at the base had been decorated before a single mention [in despatches] was awarded to the front line troops.[4]

Certainly, the commandant had his DSO gazetted on 14 January 1916. The same applied to the rank and file, and hence CSM Shephard's outburst. And he was right about the likes of ASC bakers being awarded the DCM. In 1916, one ASC sergeant was awarded the medal 'for conspicuous ability, tact and zeal in the performance of his duties as Chief Clerk in the office of the Assistant Director of Supplies, Boulogne' and another went to a staff sergeant major of the ASC 'for continuous good services throughout the campaign as Master Baker in charge of a bakery'.[5] Incidents like these made a total mockery of the awards system. On the other hand, given the restrictions on the MSM, there was nothing else with which to reward deserving men who were not serving within the combat zone.

Matters for the ordinary front-line soldier improved with the introduction of the Military Medal (MM) in March 1916. This was specifically 'For Bravery in the Field', which was inscribed on the reverse of the medal. It was initially open to just NCOs and men, but was later extended, on 1 August 1918, to include warrant officers as well. Furthermore, the MM could be given more than once, through the award of bars, to the same recipient, a reform which was also applied to the DSO, MC and RRC later in 1916. Not until early 1918, however, were recipients entitled to wear rosettes to signify bars on their medal ribands. At the same time, VC winners were granted the right to have a miniature of the cross on the riband.[6]

Some old soldiers thought little of the MM, however. Private Frank Richards of the 2nd Royal Welsh Fusiliers, winner of both the DCM and MM, besides being one of the very few to serve with the battalion throughout the war, said that this was because no financial reward went with it. Indeed, he thought cynically that it had been introduced merely to save money: 'for every DCM awarded there were fifty Military Medals.'[7] In June 1916, by royal warrant, the MM was made open to women 'under exceptional circumstances on the special recommendation of a Commander-in-Chief in the Field' for those 'who have shown bravery and devotion under fire.'[8] Among the first to receive it were five nurses in September 1916 for treating the wounded under artillery fire at No. 33 CCS at Bethune.[9] The Press, on occasion, asked why it was that nurses, who had officer status, were not entitled to the MC. The answer was that, like officials in the other uniformed women's organizations, they could not be considered as officers *per se* for legal reasons. However, the Matron-in-Chief in France, in her final report on awards to nurses, made the pointed comment: 'The Nursing Service, as a whole, have considered it a great honour to be given a medal which is awarded *solely** for bravery in the field.'[10]

There were also cases where the MM was awarded for acts carried out long before its inception. Captain Hitchcock of the 2nd Leinsters recorded in his diary on 28 September 1916: 'News came of some very belated honours for the Battalion, Capt Poole, CSM Boyer, CSM Bradley, and a few men being the recipients of the Military Medal for bravery at Premesques in October, 1914! Shortly after this action in 1914 Poole had been promoted on the field from CSM.'[11] To speed up the award of MMs, it was laid down that they could be awarded by corps commanders. 1916 also saw MC winners being allowed to put the initials after their names, a concession which was eventually extended to all other awards at the end of 1917.[12]

In spite of the introduction of new awards and reforms to existing ones, awards of the DSO, MC and DCM continued to be made to individuals for services behind the lines. The problem was that the statutes governing them did not specify that they should be for actions under fire and for junior officers and other ranks there was still nothing else available to reward other services, apart from the MSM and a Mention in Despatches. Thus, Canadian Peter Nissen, who in 1916 invented the metal hut which bears his name while working in the Engineer-in-Chief's office at GHQ in France, was awarded the DSO, which was gazetted in February 1917. The CB or CMG would have

*Author's italics.

been more appropriate, but Nissen was only an acting major at the time and was not eligible. The fighting troops did not appreciate this and continued to believe that awards which should have been made to them were being diverted to the less deserving in the rear areas. Arthur Osburn, who was a front-line doctor in France from August 1914 onwards and won two DSOs, railed against 'these sleek darlings', who,

> without ever having heard the whisper of a passing bullet, scorning mere mentions in despatches, became miraculously decorated with foreign orders and Military Crosses, and great was the bitterness and discontent amongst the ordinary fighting soldier, wet to the hips in foul mud and generally living under conditions that no sanitary inspector would consider fit for a pig on an English farm.[13]

Many of these individuals were able to obtain their awards through the half-yearly honours lists, which were published on 3 June and 1 January each year. The front-line troops' reaction is well summed up by Captain Adrian Hodgkin, commenting on that for January 1917: 'The honours list is out today; the higher officials of the Army have done well; not so the more humble ones. The list always gives rise to more ferocity among the expectant but disappointed than any Boche atrocity.'[14] There was also frustration among COs that so many of their recommendations were being turned down. The CO of the 22nd Royal Fusiliers wrote to the wife of his adjutant, Christopher Stone, after his MC recommendation for Stone had been turned down:

> It went right through to the War Office, I believe , & was recommended by everyone – All our honours list were returned, except mine [awarded DSO], & Brigadiers were told to cut them down to 7 officers a Brigade & 8 men. It is most unjust – either 150 offrs. & men did gallant deeds deserving of a decoration or they did not. It's grossly unfair to pick out 15, as starred performers, & let the other 135 extra brave men get nothing ...[15]

The resentment also encompassed mentions in despatches. Brigadier General Archibald Home, chief of staff of the Cavalry Corps noted in his diary on 21 May 1918:

> Another Gazette out and I suppose the usual recriminations will follow.
> I wish that they would do away with 'Mentions in Despatches'. It leads
> to a lot of heart burning and is really prostituted: one sees the same
> names over and over again – myself included. I shall get really hated if
> this goes on.[16]

Home himself was mentioned no less than seven times during the course
of the war.

Divisional commanders were equally frustrated and a growing number
instituted certificates which they issued to men who had performed deeds
of merit for which it had not proved possible to obtain awards. Some unit
commanders even created their own unofficial medals. Arthur Osburn used
his field ambulance's canteen profits to obtain silver and bronze medals from
Paris to reward those whose recommendations had been turned down.[17] On
other occasions, COs and other senior officers gave out rewards of money. M.
St Helier Evans of the 9th Welsh recounted an occasion in August 1916 when
some of his men successfully repulsed a German raid. The brigade
commander and the CO each gave those involved fifty francs as a reward.[18]
Another way of rewarding men was giving them additional leave. This was
often offered by formations for capturing a live German prisoner. Thus, in
December 1916 a subaltern of 2 HAC and his runner were each given ten
days leave for doing this.[19] On the other hand, there were instances when
some felt that awards were given out too unnecessarily to fighting troops.
Norman Gladden recounted that, after a successful raid by his battalion on
the Asiago Plateau in Italy in June 1918, the divisional commander personally
decorated all the NCOs who had taken part. 'We felt at the time that the
indiscriminate distribution of medals for a purely routine performance of
this sort was bound to detract from the value of awards truly earned.'[20] Cecil
Slack, himself an MC winner, echoed this in a letter home in October 1916:
'In reading the recent lists of awards one gets very disgusted at some of them,
not that they are not deserved, but because they get given for deeds which are
done every day as a matter of course.'[21] Private Jimmy Taylor of the 2nd
Worcesters even claimed that a dimwit was awarded the DCM after going
missing for twenty-four hours after taking part in a trench raid and making it back to the battalion's trenches. 'It was no wonder such decorations

were held in contempt, instead of being the inspiration and example they should have been.'[22]

Conscious of the continuing discontent among the fighting element of the army, the War Office began to institute further reforms towards the end of 1916. In October that year the MSM was extended to cover junior ranks. At the same time, the number of monthly immediate awards which commanders in the field could make was increased sharply. Then, in January 1917, the conditions of award of the MSM were redefined. It could now be given for devotion to duty in a theatre of war, and for gallant conduct not in the face of the enemy, such as saving life. In the case of the latter, a pension of sixpence per day was awarded. The third circumstance remained the 'dead men's shoes' award of the medal with annuity. Steps were also taken to restrict the awards of the DSO, MC and DCM. The Army Council considered the matter at the end of November 1916:

> In considering the selection of officers and men for honours and decorations a clear distinction should be drawn between the claims of those serving in formations in direct contact with the enemy, such as Divisions and lower formations, and those officers and men who are employed in the more distant areas of the Armies and Lines of Communication, or who are training and administering the Forces of the Crown elsewhere.[23]

Accordingly, on 1 January 1917 theatre commanders were instructed to restrict these decorations to the 'Fighting Services' and to exclude GHQs and the rear areas. In future, they were to submit two separate lists: A for the fighting services; B for the remainder. Allied to the List A awards, was the institution of immediate awards 'for Conspicious Gallantry in Action' with citations published in the London Gazette, whereas the other awards were merely listed. On 1 April, the allowance of decorations granted to Douglas Haig, which had already been gradually increased as the size of the BEF grew, was fixed at 200 DSOs and 500 MCs per month, and from May 1918 he was permitted to award as many as he liked, provided that existing standards were maintained. The other theatres of war also had allowances in proportion to the strength of British forces involved. Thus, Salonika was permitted ten DSOs and twenty MCs per month and Mesopotamia the same, although the latter's allowance was doubled in January 1918.[24] By the summer of 1917, as Padre Bickersteth, noted, 'the GOC [brigade commander] can give an MC at the Front within twenty-four hours after the brave act has been committed, and a Divisional General a DSO within forty-eight hours; only for the latter there must be two witnesses.'[25]

The intention was that those on List B should be awarded a new order which was being drawn up. This was the Order of the British Empire (OBE), which was formally instituted in June 1917. It was a blanket order to recognize 'services to the Empire', was open to women as well as men and consisted of five classes and a medal. Military recipients, it was stressed, were to be rewarded for services of a non-combatant nature. The first list was published in August 1917 and contained a mere 320 names, but the second, in January 1918, filled no less than three and a half pages of *The Times*. The impression was that the order was being devalued and, indeed, Brigadier Sir Ivan de la Bere, secretary of the Central Chancery of Knighthood, later conceded: 'There is no doubt that many of the recipients of appointments in the Order of the British Empire had not done anything sufficiently important to deserve an Order of any kind.'[26] Military recipients felt particularly bitter that their devotion to duty in theatres of war abroad should be put on the same level as profiteers at home, who had merely lined their own pockets. Furthermore, the responsibility for approving British Empire awards was in the hands of the Home Office, and civilians and military were lumped alphabetically in the same list with no indication whether the awards were for services in the field or at home. In the face of a growing outcry, the Secretary of State for War proposed to His Majesty at the end of August 1918 that a separate military division of the order be established and this was instituted at the end of that December.

In the meantime, because the Home Office regulated the number of military awards of the Order of the British Empire, those in List B often failed to receive recognition and awards of the DSO and MC continued to be made to them. The Army Council considered the problem again in September 1917. They toyed with the idea of instituting two classes for these decorations: Class I for the fighting services and Class II for the remainder. They could be distinguished by different ribands or emblems worn on the ribands. The Military Members of the Council were not in favour and there the matter rested, but there was still discontent at the

Front. The Hon. Ralph Hamilton, who was commanding an RFA brigade in France, noted on 5 January 1918:

> To-day we got *The Times* with the New Year Honours. Not a single thing for this brigade. It is very disheartening after all the hard fighting of this last year. I had put several officers in for the Military Cross, all of whom had richly earned some reward. As usual, the Staff got the rewards.[27]

However, at the end of June 1918 a committee under the presidency of the Military Secretary was tasked with re-examining the September 1917 proposals. It included among its members a battalion and a company commander, a brigade commander and a divisional commander, as well as divisional and corps staff officers. The Military Secretary admitted that up until early 1916 there had been a considerable number of awards of DSOs and MCs for services in the rear areas and it was only since the introduction of the Order of the British Empire that something positive could be done to rectify the situation. An analysis by the Military Secretary's branch of the birthday honours list published in the *London Gazette* of 3 June was shown to the committee. It covered the period 26 September 1917 to 25 February 1918, contained a total of 8,956 names, and covered all orders, decorations and medals, apart from the MM which was solely an immediate award, and the OBE, which, of course, was not in the War Office's control. The figures also included general officer promotions and brevets. During the period there had also been 25,108 immediate awards of the DSO, MC, DCM, MM and MSM. Awards to senior commanders and the staff represented just over 2 per cent of the overall total, but included all but one of the 58 CBs conferred during the period, 75 per cent of the 197 CMGs, nearly 15 per cent of the DSOs and bars, but only 0.03 per cent of the 5,385 MCs and bars. It did show that the situation was improving, but the committee considered that more could be done. While it agreed with the September 1917 review that it would not be appropriate to create two classes of DSO and MC, it did recommend that both decorations and the DCM should be restricted to 'Services in action'. This was defined as being under fire or 'in connection with air raids, bombardments, or other enemy action which at that time produces conditions equivalent to services in actual combat, and demands the same personal element of command, initiative or control on the part of individuals and, in a lesser degree only, entails the same risks'. A counter-view was taken by Major General C. H. (Tim) Harrington, the DCIGS, who argued that dividing awards into two classes would discourage staff officers from visiting the front lines, though he did concede that immediate awards should be given some distinction from those in the half-yearly honours lists.[28] Nevertheless, the Army Council approved the committee's recommendations and the new conditions for awarding the decorations were promulgated on 1 August. The policy had, however, already begun to bite. C. E. Montague working in the Press & Censorship branch at GHQ in France was told that he could not be recommended for the MC because it was restricted 'to men now fighting at the front'. He had, however, been awarded a decoration in June 1917 – the Order of the Crown of Romania for escorting a Romanian general around the front.[29] He was also later made an OBE. Not all, however, were pleased with the new ruling. Captain Thomas Heald, serving as a GSO3 with the 56th Division, commented:

> Orders have come through that one can't get a Military Cross except for an act of gallantry under fire. For continuous good service one can only get an OBE. Thousands have had the MC by now for the latter services. It does not seem at all right to change now.[30]

Brevet rank continued to be awarded to officers during the war. Although it was primarily for the benefit of Regular officers, brevets could also be given to those holding temporary commissions. The highest brevet rank was full colonel and Regular officers had to have a minimum of twenty years' service to be eligible. It was aimed at brigade commanders, who had been recommended for a division, brigadier generals RA and chief engineers, brigadier generals and colonels on the staff who had rendered good service during the previous twelve months, and Grade 1 staff officers who had been recommended for brigade command but who could not be released from their staff appointments. Brevet lieutenant colonelcies required a minimum of fifteen years' service for Regulars. Brigade commanders, brigadier generals RA, chief engineers, CREs and CRAs were eligible, as were battalion commanders recommended for brigade command, and Grade 1 staff officers who had given good service in the past twelve months. Grade 2 staff officers, 'whose retention on the Staff in the interests of the Service, has manifestly prejudiced their prospects of advancement,' were also eligible. The lowest, brevet major, required Regulars to have a minimum of five years' service. Quartermasters, too, could be rewarded by promotion up to and including the rank of lieutenant colonel and by higher rates of pay.

Brevet rank gave an officer seniority in the army, but not in his own regiment. Occasionally this could result in an unfortunate situation, as was the case with the 1st Gordon Highlanders in August 1914. The battalion was part of the 3rd Division in Smith-Dorrien's II Corps. During the Battle of Le Cateau on 26 August, the division was holding the centre of the line. In the course of the action the Germans managed to force the flanking divisions back, leaving the 3rd Division in danger of being cut off. By late afternoon it, too, was forced to withdraw, but the 1st Gordons and elements of the 2nd Royal Scots and 2nd Royal Irish on their flanks did not receive the order. Commanding the Gordons was Lieutenant Colonel F. H. Neish and his second-in-command was Major & Brevet Colonel W. E. Gordon VC, who was also an honorary ADC to the King. Once they realized that they were on their own, Neish and Gordon agreed that, because the force was a mixed one, the latter officer should take command on account of his brevet rank. By now it was 7 p.m. and the German pressure was increasing. Gordon decided that, once night had fallen, the force should withdraw from its positions. Neish apparently did not believe that they should do so without permission and insisted that an officer be sent back to the village where divisional HQ had been located. Gordon conceded and timed the withdrawal for 12.30 a.m., which allowed plenty of time for the officer, who was the adjutant, to return. In the event, the Germans were in occupation and the officer captured. The withdrawal began on time, with the men successfully leaving their positions without being detected. They had navigation problems, which slowed progress. Eventually, they ran into German troops and attempts to break through failed. Shortly before dawn the force surrendered.

Gordon felt the disgrace keenly and, once installed in the prisoner-of-war camp at Torgau, he drew up a statement in which he accused Neish of dereliction of duty. Gordon claimed that Neish had objected to the withdrawal and had gone to sleep in his trench, in effect absolving himself from his responsibilities as a battalion commander. Once the withdrawal got underway, Gordon ordered Neish to act as navigator to the column, on the grounds that Neish had always boasted of his skill at map reading and seeing in poor light. In any event, Gordon had lost his glasses. He went on to state that Neish's conduct was that 'of a wayward child determined at all costs to give trouble'. In particular, he complained at the pace Gordon was setting and demanded that the men be given a chance to rest. Finally, once they ran into the Germans, it was Neish, according to Gordon, who ordered the men to lay down their arms. There the matter rested until early 1916. Gordon was then exchanged for a German aristocrat who had been interned at Gibraltar on the outbreak of war. No sooner had he arrived back in England than he personally handed his September 1914 report into the Director of Personal Services, Major General F. C. Beatson. But with Neish still a prisoner of war, as were the other witnesses, nothing could be done about it for the time being. As for Gordon, in September 1917 he was appointed to command No. 1 (Midland) District, Scottish Command, which he did until 1920, being made a CBE for his services.

In August 1916, Neish was transferred to Switzerland, presumably because he was in poor health. From there he, too, was repatriated back to Britain. Probably at the request of the Director of Personal Services, he also submitted a statement, which was dated 3 October 1917. In it, he made no mention of ordering his men to lay down their arms and implied that it had been done on an individual basis. He did, however, say that Gordon ordered him and one or two others to come with him and evade capture. After going across two or three fields, Neish told Gordon that he could not desert his battalion and felt that it was his duty to return to his men. Gordon then thought again and also returned, as he admitted on his own statement. But still the War Office was powerless to take any action, since no other witnesses were available. Matters now took an unfortunate turn. Corporal George Mutch, who had also been captured at Le Cateau, arrived back in England, having apparently made a successful escape to Holland. In December 1917, he was interviewed by Cedric Fraser, a journalist on the *People's Journal*, which covered the Gordons' recruiting area in Scotland. In the piece that was published, Mutch is quoted as saying that it was Colonel Gordon who had ordered the men to lay down their arms. Gordon was clearly furious, since he launched a libel action for £5,000 against John Leng and Company, the publishers. A further fly in the ointment was that Neish and at least one of his brothers were shareholders in John Leng. Not until March 1919 were the preliminaries gone through and the action eventually took place in the Court of Sessions, Edinburgh, that July.

In the meantime, with all prisoners of war in Germany now repatriated, the War Office at last took action. It set up a court of inquiry. In the first instance it was to investigate the circumstances of the surrender. This, however, was standard for all officers who became prisoners of war, to ensure that their actions were justified, since Paragraph 555 of *King's Regulations* stated that any officer ordering his men to surrender was liable to be court martialled. Each merely submitted a statement to the War Office, which was considered by a standing court of inquiry, and it would seem that in every case the individual was exonerated. This clearly happened in the case of the 1st Gordons. But the court was also charged with investigating 'the allegations against Lieut. Colonel F H Neish made by Major and Bt.Colonel W E Gordon VC ADC in a report rendered by him dated 16th September 1914, and to report whether those allegations were justified'. Gordon made a request for the court of inquiry to sit after his libel action had been heard, but Neish objected, making plain that the fact that he was a shareholder in John Leng had nothing to do with the matter, since 'I have not attended a meeting of John Leng & Co Ltd for upwards of twenty-five years, nor have I any knowledge of the business of the Company or of the papers owned by it whatever ...'

As it happened, the libel action was heard first. Gordon was the first to take the stand and emphasized that he had been 'on the best of terms' with Neish 'prior to the retreat from Mons'. Under cross-examination, he stated that Neish had given the order to surrender. Another Gordons' officer, Captain A. M'D. Stewart, backed him in this, stating that 'if Colonel Neish had kept his mouth shut the column under Colonel Gordon would have broken through and got back.' Mutch also denied that Gordon had given the order, claiming that Fraser had put words into his mouth and that he had never read the articles that appeared under his name until shown them by Colonel Gordon. Neish, who had retired from the army on health grounds earlier in the year, agreed that Gordon did not give the surrender order. He also said that Mutch had consulted him over publishing his experiences and had been told by Neish to have nothing to do with journalists. When asked, therefore, why he did not write to Gordon to express his regrets over the offending article, he said that when he last spoke with Gordon, in October 1914, the latter had said to him: 'I shall not speak to you again; I will ruin you.' Neish also denied ordering his men to lay down their arms. In the event, the verdict revolved on the matter of whether Fraser had faithfully reported what Mutch had told him. The jury sided with Mutch and Gordon won his case, apparently agreeing to a settlement of £500. The court of inquiry itself sat a few days later, on 29 July 1919. Having heard the evidence from numerous witnesses, including seventeen members of the 1st Gordons (among them Corporal Mutch), who had been present at the surrender, the court retired to consider its findings. It praised Gordon for his conduct during the withdrawal, but made no mention of Neish. In the end, it concluded that 'the Column was captured owing to the chances of war'.[31] The publicity surrounding the sorry saga that had been generated by the court case did little for the Gordons' reputation. It also starkly exposed the problems that brevet rank could bring. While Gordon had assured the court of session that he had been on good terms with Neish until the withdrawal, it is difficult not to conclude that from the outset of the campaign he had a growing conviction that his commanding officer, who was six years his senior in age, was no longer fit to command troops on active service and that he could do the job much better.

The award of foreign decorations provoked much the same anguish among the fighting troops as British awards. Rowland Fielding, commanding the 1st/15th Londons, complained to his wife in the early autumn of 1918:

> These are handed over to our War office in batches, at more or less regular intervals, by all of the Allies. How many ever reach the front line? I have known perhaps half a dozen or so in my experience. Of course, the explanation is that the War Office must have its pick. Then GHQ – France must be satisfied. Then, there are the different Army Headquarters, the Headquarters of all the Corps – not forgetting the Back-area troops, the Divisions and the Brigades. It is not surprising, after so remorseless a filtering, that nothing survives so far forward as the fire-trench, except by accident, and then only if it is very small.[32]

Certainly, of the 26,893 foreign decorations handed out during the war, just over 43 per cent went to the commissioned ranks, a totally disproportionate allocation.[33] This was even though the first award, that of the French *Medaille Militaire,* went to no less than 195 other ranks for their services during 21–30 August 1914.[34] It is difficult, however, without an enormous amount of detailed research, to establish the precise proportion which fell into the hands of the staff, but browsing *War Services of Military Officers* 1919 and *The VC and DSO Book* Volumes II and III does give the impression that the staff did well from foreign decorations, with individuals often being awarded more than one. As Lieutenant Colonel H. M. Davson RFA, who was unsuccessfully recommended for the *Legion d'Honneur,* wryly put it, 'orders bred other orders'.[35] One who did receive this decoration in the summer of 1918 was George Hawes, who was now the AA&QMG of the 35th Division, which was temporarily under French operational command:

> One day, after the operations had been going on for some time, a bag of Medailles Militaires and Legion d'Honneurs arrived at Divisional Head-quarters from General Franchet d'Esperey with a request to distribute them as we thought fit! Jeffreys [divisional commander] asked me what I wanted, and I chose a Legion d'Honneur! We went round the units with the rest, and pinned them on the tunics of officers and men selected by their respective commanders. Our 'citations' or complimentary orders were issued later. A very good and quick way of decorating in the field, and very superior to our cumbersome system, when men often get their medals after they are dead.[36]

Hawes did have a point over citations. Battalion and brigade commanders found it increasingly difficult to draft their recommendations in such a way as to ensure that they would result in an award. Brigadier General F. P. Crozier recommended one of his battalion commanders for the VC after the Battle of Cambrai in November 1917, but the officer only received another bar to his DSO. Crozier complained. '"But he was only doing his duty!" I am told by the red-banded clerk-officer, who has never seen a shot fired.' Clearly, he had not phrased the recommendation in the right way.[37] Rowland Fielding explains how difficult the exercise was in a letter to his wife in September 1918:

In each individual recommendation a 'specific act' must be cited, which, if there is to be any chance of favourable consideration, must be made to 'stand out'. It must be couched in the flamboyant language of the Penny Dreadful, and the result often is that the most deserving cases get cut out by the Authorities, far behind the line, whose function is to decide these matters, and who, as a rule, have no personal or first-hand knowledge of the men or the conditions upon which they pass judgement.[38]

Guy Chapman agreed. Writing of the same period of the war, he noted: 'During the last twelve months, it had become obvious that the award of decorations was chiefly a matter of penmanship. A barren statement of facts was invariably passed over.'[39]

Evidence on the ratio of recommendations to awards given is sparse, but the AA&QMG of the 55th (West Lancashire) Division did keep some records of this nature and they indicate that it enjoyed a high success rate.[40] The division took part in the initial phase of Third Ypres and submitted 399 recommendations for awards for the period 31 July–4 August 1917. Three men were recommended for the VC. One was Captain Noel Chavasse RAMC, who was posthumously awarded a bar,* and another Lieutenant Colonel Bertram Best-Dunkley, CO 2nd/5th Lancashire Fusiliers, who was also awarded a posthumous VC. The third recommendation was also successful. Lance Sergeant Tom Mayson of the 1st/4th King's Own Liverpools lived to receive his VC and survived the war. All three were gazetted on 14 September and announced in divisional routine orders two days later. Of the remainder, the awards announced in divisional routine orders over the period 23 August–13 September 1917 were as follows:[41]

DSO – recommended, 7 plus one bar; awarded, 4 plus one bar
MC – recommended, 64 plus five bars; awarded, 49 plus six bars
DCM – recommended, 69 plus four bars; awarded, 28 plus one bar
MM – recommended, 237 plus 9 bars; awarded, 281 plus 11 bars

It is probable that some were awarded for acts outside the period, and that there were some downgradings from DSO to MC, and certainly from DCM to MM. Nevertheless, the 55th Division could feel pleased with itself for

* He was awarded his first VC at Guillemont on the Somme in July 1916.

having achieved such a success rate. It is clear that DCMs were the most difficult to obtain, probably because of the gratuity that went with them.

One of the division's outstanding performances was its sterling defence of the Givenchy–Festubert sector on the southern shoulder of the German offensive on the Lys in April 1918. Here the evidence is more precise in that the AA&QMG listed the names of all those recommended and noted what award they actually received. That such a high proportion of its recommendations came to fruition is a reflection of how highly regarded the 55th Division's action was at the higher levels of command and it is again worth giving some detailed statistics:

VC – recommended, 4; awarded, 2 (2nd Lieutenant J. H. Collin 1st/4th Royal Lancaster, 2nd Lieutenant J. Scholfield 2nd/5th Lancashire Fusiliers – the other two were downgraded to DCM)

DSO – recommended, 19 (including 7 bars); awarded, 11 (remainder were downgraded to MC)

MC – recommended, 92 (including 19 bars); awarded, 66 (excluding those downgraded from DSO). Of those unsuccessful, two were CSMs who were awarded the DCM instead, and the remainder, apart from two, were noted for future mentions in despatches. The citations of the two exceptions were deemed not to be up to the standard required for the award.

DCM – recommended, 55; awarded, 46 (excluding the two VCs and two MCs downgraded to DCM, but including one MM upgraded to DCM). Those unsuccessful were awarded the MM instead.

MM – recommended, 299 (including 20 bars); awarded, all apart from the one MM upgraded to DCM.

Overall, this represented a success rate of some 90 per cent, which was probably unusually high.

Sometimes after a battle units would be allocated a set number of awards and asked to recommend people for them. Dick Read, temporarily commanding a company in the 4th Royal Sussex, was asked to do this after the battalion had taken part in the Second Battle of the Marne, under XXII Corps, in late July 1918. The allocation was one MC, one DCM and two MMs and Read had no problem in producing names.[42] His DCM recommendation also received the *Medaille Militaire*, while Read himself was awarded the *Croix de Guerre* with Star.

The War Office also introduced other ways of recognizing soldiers' services. In July 1916 the wound stripe was introduced. It was a strip of gold Russian braid, two inches long, worn on the left forearm. One was to be awarded for each wound suffered and was retrospective to the outbreak of war.[43] Most soldiers were proud to wear them, but not all approved. Colonel Rowland Fielding called them 'un-English, besides being absurd. There are a few people who seem to make a hobby of collecting them. It is not difficult. It is only necessary to be gassed, however slightly, in order to appear on a casualty list.'[44] There was, however, a debate over whether a man suffering from shell shock should be entitled to a wound stripe (*see page 428*). Two months later, the King gave approval for a Silver War Badge, which could be worn by all members of the armed forces who had been discharged on the grounds of old age, sickness or wounds.[45]

A feeling also grew that the original BEF should receive recognition for its magnificent performance during the first months of the war. The Army Council considered the matter in February 1917 and concluded that a 1914 clasp to the international medal, which it was intended to introduce after the end of hostilities (this eventually became the Victory Medal), would suffice. However, that July it had a slight change of heart and now believed that a 'special badge' should be given to all who 'left this country in 1914 for service overseas, and to others who having left later have served in a theatre of war'. The Council's attention was focused once more by the King who told Lord Derby at the end of August that he felt that there should be a 'special distinction' for troops who had been serving abroad in 1914. It was clear to Derby that His Majesty was referring to the old BEF and it was in this context that the Army Council reconsidered the matter at two meetings, on 31 August and 1 September 1917. Some members were initially opposed on the grounds that it would create a divide between the Old and New Armies, but the CIGS, Wully Robertson, won them round. It was agreed that a medal called the 1914 Star should be awarded to all those who had served with the BEF up until midnight 22/23 November, when the French carried out a significant relief of the British troops around Ypres. The medal was quickly approved by Buckingham Palace, but there was still some discussion on who should be eligible. Sailors and Royal Marines were to be included, but the Admiralty was initially against the Royal Naval Division being entitled on the grounds that its operations around Antwerp had been independent of those of the BEF. Not until December 1917 did it have a change of heart. In the meantime, on 24 November Army Order 350 was issued, giving details of the 1914 Star. Curiously, though, there appears to have been a problem with the supplies of riband. Even though they were beginning to arrive in ordnance depots in France by mid-January 1918, there seem to have been difficulties in obtaining it. The Hon. Ralph Hamilton happened to be in Amiens on his way to leave in England in early March : 'Our train went at 11.15 and so we tried all the shops for the 1914 ribbon. Apparently it is not allowed to be sold in England, but the enterprising French are making it and selling it to the troops out here.'[46] Whether he was able to obtain it is not revealed. The German offensive, which broke on 21 March, had him hurrying back to reassume command of his RFA brigade, but he was killed before the month was out.

Not all were happy about the 1914 Star. American surgeon Harvey Cushing, who was with a base hospital at Boulogne, had an Old Contemptible as one of his patients in March 1918: 'He's very scornful of all those Mons ribbons being worn by people who were in offices at the base.'[47] This was, however, taken into account, with the bar worn on the riband of the medal and rosette on the riband alone for those had had been in the firing line. Others felt that it was unjust that the Territorial formations which had been sent out to relieve Regular garrisons overseas had been ignored. There were, too, the Indian troops which had taken part in the early operations in Mesopotamia, and, indeed, the Regular units overseas, including those involved in the capture of the German fortress of Tsingtao in China. It was for this reason that, just after the war was over, the 1914–15 Star was introduced for service in a theatre of war before the end of 1915. Likewise, those Territorials who had been serving at the outbreak of war or had rejoined after completing the minimum four years' service and had volunteered for service overseas prior to 30 September 1914, but did not qualify for the 1914 or 1914–15 Stars, were in April 1920 granted the Territorial Force War Medal.

One other form of recognition came in January 1918 with the introduction of service chevrons. The idea came from the French Army, which
was already using them.[48] All those who were or had served overseas, whether
in an active theatre of war or not, were entitled. For the period up until the
end of 1914 a red chevron was awarded. Thereafter, every year's service
overseas earned a blue chevron, the soldier becoming entitled to the first as
soon as he left Britain for overseas. Allowances were made for those who
had been evacuated sick or wounded back to Britain, as well as for a month's
home leave in every twelve months. Time spent absent without leave, in
prison or detention did not account, and neither did hospitalization for
avoidable sickness, which was clearly aimed at self-inflicted wounds and
those suffering from venereal disease. In September 1918, those involved in
conducting drafts and animals overseas became entitled, with the first
chevron being awarded after six such journeys. The chevrons were to be
worn on the right forearm.[49] When the proposal was originally discussed by
the Army Council in April 1917, the Adjutant General had commented: 'By
the time we had finished [the] only place left for decoration would be the
seat of Tommy's trousers.'[50] Nevertheless, the measure was generally
welcomed. One advantage of the chevrons and wound stripes, according
to Charles Carrington, was that one could at a glance take in a soldier's
combat record:

> Look at a man you meet on a leave-train: his cap-badge tells you he belongs
> to a good fighting regiment, but since he has four blue chevrons and no
> wound-stripe you may be confident he has a safe job down the line. His
> neighbour who had one chevron and two wound-stripes has had a very
> different war.[51]

Another injustice was over posthumous awards. The basic rule was that
the only awards which could be made posthumously were the Victoria Cross,
Albert Medal or Mention in Despatches, though the last-named did not merit
any actual medal for the recipient's next of kin. Indeed, it was not until May
1919 that those mentioned received a special certificate signed by the
Secretary of State for War, and recipients had to wait until January 1920
before a bronze oak leaf was issued to wear over the victory medal riband.
Additionally, during the first part of the war, if the officer or soldier had

been killed or had died before the theatre commander-in-chief approved the recommendation, the award was not made. But often the wheels of bureaucracy ground slowly, especially in more far-flung theatres of war, where communications were often slow. This was rectified by laying down that the award was legitimate provided that the recipient was still alive when his commanding officer made the initial recommendation. As for the rule on posthumous awards, this remained in force until the 1982 Falklands War.

The honours and awards system with which the army went to war may have suited the old Regular Army fighting colonial campaigns, but its deficiencies were soon exposed. At base was the fact that, apart from the Victoria Cross, the two awards open to officers and men for bravery – the DSO and DCM – were actually instituted to acknowledge 'distinguished' and/or 'meritorious service', which, of course, did not necessarily mean acts of gallantry on the field of battle. Likewise, when the MC was instituted, its warrant stated that it was to be awarded for 'distinguished and meritorious services in time of war'. Indeed, it was not until 1931 that the warrant was amended, with 'in action' replacing 'in time of war'. Consequently, the authorities were entirely justified in making awards for services outside the combat zone. But this served to degrade the value of the award in the eyes of fighting soldiers and aggravated the gulf that they perceived existed between them and the staff, as well as those serving in the rear areas. The War Office did begin to recognise this and, beginning with the institution of the Military Medal, made a number of reforms, which by the end of the war had produced a fairer system. The Order of the British Empire potentially solved much, especially as a way of rewarding junior officers for services at the higher headquarters and on the lines of communication. Unfortunately, the Home Office's initial policy of treating military awards on a par with those made to civilians devalued the Order in the eyes of soldiers. Wound stripes and service chevrons also helped soldiers to maintain their pride and self-respect, while the Silver War Badge protected those honourably discharged through sickness and wounds from the unwelcome attentions of those who were only too keen to accuse them of being shirkers and worse. Thus, by the end of the war much had been done to correct the seeming injustices in the system, but it could never please everyone.

sixteen

THE VERDICT

The British Army went to war in August 1914 with little realization of how the conflict would turn out. Its belief that the war on the Continent would be short was, however, shared by the other combatant nations. The original Expeditionary Force was little more than a gesture to display solidarity with the French, who viewed the Royal Navy, then the most powerful in the world, as a much more valuable asset. In truth, the army of 1914 was still orientated to defence of empire rather than war in Europe.

Pre-war planning and preparation had been carried out with care and this enabled the Regular Army to mobilize quickly and generally smoothly. The system for recalling reservists to the Colours was especially successful, allowing most units to complete their war establishments by the end of the third day of mobilization. Likewise, the movement by rail to the ports of embarkation and deployment on the Continent went with hardly a hitch. But there were some oversights. One of the most serious involved the staff, first in removing key personnel from the War Office and second in closing down the Staff College for the duration of the war. The fact, too, that there were not enough trained staff officers to fill the necessary posts on mobilization did not help. This was one of the reasons why some of the staff work was of doubtful quality during the first half of the war. Not until staff learners were given a proper education did it improve. Combined with this was the recognition that the staff could not be merely the province of Regulars. It had to draw on the brainpower and experience of civilians in uniform. Intelligence was another problem. While the army had been increasingly recognizing the need for a proper intelligence organization in the years leading up to 1914, at onset of war it was still an imperfect instrument. Matters were also not helped by Sir John French's low regard for this speciality.

Another omission was despatch riders, even though a shortage had been identified early in 1914. The immediate recruitment of them and car drivers has the authentic ring of that very singular British characteristic – muddling through. This also applied to the Territorial Force, at least in the eyes of the Regular Army. The TF, however, laboured under a number of disadvantages. Obsolescent equipment and the division of responsibility between the War Office and the TF County Associations did not help. The immediate pressure on Territorials to volunteer for overseas service in August 1914, when they had expected to be allowed time to bring their training up to scratch, also caused confusion and insecurity. They then found themselves stretched in several directions, with some elements leaving to replace Regular units on garrison duties overseas, others being deployed to guard railways, and then being sent in dribs and drabs to France. Others, too, were given a home defence role as part of the Central Force. Kitchener then accepted that TF divisions would have to be deployed to active war theatres and they began to be sent overseas in March 1915.

Pre-war legislation on the TF had, however, introduced a high degree of inflexibility. The Territorial's right to be discharged at the end of his term continued to be maintained until conscription was introduced. His right not to volunteer for overseas service restricted his employment. Likewise, his entitlement not to be transferred to another unit without his agreement also created problems. Indeed, in the 51st (Highland) Division it forced amalgamations of first-line battalions as early as 1915. There was also confusion over the purpose of second- and third-line battalions, once they were formed, with second-line battalions starved of men when they were preparing to go overseas because they were still supplying men to their first-line equivalents but were still not receiving men from the third line. In the end, the TF did gradually lose its individual character. One indication of this was that strength statistics of the TF were published separately up until August 1917, thereafter they were lumped in with those of the Regular Army, which, of course, included volunteers and conscripts.

The Territorial Force suffered, too, from that fact that initial priority for recruiting was given to the New Armies, other than those units and formations earmarked for early deployment overseas. The formation of the Kitchener armies also aggravated the Territorials' equipment problems. Yet Kitchener himself was one of the few in Britain who believed from the outset that the war would be prolonged and that a mass army would have to be created. Given the restrictions surrounding the Territorial Force and its need to complete its training, he was undoubtedly right to make the new element part of the Regular Army rather than look to an expansion of the TF. The problems facing the New Armies need not be repeated, but it was a remarkable achievement to have been able to deploy so many divisions overseas by mid 1916. Even so, the higher command, at least in France, was not overly impressed with their level of training. The delays in equipping the New Armies had not helped; nor had the fact that there was a grave shortage of military experience among junior officers and NCOs while that of more senior officers and senior NCOs was often outdated.

The training itself was now in three streams. In theory, the Reserve and Extra Reserve units supplied reinforcements for their Regular counterparts, while the second- and then third-line TF battalions did so for the first line. For the New Armies, the Local Reserve units (later the Training Reserve) fulfilled the same role. Not until the second half of 1917 was the training rationalized and a more efficient system introduced whereby recruits were streamed according to their medical category and age. It also gave back the Training Reserve to individual regiments, which at least gave recruits a better sense of belonging, although those posted to France would as often as not find themselves given a different cap badge and army number. Infantry recruit training was established at fourteen weeks for most of the war. There is, however, much anecdotal evidence that some recruits were sent out with considerably less training. It also seems clear that training standards varied widely and that some men were despatched overseas with very little idea of how to handle even their rifles. These deficiencies can probably be put down to poor instructors and, perhaps, insufficient numbers of them. It was partially for this reason that every soldier arriving in France was given refresher training, notably at the supposedly notorious Bull Ring at Etaples.

One category of recruit was undoubtedly better trained than the others. This encompassed the 'A4 boys', who, because of their age, received significantly longer training than older men. Many went on to carry out specialist training as well and there is no doubt they gave a very good account of themselves, especially during the last climactic months of the war in France and Flanders. One other aspect is worth re-emphasizing: older men, although often less obviously fit than their younger brethren, tended to have more staying power.

Conscription was inevitable. The last vestige of voluntary enlistment, the Derby scheme, was not a success and, even though the predominantly Liberal government had long set its heart against compulsory enlistment it was left with no other option. It was now that the army really found itself in competition with other sectors and the War Office became increasingly frustrated by what it saw as an unfair allocation of manpower to it. It was conscious, too, that conscription had resulted in many more lower Medical Category men being enlisted. Spurred by the Lawson Report of the beginning of 1917, a constant combing-out process was developed in an attempt to exchange fitter men in the rear areas for the less fit in the fighting arms. It was also largely thanks to General Lawson that the War Office finally accepted that women could play their part in this substitution process. One curious anomaly, which Lawson observed, was that Medical Category C, which applied to those men not fit enough to serve overseas, actually only referred to the tropics. Yet the penny did not drop with the War Office until the autumn of 1917 that there was no reason why Category C men could not be sent to France.

Labour became a major problem in France and Flanders for an army brought up on colonial campaigns in which indigenous manpower was usually readily available. To meet the growing demands, the War Office had to improvise for much of the war, as well as drawing on resources from the Empire. Even so, the labour burden was never really lifted from the shoulders of the long-suffering infantry. The formation of the Labour Corps did much to put matters on a more cohesive footing, but it was subjected to a continual combing out of its fitter men. In these circumstances, it was remarkable what it was able to achieve.

The manpower crisis reached its peak at the beginning of 1918, forcing the reduction of the number of infantry battalions in a division. But claims that Lloyd George was purposely holding back Category A men in Britain are unsubstantiated, although his assertion that the strength of the BEF in France in January 1918 compared with that of twelve months earlier was incorrect. The crisis was aggravated by the losses during the German March and April 1918 offensives, but it was remarkable how quickly shattered divisions were rebuilt. A significant number of men who joined these divisions were Category B and, with little extra training, they proved themselves capable front-line soldiers, which raises further question marks over the medical categories as they were defined in 1914. In this respect, the army showed itself to be hidebound for too long.

Conscription also produced a number of dilemmas: conscientious objectors; those of enemy alien parentage; others who did not have formal British citizenship. The government's refusal to define conscientious objection exactly compounded the War Office's problems over how to deal with those who objected to being put in uniform. Yet it did evolve a relatively humane way of dealing with the majority of COs. The exception was the absolutists, where the army found itself in a Catch-22 situation, constantly having them returned to it after they had carried out their sentences in civil jails. There was no easy solution if conscription was to be rigidly enforced. As for those of enemy parentage, the War Office was undoubtedly unfair on them, especially those who had volunteered before the introduction of conscription. On the other hand, this was government policy and the blame cannot be laid at the army's door that soldiers of enemy parentage were virtually isolated in the 30th and 31st Middlesex. With regard to those who did not hold British citizenship, there were certainly incidents of Americans joining the army prior to the USA's entry into the war, although they usually passed themselves off as Canadian volunteers. The case of the Russian Jews was rather different and caused numerous problems for the military authorities, especially once Russia left the war. There were, however, two very separate issues at stake. The first was those Russian Jews who wanted to help evict the Turks from

Palestine so that they could fulfil the dream of a Jewish homeland. The second was the growing resentment in London's East End towards Russian Jews who were taking over businesses of men who had joined the army. In the event, the two Royal Fusilier battalions of largely Russian Jews who fought in Palestine performed creditably, but the others, who were conscripted into segregated companies of the Labour Corps, were largely unwilling soldiers.

Once in a theatre of war, effort was made to post new arrivals to a unit of their cap badge, but this proved increasingly difficult as the war went on. Combing out, combined with uneven levels of unit casualties, inevitably meant that replacements had to be sent to where they were most needed. Even though there were instances of seemingly strange posting – for example, kilted Highlanders being sent to English county battalions – there is little evidence to suggest that these drafts did not settle down reasonably quickly in their new units. Much of this reason was the establishment of the battle surplus, which provided a framework on which a battalion could be rebuilt. Understanding officers and NCOs also helped the assimilation process.

With regard to officer recruitment, there was little problem during the first part of the war in obtaining the right type of material, at least in the eyes of the Regular Army. Thanks to Haldane's establishment of university and school OTCs, there was a reservoir of suitable men with at least a little military experience. They still required much training and the only suitable establishment, apart from Sandhurst and Woolwich, was the Inns of Court. The ad hoc temporary schools set up in the first weeks of the war at universities could provide little more than a crash course, as did the Young Officers companies and the most effective training that new officers received was with their men. This developed leadership qualities in a way that theoretical instruction could not. The main dilemma during the first part of the war was that the TF 'class corps', which had so much officer material in their ranks, were among the first Territorial units sent abroad. Much the same problem existed with the New Army Public Schools battalions. The establishment of the Artists' Rifles school in France was the beginning of more effective training and it would seem that the quality of instruction was better than at the schools in Britain.

The creation of Officer Cadet battalions in Britain in early 1916 marked a change in officer training. It seems, however, that it took time for the new system to bed in. In addition, the problem of trainee officers being allowed any practical experience in commanding men before they joined their units at the Front remained until the end of the war. There is no doubt that 1917 produced the greatest demand for officers, with units ordered to nominate so many candidates for commissions each month. By mid 1918, however, it seems that the crisis had passed and there is evidence of men being forced to mark time after they returned to Britain for officer training, in some cases being told that there were no longer vacancies for them. But while officer training undoubtedly improved, some Regulars remained critical of the quality of the 'temporary gentlemen' posted to their regiments, although in part this may have been influenced by the changing social nature of the officer class.

The lack of trained staff officers in a rapidly expanding army was another grave problem during the first part of the war. The army did, however, begin to accept fairly early on the value of employing temporary officers with relevant civilian experience, as least in logistics posts and the many specialities that the new warfare spawned. On the operations side, the creation of staff schools was surprisingly late, with their not being established until the end of 1915. The 'staff learner' system was also a valuable addition, not least because an effective staff officer needed a working knowledge of how arms and services other than his own functioned. Indeed, this also applied to the various schools of instruction for regimental officers and NCOs that grew up in the war theatres, which also kept them abreast of new tactics. All these innovations helped to create the efficient army of 1918.

Turning to the treatment of the soldier, discipline remains the most controversial element. Field Punishment No. 1 and the number of crimes which attracted the death sentence are not easy to accept from the perspective of ninety years on. Yet they were punishments which the Regular soldier of 1914 understood and largely accepted. What is interesting is that some of the most senior commanders had their reservations over Field Punishment. On the other hand, the army was also aware that men might be tempted to commit serious crimes in order to be awarded prison sentences, which would take them out of the danger and discomfort of the trenches. In addition, Field Punishment was seen as a means of administering a relatively short sharp shock which would deter the soldier from committing offences in the future. In some cases it did not work, especially in the case of habitual deserters. Yet, the army often displayed much leniency towards these men for a crime that did attract the death sentence, handing down more than one lesser punishment for repeat offences before eventually feeling forced to hand down the ultimate sentence. The arguments over whether it was right to execute soldiers for crimes other than murder – and whether the victims should now be officially pardoned – have been aired many times and continue to be so. Suffice to say that every soldier was made aware of the consequences of committing serious crimes and that nine out of ten death sentences were not upheld. Forty per cent of those who were executed had also previously committed similar offences. In addition, much was done to improve the court martial procedure to make it fairer for the defendant. Where there is a grey area is over those who might well have been suffering from shell shock when they committed the offence, in which case the death sentence was unjustified. Given the length of time which has now elapsed, it is difficult to make a valid judgement on many of the cases, even though the court martial proceedings of those who were executed are open to public inspection, since these need to be balanced against those where the death sentence was not upheld. Since the proceedings of the latter no longer exist, this cannot be done.

Shell shock was one of many problems with which the medical authorities had to grapple. In 1914, little was known about the condition, especially by unit MOs. Effective treatment took time to develop and for much of the war some senior officers, including medicos, had little sympathy for those who suffered from it. Yet, once diagnosed, sufferers were entitled to wound stripes. The problem was differentiating between genuine cases and malingerers and there is no doubt that genuine sufferers did slip through the net. But the RAMC enjoyed many triumphs, successfully combatting trench fever, tetanus, typhoid and the like. The lesson was learnt early on that pre-war notions of evacuating casualties to base hospitals and then treating them was much less effective than surgery as far forward as possible. The development of blood transfusion was another lifesaver. Great strides forward were also made in the development of artificial limbs and plastic surgery. Indeed, military medicine showed a radical improvement over that in South Africa fifteen years earlier. The same applies to veterinary medicine. Likewise, tribute must be paid to Fabian Ware's pioneering work on graves registration and to the support that he was given by the authorities.

The operation of the military postal system was another triumph – only in Mesopotamia was it unsatisfactory, partly because all mail to this theatre had to pass through India. Food may have been monotonous at times, but there are few incidences of troops going short and the diet was often more substantial that some were used to in civilian life. For much of the war officers enjoyed an unfair advantage over leave. In France, they could expect it twice as often, even though officially they were supposed to take their turn with the men. While it could be argued that they required more leave because of the pressure of their responsibilities, it does seem unjust that they could expect leave every six months or so while their men sometimes had to wait for up to eighteen months.

Chaplains could do much to help morale. Their organization was hampered by the fact that the Church of England enjoyed a privileged position, as the established church, and this division seems to have been actively encouraged in certain quarters. Nevertheless, efforts were made to ensure that formations of a particular religious character had chaplains of appropriate denominations attached to them. Some chaplains found it difficult to settle in the rude world that was a war theatre and could not adjust to the harshness of the life. Many others, however, performed valuable service, which included running unit canteens, helping in casualty clearing stations and with graves registration. Not least, many demonstrated a high degree of physical courage.

With regard to providing the troops with facilities for amusement, since the army went to war without any canteen facilities, the early initiatives were taken by civilians. The establishment of the Expeditionary Force Canteens in early 1915 formalized the organization, but other establishments run by such as the Church and Salvation Armies also played their part. Concert parties, both run by formations and those set up by Lena

Ashwell, were important morale boosters and from autumn 1915 the cinema became a growing attraction in the war zones. In France, troops were also allowed into *estaminets*, although the hours were strictly regulated. The army also tried to adopt a realistic approach to venereal disease, accepting that it was impossible to keep soldiers from prostitutes and that it was better to provide regular inspections of the latter to prevent infection. Unfortunately, moral outrage at home eventually put a stop to the *maisons tolerées* and VD rates accordingly rose dramatically. One other welfare aspect caused the War Office heartsearching in 1915. This was appeals by individuals and organizations for comforts, especially clothing to be sent out to the troops. The authorities considered that some, especially those involving clothing, showed the army in a poor light, with a supply system that was letting the troops down. Nevertheless, the War Office did recognize the morale value of these comforts and the establishment of the Directorate of Voluntary Organisations in September 1915 helped ensure that they went to where they were needed.

Finally, as I have shown, the honours and awards system of 1914 may have suited the pre-war Regular Army, but it was soon shown to have serious imperfections, many caused by the fact that, apart from the Victoria Cross, the rules under which those decorations that existed could be awarded did not specify that they were only for acts on the battlefield *per se*. Consequently, DSOs, DCMs and MCs were awarded for good service behind the lines, to the understandable annoyance of the fighting troops. Indeed, throughout the war, the VC and Military Medal alone were specifically for gallantry in combat. The introduction of the Order of the British Empire provided a partial solution, but, because it was controlled by the Home Office, the value of it as an award to those in uniform was diminished. For all that the War Office agonized over the problem, it never reached a satisfactory solution until after the war.

In summary, the British Army of 1914–18 was not the rigid and dogmatic organization some would like us to believe. Its massive expansion at the beginning of the war created enormous problems. Yet these were largely and successfully overcome. True, some of the solutions were ad hoc ones and had to be continually altered or adjusted, which caused a degree of turbulence. The New Warfare continually required fresh skills and there were the large casualty bills, both set against the backdrop of the fact that the manpower reservoir was sinking. As for care of its soldiers, the army put much thought and effort into their well-being and their morale did hold up. If it had not done so, then there would not have been the decisive victories in every theatre during the last months of the war. The army did make mistakes, but, in general the transition from a small Regular to vast citizen army in the space of just four years was a triumph in the face of adversity.

BRITISH ARMY ACRONYMS

AA	Anti-Aircraft; *also* Army Act
AADC	Anti-Aircraft Defence Commander
AA&QMG	Assistant Adjutant and Quartermaster General
AASC	Anti-Aircraft Searchlight Company
AASS	Anti-Aircraft Searchlight Section
AB	Army Book
ABPO	Advanced Base Post Office
AC	Armoured Car
ACC	Army Cyclist Corps
ACG	Assistant Chaplain General
ACI	Army Council Instruction
ACME	Assistant Chief Mechanical Engineer
AD	Artillery Depot
ADAPS	Assistant Director Army Postal Services
ADAP&SS	Assistant Director of Army Printing and Stationery Services
ADC	Aide de Camp
ADGR&E	Assistant Director of Graves Registration and Enquiries
ADGT	Assistant Director-General of Transportation
ADL	Assistant Director of Labour
ADLR	Assistant Director of Light Railways
ADMS	Assistant Director Medical Services
ADOS	Assistant Director Ordnance Services

ADRT	Assistant Director Railway Traffic or Transport
ADS	Advanced Dressing Station
ADTn	Assistant Director Transportation
ADVS	Assistant Director Veterinary Services
AEF	American Expeditionary Force
AF	Army Form
AFA	Australian Field Artillery
AG	Adjutant General
AGS	Army Gymnastic Staff
AHR	Army Horse Reserve
AIF	Australian Imperial Force
AIS	Assistant Inspector of Searchlights
AMB	Armoured Motor Battery
AMFO	Assistant Military Forwarding Officer
AMLO	Assistant Military Landing Officer
AMO	Administrative Medical Officer
AMS	Assistant Military Secretary
AMTD	Advanced Mechanical Transport Depot
ANSR	Army Nursing Service Reserve
AO	Army Order
AOC	Army Ordnance Corps
AOD	Army Ordnance Department
AP	Armour Piercing (ammunition)
APC	Army Pay Corps; *also* Assistant Principal Chaplain
APD	Army Pay Department
APM	Assistant Provost Marshal
APMMC	Almeric Paget Military Massage Corps
APO	Army Post Office
AQMG	Assistant Quartermaster General
ARMW	Army Reserve Munition Worker
ARO	Artillery Reconnaissance Officer
ARP	Ammunition Refilling Point
ARS	Advanced Regulating Station
ASC	Army Service Corps
ASD	Army Schools Department

A&SH	Argyll and Sutherland Highlanders
ASO	Area Searchlight Officer
ASP	Ammunition Sub-Park
AT	Army Troops
AVC	Army Veterinary Corps
BAC	Brigade Ammunition Column
BAPO	Base Army Post Office
BC	Battery Commander; *also* Base Commandant
BCA	Battery Commander's Assistant
BEF	British Expeditionary Force
BGGS	Brigadier General General Staff
BGHA	Brigadier General Heavy Artillery
BGRA	Brigadier General Royal Artillery
BGRE	Brigadier General Royal Engineers
BL	Breech Loading
BLC	Breech Loading Converted
BM	Brigade Major
BOR	British Other Rank
BRCS	British Red Cross Society
BSM	Battery Sergeant Major
BWIR	British West Indies Regiment
CB	Commander of the Most Honourable Order of the Bath; *also* Confinement to Barracks (punishment); *also* Counter-Battery
CBE	Commander of the Most Excellent Order of the British Empire
CBSO	Counter-Battery Staff Officer
CC	Confined to Camp (punishment); *also* Chief Censor
CCD	Commander of Coast Defences
CCRA	Corps Commander Royal Artillery
CCS	Casualty Clearing Station
CDS	Corps Dressing Station
CE	Chief Engineer
CEF	Canadian Expeditionary Force
CEPC	Chief Engineer Port Construction

CF	Chaplain to the Forces
CFC	Chief Field Censor; *also* Canadian Forestry Corps
CGI	Corrugated Galvanized Iron
CGS	Chief of General Staff
CHA	Commander Heavy Artillery
CHDAVC	Convalescent Horse Depot Army Veterinary Corps
C-in-C	Commander-in-Chief
CID	Committee of Imperial Defence
CIGS	Chief of the Imperial General Staff
CLC	Chinese Labour Corps
CLLE	Charger-Loading Lee-Enfield (rifle)
CLLM	Charger-Loading Lee-Metford (rifle)
CLRO	Corps Light Railway Officer
CME	Chief Mechanical Engineer
CMG	Commander of the Order of St Michael and St George
CMO	Court Martial Officer
CMP	Corps of Military Police; *also* Civil Medical Practitioner
CO	Commanding Officer; *also* Conscientious Objector
COO	Chief Ordnance Officer
CP	Censorship & Press
CQMS	Company Quartermaster Sergeant
CRA	Commander Royal Artillery
CRCE	Chief Railway Construction Engineer
CRE	Commanding Royal Engineer
CRO	Corps Roads Officer
CSIC	Cadet School Infantry Company
CSM	Company Sergeant Major
CT	Communication Trench
D of A	Director of Artillery
DAA	Director of Army Accounts
DAA&QMG	Deputy Assistant Adjutant and Quartermaster General
DAAG	Deputy Assistant Adjutant General
DAC	Divisional Ammunition Column
DACG	Deputy Assistant Chaplain General

DADAPS	Deputy Assistant Director Army Postal Services
DADAP&SS	Deputy Assistant Director of Army Printing and Stationery Services
DADGR&E	Deputy Assistant Director of Graves Registration and Enquiries
DADGT	Deputy Assistant Director-General of Transportation
DADL	Deputy Assistant Director of Labour
DADMS	Deputy Assistant Director Medical Services
DADOS	Deputy Assistant Director Ordnance Services
DADPS	Deputy Assistant Director Postal Services
DAD Roads	Deputy Assistant Director of Roads
DAD Sigs	Deputy Assistant Director of Signals
DADRT	Deputy Assistant Director Railway Traffic or Transport
DADS	Deputy Assistant Director Supplies
DADST	Deputy Assistant Director Supplies and Transport
DADT	Deputy Assistant Director Transport
DADW	Deputy Assistant Director of Works
DAG	Deputy Adjutant General
DAMS	Deputy Assistant Military Secretary
DAP	Divisional Ammunition Park
DAPC	Deputy Assistant Principal Chaplain
DAP&SS	Director of Army Printing and Stationery Services
DAPS	Director of Army Postal Services
DAQMG	Deputy Assistant Quartermaster General
DA&QMG	Deputy Adjutant and Quartermaster General
DBC	Director of Barrack Construction
DCFC	Deputy Chief Field Censor
DCGS	Deputy Chief of the General Staff
DCIGS	Deputy Chief of the Imperial General Staff
DCLI	Duke of Cornwall's Light Infantry
DCM	Distinguished Conduct Medal; *also* District Court Martial
DDAPS	Deputy Director of Army Postal Services
DDAP&SS	Deputy Director of Army Printing and Stationery Services
DDGAMS	Deputy Director-General Army Medical Services
DDGMR	Deputy Director-General Military Railways or Movements and Railways
DDGR&E	Deputy Director of Graves Registration and Enquiries

DDGT	Deputy Director-General of Transportation
DDIWT	Deputy Director Inland Waterway Transport
DDMI	Deputy Director of Military Intelligence
DDMS	Deputy Director Medical Services
DDOS	Deputy Director Ordnance Services
DDRT	Deputy Director Railway Traffic or Transport
DD Sigs	Deputy Director of Signals
DDS&T	Deputy Director Supplies and Transport
DDTn	Deputy Director of Transportation
DDVS	Deputy Director Veterinary Services
DDW	Deputy Director of Works
DEOS	Director of Equipment and Ordnance Stores
DFS	Director of Financial Services
DFW	Director of Fortifications and Works
DG	Dragoon Guards
DGAMS	Director-General Army Medical Services
DGAVS	Director-General Army Veterinary Services
DGMR	Director-General Movements and Railways
DGNS	Director-General National Service
DGO	Divisional Gas Officer
DGR&E	Director of Graves Registration and Enquiries
DGT	Director-General of Transportation
DGTF	Director-General of the Territorial Force
DGVO	Director-General of Voluntary Organizations
DHR	Director of Hirings and Requisitions
DIL	Dangerously Ill List
DIWD	Director Inland Waterways and Docks
DLI	Durham Light Infantry
DLR	Director of Light Railways
DM	Director of Mobilization
DMC	Desert Mounted Corps
DMI	Director of Military Intelligence
DMO	Director of Military Operations
DMS	Director of Medical Services; *also* Deputy Military Secretary
DMT	Director of Military Training

DNTO	Divisional Naval Transport Officer
DORA	Defence of the Realm Acts
DORE	District Office Royal Engineers
DOS	Director of Ordnance Services
DP	Drill Purpose
DPS	Director of Personal Services
DPW	Director of Prisoners of War
DQMG	Deputy Quartermaster General
DR	Director of Remounts; *also* Despatch Rider
DRF	Depression Range-Finder
DRLS	Despatch Rider Letter Service
D Rlys	Director of Railways
DRO	Director of Recruiting and Organization
DRT	Director Railway Traffic or Transport
DSD	Director of Staff Duties
DSI	Director of Special Intelligence (censorship)
DSQ	Director of Supplies and Quartering
DST	Director of Sea Transport
DTM	Director of Transport and Movements
DTMO	Divisional Trench Mortar Officer
DTN	Director of Transportation
DW	Director of Works
EEF	Egyptian Expeditionary Force
EFC	Expeditionary Force Canteen
EinC	Engineer-in-Chief
ELC	Egyptian Labour Corps
E&M	Electrical and Mechanical
EMO	Embarkation Medical Officer
FANY	First Aid Nursing Yeomanry
FAO	Forward Area Officer (Light Railways)
FAU	Friends Ambulance Unit
FCPO	Fixed Centre Pay Office
FGCM	Field General Court Martial

FLC	Fijian Labour Contingent (later Corps)
FOO	Forward Observation Officer
FP	Field Punishment
FPO	Field Post Office
FSC	Field Survey Company
FSL	Field Searchlight
FSM	Field Service Manual
FSR	Field Service Regulations
FWD	Four Wheel Drive
GBD	General Base Depot
GCM	General Court Martial
GDA	Gun Defended Area (anti-aircraft defence term)
GHQ	General Headquarters
GMP	Garrison Military Police
GOC	General Officer Commanding
GOC-in-C	General Officer Commanding-in-Chief
GRC	Graves Registration Commission
GRO	General Routine Order
GRU	Graves Registration Unit
GS	General Service; *also* General Staff
GSO	General Staff Officer: three grades, GSO1 (usually Lt Col), GSO2 (Major), GSO3 (Captain)
GSW	Gunshot Wound
HA	Heavy Artillery
HAC	Honourable Artillery Company
HAG	Heavy Artillery Group
HAR	Heavy Artillery Reserve
HBMGC	Heavy Branch Machine Gun Corps (later Tank Corps)
HC	Head Censor
HE	High Explosive
HF	Home Forces
HPD	Home Postal Depot
HS	Home Service

HSC	Hospital Ship Case (medical)
HT	Horse Transport
HV	High Velocity
IA	Indian Army
IB	Infantry Brigade
IBD	Infantry Base Depot
IE	Illegal Enlistment
IGC	Inspector General of Communications
IGT	Inspector General of Transportation; *also* Inspector General of Training
IHL	Imprisonment with Hard Labour
IO	Intelligence Officer
IOM	Inspector of Ordnance Machinery
IOR	Indian Other Rank
IS	Inspector of Searchlights; *also* Imperial Service
IW&D	Inland Waterways and Docks
IWGC	Imperial War Graves Commission
IWT	Inland Water Transport
JAG	Judge Advocate General
KBS	Kite Balloon Section (Royal Flying Corps)
KOSB	King's Own Scottish Borderers
KOYLI	King's Own Yorkshire Light Infantry
KR	King's Regulations
KRRC	King's Royal Rifle Corps
LAB	Light Armoured Battery
LACB	Light Armoured Car Battery
LAMB	Light Armoured Motor Battery
LCP	Light Car Patrol
LEE	London Electrical Engineers
LF	Lancashire Fusiliers
LG	Lewis Gun

LO	Liaison Officer
L of C *or* LOC	Lines of Communication
LR	Local Reserve
LTMB	Light Trench Mortar Battery
MAC	Motor Ambulance Convoy
MB	Medical Board
MC	Military Cross
MDS	Main Dressing Station
MEF	Mediterranean Expeditionary Force
MFD	Military Forwarding Department
MFO	Military Forwarding Officer
MFP	Military Foot Police
MG	Machine Gun
MGC	Machine Gun Corps
MGGS	Major General General Staff
MGO	Master General of the Ordnance
MGRA	Major General Royal Artillery
MLO	Military Landing Officer
MM	Military Medal
MMGS	Motor Machine Gun Service
MML	Manual of Military Law
MMP	Military Mounted Police
MO	Medical Officer
MPI	Mean Point of Impact
MPSC	Military Police Staff Corps
MS	Military Secretary
MSM	Meritorious Service Medal
MT	Mechanical Transport
MVC	Motor Volunteer Corps
MVS	Mobile Veterinary Section
NACB	Navy and Army Canteen Board
NCC	Non-Combatant Corps
NCO	Non-Commissioned Officer

NF	Northumberland Fusiliers
NTO	Naval Transport Officer
NYD	Not Yet Diagnosed (medical term)
NYDN	Not Yet Diagnosed Nervous or Neurosis (medical term for suspected shell shock)
OB	Operations Branch
OBOS	Overseas Branch Ordnance Survey
OC	Officer Commanding; *also* Officer Cadet
OP	Observation Post
OR	Other Rank
ORS	Orderly Room Sergeant
OS	Ordnance Services
OTC	Officers Training Corps
PB	Permanent Base (medical)
P&BT	Physical and Bayonet Training
PC	Principal Chaplain (non Church of England)
PCC	President of the Claims Commission
PM	Provost Marshal
PNTO	Principal Naval Transport Officer
POW	Prisoner of War
psc	Passed Staff College
PU	Permanently Unfit (medical)
PUO	Pyrexia of Unknown Origin (medical term usually applied to trench fever)
QAIMNS	Queen Alexandra's Imperial Military Nursing Service
QF	Quick Firing
QMAAC	Queen Mary's Army Auxiliary Corps
QMG	Quartermaster General
QMS	Quartermaster Sergeant
qs	Qualified for Staff

RAMC	Royal Army Medical Corps
RAP	Regimental Aid Post
RB	Rifle Brigade
RCE	Railway Construction Engineer; *also* Royal Canadian Engineers
RCO	Railway Control Officer
RDC	Royal Defence Corps
RDF	Royal Dublin Fusiliers
RE	Royal Engineers
REPS	Royal Engineers Postal Section
R&F	Rank and File
RF	Royal Fusiliers
RFA	Royal Field Artillery
RFC	Royal Flying Corps
RGA	Royal Garrison Artillery
RH	Railhead
RHA	Royal Horse Artillery; *also* Reserve Heavy Artillery
RM	Royal Marines; *also* Riding Master
RMA	Royal Marine Artillery; *also* Royal Military Academy Woolwich
RMC	Royal Military College Sandhurst
RMF	Royal Munster Fusiliers
RMLC	Royal Marine Labour Corps
RMLI	Royal Marine Light Infantry
RNACD	Royal Naval Armoured Car Division
RND	Royal Naval Division (later 63rd Division)
RO	Recruiting Officer; *also* Reconnaissance Officer
ROD	Railway Operating Division
ROO	Railway Ordnance Officer
RP	Rules of Procedure; *also* Regimental Police; *also* Refilling Point
RS	Royal Scots
RSO	Railhead Supply Officer
RTC	Reserve Training Centre
RTE	Railway Transport Establishment; *also* Railway Transport Executive
RTO	Railway Transport Officer (later Railway Traffic Officer)
RTU	Returned to Unit
RWF	Royal Welsh Fusiliers (the spelling reverted to Welch only in 1920)

S	Service
SAA	Small Arms Ammunition
SANLC	South African Native Labour Corps
SBAC	Siege Battery Ammunition Column
SBR	Small Box Respirator
SC	Staff Captain
SCF	Senior Chaplain to the Forces
SD	Staff Duties
SGS	Surveyor General of Supply
SIW	Self-Inflicted Wound
SLR	Superintendent of Light Railways
S&M	Sappers and Miners
SMLE	Short Magazine Lee-Enfield (rifle)
SMO	Senior Medical Officer
SOS	Struck off Strength
SP	Strongpoint
SR	Special Reserve
SRS	Sound Ranging Section
SS	Stationery Service
S&T	Supply and Transport
SWP	Special Works Park (later Camouflage Park RE)
TAT	Temporary Ambulance Train
TB	Temporary Base (medical)
TC	Tank Corps
TCO	Train Conducting Officer
TD	Territorial Decoration
TDO	Telephone Dug-out
TEE	Tyne Electrical Engineers
TF	Territorial Force
TFNS	Territorial Force Nursing Service
TM	Trench Mortar
TMB	Trench Mortar Battery; *also* Travelling Medical Board
TO	Transport Officer
TOS	Taken on Strength

TR	Training Reserve
TRB	Training Reserve Brigade
UOTC	University Officers Training Corps
VAD	Voluntary Aid Detachment
VADGS	Voluntary Aid Detachment General Service
VC	Victoria Cross
VD	Volunteer Officers' Decoration
VO	Veterinary Officer
VTC	Volunteer Training Corps
WAAC	Women's Army Auxiliary Corps (later QMAAC)
WD	War Department
WE	War Establishment
WHC	Women's Hospital Corps
WO	War Office; *also* Warrant Officer
WWCS	Walking Wounded Collecting Station
Y&L	York and Lancaster Regiment
YOC	Young Officers Company
YS	Young Soldier
ZMC	Zion Mule Corps

Appendix two

MEDICAL CATEGORIES

Category A – Fit for general service

A1 Men for despatch overseas in all respects, as regards training, physical and mental qualifications

A2 Recruits who should be A1 on completion of their training

A3 Returned Expeditionary Force men who should be A1 once 'hardened'

A4 Men under 19 years of age who should become A1 or A2 once they reach that age

Category B – Fit for service abroad, but not general service

B1 In Garrison or Provisional units

B2 In Labour units or on garrison or regimental outdoor employment

B3 On sedentary work as clerks or storemen only

Category C – Fit for home service only

C1 In Garrison or Provisional units

C2 In Labour units or on command garrison or regimental outdoor employment

C3 On sedentary work as clerks, storemen, batmen, cooks, orderlies, sanitary duties, etc

Category D – Temporarily unfit for service, but likely to become so within six months

D1   In command depots

D2   In regimental depots

D3   In any unit or depot under or awaiting medical or dental treatment, on completion of which will rejoin their original medical category

Category E – Unfit for service and not likely to become fit within six months

Under ACI 1606/17 of October 1917 Category C was abolished

In addition, the following categories were applied in France and Flanders:

Class A – Fit for general service

Class TB (Temporary Base) – Temporarily unfit for general service

Class PB (Permanent Base) – Unfit for general service at the Front, but fit for service on the lines of communication and in army corps areas and capable of being regraded Class A.

Class PU (Permanently Unfit) – Those in Class PB who are never likely to become Class A, but employed in the same way as Class PB.

Sources:

Statistics of the Military Effort During the Great War 1914–1920, p. 110; Lawson Report, *The Number and Physical Categories of Men Employed out of the Fighting Area in France*, National Archives, WO 32/5093

Appendix three

INFANTRY UNITS

Agricultural Companies Formed early in 1917 to help farmers. They were controlled by the Ministry of Agriculture and transferred to the Labour Corps in May 1917.

Bantam Battalions New Army units consisting of men 5ft – 5ft 3ins in height.

Cyclist Battalions TF units formed for home defence. Those cyclist units serving overseas were part of the Army Cyclist Corps.

Docks Battalions Formed from Liverpool dockers and badged King's Liverpool Regiment. The first battalion was created in April 1915 for work in the docks and a second came into being in May 1918.

Entrenching Battalions Initially formed in France in July 1915, and later in Salonika, to act as holding units for drafts en route from the base areas to their units at the front. They were also made available to the Royal Engineers as a source of labour. They ceased to exist in France by the end of 1917, but a further batch was formed in February 1918 from surplus manpower thrown up by the reduction of each division by three battalions. All had ceased to exist by the end of April 1918.

Extra Reserve Battalions These were the 6th battalions of four-battalion Regular regiments. They initially consisted of Special Reservists and fulfilled the same role as the Reserve battalions of Regular regiments. From summer 1917 they became responsible for training men above 18 years and 8 months of medical category A2.

Garrison Battalions Formed from Medical Category B men in the New Armies to relieve TF battalions on garrison duties overseas.

Garrison Guard Battalions Formed in 1918 from fitter Labour Corps men for line-holding duties. They were then transferred to infantry regiments.

Garrison Reserve Battalions Formed in summer 1916 to train and supply men to the **Garrison and Home Service Garrison Battalions**.

Graduated Battalions From summer 1917 provided specialist training for those under the age of 19 who had completed their recruit training. They were titled **Infantry Battalions**. In October 1917 they became the 51st and 52nd Battalions of 23 designated infantry regiments.

Home Service Garrison Battalions Formed for garrison duties in Britain from those unfit for foreign service.

Infantry Battalions *See* **Graduated Battalions**.

Junior Training Reserve Battalions Formed in summer 1917 to take in the surplus of 18 year-olds from the **Young Soldiers Battalions**, as well as those under 18 years and 8 months who were of medical categories B2, B3, C2 and C3.

Labour Battalions Formed in 1916 from labourers mainly for service in France. Transferred to the Labour Corps in spring 1917.

Labour Companies Formed in early 1917 by a 'comb out' of **Training Reserve Battalions**, they were immediately sent to France to work on road and railway maintenance, some also being employed in unloading railway wagons. Transferred to the Labour Corps in April 1917, with the exception of the Middlesex Labour Companies, which consisted of men of alien parentage.

Locally Raised Battalions New Army battalions raised by individuals or municipalities and more popularly known as Pals battalions. Those who raised them were initially responsible for providing uniforms, accommodation and rations.

Local Reserve Battalions Formed from the depot companies of **Locally Raised** New Army battalions. Became **Training Reserve** battalions in September 1916.

Observer Companies TF Formed to provide early warning of air raids on Britain. Absorbed by the Royal Defence Corps.

Permanent Base Battalion Formed at Etaples in November 1916 to administer men who had been found medically unfit by the Infantry Base Depots. Became an Employment Base Depot in September 1917.

Pioneer Battalions Formed during the early part of 1915 on the basis of one for each infantry division overseas for entrenching and other duties so as to relieve normal infantry of some of the more tedious labouring tasks.

Provisional Battalions Formed in summer 1915 from TF men who refused to take the Imperial Service Obligation and those not medically fit to serve overseas. They were rebadged to regiments on 1 January 1917.

Reception Battalions Established at Larkhill and Ripon in July 1918 to provide pre-training for officer cadet battalion candidates.

Recruit Distribution Battalions Formed in December 1917 from seven **Training Reserve Battalions** on the basis of one per home command to receive and post medical category B2 and B3 recruits and provided training for those with a reasonable chance of becoming B1 within three months.

Regular Battalions The battalions of the Regular Army. Most regiments had two, some had four.

Reserve Battalions Initially existed prewar and made up of Special Reservists. They were descended from the Militia and were the 3rd Battalions of two-battalion regular regiments and 5th Battalions of four-battalion regiments. Their primary role in war was to supply drafts to the regular battalions. Responsible for training Medical Category A2 men above 18 years 8 months from summer 1917.

Reserve Battalions TF Formed from third-line TF battalions in September 1916. From summer 1917 trained Medical Category A2 men above 18 years 8 months.

2nd Reserve Battalions Original Fourth New Army battalions which were converted to the training role so as to keep the **Service Battalions** supplied with men. Became **Training Reserve Battalions** in September 1916

Supernumerary Companies TF Formed from National Reserve Class II in March 1915 to provide POW camp and vulnerable point guards in Britain. Absorbed by the Royal Defence Corps on its formation in April 1916.

Senior Training Reserve Battalions Responsible from summer 1917 for training medical category B and C recruits aged over 18 years 8 months.

Service Battalions Active service battalions of the New Armies

Territorial Force (TF) Battalions Infantry battalions of the Territorial Force

Training Reserve Battalions Formed on 1 September 1916 from the **2nd Reserve** and **Local Reserve Battalions**. At the end of 1917 the vast majority of those still remaining were given regiment titles once more.

Transport Workers Battalions Began to be formed in March 1916 for dock, railway, and canal work in Britain. They were primarily used as a quick reaction labour force, which could be deployed anywhere in the country.

Volunteer Battalions Part of the volunteer force of part-time soldiers.

Works Battalions/Companies Formed in Britain in late 1915 to provide working and fatigue parties. Transferred to the Labour Corps, apart from the 30th and 31st Middlesex, in April 1917.

Young Soldiers Battalions Formed in summer 1917 from some **Training Reserve Battalions** to train soldiers aged 18 years and 1 month who were Medical Categories A4, B1 and C1. Became the 53rd battalions of twenty-three designated infantry regiments in October 1917. Three separate Young Soldiers battalions were formed in France in autumn 1918 for young men with underdeveloped physiques.

SOURCES

CHAPTER ONE

1. Hew Strachan, in French & Holden Reid, *The British General Staff*, p. 89
2. Simpson, *The Operational Role of British Corps Command on the Western Front*, pp. 21–2
3. National Archives, Kew, WO 106/50
4. David Langley, 'Bounden Duty and Service: A Royal Welch Fusiliers' Perspective of Eligibility and Liability for Service in the Great War', *Stand To*, No. 68, Summer 2003, p. 8
5. National Archives, Kew, WO 32/8207
6. Ibid., WO 32/6639,6640, and *Statistics of the Military Effort*, p. 30
7. Ibid., WO 95/1324, 1596
8. *Training and Manoeuvre Regulations*
9. *Statistics of the Military Effort*, p. 30; Ian Beckett, in Beckett & Simpson, *A Nation in Arms*, pp. 128–9
10. Germains, *The Kitchener Armies*, p. 56 fn
11. National Archives, Kew, WO 32/20745; *Statistics of the Military Effort*, p. 158
12. Ibid., WO 33/2857 and information from Jock Bruce, Joe Sweeney and others
13. Ibid., WO 33/688, WO 162/23
14. Ibid., WO 35/56A
15. Ibid., WO 162/23
16. Ibid., WO33/611
17. Ibid.
18. Fay, *The War Office at War*, pp. 20–21
19. Ibid., p. 39
20. National Archives, Kew, WO 33/665
21. Ibid., WO 33/657
22. Chapman-Huston & Rutter, *General Sir John Cowans*, Vol. 1, pp. 250–59
23. Young, *Army Service Corps 1902–1918*, pp. 47, 48
24. National Archives, Kew, WO33/611
25. Ibid., WO 33/687
26. Henniker, *Transportation on the Western Front*, pp. 15–18, 508

27. *Field Service Pocket Book 1914*, Ch. 1, para. 10
28. National Archives, Kew, WO 107/64

CHAPTER TWO

1. National Archives, Kew, WO 162/21
2. Norman, *Armageddon Road*, p. 18
3. Terraine, ed., *General Jack's Diary*, p. 21
4. National Archives, Kew, WO 163/20
5. Ibid., WO 162/21
6. Ibid., WO 95/2834
7. Ibid., WO 162/21
8. Adams, *Arms and the Wizard*, pp. 1–2
9. National Archives, Kew, PRO 30/66/9
10. Anon., *The War the Infantry Knew*, pp. 1–2
11. Macleod, *Memoirs of an Artillery Officer on the Western Front*, p. 25
12. Blacker, ed., *Have You Forgotten Yet?*, p. 7
13. Malone & Hawes, *Elegant Extracts*, p. 109
14. Ibid., pp. 113–14
15. Jourdain, *Ranging Memories*, p. 161
16. Anon., *The War the Infantry Knew*, pp. 3, 63
17. Lucy, *There's a Devil in the Drum*, p. 74
18. AO 297/14
19. Anon., *The War the Infantry Knew*, p. 7
20. National Archives, Kew, WO 95/5459
21. Jourdain, op. cit., p. 161
22. Quoted Simpson, *The Old Contemptibles*, p. 6
23. National Archives, Kew, WO 162/33
24. Van Emden, ed., *Tickled to Death to Go*, pp. 29, 31
25. Horn, *Lancer Dig In*, pp. 3–4
26. Messenger, *Terriers in the Trenches*, p. 7
27. National Archives, Kew, WO 162/21
28. Chapman-Huston & Rutter, *General Sir John Cowans*, Vol. 2, pp. 18–19
29. Ashurst, *My Bit*, pp. 27–30

30. Malone & Hawes, op. cit., p. 115
31. National Archives, Kew, WO 95/5459
32. Callwell, *Experiences of a Dug-Out*, pp. 7–8, 10–11
33. *War Office List 1914*, National Archives, Kew, WO 33/688
34. Callwell, op. cit., p. 14
35. Ibid., p. 21; Institution of Royal Engineers, *History of the Corps of Royal Engineers*, Vol. 5, pp. 526–7
36. Bond, *The Victorian Army and the Staff College*, p. 308
37. Anglesey, *A History of the British Cavalry*, Vol. 7, p. 77; Home *The Diary of a World War 1 Cavalry Officer*, p. 13
38. Marshall-Cornwall, *Wars and Rumours of Wars*, pp. 13–14
39. Casson, *Steady Drummer*, pp. 22–34
40. Andrew, *Secret Service*, pp. 127–130; Occleshaw, *Armour Against Fate*, pp. 31–3
41. National Archives, Kew, WO 339/10938
42. Anglesey, op. cit., p. 77 & fn
43. Marshall-Cornwall, op. cit., pp. 14–16
44. Andrew, op. cit., p. 135
45. Bond, op. cit., p. 309
46. National Archives, Kew, WO 106/50
47. Watson, *Adventures of a Despatch Rider*, pp. 4–10
48. Anon, *The War the Infantry Knew*, p. 15
49. Rawlinson, *Adventures on the Western Front*; Rolls-Royce *Cars in War*, Rolls-Royce Ltd, London, 1919; Maze, *A Frenchman in Khaki*, p. 76
50. Hamilton, *The War Diary of the Master of Bellhaven*, pp. 1, 3–4
51. National Archives, Kew, WO 339/21582
52. Fuller, *Memoirs of an Unconventional Soldier*, pp. 31–4
53. Anon, *The War the Infantry Knew*, p. 8
54. Kipling, *The Irish Guards in the Great War: The First Battalion*, p. 29
55. National Archives, Kew, WO 95/4116
56. Ibid., WO 95/4043
57. Henniker, *Transportation on the Western Front*, pp. 19–25
58. Henniker, op. cit., pp. 25–6
59. National Archives, Kew, CAB 45/129
60. Ibid., WO 95/1416
61. Ibid., WO 162/21
62. *Military Operations: France and Belgium, 1914*, Vol. 2, p. 164 fn1
63. Severn, *The Gambardier*, pp. 17, 26–7
64. National Archives, Kew, WO 33/702
65. Adams, op. cit., p. 15
66. *Military Operations: France and Belgium 1914*, Vol. 2, p. 16 fn1
67. National Archives, Kew, WO 95/4185, 4186
68. Ibid., WO 95/4116
69. Lucy, op. cit., p. 155
70. National Archives, Kew, WO 79/63
71. Ibid., WO 95/4185
72. Ibid., WO 95/4116
73. Davson, *Memoirs of the Great War*, pp. 1–4
74. Lucy, op. cit., p. 267
75. Letter dated 1 December 1914, National Archives, Kew, PRO 30/57/51
76. Ibid., WO 95/4185
77. Ibid., WO 95/3929
78. Ibid., WO 95/3119, 3118
79. Ibid., WO 95/2244, 2488
80. Letter to Kitchener, 24 September 1914, Ibid., PRO 30/57/51
81. Middlebrook, *Your Country Needs You*, pp. 30–31
82. National Archives, Kew, WO 107/19
83. Home, op. cit., pp. 53, 54
84. Letter dated 23 February 1915, National Archives, Kew, PRO 30/57/51
85. Norman, op. cit., p. 102
86. Letter dated 23 February 1915, National Archives, Kew, PRO 30/57/51
87. Cavan's handwritten account in Ibid., WO 79/71; Middlebrook, op. cit., pp. 34–5

CHAPTER THREE

I am most grateful to Charles Fair and Jock Bruce for their valuable comments on an earlier draft of this chapter.

1. Latham, *A Territorial Soldier's War*, p. 4
2. National Archives, Kew, WO33/692
3. Ibid., PRO 30/66/9
4. Ibid., WO33/692
5. Germains, *The Kitchener Armies*, p. 56
6. War Office AG1 letter dated 21 August 1914, National Archives, Kew, WO 70/50; Germains, op. cit., p. 64
7. Nicholson, *Behind the Lines*, pp. 19–20
8. Bond, ed., *Staff Officer*, p. 25
9. Anon, *Tale of a Territorial*, p. 28
10. Reith, *Wearing Spurs*; p. 27, National Archives, Kew, WO 70/50
11. Germains, op. cit., p. 64
12. Latham, op. cit., p. 6
13. *Tale of a Territorial*, op. cit., p. 30
14. Letter dated 7 August 1914, National Archives, Kew, WO 50/70
15. Goodland, *Engaged in War*, p. 5
16. National Archives, Kew, WO 162/21
17. Goodland, op. cit., pp. 3,8
18. National Archives, Kew, WO 95/3118
19. Ibid., WO 162/23
20. Walker, *The Honourable Artillery Company in the Great War*, pp. 19–21
21. Hawkings, *From Ypres to Cambrai*, pp. 11–12
22. AO 186/15
23. National Archives, Kew, WO 364/3708, WO 372/18; Silvester, *Dancing is My Life*, pp. 16–30; Errington, *Inns of Court Officers Training Corps During the Great War*; Stagoll Higham, *The Regimental Roll of Honour and War Record of the Artists' Rifles*
24. National Archives, Kew, WO 33/788
25. Lewis, *Remembrances of Hell*, p. 23
26. National Archives, Kew, WO 70/50
27. Ibid., WO 32/18617, WO 95/5640; Army Council Military Members Meeting 13 August 1914 in WO 163/44
28. Reith, op. cit., p. 30
29. Nicholson, op. cit., pp. 47–8
30. Andrews, *Haunting Years*, p. 21
31. Rifleman, *Four Years on the Western Front*, pp. 2–3
32. Behrend, *Make me a Soldier*, p. 36

33. National Archives, Kew, WO 32/5266
34. War Office Instruction dated 30 September 1914
35. Glover, *The Fateful Battle Line*, p. 16
36. Malone & Hawes, *Elegant Extracts*, pp. 117–18
37. Ibid., pp. 127–8
38. Behrend, op. cit., p. 36
39. Hawkings, op. cit., p. 8
40. Latham, op. cit., p. 23
41. Glover, op. cit., p. 37
42. Macleod, *Memoirs of an Artillery Officer on the Western Front*, p. 141
43. Andrews, op. cit., pp. 88, 95
44. Behrend, op. cit., pp. 77–8
45. Baynes, *Far from a Donkey*, p. 128
46. National Archives, Kew, WO 162/21
47. Army Council Meeting of 28 October 1914, Ibid., WO 163/45
48. Army Council Meetings 9, 20 January 1915, Ibid.
49. War Office Instruction dated 13 January 1915
50. Letters to Kitchener dated 21 April and 5 June 1915, National Archives, Kew, PRO 30/57/51
51. Burgoyne, *The Burgoyne Diaries*, p. 171
52. Mitchinson, *Gentlemen and Officers*, p. 134
53. *Army Lists*, September 1915 – May 1916
54. War Office Instruction dated 4 July 1915
55. National Archives, Kew, WO 70/50
56. Ibid., WO32/18617, 18620
57. Ibid., WO 70/50 and AO187/15
58. Carlisle, *My Own Darling*, p. 30
59. National Archives, Kew, WO 70/50, WO 95/5460
60. Harbottle, *Civilian Soldier 1914–1919*, p. 45
61. Andrews, op. cit., p. 180
62. AO 188/15, AO 249/15 and National Archives, Kew, WO 32/5452
63. Beckett, in Beckett & Simpson, *A Nation in Arms*, pp. 136–8; Mitchinson, The 'Transfer Controversy', *Stand To*, No. 33, Winter 1991; Woodward, *The Military Correspondence of Field-Marshal Sir William Robertson*, pp. 34–5; National Archives, Kew, WO 95/128 and information from Tom Tulloch-Marshall
64. National Archives, Kew, WO 70/50 and information from Charles Fair and Jill Knight
65. Letter French to CIGS dated 13 February 1916, National Archives, Kew, WO 32/5273
66. Ibid., WO 95/5454. *Great Britain and London AA Defences and Air Raids*, AIR 1/1190/204/5/2596, and Jock Bruce

CHAPTER FOUR

1. Quoted Germains, *The Kitchener Armies*, pp. 44–5
2. National Archives, Kew, PRO WO 293/1
3. Ibid., WO 162/21
4. Ibid., WO 293/1
5. Ibid., PRO 30/57/50
6. Ibid., WO 162/3
7. Germains, op. cit., p. 67
8. Ibid., pp. 70–71
9. Baynes & Maclean, *A Tale of Two Captains*, p. 65
10. National Archives, Kew, WO 32/11343
11. Simkins, *Kitchener's Army*, pp. 83–4

12. Germains, op. cit., pp. 71–4
13. Sheffield & Inglis, eds., *From Vimy Ridge to the Rhine*, p. 23
14. Quoted Germains, op. cit., p. 77
15. Stanley, *The History of the 89th Brigade 1914–1918*, pp. 3–18
16. Simkins, op. cit., p. 79
17. Ibid., pp. 96–99; Jones, *Mametz*, pp. 28–30 on appointment of brigade commanders, *Welsh Army Corps 1914–1919: Report of the Executive Committee*
18. *Welsh Army Corps*, op. cit.; Jones, op. cit., pp. 32–4
19. Adams, *Arms and the Wizard*, p. 46
20. Denman, *Ireland's Unknown Soldiers*, pp. 23–4
21. Simkins, op. cit., pp. 94–6
22. Denman, op. cit., pp. 24–6
23. Simkins, op. cit., pp. 113–16
24. Denman, op. cit., p. 36
25. Ibid., p. 62
26. Quoted Allinson, *The Bantams*, p. 39
27. Ibid., pp. 45–6
28. Turner, *Dear Old Blighty*, p. 34
29. Quoted Allinson, op. cit., p. 62
30. Largely drawn from Page, *Command in the Royal Naval Division*; and Sellers, *The Hood Battalion*
31. Quoted Germains, op. cit., p. 108
32. Drury, *Camp Follower*, pp. 7–8
33. Institution of Royal Engineers, *History of the Corps of Royal Engineers*, Vol. 5, p. 134
34. Chapman-Huston & Rutter, *General Sir John Cowans*, Vol. 2, pp. 20–22
35. National Archives, Kew, WO 106/364
36. Quoted Germains, op. cit., p. 110
37. Letter dated 25 October 1914, from Cook, *1914: Letters from a Volunteer*
38. Coppard, *With a Machine Gun to Cambrai*, p. 3
39. Quoted Simkins, op. cit., p. 240
40. Ibid., p. 239
41. Casson, *Steady Drummer*, p. 36
42. Tucker, *The Lousier War*, p. 13
43. Quoted Simkins, op. cit., pp. 249–50
44. Lewis, *Remembrances of Hell*, p. 23
45. Quoted Simkins, op. cit., p. 260
46. Quoted Chapman-Huston & Rutter, op. cit., p. 34
47. Quoted Simkins, op. cit., p. 262
48. Baynes & Maclean, op. cit., p. 66
49. Simkins, op. cit., p. 263
50. Stanley, op. cit., p. 27
51. Hughes, op. cit., p. 36; Simkins op. cit., p. 265
52. Nettleton, *The Anger of the Guns*, p. 27
53. Stanley, op. cit., p. 29
54. Minute dated 14 September 1914 and letter to home commands dated 9 September 1914, National Archives, Kew, WO 107/17
55. Simkins, op. cit., pp. 296–7
56. Liddell Hart, *The Memoirs of Captain Liddell Hart*, pp. 12–13
57. Frankau, *Self-Portrait*, pp. 131–2
58. Chapman, *A Passionate Prodigality*, pp. 13–14
59. Baynes, *Far from a Donkey*, p. 160
60. Letter to home commands dated 11 August 1914; National Archive, Kew, WO 162/3

61. Ibid., WO 162/24

62. War Office Instruction, No. 22 of November 1914

63. Crozier, *A Brass Hat in No Man's Land*, pp. 29–31

64. Harris, *Billie*, p. 14

65. Hankey, *A Student in Arms*, pp. 46–9

66. Baynes & Maclean, op. cit., pp. 68–9

67. *Military Operations: France and Belgium 1914*, Vol. 2, p. 17 fn1

68. National Archives, Kew, WO 79/73

69. Ibid., WO 32/11333

70. Ibid., letter Ministry of Munitions to War Office, 25 April 1916

71. Callwell, *Experiences of a Dug-Out 1914–1918*, p. 69

72. Eberle, *My Sapper Venture*, p. 34

73. Clapham, *Mud and Khaki*, p. 185

74. Shephard, *A Sergeant-Major's War*, p. 69

75. Ashley, *War-Diary of Private R. S. (Jack) Ashley 2472*, p. 18

76. Lucy, *There's a Devil in the Drum*, p. 342

77. Osburn, *Unwilling Passenger*, p. 248

CHAPTER FIVE

1. AO 217/15

2. Gladden, *The Somme 1916*, p. 18

3. Fielding, *War Letters to a Wife*, p. 75

4. Anon, *The War the Infantry Knew*, p. 245

5. Davson, *Memoirs of the Great War*, pp. 56, 65

6. Allinson, *The Bantams*, pp. 233–47; Babington, *For the Sake of Example*, pp. 90–91; Middlebrook, *Your Country Needs You*, p. 75; Oram, *Worthless Men*, pp. 92–4

7. Moynihan, *People at War 1914–18*, p. 199

8. Rae, *Conscience and Politics*, p. 57

9. National Archives, Kew, WO 106/373

10. ACI 551/16

11. National Archives, Kew, Director of Labour War Diary entry 4 March 17, WO 95/83

12. Quoted Rae, op. cit., p. 141

13. Graham, *Conscription and Conscience*, p. 64

14. Catchpool, *On Two Fronts*

15. Read, *Of Those We Loved*, pp. 276, 278–80

16. I am most grateful to Maggie Tyler for sharing the information she has collected on these relations of her husband.

17. National Archives, Kew, HO 45/10818/317810

18. Ibid., WO 32/11349

19. Ibid., WO 158/966

20. Ibid., WO 32/4773, Frank website

21. Ibid., WO 32/11351

22. Ibid., WO 162/28

23. Ibid., WO 32/11353

24. Ibid., WO 73/108, WO 162/6, WO162/338

25. Ibid., WO 32/4774

26. War Cabinet meetings 13 February, 7 March, 25 March 1918 CAB 23/5 Ibid

27. Ibid., WO 32/11353

28. Malone & Hawes, *Elegant Extracts*, p. 163

29. National Archives, Kew, WO 73/109, WO 95/4456, WO 162/6

30. Ibid., WO 32/5091, 5093

31. AG Memorandum and Secretary of State covering note dated 7 June 1917, WO 32/5917 Ibid

32. Fussell, *The Ordeal of Alfred M Hale*, pp. 36–64

33. War Cabinet meeting 19 January 1917, CAB 23/1 National Archives, Kew

34. Ibid., WO 95/5460

35. Mellersh, *Schoolboy into War*, p. 125

36. Hanbury-Sparrow, *The Land-Locked Lake*, pp. 208–9

37. Andrews, *Haunting Years*, pp. 213–4

38. Drury, *Camp Follower*, p. 165

39. National Archives, Kew, WO 162/7

40. Ibid., WO 95/5459

41. Chapman-Huston & Rutter, *General Sir John Cowans*, Vol. 2, pp. 182–5

42. National Archives, Kew, WO 95/5459

43. Latham, *A Territorial Soldier's War*, p. 59

44. Macleod, *Memoirs of an Artillery Officer on the Western Front*, p. 174

45. Ibid., pp. 57–60

46. Hodges, *Men of 18 in 1918*, pp. 22–40

47. National Archives, Kew, WO 162/6

48. Ibid., WO 380/17

49. Kiernan, *Little Brother Goes Soldiering*, pp. 21–33

50. National Archives, Kew, WO 95/5460

51. Ibid., WO 95/5459

52. Ibid., WO 32/18622, AIR 1/1190/204/5/2596

53. Moynihan, op. cit., p. 197

54. Robert J. Williams, *Notes on the West Bromwich Volunteer Rifle Corps 1914–1919* Military History Society Bulletin, Vol. XXVIII, No. 111, February 1978

55. National Archives, Kew, WO 161/105

56. Liddell Hart, *Memoirs*, pp. 28–9

57. Young, *Army Service Corps 1902–1918*, pp. 140–2

58. National Archives, Kew, WO 161/105

59. Peacock, *Tinker's Mufti*, p. 68

60. ACI 1606/17

61. Anon., *The War the Infantry Knew*, pp. 359, 412, 414

62. National Archives, Kew, WO 32/9553

CHAPTER SIX

1. National Archives, Kew, WO 95/2257, 1693

2. Panichas, *Promise of Greatness*, p. 39

3. Tucker, *A Lousier War*, pp. 14, 16

4. National Archives, Kew, WO 106/1518

5. Nettleton, *The Anger of the Guns*, pp. 123–8

6. National Archives, Kew, WO 158/794

7. Ibid., WO 95/930

8. Ibid., WO 95/737

9. Terraine, ed., *General Jack's Diary*, p. 288

10. Malone & Hawes, *Elegant Extracts*, p. 123

11. Seton, *Footslogger*, pp. 155–6

12. Bickersteth, *The Bickersteth Diaries*, pp. 112, 237

13. Letters 7 December, 21 November 1914, National Archives, Kew, WO 159/15

14. Mike Hibberd, *Development of Trench Mortars and their Tactical Use in the First World*, War lecture given at BCMH Summer Conference, July 2003

15. National Archives, Kew, MUN 5/382/1600/8 and Smith, *Four Years Out of My Life*, pp. 8–9

16. Rawlinson, *Adventures on the Western Front*, pp. 233–315

17. National Archives, Kew, WO 162/21 and Smith–Dorrien letter to von Donop 6 Dec 14, PRO 159/14

18. Saunders, *Weapons of the Trench War 1914–18*, p. 33

19. Macleod, *Memoirs of an Artillery Officer on the Western Front*, p. 67

20. Hibberd lecture, op. cit.

21. Ibid., and Saunders, op. cit., p. 35

22. Behrend, *Make me a Soldier*, pp. 95–6

23. Hibberd, op. cit. ; Saunders, op. cit., pp. 124–135

24. Macleod, op. cit., p. 87

25. 32nd Division TM Association, *Artillery and Trench Mortar Memories*, p. 19

26. Rees, *A Schoolmaster at War*, pp. 34–5

27. 32 TM Association, op. cit., pp. 54

28. Institution of REs, *History of the Corps of Royal Engineers* Vol. V, pp. 506–7

29. Hampson, *A Medical Officer's Diary*, p. 85

30. Casson, *Steady Drummer*, p. 64

31. Eberle, *My Sapper Venture*, p. 29

32. Gillespie, *Letters from Flanders*, p. 187, Hitchcock 'Stand To', p. 53; Lucy, *There's a Devil in the Drum*, p. 314

33. Hitchcock, op. cit., p. 211, Fletcher, *Letters from the Front*, p. 7

34. RE Institution op. cit., p. 515

35. Saunders, op. cit., p. 150

36. Norman, *Armageddon Road*, p. 124

37. Taken largely from Saunders, op. cit., pp. 1–27, 78–86 and Stigger, Philip, Note No. 1668, *Numerous Matters Relating to Grenades*, JSAHR No. 236, Summer 2003

38. AO 403/15

39. Shephard, *A Sergeant-Major's War*, p. 127

40. Talbot Kelly, *A Subaltern's Odyssey*, pp. 128–9

41. Terraine, op. cit., pp. 219–20; Nettleton, *The Anger of the Guns*, p. 81

42. Bickersteth, op. cit., pp. 54–5

43. National Archives, Kew, WO 106/403

44. Anglesey, *A History of the British Cavalry* Vol. 8, p. 159

45. Ibid., p. 162 fn

46. Home, *The Diary of a World War 1 Cavalry Officer*, p. 160

47. Stephen Badsey, *Cavalry and the Breakthrough Doctrine* in Griffith, ed., *British Fighting Methods in the Great War*, p. 161; Anglesey, op. cit., p. 163

48. Home, op. cit., p. 162

49. Hampson, op. cit., p. 74

50. Rawlinson, *The Defence of London 1915–1918*, pp. 5–6

51. *Reports on the Metropolitan Observation Service* National Archives, Kew, AIR 2/88

52. Panichas, op. cit., p. 261

53. This section is drawn largely from National Archives, Kew, WO 162/5 Appendix IX, Farndale, *Western Front*, pp. 364–6; Farndale, *The Forgotten Fronts and the Home Base*, pp. 362–8; Institution of REs op. cit., pp. 55–68, 488–98

54. Innes, *Flash Spotters and Sound Rangers*, p. 212

55. GHQ BEF GRO dated 13 November 1916

56. Above section largely drawn from Chasseaud, *Artillery's Astrologers*; Innes, op. cit; Institution of REs, op. cit., pp. 526–38; Farndale, *Western Front*, pp. 372–9; Lecture by John Peaty at BCMH Summer 2003 Conference, July 2003

57. Talbot Kelly, op. cit., p. 86

58. *London Gazette*, No. 31284, dated 10 April 1919

59. Based largely on National Archives, Kew, WO 95/120 and 127, Hartcup *Camouflage*, Institution of REs, op. cit., pp. 483–7

60. Drury, *Camp Follower*, p. 127

61. Carrington, *Soldier from the Wars Returning*, p. 126

62. Hammerson, *No Easy Hopes or Lies*, pp. 224–5

63. Greenwell, *An Infant in Arms*, pp. 184–5

64. Ibid., p. 195

65. Gray, *The Spirit of the Bayonet*, pp. 13–15. I am most grateful to the author for showing me his manuscript.

66. Hart-Davis, *Siegfried Sassoon Diaries 1915–1918*, pp. 59–60

67. National Archives, Kew, WO 95/55

68. Ibid.

69. Samuels, *Command or Control?*, p. 122

70. Baynes, *Far from a Donkey*, p. 212

CHAPTER SEVEN

I am extremely grateful to Ivor Lee, who probably knows more about Labour 1914–18 than anyone else, for reading this chapter in draft and, providing valuable comment.

1. National Archives, Kew, WO 95/4174

2. Burgoyne, *The Burgoyne Diaries*, p. 123

3. Young, *Army Service Corps 1902–1918*, pp. 55–6, 236–7

4. Eades, *The War Diary and Letters of Corporal Tom Eades*, p. 1

5. RE Institution, *The History of the Corps of Royal Engineers*, Vol. 5, pp. 232, 539–43

6. ACI dated 23 March 1915

7. Ashley, *War Diary of Private R S (Jack) Ashley 2472*, pp. 16–18

8. National Archives, Kew, Letters 10,12 July 1915 WO 158/293

9. Wolff, *Subalterns of the Foot*, p. 62

10. Ibid., p. 128

11. Ibid., p. 138

12. National Archives, Kew, WO 95/3976A A&Q LOC War Diary entry 17 Nov 16

13. Mitchinson, *Pioneer Battalions in the Great War*, p. 66

14. Anglesey, *A History of the British Cavalry*, Vol. 8, p. 181

15. Ibid., p. 111

16. Blacker, ed., *Have You Forgotten Yet?*, pp. 89–103

17. National Archives, Kew, WO 32/5145

18. Ibid., WO 159/15

19. Burgoyne, op. cit., p. 96

20. National Archives, Kew, WO 95/2110, 2032, WO 107/69, 72

21. Maude, *The 47th (London) Division 1914–1919*, p. 221

22. National Archives, Kew, WO 95/43

23. Ibid., WO 95/947

24. Ibid., WO 95/905

25. Mitchinson, op. cit., p. 216, Note 4

26. National Archive, Kew, WO 95/26

27. Ibid., WO 95/4803

28. Wolff, op. cit., p. 121

29. National Archives, Kew, WO 95/337

30. Ibid., WO 95/4059

31. Ibid., WO 95/559

32. A Rifleman, *Four Years on the Western Front*, p. 134

33. National Archives, Kew, WO 95/5499

34. Ibid., WO 95/5468; Young, op. cit., p. 56; RE Institution, op. cit., pp. 591–2, 595, 597

35. Ibid., WO 95/337, WO 162/14

36. Ibid., WO 32/11374, WO 107/39

37. Chapman, *A Passionate Prodigality*, p. 46

38. Prior & Wilson, *Command on the Western Front*, p. 156

39. National Archives, Kew, WO 95/3975 A&Q LOC War Diary entries 14 May, 24 July, 26 July 1916

40. Ibid., WO 95/517

41. Maude, op. cit., p. 221

42. National Archives, Kew, WO 162/6, WO 95/4174

43. Ibid., WO 162/6, WO 73/106

44. Wylly, *The York and Lancaster Regiment*, p. 283

45. National Archives, Kew, NATS 1/299

46. Ibid., AAG War Diary 27 June, 30 September 1916 WO 95/26

47. Ibid., WO 106/33

48. Ian Gallacher, 'Invisible Army' *Military Illustrated* No. 127. I am grateful to Tim Newark, the Editor, for sending me a copy of this.

49. National Archives, Kew, WO 95/83; Young, op. cit., p. 207

50. Ibid., WO 95/83

51. Ibid., Historical Record 1 TRB WO 95/5459

52. ACI 84/15

53. National Archives, Kew, WO 106/373

54. Ibid., WO 95/26

55. ACI 611/17

56. National Archives, Kew, WO 95/83

57. Purdom, ed., *Everyman at War*, pp. 262–8

58. National Archives, Kew, WO 95/4174

59. Information from Ivor Lee

60. National Archives, Kew, WO 106/33

61. Maude, op. cit., p. 221

62. National Archives, Kew, WO 107/69

63. Nicholson, *Behind the Lines*, pp. 205–6

64. National Archives, Kew, WO 107/69, 72

65. Ibid., WO 95/243, 337, 408, 492, 558

66. Ibid., WO 107/69, RE Institution, op. cit.

67. Nettleton, *The Anger of the Guns*, p. 104

68. Hampson, *A Medical Officer's Diary*, p. 114

69. Information largely from Ivor Lee

70. National Archives, Kew, WO 95/4944

71. *Statistics of the Military Effort*, pp. 64(ii), 65

72. Page, *Command in the Royal Naval Division*, pp. 150–61

73. National Archives, Kew, WO 95/5494

74. Ibid., WO 95/905, 95/930

75. Ibid., WO 95/753

76. Ibid., WO 95/409

77. Ibid., WO 95/26

78. Ibid., WO 95/187

79. Ibid., WO 95/26, 83

80. Ibid., WO 95/83

81. Ibid., WO 95/429

82. Ibid., WO 106/33

83. Figures from Ivor Lee

CHAPTER EIGHT

I am much indebted to Krisztina Robert, who is currently writing a study of women in uniform during the Great War, for her advice on sources and valuable comments on a draft of this chapter.

Much of the framework for this chapter is drawn from the entry *Women's War Work: United Kingdom* in the Twelfth Edition of the Encyclopaedia Britannica Vol. XXXII, London and New York, 1922. This was written by Agnes Conway, Honorary Curator of the Women's Work Section of the Imperial War Museum, who was able to gather information from the relevant organizations before they were disbanded.

1. Mitchell, *Women on the Warpath*, p. 152

2. Letter dated 17 April 1915, National Archives, Kew, WO 107/14

3. Marwick, *Women at War*, p. 40

4. ADMS Boulogne War Diary, National Archives, Kew, WO 95/4010

5. Chapman-Huston & Rutter, *General Sir John Cowans*, Vol. 2, pp. 84–8; Cowper, *A Short History of Queen Mary's Army Auxiliary Corps*, pp. 10–11

6. Chapman-Huston & Rutter, op. cit., pp. 132–4; Young, *Army Service Corps 1902–1918*, pp. 93–4

7. Beardwood, *FANY at the Western Front*, pp. 3–5

8. Mitchell, op. cit., pp. 125–138; Marwick, op. cit., pp. 105–7

9. Lawrence, *Sapper Dorothy Lawrence*

10. Mitchell, op. cit., pp. 145–9, Turner, *Dear Old Blighty*, pp. 50–51

11. Charteris, *At GHQ*, p. 162

12. Marwick, op. cit., p. 85

13. Cowper, op. cit., pp. 15–16

14. National Archives, Kew, WO 32/5251

15. Ibid., WO 32/5093

16. Drawn largely on Cowper, op. cit., pp. 17–21

17. GSO, *GHQ*, pp. 162–3

18. Charteris, op. cit., p. 224

19. ACI 1185/18

20. Whitehead, *Doctors in the Great War*, p. 114

21. National Archives, Kew, WO 32/5254; Marwick, op. cit., p. 93

22. Tennent, *Red Herrings of 1918*, p. 17

23. *Statistics of the Military Effort*, p. 194

CHAPTER NINE

1. National Archives, Kew, WO 95/4186

2. Ibid., WO 95/5467

3. Ashurst, *My Bit*, pp. 32–3

4. Gladden, *The Somme 1916*, pp. 57–75

5. Thomas, *A Life Apart*, pp. 44–5

6. National Archives, Kew, WO 95/4186

7. Bird, *Honour Satisfied*, pp. 8–14

8. Gladden, *Ypres 1917*, p. 27

9. Rifleman, *Four Years on the Western Front*, pp. 255–6

10. Terraine, ed., *General Jack's Diary*, pp. 176, 182

11. National Archives, Kew, WO 95/4186

12. BEF GRO dated 8 March 1918

13. Cardinal-Harford, Major J., *They had Lied about their Age* from *I Was There* Vol. 4, pp. 2207–9; Waverley Book Company, 1938–9 and National Archives, Kew, WO

95/26. I am most grateful to Terry Carter for drawing my attention to the Cardinal-Harford article.

14. Defending Officer's copy of Summary of Evidence, including draft of his summing up for the defence. I am very grateful to Mike Hibberd for giving me a copy of this.

15. National Archives, Kew, WO 95/4018, 4186

16. Roskill, *Hankey: Man of Secrets*, p. 469

17. *Statistics of the Military Effort*, p. 85; Woodward, *Lloyd George and the Generals*, pp. 234–7

18. Maurice, *The Maurice Case*, p. 63

19. Figure based on *Statistics of the Military Effort*, p. 123

20. National Archives, Kew, WO 162/6

21. Denman, *Ireland's Unknown Soldiers*, p. 137

22. Chapman, *A Passionate Prodigality*, p. 223

23. Maurice, op. cit., p. 77

24. National Archives, Kew, AAG War Diary WO 95/26, WO 95/1626

25. Ibid., WO 95/5459

26. Hodges, *Men of 18 in 1918*, p. 40

27. Taylor, *The Bottom of the Barrel*, pp. 47–8

28. National Archives, Kew, WO 95/1626

29. Fay, *The War Office at War*, p. 154

30. *Statistics of the Military Effort*, pp. 64(iii), 267

31. Ibid., pp. 64(iii), 65

32. Maurice, op. cit., pp. 82–3

33. Ibid., pp. 96–7; Jeffery, *The Military Correspondence of Field Marshal Sir Henry Wilson 1918–1922*, ed., p. 41

34. Quoted Woodward, op. cit., p. 303

35. Blake, *The Private Papers of Douglas Haig 1914–1919*, p. 308

36. *Statistics of the Military Effort*, p. 364

37. National Archives, Kew, WO 95/3011, 95/3012, WO 162/6

38. Ibid., WO 95/2594

39. Crozier, *A Brass Hat in No Man's Land*, pp. 215–6

40. National Archives, Kew, WO 95/2606

41. Ibid., WO 95/128

42. I am very grateful to Charles Fair for sharing the fruits of his research with me.

43. National Archives, Kew, WO 95/1895

44. Ibid., WO 95/1895

45. Moynihan, *People at War 1914–1918*, pp. 210–11

46. *Statistics of the Military Effort*, pp. 65–6

47. Jeffery, op. cit., p. 47

48. Woodward, op. cit., pp. 329–30

49. Blake, op. cit., pp. 325–6; Jeffery, op. cit., p. 50; Woodward, op. cit., pp. 331–2

CHAPTER TEN

1. Keith Simpson in Beckett & Simpson, ed., *A Nation in Arms*, p. 64

2. Wedderburn-Maxwell, *Young Contemptible*, pp. 4–6

3. Law, *A Man at Arms*, pp. 39–40

4. Talbot Kelly, *A Subaltern's Odyssey*, pp. 34–5

5. Errington, *The Inns of Court Officers Training Corps during the Great War*, pp. 11–13

6. Graves, *Goodbye to All That*, pp. 61, 71

7. Behrend, *Make me a Soldier*, pp. 22–5

8. Lytton, *The Press and the General Staff*, pp. 3–4

9. Described by Sherriff in Panichas, ed., *Promise of Greatness*, pp. 136–7

10. Haig-Brown, *The OTC and the Great War* Appendix

11. Tyndale-Biscoe, *Gunner Subaltern*, pp. 6–8

12. Institution of Royal Engineers, *History of the Corps of Royal Engineers*, Vol. 5, pp. 31–4

13. Gibbon, *Inglorious Soldier*, pp. 4–28

14. Gillespie, *Letters from Flanders*, pp. 2–11; Slack, *Grandfather's Adventures in the Great War*, p. 13

15. Sheffield & Inglis, ed., *From Vimy Ridge to the Rhine*, pp. 24–7

16. Quoted Anglesey, *A History of British Cavalry*, Vol. 7, p. 107

17. Mitchinson, *Gentlemen and Officers*, p. 85; Rifleman, *Four Years on the Western Front*, p. 69

18. National Archives, Kew, PRO 30/57/49

19. Ibid., WO 162/24

20. Anon., *The War the Infantry Knew*, pp. 89, 109

21. Crozier, *A Brass Hat in No Man's Land*, pp. 153, 187, 253

22. Anglesey, op. cit., p. 107; Creagh & Humphris, *The VC and DSO Book*, HMSO *Services of Military Officers 1919*

23. Graves, op. cit., pp. 80–1

24. National Archives, Kew, WO 162/2

25. Nicholson, *Behind the Lines*, p. 46

26. National Archives, Kew, WO 95/128

27. Letter dated 25 November 1914; Ibid., PRO 30/57/51

28. BEF GRO dated 24 December 1914

29. Anon, *A Soldier's Diary of the Great War*, pp. 101–110

30. Walker, *The Honourable Artillery Company in the Great War*, pp. 28–9; Burgoyne, *The Burgoyne Diaries*, p. 112, whose 2nd Royal Irish Rifles received eight of them.

31. Mitchinson, op. cit., p. 86

32. Rifleman, op. cit., pp. 69, 72–4, 114

33. Lewis, ed., *Remembrances of Hell*, p. 72

34. Andrews, *Haunting Years*, p. 146

35. Carlisle, *My Own Darling*, pp. 12–15

36. AO 174/14 and Appendix XII to Army Orders 1914

37. Quoted Simkins, *Kitchener's Army*, p. 300

38. Chapman, *A Passionate Prodigality*, p. 13

39. Letter to Kitchener, 29 November 1914, National Archives, Kew, PRO 30/57/73

40. Stanley, *The History of the 89th Brigade*, p. 30

41. Errington, op. cit., p. 22

42. Denman, *Ireland's Unknown Soldiers*, pp. 42–5, 59–60

43. National Archives, Kew, WO 32/18556

44. Carr, *A Time to Leave the Ploughshares*, p. 13

45. Errington, op. cit., pp. 42–3

46. Mellersh, *Schoolboy into War*, pp. 31–4

47. Waugh in Panichas, op. cit., pp. 335–7

48. ACI dated 24 April 1915

49. Baynes & Maclean, *A Tale of Two Captains*, p. 73; Carrington, *Soldier from the Wars Returning*, pp. 76–8

50. ACIs dated 2 and 20 October 1915

51. Morten, *I Remain, Your Son Jack*, pp. 42, 81, 84–5, 107–8

52. Baynes, *Far from a Donkey*, p. 125

53. Fraser-Tytler, *With Lancashire Lads and Field Guns in France*, pp. 21–2

54. Mellersh, op. cit., pp. 48–60

55. Gore-Browne letter dated 29 March 1916; Gore-Browne Letters

56. Latham, *A Territorial Soldier's War*, pp. 38–9; Foster in Panichas, op. cit., p. 309
57. AO 429/15
58. Terraine, ed *General Jack's Diary*, p.105, Malone & Hawes, *Elegant Extracts*, pp. 143–4, Moynihan, ed., *God on Our Side*, p. 145
59. Turner, *Gallant Gentlemen*, p. 280
60. Quoted Anglesey, op. cit., p. 87
61. National Archives, Kew WO 106/373
62. Ibid., WO 95/2427
63. Errington, op. cit., pp. 25–8
64. Worden, *Yes Daddy but there has been Another War Since Then*, pp. 25–7
65. Quoted Shepperd, *Sandhurst*, p. 126
66. ACI 497/18
67. Errington, op. cit., pp. 29–30
68. Nettleton, *The Anger of the Guns*, pp. 16–58
69. Shephard, *A Sergeant-Major's War*, pp. 135–41
70. West, *Diary of a Dead Officer*, pp. 17–42, Collins *Last Man Standing*, p. 72
71. Read, *Of Those We loved*, pp. 283–4; Peacock, *Tinker's Mufti*, p. 43; Hartley in Panichas, op. cit., p. 256; Glover, ed., *The Fateful Battle Line*, pp. 150–52
72. *Manual of Military Law*, 1914, p. 471
73. National Archives, Kew, WO 339/62717. I am very grateful to Tom Tulloch-Marshall for bringing this file to light.
74. Ibid., WO 339/90293
75. Ibid., WO 163/23, pp. 107–9
76. Ibid., WO 162/5
77. Ibid., WO 162/6
78. Harbottle, *Civilian Soldier*, pp. 75–79
79. Graves, op. cit., p. 218; Hawkings, *From Ypres to Cambrai*, p. 111
80 Scrivenor, *Brigade Signals*, pp. 22–3
81. Walker, op. cit., pp. 289, 474
82. Nicholson, op. cit., p. 223; Terraine, ed., op. cit., p. 195; Slack, op. cit., p. 169
83. Graves, op. cit., p. 218; Collins, op. cit., pp. 77, 79
84. Andrews, op. cit., pp. 266–85; Morgan, *Our Harry's War*, pp. 184–6
85. ACI 785/18
86. National Archives, Kew, WO 162/5
87. Walker, op. cit., pp. 99–100
88. Lucy, *There's a Devil in the Drum*, pp. 352–4
89. GHQ BEF GRO dated 2 September 1918
90. Thomas, *A Life Apart*, p. 67
91. Hanbury-Sparrow, *The Land-Locked Lake*, p. 293; Rees, *A Schoolmaster at War*, p. 79
92. Campbell, *In the Cannon's Mouth*, p. 13, Dolden *Cannon Fodder*, p. 91
93. Crozier op. cit., p. 157; Terraine, ed., op. cit., p. 247; Peacock, op. cit., p. 51; Glover, ed., op. cit., pp. 150–53; Eberle, *My Sapper Venture*, pp. 101–2
94. Graves, op. cit., p. 218
95. *Statistics of the Military Effort of the British Empire*, p. 707; Sheffield, *Leadership in the Trenches*, pp. 31–3
96. Turner, op. cit., p. 286

CHAPTER ELEVEN

1. Quoted Brown, *Tommy Goes to War*, p. 169
2. Statistics taken from Nicholas Evans, *The Deaths of Qualified Staff Officers 1914–18*, JSAHR No. 313, pp. 29–35
3. Callwell, *Experiences of a Dug-Out 1914–1918*, pp. 39–40
4. Roskill, *Hankey: Man of Secrets*, p. 219
5. Woodward, *The Military Correspondence of Field-Marshal Sir William Robertson*, p. 11
6. Magnus, *Kitchener*, pp. 350–51
7. Woodward, op. cit., p. 12
8. Roskill, op. cit., p. 237
9. Callwell, op. cit., pp. 137–8
10. Woodward, op. cit., p. 128
11. Fay, *The War Office at War*, p. 182
12. Roper, *The Records of the War Office and Related Departments, 1660–1994*, p. 110
13. Carrington, *Soldier from the Wars Returning*, p. 111
14. Devonald-Lewis, *From the Somme to the Armistice*, p. 124
15. Hamilton, *Monty*, p. 123
16. Eden, *Another World 1897–1917*, p. 167
17. Gore-Browne letters
18. Scrivenor, *Brigade Signals*, pp. 51–2
19. Kelly, *39 Months with the 'Tigers'*, pp. 32–3
20. Rogerson, *The Last of the Ebb*, p. 6
21. Hamilton, op. cit., p. 123
22. Fuller, *Memoirs of an Unconventional Soldier*, pp. 51–2
23. Carrington, op. cit., p. 104
24. Chandos, *From War to Peace*, pp. 134–5
25. Chapman, *A Passionate Prodigality*, p. 141
26. Home, *The Diary of a World War 1 Cavalry Officer*, p. 105
27. Wolff, *Subalterns of the Foot*, p. 244
28. Farndale, *History of the Royal Regiment of Artillery: Western Front 1914–1918*, pp. 343–7
29. Law, *A Man at Arms*, p. 73
30. Institution of REs, *History of the Corps of Royal Engineers*, Vol. 5, pp. 153–67
31. Bridges, *Alarms & Excursions*, p. 165
32. Home, op. cit., p. 153
33. GSO, *GHQ*, pp. 35–6, 51
34. Page, *Command in the Royal Naval Division*, p. 80
35. Chapman, op. cit., p. 199
36. Terraine, ed., *General Jack's Diary*, pp. 139, 226
37. Siepmann, *Echo of the Guns*, p. 71
38. Terraine, op. cit., pp. 295–6
39. Nicholson, *Behind the Lines*, pp. 103–4
40. Panichas, *A Promise of Greatness*, p. 212
41. Bond, *Staff Officer*, p. 219
42. National Archives, Kew, WO 32/5153
43. War Office Instruction dated 23 August 1914
44. Ibid., dated 5 October 1914
45. AO 92/16
46. National Archives, Kew, WO 359/16
47. Hitchcock, *'Stand To'*, p. 91; Fletcher, *Letters from the Front*, p. 100
48. Baynes & Maclean, *A Tale of Two Captains*, p. 248
49. Moynihan, *People at War 1914–1918*, p. 158
50. Collins, *Last Man Standing*, p. 113
51. Fuller, op. cit., p. 53

52. Nicholson, op. cit., p. 135

53. Charteris, *At GHQ*, p. 58

54. Burgoyne, *The Burgoyne Diaries*, p. 51

55. Malone & Hawes, *Elegant Extracts*, p. 128

56. Eberle, *My Sapper Venture*, p. 30

57. Hamilton, *Monty*, pp. 97–8, 102 and Fuller, op. cit., p. 52

58. Charteris, op. cit., pp. 209–10

59. Chapman, op. cit., pp. 141–2

60. Fletcher, *Letters from the Front*, pp. 85–6

61. Farrar-Hockley, *Goughie*, p. 231

62. Letter dated 7 November 1915 National Archives, Kew, WO 107/15

63. Nicholson, op. cit., pp. 184–5

64. Powell, *Plumer*, p. 157

65. *Notes for Commanding Officers*, pp. 349–59

66. Fuller, op. cit., pp. 60–2; Kentish, *This Foul Thing Called War*, pp. 62–4; Rees, *A Schoolmaster at War*, p. 100

67. Bird, *Unversed in Arms*, pp. 69–79

68. Fraser, *In Good Company*, pp. 62, 79

69. Lytton, *The Press and the General Staff*, p. 50

70. Chapman, op. cit., p. 161

71. Griffith, *Up to Mametz*, p. 208

72. Home, op. cit., p. 97

73. Haig, January 1917 diary annex *Summary of Schools of Training for the British Expeditionary Force, During Winter 1916–17*, National Archives, Kew, WO 256/15

74. Bond, *Staff Officer*, pp. 131–2. Guinness mistakenly referred to Currie by the initials R.C.

75. Bond, *The Victorian Army and the Staff College*, pp. 303–4; Corrigan, *Mud, Blood and Poppycock*, p. 211, ACI 1379/17

76. Nettleton, *The Anger of the Guns*, pp. 111, 113

CHAPTER TWELVE

1. National Archives, Kew, WO 95/4092

2. *Statistics of the Military Effort*, pp. 30, 363, 669

3. Terraine, ed., *General Jack's Diary*, p. 60

4. Blake, *The Private Papers of Douglas Haig*, p. 291

5. Fielding, *War Letters to a Wife*, pp. 175–6

6. Talbot Kelly, *A Subaltern's Odyssey*, pp. 82–3

7. Hitchcock, *'Stand To'*, p. 255

8. Fielding, op. cit., pp. 175–6

9. Lucy, *There's a Devil in the Drum*, p. 93

10. Osburn, *Unwilling Passenger*, p. 183

11. Nettleton, *The Anger of the Guns*, pp. 166–7

12. National Archives, Kew, WO32/5460

13. Burgoyne, *The Burgoyne Diaries*, pp. 24–5

14. Slack, *Grandfather's Adventures*, p. 168

15. Thomas, *A Life Apart*, pp. 113–7

16. Crozier, *A Brass Hat in No Man's Land*, pp. 60–62

17. Chapman, *A Passionate Prodigality*, pp. 73–4

18. Quoted Babington, op. cit., p. 120

19. Nettleton, op. cit., p. 166

20. Martin, *Poor Bloody Infantry*, p. 92

21. Bickersteth, *The Bickersteth Diaries*, p. 198

22. *Statistics of the Military Effort*, pp. 658–9, pp. 667–8

23. National Archives, Kew, WO 154/2 and /3

24. Scott, *'Dishonoured'*; Bridges, *Alarms & Excursions*, pp. 85–8

25. Osburn, op. cit., pp. 82–3

26. Oram, *Worthless Men*, p. 121

27. Circular memorandum accompanying GHQ France GRO 585 dated 31 January 1915

28. *Notes for Commanding Officers*, p. 408

29. Figures based on Oram, op. cit., p. 120

30. *Statistics of the Military Effort*, p. 64 (xix)

31. National Archives, Kew, WO 154/8

32. John Peaty, *Haig and Military Discipline* in Bond & Cave, *Haig's Command*, p. 199

33. Putkowski & Sykes, *Shot at Dawn*, pp. 295–7

34. *Statistics of the Military Effort*, p. 155

35. Quoted Oram, op. cit., p. 91

36. *Notes for Commanding Officers*, p. 423

37. Putkowski & Sykes, op. cit., p. 22

38. Ibid., p. 23

39. Dearden, *Medicine & Duty*, pp. 155–7, 170–71

40. Bickersteth, op. cit., pp. 189–191; Babington, op. cit., p. 122; Putkowski & Sykes, op. cit., p. 178

41. National Archives, Kew, WO 71/537; Devonald-Lewis, *From the Somme to the Armistice*, pp. 95–6

42. Babington, op. cit., p. 143; Putkowski & Sykes, op. cit., p. 191

43. Quoted Babington, op. cit., p. 124

44. Ibid., p. 92

45. Quoted Carver, *Britain's Army in the Twentieth Century*, pp. 129–30

46. Delamain, *Going Across*, p. 62

47. Martin, op. cit., pp. 92–3

48. Oram, op. cit., p. 101; *Statistics of the Military Effort*, p. 669

49. Crozier, op. cit., pp. 81–4; Putkowski & Sykes, op. cit., pp. 68–9

50. Chapman, op. cit., p. 209

51. Siepmann, *Echo of the Guns*, p. 99

52. Devonald-Lewis, op. cit., p. 162

53. Collins, *Last Man Standing*, p. 162

54. I am most grateful to Joe Devereux for this information.

55. Babington, op. cit., pp. 104–5; Putkowski & Sykes, op. cit., pp. 142–3; Corns & Hughes-Wilson, *Blindfold and Alone*, pp. 325–32

56. National Archives, Kew, ADM 156/24, WO 339/87122; Babington, op. cit., pp. 95–103; Putkowski & Sykes, op. cit., pp. 150–55

57. Babington, op. cit., pp. 136–42

58. National Archives, Kew, WO 32/4675

59. Osburn, op. cit., p. 350

60. Glover, ed., *The Fateful Battle Line*, p. 87

61. Osburn, op. cit., p. 350

62. F. W. Harvey, *Homosexuality and the British Army during the First World War*, JSAHR Winter 2001

63. Ibid.; and Seton, *Footslogger*, pp. 142–53

64. Taylor, *The Bottom of the Barrel*, p. 118

65. Kiernan, *Little Brother Goes Soldiering*, p. 106

66. Putkowski, *British Army Mutineers*, p. 129

67. Ibid., pp. 21–2

68. Ibid., pp. 147–8; and National Archives Kew, WO 95/4435

69. Ibid., p. 147; WO 95/2606

70. Ibid., p. 100; WO 95/4851

71. Ibid., pp. 151–2; WO 95/1979

72. Ibid., pp. 154–6, WO 95/3217

73. National Archives, Kew, WO 32/5455

74. Putkowski, op. cit., pp. 24–6; Corns & Hughes-Wilson, op. cit., pp. 389–94

75. National Archives, Kew, WO 256/22

CHAPTER THIRTEEN

1. Osburn, *Unwilling Passenger*, p. 20

2. Herringham, *A Physician in France*, p. 50

3. Hampson, *A Medical Officer's Diary*

4. McConachie, *The Student Soldiers*, pp. 124–36

5. Herringham, op. cit., p. 53

6. Whitehead, *Doctors in the Great War*, p. 35

7. Bridges, *Alarms & Excursions*, p. 182

8. Cushing, *From a Surgeon's Diary 1915–1918*, p. 114

9. Whitehead, op. cit., p. 76

10. *Notes for Commanding Officers*, pp. 325–6

11. Panichas, ed., *Promise of Greatness*, pp. 183–5

12. Osburn, op. cit., p. 262

13. Luard, *Unknown Warriors*, p. 178

14. Geoffrey Noon in Griffith, ed., *British Fighting Methods in the Great War*, p. 96

15. Terraine, ed., *General Jack's Diary*, p. 84

16. Talbot Kelly, *A Subaltern's Odyssey*, p. 122

17. Noon in Griffith, op. cit., p. 95

18. Burgoyne, *The Burgoyne Diaries*, p. 61

19. Noon in Griffith, op. cit., pp. 92–3

20. Norman, *Armageddon Road*, pp. 100–101

21. Hampson, op. cit. diary entry 28 November 1914

22. Whitehead, op. cit., pp. 221–3

23. Herringham, op. cit., pp. 103–8

24. Ibid., p. 125

25. Cushing, op. cit., pp. 300–1

26. Whitehead, op. cit., pp. 232–3; Herringham; op. cit., pp. 104–8

27. Fielding, *War Letters to a Wife*, p. 213

28. Dolden, *Cannon Fodder*, p. 145

29. Burgoyne, op. cit., p. 25

30. Baynes, *Morale*, p. 56

31. AAG War Dairy 16 January 1915, National Archives, Kew, WO 95/25; Burgoyne, op. cit., p. 82

32. Dugdale, *'Langemarck' and 'Cambrai'*, p. 41

33. Greenwell, *An Infant in Arms*, p. 157

34. Worden, *Yes Daddy*, p. 85

35. GHQ BEF GRO dated 9 January 1915

36. Whitehead, op. cit., pp. 196–7

37. Herringham, op. cit., pp. 69–75; Luard, op. cit., p. 181fn

38. Luard, op. cit., p. 157

39. Whitehead, op. cit., p. 201

40. Luard, op. cit., pp. 192–244

41. Henniker, *Transportation on the Western Front*, pp. 55–63

42. Osburn, op. cit., p. 209

43. Panichas, op. cit., p. 187

44. Dolden, op. cit., pp. 52–54

45. Lewis, *Remembrances of Hell*, pp. 56–7

46. Latham, *A Territorial Soldier's War*, p. 55

47. Cushing, op. cit., p. 296

48. Ware, *'A Rose in Picardy'*, p. 17

49. Herringham, op. cit., pp. 90–91

50. Glover, *The Fateful Battle Line*, pp. 61–4

51. Rifleman, *Four Years on the Western Front*, pp. 250–51

52. Noakes, *The Distant Drum*, pp. 113–5

53. Tyndale-Biscoe, *Gunner Subaltern*, p. 100

54. Drury, *Camp Follower*, p. 54

55. Ashurst, *My Bit*, pp. 106–9

56. GHQ BEF GRO dated 13 November 1914

57. Herringham, op. cit., pp. 91–3; Whitehead, op. cit., pp. 243–4

58. This section draws mainly on Babington, *Shell-Shock*, pp. 29–135; Herringham, op. cit., pp. 133–142; Holden, *Shell Shock*, pp. 7–71; Whitehead, op. cit., pp. 168–70

59. Osburn, op. cit., p. 169

60. Fraser-Tytler, *With Lancashire Lads and Field Guns in France*, p. 94

61. Osburn, op. cit., p. 345

62. National Archives, Kew, WO 32/17700

63. Lucy, *There's a Devil in the Drum*, pp. 349–52

64. National Archives, Kew, WO 163/23 Precis 928

65. Ibid.

66. Babington, op. cit., p. 76

67. Nettleton, *The Anger of the Guns*, pp. 63–4

68. Ware, *The Immortal Heritage*, pp. 24–5

69. National Archives, Kew, WO 32/5846

70. Fraser-Tytler, op. cit., p. 226

71. Ware, op.cit., pp. 39–40fn

72. National Archives, Kew, WO 32/5846

73. Bickersteth, *The Bickersteth Diaries*, p. 109

74. Moynihan, *God on Our Side*, pp. 136–7

75. Hitchcock, *'Stand To'*, p. 188

76. National Archives, Kew, WO 95/4944

77. Leckie, *A Centaur Looks Back*, p. 73

78. Chapman-Huston & Rutter, *Sir John Cowans*, Vol. 2, pp. 100–101

79. Ibid., pp. 97–9

CHAPTER FOURTEEN

1. FSR II Ch XII; Kennedy & Crabb, *The Postal History of the British Army in World War 1*, pp. 1–11, 35

2. National Archives, Kew, WO 161/114

3. Burgoyne, *The Burgoyne Diaries*, p. 38

4. Carrington, *Soldier from the Wars Returning*, p. 159; Kennedy & Crabb, op. cit., p. 35

5. National Archives, Kew, WO 161/114

6. Kennedy & Crabb, op. cit., pp. 21–2

7. Ibid., pp. 21, 135

8. Drury, *Camp Follower*, p. 208

9. Anon, *The War the Infantry Knew*, p. 96

10. Lucy, *There's a Devil in the Drum*, p. 317; Clapham, *Mud and Khaki*, p. 171; Pollard, *Fire-Eater*, p. 96; Harbottle, *Civilian Soldier 1914–1919*, p. 39

11. Harris, *Billie*, p. 120

12. Greenwell, *Infant in Arms*, p. 41; Dolden, *Cannon Fodder*, pp. 99, 136, 181; Greenwell, op. cit., p. 190

13. Fuller, *Troop Morale and Popular Culture in the British and Dominion Armies 1914–1918*, p. 72

14. Page, *Command in the Royal Naval Division*, pp. 76–7; Carrington, op. cit., p. 168; Baynes & Maclean, *A Tale of Two Captains*, pp. 148–9

15. Lewis, *Remembrances of Hell*, pp. 75–6; Fielding, *War Letters to a Wife*, p. 95

16. Blake, *The Private Papers of Douglas Haig*, p. 273

17. Fay, *The War Office at War*, p. 106

18. National Archives, Kew, WO 162/6

19. Young, *Army Service Corps 1902–1918*, p. 29

20. Chapman-Huston & Rutter, *General Sir John Cowans*, Vol. 2, pp. 56–9

21. Letter dated 16 December 1914, National Archives, Kew, WO 107/13

22. Lewis, op. cit., p. 39; Burgoyne, op. cit., pp. 74, 96; Clapham, op. cit., p. 96

23. Tyndale-Biscoe, op. cit., p. 83; Beatson, *The Motor-Bus in War*, p. 44; Letter dated 28 December 1917 in Sommers, *Temporary Crusader*, Tyndale-Biscoe, op. cit., p. 150; Gladden, *Across the Piave*, p. 14

24. Lewis, op. cit., p. 74; Rifleman, *Four Years on the Western Front*, p. 125

25. Chapman-Huston & Rutter, op. cit., pp. 60–63

26. Ibid., p. 66

27. Griffith, *Up to Mametz*, pp. 50–55

28. Haig Diary annex January 1917, *Summary of Schools of Training for the British Expeditionary Force, During Winter 1916–17*, National Archives, Kew, WO 256/15

29. Ibid., WO 95/4946

30. Chapman-Huston & Rutter, op. cit., pp. 70–77, 189–190

31. National Archives, Kew, MUN 4/6622, p. 379

32. Tyndale-Biscoe, op. cit., p. 114

33. Chapman-Huston & Rutter, op. cit., pp. 77, 166

34. Martin, *Poor Bloody Infantry*, p. 79

35. *Notes for Commanding Officers*, pp. 434–5

36. Anon., *The War the Infantry Knew*, p. 206

37. Fletcher, *Letters from the Front*, p. 35; Douie, *The Weary Road*, p. 207; Carrington, op. cit., p. 94; Baynes & Maclean, op. cit., pp. 119–20

38. Rifleman, op. cit., p. 281

39. Chapman-Huston & Rutter, op. cit., pp. 252–3

40. National Archives, Kew, MUN 4/6622, p. 381

41. Moynihan, *God on Our Side*, p. 12

42. BEF General Routine Order dated 19 December 1916

43. Drury, op. cit., p. 121

44. Diary entry 30 March 1916, National Archives, Kew, WO 256/9

45. Ibid., WO 32/14826

46. The Rev. P. Middleton quoted by Baynes, *Morale*, p. 206 fn

47. Bickersteth, *The Bickersteth Diaries*, p. 169

48. Moynihan, op. cit., p. 209

49. Ibid., pp. 24, 35

50. Ibid., pp. 158–61

51. Bickersteth, op. cit., p. 78; Housman, *War Letters of Fallen Englishmen*, p. 79; Moynihan, op. cit., pp. 84, 85

52. Osburn, *Unwilling Passenger*, p. 339; Hodges, *Men of 18 in 1918*, p. 109

53. Davson, *Memoirs of the Great War*, p. 82

54. Nettleton, *The Anger of the Guns*, p. 161; Baynes & Maclean, op. cit., pp. 125, 139, 148

55. Moynihan, op. cit., p. 106

56. Bickersteth, op. cit., pp. 106–8

57. Terraine, op. cit., p. 83fn

58. *Women's War Work: Britain*, Encyclopaedia Britannica, Vol. XXXII, 1922, p. 1059

59. Fielding, op. cit., pp. 194–5; Gladden, *Ypres 1917*, p. 44; Noakes, *The Distant Drum*, p. 114

60. Behrend, *Make me a Soldier*, p. 87

61. Memo to QMG dated 16 July 1915, National Archives, Kew, WO 107/15

62. Memo dated 23 April 1915 and letter dated 17 April 1915, Ibid., WO 107/14

63. Chapman-Huston & Rutter, op. cit., pp. 69–70

64. Greenwell, op. cit., p. 16; Terraine, op. cit., p. 204

65. Hampson, *1914 to 1919*, p. 61 diary entry 27 Oct 14

66. Burgoyne, op. cit., pp. 131–2

67. Wolff, *Subalterns of the Foot*, pp. 23–4

68. Steuart, *March, Kind Comrade*, p. 182

69. Fraser-Tytler, *With Lancashire Lads and Field Guns in France*, pp. 124, 136, 142, 183; Harbottle, op. cit., p. 70; Fielding, op. cit., p. 207

70. Poperinghe, Town Major War Diary entry 15 June 16 National Archives, Kew, WO 95/4042

71. Ellis, *Eye-Deep in Hell*, p. 134

72. ACI dated 14 March 1915

73. Crozier, *A Brass Hat in No Man's Land*, p. 50

74. Ashhurst, *My Bit*, pp. 48–9; Wedderburn-Maxwell, *Young Contemptible*, p. 18

75. Winter, *Death's Men*, p. 151

76. Peter Liddle, *The British Soldier on the Somme*, Strategic & Combat Studies Institute Occasional Paper No. 23, 1996

77. Winter, op. cit., p. 150

78. Ibid., p. 152

79. National Archives, Kew, WO 32/5597

80. Gladden, *The Somme 1916*, p. 25; Bickersteth, op. cit., p. 84; 32nd Division TM Association, *Artillery & Trench Mortar Memories*, p. 153

81. Fuller, op. cit., p. 95

82. Gillespie, *Letters from Flanders*, p. 75; Hampson, op. cit., p. 75; Harbottle, op. cit., pp. 45–6; Bickersteth, op. cit., p. 207; Fuller, op. cit., p. 98

83. Maude, *The 47th (London) Division 1914–1919*, pp. 223–4

84. Encyclopaedia Britannica, op. cit., p. 1059

85. *Notes for Commanding Officers*, pp. 185–93

86. Harris, op. cit., p. 106, 32nd Division TM Association, op. cit., pp. 202–3

87. Fuller, op. cit., p. 115

88. Luard, *Unknown Warriors*, p. 303; Fuller, op. cit., pp. 110–11

89. National Archives, Kew, WO 95/5000

90. Ibid., WO 293/1

91. Ibid., WO 154/4

92. Encyclopaedia Britannica, op. cit., p. 1062

93. National Archives, Kew, WO 107/14

94. Ibid., WO 107/15

95. Encyclopaedia Britannica, op. cit., pp. 1062–3

96. Steuart, op. cit., p. 179; Cushing, *From a Surgeon's Diary 1915–1918*, pp. 281–3

97. Rogerson, *The Last of the Ebb*, pp. 104–5; Wedderburn-Maxwell, op. cit., p. 5

98. Wintringham, *With the Lincolnshire Yeomanry in Egypt and Palestine, 1914–1918*, pp. 31–33

99. Bridges, *Alarms & Excursions*, p. 145; Delamain, *Going Across*, p. 161

CHAPTER FIFTEEN

The basic history of awards and decorations is taken from *Review of New Orders, Decorations, etc*, published by the Military Secretary in June 1920 and found in National Archives, Kew, under WO 32/5420.

1. Shephard, *A Sergeant-Major's War*, p. 57

2. Chapman-Huston & Rutter, *General Sir John Cowans*, Vol. 2, p. 290

3. Chapman, *A Passionate Prodigality*, p. 144

4. Lieutenant Colonel E. R. Pratt, OBE MC, *The Origin of a Fuse*, www. hellfire-corner. demon. co. uk/ fuse. htm

5. Young, *Army Service Corps 1902–1918*, p. 374

6. GHQ France GRO dated 3 February 1918

7. Richards, *Old Soldiers Never Die*, pp. 152–3

8. National Archives, Kew, WO 32/4959

9. Luard, *Unknown Warriors*, p. 110

10. National Archives, Kew, WO 222/2124

11. Hitchcock, *'Stand to'*, p. 184

12. AO 13/18, issued 30 December 1917

13. Osburn, *Unwilling Passenger*, p. 251

14. Wolff, *Three Subalterns of the Foot*, p. 140

15. Sheffield & Inglis, ed., *From Vimy Ridge to the Rhine*, p. 71

16. Home, *The Diary of a World War I Cavalry Officer*, p. 172

17. Osburn, op. cit., p. 304

18. Delamain, ed., *Going Across*, p. 57

19. Walker, *The Honourable Artillery Company in the Great War*, p. 300

20. Gladden, *Across the Piave*, p. 110

21. Slack, *Grandfather's Adventures in the Great War*, p. 106

22. Taylor, *The Bottom of the Barrel*, pp. 72–3

23. Army Council Meeting, 29 November 1916, National Archives, Kew, WO33/881

24. *Statistics of the Military Effort*, p. 558

25. Bickersteth, *The Bickersteth Diaries 1914–1918*, p. 184

26. Quoted Turner, *Dear Old Blighty*, p. 223

27. Hamilton, *The War Diary of the Master of Bellhaven*, p. 432

28. National Archives, Kew, WO 32/5400

29. Elton, *C E Montague*, pp. 188–90

30. Wolff, op. cit., p. 250

31. National Archives, Kew, WO 141/37; A. J. Peacock, *A Serious Misfortune: The 1st Gordon Highlanders in August 1914, Gun Fire* (Northern Branch of the Western Front Association) No. 22. I am grateful to Hedley Mallock for drawing my attention to this article and sending me a copy.

32. Fielding, *War Letters to a Wife*, pp. 317–8

33. *Statistics of the Military Effort*, p. 557

34. AO 466/14 dated 5 November 1914

35. Davson, *Memoirs of the Great War*, p. 146

36. Malone & Hawes, *Elegant Extracts*, pp. 171–2

37. Crozier, *Brass Hat in No Man's Land*, p. 187

38. Fielding, op. cit., p. 316

39. Chapman, op. cit., p. 266

40. Jeudwine Papers, Liverpool Record Office, 356 FIF Serial 16. I am grateful to Michael Orr for making me aware of these papers and to Sarah Starkey for providing photo-copies of the relevant documents.

41. National Archives, Kew, WO 95/2909

42. Read, *Of Those we Loved*, pp. 384, 391

43. AO 249/16 dated 6 July 1916

44. Fielding, op. cit., p. 318

45. AO 316/16 dated 12 September 1916

46. GHQ France GRO dated 15 January 1918; and Hamilton, op. cit., p. 466

47. Cushing, *From a Surgeon's Diary*, p. 315

48. National Archives, Kew, WO 163/22 Precis 873

49. AO 4/18 and Ray Westlake, *Overseas Service Chevrons, Stand To*; No. 48, p. 25

50. Fay, *The War Office at War*, p. 58

51. Carrington, *Soldier from the Wars Returning*, p. 158

BIBLIOGRAPHY

NATIONAL ARCHIVES, KEW

In particular:

CAB 23 / 1-5, War Cabinet papers from June 1916

WO 32, 33, 95, 107, 162

WO 123 / 56–60 Army Orders 1914-18

WO 123 / 199–201 General Routine Orders, GHQ France 1914–1919

WO 163 / 20–23 Army Council Minutes of Proceedings and Precis, 1914–18

WO 163 / 44–46 Army Council Military Members Meetings August 1914 – January 1916

WO 293 / 1–9 War Office and Army Council Instructions August 1914 – December 1918

Official / Semi-Official Publications

Army Lists

Chronology of Events Connected with Army Administration 1914, 1915, 1916, 1917, 1918

Field Service Pocket Book, HMSO, London, 1914

Field Service Regulations Part II: Organisation and Administration (reprinted with amendments to October, 1914), HMSO, London, 1914

Hart's Annual Army List for 1915, two parts (reprinted by Naval & Military Press, 1996)

History of the Great War: Military Operations (the official history of the war on land, with numerous volumes covering all theatres)

Infantry Training, HMSO, London, 1914

Instructions for the Training of the British Armies in France, January 1918 (SS.152)

Instructions Regarding Recommendations for Honours and Awards, Military Secretary's Branch, 1918

The King's Regulations and Orders for the Army, 1912: Reprinted with Amendments Published in Army Orders up to 1 August 1914, reprinted HMSO, 1918

Notes for Commanding Officers Issued to Students at the Senior Officers' School, Aldershot, 1917

Statistics of the Military Effort of the British Empire During the Great War 1914–1920, War Office, 1922 (reprinted by Naval & Military Press, 1999)

Training and Manoeuvre Regulations, 1913, HMSO, 1913

War Office Administrative Directory, HMSO, London, 1914, 1918

Welsh Army Corps 1914–1919: Report of the Executive Committee, Western Mail, Cardiff, 1921

Published Works

Adams, R. J. Q., *Arms and the Wizard: Lloyd George and the Ministry of Munitions, 1915–1916*, Cassell, London, 1978

Agate, Captain James E., *L of C (Lines of Communication): Being the Letters of a Temporary Officer in the Army Service Corps*, Constable, London, 1917

Allinson, Sidney, *The Bantams: The Untold Story of World War 1*, Howard Baker, London, 1981

Andrew, Christopher, *Secret Service: The Making of the British Intelligence Community*, Heinemann, London, 1985

Andrews, William Linton, *Haunting Years: The Commentaries of a War Territorial*, Hutchinson, London, nd

Anglesey, The Marquess of FSA, *A History of the British Cavalry – Volume 7: The Curragh Incident and Western Front, 1914*, Leo Cooper, London, 1996

Anglesey, The Marquess of FSA, *A History of the British Cavalry – Volume 8: The Western Front, 1915–1918, Epilogue, 1919–1939*, Leo Cooper, London, 1997

Anonymous (Capt Duncan Bell MC), *A Soldier's Diary of the Great War*, Faber, London, 1930

Anonymous, *The Tale of a Territorial: Being a Record of Experiences at Home and Abroad during the years 1914, 1915 & 1916*, Perkins & Co, Wellingborough, c.1917

Anonymous (Dr J. C. Dunn DSO MC), *The War the Infantry Knew 1914–1919: A Chronicle of Service in France and Belgium with the Second Battalion His Majesty's Twenty-Third Foot, The Royal Welch Fusiliers*, King, London, 1938

Ashley, R. S., *War-Diary of Private R S (Jack) Ashley 2472, 7th London Regiment 1914–1918*, Philippa Stone, London, 1982

Ashurst, George, *My Bit: A Lancashire Fusilier at War 1914–1918*, Crowood Press, Marlborough, 1987

Babington, Anthony, *For the Sake of Example: Capital Courts-Martial 1914–1920*, Leo Cooper, London, 1983

Babington, Anthony, *Shell-Shock: A History of the Changing Attitudes to War Neurosis*, Leo Cooper, London, 1997

Barnett, Lieutenant Colonel George Henry CMG DSO, *With the 48th Division in Italy*, Blackwood, Edinburgh and London, 1923

Barrie, Alexander, *War Underground: The Tunnellers of the Great War*, Spellmount, Staplehurst, 2000 paperback edition

Barton, Edith M. and Cody, Marguerite, *Eve in Khaki: The Story of the Women's Army at Home and Abroad*, Nelson, London, c.1918

Baynes, John, *Morale: A Study of Men and Courage*, Cassell, London, 1967

Baynes, John, *Far from a Donkey: The Life of General Sir Ivor Maxse*, Brassey's, London, 1995

Baynes, John and Maclean, Hugh, *A Tale of Two Captains*, Pentland Press, Edinburgh, 1990

Beatson, A. M., *The Motor-Bus in War: Being the Impressions of an ASC Officer During Two and a Half Years at the Front*, Fisher Unwin, London, 1918

Beckett, Ian F. W. and Simpson, Keith, eds., *A Nation in Arms: A Social Study of the British Army in the First World War*, Tom Donovan, London, 1985

Behrend, Arthur, *Make me a Soldier: A Platoon Commander in Gallipoli*, Eyre & Spottiswoode, London, 1961

Behrend, Arthur, *As from Kemmel Hill: An Adjutant in France and Flanders 1917 & 1918*, Eyre & Spottiswoode, London, 1963

Bet-El, Illana R., *Conscripts: Lost Legions of the Great War*, Sutton Publishing, Stroud, 1999

Bickersteth, John, ed., *The Bickersteth Diaries 1914-1918*, Leo Cooper, London, 1995

Bird, Antony, ed., *Honour Satisfied: A Dorset Rifleman at War 1916–1918 – 2nd Lieutenant Frank Warren*, Crowood Press, Swindon, 1990

Bird, Antony, ed., *Unversed in Arms: A Subaltern on the Western Front: The First World War Diary of PD Ravenscroft MC*, Crowood Press, Swindon, 1990

Blacker, John, ed., *Have You Forgotten Yet? The First World War Memoirs of C P Blacker MC GM*, Leo Cooper, Barnsley, 2000

Blake, Robert, ed., *The Private Papers of Douglas Haig 1914–1919*, Eyre & Spottiswoode, London, 1952

Bond, Brian, *The Victorian Army and the Staff College, 1854–1914*, Eyre Methuen, London, 1972

Bond, Brian, ed., *Staff Officer: The Diaries of Lord Moyne 1914–1918*, Leo Cooper, London, 1987

Bond, Brian et al., *'Look to Your Front': Studies in the First World War by The British Commission for Military History*, Spellmount, Staplehurst, 1999

Bond, Brian and Cave, Nigel, ed., *Haig: A Reappraisal 70 Years On*, Leo Cooper, Barnsley, 1999

Bourne, J. M., *Britain and the Great War 1914–1918*, Edward Arnold, London, 1989

Bowser, Thekla FJI, *The Story of British V.A.D. Work in the Great War*, Andrew Melrose, London, c.1918

Brereton, J. M., *The British Soldier: A Social History from 1661 to the Present Day*, Bodley Head, London, 1986

Bridges, Lieutenant General Sir Tom KCB KCMG DSO, *Alarms & Excursions: Reminiscences of a Soldier*, Longmans Green and Co., London, 1938

Brion, Wilfred R., *The Long Week-end 1897–1919: Part of a Life*, Fleetwood Press, Abingdon, 1982

Brown, Ian Malcolm, *British Logistics on the Western Front, 1914–1919*, Praeger, Westport Conn and London, 1998

Brown, Malcolm, *Tommy Goes to War*, Paperback edition, Tempus Publishing, Stroud, 2001

Burgoyne, Gerald Archilles, *The Burgoyne Diaries*, Thomas Harmsworth, London, 1985

Callwell, Major General Sir C. E. KCB, *Experiences of a Dug-out, 1914–1918*, Constable, London, 1921

Campbell, P. J., *The Ebb and Flow of Battle*, Hamish Hamilton, London, 1977

Campbell, P. J., *In the Cannon's Mouth*, Hamish Hamilton, London, 1979

Carlisle, Christopher, *My Own Darling: Letters from Montie to Kitty Carlisle*, Carlisle Books, London, 1989

Carr, William, *A Time to Leave the Ploughshares: A Gunner Remembers, 1917–18*, Robert Hale, London, 1985

Carrington, Charles, *Soldier from the Wars Returning,* Hutchinson, London, 1965

Carstairs, Carroll, *A Generation Missing,* Heinemann, London, 1930

Carver, Field Marshal Lord GCB CBE DSO MC, *Britain's Army in the Twentieth Century,* Macmillan in association with the Imperial War Museum, London, 1998

Casson, Stanley, *Steady Drummer,* Bell, London, 1935

Catchpool, Corder, *On Two Fronts: Letters of a Conscientious Objector,* Allen & Unwin, London, 1940 edition

Chandos, Oliver Lyttleton Viscount PC DSO MC LLD, *From War to Peace: A Study in Contrast, 1857-1918,* Bodley Head, London, 1968

Chapman, Guy, *A Passionate Prodigality: Fragments of an Autobiography,* MacGibbon & Kee edition, London, 1965

Chapman-Huston, Major Desmond & Rutter, Major Owen, *General Sir John Cowans GCB GCMG: The Quartermaster-General of the Great War,* 2 volumes, Hutchinson, London, 1924

Charteris, Brigadier General John CMG DSO, *At GHQ,* Cassell, London, 1931

Chasseaud, Peter, *Artillery's Astrologers: A History of British Survey and Mapping on the Western Front 1914–1918,* Mapbooks, Lewes, 1999

Clapham, H. S. *Mud and Khaki: The Memories of an Incomplete Soldier,* Hutchinson, London, 1936[?]

Collins, Norman, *Last Man Standing: The Memoirs of a Seaforth Highlander during the Great War,* Leo Cooper, Barnsley, 2002

Cook, Don, ed., *1914: Letters from a Volunteer,* privately, 1984

Coppard, George, *With a Machine Gun to Cambrai,* Imperial War Museum & HMSO, London, 1969

Corns, Cathryn & Hughes-Wilson, John, *Blindfold and Alone: British Military Executions in the Great War,* Cassell, London, 2001

Corrigan, Gordon, *Mud, Blood and Poppycock,* Cassell, London, 2003

Cowper, Colonel J. M. TD WRAC(Retd), *A Short History of Queen Mary's Army Auxiliary Corps,* privately, c.1967

Creagh, General Sir O'Moore & Humphris E. M., *Distinguished Service Order,* 2 volumes (1886–1915, 1916–1923) Naval & Military Press, Uckfield reprint of original 1924 edition

Croft, Lieutenant Colonel W. D., *Three Years with the 9th (Scottish) Division*, John Murray, London, 1919

Crozier, Brigadier General F. P. CB CMG DSO, *A Brass Hat in No Man's Land*, Cape, London, 1930

Cumming, Hanway R., *A Brigadier in France 1917–1918*, Jonathan Cape, London , 1922

Cushing, Harvey, *From A Surgeon's Diary, 1915–1918*, Constable, London, 1936

Dallas, Gloden and Gill, Douglas, *The Unknown Army: Mutinies in the British Army in World War 1*, Verso, London, 1985

Darlington, Colonel Sir Henry KCB CMG TD DL, *Letters from Helles*, Longmans, Green, London, 1936

Davies, Frank and Maddocks, Graham, *Bloody Red Tabs: General Officer Casualties of the Great War, 1914–1918*, Leo Cooper, London, 1995

Davies, W. J. K. BA AKC, *Light Railways of the First World War: A History of Tactical Rail Communications on the British Fronts, 1914–18*, David & Charles, Newton Abbot, 1967

Davson, Lieutenant Colonel H. M. CMG DSO, *Memoirs of the Great War*, Gale & Polden, Aldershot, 1964

Dearden, Harold (Late Captain RAMC), *Medicine & Duty: A War Diary*, Heinemann, London, 1928

Delamain, Frank, ed., *Going Across or With the 9th Welch in the Butterfly Division: Being Extracts from the War Letters and Diary of Lieut M St Helier Evans*, R. H. Johns, Newport, Mon, nd

Denman, Terence, *Ireland's Unknown Soldiers: The 16th (Irish) Division in the Great War, 1914–1918*, Irish Academic Press, Blackrock, 1992

Devonald-Lewis, Richard, ed., *From the Somme to the Armistice: The Memoirs of Captain Stormont Gibbs MC*, Kimber, London, 1986

Dolden, A. Stuart, *Cannon Fodder: An Infantryman's Life on the Western Front 1914–18*, Blandford Press, Poole, 1980

Douie, Charles, *The Weary Road*, John Murray, London, 1929

Drury, The Rev. William Edward, *Camp Follower: A Padre's Recollections of Nile, Somme and Tigris during the First World War*, Exchequer Printers, Dublin, 1968

Dugdale, Captain Geoffrey MC, *"Langemarck" and "Cambrai": A War Narrative 1914–1918*, Wilding & Son, Shrewsbury, 1932

Eades, Frances, ed., *The War Diary and Letters of Corporal Tom Eades 1915–1917*, Cambridge Aids to Learning (Publishing) Ltd, Cambridge, 1972

Eberle, Lieutenant Colonel V. F. MC, *My Sapper Venture*, Pitman Publishing, London, 1973

Eden, Anthony, *Another World 1897–1917*, Doubleday, New York, 1976

Ellis, John, *Eye-Deep in Hell: The Western Front 1914–1918*, Croom Helm, London, 1976

Elton, Oliver, *C. E. Montague: A Memoir*, Chatto & Windus, London, 1929

Empson, C. C., *Empsons' War: A Collection of Letters*, Pentland Press, Edinburgh, 1995

Errington, Lieutenant Colonel F. H. L. CB VD, *The Inns of Court Officers Training Corps During the Great War*, Printing Craft Ltd, London, nd

Fairlie, John A., *British War Administration*, OUP, New York, 1919

Falls, Cyril, *War Books: An Annotated Bibliography of Books about the Great War*, Greenhill Books edition, London, 1989

Farndale, General Sir Martin KCB, *History of the Royal Regiment of Artillery: Western Front 1914–18*, The Royal Artillery Institution, London, 1986

Farndale, General Sir Martin KCB, *History of the Royal Regiment of Artillery: The Forgotten Fronts and the Home Base 1914–18*, The Royal Artillery Institution, London, 1988

Farrar-Hockley, Anthony, *Goughie: The Life of General Sir Hubert Gough GCB GCMG KCVO*, Hart-Davis, McGibbon, London, 1975

Fay, Sir Sam, *The War Office at War*, Hutchinson, London, 1937

Fielding, Rowland, *War Letters to a Wife: France and Flanders, 1915–1919*, Medici Society, London, 1929

Fletcher, David, *War Cars: British Armoured Cars in the First World War*, HMSO, London, 1987

Fletcher, Ian, ed., *Letters from the Front: The Great War Correspondence of Lieutenant Brian Lawrence, 1916–17*, Parapress, Tunbridge Wells, 1993

Frankau, Gilbert, *Self-Portrait*, The Book Club edition, 1941

Fraser, David, ed., *In Good Company: The First World War Letters and Diaries of The Hon William Fraser Gordon Highlanders*, Michael Russell, Salisbury, 1990

Fraser-Tytler, Major Neil DSO RHA(TF), *With Lancashire Lads and Field Guns in France, 1915–1918*, Heywood, Manchester 1922

French, David and Holden Reid, Brian, ed., *The British General Staff: Reform and Innovation, 1890–1939*, Frank Cass, London, 2002

Fuller, Major General J. F. C., *Memoirs of an Unconventional Soldier*, Nicholson & Watson, London, 1936

Fuller, J. G., *Troop Morale and Popular Culture in the British and Dominion Armies 1914–1918*, Clarendon Press, Oxford, 1990

Fussell, Paul, ed., *The Ordeal of Alfred M Hale: The Memoirs of a Soldier Servant*, Leo Cooper, London, 1975

Germains, Victor Wallace, *The Kitchener Armies: The Story of a National Achievement*, Peter Davies, London, 1930

Gibbon, Monk, *Inglorious Soldier*, Hutchinson, London, 1968

Gillespie, A. D., *Letters from Flanders*, Smith, Elder & Co, London, 1916

Gladden, Norman, *Ypres 1917: A Personal Account*, William Kimber, London, 1967

Gladden, Norman, *Across the Piave: A Personal Account of the British Forces in Italy, 1917–1919*, HMSO, London, 1971

Gladden, Norman, *The Somme 1916: A Personal Account*, William Kimber, London, 1974

Glover, Michael, ed., *The Fateful Battle Line: The Great War Journals and Sketches of Captain Henry Ogle MC*, Leo Cooper, London, 1993

Glubb, John, *Into Battle: A Soldier's Diary of the Great War*, Cassell, London, 1978

Goodland, Stanley, *Engaged in War: The Letters of Stanley Goodland, Somerset Light Infantry 1914–1919*, Twiga Books, Gomshall, 1999

Graham, Dominick, *Against Odds: Reflections of the Experiences of the British Army, 1914–45*, Macmillan, Basingstoke, 1999

Graham, John W. MA, *Conscription and Conscience: A History 1916–1919*, Allen & Unwin, London, 1922

Graves, Robert, *Goodbye to All That*, Cassell, London, 1957 edition

Gray, John G., *Prophet in Plimsoles: An Account of the Life of Colonel Robert B Campbell*, Edina Press, Edinburgh, 1977

Greenwell, Graham H., *An Infant in Arms: War Letters of a Company Officer 1914–1918*, Allen Lane, London, 1972 edition

Griffith, Ll. Wyn, *Up to Mametz*, Faber, London, 1931

Griffith, Paddy, ed., *British Fighting Methods in the Great War*, Frank Cass, London, 1996

'GSO' [Frank Fox], *GHQ (Montreuil-sur-Mer)*, Philip Allan, London, 1920

Haig-Brown, Captain Alan G., *The OTC and the Great War*, Country Life, London, 1915

Hamilton, Nigel, *Monty: The Making of a General 1887–1942*, Hamish Hamilton, London, 1981

Hamilton, Lieutenant Colonel The Hon. Ralph G. A. (Master of Bellhaven), *The War Diary of the Master of Bellhaven 1914–1918*, John Murray, London, 1924

Hammerson, Michael, ed., *No Easy Hopes or Lies: The World War 1 Letters of Lt Arthur Preston White*, London Stamp Exchange, London, 1991

Hanbury-Sparrow, Lieutenant Colonel A. A., *The Land-Locked Lake*, Arthur Barker, London, 1932

Hankey, Donald, *A Student in Arms*, Melrose, London, 1916

Harbottle, George, *Civilian Soldier 1914–1919: A Period Relived* published privately, no date

Harris, Ruth Elwin, *Billie: The Nevill Letters 1914–1916*, Julia Macrae Books, London, 1991

Hartcup, Guy, *Camouflage: A History of Concealment and Deception in War*, David & Charles, Newton Abbot, 1979

Hart-Davis, Duff, ed., *End of an Era: Letters & Journals of Sir Alan Lascelles from 1887 to 1920*, Hamish Hamilton, London, 1986

Hart-Davis, Rupert, ed., *Siegfried Sassoon Diaries 1915–1918*, Faber, London, 1983

Hawkings, Frank, *From Ypres to Cambrai: The Diary of an Infantryman, 1914–1919*, Elmfield Press, Morley, 1974

Haworth, Christopher, *March to Armistice 1918*, Kimber, London, 1968

Hay, Ian, *The First Hundred Thousand*, Richard Drew, Glasgow, 1985 edition

Henniker, Colonel A. M. CBE RE (Retd), *Transportation on the Western Front 1914–1918*, HMSO, London, 1938

Herringham, Major General Sir Wilmot KCMG CB, *A Physician in France*, Arnold, London, 1919

Hesketh-Prichard, Major H. DSO MC, *Sniping in France: With Notes on the Scientific Training of Scouts, Observers, and Snipers*, Leo Cooper edition, London, 1994

Higham, Major S. Stagoll VD, *The Regimental Roll of Honour and War Record of the Artists' Rifles (1/28th, 2/28th and 3/28th Battalions The London Regiment TF)*, Howlett, London, 1922

Hitchcock, Captain G. E. MC, *"Stand To": A Diary of the Trenches 1915–1918*, Hurst & Blackett, London, 1937

Hodges, Frederick James, *Men of 18 in 1918*, Arthur Stockwell, Ilfracombe, 1988

Holden, Wendy, *Shell Shock*, Channel 4 Books, London, 1998

Holmes, Richard, *Tommy: The British Soldier on the Western Front 1914–1918*, HarperCollins, London, 2004

Home, Brigadier General Sir Archibald KCVO CB CMG DSO CderLH, *The Diary of a World War 1 Cavalry Officer*, Costello, Tunbridge Wells, 1985

Horn, Trevor MC, *Lancer Dig in: 1914 Diary The Marne*, Ellisons' Editions, Orwell, Cambs, 1983

Housman, Lawrence, ed., *War Letters of Fallen Englishmen*, Gollancz, London, 1930

Innes, John R. compiler, *Flash Spotters and Sound Rangers: How they Lived, Worked and Fought in the Great War*, Allen & Unwin, London, 1935

Institution of Royal Engineers, *History of the Corps of Royal Engineers*, Volumes 5–7, Institution of Royal Engineers, Chatham, 1952

✓ James, Brigadier A. E., *British Regiments 1914–1918*, Naval & Military Press edition, Heathfield, East Sussex, 1998

Jeffery, Keith, *Ireland and the Great War*, Cambridge University Press, 2000

Jeffery, Keith, ed., *The Military Correspondence of Field Marshal Sir Henry Wilson 1918–1922*, Bodley Head for Army Records Society, London, 1985

Jones, Colin, *Mametz: Lloyd George's 'Welsh Army' at the Battle of the Somme*, Gliddon Books edition, 1990

Jones, Paul, *War Letters of a Public-School Boy*, Cassell, London, 1918

Jourdain, Lieutenant Colonel H. F. N. CMG, *Ranging Memories*, John Johnson, University Press, Oxford, 1934

Kelly, D. V. MC, *39 Months with the 'Tigers', 1915–1918*, Ernest Benn, London, 1930

Kennedy, Alistair and Crabb, George, *The Postal History of the British Army in World War 1 – Before and After, 1903 to 1929*, privately, 1977

Kentish, Basil, *This Foul Thing Called War: The Life of Brigadier-General R J Kentish CMG DSO (1876–1956)*, The Book Guild Ltd, Lewes, 1997

Kiernan, R. H., *Little Brother Goes Soldiering*, Constable, London, 1930

Kipling, Rudyard, *The Irish Guards in the Great War: The First Battalion*, Spellmount, Staplehurst, 1997

✓ Latham, Bryan, *A Territorial Soldier's War*, Gale & Polden, Aldershot, 1967

Law, Francis, *A Man at Arms: Memoirs of Two World Wars*, Collins, London, 1983

Lawrence, Dorothy, *Sapper Dorothy Lawrence: The Only English Woman Soldier Late Royal Engineers, 51st Division 179th Tunnelling Company BEF*, John Lane, London, 1919

Leckie, Lieutenant Colonel V. C. DSO, *A Centaur Looks Back*, Hodder & Stoughton, London, 1946

Lee, John, *A Soldier's Life: General Sir Ian Hamilton 1853–1947*, Macmillan, London, 2000

Lewis, David, R. ed., *Remembrances of Hell: The First World War Diary of Naturalist, Writer and Broadcaster Norman F Ellison - 'Nomad' of the BBC*, Airlife, Shrewsbury, 1997

Liddell Hart, Captain B. H., *The Tanks: The History of the Royal Tank Regiment and its Predecessors Heavy Branch Machine-Gun Corps, Tank Corps and Royal Tank Corps 1914–1945*, Vol. 1 Cassell, London, 1959

Liddell Hart, B. H., *The Memoirs of Captain Liddell Hart*, Vol. 1, Cassell, London, 1965

Luard, K. E. RRC, *Unknown Warriors*, Chatto and Windus, London, 1930

Lucy, John F., *There's a Devil in the Drum*, Faber, London, 1938

Lytton, Neville, *The Press and the General Staff*, Collins, London, 1920

Magnus, Philip, *Kitchener: Portrait of an Imperialist*, Dutton, New York, paperback edition, 1968

Malone, Edmund and Hawes, George, *Elegant Extracts: A Duobiography*, Lovat Dickson & Thompson, London, 1935

Martin, Bernard, *Poor Bloody Infantry: A Subaltern on the Western Front 1916–1917*, John Murray, London, 1987

Marshall-Cornwall, James, *Wars and Rumours of Wars: A Memoir*, Leo Cooper, London, 1984

Marwick, Arthur, *Women at War 1914–1918*, Croom Helm, London, 1977

Marwick, Arthur, *The Deluge: British Society and the First World War – Second Edition*, Macmillan, London, 1991

Maude, Alan H., ed., *The 47th (London) Division 1914–1919*, Amalgamated Press, London, 1922

Maurice, Nancy, ed., *The Maurice Case: From the Papers of Major-General Sir Frederick Maurice KCMG CB*, Leo Cooper, London, 1972

Maze, Paul DCM MM, *A Frenchman in Khaki*, Heinemann, London, 1934

McConachie, John, *The Student Soldiers*, Moravian Press, Elgin, 1995

Mellersh, H. E. L., *Schoolboy into War*, Kimber, London, 1978

Messenger, Charles, *Terriers in the Trenches: The History of the Post Office Rifles*, Picton Publishing, Chippenham, 1982

Middlebrook, Martin, *Your Country Needs You: Expansion of the British Army Infantry Divisions, 1914–1918*, Leo Cooper, Barnsley, 2000

Mitchell, David, *Women on the Warpath: The Story of the Women of the First World War*, Cape, London, 1966

✓ Mitchinson, K. W., *Gentlemen and Officers: The Impact and Experience of War on a Territorial Regiment 1914–1918*, Imperial War Museum, London, 1995

Mitchinson, K. W., *Pioneer Battalions in the Great War: Organized and Intelligent Labour*, Leo Cooper, Barnsley, 1997

Morgan, Henry, *Our Harry's War: 1553 – Sgt G H Morgan Royal Warwickshire Regiment 1914–1918*, Rydan Publishing, Little Sandhurst, Berks, 2002

Morris, A. J. A., ed., *The Letters of Lieutenant-Colonel Charles à Court Repington CMG, Military Correspondent of The Times, 1903–1918*, Sutton Publishing, Stroud for Army Records Society, 1999

Morten, J. C., *I Remain, Your Son Jack: Letters from the First World War*, Sigma Leisure, Wilmslow, 1993

Mottram, R. H., Easton, John, Partridge, Eric, *Three Personal Records of the War*, Scholartis Press, London, 1929

Moynihan, Michael, ed., *People at War 1914–1918*, David & Charles, Newton Abbot, 1973

Moynihan, Michael, ed., *God on Our Side: The British Padre in World War 1*, Leo Cooper, London, 1983

Myatt, Frederick, *The British Infantry 1660–1945: The Evolution of a Fighting Force*, Blandford, Poole, 1983

Nash, Paul, *Outline: An Autobiography and Other Writings*, Faber, London, 1949

Nettleton, John, *The Anger of the Guns: An Infantry Officer on the Western Front*, William Kimber, London, 1979

Nicholson, Colonel W. N., *Behind the Lines: An Account of Administrative Staff Work in the British Army 1914–1918*, Strong Oak Press with Tom Donovan Publishing, Stevenage, c.1990 (originally published by Cape, 1939)

Noakes, F. E., *The Distant Drum: The Personal History of a Guardsman in the Great War*, privately, nd

Norman, Terry, ed., *Armageddon Road: A VC's Diary – Billy Congreve*, Kimber, London, 1982

Occleshaw, Michael, *Armour against Fate: British Military Intelligence in the First World War*, Columbus Books, London, 1989

'O.E'. *Iron Times with the Guards*, John Murray, London, 1918

Oram, Gerard, *Worthless Men: Race, Eugenics, and the Death Penalty in the British Army during the First World War*, Francis Boutle, London, 1998

Osburn, Arthur DSO MRCS LRCP, *Unwilling Passenger*, Faber, London, 1932

Page, Christopher, *Command in the Royal Naval Division: A Military Biography of Brigadier General A M Asquith DSO*, Spellmount, Staplehurst, 1999

Panichas, George A., ed., *Promise of Greatness: The War of 1914-1918*, Cassell, London, 1968

Peacock, Basil, *Tinker's Mufti: Memoirs of a Part-time Soldier*, Seeley Service, London, 1974

Pollard, Captain A. O. VC MC DCM , *Fire-eater: The Memoirs of a VC*, Hutchinson, London, 1932

Pound, Reginald, *The Lost Generation*, Constable, London, 1964

Powell, Geoffrey, *Plumer: The Soldier's General*, Leo Cooper, London, 1990

Prior, Robin and Wilson, Trevor, *Command on the Western Front*, Blackwell, Oxford, 1992

Purdom, C. B., ed., *Everyman at War*, Dent, London, 1930

Putkowski, Julian, *British Army Mutineers 1914–1922*, Francis Boutle, London, 1998

Putkowski, Julian and Sykes, Julian *Shot at Dawn: Executions in World War One by Authority of the British Army Act*, (new and revised edition) Leo Cooper, London, 1992

Rae, John, *Conscience and Politics: The British Government and the Conscientious Objector to Military Service 1916–1919*, Oxford University Press, London, 1970

Ramsay, M. A., *Command and Cohesion: The Citizen Soldier and Minor Tactics in the British Army, 1870–1918*, Praeger, Westport, Conn and London, 2002

Rawlinson, Lieutenant Colonel A. CMG CBE DSO, *The Defence of London 1915–1918*, Melrose, London, 1923

Rawlinson, Lieutenant Colonel A. CMG CBE DSO, *Adventures on the Western Front, August 1914 –June 1915*, Melrose, London, 1925

Read, I. L., *Of Those We Loved*, Pentland Press, Bishop Auckland, 1994

Rees, Major R. T., *A Schoolmaster at War*, Haycock Press, London, 1937[?]

Reith, John, *Wearing Spurs*, Hutchinson, London, 1966

Richards, Frank, *Old Soldiers Never Die*, Faber & Faber, London, 1933

'A Rifleman' (Aubrey Smith), *Four Years on the Western Front: Being the Experiences of a Ranker in the London Rifle Brigade, 4th, 3rd and 56th Divisions*, Odhams, London, 1922

Rogerson, Sidney, *The Last of the Ebb*, Arthur Barker, London, 1937

Roper, William, *The Records of the War Office and Related Departments, 1660–1994*, Public Record Office, Kew, 1998

Roskill, Stephen *Hankey: Man of Secrets Volume I 1877–1918,* Collins, London, 1970

Samuels, Martin, *Command or Control? Command, Training and Tactics in the British and German Armies, 1888–1918,* Frank Cass, London, 1995

Saunders, Anthony, *Weapons of the Trench War 1914–1918,* Sutton, Stroud, 1999

Scott, Peter, T. *"Dishonoured": The "Colonels' Surrender" at St Quentin. The Retreat from Mons. August 1914,* Donovan, London, 1994

Scott, Ralph, *A Soldier's Diary,* Collins, London, 1923

Scrivenor, J. B. ISO, *Brigade Signals,* Blackwell, Oxford, 1932

Sellers, Leonard, *The Hood Battalion Royal Naval Division: Antwerp, Gallipoli, France 1914–1918,* Leo Cooper, Barnsley, 1995

Seton, Graham (Lieutenant Colonel G. S. Hutchison DSO MC), *Footslogger: An Autobiography,* Hutchinson, London, 1931

Severn, Mark, *The Gambardier: Giving some Account of the Heavy and Siege Artillery in France 1914–1918,* Ernest Benn, London, 1930

Sheffield, G. D., *Leadership in the Trenches: Officer-Man Relations, Morale and Discipline in the British Army in the Era of the First World War,* Macmillan, London, 2000

Sheffield, G. D. and Inglis, G. I. S., eds., *From Vimy Ridge to the Rhine: The Great War Letters of Christopher Stone DSO MC,* Crowood Press, Ramsbury, 1989

Shephard, Ernest, *A Sergeant-Major's War: From Hill 60 to the Somme,* Crowood Press, Ramsbury, 1987

Shepperd, Alan, *Sandhurst: The Royal Military Academy and its Predecessors,* Country Life Books, London, 1980

Siepmann, Harry, *Echo of the Guns: Recollections of an Artillery Officer 1914–18,* Robert Hale, London, 1987

Simkins, Peter, *Kitchener's Army: The Raising of the New Armies, 1914–1916,* Manchester University Press, 1988

Simpson, Keith, *The Old Contemptibles: A Photographic History of the British Expeditionary Force August –December 1914,* Allen & Unwin, London, 1981

Silvester, Victor, *Dancing is My Life: An Autobiography,* Heinemann, London, 1958

Slack, Cecil Moorhouse, *Grandfather's Adventures in the Great War 1914–1918,* Arthur Stockwell, Ilfracombe, 1977

Smith, Lesley, *Four Years Out of My Life,* Philip Allan, London, 1931

Smithers, Roger, ed., *Imperial War Museum Film Catalogue Volume One: The First World War Archive,* Flicks Books, Trowbridge, 1993

Sommers, Cecil, *Temporary Crusaders,* Bodley Head, London, 1919

Stanley, Brigadier General F. C., *The History of the 89th Brigade 1914–1918*, Liverpool Daily Post, 1919

Steuart, R. H. J. SJ, *March, Kind Comrade*, Sheed & Ward, London, 1931

Summers, Anne, *Angels and Citizens: British Women as Military Nurses 1854–1914*, Routledge & Kegan Paul, London, 1988

Talbot Kelly, R. B., *A Subaltern's Odyssey: Memoirs of the Great War 1915–1917*, William Kimber, London, 1980

Taylor, F. A. J. (Tanky), *The Bottom of the Barrel*, Regency Press, London, 1978

Tennent, R. J. MM, *Red Herrings of 1918*, privately published, no date

Terraine, John, ed., *General Jack's Diary 1914–1918*, Eyre & Spottiswoode, London, 1964

32nd Divisional (RA) Trench Mortar Association, *Artillery & Trench Mortar Memories,* Unwin, London, 1932

Thomas, Alan, *A Life Apart*, Gollancz, London, 1968

Trapmann, Captain A. H., *Straight Tips for 'Subs'*, London, 1915

Travers, Tim, *The Killing Ground: The British Army, the Western Front and the Emergence of Modern Warfare 1900–1918*, Allen & Unwin, London, 1987

Tucker, W. A., *The Lousier War*, NEL paperback edition, London, 1974

Turner, E. S., *Gallant Gentlemen: A Portrait of the British Officer 1600-1956*, Michael Joseph, London, 1956

Turner, E. S., *Dear Old Blighty*, Michael Joseph, London, 1980

Tyndale-Biscoe, Julian, *Gunner Subaltern: Letters written by a Young Man to his Father during the Great War*, Leo Cooper, London, 1971

Van Emden, Richard, ed., *Tickled to Death to Go: Memoirs of a Cavalryman in the First World War*, Spellmount, Staplehurst, 1996

Vansittart, Peter, ed., *John Masefield's Letters from the Front 1915–1917*, Constable, London, 1984

Walker, Major G. Goold DSO MC, ed., *The Honourable Artillery Company in the Great War 1914–1919*, Seeley, Service, London, 1930

Ward, Irene DBE MP, *F.A.N.Y. Invicta*, Hutchinson, London, 1955

Ware, Fabian, *The Immortal Heritage: An Account of the Work and Policy of the Imperial War Graves Commission During Twenty Years, 1917–1937*, Cambridge University Press, 1937

Ware, Gwen *'A Rose in Picardy': The Diaries of Gwen Ware, 1916–1918*, Farnham & District Museum Society, 1984

Watson, Captain W. H. L., *Adventures of a Despatch Rider*, William Blackwood, Edinburgh, 1915

West, Arthur Graeme, *Diary of a Dead Officer: Being the Posthumous papers of Arthur Graeme West*, The Herald, London, 1918

Westlake, Ray, *Kitchener's Army*, Spellmount, Staplehurst, 1998

Whitehead, Ian R., *Doctors in the Great War*, Leo Cooper, Barnsley, 1999

Wilkinson, Alan, *Destiny: The War Letters of Captain Jack Oughtred MC, 1915–1918*, The Hutton Press, Beverley, Yorks, 1996

Wilson, Trevor, *The Myriad Faces of War: Britain and the Great War, 1914–1918*, Polity Press, Cambridge, 1986

Winter, Denis, *Death's Men: Soldiers of the Great War*, Allen Lane, London, 1978

Wintringham, Colonel J. W. CBE MC DL JP, *With the Lincolnshire Yeomanry in Egypt and Palestine, 1914–1918*, Lincolnshire Life, Grimsby, 1979

Wolff, Anne, *Subalterns of the Foot: Three World War 1 Diaries of Officers of the Cheshire Regiment*, Square One Publications, Worcester, 1992

Woodward, David R., *Lloyd George and the Generals*, Associated University Presses, East Brunswick NJ, London, Mississauga, Ontario, 1983

Woodward, David R., ed., *The Military Correspondence of Field-Marshal Sir William Robertson, Chief Imperial General Staff December 1915 – February 1918*, Bodley Head, London (for the Army Records Society), 1989

Worden, Alan Fletcher MC, *Yes Daddy But There has been Another War Since Then*, P R Macmillan, London, 1961

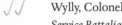

Wylly, Colonel H. C. CB, *The York and Lancaster Regiment: The Territorial and Service Battalions 1758–1919*, Vol. 2 privately, 1938

Young, Michael, *Army Service Corps 1902–1918*, Leo Cooper, Barnsley, 2000

Journals

Journal of the Society for Army Historical Research (JSAHR)

Stand To Journal of the Western Front Association

Unpublished

Macleod, Rory, *Memoirs of an Artillery Officer on the Western Front*, no date (typescript copy held at West Hill Library, Wandsworth, London SW18)

Davies, Emlyn, *Taffy Goes to War*, presented by the Knutsford Secretarial Bureau, c.1975

Gore-Browne, Eric, letters August 1915 – September 1916 (Author's Archive)

Gray, Paul Richard, *The Spirit of the Bayonet*

Simpson, Andrew, *The Operational Role of British Corps Command on the Western Front, 1914–1918*, PhD thesis University College, London, 2001

Wedderburn-Maxwell, John, *Young Contemptible*, c.1985 (Author's Archive)

Websites

Baker, Chris, *The Long, Long Trail*, http://www.1914-1918.net/home.htm

Beardwood, Lynette, *FANY at the Western Front*, http://www.fany.org.uk/ww1

Chappell, Brad, *The Regimental Warpath*, http://members.tripod.com/regtwarpath/

Commonwealth War Graves Commission, http://www/cwgc.org

Frank, Benis M., *The Jewish Company of the Shanghai Volunteer Corps Compared with Other Jewish Diaspora Fighting Units*, http://raven.cc.ukans.edu/kansite/ww_one/comment/svc.htm

Hampson, Travis MC, *1914 to 1919: A Medical Officer's Diary and Narrative of the First World War*, http://web.ukonline.uk/xenophon/contents.htm

Shot At Dawn Campaign, http://www.shotatdawn.org.uk

Western Front Association, http://www.westernfrontassociation.com/

INDEX